Rock n Roll:

IT'S BETTER THAN WORKING FOR A LIVING

Rock n Roll:
It's Better Than Working For A Living

by

Mick (Michael) Tyas

Rock 'n' Roll: It's Better than Working for a Living, Mick Tyas

Donnalnk Publications, L.L.C. Editors: Mr. Philip Bartholomew, Mr. Quante Bryan, and Ms. Shelby Catalano; ZenCon an Art of Zen Consultancy Editor and Layout Designer, Ms. Dana Queen; Cover design, Sprinkles on Top Studios, Ms. Sarah Foster.

This book is intended to provide general information on a particular subject and is not an exhaustive treatment of such subjects. This is a work of nonfiction from the author's perspective and memory of facts and events. Much of the vernacular in this title is minced with slang and varied forms of English, editorial review provided creative liberty and the publisher takes exception for remaining misnomers, errors or omissions. Names have not been changed. Without limiting the foregoing, the author and publisher does not warrant the content will be error free or will meet any particular criteria. Neither the publisher nor author advocate drug use.

© 2014 – Donnalnk Publications, L.L.C.

ALL RIGHTS RESERVED. No part of this work covered by the copyright herein may be reproduced, transmitted, stored, or used in any form or by any means graphic, electronic, or mechanical, including but not limited to photocopying, recording, scanning, digitizing taping, Web distribution, information networks, or information storage and retrieval systems, except as permitted under Section 107 or 108 of the 1976 United States Copyright Act, without the prior written permission of the publisher.

For information about permissions to reproduce selections from the book write to Permissions, Donnalnk Publications, L.L.C., 4405 S. Kirkman RD, Suite B-208, Orlando, FL 32811 or email: permissions@donnaink.org or call 01-888.564.7741.

For information about special discounts for bulk purchases, please contact Donnalnk Publications, L.L.C. Special Sales, 4405 S. Kirkman RD, Suite B-208, Orlando, FL 32811, Orlando, FL or email: special_markets@donnaink.org or call 01.888-564.7741.

Donnalnk Publications, L.L.C.
4405 S. Kirkman
Suite #B-208
Orlando, FL 32811
(888) 564-7741 (office)
(703) 373-9552 (fax)
www.donnaink.org

The Library of Congress has catalogued this title as follows:
  Tyas, Mick, 2014-
    Rock 'n' Roll: It's Better than Working for a Living | Mick Tyas. 1st edition.
    ISBN: 978-1-939425-64-5 (alk. paper)
    p. cm. 488
[1. Tyas, Michael (Mick), 2014 - Rock 'n' Roll. 2. Rock 'n' Roll-International-Biography. 3. Rock 'n' Roll-United Kingdom-Biography. 4. Rock 'n' Roll-United States-Biography. 5. Music-United Kingdom-Biography. 6. Music-United States-Biography. 7. Drugs and Addiction-United Kingdom-Biography. 8. Drugs and Addiction-United States-Biography. 9. Artists-United Kingdom-Biography. 10. Artists-United States-Biography.]

Printed in the United States of America.

2014941264 - reprint

12 11 10 9 8 7 6 5 4 3 2 1

Contents

Contents _____ i

Foreword _____ v

Acknowledgement _____ vii

Dedication _____ ix

Memorium _____ xi
    It's Better Than Working for a Living

Epigraph _____ xv

Prologue _____ xvii
    The Story

Chapter One _____ 1
    Working for a Living

Chapter Two _____ 7
    In The Beginning

Chapter Three _____ 25
    The Worst Journeys

Chapter Four _____ 33
    The First Worst Journey

ROCK 'N' ROLL
It's Better than Working for a Living

Chapter Five _____ 35
    Maybe the Last Worst Journey

Chapter Six _____ 39
    1975

Chapter Seven _____ 57
    1977

Chapter Eight _____ 135
    The Wall

Chapter Nine _____ 157
    Lorelei, West Germany

Chapter Ten _____ 173
    My Festival Work

Chapter Eleven _____ 189
    1983

Chapter Twelve _____ 201
    1984

Chapter Thirteen _____ 217
    1985 Serious Rock 'n' Roll!

Chapter Fourteen _____ 269
    The Mayhem Continues

Chapter Fifteen _____ 333
    Monsters!

Chapter Sixteen _____ 339
    Was This The End?

Chapter Seventeen _____ 341
    1989 Life after Death

Chapter Eighteen	347
Meanwhile – Back in the Kremlin	
Chapter Nineteen	355
Into The Nineties	
Chapter Twenty	365
What Next?	
Chapter Twenty–One	371
Is This The End?	
Chapter Twenty–Two	373
Back Home 1992 to Present	
Part II	415
Festivals	
Chapter Twenty–Three	417
Some Festival History	
Chapter Twenty–Four	421
National Jazz and Blues Festival	
Chapter Twenty–Five	425
The Woodstock Festival	
Chapter Twenty–Six	437
Altamont Free Concert	
Chapter Twenty–Seven	443
The Isle of Wright Festivals	
Chapter Twenty–Eight	447
The Glastonbury UK Festivals	
Chapter Twenty–Nine	453
The Next Big British Festival	

Chapter Thirty _____ 457
       Concert Histories

The Author _____ 463

Visit the Author _____ 465

Foreword

If you, like me, always wanted a backstage pass and couldn't wrangle one, here you go. Mick Tyas, who has a worldwide career with the top names in the music business, is opening the back door to give you a full no-holds-barred expose of what went on when you were trying to get those front row seats.

Like many of us, Mick started out in a day-to-day, hum-drum job as a teenager, but then broke free and ran to London (as we all wanted to do in the sixties, early seventies). He realized his destiny was in Rock 'n' Roll. He has now written, as a sound engineer, about his tours of America and the rest of the World.

When I met Mick in 1974, he was tall, lean and had hair down to his waist. He already had many gigs under his belt. I was mesmerized. He took me along with him to dozens of shows and I remember loving having access to private sections of The Royal Albert Hall and The Rainbow Theater in London, to name but a couple. Mick has now revealed some of these secret places in this book.

Read on and you will discover his many mad journeys and outrageous experiences with some of the biggest names in rock history such as The Rolling Stones, Rush, Lou Reed, Rod Stewart, Whitesnake, Thin Lizzy, Iron Maiden, Motley Crue and Kiss. Also, find out about his encounters and dealings with up-market

ladies like Bette Midler and Liza Minnelli as well as pop icons like Neil Sedaka and Paul McCartney, to name a few.

Knowing Mick, as I do, I know he wrote this book not to impress anyone, but to share some wild days and nights over his 40 years on the road. It's a bit like a Bill Bryson with sex and drugs!

Since his touring days, Mick has worked steadily at the top venues in London such as The Marquee and Shepherds Bush Empire as well as for MTV and the BBC. He now resides in Colorado and London. And is still rockin'!

> Roz Bea
> Managing Director
> The Video Pool
> London

Acknowledgement

Acknowledgements to all the people who gave me a chance in the business and help me live such a wonderful life. You know who you are, thank you.

Dedication

Dedicated to the life of Salli Jane Holgate, the most exciting and loving person I ever met.

Memorium

In memory of Steve Gadd, who kept me laughing for so many years on the road.

Rock n Roll:
IT'S BETTER THAN WORKING FOR A LIVING

Epigraph

I don't believe in been serious about anything. I think life is too serious to be taken seriously."
~Ray Bradbury

Prologue

THE STORY

I haven't done a tour in the Rock 'n' Roll business for over twenty years now, so what you are about to read is definitely ancient history. When I started in the business in the early 1970s, none of us really had any clue what we were doing. There were no colleges teaching audio courses or how to be a roadie. We were just a bunch of hippies who thought being in a band, or even working as a roadie, was actually ***better than working for a living***. We were basically making it up as we went along.

A few years earlier, I'd taught myself to play drums, and eventually I taught myself how to be a sound engineer. Albeit, with no drum lessons and no electronics background, my technical abilities in both sports were somewhat limited. I think I was a half-decent drummer and a pretty good sound engineer (so I've been told), but I still can't say I know much more technically about the job than when I first started doing it. Although I haven't toured with a band for twenty years, I'm still in the business, and I know what is required of engineers in this day and age. There is less money thrown at the job, the parameters of the job are different, and there is definitely more competition for the jobs.

The pioneer days of Rock 'n' Roll touring were from 1969 onwards. The next twenty-five years or so were to mold the business

we see now. There are two schools of thought: some say that the Rock 'n' Roll business as we know it started with the Woodstock concert in 1969. Others say the Rock 'n' Roll touring business started at the end of the last chord, of the last song, of The Beatles concert at Shea Stadium in New York in 1965.

Such was the chaos to that point.

I just feel so lucky to have been part of that first twenty-five years of history in the Rock 'n' Roll business; it was wild. It was wacky. And, it was weird. Sometimes, it was just downright wrong, but I'd like to share some of it with you.

It all starts very quietly in the North of England . . .

Chapter One

WORKING FOR A LIVING

It's January 1958, I'm eleven years old and have just been given my first record player for my birthday. It included three 12inch vinyl singles: *Come On Let's Go,* by English Rock 'n' Roll singer Tommy Steele; a skiffle single by an English guy called Lonnie Donegan, the name of which escapes me; and a single by a woman called Shirley Bassey for my Mum to play. About seventy miles away in Liverpool, John Lennon is forming his first band, something that will change the face of popular music forever. If he hadn't decided to form a band, I probably would not be writing this book. Show business was about to be turned into the "music business" or the "Rock 'n' Roll business" or whatever.

As most pre-pubescent children do, I really loved pop music. We were stuck with white American Rock 'n' Roll and pale British imitations, which was not very exciting. Nearly fifty years later, I am now an avid collector of '50s and '60s Rock 'n' Roll. Until September 1962, when 'The Beatles' first British EMI single was released, there was not much invention in pop music. By the time *Please, Please Me* was released in 1963 everybody wanted to be in a band, including me. I bought an old acoustic guitar but gave up on that after about two months. It was taking

ROCK 'N' ROLL
It's Better than Working for a Living

too long. I couldn't wait. I had to be able to play next week. So . . . I sold the guitar and bought a little old Olympic drum kit. This had to be easier, and strangely enough, it was. Very quickly, I was able to pick up the rudiments of making each limb on my body do a different thing, all at the same time. All my practice still left me time for that other pre-pubescent occupation . . . GIRLS.

In the six years from January 1958 to the end of 1963, as with every kid growing up from eleven years old to seventeen, a lot happened during that time. I'd left school at fifteen, much to my teacher's and parents' disgust. He, and they, thought I was academically solid. I loved music. I loved cars. I loved girls and I also loved money. I wanted all of the things I loved. So, I convinced my parents I would leave school and get a good job. I did get a good job. I didn't totally let my parents down. Although, I think they had a few misgivings during the next few years.

I got a job in an accounts office. It paid well enough for me to be able to buy a little old car. It was not exactly what you would call a "babe magnet," but it served its purpose over the next two years.

I had to go to night school two nights a week, on Wednesday and Thursday, to do an accountancy course which was one of the stipulations of the job. Unfortunately, Wednesday clashed with a gig night at the local dance hall. I started missing some of the night school classes to go to gigs.

I saw *The Rolling Stones, The Beatles, Gerry and The Pacemakers* and lots of other bands destined for stardom there. Unfortunately, this was to be the beginning of the end of my accountancy career and the beginnings of my musical career. I started growing my hair long, which in those days was totally un-acceptable in such a job. And, there was another influence in my life at the time, which is quite prevalent in this book . . . DOPE! I met

some guys from the local art school, who of course had long hair and smoked marijuana and were pulling the chicks like you wouldn't believe. I had to have some of their action, and this really was getting close to the end of my accountancy career.

By the beginning of '65, I had left the office job and got a job driving a delivery van for a company my Aunt worked for. I was finally able to grow my hair. I went to every gig possible. I started a band with my longtime friend Brian, who I still talk to. And, I was getting the women also. For me, this was more like it.

The dope smoking had not become any sort of major habit, instead it was just a casual thing (luckily) as we were getting much more serious about the band. We wanted to play Rock 'n' Roll music. In the North of England in 1965, the only places a small local band could play were the working men's clubs, which were full of "old" people. Apart from that, were the odd youth club dances who also wanted to hear pop music but not *Chuck Berry, Bo Diddley, Buddy Holly*, and etc. So, the band's progress was beginning to stall somewhat, but we still went to gigs all over the place and I had the wheels. We visited *Sheffield, Leeds, Bradford, Manchester* . . . in fact, every major city in the North of England where there was a good rock club . . . we were there.

This was now 1966, obviously a classic 1960s year. England won the World Cup for soccer and British bands ruled the world. Brian and I used to go to the *Esquire Club* in Sheffield every Saturday night. Lots of big acts played the Esquire—*Rod Stewart, Joe Cocker*, the *Stones, Small Faces*, and blues legends like *John Lee Hooker, Muddy Waters* and *Howlin' Wolf*. One Saturday night, I met the love of my life: blond, statuesque . . . the beautiful Marcia who was just 16 years old! I think we went out for about 6 months and then she dumped me. There were far too many inter-

esting men in Sheffield at that time, but I met her 40 years later and she didn't have quite the same appeal as she did at 16.

For the next four years, my musical career went along okay in the North of England. I played with various bands and had to play at the working men's clubs. At times, I had to wear a suit. I went on a couple of tours of American air bases in Germany with a couple bands and made good money. My parents were still worried about me, but I had a steady girlfriend after the devastation of losing Marcia.

Joan was a very tall redhead, very striking-looking, very sensible. She was an art school student and thus . . . an incredibly hip chick.

I was having quite a serious relationship with Joan and we became inseparable. I took her home to meet my parents and she took me home to meet hers. On Thursday nights, Joan's parents would go out to their local club, so I would go round to keep Joan company and play the newest *Led Zeppelin* albums. We would eventually end up rolling about on the living room carpet in sexual ecstasy, cutting it so fine some weeks that we were still trying to scramble into our clothes as her parents car came up the drive.

By 1970, I got "itchy feet" and wanted the big time, and that, of course, meant moving to London. Unfortunately, Brian couldn't afford "itchy feet," as he had a wife and baby by this time. I had to have more action and better drugs though, so I put the drum kit in the car and set off to follow my now "ex" girlfriend Joan to the big city. We were "ex" as she had spotted those bright lights and streets of gold a few months earlier than I. She had gotten herself a secretary's job at EMI records in London, which was the biggest record company in the country. She'd also managed to find herself a minor rock star--very minor--and better drugs. She'd even got an apartment in London. Unfortunately, she didn't want

to share it with me, as she was too involved with her minor rock star. But, she did let me sleep on her floor for a few months whilst I went in search of those streets manufactured out of that expensive glittery stuff.

Anyway, the short story is, I ended up going back to the North of England after six months. It was hard work for a boy from the sticks to get involved in the London music scene with no money, nowhere to live and not many contacts.

I wasn't to be beaten and hatched a plan . . . what I needed was money and contacts. I managed to make some money back in the North by playing in a little local band that played all the top forty records. They were the worst band I had ever heard, but they were booked every night of the week and made a whole load of money. It wasn't exactly the *Rolling Stones*, but I was making a pretty good living and my Mum was happy. Of course, I had come back home from the ravages and deprivation of the big city; unfortunately, I had to tell her I was going back, and I did, almost six months to the day I had left. And, once again my "ex" let me sleep on the sitting room floor. *Minor Rock Star* was still pretty minor, but she had met lots of people around the Notting Hill area of London. Lots of people who were going to be useful to me in making a living in the music business!

Chapter Two

IN THE BEGINNING

There was *Light and Sound!*
In the beginning, as you've noted in Chapter One, I was a 15 year old boy who dreamt of being a rock star but hadn't quite been made it. Like lots of others, I fell by the wayside, but I still managed to get into the business!

So this is the beginning of my professional career as a roadie and/or sound engineer. My ex-girlfriend Joan, on whose floor I crashed in London, had acquired herself a minor rock star who played guitar in a minor rock band in England called the *Pink Fairies*. Joan introduced me to a guy . . . Ian, who was a really nice guy, and one of the *Pink Fairies*. I asked Ian if he would take me along on some local gigs as extra help, which he agreed to do along with another roadie, Dave.

The *Pink Fairies* never made any money, as they were never really in the mainstream of the music business. They were always performing "alternative" gigs at festivals and street gigs at carnivals. So I never made money when I went out with Ian and Dave. Instead, I just smoked a lot of dope and took a lot of speed. I did gain some experience and met some interesting people.

It didn't look too great on the CV but neither did my couple of months with a loser band called *Help Yourself* who had just gotten a record deal with United Artists. They had a few semi-famous

friends, and spent a couple of years renting Headley Grange, near Guilford in Southern England. It was a huge early 19th century manor house where Led Zeppelin recorded *Houses of the Holy*. Sadly, it didn't deal up the same results for *Help Yourself*. They invited their friends down from London all the time with various hangers on. They spent lots of money on nothing (very much) except truckloads of drugs. *Help Yourself* spent most of the time getting fucked up. I did do a couple of gigs with them, but they were very forgettable affairs.

So, the back end of 1972 and early '73, I was working at Maurice Placquet's equipment hire store in West London. It was a great job--didn't pay a whole lot, but I met a whole lot of people and learned a little more about equipment and sound systems. This was an era where sound systems were developing into something resembling what we use today—especially WEM systems, developed by a legend in the British Music business called Charlie Watkins.

Charlie had been an innovator and had supplied systems for all the early festivals--very small by today's standards, but Charlie was the first. He titled his new system WEM Festival Stacks.

The hire shop I worked at had a whole load of this type of PA system. It was managed by Peter Edmonds--an original roadie with *Jimi Hendrix*. He is the man who gave me my first chance in the audio business and probably one of my first gigs as a sound engineer was when I asked Peter if I could help out at *Rainbow Theater* in North London. They were supplying a huge WEM Festival system for a big *Gary Glitter* spectacular called *Remember Me This Way*. It seems a bit of an ironic title these days, after all this guy's problems with the law in various countries around the world.

MICK (MICHAEL) TYAS

The Rainbow in Finsbury Park in London had been refurbished and renamed after its closure in the late '60s when it had been a favorite venue. It was formerly titled, Finsbury Park Astoria on the '60s pop package tour circuit. It was huge inside and was one of my favorite venues. Today, it is owned by some religious group or other, which somehow loses its emphasis.

I was about the 5th man on the sound crew at that show. I really didn't know much about how all the equipment worked—it was a start. Later on that year, Peter was to send me out on tour with one of my childhood heroes, as a real sound engineer, and how good that was.

When my boss, Peter, let me go out on that first tour, I was to mix monitors while an experienced engineer called Peter Carr who mixed the "front of house" sound. I had been practicing with a WEM Audiomaster, which was the state of the art mixing console at the time. I knew the basics of how to get noise in and out of the console. I had lots of confidence but not much knowledge. Peter believed I had a reasonably "good ear" and I guess it couldn't have been that bad, seeing as I have been in the business for nearly forty years now.

That first tour in 1973 turned out to be with Neil Sedaka. I grew up hearing Neil Sedaka songs from 1958 when I got my first record player. To actually be working with the guy whose voice I heard singing *Happy Birthday Sweet Sixteen* and *Oh Carol* on old radio shows in the early sixties was fantastic. For this to be my first ever tour made it even more so. In writing this today, it feels like only yesterday.

Uncle Neil, as the band and crew affectionately called him, was a fantastic individual. I didn't really know what I was doing at the time *and I guess not much has there changed in nearly forty*

ROCK 'N' ROLL
It's Better than Working for a Living

years. Neil was so professional. He was very easy to work with. He made my job an absolute pleasure. I even was under the impression he was nursing me through the first few gigs to help me get up to speed for the profession. This guy hadn't done a gig in ten years, but he sure knew what he was doing. Neil definitely was teaching me the job! That tour was a real milestone in my life. Of course, I have nothing but fond memories.

One of these was the friendship I struck up with the bass player from Neil's English backing band . . . Mr. Dave Wintour.

Dave and I both liked amphetamines. Dave used to turn up at gigs with bags full of "bombers" and "dexys" (Durophet and Dexadrine). He and I would be "speeding our brains out" for an entire show, but if we believed we were the only druggies on that tour, we were sadly mistaken.

I remember Dave telling me he had been invited to a dinner party at Neil's Hyde Park Square apartment in a very swish part of London. This was on a night off during tour. After dinner, port, and brandy, Uncle Neil surprised his guests when he brought out a block of compressed green stuff. He proceeded to entertain his guests with stories of his time in the business since 1955. I wish I could have been there.

Dave later played with the likes of *Eric Carmen, Roger Daltrey* and *Ian Gillan*, to mention only a few. I haven't seen Dave since that tour, but along with Uncle Neil, he was a diamond in a business where it's difficult to find anyone who is really genuine.

The guitarist in that band was Andy Summers, who later went on to found big 1980s British band *The Police*.

A little while after this tour, Peter left that hire company to start his own sound company with a couple of associates. He asked me if I wanted to work for him, which I did. Probably the first thing I ever did for Pete's company was *Queen's* first headlining

European tour. This was now 1974, and a guy called Peter Street (everyone was called Peter in Peter's company except me I think) set off from London in a seven and half ton truck with the PA and monitors in it. We got the car ferry from Immingham (England) to Gothenburg (Sweden) and arrived in "Goteburg" (Swedish pronunciation) the night before the first gig. We then had to drive across Sweden to Stockholm to get another ferry to Finland for one show in Helsinki. When you play gigs in Scandinavia, it is all ferries—and some are pretty spectacular.

So, after the gig in Helsinki, we had six days to drive back to Brussels. Just a word here about Scandinavia—first, Swedish women . . . many blond Swedish women are really beautiful, but why is it they have complexions that would give Keith Richards a run for its money?

Next beer!

In Sweden, there were three classes of beer; today there are three and a half but it's still pretty stupid. Class 1, was fractionally weaker than lemonade; Class 2, we used to call "near beer"--it tasted like beer, but it was almost alcohol free; and Class 3, was regular beer that they tried to keep away from the locals and could only be bought in private clubs and bars. They also now have Class 2 1/2, which is neither here nor there nor beer.

And, they have ridiculous laws, which obviously do not work—because if people want a drink, they'll find a drink. The reason being is they have big problems with alcoholics and alcohol related suicides. Which is not surprising, they probably top themselves trying to find a drink. With these laws in place, it makes the ferry journeys between Sweden and other countries-- like Finland and Denmark, which don't have these restrictions— pretty wild affairs, especially the overnight ones.

ROCK 'N' ROLL
It's Better than Working for a Living

I was once on a ferry journey between Fredrickshavn in Denmark, and Gothenburg in Sweden, on a Sunday evening. The ferry was like a war zone. It was absolutely full with young Swedes on their way home after a weekend's boozing in Denmark. And, they were casualties, every one of them. They even had to stop the journey in mid-crossing for two hours after it was suspected one of them had fallen overboard. We should have been so lucky, but in the end, he was found lying under one of the lifeboats, completely wasted, and oblivious to the panic.

One boring night in a Stockholm hotel room, I turned on the TV to see if there might be anything I might watch. There was no satellite or cable TV, just the local garbage and Swedish TV closed down about 10:30 p.m., even in the 1970s.

What I saw was a black and white movie about two guys going on a fishing trip. All very innocent until they came to their cabin out in the wilderness and decided they would have a quick drink before they went out with the poles for the day. They both had large stone jugs full of some dubious brew, which was obviously an integral part of their fishing equipment. What followed was about thirty minutes of watching these two fishermen drink themselves into a stupor from their stone jars. It went on through the day, into the night and eventually they passed out completely fucked up. The next screen was a blank screen with one word on it in large letters: DEATH! Not much fishing was done that day. They had drunk themselves to death. What prime time entertainment, an anti-alcohol movie. What a fucked up country.

Over the years working for a UK based sound company you end up doing the same gigs around Europe quite a few times a year with different bands. Therefore, you get to know the promoters, local crews and the local female company—always a necessity when touring so much. In Stockholm, a few of us regulars

on the European circuit knew who the local girls were. After one show, one girl who I had seen many times before invited me and some of the other guys back to her house (parents' house) for a party. Luckily, we had a day off the next day, so I think it was four crew and four of the local ladies piled into our rented Volvo estate car.

The leader of the gang of four ladies mentioned that she had no liquor at the house so we should buy some on the way. She asked if whiskey would be acceptable, at which we agreed. We were confused as to how she was going to find a bottle of Chivas Regal at 1:00 a.m. in Stockholm, when you couldn't buy a bottle of beer in a liquor store, not that they had any liquor stores. She gave directions as we drove off into the night, to the Docks!!!!! She stopped us at the side of this huge ferry "parked" at the side of the quay and told us to turn off all the lights and keep very quiet. She got out of the car and looked around very carefully to see she wasn't being followed and quietly ran up the gangplank to the deck of the ferry. Once more she turned to make certain no one saw her. What was she up to?

I was getting as paranoid as if I were doing some big dope deal in the middle of a hot area with a big flashing "Bust me" sign on my head. It reminded me of some Cold War movie or other. After what must have been about an hour of the remaining seven of us being squashed into the Volvo, the girl reappeared walking down the gangplank of the boat and quickly got in the car and said, "Drive! Quick!" I was almost in a panic.

"What the fuck is going on?" I said.

"I have bought whiskey" she said and produced from under her coat a bottle of Chivas Regal. "It was £30 at the time and about £75 today.

ROCK 'N' ROLL
It's Better than Working for a Living

At which I had to reply: "What the fuck is all that about?"

Thinking of the guys in the "horror" movie with their stone jars of "rotgut" reminds me of another incident that happened in a Scandinavian country. This time it was Finland.

Now the Finns are quite strange people. They have the brusqueness of most Scandinavian people but living next door to Communist Russia for so many years had given the place a really strange vibe. I could never get on with Finland at all.

In 1976, I was on tour in Finland with British pub rock band *Dr. Feelgood*. Now, this band had a black sound engineer, an Afro Caribbean or African American, as they would call them in the US these days, except he was English.

Many black people, especially the younger ones who live in urban areas in the UK these days, have very big problems with their attitude towards society. They still carry huge chips on their shoulders about how they are still discriminated against. Some are also very aggressive. I'm not going to argue that point one way or another but just to say that Geoff, the black engineer, was none of these things . . . as someone once said to me, "He is probably one of the whitest black men I have ever met." Geoff was a lovely guy.

We were in a hotel in "Bumbfuck," Finland. When we got up that morning it was a hot summer's day. Well . . . in Finnish terms it was summer so there was daylight. Geoff and I decided to walk into the local town, which involved walking around this small lake in front of the hotel into town. This was an idyllic setting. There were park benches all around the lake with people just sitting and watching the world go by. I noticed as we passed one of the benches there were three middle aged guys on it talking very loudly. I also saw resting on the seat at the side of one of the guys a double barreled shotgun and a large stone jar. Thinking back to the movie, this would be what was making them talk so loudly--they were all drunk as skunks. As we walked past them there conversation became more animated.

Geoff and I both knew what was happening; they had never seen a black man before in "Bumbfuck," so we walked a little faster. Looking half-back at the three guys, their animation had reached a point where one of them had picked up the shotgun and we heard a click as he cocked the trigger. It was at this point when Geoff and I both decided we needed some jogging practice, fast jogging! We cleared the area pretty quickly and never did hear a shot.

I have had three experiences of guns being aimed at me whilst on the road. The first was at the *Lorelei Festival* in Germany in 1978, which gets its own chapter later on. The second was the experience in Finland. The last was in Belfast, Northern Ireland on a *Rory Gallagher Tour*. Rory was an Irish Blues guitar legend who died in 1995.

Back on the first ever *Queen* European headlining tour . . . Peter Street was attempting to drive the 14' high, seven and a half ton truck under a 12' high bridge in Southern Sweden. We were on our way to the ferry that would take us to Germany. Unfortunately, I don't think Peter understood the exchange rate between meters and feet at the time. We had to hire a secondary truck in Sweden, as Peter had managed to rip the roof off completely without damaging too much equipment. So . . . we set off a second time for Belgium for the next gig, three days later.

I now want to move on to another highlight from 1973 / 4. Number two in the singles charts in the UK in December 1973, was a catchy little number entitled *My Coo Ca Choo* by *Alvin Stardust* aka *Shane Fenton*, aka *Bernard Jewry*. He was an old Rock 'n' Roll musician from the 1960s who had re-invented himself; this was to be my next assignment.

By March 1974, his second single entitled *Jealous Mind* was No.1 in the charts. Suddenly, money was no object to this production. This was going to be glamorous, although it didn't start too glamorous.

Peter, the owner of the company, sent Peter Carr and me out on the tour. Once again, it was starting in Scandinavia only in Denmark this time. And once again, we had to drive a seven and a half ton truck - this was now pretty normal on "biggish" tours.

We had a brand new truck from a company in the North of London in a town called Watford. It was going to be pretty well laden as we were taking quite a large amount of PA.

We were booked on a ferry from Harwich in England to Ejsberg in Denmark--about noon time I think. So, after loading the truck the day before, I drove it home to my apartment in South London as we would have to make an early start in the morning.

I jumped in the cab the next morning at the ungodly hour of 7:00 a.m., put the key in the ignition and nothing happened, it wouldn't turn. The steering lock was jammed. I called the breakdown service but couldn't get hold of them until 8:00 a.m. (No 24/7 service in those days.). I'd also called Peter to tell him I would be late picking him up, which didn't bother him as he was still in bed with his new Spanish girlfriend. And, he was still there in bed when I eventually picked him up about 1:00 p.m.

We eventually made it to Denmark on the evening ferry, and we had two rather boring weeks of gigs around Scandinavia, except for being harassed by Swedish Border guards (No European Union then.). The more aggressive Finns gave us a bit of a "going over," when we disembarked from the overnight ferry in Helsinki.

It was a really fucking cold morning with about a foot of snow on the ground, and the Customs guys made the band and the crew put all their baggage in this garden shed on the dockside. They then pushed this lovely Golden Retriever dog into the shed and left him in there for about ten minutes and then let him out. The dog nonchalantly walked away and the Customs guys said we could take our bags. The sniffer dog didn't find any dope; he just pissed on one guy's suitcase.

As much as I hate the Finnish people, I quite like the country. It feels as if it is somewhere very cold, even in summer—which it is, of course—as the northernmost part is within the Arctic Circle. I remember coming out of a club in the Northern city of Oulu about 2:30 in the morning and it was bright with sunshine. Finland is not a good place for vampires in summer.

Finland also feels quite foreign, although it has big modern European cities, when you drive north it starts getting pretty wild. Parts of it cannot be reached by road in the winter. You see places where suddenly the road widens to four lanes in each direction for a mile, even though there is no traffic on the road--even in summer. These are actually landing strips so planes with skis attached can reach these remote areas in winter.

ROCK 'N' ROLL
It's Better than Working for a Living

We were doing a gig in the northeastern town of Joensuu one day, and we were driving the next day to a place called Lapeenranta, about 200 miles from the capital, Helsinki. The town is actually closer to St. Petersburg in what was then Communist Russia than it is to the Finnish capital. This was a really strange feeling in 1974, as there was still a Cold War on between the US and Western countries and Communist Russia. In one section of the journey, the road ran parallel to the Russian border, literally 100 yards away. It was all very strange but also quite exciting for a young guy from Northern England, who'd never really been anywhere very much.

We finished the European leg of the tour in Finland, probably one of the furthest points of Europe from London that you could visit at the time. It was at least two ferry rides and two days journey home. This came as no surprise as agents seem to like to have a laugh with you at the end of the tour by making the last show as far away as possible from your base. You never quite get used to having to drive back from Lisbon or Athens or Prague.

When we started the English leg of the tour the second single, *Jealous Mind*, had hit No.1 in the singles charts. Another couple tunes . . . *Red Dress* and *You, You, You* quickly followed. *Mr. Stardust* was now big news, and we set out on what was a forty-two date tour; I didn't even know there were forty-two 2,000 seater gigs in England.

We played a varied selection of city halls, theatres, end-of-the-pier dance halls and scout huts. There were no real outrageous events on this tour. I just remember it as being a really good tour. There was plenty of money about, and I managed to make a little. Plenty of people wanted to know you, as Alvin was the No.1 act in the country at the time. He, himself was a bit of a dick, but I have met many worse in the business.

MICK (MICHAEL) TYAS

Some of the gigs we played were quite memorable though. Dunstable Civic Hall was a wood paneled, oval-shaped concert hall with fantastic acoustics for an acoustic orchestra, but disgusting for a "rock" band. When you spoke on stage you could hear every word as clear as a bell at the back of the room without any amplification.

We played some beautiful old theaters also, such as the outstanding Rainbow in London already been mentioned earlier; the beautiful old Sunderland Empire in the Northeast of England, which was stuck in a 1930s time warp – thankfully – it was lovely; the Coventry Theater, which was bombed to bits in the Second World War but rebuilt with a load-in door big enough to drive a truck onto the stage; the Hastings Pier Pavilion where you had to push all the equipment the full length of the pier to the dance hall at the end where a legendary, one-armed, local crew guy was there for eons (whose name I never knew); and the Blackpool Winter Gardens with it's beautiful late 19th century rococo interior.

West Runton Pavilion near Cromer in Eastern England looked like a converted scout hut. Another classic gig was the Top of The World in Stafford. I must admit I never expected the Top of the World to be in Stafford, UK if you get my drift. This was an old 1950s dance hall on the top floor of this building with a nightclub on the first floor.

I remember this gig being a real pain in the butt due to the fact all the equipment had to be taken up two floors in a small elevator, which took hours. It had a small stage at one end of the hall with the dressing rooms right next door, which could be accessed from the dance floor by the general public.

After the show there, a disco going on and the band had gone off into the crowd to find some women whilst we had to do the endless load-out down the elevator. When we eventually finished, we went back upstairs to the dance hall for a quick beer before we left. I got a beer and sat in the dressing room. I'd been in there about five minutes when the door opened and in walked or staggered this gorgeous, tall chick in a long silver evening dress. As soon as she saw I was one of the crew, she took off her dress and everything else without saying a word, though I don't recollect there was much more to take off. She expertly removed my jeans and dragged me to the floor and after a few minutes of wrestling on the floor the door opened again and in walked a couple of the band members.

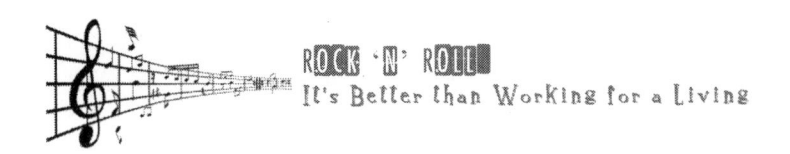

"Whoops! Sorry, Mick," was all the bass player said, and he walked out. After half an hour I had to leave the girl from the "Top of The World," but she was fun.

This knee-trembling, erotic experience was quite a rare occurrence on this tour, despite women forming probably 80% of the audience at these shows. They were mainly middle-aged housewives out for a night out with the girls and not interested in drug-taking, long-haired hippie crew guys, but it was a really good tour. After this very successful tour for me, and after three No.1 singles for Mr. Stardust, the shrewd Jewish management headed by a guy called Michael Levy[1] decided that spending money on renting sound systems was just wasteful.

An old friend of Alvin's from his Shane Fenton Rock 'n' Roll years named Stewart Mercer who owned an English guitar amp-

---

[1] An accountant who in later years had some very dodgy financial dealings whilst being part of the 1998 Labor Government in the UK. He now sits in the House of Lords as Baron Levy, a peer of the Realm, as you would imagine.

lifier manufacturing company. He was approached to build a PA system to use on a big tour of cabaret venues, which was lined up. Stewart, although quite a successful builder of guitar amplifiers known as Carlsboro, had no idea really about building a PA system. He was asked if he could provide it for free, which seemed pretty stupid, but good publicity for Stewart's company.

I was asked if I wanted to work for Alvin directly, rather than through the sound company. They made me a great offer I couldn't refuse. They didn't tell me about the Carlsboro PA system, which I would eventually spend more time taking bits back to factory to have repaired than actually operating it. I also had to have a second man on the PA crew. I was asked to go down to the very swish management office on York Street in Central London to meet a prospective candidate who had been interviewed.

I consequently arrived the next day to meet a certain Francis Xavier Gallagher. Now, Francis Xavier had a Scottish accent you could stir with a spoon. He also had the most wicked sense of humor. He took lots of speed and smoked lots of dope. We were going to get on fine. He also knew his job, having just finished touring with Suzi Quatro. Frank later moved to the US in the late seventies, and went on to mix *Talking Heads* and *Tom Tom Club*, for the next thirty-four years, which he still does.

There used to be a bunch of what you would call supper clubs—night clubs I suppose, but with a working class clientele. These were quite large places with capacities of around two to two and a half thousand people. They were situated mainly in Northern industrial towns in the UK, but there were a couple in the more affluent South. These places were mainly owned by three companies: Baileys (probably being the largest) along with Top Rank and the Fiesta Clubs. It was into these clubs management now booked Alvin Stardust. Frank and I were about to have some fun and also get into a fair bit of trouble.

"No jeans! Suit and tie required. NO LONG HAIR!!!" Those were the rules of admission to these clubs. Can you believe it? Actually, the jeans and the suit and tie, yeah that is fair enough if you want to run a smart club, but "NO LONG HAIR"? If they said that now, in the 21st century, no one would go. Those companies would be dragged through court for discrimination.

I had waist-length straight hair. Frank and I wore jeans and T shirts; we were workers and Rock 'n' Rollers. We had to load and unload PA systems and rig them in dirty clubs. And, some of them, of course, were pretty dirty under the surface, but we were in trouble with the club managers every week.

Alvin would play a week's residency at each one of these clubs and we had trouble just about every night. The band was a cheap bar band from the North of England and used to playing some of these places; some of which were pretty horrible and frequented by pretty horrible people. Frank and I ran into a little bit of trouble with some of these people who were jealous we were walking around these clubs in T shirts and jeans with waist-length hair. The band said we would get into trouble and we did. Some of the male members decided to start a fight with us to satisfy their anger at having to wear a suit and tie while we were wandering around in T shirts and jeans eyeing up their women.

The club management always complained to Alvin's manager, but was told our crew dress as they like or Alvin doesn't play. We had power in those days and used it to the maximum. Alvin never used to go on stage before 10:00 p.m. So Frank and I would take a gram of amphetamine sulphate and go down to the local bar and get pretty drunk most nights before we went to do the show. We usually had a really good time; even the security staff tried to give us a hard time but were told to "cool it" by the management and to leave us alone.

This went on for about sixteen weeks in the summer of 1974. Apart from being a little weird for the locals, it was all a little weird for us, as we were Rock 'n' Roll people working in this cabaret environment. There were a couple of funny things that happened to us though.

I would have my sound console set up out in the auditorium and cordoned off with barriers to stop inquisitive hands touching it. You would get the usual amount of local dickheads with questions like, "Do you need a pilot's license to fly that?"

My reply would be, "Sure do . . . now do you like sex and travel? Well, fuck off!"

I would have to call security to protect us when they wanted to fight after that remark, it was great fun. One night, halfway through the show, I was watching the stage seated behind my console when I heard a strange noise, like someone with a really deep voice trying to sing, which is what it actually was . . . I didn't realize for a few minutes that it was. The sound console obviously was out in the auditorium where you could hear to mix the sound, but space was so tight in some of these clubs, as in this particular case, I was positioned in a walkway. A fire lane had to be kept clear, so I was squeezed in, surrounded by crowd control barriers. I had a Revox reel-to-reel tape machine fitted with a Vari speed device whereby a signal from a microphone on stage was fed into the machine on a record setting, and with the help of the Vari speed control, I could speed up the signal coming from the playback head of the machine to raise the pitch of the signal.

This was returned into the console and mixed with the original signal, so you would have double tracking of Alvin's voice. It is known as ADT or automatic double tracking. In this instance, Alvin's vocal on the records was speeded up to make it higher pitched, but he couldn't sing live at this pitch, hence the Vari speed to speed up the tape made his voice higher. These days it is all done digitally, but in 1974 / 5 this was the cutting edge in vocal effects. That is, until a member of the audience stands next to the desk, leans on the barrier and an elbow catches the tape spool and slows it down. Then Alvin Stardust turns into Darth Vader. I don't think anyone noticed except me, when I had to pull down the volume of the higher pitched vocal and replace it with the original vocal signal. That was the end of that effect for the show as the tape machine wound about twenty-five miles of recording tape onto the floor.

After the cabaret tour, we went on to do some more "one nighter" shows early the following year, but the hits seemed to have dried up for Alvin and also the money for financing the touring. By the middle of 1975, the touring stopped. It was quite fun for a time though for a new boy in the business.

Chapter Three

THE WORST JOURNEYS

Touring with a Rock 'n' Roll band is probably the most glamorous and exciting part of the job as sound engineer. As much as I loved traveling the world for thirty years; I loved even more coming home and seeing England's green and pleasant lands through that airplane window. Unfortunately, that's all changed since I stopped touring; perhaps it's because I'm now spending more time here. Personally though, and not to get too political, I believe the place has been ruined by politicians, do-gooders, tree huggers, bankers, the Flat Earth Society, Greenpeace and people in general. It would be a much better place without people.

Although traveling to places like the US, Canada, Australia, New Zealand, Japan, South America and just about every European country and actually getting paid quite a lot of money for doing it seemed to me like the dream job when I first started in the early seventies. Over time, you become blasé as the gloss wears off. It's not because you've been to a certain place so many times before – it just happens.

Over the thirty-nine years I've been in the business, I've done twenty-eight tours of America. I still love going there enough to have now bought a lump of Colorado for myself.

ROCK 'N' ROLL
It's Better than Working for a Living

There are two factors which make traveling to all these places a pain in the butt these days, whereas in the early days of touring there was only one pain and that was the complete and utter tedium!!!

You could try reading *War and Peace* or *The Decline* and *Fall of the Roman Empire* all the way to Australia, but you would probably need a week in a dark room to get over the eye strain. Of course, we were able to smoke and drink as much as we liked back before the world went "politically correct" stupid.

On these long flights, also, when we got a little frazzled we could always pop into the toilets for a quick line of coke. Of course, in these days of CCTV on planes and searches before you board, you would probably get a firing squad or be questioned for 48 hours at a high security police station before you were sent on your way to Australia or to jail. Therein lays the second pain in the butt about flying around the world these days: security.

I know we can't do without it, and it has to be implemented so as to try and deter every faction of towel-headed lunatic who wants to meet the Angel of Death on flight BA652 to New Delhi, but it now turns a six-hour flight to New York into twelve hours, three hours for check-in and security checks, six hour flight and at least another three hours of queuing and security checks when you land. That's without flight delays and traveling to and from the airport of course.

I'm going to start my own personal history of touring, not at the start, back in the early '70s but about fifteen years later in 1987. This was one nightmare journey which makes that current flight to New York look like a walk in Central Park.

MICK (MICHAEL) TYAS

It was fall 1987, and I was in Australia with Iron Maiden. Being fall in the UK, it was springtime in Australia. The weather was just getting really warm. We were just at the end of a three week tour where we had played all the usual cities: Sydney, Melbourne, Adelaide, Canberra, Brisbane and Perth. You can't really play much more than that or you start getting into some interesting places away from the coast where lots of the folks haven't even seen a white man. But seriously, it takes three weeks just to do those six or seven shows because nobody wants to travel that far and then rush around the country. It's much nicer to take time out in between gigs and relax a little, as the local promoter always pays for the hotels anyway. So why not?

We had been away from home for ages having just done three months in the States, which was our third trip there that year. And, we landed in Australia after a two week tour of Japan. Two weeks in Japan sounds exciting and exotic. I suppose to the average man in the street it is especially when getting paid for it, but I personally hated it. It's a long way from home, it's expensive and it feels very foreign. Try buying drugs there, I'll tell you what happened to me when I did, in another chapter.

I quite like Australia, especially when I have arrived there from somewhere like Japan. It is where I can go into the Southern Cross Hotel, somewhere at the top of George Street in Sydney, and get a pot of tea and a full English breakfast . . . what a treat. The last gig in Australia was at the Horden Pavilion, a 1920s-built venue right next to Sydney Cricket grounds. We had a good day and everyone was looking forward to going home the next day; however, we had heard a rumor some of the ground crews at Sydney International Airport were going on strike the next day. I think that's called Murphy's Law--you go around the world for a year and the day you want to go home, the fucking airports on strike.

ROCK 'N' ROLL
It's Better than Working for a Living

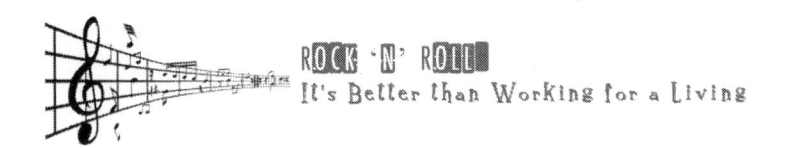

We were assured by the tour manager we would still make it out of the country. It wasn't until later on in the day we were informed nothing would be leaving Sydney airport the next day. Instead, we had to leave from Brisbane, which was a twelve hour overnight drive away. It would have been okay, as we were to leave after the show, sleep the whole journey and wake up at the Brisbane airport in the morning, but this was where the nightmare was about to begin.

Usually, on overnight journeys to the next gig we would have sleeper buses with anywhere from six to twelve bunks, two lounges, a toilet, shower and etc. This being a last minute changes of plans after the gig, due to the airport strike, no sleeper buses could be found in Sydney. The promoter wanted us out of there as cheaply as possible, so the twenty-five or so crew that we were was put on what I can only describe as a regular bus. There were no luxuries, only seats, an engine and a few crates of beer. It was what it was for twelve fucking hours! There was no video to watch, no toilet, and loads of people who drank lots of beer so we were forever stopping to let the piss heads empty their bladders. This didn't make for ideal conditions to sleep in. We were all in regular upright seats. I had to sit next to this Irish member of the set building team called Paddy. How original is that?

About three hours into the journey, Paddy had drunk probably more than his own weight in Guinness. He was involuntarily falling asleep next to me with his open can of Guinness still in his hand. I had to wake him up to tell him he was falling asleep with a full and opened can of beer in his hand. It was perilously clasped in his left hand; one slight flip of ninety degrees would bath my groin in Guinness. He insisted he was going to drink it, yet he kept closing his eyes to sleep and I kept waking him up. He just refused to let the can from his grasp. After this went on for about an hour or so, I must have eventually fallen asleep. And, yep, you guessed it: a little while later, I screamed out as Paddy anointed my nuts in Guinness.

I'm not going to relate any more of the horrendous bus journey; it's safe to say Paddy and I didn't speak for quite a while after that incident.

Our revised flight schedule from Brisbane Airport the next morning was something of a "Magical Mystery Tour," which would have been really interesting if you were on vacation. However, to twenty-five weary, unwashed, unkempt road crew it wasn't very good news.

There was no direct flight leaving Brisbane for the UK as the strike had spread to Brisbane and all the people on strike worked for Quantas, the only airline flying to the UK from Brisbane.

We managed to get an Ansett flight to Auckland, New Zealand. Whether this was a good move or not remains a question in my mind to this day; still, off we went on the two-and-a-half-hour flight to Auckland. Arriving in Auckland, we all looked at our new tickets, which had just been handed to us by Tony our tour manager. This is where it all starts getting a little hazy. I know we had had quite a long stopover in Auckland, maybe three or four hours, but it was the next leg of the journey that interested me, and that was to Honolulu, Hawaii.

Now, I had been to Hawaii before. It is a fabulous place if you are doing one gig with a few days to chill after the show, which is what we did with Maiden when we were there last time. However, a stopover in the middle of a flight home, three quarters' way around the world and then being stuck in the terminal . . . it's just a place you do not want to be. Plus, I learned to get to Hawaii from Auckland, the plane has to go to Sydney (Where we had just come from twenty four hours ago.), as there are no direct flights to Hawaii from Auckland.

I was assured by the tour manager this was the only way back to London as we were trying to get thirty people back home within less than twenty-four hours' notice of no flights taking off from Sydney. You could stopover in Sydney, as it was baggage handlers on strike. So, as long as you did not have to change planes, you could still land and take off from Sydney. So, we were back in Sydney nearly 24 hours after we left and eight hours later we were approaching Honolulu. At this point, I must impress on you my memory of this section of the journey is very sparse, as I was having trouble recalling what day it was.

I had no idea what time it was in London. I know, local time, it was early evening. One redeeming characteristic is as we disembarked from the Air New Zealand flight we were laid as usual by some locals. Afterward, we proceeded to the transit lounge on our way to hang out for about an hour before catching our early evening flight to LOS ANGELES!!!!!!!!!!!!!!!

How wacky was all of this. It must have taken many hours of phone calls by Tony in his Sydney hotel room to get this itinerary sorted. And, where would our luggage finish up? Would we ever see it again? It looked like the definite result had to be breakfast in Brisbane, dinner in Los Angeles, baggage in Bombay, but we were mostly to be surprised.

Talking of hanging out in airport transit lounges, there was the famous interview with Charlie Watts from the Rolling Stones in the mid-nineties, where he was asked by a reporter "What it had been like playing in the Rolling Stones for 30 years?"

His reply being, "Five years of playing and 25 years of hanging about."

There was never a truer sentence summing up the touring experience.

An hour later, we were taking off for our six hour flight to Los Angeles. Trying to make sense of my flight ticket I realized we only had another hour to wait at LAX before we would be on the late evening British Airways flight to London.

By this time, I was actually feeling physically okay. We had been through three time zones and I had been asleep and awake on and off. It didn't really matter whether it was breakfast or dinner time because I had a large vodka.

The flight, landing and passage through LAX passed off without a hitch. We were sat on the BA 747 on the tarmac at LAX waiting for take-off. There was a certain party atmosphere in the air tinged with much inane gibbering from most people. And, as we took off and the bar opened, I decided two or three hours of heavy drinking was probably the way to go, followed by eight hours sleep before we got to Heathrow. I don't think it quite worked out like that from my very vague memory. I think I was probably asleep within an hour of taking off.

Arrival at Heathrow airport in London was treated as some sort of huge victory. A huge cheer with sighs of relief went up from the whole entourage as we hit the tarmac. It was as if we had been given a military logistics exercise to navigate our way from Australia to England on a route that nobody would have guessed we would have taken. It was nearly over as we disembarked and headed for Immigration and Customs.

I thought if any one of these spooks working for Customs and Excise says more than two words to me, he's going to get the sharp end of my tongue, after what we had been through.

We were home and through immigration without a second look and headed in trepidation to Baggage Claim. This was going to be interesting. As always, at Heathrow Airport you could literally spend half of your life waiting for your bags to come off the airplane. This time was no exception, but amazingly only one piece of baggage was lost and I believe that was returned to its owner the next day.

So that was it, forty-two hours in total from Sydney to London, the worst journey of a few worst journeys I had ever done (I think?).

Chapter Four

THE FIRST WORST JOURNEY

This first worst journey was unfortunately all my own fault. I was just being greedy, although I would sooner think of it as, "Making hay while the sun shone."

An old lag called Ian Horne, who had mixed the sound for Paul McCartney's very successful '70s band (Wings), was a pretty well-respected sound engineer. He was doing the mix for the then "new" UK skinhead band, Madness. They were becoming really successful in the UK and I was doing the onstage monitor mix. We were scheduled to do this six-week tour of the UK with Madness. We had just finished eight weeks around Europe with Ian Dury and The Blockheads, which was another of Ian's clients Ian got me in to do the monitor mix for.

It was the fall (autumn) of 1981. I was getting lots of work and making good money; Ian Dury was also due to go off to Australia on a very lucrative three week tour and obviously wanted Ian Horne and I to go along to do the sound. No problem there. I had never been to Australia, so it all sounded pretty cool. The money they were offering was outrageous; it was nearly three times more than I had ever been paid before. It would be the last tour I did before Christmas that year, so it looked as if my girlfriend

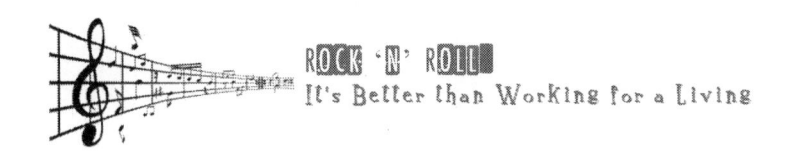

Salli and I would have a very merry Christmas. I actually got paid enough to buy her a £750 silver fox fur coat for Christmas, which was quite a lot of money in 1981.

In the euphoria of having all this work and making all this money over the next two months, one problem loomed on the horizon. The last show of the Madness tour was at the Dominion Theatre in London on a Tuesday. The first day of Ian Dury's Australian tour was on the Thursday, the same week!

Now, both Ian Horne and I decided we could do this, even though we might have a bit of jet lag at the first gig, but we could do it. A BIT OF JET LAG!!!!!!!!!

Ian Dury and the band had gone out to Australia a week before the first gig. And, you really do need that long after what was a 24-hour flight, but Ian Horne and I were convinced we would be okay. We realized a few days before the last Madness gig that when we left on the Wednesday morning we would actually arrive at 7:30 a.m. the day of the first gig in Australia!

We had committed. After getting home at about midnight from the last Madness gig, we were at Heathrow Airport at 10:00 a.m. the next morning. This was to be a journey of a lifetime, if we lived through it.

As we got on the plane, Ian said to me, "Don't worry, I've got a gram of Racket (cocaine) for the journey." I wasn't sure if a gram of cocaine was really what was needed for a twenty-four hour flight to Australia. I now know it definitely wasn't. Still . . . we had to make the best of a bad situation, so off we went.

Chapter Five

MAYBE THE LAST WORST JOURNEY

In 1991, I was working in the US with American hip hop band Color Me Badd, who was quite a nice bunch of young guys. They brought out a couple of pretty iffy singles but were starting to make some good money. They got themselves a good support act slot on Paula Abdul's big nationwide tour of 1990/91.

I managed to make a deal with their management, as they were looking for an experienced sound engineer. I stayed for 18 months, doing the Paula Abdul tour with them, and also some of their own shows. It was an easy job and I was making excellent money.

We came to the last show before Christmas 1991, which was at the Desert Sky Pavilion--in the desert. Obviously, just outside of Phoenix, Arizona, it was *hot*, even at the end of December. This being the last show before Christmas on the 22nd of December everyone was making arrangements to leave after the show or the next day to fly home, which included various parts of the US and of course, me, back to the UK.

Luckily, with Color Me Badd being the support act, they were off stage at 8:30 p.m.; so I was able to get a flight after the show. Trying to fly anywhere in the US three days before Christmas is an absolute nightmare. It is as if the whole of the population has decided to go somewhere else for Christmas and is passing through the same airport as you.

I actually left Desert Sky Pavilion at 8:35 p.m. It was exactly five minutes since the band had played the last chord of *I Wanna Sex You Up*, whatever that means (Well, you could probably take a wild guess.).

I had a cab waiting outside of the stage door. So . . . I was off and it was only a fifteen-minute drive to the airport if I could keep the driver driving, instead of talking about his relations in England. I find it very strange that every American cab driver has relations that live in England. Even the Mexican cab drivers in Los Angeles do or else they're just making conversation. With a 10:30 p.m. flight to New York via Las Vegas, I would arrive at the JFK airport in plenty of time for a morning flight to London. WRONG!

The departure lounge at Phoenix Sky Harbor airport resembled a crowd scene from the movie, *The Ten Commandments*. It was complete with priests, beggars and prostitutes.

When I, at last, managed to get my baggage checked in, I had to run like hell to get to the departure gate in time. In time, that was, to wait for another one-and-a-half hours before we embarked and eventually got off the ground. Of course, all this meant that unless this very aged Boeing 727 hit Mach 3 over Tucson, I was going to miss my connecting flight from Vegas.

I needn't have worried; Las Vegas International Airport was more like Super Bowl Sunday. I had never seen so many people in an airport at the same time. I hurried to check out the departure screens. The Vegas-to-New York flight was delayed by two hours, which didn't come as any great surprise. I had made it with half an hour to spare without the delay. Even with these delays, I would still catch my flight to London.

What I was to find was that the American airline system had not finished with me yet. As I made my way down the endless moving walkways, I noticed on the departure screens another hour had been tagged on to the departure time of the New York flight I was booked on. I decided then and there that the cocktail lounge was going to be my next destination. This was now getting depressing.

Three large Jack Daniels later and I felt much better. I became invigorated by the thought of boarding the aircraft and actually being on my way again. I think this euphoria lasted roughly ten minutes. In fact, until the massed horde of fellow eastbound travelers and I, were informed the in-bound flight which was to become our outbound flight to New York had still not arrived from Los Angeles. This meant at least another hour delay; so it was now four fucking hours and counting!

As luck would have it, the plane arrived shortly after the announcement. Personally, I think it had been parked around the corner all the time waiting for the announcement. We did, at last, get to board our flight, but this was by no means the end of the nightmare. It was another good half hour before the mighty Rolls Royce engines roared and we sped down the runway hopefully heading for the stratosphere.

One of the reasons for our last delay had been because of all the American airlines' favorite trick for not losing any revenue due to "no show" passengers and that is overbooking aircraft seats. This over-sell trick is now used by almost every airline in the world, except JAL and all Nippon Airways who are much too honorable to sell a seat twice.

ROCK 'N' ROLL
It's Better than Working for a Living

This practice started in America, and surprisingly, this hit-and-miss method of filling an aircraft works pretty smoothly 99% of the time. And, if there are a few too many passengers on a particular flight, they are offered various incentives by the airline to catch the next flight.

I've seen these incentives vary from 200 dollars and an overnight stay in a 4-star hotel to 750 dollars and a return flight to anywhere in the continental US. This night, everybody and his nearest relations were flying, and it was Christmas and they all wanted on this flight.

The ensuing thirty minutes were like a cross between some bizarre marketing ploy by the airline and an auction. Offers were made and rejected. Then re-offered and re-rejected. If I recall, the only offer that wasn't made was an all expenses two week holiday in Tahiti with a supermodel.

Finally, four hours and thirty minutes late, we left Vegas for New York. I was now in grave danger of missing my flight to London and was having horrific thoughts of having to spend Christmas on my own in New York.

I did miss my flight, by ten minutes. New York ground staffs were supposed to inform British Airways I was inbound from Vegas for B.A. to hold the flight. However, B.A. was never informed so they didn't. It left on time, probably the only fucking flight that day to leave American soil on time! Murphy's bloody law again, and thank you, New York, and up yours!

I was calmed down by the "angels" of the B.A. ground crew. They were really efficient and impressive and found me a seat on the 7:30 p.m. flight that evening. It was the last seat and the last flight!

I went to the bar. I was going to be home for Christmas; just the flight was late, of course!

Chapter Six

1975

After the euphoria and the hedonism of the Alvin Stardust job, 1975 was to turn into a bit of a disappointment with regard to my career as a sound engineer. Not that I even regarded it as a career yet. It was great fun doing a job other guys envied, even though I hadn't a clue about the job three years ago. It was much better than working for a living and the next couple of years shaped the rest of my life.

I had managed to get work with this small sound company that was picking up quite a lot of work. They did gigs and small tours with the likes of John Cale (what a weirdo) and Nico who previously had played a treadle sewing machine in '60s New York cult band Velvet Underground.

It was in fact a harmonium she used to play, but it looked like a 1930s sewing machine. It even sounded like one on some songs--but no matter. None of it could hide the fact this woman had the biggest feet on any woman I had ever seen, they were enormous!

Both these Artistes had in fact been in Velvet Underground. Quite frankly, both of them were a few miles short of a freeway. This was a band that was one of David Bowie's favorite bands in the '60s. Who himself, at times, has had various run-ins with sanity, I believe.

ROCK 'N' ROLL
It's Better than Working for a Living

I did, in fact, a couple of years later, do a tour with yet another member of the infamous Velvet Underground. This guy was a little more manic than the other two aforementioned members of the band. This was a guy called Lou Reed.

Most of these bands came out of New York in the '60s, '70s and even up to the present day were not like their counterparts on the West Coast. Their music was mainly fuelled by Acid (LSD). The New York bands' music was mainly fuelled (If such a word can be used for what this drug does to you.) by Smack (heroin) as one of the Velvet Underground's songs points out, which is rather catchy-named *Heroin*.

Lou Reed was slightly different in his tastes than the others in the band, in that he was a speed freak. He enjoyed Smack and speed together. I cannot really imagine how that makes you feel, although my girlfriend and I used to do downers (barbiturates) and speed together, which had quite interesting affects. You didn't so much get high, as sideways. I can recommend it as an interesting way to get through a boring weekend.

One of the problems with touring with Lou Reed in the late '70s was that he was going through his intravenous Methedrine (speed) phase. This meant before he went on stage every night he would inject himself with a large amount of Methedrine and then bounce about intensely on stage for about one and a half hours.

I thought it was a pretty good show. I liked his songs and I thought it was a good set the first time I saw it. BUT he would come back and do an encore for about another one-and-a-half to two hours every night; obviously after being back in the dressing room pumping himself with another armful of Methedrine.

The punters loved it. The crew hated it. We were doing outdoor shows around the South of France, which would start in beautiful, hot sunshine about 6:30 p.m. and end in the freezing cold about 10:30 p.m. The band was dead on their feet every night, as nobody gave them or me any Methedrine!

It was strange how Lou's career went after those manic times. He disappeared in the '80s to reappear as what you would call a respectable artist in the '90s with the re-release of his '70s song *Perfect Day*. It was even taken up by the BBC in the UK in 1997 for a day of nationwide charity fund raising. Funny old world, isn't it?

Around 1975 and into 1976, I had also done gigs with Ronnie Lane from the British '60s band the Small Faces. They later became The Faces and teamed up with Rod Stewart. These were Ronnie Lane's gigs with his own band after he left The Faces resulting in two shows in a circus tent on Clapham Common, South London.

When I was delivering some pieces of equipment in the afternoon and just walking out of the tent, this chick grabbed me. She dragged me under the raised seating at the back of the tent and proceeded to take off her clothes after dragging down my jeans.

I won't go into lurid detail of what happened next, but it turns out that she was the bass player's girlfriend and had just got bored and drunk I think. During the sound check she spotted me and said I looked like a nice guy so came over to talk to me. Well, I don't remember much talking going on, but it was quite a pleasant afternoon.

One of the first gigs I went out on as crew chief and FOH sound engineer was with a new British band called Pilot. The company sent me out with a guy called Pete Rush, a monster of a man--6'7" tall, 270 pounds. He didn't know much about the sound business--mind you, neither did I--but he was a really good worker. He took huge amounts of speed. You'll hear more of him, later.

Pilot was doing a few promotional gigs, as they had never done any live gigs before. The first of these was in a weird little town in the West of England called Warminster. Pete and I loaded the truck in the morning and set off for Warminster about 11:30 a.m. By the time we got to the gig, it was about 2:00 p.m., which gave us plenty of time to set up the system before the band arrived. As we were unloading the truck I was getting a little concerned as I hadn't seen the multicore cable come off of the truck. The multicore is where all the mics are plugged in at the stage end to plug into the mixing console out in the audience. As the truck was emptied, it hit me: "Fuck me!" I'd forgotten the multicore.

Going back to London to pick it up was not an option; it was over 100 miles. Calling the company to ask someone to bring it out to us was going to be really embarrassing and would probably get me fired, but it was the only choice.

I was just going off to look for a pay phone when the band's roadies appeared and told us the gig may be cancelled as one of the band was ill or had broken his leg or something. I can't exactly remember what it was now, but thirty minutes later the tour manager called and told us the gig had been cancelled.

The next day, we unloaded the truck at the warehouse and made no mention of the missing multicore. We just mentioned we were really pissed off because the gig had been cancelled. I had gotten away with it, maybe my first big mistake in the business and I had gotten away with it.

Strangely enough, I never did anymore gigs with Pilot, so maybe someone did *suss* my mistake and didn't mention it.

Afterwards, I did a couple of small tours with a much-respected singer/songwriter called Roy Harper. He was a really nice guy, but one of the most boring songwriters ever. Roy was very much in demand on the University circuit in the 1970s. The massed throngs of future scientists, doctors and politicians would listen for hours to his rambling songs of social commentary. Ten minutes was enough for me, but my mate Paul had to sit there for hour after hour mixing the stuff.

One thing that really annoyed me about Roy Harper was that after the last song and the endless encores, he would go off stage. Then, ten minutes later, he would come out of his dressing room and sit on the edge of the stage. Generally, he got in the way of the derig to sign autographs. And there would always be a crowd of the more intellectual element of the audience left who were interested in what Roy had to say about the current social issues. His general outlook on the world and what his songs actually meant. What his songs actually meant was that he was getting a big fat pay check every night and they were paying it!

There was one standout gig I remember that I did with Roy, and that was an outdoor show on the grounds of Oystermouth Castle on the Gower Peninsula in South Wales. It was a beautiful place for a gig. It was a lovely hot summer's day and there were some excellent local Welsh bands on during the day.

Paul and I were primarily there to do the Roy Harper gig. Roy didn't go on until 7:30 p.m. so we had all day to kill. Having been there since 9:00 a.m., by late afternoon I was getting somewhat wasted. I had tried out many of the excellent local brews on offer and even bumped into another crew guy who I knew who had some speed. So, after partaking of some of his excellent white powder, I headed over to the backstage bar to top up my drink, which I must have done many times in the following hours.

ROCK 'N' ROLL
It's Better than Working for a Living

I remember talking to a very pretty, young, blonde Welsh girl for quite a long while. I couldn't understand a fucking word she was saying, but that didn't matter. The next thing I can remember was that we were in a cornfield and I could hear the music, but there were no other people around. The blonde was naked and I had my jeans around my ankles. It was such a beautiful sunny day, I could not think of anywhere else I would have like to have been.

Then, all too soon, I heard someone calling my name. My sound buddy Paul appeared and frantically dragged me away from the vision in the cornfield shouting, "Hurry up Roy's going on stage!" I hurriedly dressed myself and made for the stage turning once to see my naked nymph still lying in the cornfield. That was the last I saw of her.

I made it back for the start of the gig, which was the usual boring stuff. At the end of the show I went looking for my naked nymph, but she'd disappeared. She obviously got bored and headed off looking for another conquest. What a beautiful day, what a sweet girl. If you're out there, you made my day, one of the nicest days I have ever had whilst being in the business.

I did actually meet Mr. Harper again, about two years ago on a gig I was doing at the Shepherds Bush Empire in London. I mentioned to him that I had done some tours with him in the '70s, working with an engineer called Paul Weston, at which Roy said, "I thought your face was familiar to me."

It was then I remembered that Paul Weston, the guy I had been working with, had moved in with Roy's wife while Roy was away on an American tour. As far as I know, he was still there in Roy's house in Brighton on the South coast thirty-three years later! Whoops!

MICK (MICHAEL) TYAS

Another rather boring job I undertook was as a keyboard roadie with British keyboard player Dave Greenslade at the end of 1975. Now, what I knew about keyboards you can write on the head of a pin. Somehow I managed to talk my way into the gig and it did have its advantages. The biggest one being I was able to take the band's truck home still loaded with all their equipment to use it as my personal transport.

All the roadies at that time used to hang out at a pub in Fulham, London, called the Greyhound. On a good night you would see a dozen seven and one-half ton trucks outside. You really were among the elite if you worked for a band, and you had the truck all the time. It doesn't sound it now, but you were cool if you did. And, you could really pull the chicks if you were that cool.

I had a nice little harem of chicks in the Greyhound, at the time. There was Sophie, who I think was in love. I don't think I was ready for love, which is probably why I dumped her. She later moved to South Africa.

There was Panstick Sharon, who was a real man eater. She had the biggest tits I had ever seen. There was a little blonde American girl called Roz, who had just arrived in this country. She talked incessantly, took lots of speed, and made lots of friends. She was good fun and is still in London, and we're still friends. The Greyhound was also where I met Salli Jane and Salli crops up throughout this saga.

Around this time, I also got some work with a funny little British band called Stackridge. This was mainly because the keyboard player was also in the band Greenslade I also worked for.

ROCK 'N' ROLL
It's Better than Working for a Living

I remember one particular gig with this band. It was possibly because I have never been so fucked up on the morning of a gig. I needed another sound guy to work with on these gigs, so I gave Frank (from my Alvin Stardust days) a call and asked him if he wanted some work. He agreed to come and do the gigs with me.

My girlfriend Salli and I were going through one of our extremely crazy periods. She was taking as many drugs as possible of differing varieties all at the same time, which was not clever, but it seemed to have the desired effect. One evening, we really got whacked out on booze, speed and downers. By seven in the morning we were still bouncing off walls and anything else in sight.

It was about that time, I realized I had a gig to do that day with Stackridge in Bristol about 80 miles from London. I was to pick up Frank at about 10:00 a.m. in North London. Salli and I were both high as kites. Still, I made an attempt to get myself together, which turned out to be virtually impossible. Two or so hours later I realized we were both still blind drunk. I thought a shower might help, and then we did our last line of speed. I called Frank to tell him we were going to be late and that we would be setting off in about half an hour. Salli was going to come with me.

I asked Frank if he knew anyone who had any speed, as I thought that was going to be the only thing that would get me through the day. He did! How the fuck I drove through London up to Frank's house I will never know. All Salli and I could do was laugh all the way there. We got to Frank's house about 12:30 p.m. I was two-and-a-half hours late and he opened the door and looked at us and said, "What the fuck have you two been doing? Have you seen the state of yourselves?"

"Right, let's go get these fucking pills, you need help," he said. We got a bag full of "blueys" (I believe their pharmaceutical name was Duromin and they were slimming pills) and I took two straight off. Then we set off for Bristol. By the time we got to the freeway, the pills had set me buzzing again and I was just laughing and talking constantly. I remember at one point in the journey, I kept lifting Salli's top up and Salli would wave her tits at cars passing in the opposite direction.

As you can probably deduce from those actions, we were still in trouble. Frank's face showed concern as he gave me another couple of pills. By about halfway through the journey I had calmed down a little when Frank said, "Fuck me, there's the band."

The band had just passed us in their car on the way to the 4:00 p.m. sound check, and it was 2:30 p.m. and we weren't even at the gig yet. We just waved and pointed at the truck, breakdown!!!

We arrived at the gig about 4pm and the band were there waiting for us. "Yeah, we had a really bad breakdown!" I'm not convinced they ever believed us, looking at the state of us, but after a few more pills we got through a sound check.

What the fuck it sounded like, I have no idea. After I lay on a bench in the dressing room I must have passed out because Frank had to come and wake me up at 8:00 p.m. as the band were going on stage. And, what the show sounded like, once again I have no fucking idea.

It was over and we loaded the truck and drove back to London almost in silence, I dropped Frank at his house and as he got out, he gave me a look that said, "Boy, you were fucking lucky today!"

By the time 1976 came around, I was getting some better work, mainly from a couple of former Emerson, Lake and Palmer roadies who had formed their own sound company. And, 1976 turned out to be a really busy year for me doing gigs and tours

ROCK 'N' ROLL
It's Better than Working for a Living

with Dr. Feelgood, Irish blues guitarist Rory Gallagher, a lovely girl singer called Elkie Brooks, '60s British rockers The Pretty Things and one of the nicest bunch of people I have ever worked with, AC/DC.

Dr. Feelgood was a good old English Rock 'n' Roll band that came out of the British pub rock scene of the mid '70s; they were hard drinking, hard playing, and spawned a strange guitarist called Wilco Johnson. He later went off to form his own band. There are two classic stories about the Dr. Feelgood tour that I remember.

In Paris, we were all taken out to dinner by the local promoter on a night off before the gig. After the dinner, most of the band and crew decided to carry on drinking down in the Monmartre district where many of the bars are open till dawn. One person who didn't come with us was the bass player called Sparko. He'd decided to go off on his own down the Pigalle area or somewhere else to find some Sparko style of entertainment.

The next day when everyone was suffering with the ugliest hangovers you could ever imagine, someone asks Sparko where he "ended up last night." He told us he spent most of it in a club specializing in "mutant sex shows." Feeling pretty ill already, what he described made me dash for the nearest toilette. Apparently, Sparko had a desire for mutant women. He liked ones with one leg, ones with no legs, and ones with three heads. . It didn't matter, the weirder the better. Well, whatever gets you through the night!

The opening act on the tour was an American band called the George Hatcher Band. It was their first time in Europe, maybe the first time out of Carolina. Once again a night off before the gig somewhere in France, a few of the crew and the guys from the George Hatcher Band were sitting drinking in the hotel bar.

There were a few locals in, also. George decided to go and chat to this French girl at the bar and boy, did his Southern drawl do the trick! Within 15 minutes, George was dragging the girl up the stairs toward his hotel room! We were all sitting there suitably impressed with George's technique and commenting what a good looking chick she was as well, when the Irish lighting director, Peter, who we guessed was a bit of an expert in these matters said, "That's a guy!"

Although knowing the French were very good at that sort of behavior, none of us really believed it. She was very pretty. Within minutes George came screaming down the stairs yelling, "She's got fucking balls!"

I should laugh!!!!

All will be revealed later!

The Rory Gallagher tour I did in Ireland in 1977 was my first experience of ever coming face-to-face with a firearm. That is, apart from a BB gun someone once pointed at me when we were playing Cowboys and Indians in the woods around my home when I was about nine years old. Fucking hell! Nothing changes very much does it? Except they probably play Cowboys and Indians with machetes and real guns now.

Rory Gallagher was a lovely guy, an alcoholic and an excellent guitar player. We were staying in a hotel called the Greenan Lodge Hotel, which was a quiet little hotel in West Belfast. Belfast, at the time, was in the middle of some of the worst violence in the conflict in Northern Ireland, in years, with the British Army on the streets of the city.

ROCK 'N' ROLL
It's Better than Working for a Living

We were once again sitting in a hotel bar with members of the band and crew and a few locals, when we heard what we thought was machine gun fire.

"Fuck me, what was that?" one of our guys shouted.

"Sounded like machine gun fire," one of the locals had replied . . . "Nothing to worry about, just one of the boys having a bit of a go."

I could never work out who was on whose side that night. Were "the boys" on the locals' side or on the other side, and in that case, which side were we on? I'd have preferred to be on "the boys's" side, if they had fucking machine guns!

Being a somewhat sensitive subject, I decided it was probably a good idea not to pursue that particular question and have another drink instead. The hotel suffered serious damage when it was blown up by the IRA in 1981. I guess "the boys" weren't on our side that night or the locals' side, or maybe they were! Who fucking knows?

Not content with one scary incident in twenty-four hours, we proceeded to get ourselves into another one. After a rather nervy gig at the Ulster Hall in Belfast . . . the crew were nervy anyway as we were all English. The English were not 100% popular with all people in Belfast at the time; and possibly not popular with "the boys."

After the show, one of our crew offered this pretty chick a ride home in our van on our way to our hotel. He hoped to get her to come to the hotel I think, but she insisted on being taken home. So . . . off we went to drop her off at home.

I didn't feel particularly comfortable with this--driving around the very dark streets of Belfast in the middle of the night--but no one else seemed worried. I kept my mouth shut in case everyone started feeling as paranoid as I felt.

We turned off the main Falls Road, which was a hard line Republican (The ones that don't like the English.) area, into scary dark streets of bombed out houses. Our guide then told us we could drop her on the next street corner, which was really in the middle of a bomb site with just a few lights in occupied houses. She gave us instructions to get back to the main road and the way to our hotel, which sounded like an amazingly complicated route.

We decided to get out of the area as quick as possible as it was not the place for a bunch of English guys to be driving around in a van in the middle of the night. Then we got lost!!! This was not good!

We eventually found our way out of the housing estate onto a pretty well-lit main road, but now well and truly lost. We saw ahead of us three British soldiers on duty on a street corner.

"Ask those soldiers the way to the hotel," someone suggested. We pulled up to the kerb behind the three soldiers. "Which way to the Greenan Lodge Hotel mate?" someone shouted to them. Wrong! Very fucking wrong!

Three HK33 assault rifles were immediately pointing straight at us and could have taken us all out with one burst. "Don't ever fucking do that again you stupid fucking cunts; now get the fuck out of here as quick as possible." Which I thought was a little bit of an overreaction on their part at the time, but some people in that country made it their job to kill as many British soldiers as possible, so I guess they had just cause to be jumpy.

I'm still suspicious of the pretty chick from the gig that we gave a ride home to. I think she may have been a Republican plant to take these "British infidels" into the heart of Republican territory and get them lost and then maybe "the boys" would find us and make us disappear!!!

ROCK 'N' ROLL
It's Better than Working for a Living

Or maybe she just wanted a lift home!

I believe my favorite people in the Rock 'n' Roll industry was AC/DC; I did a tour with them in 1977. I was still pretty new at that time and they'd been around since about 1973 also - so we had about the same amount of experience. The tour I did was mainly a tour of universities and old dance halls in the UK. What a whole load of fun it turned out to be. The band at that time consisted of the founder members, the Young brothers, Malcolm and Angus; Mark Evans on bass; Phil Rudd on drums; and one of the greatest guys in the business, Bon Scott on vocals.

We were doing a gig at a horrible little club in Plymouth in the West of England called Van Dyke's. After the show, whilst we were de-rigging the equipment, the promoter made the big mistake of paying our local crew before we'd finished the load out. Of course, as soon as they'd been paid, they left. In doing so, they left us with two flights of stairs to carry all the equipment down between the five of us. This, of course, was taking forever and I think there were three local security guys left behind to make certain we didn't steal anything. They were also in a hurry to get home. They began to threaten us with physical violence if we didn't hurry up and finish the load out, which wasn't very pleasant until drummer Phil showed up back at the gig. Apparently, he'd left his camera behind in the dressing room and quickly discovered it in the possession of one of these local gorillas, so the conversation went thus: "Weren't considering stealing that fucking camera there pal, were you? Because if you were, I'll break every bone in your fucking body; and . . . what's all this about threatening these guys? They're just trying to do their job, so if any of you come near them, I'll take you all out."

Phil was about 5'8" and about 140 pounds. These three jokers were each about 6'4" and 300 pounds, but they hadn't had the training Phil had in the back streets of Melbourne; also various Oriental fighting academies. Phil stayed behind until we had finished the load out and not one of those gorillas came near us. What a guy!

All of AC/DC were pretty tough guys. Angus and Malcolm were no wimps. Singer Bon Scott, who had originally been their driver, had a list of minor convictions in Australia and had been refused entry into the Australian army for being "socially mal-adjusted." He had even worked in a brothel as a "bouncer." You probably won't be surprised to hear that some of his salary was paid in sampling the delights of the goods on offer.

Although these people put forward a very hard image, they were some of the nicest people I have ever met in the business. They would share with you anything they had.

This brings me to another evening in a hotel somewhere, which may have been Southampton on the south coast of England. We were not traveling in crew buses and doing overnight drives to the next gig. Instead, we were staying in hotels, which unfortunately made for long days and early mornings. We must have gotten back to the hotel at about 1:00 a.m. and probably had to be up again at about 8:00 a.m. to drive to the next gig.

I had a single hotel room to myself, which was very rare. To keep costs down on a tour you usually had to share a twin room with another one of the crew. But because there was an odd number of us, you got a single room every fifth day. I was just going to bed about at 2:00 a.m., when there was a knock on the door. I opened it, surprised to see Bon standing there.

"Hi Bon, I was just going to bed."

"Would you fancy a quick one before you do?" and he held up a bottle of vodka and a small white wrap, which as I feared contained a gram of coke. Now, you do not have a "quick one" with a bottle of Vodka and a gram of coke. Thinking sensibly, of course, I should have graciously declined his offer, but when a guy like Bon turns up at your door and wants to share it with you, you can't help but want to keep him company. He was that nice a guy, so we talked and we talked and we talked.

I think Bon left at about 6:00 a.m. I was totally fucked up, but happy. I was going be a terrible mess the next day or the same day or whatever fucking day it was, but it really didn't matter. That night, I got to know one of the nicest people in the Rock 'n' Roll business.

Bon Scott died on February 19th, 1980 in East Dulwich, London, after a night of partying. The band was at their zenith, their last album with Bon; *Highway to Hell* was huge all over the world and it now seems a fitting testament to a lovely guy. The official coroner's report stated that he simply "Drank himself to death." I prefer to think that he "Partied himself to death." That was the way Bon did things.

As Angus Young was quoted as saying when he heard of Bon's death. ". . . if there was a town out there, he painted it and if he missed one, he went back again." There is a piece of film exists made by the BBC at an AC/DC gig at a university somewhere on that tour, which has Bon and myself in the same shot. That is one of my prize possessions.

R.I.P. mate!

MICK (MICHAEL) TYAS

The end of 1976 was really the end of my apprenticeship. I'd had my fun, but now I thought I was a good enough sound engineer to mix it with the big boys, and I was. There were still lots more fun to come and also some pretty tough times.

Chapter Seven

1977

This six year period is really where I came of age in the business and I also did a hell of a lot of work. I suppose I was doing on average about six tours a year, these were all European tours. I hadn't yet achieved the Holy Grail of touring and done an American tour as yet. This left me feeling maybe a little in adequate or even naive when out socially with other roadies and engineers. This was especially true at The Golden Lion pub on Fulham Broadway in London, which was infamous as the preferred drinking hole for these people, which I was introduced into by my then permanent girlfriend, Salli Jane.

I met Salli Jane when she was a 21 year old girl from the sticks, bathing in the bright lights of London Town. She was slowly and ever so surely heading for the depths of despair that drink and barbiturate use can take you into. What I didn't know at the time was that Salli was such a strong person and could beat those things. She re-invented herself and had now emerged as a flourishing flower and life and soul of the party in the Golden Lion.

If you work it out that it was usually taking on average about six weeks to do a European tour. I was away from home about 36 to 40 weeks a year, which obviously in the coming years was going to put a huge strain on my personal relationship with Salli Jane. So, it was to be for the next twenty years and we both made lots of mistakes, but we had never lived this life before so we just didn't know.

Now here is a wonderful idea!

You should get a trial run at life before you actually have to live it. A little like downloading software for your computer, where you get a thirty day free trial of the software with not all the functions available to you, and then you decide if you want to buy the full version with all the functions working. It would probably have to be a little longer than thirty days with life though.

You could start at say twenty years of age.

Be able to choose your sex.

Be able to choose your girlfriend or boyfriend.

Decide whether you had a job or not.

Decide whether you had a drug habit or not.

Pick your own personality, etc.

Then see what you can make of that lot!

If it didn't work out too well, you could then decide not to buy and go back to the beginning and choose not to have a life or be born normally or, buy the whole package if it was working well and start from the beginning and live the life.

I think the rules need a little tinkering with yet,

BUT!

Fuck me! I think I've just invented a new video game!

Or, is it Monopoly with a twist?

The tour I did in February 1977 with Canadian rock band Rush was the first tour I had been on where we had a sleeper bus or crew bus for overnight journeys between gigs. These were a new concept in the UK, but with the onset of bands having more and more equipment, it was getting logistically impossible to have enough time in a twenty-four hour period to rig, do the show, de-rig and get a night's sleep in a hotel and then drive to the next show, so why not have a moving hotel and wake up at the gig?

I was on the Rush tour as I had just got a job with a London sound company called TFA Electrosound. They were providing sound equipment for Rod Stewart, Paul McCartney, Bob Marley, Tom Petty, Kiss, Aerosmith, Abba and countless other worldwide acts. I also had premises in Los Angeles, so for me this was a huge step up in the right direction.

When we started this tour on the bus, I didn't know that buses existed with bunks and toilets and kitchens in them. They'd been using them in the US for many years, obviously because of the huge distances you can travel by road. The most famous of these were the Silver Eagles, which was a design dating from the 1950's. These are now becoming collectors' pieces.

Unfortunately, we didn't have a Silver Eagle; ours was more of a Rubber Chicken. It was nice and new. It was also actually an executive bus with the tables removed and little stools put in the middle of the two sets of opposing seats to make a "couchette," where if you laid next to your friend you could spread across the two seats. It did have tea and coffee and a small portaloo in a cubicle at the back. It didn't really work as you still had to have a hotel, you couldn't really spend every night on your "couchette" and the idea of a sleeper bus is to cut out hotels on back to back gigs, so it was hopeless. Sleeper buses now of course are fitted with every conceivable high tech gadget including GPS systems, satellite TV, Internet and etc.

ROCK 'N' ROLL
It's Better than Working for a Living

There *was a bus back in 1981* in the UK that was like the American ones. It was even better than some, well, better than many of them. It was BRITISH, not American. It was owned by a company called Edwin Shirley Trucking, who were the original and biggest Rock 'n' Roll trucking company in Europe. The bus didn't have GPS or satellite TV or Internet, because they hadn't been invented yet, but it was very luxurious and huge inside. There was a front lounge, a back lounge, separate Hi Fi and TV, video and game consoles. It was the same for the "good" American buses. It had twelve really big bunks in a separate bedroom area, a kitchen, microwave oven, toilet and washroom. They had something extra, I still cannot recall seeing on any other sleeper bus to this day, and that was a separate shower! I knew they had showers and tubs in mobile homes, *Why not on a bus?*

We had this bus on the Weather Report tour in 1981. I was itching to try out the shower whilst doing 70mph down the freeway. The driver said nobody had actually done this on the bus as far as he knew but couldn't see a reason why you couldn't as long as the water tank was full. I must say in retrospect, he didn't seem overly enthusiastic about the idea, and after I had actually taken a shower I can't really blame him.

We were driving after the gig, which was somewhere in Italy, and after a few beers I decided I would take a shower. I went in the shower cubicle, took off my robe and turned on the shower. It was fantastic! It was really powerful and better than my shower at home. You did have to brace yourself every so often as the bus took a bend, but it was cool as long as you held on tight.

Why don't they have showers on airplanes? In First Class at least, it would be perfect after a twenty-two hour flight to Australia, especially considering the amount of cash it costs to fly First Class. The answer probably lies in the next couple of lines.

MICK (MICHAEL) TYAS

About five minutes into my shower at 70mph there was a banging on the door and a voice shouting . . . "Mick turn off that fucking shower quick."

It sounded as if there was a bit of panic outside so I turned off the shower and opened the door. I was just in time to see little waves of water sloshing up and down the center aisle of the bus.

All the carpets were soaked and water was running down the couple of steps into the driver's cabin. He had quickly pulled to a halt in a service area.

The driver was a really nice guy. Anyone else in that situation would have gone crazy as I had just ruined the carpets in his brand new bus. We all agreed there was a slight design flaw in the shower system that really did not allow for using the shower at 70mph. Because it was a regular domestic shower tray and the shower was powerful, there was too much water sitting in the tray. It began sloshing over the edges and into the bus as it cornered. The drain couldn't handle the amount of water. The problem could have been solved by fitting better drainage and cutting down the water pressure but we really didn't want to fuck with his bus anymore. The carpets all dried out after a couple of days without any real damage. We resolved to only use the shower whilst we were stationary.

Taking into account the Rush tour was my first really big tour it was surprisingly uneventful. It was pretty hard work as we had more sound equipment than I had ever worked with before as we were doing much larger gigs than I had ever done before.

One show that does stand out to me, as this was probably the largest gig I had ever done in my career and that was in a place called The Bingley Hall in the Midlands in the UK. Hall stands in the middle of the County Showground and if I remember had a

ROCK 'N' ROLL
It's Better than Working for a Living

capacity of around 5000 people and it was a barn! Literally! They called it an exhibition hall, which was slightly embellishing the facts a little here. It was, in fact, used mainly as an indoor cattle market, as one could deduce by the overpowering smell of cow shit.

I also don't think I have ever been so cold at a gig. It was even cold in the middle of summer. No point in putting heating in for the cows, the place would just smell even worse. Ah! The glamour of Rock 'n' Roll.

Speaking of cow sheds, it wasn't the biggest cowshed I had ever been in. The biggest is in San Francisco, it is called The Cow Palace. Luckily its name does give you prior warning of what you are about to experience. Unfortunately, if you do a gig there just after a rodeo or a "cow show" or whatever they have for cows, it smells like shit, lots of shit!

The Cow Palace holds 15000 people (and 3000 cows). It is huge. And, it has been a Rock 'n' Roll venue since the early 1960's when The Beatles and The Rolling Stones were the first big acts in there. Since then everybody has played there. I think I did it with Iron Maiden a couple of times, Motley Crue and Kiss. It's regarded as a very prestigious gig, along with Madison Square Gardens and Long Beach Arena.

Back in the UK, Bingley Hall was also a prestigious gig for bands in the 1980's and 1990's., God knows why. It is such a shit hole. While we are on the subject (of shit), there is another one of these "Cow Venues," which is on the main arena touring circuit in the US. This one is some place in New Mexico. It could be Albuquerque I think. The last time I was there was in high summer and boy was it high you could smell it a mile before you got there.

Now, I don't remember the name of this place. I think I think it must have been called "The Cow Shit Shed" or something very similar.

The Rush tour plodded on through Europe for about five weeks. I have to say it was not the most exciting tour I had ever been on. I thought, *This next step up to bigger bands and bigger venues better work.* Of course, more money seemed to be going according to plan. I did have a slight problem though; I had to spend more money.

As all these guys who worked for these bigger bands were taking "Charlie," "Coke," or "Racket." In laymen's terms . . . cocaine! I had really only taken good old cheap and cheerful, "speed," "Blues," "Dexys," and everybody's Friday night favorite Amphetamine Sulphate, which was cheap and readily available. You could drink a brewery dry without getting drunk or so you thought. But at these next level gigs, these boys took cocaine.

This was more sophisticated drug taking but it was also bloody expensive. It was a little too subtle for my taste. Ten pounds or sixteen dollars for a gram of sulphate and you could rage until dawn and lunch and dusk and maybe the next dawn. Fifty pounds for a gram of Coke and it could easily be all gone in an hour (Especially if your friends helped, and it was a social thing.). There was just no mileage in it at all, but it was peer pressure. We did it because most of the musicians did also. We were going to be as cool as them. Unfortunately, they made a hell of a lot more money than we did.

ROCK 'N' ROLL
It's Better than Working for a Living

Something I had discovered on the Rush tour was that most of the band crew, the Canadians, were taking "Smack" (heroin). Now kids, there is no future in that at all. Heroin is not a fun drug and how they ever managed to do their gig is beyond me. Having taken it twice in my life, once knowingly and once unknowingly, I can tell you it is no fun at all. I like drugs that make you have fun, not turn you into a stoned, wreck.

I got back from the Rush tour and was at home for about three weeks before I was asked to go on another European tour, this time with American Progressive Rock band Kansas, who I must admit I had never heard of.

We were doing the same European circuit that I had just done with Rush plus some European festivals. Afterward, we were back home again this time for only a couple of weeks until I was back out again with yet another American band, Cheap Trick.

I had never worked with so many Americans before. In fact, I don't think I had even met as many Americans before. I now understood why English crews were considered the best in the World, even better than Americans. How wild is that?

The reason being, most American crew guys talked a good gig . . . some of them talked far too much of a good gig. I must say at this point, I don't include every American engineer or crew guy that I have known; I have known some really good guys and still do. I'm afraid the English just deliver the goods better and with a sense of humor.

In 1978 I did this tour with a real life "All American," Mr. Ted Nugent! Ted used to be known as the "Wildman of Rock n Roll." Yeah right! He was about as wild as my Mum at the British

Heart Foundation Charity weekly lunch. Never drank alcohol or took drugs in his life, how wild is that? He was mainly known as a wild man because of his exploits with the guitar. Or course, his reputation for shooting harmless animals with anything from a bow and arrow to an armored assault vehicle (Tank!) helped out.

At one show after the sound check all the crew was sitting in the catering room having dinner before the show. Ted walked in and announced . . . "Hi guys, I think I'll have dinner with you guys tonight, if that's okay?" and sat down at one of the tables with us.

At this point, one of the caterers asked one of the lighting guys what he'd like for main course. At this, the lighting guy replied . . . "Could I have the vegetarian option please?"

"Vegetarian!" screamed Ted, "I ain't eating with no vegetarians!" and he stormed out.

Ah Ah! What a dickhead!

On the Iron Maiden "Seventh Tour of a Seventh Tour" in 1988, on some of the gigs on the American section of the tour, Guns and Roses was the opening act. This was literally a couple of weeks before their "Appetite for Destruction" album went stratospheric. We were somewhere out in the Midwest, once again having dinner before the show. This time local caterers were in the venue who, of course, didn't know us personally. To prevent anyone just walking in and demanding to be fed we each had to collect meal tickets from the Production office to present to the caterers. After presenting our meal tickets and picking up our food we sat down in a rather sparsely populated catering room.

Myself and one of the other sound guys were just finishing off our dessert course when Axl Rose, lead singer from Guns and

ROCK 'N' ROLL
It's Better than Working for a Living

Roses, walked in with one of their crew. He sidled over to the caterers and asked, "What's for dinner?"

"Could I see your meal ticket please sir?"

"Meal ticket? . . . Meal ticket?" questioned Axl very aggressively.

"I don't need no meal ticket; don't you know who I am?"

By now this little scenario was now catching our attention. It was looking like it could be good entertainment, especially seeing as Mr. Rose was getting a bit of a reputation in the business for his tantrums.

"Yeah, don't you know who he is?" piped up his associate.

I still don't know to this day whether the crew guy was serious, which would have made him just as much of a dickhead as his employer of course. Or whether he was taking the piss out of him, in which case the man was pretty cool and probably unemployed by the next day.

"I don't give a flying fuck who you are!" or words to that effect, "You still need a meal ticket," was the cool reply Axl got from the caterer.

At that the two desperados noisily turned to leave the catering room. Now, about ten of the Iron Maiden crew sniggered in the background as Axl made a big deal out of trying to knock over a couple of chairs on his way out, but not really daring to. He made himself look a complete tit and prompted howls of laughter from the assembled crew.

Production Manager Dick Bell and I had finished our dinner. We were on our way back to the production office after the little cabaret in the Catering Room. When we came upon Axl and his tour manager, they were having a heated conversation outside the Guns and Roses dressing room. Axl was obviously berating the tour manager for not telling him about the meal ticket protocol and explaining he was too big a star to need a meal ticket anyway; the tour manager ass lickingly apologizing to him.

Dick and I quickly realized there was still mileage left in this situation and as we passed the two squabbling Americans. We managed, in our loudest possible voices, to extol the qualities of the beautifully tender pork chops and the unbelievably tasty apple sauce. At which point there was a quick silence from the Americans as we turned the corner into the Production office and quickly burst into tears of laughter.

To return to Ted Nugent for a moment, he turned up at the sound check one day with a new song he had written that morning in his hotel room. Now you have to understand that the band he had on the road, were only young guys that he had found playing in a bar in his hometown. These guys were incredibly impressed by being picked by the big star Ted Nugent to be his backing band. What they didn't know was that they were chosen because they were cheap. They were not chosen for their musical ability. Okay, they could play but so can half of the planet. So they were given a plane ticket around the world and a few hundred bucks a week (There was rumor of it been no more than $500 a week.) and they were Rock 'n' Roll stars. With this in mind, anything Ted did or said was the Gospel to them. Ted was a God (or thought he was). So today, Ted turned up with a song called, *Heads will Roll*.

This song was never going to be a Rock 'n' Roll classic. It is very hard to put over in print exactly what it sounded like, but it went something like this:

"Heads will roll"

Repeat,

ROCK 'N' ROLL
It's Better than Working for a Living

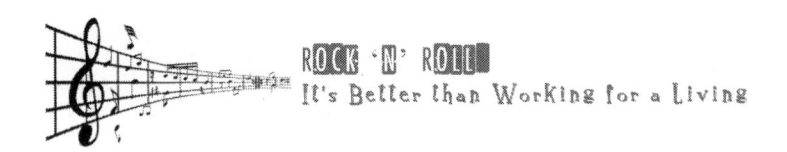

Repeat,

"If you don't get outta my way, heads will roll"

Repeat this verse twenty five times with ten guitar solos in there somewhere and you have the makings of the worst fucking Rock 'n' Roll song you have ever heard in your life. The band loved it, like it was divine poetry, we all just groaned.

The guy who did the sound mixing for Ted Nugent was an American guy called Dancer (Never knew his real name.). He had been mixing the sound for Ted since day one of Ted's illustrious career. He was a pretty alright guy, a little big mouthed but he was fine.

One day I wandered out to the crew bus during the sound check, as I wasn't doing any mixing on this tour just rigging the PA, and Dancer was on the bus watching a movie. I sarcastically said to Dancer, "I thought being the sound engineer meant you had to be in the venue mixing the sound during a sound check."

"Don't be fucking stupid," said Dancer," I hear enough of that fucking shit during the show without having to sit through it at the sound check."

That about sums up a Ted Nugent tour.

1978 actually started with a tour with a strange little woman called Bette Midler. I knew who she was of course. I wasn't particularly interested in doing the tour as it didn't seem very Rock 'n' Roll to me at the time. Which, which I suppose it wasn't, but it actually turned out to be pretty cool in the end.

The sound crew had to fly to Hamburg for the first show of the European Tour. This is when it all started getting a little bit cooler. I found out we weren't doing the whole tour by bus, we were doing quite a bit of flying between gigs, which suited me just fine at the time. I used to enjoy flying in those days.

We turned up the next morning at the Congress Center in Hamburg for the load in and rigging for the first gig. I met the American crew who had come over for the tour. They all seemed to be pretty nice guys and had a pretty good sense of humor for an American crew. Still, I thought you probably needed it working with Bette Midler, who had a bit of a reputation for been quite feisty.

Sound check came and went. I was doing the onstage monitor mix, so I had personal contact with the Artist during the show. I was introduced to Bette, who was a bit of a strange looking little woman, big hair, big mouth and even bigger tits, but she was pleasant. I had no problems at the sound check.

When we came to do the actual show things changed somewhat, it was an interesting show, not exactly Rock 'n' Roll, more Cabaret with comedy. There was music hall stuff, big band, dancing girls . . . pretty wacky stuff; and, Mildew had changed into a monster!

Mildew being the affectionate nickname given to Bette by the crew. However, affection was the least of the things I was feeling about ten minutes into the show.

"I can't here this; I can't here that, turn this up, turn that up, turn this down!"

What the fuck is going on with this woman? I thought.

She wanted everything changing in the mix, song after song this went on for. Things eventually calmed down and she seemed happy. There is a bit of a psychological thing that goes on between you and the Artiste when mixing the monitors onstage. You can acknowledge the Artiste wants something changing in the mix, but know for yourself it really ought not to be changed. Sound engineers really do develop an ear for it over the years, which possibly makes for a good monitor engineer or an average monitor engineer.

You have to convince the Artists you have changed it as they said and it does sound better even though you just run your fingers around the button without doing anything. This approach wasn't working so well this woman.

The next morning we got on the plane to Copenhagen for the next gig and I couldn't believe it, Mildew came and sat next to me. My God, I thought that's all I need at nine o clock in the morning; her bitching about the sound all the way to Copenhagen. What she told me was to make me feel even more loathsome. She told me she didn't really have a problem with the sound, she was just testing me to see how I would react to the situation and to see if I knew what I was doing. Apparently, I passed the test with flying colors.

She had obviously had some engineers who hadn't passed the test. Instead, they reacted by openly wanting to strangle her. What she didn't realize was that my initial reaction was much the same, but she kept talking and eventually talked me down.

We talked about lots of other stuff during the flight. She finished by making me promise to lend her the book I was reading, which was *The Human Factor* by Graham Greene, as she was a big fan of the writer.

Mildew was certainly a bit of a charmer. I think I became a bit of a fan of hers.

About a week into the tour, we had a day off in Munich and Mildew asked if anybody wanted to go to the Barry Manilow show as he was playing in town that night. I'd never seen "ole big nose" so thought it might be a bit of a laugh, so the tour manager organized backstage passes for us all, and it did turn out to be a bit of a laugh.

We were stood backstage and watched the big opening. The big orchestra struck up as the curtains opened and duly knocked over every mic stand and music stand in the front row of the orchestra. As Barry walked on in all his glory, most of the band and the crew were scrambling about on the floor picking up their music and mics. It was a truly wondrous fuck up.

By the end I couldn't fault the Bette Midler tour, it probably still goes down as one of the best tours I have ever done. Nice folks, easy schedule, well looked after, five star hotels and a couple of firsts for my own career. This was the first "first" . . .

The first time I had done a show at the world famous London Palladium theatre. I couldn't believe how small it was. Everyone had played there from Marlene Dietrich in the 1930's to The Beatles in the 1960's. There was so much history there, it was pretty cool and we did five nights there.

The second "first" as it were, was when Mildew called me into her dressing room before the last show in Frankfurt. I just thought, "She started the tour by bitching at me . . . don't tell me she's going to finish it bitching."

When I went into her dressing room, first she gave me a glass of champagne, then a big kiss, then a big thank you and lastly a thousand dollar bonus.

What a lovely girl!

The company I was working for at the time was a very well established sound company in the UK and owned by a guy called Ricki Farr. He had made his money from being involved in the production of The Isle of Wight Festivals in the UK in 1969 and 1970. Both drew huge audiences with the appearance of Bob Dylan in 1970 and Jimi Hendrix in 1969. Attendances were rumored to be in the region of 600,000 people.

Ricki was the son of a British boxing champion of the late 1930's and early 1950's, Tommy Farr. Ricki was a pretty tough guy himself. His business took off quite rapidly in the early 1970's. He was taking on the big boys in the American market.

In 1975, having secured his first big American tour, but not having any equipment in the US, he decided to ship a container load of sound equipment over to New York for an Alice Cooper tour. Unfortunately, before the tour got off the ground Mr. Cooper booked himself into the Betty Ford clinic for an extended rehabilitation period.

Being a very shrewd businessman Ricki quickly decided to ship his sound equipment to Los Angeles. He realized he had a big sound system immediately available and could undercut the big American companies. Through his contacts in the business he very quickly picked up the Rod Stewart tour and never looked back, Electrosound US was born.

By the time I joined the company in February 1977, Electrosound in the UK were getting lots of tours with big American acts. Included were Alice Cooper, The Beach Boys, Tom Petty, Aerosmith, Ted Nugent, and others. The Electrosound engineers were tempted by moves to the US, where the business was much bigger and the rewards much greater when working out of the Los Angeles shop.

Many of the English guys I knew went over to LA to work as it was a time in the business when the best engineers in the business were English. Everybody wanted them in the US. For some reason, which totally escapes me now, and it is something I have never been able to figure out for many years, was . . . why I didn't go.

The lifestyle and culture were perfect for my girlfriend Salli Jane. She loved America. For some reason she didn't want to go. She did say she didn't want to leave our seven cats behind, but, she wouldn't have had to. Who knows? It was probably the biggest mistake we ever made, and we made quite a few in 27 years.

In the end I was quite happy working for Electrosound in London. I did lots of tours. I made lots of money. And, I was getting a really good reputation. I was in demand.

For a change I'm going to tell you about a tour I didn't do. Believe me it was no great loss, as I had virtually the same experiences twelve years later. It was a Bob Marley and The Wailers European tour. It would have been extremely prestigious tour to do, but I was still a bit of a new boy at Electrosound. And, I figureed they wanted someone with a little more experience to go out on it.

So a very experienced old mate Steve "Flaky" Flewin went out on it. He got the nickname "Flaky" as he did like his "weed." He gave off a bit of an aura of been stoned most of the time and a bit of an incompetent. He was actually very laid back, a very clever man, and an excellent engineer. And, he is a lifetime friend. So, this tour should have been a breeze for him with a bunch of stoned Jamaican session musicians and lots of weed around.

Steve was doing the onstage mix and was the perfect person to deal with these guys. The only problem was that they did not want a white face behind the mixing console! Racism in the music business at that time was a very rare phenomenon. In fact, it was pretty much unheard of. It may have been kicking off all over the world for many years, but the music business always seemed pretty insulated from it. It may sound somewhat reminiscent of the hippies of the 1960's, but we all seemed to be one family in the business. We were all in it together and oblivious to the "real" world outside.

It did smack a little of a fantasy existence but, they were hedonistic times. Everybody wanted to be in the music business. It had different rules to normal living and it was exciting, vibrant and financially rewarding.

Flaky had a great attitude when it came to dealing with Artistes and rock stars or whatever you want to call them. Knowing these people had egos as big as their bank balances; he would be laid back, friendly, decisive and he gave them what they wanted. He made Artistes feel as if he was their best mate. Unfortunately, this was not what Mr. Marley and his crew wanted. Well . . . not from a WHITE man anyway. I can only imagine how many hoops he had jumped through trying to please these people. In the end he decided he could never make it work with them. He decided to resign and go home. He let someone else take over mixing monitors and he even hitchhiked from Stockholm! That's how pissed off he was.

I did witness a similar situation 12 years later and this was a tour I did do! Ziggy Marley, son of Bob! A different time, a different generation, same old fucking attitude! In three weeks on the road in Europe, I don't think one of the band members actually spoke to me. They had a four Jamaican crew on the road with them, who I have to say were all absolutely fucking useless. They didn't have a fucking clue what they were doing. They were just friends of the band or thought they were and all completely fucking expendable.

It really was quite an uncomfortable vibe on the tour. We really just got our heads down and did the work we had to do. The Jamaican "crew" did absolutely nothing, apart from winge and complain. On the bus it was like a day in a small town in the Deep South of America in the early 1960's. The black guys sat at the back and we sat at the front of the bus. When we tried to be friendly, which we did all the time, and sit with them . . . they would move and go sit down the front.

It really was a very uncomfortable three weeks. We were only spared when Ziggy got fed up with Europe or vice versa. He cancelled a couple of weeks of European shows and went back to do some shows in America. Good fucking riddance!

To show the other side of the coin and prove there is no room for those attitudes in the music business or anywhere else for that matter . . . the same year I did a European tour with black American funk band. They were The Commodores from Tuskegee, Alabama. I'd never actually heard of The Commodores myself, not been into that funky soul stuff, but they were big apparently. Also, as can be seen from the photograph a couple of them had very big hair also.

I first met The Commodores when myself and a guy called Jack Armstrong (Who had been doing FOH sound for them in the US and who worked for Electrosound US.) flew out to do a festival in Saarbrucken in Germany with them. Once again, I was doing the onstage monitor mix, and I couldn't believe it when

ROCK 'N' ROLL
It's Better than Working for a Living

these six black guys dressed in matching sparkly jump suits got on stage. They were wearing what we would call today, "bling, bling." Gold chains, bracelets and rings . . . They weren't exactly what you expected to see in a muddy field at an outdoor festival in what was then West Germany. They whipped up a storm and the crowd went bananas. The show was so slick and professional; it was probably one of the easiest gigs I have ever done. After the show the singer came up and introduced himself to me. "Hi I'm Lionel Ritchie, nice to meet you." He seemed like a pretty good guy!

So next day, we flew up to Stockholm to start the tour properly. There I met Rudy, who was production manager for the band. He was the only white guy in The Commodores organization. Basically Rudy was in charge of all the crew. It was quite a big crew for those days. There were sixteen people in all and we were all on one bus, which was very crowded.

Some very cheap bus company called Trathens, were supplying the bus. They were to become famous for having the worst busses in the Rock 'n' Roll industry. What they did was convert one of their regular "Executive" buses (which were just seats and tables inside), into a sleeper bus with sixteen bunks in it. It may not sound to be many people, but sixteen people living and sleeping on one bus for sometimes four or five days at a stretch was pretty horrendous.

The bus was called a "Nightliner" by the company. One of our crew remarked after spending a couple of nights on it, "It's more like a Binliner than a Nightliner."

In America, the Silver Eagles had usually a maximum of ten people on one bus. Usually, eight is more routine, which makes it pretty damn comfortable. However, we were stuck with our Binliner.

We did shows in Stockholm, Goteborg; Oslo, Norway and then down in Denmark, Copenhagen with a night off in Copenhagen.

A night off in Copenhagen was always very dangerous due to the excellent local brews they manufacture. Although, maybe not quite as dangerous as a night off in Amsterdam.

A few years before on my first trip to Denmark on an Alvin Stardust tour, I'd discovered a concoction called Elephant Beer. Never was a beer so perfectly named because the next day after drinking it, you really did feel like an elephant was standing on your head.

This rather potent brew, made by Carlsberg, was relative to another of their elixirs called Special Brew. And, it is very special. The two beers are very similar in the results they produce. After a few intense hours of consumption, unless you have something to take the edge off, like say . . . three days in a darkened room, you could be in big trouble.

They are both very strange brews, as there is another consequence you have to look forward to after imbibing copious amounts of the liquid. They seem to make you want to sit down in the street, not fall down, just sit on the sidewalk and start talking in some strange alien language no one on Planet Earth seems to understand.

This happened to me the first time I drank about twelve bottles of it in a bar in Ejsberg. I ended up sitting on the sidewalk with my feet in the gutter outside this club about two in the morning.

Spookily, on this day off on The Commodores tour, we went to a club in Copenhagen we had been told about. It was alleged it was a great place to pick up chicks; that is, as long as you didn't drink Elephant beer!

I was having a great time I was acting out my role as *Mr. International Rock 'n' Roll Playboy*. We were, of course, really only a bunch of drunken British Rock 'n' Rollers. Yet, we'd managed to interest a few of the local chicks and all was looking very promising.

Then the next thing I knew, BANG! It was five in the morning. Here I was, sitting out on the sidewalk in the pouring rain, with my feet in a puddle of water in the gutter.

What was it with that shit? It happened every time!

Copenhagen I found to be a very sociable and welcoming town. It's kind of the border town between Central Europe and Scandinavia. It's not quite as old and boring and dirty as Central European towns. It's not as weird as places in Scandinavia like Stockholm where all the beautiful women have holes in their faces from being quite a bit nearer to the Sun than we are in the summer. Or rolling in the snow and beating themselves and each other with sticks in winter.

I have always had a taste for a nice smoke whilst on tour. Such as, some good weed whilst in America or some pungent hash in Europe. It was nice just to relax after a long stressful fourteen hour day dealing with rock stars and managers and promoters and lots of other people with obscure titles. Most of these folks, without the business would be much easier entities to work with.

A Market Stall in Cristiana

Usually people on tour interested in purchasing post- or pre-gig relaxants would rely on local knowledge to acquire such substances. So, the local crews at each gig were usually the best point of contact for acquiring goods they had in mind. Copenhagen was no exception, although at first it was not a city I had associated with being able to buy good dope. The boys that would work the shows at The Tivoli Theatre or the KB Hallen were usually able to oblige. They had this wonderful source of supply in an area known as Cristiana.

Cristiana is located in what is basically a poor area of Copenhagen. There are tall red brick blocks of apartments built around a large open green space. Once a military establishment, it appears a couple of manufactured homes or community centers are housed

ROCK 'N' ROLL
It's Better than Working for a Living

in the middle of the complex. The whole area is an enclave inhabited by hippies, Artistes, poets, musicians, drug dealers and Hells Angels. In fact, anyone who likes to live by their own rules rather than ones set out by society might be found in Cristiana.

It is officially recognized by the National Government as a commune. The residents largely live by their own rules. Over the years they have been both ignored and encouraged by National authorities. Even after forty years of tumultuous existence, they still sell dope on the aptly named street called Pusher Street! It appears that Cristiana is still a no go area for the local police force.

There are, and were, such separatist groups and societies throughout the world. In London, in the 1970's, the whole of the Notting Hill Gate and North Kensington areas were populated by hippies, musicians, poets and, of course, drug dealers. It was cleaned up in the 1980's and is now one of the most expensive areas to live in the whole of London.

On a more radical scale is Kuba, Istanbul, which is a very poor area of the capital. Unfortunately, it is now the home to extremists and radicals much like the slums of Buenos Aires. Cristiana; however, goes on much the same as it did back in the 1980's, which is when I actually visited there. I was taken to Christiana by one of the local promoter's boys who thought I might like to go and see it for myself. Rather than send someone else to collect the goods as it were; I'm pleased I did go, but I only ever went there the one time.

We drove around the back of one of the large apartment blocks into the square. At the back, where the community centres were, my guide told me that they were actually built by the local town council for the inhabitants of the apartments. It was all beginning to make sense as to what was going on as we pulled up outside of one of the wooden buildings. My guide went inside and told me to wait in the car. There was quite a lot of barking going on from what sounded like very large dogs. He then beckoned me from the open door to come into the building. It did look like a scout hut or youth club until you went inside, some youth club!

There I saw the big dogs. They were big German shepherd dogs, with big teeth and with big owners who had big glasses of beer in their big hands and big blocks of green stuff on the table as well as a big knife to cut it with! We had a beer. My guide negotiated some deal with the very big guy who had Hells Angels patches all over his leather jacket. He handed him a wad of kroner and in turn received a lump of his green stuff sliced expertly from the block by the big biker. We then said our thanks and waved goodbye, which was greeted by a grunt and the scary sound of the dogs when we closed the door.

I hear now that all the bikers have left or been thrown out of the community. They had been trying to muscle in on the peaceful locals' control of their own marijuana trade with strong arm tactics and the big dogs. I had bought drugs openly like that once before, but it was downstairs in the hash cafe of the Paradiso club in Amsterdam. Half a dozen guys would be at different tables, each with a different variety of weed or hash. One could peruse the goods on offer and even sample the wares before buying. It was an altogether more laid back atmosphere than in the scout hut in Cristiana.

My local guide told me it was such a large community in Cristiana, that in some way or another everyone in the community was involved with drugs. They were either users or suppliers. He stated, "Many years ago the local authorities decided rather than cause a major war between locals and themselves in trying to evict the "heads" to clean up the neighborhood, they just decided to

ROCK 'N' ROLL
It's Better than Working for a Living

overlook the issues." Also, rather than shift the problem to somewhere else in the city, they allowed them to live in the small square mile area as long as they didn't cause any trouble to anyone else. Consequently, the local police were told not to hassle people in Cristiana as long as there was no "serious" crime to attend to . . . to just stay out of their way.

What an extremely sensible way to deal with a drugs problem! In fact, there is no problem there at all.

We carried on into Central Europe on The Commodores tour on our horrible overcrowded bus and then into Germany where the band could draw very large audiences due to the large number of US military personnel stationed in the country. We were on our way to Nuremberg from Frankfurt overnight, which was a distance of about 180 miles. We'd been on the road two hours and most people had gone to their beds. I think there must have been two or three night people still awake in the front lounge when the bus driver pulled into a truck stop to use the toilets. It was strictly forbidden to use the portable toilet on the bus for solids.

I was in my bunk and must have fallen asleep before we set off again as the next thing I remember it was about 8 a.m. I heard someone walking between the bunks calling out; "Simon, Simon, where the hell are you?" He managed to wake everyone else up on the bus except Simon!

We were at the gig in Nuremberg. The way the setup works is that the lighting crew, of whom Simon was the boss, always handled lighting rigs first. It is a good couple of hours before the sound crew begins setting up. The band's backline equipment goes in last.

So at 8 a.m. the lighting crew must have just been going into the gig and were looking for their leader. He was nowhere to be found on the bus. I went back to sleep again and got up about 10 a.m. and went into the gig and noticed that there was still no Simon. There is a golden rule when travelling overnight on a crew bus, if it stops in the middle of the night and you get off, make sure somebody knows you have got off. This way, the crew knows to make certain you got back on again and also lets the driver know. Simon was standing at a truck stop about 100 miles from Nuremberg at 4 a.m. with no bus in site anywhere. He had no jacket and it was pretty cold in Southern Germany at that time year at night.

Personally, I didn't give a flying fuck where he was. He was not one of my favorite people, after hitting on my girlfriend for a couple of months. After an overnight stay in a hotel and a 300 dollar taxi ride he wandered into the gig about 2 p.m. and then tried to blame the bus driver for leaving him. He tried to get the driver to pay his overnight expenses at which he was told to get over it. Silly ass!

1978 was not proving to be as busy a year as I thought it would be. I did another five week European tour with that wild man of the catering room Mr. Ted Nugent, but I'm afraid after the last one I found it very difficult to take it seriously.

During the summer I did three festivals. One was a three day affair in Holland called Pinkpop. The other two were at an old English stately home called Knebworth House. One was with Peter Gabriel and Frank Zappa. The other was with Genesis, Tom

ROCK 'N' ROLL
It's Better than Working for a Living

Petty and Jefferson Starship (Of whom more will be heard in the Festivals chapters of my memoir.).

In 1979, I was booked to do a European Tour with British post-punk band; Ian Dury and The Blockheads. Ian Dury, who contracted polio when he was a child, was the least likely of pop stars. A working class boy from the back streets of the East End of London; he had a working class image and some excellent songs made him big news in Europe in 1979.

Ian was basically a really nice bloke. Because of his illness he had been forced to wear a caliper on his right leg for all of his life in order for him to stand and walk. This had given him a bit of an inferiority complex throughout his life. With his new found fame and record companies competing to sign him, he was suddenly getting spoilt. Money was no longer a problem for him and he had as much as he wanted. That all made for one confused and irritable and sometimes even obnoxious person.

We did a really long European tour that spring and summer from the north of Finland to the south of Italy. It was a really good tour for sightseeing. I was just rigging the equipment because the band had their own engineers (Using the term somewhat loosely.). There was lots of time for sightseeing and my girlfriend Salli came out for the Scandinavian leg of the tour as she had never been to Scandinavia before. It turned into quite a nice little vacation for her.

Looking back my career was not so much a career in the music business; it was more of a career in organizing Salli's vacations and sightseeing commitments around the world . . . as she did come out on many tours.

That particular Ian Dury tour was lots of hard work but it was also lots of fun as can be seen in the "Worst Journeys" segment. I got lots of work from them in the future in some very interesting places. I think the Australian tour was probably the most entertaining of all.

As I said, Ian did have a bit of a chip on his shoulder as regards his incapacity and the fact he thought everyone regarded him a cripple. His incapacity did make for some amusing incidents and others, but then some others not quite so amusing. On the next leg of the tour, the monitor engineer had been fired, which was no surprise to anyone. I took over doing onstage monitors for Ian.

Despite all his hang-ups, he was not a difficult guy to deal with during the show, just a little cantankerous. Usually, we would start the show and everything would be going along fine when suddenly he would shout down the mic, "Tyas! Tyas! What's going on?" Of course, nothing was going on, nothing had changed . . . it was just Ian craving some attention. As a monitor engineer, with most bands you have to be the singer's best friend, and always awake to their whims. With Ian it happened every night, "Tyas! Tyas!" After a few shows of working with Ian as the monitor engineer, I found a good thing every night was just to dive down behind the monitor board when he shouted.

I knew nothing was wrong on stage. Due to his immobility, he could just hobble along very slowly. I knew he wouldn't come looking for me and it caused a great deal of amusement to the rest of the crew. Ian's immobility always caused a great deal of amusement with the band and crew, which I thought was very cruel at first. This might have contributed a great deal to his insecurity and inferiority complex, but in the end I had succumbed to the joke as well.

ROCK 'N' ROLL
It's Better than Working for a Living

One of the more amusing times was always when he got a little excited on stage or when he got a little drunk before he went on stage, which happened quite often. He always did try to move around a little whilst he was stood at the center mic position and even try to do a little dance. The inevitable usually happened. He fell over!

I must point out that these incidents in themselves were not any serious threat to his health. Some of the time, you almost thought he was falling over on purpose. When he did fall over, due to his incapacity, he couldn't get up again. This once again caused great amusement among the crew. Ian always had to have a minder, to help him do almost everything; including helping him to get up if he fell over on stage. Fred Rowe aka "Spider" had known Ian since they both lived in the same apartment block in South London in the early 1970's.

Fred had been a minor criminal in a past life but he was now Ian's minder. He stood at the side of the stage every night in case Ian fell over. Ian kept falling over more and more. In the end Spider just said, "Get up yourself you stupid bastard," and left him in the middle of the stage lying on his back, legs kicking and arms flailing about. This caused the crew to fall about themselves in howls of laughter and the punters seemed to love it as well, maybe that's why he kept doing it.

The next incident where Spider had to step in was not so savory. On the Australian tour in 1981, we were staying at The Sebel Town House Hotel on Double Bay Beach in Sydney which was a very nice, new 4 star hotel and really was right on the beach.

Also staying at the same hotel was an English actor called Warren Mitchell, a very well-known actor, who used to play an East End of London bigoted, racist, working class guy (In a time when you were allowed to portray such people.), called Alf Garnett, in the British TV comedy, *Till Death Us Do Part*.

Ian was really pleased to meet Warren Mitchell, being a big fan of the show. The second night at the hotel we were all in the bar and Ian was chatting with Warren Mitchell. They were planning having dinner tomorrow night after the show. A few minutes later, their voices became a little raised in volume and the next thing we knew Warren Mitchell jumped up and screamed, "He fucking spat at me." Apparently, there had been some disagreement between Ian and Warren. Ian adopted one of his usual childish mannerism and spat in Warren Mitchell's face. Ian was of course blind drunk, but quickly Spider had to wrap his huge arms around Ian, who was shouting and swearing, and carry him up to his room. Spider locked Ian in his room for the rest of the night, where he carried on shouting and swearing until he passed out. I don't think they ever did have dinner.

The gigs on the Australian tour were largely forgettable apart from probably the first one. The band went out to Australia about a week or more before the first gig to acclimatize after the long flight. The other sound guy (Who was also called Ian.) and I went out the day before the first gig. In fact, it was two days before due to time zones.

We were only in that position due to our commitments to another band to do the last show of their tour in London, and our own greed of course.

We actually arrived in Sydney at 7.30 a.m. on the morning of the first gig after twenty-three hours, three stops, a gram of cocaine, and being drunk and sober so many times I didn't know whether I wanted a Jack and Coke or a bowl of Corn Flakes.

We had made a few mistakes on the way, like taking cocaine on a flight. This, of course, makes you drink, so you start getting dehydrated very quickly. Then, you get off the plane in Bangkok to go into the transit lounge for more alcohol. We had to walk across the tarmac where the outside temperature was over 100 degrees Fahrenheit, but we had made it with maybe a few brain cells still in working condition.

I don't know what we looked like to the Australian immigration officials, who are not known for their sense of humor. I felt as though I looked like Johnny Depp in one of the scenes in the movie "Fear and Loathing in Las Vegas." The one where he wakes up in the hotel room which is flooded and he has a large fishes tail strapped around his waist. For some unknown reason they let us into the country and we got a cab to the hotel. The cab driver actually knew where it was! This was a minor miracle as Sydney is like New York in that respect.

Cab drivers very rarely speak English as they are all from Turkmenistan or these days China and Hong Kong. First, the only English they know is; Manchester United and Bobby Charlton or David Beckham. Secondly, they never know where anywhere is!

We got to the hotel and after checking in went immediately to Ian Dury's manager, Peter Jenner's room. My fellow sound engineer and traveling companion said he needed a joint to take the edge off of the last twenty-four hours. Once again a week in a dark room would have done it for me.

Eventually, when I got to my room I think I lay down and twitched for a few hours. Then I got up, then I lay down, then I got up, then I lay down, then I gave up and had a shower. When I was done, I felt exactly the same after the shower but slightly wetter.

I think we eventually went down to the gig with some purpose about midday. Looking back now this whole fucking fucker of a day felt like I was still in "Fear and Loathing in Las Vegas."

Ian, the FOH engineer, and I arrived at the gig at the old Capitol Theatre to find the PA and lights and the backline all set up. Backline crew had also been here a week so they had gotten over their jetlag, whereas we were just a mess. The Aussie sound crew was really helpful though and I had a guy called Harry Parsons helping me with the equipment, as it was all new to me. Harry was apparently a legend in the Australian audio industry but now pursues more leisurely activities up on the Gold Coast.

Even in my confused state, I managed to get some noise out of the monitor system. I thought it sounded fine. What would I know though? I'd been up and down. Drunk and sober so many times in the last forty eight hours, I was just happy it made noise at all.

The band arrived about 4 p.m. for the sound check. They collectively burst out laughing when they saw the state of Ian and me. If I looked how I felt, I'm not surprised.

Jenny was Peter Jenner's assistant. She came up to me when we arrived and pressed a paper wrap in my hand. "Here's a present from Peter," she said . . . "Might get you through the day."

When I opened it and tasted it, it was a gram of amphetamine sulphate and it was just what I needed. I went into the bathroom and put out a big line on the cistern. It hurt! Something similar to snorting broken glass I should imagine. It was good though, and it really fucking worked!

I breezed through the sound check smoking about thirty cigarettes in about half an hour and drinking about ten bottles of beer. I was just managing to do the job on instincts, adrenalin and speed, but it was getting it done. That was, until I stopped working after the sound check, then I started going down again. There was only one thing for it, more speed, more beer and more cigarettes. By the time we came round to doing the gig, I was almost in party mood, except I was going down again. So! Two minutes before the show, I did the last line of speed I had left, took six bottles of beer with me on stage and I was off.

The show went really well. I was ready to go out drinking all night, so I went in the dressing room, poured myself a big Jack and Coke. I waffled away for half an hour to anyone who would listen, then felt a little weary. I sat down on the floor in the corner of the room, AND PASSED OUT! Probably not for very long, but the next thing I knew I was been bundled into a cab back to the hotel, but I was still considering if I wanted to go out drinking or not.

Soon as I got in my hotel room I thought that might not have been the greatest idea I had ever had.

I just laid and twitched for the next twelve hours.

The Australian tour turned out to be a very leisurely affair. We only did six gigs and after eventually recovering from the jet lag it turned into very easy money with a few promoters' dinners thrown in as well as a bit of sightseeing. The weather was really beautiful.

MICK (MICHAEL) TYAS

We flew to New Zealand for three gigs, in Christchurch, Auckland and Wellington. Where Australia was a thoroughly modern country and their big cities could have been anywhere in the world, New Zealand was an altogether different world.

In New Zealand it was still 1958! There were still lots and lots of 1930's, 40's and 50's English and American cars on the roads. In fact, the guy who ran the sound company had a beautiful Cherry Red 1930's Buick Coupe. It was the type of thing you would see in a gangster movie.

Even the TV stations also closed down at 10. 30 in the evening! So one night in Christchurch I went for a walk in the city center about 11 p.m. and the place was deserted. I haven't been there for over twenty years but I believe it may have actually made it into the 21st century now, just!

I flew back to Sydney from Auckland in a Quantas Airlines 747. I was considering putting this little story in the "Worst Journeys" section of this book, but the journey itself was actually fine. It was just the end of it that was memorable. It was only a four hour flight to Sydney. I had got myself a window seat in an exit row with the two fold up crew seats opposite, so there was plenty of leg room. It was a lovely fine day as we came into Sydney Kingsford Smith Airport. There were two cabin crew sat opposite me in their seats. As we came in to land, we were low enough for me to look out of the window and see the white marker line running along the edge of the runway, when suddenly!

There was an almighty roar. The nose of the plane pointed skyward and the plane accelerated into a high banking curve. Everyone was thrown back in their seats. So violent was the acceleration I quickly looked over at the two crew members sitting opposite. One of them was making a strange face at the other one, as if to say . . . "What the fuck is going on?" The pilot came on the PA and apologized for the violent behavior of the plane and informed us that, "They had had to abort the landing for technical reasons." I looked out of the window. We were just climbing in a steep curve and crossing the runway we were supposed to land on. Right where we were supposed to have landed another Quantas Airlines 747 was just taxiing off of the runway towards the terminal buildings. If we had have landed, we would have gone straight into the other 747 at 160 mph. Pretty scary stuff!

Someone once told me there was a video of this incident, but I've never been able to find it. Apparently, what it showed was the 747 in front of us on the tarmac that had just landed. It failed to clear the runway as the air traffic controllers had expected. It could have been a very ugly mess.

That Australian tour was at the end of 1981. Earlier in the year we had played The Roskilde Festival just outside of Copenhagen in Denmark. This festival was quite well renowned for its somewhat changeable weather conditions. It sometimes can be very wet. This year it was.

The stage is covered by this large orange tent type structure. It looks like half a circus tent, which is more or less what it is as can be seen from the picture below. This roof is actually the Rolling Stones old touring tent which was used on their outdoor shows in the mid-seventies and at the 1976 Knebworth Festival. It is still used at the Roskilde Festival to this day, albeit somewhat larger. The amazing thing is with this tent, roof, whatever you want to call it, it is absolutely useless.

The Roskilde Festival, Copenhagen, Denmark.

Ian Dury was headlining this festival. The rain had been hammering down all day. Robert Palmer had just finished his set. I was stood behind the monitor board stage left when I felt a few spots of rain. Then a little more, and then suddenly, it was as if someone had turned on the faucet at the gentle rate of about a quarter of a gallon a minute directly onto the monitor board. Being aware water and electricity don't mix too well, we quickly moved the monitor board and cut the power. We started dismantling it, input channel by input channel. Each input channel controlled a specific microphone on stage and there were forty of them.

There is only one way to dry out a rather soggy mixing console and that is carefully with a towel and a hair dryer; taking care not to get the dryer too close to the circuit boards and turn a flood into a fire. As we were drying out the channels, the band walked past us onto the stage. That was not a good sight, as we had no monitors, but by the end of the first number we had four

ROCK 'N' ROLL
It's Better than Working for a Living

channels back in the board and working, which meant we could hear... Kick, Snare, Hi Hat and 1st Tom. Reassembling a mixing console whilst it is powered up is quite scary with electricity and water around. By the end of the band's set we had all the channels working. Outdoor shows are fantastic on a hot summer's day, but when it's raining it feels like the most miserable place on earth.

I last saw Ian Dury at Shepherds Bush Empire Theater in London, where I was working, April of 1999. This was on the last tour he ever did. It was more or less the same band, so it was nice to see old friends again. There seemed to be a bit more of a subdued atmosphere around the band on that tour. Sadly Ian died of cancer eleven months later on 27th of March 2000. He is buried in Golders Green Cemetery in North London.

Unfortunately, I never made it to the funeral but with typical Rock 'n' Roll humor I was told later, "It was so popular, and so many people turned up, they could have done two nights!"

Another connection I had with Ian Dury was a guy called Pete Rush, who, as you have heard earlier was one of the first sound guys I ever worked with in 1974.

Pete was a giant, about 6'7" tall, with an appetite for amphetamines as big as his frame. He could easily work his way through half an ounce of speed in a day, and then never sleep for a week. Sleep was a waste of party time for Pete anyway. He was a lovely guy, totally useless as a sound guy, but nevertheless a real friend.

With Pete being such a scary monster, he eventually got the job as Ian Dury's minder in the early 1990's. This job suited him to a tee. He was such a gentle giant, except when he was half way down a bottle of Jack Daniels and half way through half an ounce of speed ... then the monster reared it's very ugly head. One of these times was when he was back in his home town of Bournemouth on the south coast of England. I never actually found out why he was back there, but allegedly there was a large ruckus in a local night club one night and Pete was there. He managed to get himself arrested.

There was one story I had heard about that night. When he was arrested and taken to the police station, instead of accepting his fate of spending the night in custody, he tried to fight his way out of the police station. He almost succeeded. Unfortunately, Pete died of a heart attack before he made it out. I can just see him now; Pete really did know how to go out with a bang.

Ian Dury's last album entitled *Ten More Turnips from the Tip* was released posthumously in 2002. There is a track on it titled, *The Sulphate Strangler*. It is dedicated to the monster that was Pete Rush. I had lots of time for Ian Dury and Pete Rush. R.I.P.

I worked on a couple of European festivals in 1979. One was Pink-pop in Holland with Canadian band Rush, Dire Straits, Elvis Costello and etc. I had done a few shows with Elvis Costello before as his management hired TFA Electrosound, a company I was doing lots of work for.

Elvis Costello's sound guy was a guy called Steve Moss or The Bishop. This was on account of his rather circular hair growth with the hole in the middle. Steve was a renowned member of The Drinking for England Club and would daily have breakfast, lunch, dinner and supper in the nearest pub or bar. Unfortunately, this habit caught up with him by the time he was fifty years old when he developed a very nasty strain of diabetes, but I do believe from the last report I had he is still of this planet.

I was to spend a couple of weeks with Steve that summer. We drove out in a seven and a half ton truck to just outside of Grasse

ROCK 'N' ROLL
It's Better than Working for a Living

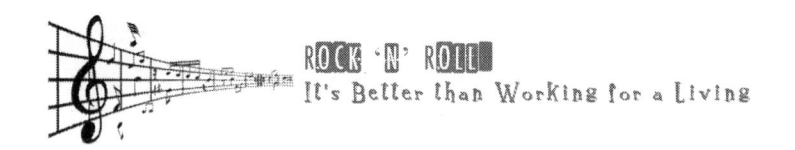

on the French Riviera with a sound system and Elvis Costello's band equipment. We were to do two weeks of rehearsals and three shows with Elvis Costello as preparation for recording a new album. We were rehearsing in this huge villa half way up the side of a mountain just outside of the sleepy village of Grasse. The villa had been rented for some enormous amount of money for these rehearsals and was paid for by the record company, of course. The villa next door, which was about half a mile away, was owned by the then Rolling Stones bass guitarist, Bill Wyman.

What I remember about this villa we were staying in was it had a Roman sunken bath in the floor in the living room in front of this huge open fireplace. That could have been the source of much exotic fun with your friends on a cold winter's evening. Anyway, I don't recall much rehearsing been done as usually happens in these circumstances. They're usually more of a jolly up for the band before they have to get down to hours and hours and hours in a recording studio. I just remember much drinking and making merry.

So we stayed there for two weeks and then there were three low profile shows planned on the way back to England. These being in Perpignan, which is just before you go over the border into Spain; in Sitges, just outside of Barcelona, which is a major gay resort on the coast; and Porto in northern Portugal. I never did find out who thought Northern Portugal was on the way home from the South of France to the UK.

Sitges is a really nice little seaside resort on the Catalonian coast only 20 miles from Barcelona. The only problem I have with it is that it's full of Gay people. Whoops! Mustn't be homophobic. Anyway, we stayed there overnight and the next morning Steve and I set off in our seven and a half ton truck to drive the seven hundred miles to Porto on the Atlantic coast of Portugal. That sounds like a long drive, which it was, but we did have three days to do it in so it was fine. You do pass through some beautiful countryside, so it was going to be pretty cool.

Steve drove for about one hundred and fifty miles of the first day's drive. Then, I drove for about the last one hundred miles that day. The next day we had about two hundred and fifty miles to go to the Portuguese border, which I had to drive. Poor old Steve couldn't seem to stay awake in the driver's seat, which may have been something to do staying up until 3 a.m. sampling the wines of the region with the local residents.

We stayed overnight in Spain and set off the next lunchtime to drive into Portugal. Then we had another two hundred miles to Porto, with Steve at the wheel. When we got into Portugal, Steve being an expert on national alcoholic beverages stopped at the first liquor store and bought a bottle of Port. Which is something we had to do of course; Steve then asked me if I wouldn't mind driving for a little while whilst he tasted a little sample of the Port he had just bought. In fact, he managed to drink three quarters of the bottle before he fell asleep completely paralytic in the sleeper bunk in the back of the cab of the truck.

That was the last I heard from Steve until we got to Porto, so out of about a seven hundred and twenty mile drive, he managed about one hundred and ten miles. What a buddy!

I hadn't really been enjoying this trip very much so far. The gigs were awful. I had spent far too much money. I had done too much driving. The truck tires were let down in Southern France by the locals, as we had been illegally parked, which delayed us for almost a day. Worst was to happen after the show in Porto. The local Portuguese promoter took all the band and crew out for a beautiful seafood meal after the show. I had some wonderful steamed Sea Bass. It was so lovely I saw it again next morning and it didn't look so lovely.

I had the worst food poisoning I have ever had in my life. It was coming out both ends. Nevertheless Steve and I set off to drive the twelve hundred miles back to London. I maybe should have called in the local hospital on the way and got some potion for it as I imagine they have quite a lot of it around there. Instead, we set sail and I had to suffer it for all of the two and a half days it took to drive back to the UK.

I just realized this little piece should have been in the Worst Journeys section of the book also, because it was certainly one of them!

The saving grace after all that mayhem and stupidity of the trip to the South of France was once again doing a Commodores tour. This time, it was beautifully organized. The band, as always, was the ultimate professionals. They always said thank you to you for your work after the show. That really is all you're looking for after a very hard days' work and I had nothing but respect for these people.

Rudy the production manager, the only white guy in the organization, wanted me to go on The Commodores next American tour with them. So did I and so did Mr. Lionel Richie. For some unknown reason I never made it. As with most decisions in the Rock 'n' Roll business, it would have been made by an accounttant, not by a production manager or even a mere musician. The accountant's logic would be, "Why take a monitor engineer to America, when there are thousands that already live in America. Why waste probably eight hundred pounds in extra airfares?"

1978 PLATINUM TOUR

GET NATURALLY HIGH WITH THE COMMODORES!

The Sixth Commodore - the Little White Guy on the right!

Unfortunately, accountants have run this business for many years now. And, it's only getting worse.

Rudy was actually telling me stories of what it was like touring the US with The Commodores. They were a huge band at the time and could fill ten to fifteen thousand seat arenas nationwide. He told me one thing you have to realize is, there are some venues in some States, where you can look around during the show and see you are the only white face in the building. Such was their popularity with the black community. Once you got down to Mississippi and their home state of Alabama you could be there for four weeks as they did so many shows there.

ROCK 'N' ROLL
It's Better than Working for a Living

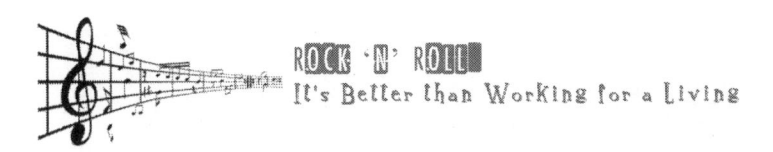

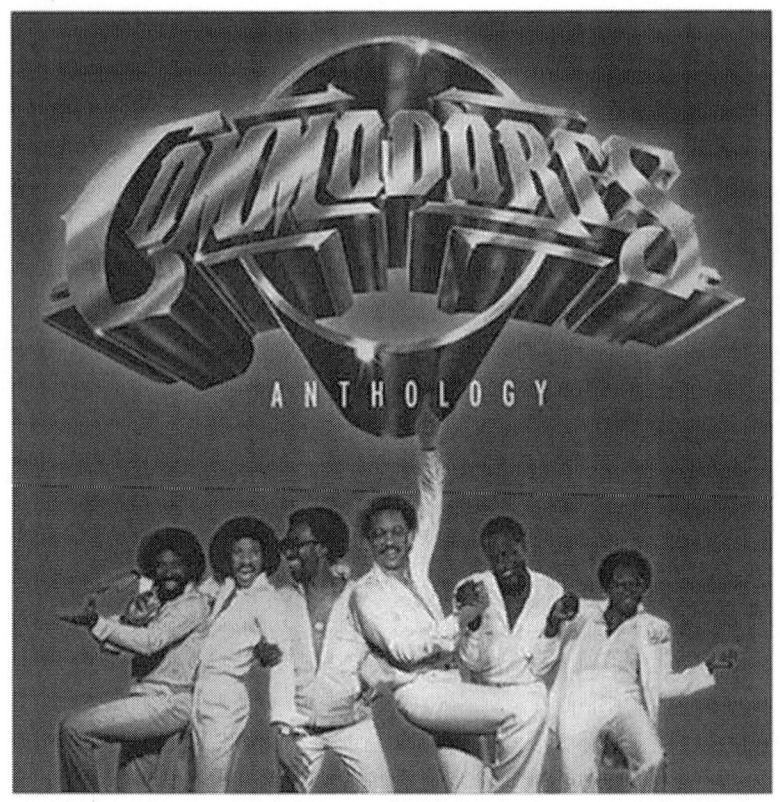

The Commodores!

This was never going to worry me, of course, because opposite you will see a picture of an album cover. On that album cover you will see five black guys, but there are six guys in The Commodores. You'll note the photographer cut the drummer Clyde out of the photograph, but on the right hand side there is a long haired white guy feverishly working behind a sound console . . . that's me!

I never saw this album cover for many years and as it was a limited edition promotional album. It's also pretty rare, but Rudy got hold of a copy of it in about 1990 and sent it to me. He told me that, after the band saw that photo I was always regarded by them as the sixth Commodore and not the drummer Clyde.

Lionel Richie turned out to be a really nice guy and our respective careers seemed to keep running into each other in the 1980's. This was before his solo career took off. There was one hilarious incident on that last tour I did with The Commodores in 1979. Lionel Richie used to play one of their big hits, *Three times a Lady* on a white six foot grand piano, perched behind the band's backline of amplifiers on an industrial scissor lift. At the big UK gig, of the tour at Hammersmith Odeon in London, he started the song seated at the piano. As he started playing the scissor lift would lift him and the piano into the air about fifteen feet above the stage. Dry ice clouds were flowing around it and it all was very celestial looking. This being the biggest gig of the tour, of course, Murphy's Law had to be taken into account or "If it could fuck up, it will fuck up." It did!

It usually did in one way or another, Lionel had to have a speaker up there to hear what the rest of the band was playing and obviously, mics for the piano and his voice. Every night when the lift came down, it would cut either a mic or a speaker cable with a nasty crack. This night it looked as if the cables were going to survive. It was going well to say it was a big prestige gig, but that big lift was always an accident in waiting. It consisted of two jacks that worked in a scissor motion supposedly . . . usually. But the piano on its way down didn't look quite horizontal tonight, moments later one jack stopped completely and the piano and Mr. Richie were stranded at a crazy sloping angle. The words, "safety net," "parachute," and "safety wire" was bandied about, but they had none of those. Somehow, the stage crew inched the lift down and a pretty relieved Lionel Richie jumped off about six foot from the ground. I did get a photo of this great scene, but sadly I've been unable to find it after all this time. It is a shame because could have been worth some money.

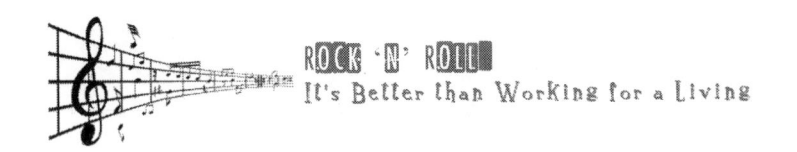

I didn't see Lionel Richie again until the mid-eighties at one of his shows at Wembley arena in London. I wasn't working on the show, but Salli and I were given backstage passes by Lionel's management. I was able to call in his dressing room and say hello and was greeted by Lionel with, "My man, how you doin?"

I wasn't his first visitor though. As we walked through the backstage area, Prince Charles and Princess Diana walked past us on the way from his dressing room. We were really mixing with Royalty that night.

I was asked if I was interested in working for Lionel again as monitor engineer in 1984. I turned down the offer. God knows why, it was more money than I was getting at the time, but I was in the middle of a Whitesnake tour and that seemed a better bet, so I turned down the offer.

What fucking drugs was I on at that time?

I guess I must have been in the middle of my Heavy Rock period as I was offered the job once more in 1986, whilst I was on an Iron Maiden tour, again I turned it down. What the hell was I thinking at that time? What I was thinking was that Iron Maiden, Motley Crue, Whitesnake and etc. was the epitome of SEX, DRUGS and ROCK 'N' ROLL. To quote Mr. Ian Dury, "I was getting paid for it!" And, Mr. Lionel Richie was cabaret and Vegas. Nothing wrong with Vegas but it is one of the most fucked up cities I have ever been to.

Of course, if I had have taken the sensible route and gone to work for Mr. Richie, I would probably still be there making $200,000.00 dollars a year. I don't think I would have had anywhere near the fun and experiences, both good and fucking awful . . . that I had in the upcoming METAL YEARS.

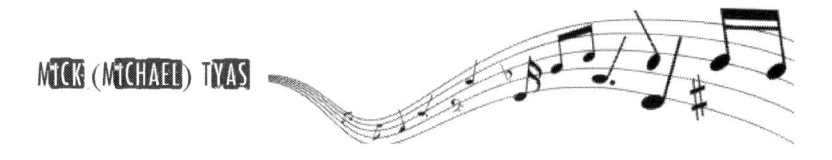

One person I would definitely still not be working for now was that pseudo Scots Londoner, Rod Stewart. I think it was that same year, 1984, when Danish engineer called Lars whom I had met seven years before at TFA Electrosound, called me and said he was back in England. He had been in America for about five years, and he was mixing the sound for Rod Stewart. Lars said he was only over on a quick break during some off time on the tour. While he was here, he decided to call me as he needed my help. Rod had fired his long time monitor engineer, for the twelfth millionth time.

Davie Bryson had been Rod's monitor engineer since the beginning of time. This firing was not an unusual occurrence. It was done at least once or twice on every tour. Davie would be fired or he would resign. This time according to Lars, it was a huge bust up and he was convinced Davie would never ever be allowed back on this or any other Rod Stewart Tour.

Lars wanted me to go back to LA with him in a week's time, telling me I was the only engineer that could actually make Rod happy, as I was one of the best in the world. "Come back with me on Saturday, and name your price."

I was a fingernail's width away from going back to LA with him when Lars hit me with a hammer blow. "Rod is not happy. He is finding fault with everything. He doesn't want to be here. He wants to be at home with his wife on his beach, driving his cars and not on tour. I need one of the best engineers in the world to keep him sweet." My dream was shot down in this single sentence. I had decided earlier to go to LA with Lars and take the job and had dreams of wealth and sunshine and glamour. Rod was

ROCK 'N' ROLL
It's Better than Working for a Living

always on tour. I was also dreaming of living in Los Angeles, but in that one sentence from Lars were a million and one reasons never to take a job as monitor engineer for Rod Stewart. I heard Davie was back within the month.

Lionel Richie and I though kept bumping into each other around the world. It was almost as if fate had decreed I should have taken the job. In 1986, I was in Hiroshima Japan on an Iron Maiden Japanese tour when, after the show we went back to our hotel and decided to go up to the rooftop bar for a few drinks. As we walked in, I saw a couple of black guys sat on a sofa at the other side of the room; I only noticed them as you don't see that many African Americans in Japan. As we sat down at the bar and ordered our drinks, this voice came from across the room, "My man, what are you doin' here?" Mr. Lionel Richie, once more; so we sat and had a long conversation about life and where we'd been since we last met. This time, he offered me the job himself. I said I would get back to him, when he got back to the US. I didn't!

What the fuck was I thinking of in those days? I know what I was thinking of . . . my nose and my dick!

In 1988, at the Iron Maiden American Tour in Le Parc Hotel, Hollywood, California I was going up in the elevator to my room. The doors opened at a floor, which wasn't the floor I wanted. This black guy and what looked like his wife (or maybe not) were just walking past the elevator down the corridor to their room and the man looked into the elevator as he passed. I saw a hint of recognition and he shouted, "My man, how you doin?" then the doors closed.

This time he didn't offer me the job.

Turning that job down twice was definitely the worst decision I have ever made in my whole professional life. Bar none!

Lars, who offered me those jobs with Rod Stewart, and Lionel Richie, started at the sound company in London at exactly the same time as me. I always got the impression he possessed slightly more ambition than I did in the Rock 'n' Roll business. I have to admit, I was certainly in it, or wanted to be in it, for the glamour . . . and sex and drugs and rock n roll. Of course, it was better than working for a living. Lars gave the impression he had a Master Plan. He was in it to make as much money as possible and basically take over the world, which wouldn't have been a bad plan at all. I could have subscribed to that, but unfortunately the sex and drugs always seemed to get in the way with me.

Lars had managed to hustle himself into the Rod Stewart and Lionel Richie jobs. That's what he did. He hustled. He was a hustler. He wasn't the best engineer in the world. I still regard myself as been a better engineer than he ever was or in fact . . . is.

Apologies here to Lars, "I've just got better ears than you mate." But he was an excellent hustler and that is what you had to be in the business in the late 1970's and early 1980's.

Lars's big break finally came in 1978. The company finally got the contract for the long awaited headlining tour by Swedish band Abba. As John Lennon would have said were bigger than God at that time. The obvious choice for monitor engineer on the tour was of course Lars. Being Danish, and Abba being Swedish, they more or less spoke the same language. Although, in the real world the Danes and the Swedes are not particularly fond of one another; however, in the rock n'; roll business, and particularly in

ROCK 'N' ROLL
It's Better than Working for a Living

Lars's career, this must have been a defining moment and probably the best present he ever had.

The biggest band in the World is a band that speaks Swedish! Who would have thought it? The Abba phenomenon was really just as the word says . . . phenomenal. In a couple of years, they were the biggest thing on the planet. One show I did with them in 1979 at Wembley Arena in London showed me how big it was all getting. Merchandise companies were falling over themselves to be associated with Abba. They had jeans sponsorship, shirt sponsorship, shoe sponsorship, sock sponsorship; this was before sponsorship in the Rock 'n' Roll business had even appeared on the horizon. Today, of course, it is commonplace. They didn't have to pay for anything. They would go on tour and it would cost them nothing. The sponsorship would cover all costs. They just banked their millions. We got free jeans, shirts, shoes and socks, seems fair doesn't it?

Lastly, and I'm not bitter about this, okay I am, still, after thirty plus years. I was the best monitor engineer at the company at that time, but Lars got the Abba job because he spoke Swedish or Danish or whatever it was. His mixing skills were not as good as mine. Lars designed some floor monitors for the tour, which were ultra-low profile, so you could see the two singer's legs (Girls they were!) when you sat in the audience. Whereas if you see normal floor monitors on a stage, they are usually at the best the size of a small packing case. At worst, they are the size of a garden shed, which of course would have blocked the view of Frida's and Agnetha's legs. So it was quite an agreeable idea to design something smaller.

Lars built these small boxes about six inches high with, if I recall correctly about ten 5" speakers in each box. 5" speakers being the size of speaker you would find in an old 70's transistor radio. About six of these boxes sat on the front of the stage facing the band. They looked like 1970's radio speakers and they certainly sounded like them. They were garbage, but the band loved them because you could see the girl's legs. I'm not going to argue with that. Lars was off and running on his quest for world domination.

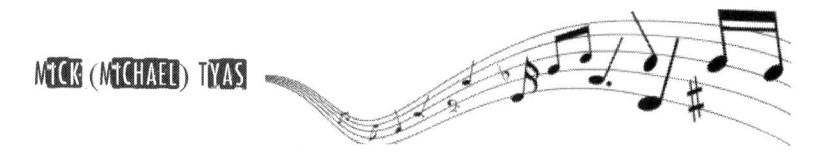

There is one other connection I had with Abba, which didn't manifest itself until a couple of years later. Agnetha was the "older" of the two girls in Abba. She was probably in her mid-thirties at the height of Abba's fame, nevertheless a good looking woman. In 1980, our sound company was employed by local Stockholm promoter. He was joint manager of Abba; a generally good guy, Thomas Johannsen employed us to provide our services for a big tri-nation Scandinavian gig at the ice stadium in Stockholm.

The line-up consisted of Denmark's biggest band, Gasoline and a pretty awful rock band from Finland called The Hurriganes . . . who for some totally unknown reason, still exist today. Headlining the gig was a Swedish singer / songwriter called Ulf Lundell, who had the balls to call himself the Swedish Bob Dylan. Not quite I'm afraid. In fact, nowhere near, but, he was incredibly big in Sweden . . . then again so were Volvos.

The band itself all seemed to be competent musicians, but one guy who stood out in the band was the drummer. Not for the fact he was an incredible drummer, but the fact he was probably the ugliest human being on the planet at that time. Fat as fuck, spotty, as if he had some flesh eating disease, which obviously wasn't eating it fast enough looking at his size. He was the type of person you would cross the road to avoid in case you got infected as you passed by. Shame really, I guess we can't all be pretty. He was only a young guy too. In fact, he was so young that I found out later in the day he was the son of the beautiful Agnetha from Abba. Obviously, from an earlier life, and a different galaxy I feel.

I have to finish this revue of my 1979 year quite late really. In fact, the end starts, if you know what I mean, on the day before Christmas. One of the biggest American bands in the UK at the time was Blondie. It was to the old Roxy cinema, formerly the Odeon cinema in Harlesden, North London we went the day before Christmas for rehearsals with the band. It was a pretty strange day, the 24th of December to start rehearsals for a tour. It was a pretty strange time to start a tour, but they were quite a strange band also.

The English sound and lighting crew were not altogether happy at having to do rehearsals up until 9 p.m. on Christmas Eve. It didn't get us off to a very good start with Blondie's management.

You can imagine how we felt. Imaging how the American crew felt sitting in a London hotel room on Christmas Day with their families over three thousand miles away. We then had to leave on the bus on the 26th of December to drive the ninety miles to Bournemouth on the South Coast of England to be ready for the first gig on the 27th. How fucking stupid was that? We could have stayed at home another day and driven down on the day of the gig.

Blondie first surfaced in the early 1970's with the emergence of guitarist Chris Stein. He had been around various New York club bands along with his girlfriend, Debbie Harry . . . a supposed former Playboy Club Bunny. Of course, by the time we got to work with them in 1979, they had had two or three big records in the charts. My own favorite being a remake of an old 1960's track called *Denis*.

The band at this time consisted of drummer Clem Burke and still does. English bass player Nigel Harrison from Stockport near Manchester; when the band disbanded in 1982, he went on to get a job as an A and R man at Capitol Records in LA. He also allegedly insulted just about everyone in the music business within a three thousand mile radius of Los Angeles. On keyboards was a guy called Jimmy Destri, who apparently is still involved with the band. He is also a drugs counselor these days. He probably even counseled his mate Frank Infante the second guitarist in the band, because in 1979 he certainly looked as though he needed it. It was definitely one of the best impressions I have ever seen of "a man barely alive."

Chris Stein, lead guitarist, was the leader of the band and boyfriend of Debbie Harry. He was a very lucky man as he wasn't the best looking guy on the planet. Being the boss he could have always fired her I suppose if she ran off. She really didn't need him; she was the "Star" of the show. Nobody came to see that ugly bastard.

They weren't the friendliest of bands on the road. Although Debbie did eat with the crew in catering quite a lot of the time on gig days. I believe one of the big problems with this band was that they came from that pre-Punk time of the early 1970's, with other bands like Talking Heads and the New York Dolls. They used to play the seedy clubs around New York City at the time and even earlier bands like Lou Reed and his Velvet Underground. Lots of the bands at this time were into "Smack." That over used and definitely over-rated drug called "Heroin." How anyone can get addicted to a drug that makes you feel as bad as you do when

ROCK 'N' ROLL
It's Better than Working for a Living

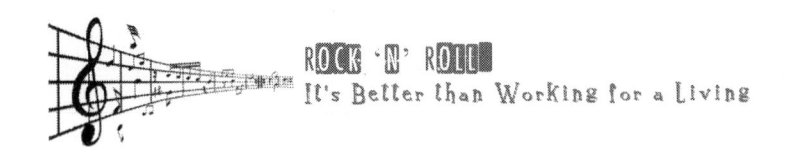

you've taken Smack I will never know. How a musician can take Smack and play is beyond me. It makes you terribly introverted and anti-social and SICK!

I like to hear bands that are enjoying themselves and making enjoyable music. Much better than stuff that sounds as though they are going to slit their own wrists when they put their guitar down and expect you to do the same. This whole thing goes back a long way. Listen to some of The Doors stuff from the 1960's. No wonder Jim Morrison topped himself playing in a band like that. Also, from a little closer in time to the late 1990's and early 2000's . . . Nick Cave and The Bad Seeds. What the fuck was that all about?

Quite possibly the most miserable band I have ever heard. How Blondie as a band managed to sound so fresh and happy sounding was quite an achievement as I knew that at least three of that band was heavily involved with Smack. Debbie? I don't know, maybe she got induced into it at some point, all I can say is . . . they were not the happiest and friendliest bunch of people I had ever met.

Thank God for the emergence of Punk and speed and cocaine and that old favorite; Alcohol again, happy, jump about music and drugs. Actually, thinking about it a little longer, the band weren't that miserable and moody. Rather only Stein, Harrison and Infante who I think may have been the instigators of bad habits. Definitely, the happiest person in the band was Clem the drummer. He was the most sociable. He came around to our apartment for dinner one night when we were in London. We kept in touch for a few years after that.

The tour itself was pretty good; except the band engineers were so full of crap their eyes were brown. As with many American engineers of that time, they knew all the numbers and talked a good gig, but actually couldn't deliver a letter. That is why all the big American bands of the time employed the British engineers and many still do.

We did some interesting gigs though; we did a week in Hammersmith Odeon in London. This was excellent as it was less than three miles down the road from where we lived in West London. As the tour started at such an unusual time of year, (i.e., Christmas) we were actually doing a gig on New Year's Eve and in of all places; Glasgow, Scotland, which is famous for its mad New Year's Eve celebrations called Hogmany. 99% of the population gets drunk, so I was expecting the local crew would be absolutely blind drunk and useless, but it didn't quite turn out like that.

The gig was in the Glasgow Apollo a late 1920's cinema formerly known as Green's Playhouse. It was converted to a music venue in the early 1970's. It must have been an amazing cinema in its early days. There were two huge balconies and a capacity of over four thousand people. It was one of the biggest cinemas in the UK in 1927. It also had a full size ballroom on the 4th floor.

A few years after it opened as a music venue the top balcony, known as the Gods, had to be closed as it had become structurally unsafe. The rest of the fabric of the building was quickly going the same way. It had a strange stage that was built twelve feet high from the ground level, which meant any performer suffering with vertigo, was going to spend most of the show pinned to the back wall of the stage. I eventually realized if it hadn't been built that high instead of at ground level, if you sat in the Gods in the early days you would have been looking down almost vertically at the stage. Even when they closed the Gods, it was still an amazing site. If you stood on the stage when there was a good rock band playing and looked out at the audience, you saw the balcony actually going up and down with people jumping up and down, which they always do in Glasgow. You could see the lights suspended under the balcony swaying back and forth. I actually sat up there during a set by British rock band Status Quo once. It scared the living daylights out of me. It was actually moving up and down and felt as if it would collapse at any minute. It probably would have eventually if they hadn't closed the old place down in 1985. That night with Blondie playing, it was certainly rocking!

The old gig had one major flaw, amongst many other minor ones, and that was you had to load in and out from a small alleyway at the side of the venue. On this particular New Year's Eve the BBC were recording the gig. So apart from our trucks there were a couple of big BBC recording trucks all trying to get in the small alley.

My birthday is New Year's Day. As well as being New Year's Eve that night, there was a little celebration for my birthday. Unfortunately, the crew bought me a quart jug of Jack Daniels, which was a huge mistake as I tried to drink my way through the whole bottle during the show.

New Year's Eve in Glasgow is famous for its New Year's Eve drunken celebrations. We were expecting the local crew guys to be so inebriated as to be totally useless as I said, but respect to them, they were fine. It was me that was the problem!

Unfortunately, I was going through a time in my career where my ego had developed more than my brain and I wasn't able to keep it in check. As was the case on this particular evening; I was just too fucking drunk to be able to do anything about it. As soon as I walked out of the loading door after the show, and so the BBC guys had fucked off to their hotel to indulge in their own New Year's Eve celebrations, and left their trucks right up tight to the loading doors leaving us very little room to load our trucks, a red mist descended in front of my eyes. I went back into the gig and grabbed a mic stand. Charging out of the door like an ancient warrior, in a drunken rage, I attacked the first BBC truck smashing its headlights and ripping off the windshield wipers while screaming "You fucking BBC bastards." I then meted out the same treatment to the second truck.

The whole frenzied attack was over in about forty-five seconds. Looking back at it now, it must have looked to onlookers like video footage from a Police CCTV camera in what could have been any number of the UK's big city centers . . . after all the binge drinking kids are thrown out of the bars and clubs. The amazing fact about the whole incident was that nobody tried to stop me doing it. Maybe they thought I was too scary to approach; or more likely, they knew I was just a complete fucking idiot. The entire incident would eventually come back to haunt me when word got back to the office. Amazingly I never heard any more about this incident from anybody. Maybe when the BBC dicks discovered the damage they thought that local drunken hooligans had done it.

It may not seem like it but Rock 'n' Roll is a pretty dangerous business to be in or it was anyway. Today's engineers and technicians are probably a little more protected by health and safety regulations. I couldn't really see another ridiculous situation happening like what happened at the Lorelei Festival in 1978, which had a whole chapter to its self-earlier on. Accidents can happen and one such occurrence happened on the Blondie tour.

Ed the American pyrotechnics technician on the tour decided to plug in his little flash pots on the front of the stage one day before, of course while ensuring the control unit that fires them was unplugged and disarmed. His little pots were each the size of an ashtray and contained some gunpowder or flash powder or some such stuff that explodes and catches fire when you put an electrical current through it. Unfortunately, that is exactly what happened when he plugged one in. As nasty enough a mess as that would have made with his head bending over it, whilst plugging it in he was also carrying another six. They caught and went off and burnt most of his hair burnt most of the skin off of his arms and gave him a very good suntan. That, sadly for Ed was the end of his European adventure.

There have been quite a few accidents over the years in the business, but they seem to have been mainly falling accidents. I once knew a guy who fell from a speaker tower at a gig, only a fall of about twenty feet. He banged his head severely when he landed; he later died in the hospital. Then there was a guy who fell down an elevator shaft at a gig in England. Unfortunately, the elevator shaft was where the stage should have been. The guy was up on the lighting rig about thirty feet in the air when he actually jumped from the rig. Normally falling thirty feet, you would expect to break a leg maybe at the most. In this arena the seating, the floor and the stage went up and down on hydraulic rams. One of the local guys had dropped the stage down while this lighting guy was up on the rig.

What actually happened was the lighting rig was suspended from the roof, so it was in the same place whether the stage was in the up or down position. It was only about eight feet off of the ground when the lighting guy climbed on to it to do some work. Then the local guy lowered the stage, which the lighting guy never saw him do. After finishing his work on the rig, without looking, thinking he was still eight feet off of the ground, he jumped on to a stage that was now over twenty feet lower than it was when he climbed onto the rig. Realizing his mistake, as he fell, he tried to reach the bleachers seating, which was now higher than the stage. Between the stage and seating there should have been some sections of floor to block off the hole where the hydraulic rams were under the stage. These sections had not yet been put in place. The guy fell down the shaft in between the stage and the floor . . . about sixty feet.

Dangerous stuff this Rock 'n' Roll! I guess I must have been pretty lucky with injuries or careful over the years as the only injury I was to suffer to break my right big toe, twice, in thirty years.

The first time was in 1976, when a guitar amp fell off the back of a truck and landed on my right foot. The second time was ten years later in more bizarre circumstances on a Motley Crue tour. After a really long tiring day, as they all were on this tour, we were on the bus on the way to the next gig. I'd had a couple of lines of cocaine, about a dozen beers and a couple of joints. I felt no pain when I went to my bunk about 2.30 a.m.

Unfortunately, after drinking all that beer I had to get up an hour and a half later to go visit the toilet. I was in a second bunk up so I had to jump down to the floor. I don't know how fast the bus was going but as I jumped down out of my bunk the bus took a right hand bend pretty quick. In the time from me leaving my bunk to landing on the floor, the bus had moved, whilst relatively speaking I was in the same place in midair. Instead of landing on the floor in the aisle, I landed with my right foot on the edge of the bunk opposite. It really fucking hurt!

I quickly staggered down the bus to the toilet and then quickly back to my bunk as the big toe on my right foot was really hurting. I fell asleep again pretty quickly. Four hours later I woke up, the bus had stopped and we were at the next gig. My toe was really

ROCK 'N' ROLL
It's Better than Working for a Living

fucking hurting, so I put on the light in my bunk and saw then that the nail on my big toe was hanging half off. The bunk looked as if Freddie Kruger had visited in the night – it was covered in blood!

After a trip to a local medical center to rip the big toe nail off and get it dressed; I was on light duties for three weeks as I couldn't get a shoe on my foot. That was a really fucking nasty injury.

After my drunken outburst of violence against the BBC trucks at the Blondie gig in Glasgow, I wasn't aware I had any problem whatsoever. Salli had seen my temper and mixed with the alcohol and the ego, I think I was very lucky to get away with that. It wasn't the first time my temper and ego and alcohol had got the better of me. I do remember something happening on one of those Commodores tours.

An old associate of mine, Mick Williams and I and a young upstart at the company Rory Orr were out in Europe on the first Commodores tour we ever did. We were a good crew and we knew it. We got all the good tours from the company and were perhaps a little big headed about it. I think we were one of the best sound crews in the business at the time. This Commodores tour was a breeze for us and the band and management loved us. We always indulged quite heavily in the Rock 'n' Roll lifestyle lots of cocaine, alcohol and, well, you get the picture by now.

One night, after a gig in some sports hall somewhere, in what was then West Germany, we did as we always did. When the band left, we raided the dressing room for left over remnants of the band's rider, beer, wine, spirits and believe or not food also. This one night we went in there and there was nothing. The promoter had taken it all. Now that was not good form. It was an unwritten rule, you always left the food and drink in the dressing room for the crew after the band had left. I was furious and maybe already a little drunk. I picked up a fire extinguisher and sprayed it all around the room, then closed the door and ran away before anyone saw us.

Next day we heard from the promoter, someone had been in the dressing room after the gig and let off a POWDER extinguisher. As a result the room was inhabitable. The promoter would have to pay for it to be redecorated. He never did find out who did it. I had gotten away with it again, but I was getting way out of order and I didn't really know it. It took Salli to sit me down on one tour when she came along for a few days, to tell me. She said if I didn't calm down someone on the tour was going to kill me or would have liked to have done as I was getting so obnoxious and out of order.

But not quite as out of order as someone else I knew. Actually this was someone else I didn't know, but someone who I had heard of. This was a guy called George McQuaid. As you can guess from his name, he was Scottish. As I have mentioned earlier on in this chapter, the Scottish do have a long standing reputation for their intake of alcohol. George was no exception. Unfortunately, George was on his first tour for the company and he wasn't getting off to a very good start. The tour was, in fact, the Judas Priest tour of 1980. This is the same tour where Simon the lighting designer had been left at a truck stop in the middle of the night.

We all left London on the crew bus from the company's headquarters in South London. We were bound for the afternoon

ROCK 'N' ROLL
It's Better than Working for a Living

ferry from Dover to Zeebrugge in Belgium for our overnight hotel stay before the first gig in Amsterdam the next day.

On these ferry journeys it was customary for the crew to spend most of their time, which was usually about four hours on journeys from the UK to mainland Europe, in one of a number of bars or duty free shops where the staple diet of cigarettes and alcohol could be bought at much cheaper prices than in the UK. When we arrived at the port of Zeebrugge, we all trooped back onto the bus for the three hour journey to Amsterdam. It was then, it appeared one of us had spent more time and more money than most of us in the bars and duty free shops. Mr. McQuaid sounded distinctly worse for wear.

On these long bus journeys, people watched videos, played video games, played cards or something and some slept, whatever got you through the journey. On this particular journey, a cribbage school started at the back of the bus. It proved very popular with those of us educated enough to understand the game. Unfortunately, Mr. McQuaid was not one of those. He just carried on drinking, and trying to strike up a conversation with anyone who would listen to his drunken ranting. He was beginning to rant more and more as people tried to ignore him, but he was also getting very abusive. He then decided to pick on the cribbage school. He tried to tell them they should be playing a proper game like poker. He was more or less ignored and told to try to behave as some people just wanted to quietly play the game. To a very irate George, this was like a red rag to a bull. It made him even more abusive and obnoxious. He decided he wanted to fight the participants of the cribbage school one by one or all at once. Once again they just ignored him, which further enraged him. He pulled a cigarette lighter from his pocket and tried to set one of the guy's hair on fire.

MICK (MICHAEL) TYAS

This journey should probably have been another one put under the "Worst Journeys," headings as it was rapidly developing into a bloody nightmare.

The paralytic, abusive Scotsman eventually passed out and left us to enjoy the delights of our bus driver circumnavigating Amsterdam at least three times in a vain effort to locate our hotel. Remember no satellite navigation in those days' only maps. He didn't even have one of them.

We had been on the road getting on for about twelve hours and it was about 1:00 a.m. before the driver eventually found the hotel. Thankfully, the hotel bar was closed, which gave most of us the incentive to crash out as we had an 8:00 a.m. call the next day. Of course, the delights of Amsterdam are open 24/7. So the hardcore decided to sample a few of the delights of the European capital, if not the world capital of sex and drugs. This included the obnoxious Scotsman and we had to give him an A for stamina.

Next morning promised even more chaos than the previous day, if that were possible. Most of us were in a reasonable state, well as reasonable as you can be at 7.45 a.m. There were a few very hurting people on the bus that morning. Of course, you always say . . . "Never again!" but . . . do you ever listen to yourself? Of course not! I was just proud not to be one of them.

We were also about to be treated to another "Mystery Tour" by our exalted bus driver as he tried to navigate the streets of Amsterdam, and find the gig. He really was the worst fucking bus driver I have ever met. The biggest shame is I can't remember his fucking name. I can't find anyone else that remembers either, because he really does deserve a name check. I remember the company he worked for, they were called Trathens Coaches. They themselves became famous in the business for being the worst

ROCK 'N' ROLL
It's Better than Working for a Living

fucking bus company in the whole world. So, he was definitely working for the right company.

There was one notable absence on the bus that morning . . . the obnoxious Scotsman. We all thought he was just so hung-over after his exploits the previous night and couldn't get up or dare not face the rest of the crew in the cold light of the morning after. Apparently, he'd been fired overnight before he even got to the first gig! Now that is some achievement to get fired before you even get to a gig. In this rarified occupation and little fantasy world we lived in – in the business, much of the time it isn't how good an engineer you are, but more so are you able to keep yourself under control. Given the nature of the job; believe me I should know.

So! Big Scotty went home and Big Paddy flew out to replace him and met us at the gig. Big Paddy being Tony Kelly, aka Murph; Tony had been at the company longer than me and thought he was the best monitor engineer in the company. Well . . . so he told everyone. Apart from been totally disillusioned about his status, Tony also had another problem and strangely enough it was the same problem that Big Scotty had . . . ALCOHOL! Luckily, Tony wasn't violent when he was drunk. He just talked and talked and talked and then talked some more and some more and more. I quite liked Tony when he was sober and although not the best monitor engineer in the company, he was still a clever engineer. When he was drunk, which was quite often, you just had to run and hide. He would just talk until you lost the will to live. I have to admit though he was pretty well behaved on this tour. I think he knew he had to be as he had been given some warnings by the company in the past.

So, we eventually went off to do some gigs around Europe. It was all going really well. Good band to work for, easy to please and genuinely nice people. Rob the singer, the most raving queen you would ever meet, except for Freddie Mercury probably. With an amazingly high voice that would cut glass, it was a treat for any sound engineer.

If there is one memory that stands out for me on that tour, it is seeing Rob sitting in his dressing room after the gig talking to my girlfriend about dresses and makeup. He was telling her how they should go out shopping together one day during the tour.

METAL!

I had a lot of time for Judas Priest.

We did eventually get some payback on that dickhead of a bus driver on that tour. When we eventually got back into London, we were all discussing where we wanted the driver to drop us off. Obviously, there has to be a small number of destinations where people could get off near to their homes or forms of public transport or places to grab a cab. I think we narrowed it down to about three stops. If I would have had my way I would have made the driver take each one of us home personally, but we had a secret plan anyway, to teach him a lesson.

I believe that one of the lighting guys and me were the last off of the bus near King's Cross Rail Station in Central London. Just as we were pulling up at the station the lighting guy went into the bathroom on the bus for a quick leak. We then got our baggage out of the trunk and disappeared into the crowds as quickly as possible. When we were safely out of sight of the bus I asked the lighting guy, "Did you do it?"

"Yep" he replied.

What he'd done, at the last minute, was let off a large, probably weapons grade. Sulphur Stink Bomb in the bus toilet. By now the guy would be driving along one of the busiest roads in

London, unable to stop in the ridiculously busy traffic of Central London with the most horrible stinking smoke pouring out of the bathroom, I just wish we could have seen it.

Strangely enough never heard of that guy again, what a fucking shame!

To round off the end of the 70's I want to mention a guy called Bob Geldof. Geldof was lead singer in the moderately successful Irish band the Boomtown Rats. He left Southern Ireland for London in 1976. I had never heard of them until late 1977 and by this time they were having singles in the Top 40 on a regular basis through into 1978 and 79. I first came across them in the summer of 1979, when I was asked to do a one off show with them in Utrecht in Holland after an appearance at the Pinkpop festival.

I thought they were an excellent post-punk band with some good songs. They had a really mouthy lead singer. Although the gig went really well, I could have never worked with that singer on a regular basis. Of course, after forsaking the band for his charity work and organizing the famous Band Aid concerts in both the US and UK in 1985; his mouthy, confrontational style of dealing with business went on to help many thousands of starving people around the world and earned himself a knighthood.

I can't really say any more than, "Never liked the man." I'm not on my own in that respect, but didn't he do well?

1980/81 was a really defining time for me. I was becoming a sought after engineer. I was never out of work; I could have worked twelve months a year and is almost did. I was making lots of money. I was also spending lots of money. I had a beautiful girlfriend, who was also managing to spend lots of money.

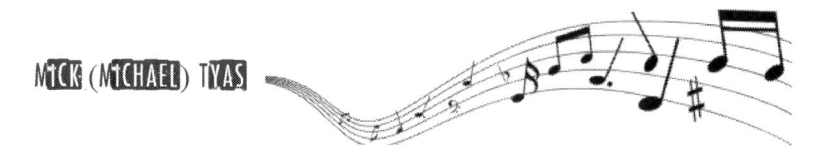

My reputation was building and my bank balance was building. Unfortunately, so was my ego and so were my tastes. On the surface everything was rosy, my relationship with Salli Jane was let's say, interesting. There was never a dull moment. There never was to be for the rest of our time together and apart for that matter. Unfortunately, I think we were both caught up in the hedonistic lifestyle available in the Rock 'n' Roll business. We both caught the bug at the same time. It was pretty good fun, well, most of the time it was.

Some of the bands and Artistes I worked with in 80/81 were the aforementioned Blondie, Average White Band, Foreigner, Kansas, Blackfoot, 38 Special and the jazz rock band Weather Report. The only interesting thing I can think of to say about this band was that we did a gig, which was a semicircular cone, a tit shaped building I suppose you could call it. This building was built right at the beginning of the causeway you have to drive across to get to the watery city of Venice. On the side of the building, there was a ladder you could climb, which went right up to the nipple of the tit (Although there wasn't really a nipple of course.). It was such a beautiful hot summer's day we climbed right to the top of the tit and we were able to see right across the lagoon to St. Mark's cathedral in the centre of Venice.

It was an incredible view, but that was about as interesting as that tour got. That is, apart from the fact I did share my bunk on the bus that night with this beautiful little Italian girl who I had picked up at the gig. She insisted on sleeping in my bunk with me. Who would I be to complain? It was quite handy she was small though as there wasn't much room in those bunks for tumbling about.

That night we were actually on our way to a gig in Ljubljana, which is now in Slovenia I believe. Back then it was in some other country. God knows what! That also meant we had to cross the border of course from Italy into whatever country Ljubljana was in.

I have it now! It was in the slightly Communist country of Yugoslavia in those days. That meant we couldn't really risk taking any extra passengers especially, unfortunately, very pretty ones without passports. So, I had to tell the little girl she had to get out at the border before we attempted to cross into Yugoslavia.

She was heartbroken and really wanted to come with me, but she had to get off the bus at the border. It was really sad to see her stood at the side of the road in the middle of the night as we crossed the border. I often wondered how she got back to Venice from being dumped in the middle of nowhere, probably the same way as she had got there. She was a very resourceful girl.

As you can see many of these bands I've listed are American. I was working with a lot of Americans at the time. One of these bands was REO Speedwagon from the wonderfully named town of Champaign-Urbana in Illinois. The band had three or four Top 40 hits in the early eighties and then disappeared after about 1985. Not a sad loss really, but they had the most amazing road crew. "Amazing" being one word, whereas two others may have been more appropriate; they being the two that make up the much used and very descriptive English colloquialism: "Useless tossers."

At the end of the gig after the last encore, of which there were many as I recall, and the band were taking their 25th bow. The crew would come on stage with a dressing gown each and wrap it around their "favorite" band member just so he didn't catch a chill on his way back to the dressing room. Then as the house lights went on and we descended on the stage to de-rig mics and cables and all the rest of the sound system, the band's crew was nowhere to be seen. Eventually, after about half an hour they appeared on the stage to start de-rigging the band's amps and stuff, each dressed in their OWN fucking monogrammed dressing gown. Incredible! They looked as though they had just been woken up and got out of bed. They had obviously been hanging out in the dressing room with the band celebrating their mutual success. Their success as a road crew was nonexistent and they were a bunch of completely "useless tossers" as already stated.

There are a couple of English bands I worked with in this period, and one of these was Adam and The Ants. A post punk, New Wave band fronted by singer Adam Ant aka Stuart Goddard. I must admit I hated them and thought it was the worst band I had worked with in years. However, for three or four years in the early 1980's they were incredibly successful, which really just sums up how much I had my finger on the pulse of popular music. Well, I don't think I have ever had my finger on the pulse of popular music, even when I thought it was popular it probably wasn't.

Anyway, I did a six week tour of Europe with this lot, must of whom had never been on tour before, so that was going be interesting. I guess we all had to start somewhere or sometime and it was weird, I was starting to act like the experienced old lag. Well, I had been in the business now, in some form or another for getting on for ten years. This was a lifetime of experience in those days as Rock 'n' Roll touring as we now know it, or at least in the format that we now know it, was always said to have started after the last chord of the last encore song of The Beatles concert at Shea Stadium in August 1965. Such was the chaos of the organization, although it took a few more years of tinkering before anything recognizable as a real organized tour took to the road.

Adam and The Ants couldn't believe the glamour of playing in a different sports hall or theatre every night. That's where the big problem lay of course. They believed all the hype and really thought they were a great band, poor disillusioned fools. On stage where the real work was done, they failed to grasp the facts. The band was not going to sound the same as it did when they were sat at home listening to the records on their HiFi or in the recording studio. There were basic rules and parameters that restricted you as to what you were able to achieve on stage as compared to being in a recording studio. Most of those rules dictated by the laws of physics; it was those bloody acoustics! Nasty little creatures.

I had a lot of problems on that tour, which turned into a lesson called; teach yourself gigging in six easy weeks. Nevertheless, I was asked to go to America with them for three weeks on their first promotional tour of the States. It wasn't going to be fun, but at least the bits in between the gigs might be interesting. That's exactly how it turned out. We did a mixture of small clubs and a few TV shows, all of which were a complete nightmare. As I recall, we did Boston, Philadelphia, Washington, San Francisco, Los Angeles, New York and maybe a couple more, all instantly forgettable, except a couple.

Boston, the first gig, was in a tiny club I already knew called The Paradise Club, which still exists today. The problem with playing these little clubs in the US is that, you have to use the house PA and lighting systems. Small clubs worldwide suffer from the lack of investment in the upkeep of these house systems (The only decent ones I've seen have been in Japan, where it would have been a smirch on their honor if it didn't all work properly.).

So you go in these clubs with a touring band and there either isn't enough PA or monitors or half of it isn't working. You are on a loser from the off. Of course, you try to explain the situation to the band and management and everybody says, "Well, we'll just have to compromise and do the best we can." I don't ever remember any band compromising.

I once did a small, though very famous club in Brooklyn, New York called Lamour's with Iron Maiden as a warm up gig for a big American tour. Everybody in the organization, band, management and crew knew this club held about six hundred people as opposed to the six thousand plus they normally played to in arenas. We also explained to the band the stage was about twenty feet wide and ten feet deep. Putting the normal backline on stage would be impossible. So, all agreed they would compromise and put one Marshall Stack each on stage. Unfortunately, Nicko couldn't make his drum kit any smaller.

I knew that only half of the clubs monitor speakers were in working condition, so this wasn't going to be easy. Even with just three Marshall Stacks on stage, as I really didn't have enough monitor speakers, but everybody knew the problems so we just all had to make the best of what we had. Some of us compromised more than others and some of us were just simply compromised!

It's a good job that the local drugs were good that day, because eight Marshall stacks, instead of three and the huge drum riser on the stage left me furious by the end of the set. I was a gnat's gonad away from resigning. Compromise my ass!

ROCK 'N' ROLL
It's Better than Working for a Living

Back to Adam and his Ants in the Paradise Club in Boston; it really was a small club, about five hundred capacity I would guess at the time. I believe it's quite a bit bigger these days. I liked it for some reason. They had this resident girl sound person, not terribly pretty but really helpful and she had the best cocaine ever. She would take you into her little office under the stairs. It really was little. You could hardly stand up in there, but we were in there for hours jawing about everything under the Sun. Considering it was an Adam and The Ants gig, it was a really nice day.

The second gig of the tour was in New York in this sleazy little club called The Ritz on the second floor of this old building on 11th St in the East Village. This was originally a ballroom called Webster Hall. In fact, since 1986 when The Ritz moved to new premises at the former home of Studio 54 on W54th St, Webster Hall has been reborn as a ballroom again.

When we were there in 1981, it was a dowdy replica of its once art deco splendor but there were still a few ghosts around the place. The likes of Elvis Presley, Frank Sinatra, Tina Turner and James Brown had all played this place at various times in its history.

I called my old mate Frank Gallagher when I arrived in New York. He'd been living there for a couple of years after getting the job as sound engineer for Talking Heads (A legend in their own lunchtime in New York.). He still bloody works for them thirty years later, although it now seems to be more of a hobby. He married the wardrobe girl who worked for Kiss and moved to San Francisco. They now run a children's fashion store. Very suitable employment for an ex Rock 'n' Roller I think. Anyway, Frank came down to the Ritz to see me. By this time my girlfriend, Salli had arrived from England, so we would be having a big reunion that evening.

MICK (MICHAEL) TYAS

The Ritz had a small, but quite high stage. Nothing had really changed backstage since probably the days of Prohibition in the 1920's when the Ritz was also a privately run club. It was a famous Speakeasy where people with enough money were unable to notice the Federal ban on the sale of alcohol. It was also rumored to be owned at this time by notorious gangster; Al Capone.

Either side of the stage are men's and women's bathrooms. Men's on the right of the stage, women's on the left. To get backstage from the front of house, you have to go into one or other of the toilets and through a door in the back then up a flight of stairs to the dressing rooms. Many old dance halls and music halls were designed in this manner.

Before the Adam and The Ants set, Frank pulled out a little wrap from his pocket and asked me where we could go to partake of his little treat. I couldn't think of anywhere else, private, except the toilets, "Let's go in the women's then" said Frank. So we went through the door on the left of the stage and into the women's toilets. They really looked as if they hadn't been updated since 1930, probably still haven't. Frank produced a small coke spoon, stuck it into the wrap and then stuck it under my nose, a quick sniff and I realized Frank had got his hands on some quality merchandise and he did the same again.

Just at that moment the door from the front of house opened, which was really annoying. Standing there was this guy in the dark blue uniform, unmistakable, as a New York cop! Shit! We were in trouble now; I thought we were both heading for San Quentin. "Excuse me, sorry to disturb you guys," the cop said. He walked past us towards the dressing rooms. Unbelievable, what a guy, he took no notice of us whatsoever, but we didn't wait around for him to come back that way.

ROCK 'N' ROLL
It's Better than Working for a Living

After the show of course, we all went out of a good drink and to catch up as I hadn't seen Frank in quite a while. It was also Salli's first time in New York. Frank took us to a favorite haunt of his, The Peppermint Lounge uptown on W45 St. It opened in 1958 and was the first real "rock" club in New York City. It was the birthplace of 1960's dance craze . . . The Twist. It was also the first club to ever feature Go Go dancers. The Peppermint Lounge was the haunt of many famous people in the 1960's including Jackie Kennedy, Marilyn Monroe, Frank Sinatra, Truman Capote, Judy Garland, Noel Coward and even the elusive film star, Greta Garbo.

It wasn't really famous for the bands that played there, although The Beach Boys, Chubby Checker, The Isley Brothers and Liza Minelli all played there. It was more famous as an exclusive after hours hang out. There was one very famous musician who played it quite regularly in the 1960's. Joey Dee and The Starlighters was the resident band at the Peppermint Lounge and even had a No.1 single, which was aptly called, *The Peppermint Twist*. They had a young guy on guitar that had just moved to New York from Tennessee by the name of James Marshall Hendrix, who of course went on to much bigger things.

Being engineer for one of New York's most famous bands, Frank of course, had a pass to the VIP lounge at The Peppermint, which I thought was pretty cool. I had heard of The Peppermint Lounge. I even had a copy of Joey Dee and The Starlighters single. I had always wanted to visit this famous club, never thinking I would be snorting cocaine off of a glass table top in the VIP lounge with lots of other VIPs I had never heard of.

I think the place closed about 3 am so as it was still "early." Frank decided to take us to another club down in the "Village," but not before a strange thing happened. We came out of the

Peppermint Lounge and right next door was a Kebab take out joint, which of course was still open and as we walked past a voice screamed . . . "Oi."

Somewhat startled I turned thinking someone had been murdered, but instead I saw an old friend of ours from London called Graham Reynolds. He was standing there with a huge doner kebab in his hand. Graham had been in the club all night, not in the VIP lounge of course as he was only a "roadie." Graham was roadie with British metal band Motorhead and had been in the club with another old reprobate we knew from way back, bass guitarist and founder of Motorhead, Lemmy. We tried to get Graham to come down the Village with us, but Graham was too drunk, too wired, too fucked up and too hungry!

I never did know the name of the place that Frank took us to in the Village, but I remember it as being a little like a large café. It was dark and pretty empty, but we did bump into Lemmy there who had decided to go on to another round of drinking and amphetamines, leaving the lightweight Graham in the Kebab shop. As we were all pretty much off our tits by then, it didn't really matter if there was anyone else in the club or not, as long as they sold alcohol.

Lemmy joined us at a table. We were all talking "at" each other as fast as was possible and drinking as many drinks and smoking as many cigarettes as possible. Suddenly, I saw this apparition at the bar. Of course, I was with my girlfriend, but that didn't really seem to bother me in my less than sober state. I went up and spoke to this beautiful tall long blond haired woman and asked her if she wanted to join us at our table, to which she replied coyly, "Yeah, might do."

ROCK 'N' ROLL
It's Better than Working for a Living

It was definitely lust at first sight; I wasn't really bothered that Salli, Frank and Lemmy were sat at the table watching me all this time. Anyway, I went back to our table. Salli never said a word to me, which in normal circumstances would have been unusual, after watching her boyfriend chatting up another woman and strangely enough no one else said anything either.

Then the blond Goddess came over to our table, introduced herself and SAT ON MY KNEE!!! Whoa!! What a night this was going to be, I had visions of sex and debauchery with not only my girlfriend but with this gorgeous stranger also. These thoughts were all being fuelled by the fact Salli hadn't objected to this woman sitting on her man's knee and rubbing his groin, I was very excited. Just then Lemmy got up and came around the table and whispered in my ear. Lemmy had a worldwide reputation as a serial womanizer. I thought he was after a little of the upcoming action, then he said: "It's a fellah!"

I didn't even question this statement, which in my euphoric state, I thought I might have done, but I didn't.

I jumped up immediately and yelled: "Hey, get the fuck away from me!" The "Goddess" jumped about six feet in the air and came back with a with a suitable New York retort, "And fuck you too asshole" and stormed off.

Salli, Lemmy and Frank were almost rolling on the floor laughing, how come they had spotted it and I hadn't? Talk about blinded by the light. I had had enough and wanted to go back to the hotel, my carnal fantasies were in tatters. Still, it could have turned out a whole lot worse.

I still don't know to this day, was it a setup?

1981 was going to be a really busy year for me. Of course, working in a freelance capacity for a sound company, you could actually say no to a certain tour or gig if you were offered it. There weren't many of us about in those days, so there was work aplenty. Today, you can go to a college for six months and come out a sound engineer or rather with a piece of paper that says you are a sound engineer. In 1981, the only way to learn how to be a sound engineer was to do it, so I did. I did every gig or tour I could get my hands on from 1973 onwards and this year was no exception, I accepted everything I was offered and a strange collection of gigs and tours it turned out to be.

Billy Connolly was a rough, loud Scottish standup comedian and also a musician who played guitar and banjo. He'd dumped his frumpy first wife from Scotland, who he married when he was quite young and took up with a beautiful blond English TV personality called Pamela Stephenson. They were the Talk of the Town in 1981.

Billy went out on tour in 1981. A guy called Steve Cox and I was asked to do the tour. It was a bit of a low budget affair, sometimes staying in one hotel in the North West of England and traveling every day to the big cities in the area like Manchester, Liverpool, and Sheffield etc. They were only a two hundred mile round trip every day at the most, but that becomes a little bit of a pain after you finish loading out at 1:30 a.m. and don't get back to the hotel until 3:00 a.m. Then find that Billy has kept the bar open and end up drinking until 6:00 a.m. every morning. Billy liked a drink and lots of other things also. Of course, Billy went on to do quite a lot of TV work in America, but they never did get off on his standup comedy. It was a shame really, I never actually liked the guy very much, but at the time I would have rated him along with Bill Hicks.

Chapter Eight

THE WALL

In 1981 the Berlin Wall had been in existence for almost twenty years. It separated the Russian occupying forces, the East German collaborators and the unfortunate citizens of East Berlin and East Germany from us in the West.

One of my hobbies at this time was reading spy fiction novels and also spy fact. This was a busy time for writers like John Le Carre, Len Deighton and Tom Clancy. I read everything they wrote. I knew the names of all the districts in Moscow and the names of the streets. Even the KGB prisons in Moscow and East Berlin.

In the summer of 1981, I was asked if I wanted to do a big show with English progressive rock band, Barclay James Harvest. They were doing an outdoor show on the lawns in front of the steps of the Reichstag in West Berlin. This is the historic old parliament building of the German government, up until the end of World War II, when it was almost totally destroyed by Allied bombs and shells. I was first on the bus.

I had been to Berlin many times before on tour with various bands but I had never seen the Berlin Wall close up. I had seen it from the air whilst coming into land at Templehof airport. It cut through the center of Berlin like a huge wound in the landscape, but the Reichstag backed right up against the Wall. When the Wall was built in 1961, The Brandenburg Gate formed the border between East and West in this part of Berlin. The Wall swung round to the left behind the Reichstag. The Russians really couldn't have built it any closer to the Reichstag or it would have been part of the Wall.

The stage was built on the grass in front of the main entrance to the building. If you looked to the right of the building or even walked down the right hand side of the building you would actually come face-to-face with the Vopos. They were the despised East German border guards. The Vopos stood on their thirty foot high raised platforms looking suspiciously over the wall with binoculars at all this strange action taking place on the Western side. We even waved to them and they waved back! Just wishing they could get over that bloody wall I should think. They would probably have been shipped off to Siberia for twenty years of hard labor in the Gulags if they had been spotted waving to us by their Kommandant. The stage had been erected specifically to one side of the front of the building, so it could be seen by the Vopos from the wall, just to show what they were missing I guess. All this Western decadence and, Barclay James Harvest.

I felt the gig itself was somewhat overshadowed by this historic location.

Barclay James Harvest was formed in the North of England in 1966 and was regarded as one of the most "progressive" of the Progressive Rock bands of their era. With one song lasting the length of one side of an album sometimes and twenty-five minute guitar solos, I guess they must have sold quite a few albums in the UK over the years. Their popularity was somewhat limited, mainly because they were so fucking boring! The Germans, though, did like a good Progressive Rock outfit. The evidence being in their own bands of the time, like Amon Duul, Kraftwerk, Tangerine Dream and countless others; the highlight of my day however, was being allowed into the Reichstag. Still bearing some of the scars of World War II, that's the Reichstag . . . not me, it was a magnificent building inside and pretty well completely restored. There was still work in progress. Being allowed into what were allegedly Hitler's offices for a short while was a bit of a buzz. I wanted to go down into the cellars, but unfortunately that was "verboten." I'll bet there was something interesting stuff down there.

I did actually make a couple of journeys into East Berlin on days off on tour, in 1987 and 1989, literally weeks before the Berlin Wall was demolished.

The first time I went over to the East was on an Iron Maiden tour in 1987. The band always used to try and get days off in interesting places. Being an avid spy novel reader, I thought Berlin was a fantastic place for a day off. West Berlin in those days was a fabulously decadent, bright and cosmopolitan Western city, but once you went over to the East, everything was very different. Four of us that day decided to go into East Berlin for a few drinks in an East German "pub," which I believe is as good an excuse as any for visiting a Communist state. Like all good spies, we decided to take the U Bahn underground rail system, which was now a rather weird railway as some of the West German trains ran through the East without stopping due to the nature of the route. Whereas you could get a train from downtown West Berlin to Friedrichstrasse station, which although in the Eastern sector, the Communists authorities allowed the West German trains in mainly for tourists and for spies such as ourselves that had business in the East. It was all a pretty strange sight as the bright new West

ROCK 'N' ROLL
It's Better than Working for a Living

Berlin trains plastered with advertising pulled into the drab Friedrichstrasse station.

After we'd gone past the Vopos checkpoint, who didn't give us a second luck, obviously we were well "under cover." We walked down the main street, which looked surprisingly clean and tidy, and spied what we thought looked like a pub, and it was. No neon signs or advertising but it's amazing, it seems whatever country you are in anywhere in the world, spotting a hostelry that sells alcohol is the easiest thing in the world. Now this place really was spy territory, grubby curtains in the windows, three electric light bulbs of about 25 watts each in the whole bar. They turned the whole scene inside into sepia tones. There was a distinct lack of color. It was like walking into a bar in Montana, two hundred miles from the nearest town. The place just went silent when four long haired Englishmen walked in. I must admit it was a little weird, but I have been in scarier places and as soon as we went over to the bar and ordered "vier grosse bier bitte" the place carried on as before.

We found a free table in the gloom. Even if you didn't smoke, you were liable to catch some terminal lung disease in this bar as you could hardly see the person sat across from you in the thick fog of cheap Russian cigarette smoke. The beer was excellent and I sat there imagining a spy sat in every dark corner. It is quite possible of course that there could have been a couple of East Berlin undercover Vopo officers in there, as it was the first bar the Westerners came to when they left the station.

We sat there for about three hours and drank about five or six rounds of these excellent "grosse biers." By this time we were well and truly under the influence and happy to be so. We had to leave and catch the Ubahn back to the West, so we wished everyone in the bar "eine sehr gute nacht" which was returned by all our new friends in the bar. We staggered off for the West. We had spent the equivalent of about $10 between all of us that afternoon and we met some really friendly East Berliners who wanted to know about London and New York and Los Angeles. I had imagined myself as a spy, albeit a pretty drunken spy. What a wonderful day!

The second time I went into East Berlin was literally weeks before the fall of the Wall. This time, we were on an extremely low budget tour and five of us (Two sound guys, two lighting guys and one guy for the band equipment.) were driving ourselves on the tour in a large Ford Station Wagon. I think the name of the Artiste was a guy called Linton Kwesi Johnson. He was a kind of West Indian poet, with his words put to music. It was the spoken word and not singing, but it was all instantly forgettable. Anyway, once again we had a day off in West Berlin and it was summer 89. So, being a nice sunny morning we decided to take a tourist trip into East Berlin but this time we were going to go by car. This would be extremely interesting as we had already had a run in with the Vopos on the way into West Berlin. There was only one way to drive over to East Berlin and that was through the infamyous Checkpoint Charlie on Freidrichstrasse, just down the road from the train station where I had previously crossed into East Berlin.

Once again, we looked like a bunch of hippies with attitude, driving a big Western car. The Vopos didn't usually bother Westerners it was just the East Berliners they were after who trying to get out, so we weren't particularly worried about going in and thousands of tourists did it every day. We were very friendly to the rather serious and grumpy looking guards. I suppose you'd be rather grumpy if you had to do that job and live there in those days on a dollar a day. When the guard stopped us at the barrier going into the Eastern sector he took a cursory look at our passports, satisfied we weren't American (They didn't like Americans in those days, not much has changed really has it?) or West German smugglers, be it drugs or people, we thought he was happy to let us go. Then he ordered; "open ze ashtray," which the guy who was driving did and in the same instant I felt in my pocket to see if I had five deutsche marks handy so as to call my mother and tell her to get the family lawyer on the first plane to Berlin, because I thought I was gonna need him!

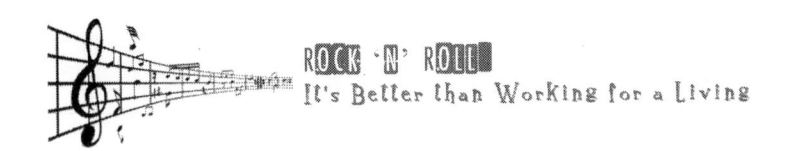

In the ashtray were lots of cigarette butts and the remains of a ripped up Rizla cigarette rolling paper packet. It was ripped up the way you would rip it to make a roach (filter) for a joint.

"You have marijuana?"

"No, no, no, no, no, no, no, definitely no!" We said, far too many times to be believable. How the fuck was he going to believe that? I had visions of strip searches in a freezing cold room and spending a night in a rat infested East German prison, which would have been the not so glamorous side of been a spy, but he waved us on????????

"OK. Thank you."

After our little drama at the border, we decided to take a small drive around downtown East Berlin, which I must admit looked much grimmer than last time I was there.

We were a little conspicuous in our big Ford Station Wagon, so we decided to park and take a stroll. Then again there weren't that many people strolling. Guessing the locals stayed inside and tried to keep out of trouble. Nevertheless we headed for a multi-story parking garage, driving down this big wide boulevard with huge stone palatial 19th houses on either side of the road, which now probably housed about 50 families each. The incongruous sight in this elegant street of houses, of piles of coal and logs stacked on the wide sidewalks. Guess that was the Communist ethic, back to basics, no central heating for you.

We drove into the parking garage to see it mostly full of the East German's favorite car, The Trabant. With an engine the size of a lawnmower engine and cardboard body (allegedly), the size of a shoe box. There was allegedly a fifteen year waiting list to acquire one of these beauties in the old Communist days, mainly because unless you were President of the country or a State sponsored drug dealer, you couldn't get any other make of vehicle. We parked the station wagon in between two Trabants on the first floor and then discovered our error.

Although this was a multi-story parking garage with a capacity to probably park two thousand cars. It was built to park the same car, The Trabant! Consequently, the spaces in the garage were all Trabant size. We had parked between two Trabants and found the station wagon was not Trabant size. It was much larger. So, although we got into the space, we couldn't actually open the doors when we were in it. We quickly gave up on the idea of a stroll and drove back down the elegant boulevard and back over to the West slightly disappointed. We also felt very lucky we weren't spending the night in Hohenschönhausen, which was an infamous detention center run by the Stasi, the dreaded East German secret police

As I wrote earlier, we had had an earlier run in with the local Vopos on the road to Berlin. When the city of Berlin was split into two Berlins after World War II by the US/British/French on one side and the Russians on the other, it wasn't just Berlin that was split in two; it was the whole of Germany. We had the West and the Russians had the East, obviously. Unfortunately, for many

Berliners, Berlin was in the East so when West Berliners wanted to visit the rest of the Free World, they had a problem . . . sixty miles of Russian occupied East Germany. Of course, the Russians didn't want all these capitalist Westerners giving any of the occupied population of the East any big ideas about making a run for freedom and making their own money. The Russian and East German States wanted their money, so under pressure from the rest of the Free World a corridor had to be created to allow Westerners to visit capitalist West Berlin and vice versa. Ok! Political lesson over.

What happened was that the Russians and East Germans dug up the Bundesautobahn which ran between Hannover and Berlin at the town of Marienborn in the East and Helmstedt in the West. They put a border checkpoint there eventually rebuilding it in the 1970's to the size of a small town. Putting this checkpoint in and one at the Berlin end at Dreilinden / Drewitz, this autobahn "corridor" allowed Westerners and West Berliners access to the Free World. Of course, no Eastern Bloc citizens or East Berliners were allowed on it.

Driving to Berlin for a gig was a nightmare, you could wait anything up to six hours at a time to get through the East German passport control, causing huge gridlock on the West German side, but the East Germans weren't in any hurry to let people into their "country."

It was always rumored that vehicles joining the corridor at the East German border post, were timed on their journey down the corridor to make sure they didn't make an excursion into the East German countryside. There were exits off the freeway, but you weren't allowed to use them. You were; however, allowed to stop at the two or three truck stops on the road and these were the undoing of many a Rock 'n' Roll road crew.

The truck stops were called Intershops; they were Communist hard currency stores and restaurants. They sold Western cigarettes, perfumes, alcohol, chocolate and lots of other duty free goods you would normally see in an airport today. The prices in the Intershops were vastly discounted compared to prices in the West, an example would be a litre bottle of Remy Martin VSOP brandy that would cost you maybe $50 in Western Europe, would cost you $10 at the Intershop consequently there were always lots of people with big headaches at the gig the next morning.

The story of gigging in Berlin is almost finished, but I'll finish it with the story of the drive to Berlin in the Ford station wagon.

The freeway where it went through East Germany was never too well maintained by the East Germans. Obviously, they thought we have to allow these despicable capitalists to transit through our country, but we don't have to make it comfortable for them. All the times I had traveled down that road, I never ever saw anybody working on it.

It really was a mess. It made the streets of New York look like a bowling green. There were pot holes in it big enough to swallow a medium sized car and there was a speed limit of 50mph on it. 50mph really was optimistic on this road unless you had wings fitted and a parachute in the back seat.

So we set off in our big Station Wagon traveling after the last gig from Hannover to Berlin for a gig in some weird little theater, of which Berlin had lots. It was somewhat similar to the seedy little place you can see in the movie Cabaret. We had been traveling about two hours and we were on the East German autobahn . . . the dreaded "corridor."

Surprisingly, we sailed through the East German passport control. Well, "sailed through" was a relative term compared to the four to six hours it could take sometimes. I think we did it in about an hour and it was as dark as hell. No lights in East Germany, no fucking electricity in this part of East Germany!

After another couple of hours of bouncing around, which wasn't too bad in our softly sprung Capitalist luxury vehicle; fuck knows what it was like driving a Trabant down that road. I should think you'd be lucky to get out without any serious head injury and a fully functioning road vehicle (I almost said car then!) The road suddenly seemed to smooth out a little, which was very unusual for that road. We were nearing the civilization of West Berlin. I was driving at the time and thought I had had enough of the 40mph crawl we had had to travel at for the last two hours. I decadently put my foot down hoping to get to a bar before they all closed, absent mindedly forgetting that West Berlin was a twenty four hour city of course. Within seconds I hit the dizzying speed of 70mph, cool!

What the fuck was that!!!!!

I thought we had been nuked; there was the brightest light I had ever seen in my life that went on for a quick second straight in front of me. It blinded me momentarily so I couldn't see the road.

I slammed the brakes on immediately, literally two minutes later two Vopo patrol cars came up behind us. They were very smart looking Ladas I might add, obviously the pride of the fleet.

"You were driving at 112Kph, which is illegal on this road, the speed limit is 70Kph. There is an instant speeding fine of 20 US dollars or the equivalent in British pounds or West German Deutsche Marks, can you pay this?"

"Ja" I told him, "no problem." I gave him 30 dollars, as I was feeling particularly generous and it was probably the cheapest ticket I had ever had.

It was always a good idea to carry dollars in East European countries, as it was more or less equivalent to gold dust to the locals.

"Keep the change," I told him

The Vopo wrote me a receipt for 20 dollars wished me "dankeschon and gute nacht." They drove off into the night, two happy little Vopos.

Three things struck me about that incident. (1) Two policeman hiding in the trees on a major highway with a laser or whatever it was, a speed trap light bright enough to blind a driver and maybe cause him to drive off the road, would not be allowed in any Western country. (2) I later realized why that stretch of road was so smooth; it was East German psychology, very Communist thinking. After 50 miles of a diabolically pot holed road, suddenly when the traveler is only ten miles from civilization make the road as smooth as a bowling green and the driver will think exactly like I did, fuck this, ten miles to go, let's get there! A perfectly laid trap.

The third thing that struck me was this: I had probably given those two Vopos a tip equal to both their weeks' wages put together and that made me feel really good.

I haven't been to Berlin since 1989, but I still have a piece of the Berlin Wall sitting on my desk. I must go back soon and see if it's as inhumane as it always used to be.

I did one landmark tour in 1981; well it was a landmark for me. This was with Liza Minelli, who I found out earlier was the daughter of Judy Garland. Ms. Garland had been a pretty famous singer and film star, starting as a child protégée in the mid 1920's through until her death in 1969. She suffered from amphetamine and barbiturate addiction during her working life due to the pressure of the work she was put under. Uppers to get her going and keep her going during the day; downers to put her to sleep at night; she eventually died of a barbiturate overdose at the age of forty seven. It would appear that Liza had been rumored to have been "her mother's daughter," which I could never have believed at the time, as she was an international superstar both as a singer and an actress . . . we shall see!

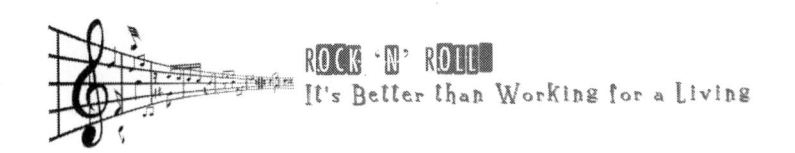

I agreed to do the Liza Minelli tour as I don't think I had worked with anyone so famous. At the time, I was doing as much work as I could for a few reasons . . . 1) to feed a my blossoming drug habit; 2) to feed a girlfriend with a blossoming shopping habit and an aversion for work; and 3) to try and carry on learning how to be a sound engineer. After seven years, I still didn't have a fucking clue what I was doing. I knew how to make a sound system work. I knew how to EQ microphones to make the band sound good, but when people started talking about watts, ohms, impedance, balanced lines, and line inputs . . . I was lost. The only balanced lines I knew were the ones I put up my nose.

The American guys working with Liza were old pros. The front of house engineer had been Frank Sinatra's sound engineer for the last ten years for God's sake. Of course, these days all the bright new engineers learn their sound engineering at college. When I started the only thing you learned at college were bookkeeping, history and geography. You learned how to be a sound engineer when someone sat you behind a mixing console and said, "You can mix the band can't you?"

"Yeah, no problem!"

A Liza Minelli tour didn't sound very Rock 'n' Roll to me at the time, but I took it on. It was one of the best decisions I ever made in my career, which was good because I made some fucking God awful ones years after.

The first gig was in Copenhagen. We got into town the night before. We were, of course, obliged to go out to a bar and drinks gallons of Elephant Beer. So, as usual in Copenhagen, the next morning I woke up with what felt like an Elephant's foot on my head.

Liza's crew though were really nice people and so professsional. Not professional like most American engineers in Rock 'n' Roll are . . . where they regard themselves as knowing everything about anything and waste no time telling you so, when the fact is they have their heads up their own ass. In those cases, it would be advantageous to everyone if they just shut the fuck up.

No, these people were nice people. These people knew their shit. They were also adults and acted like adults, rather than children let loose in a computer store. They were people you could invite over to dinner without worrying about their behavior and if they were going to leave white powder all over the cistern in your bathroom. They were very sympathetic when we all turned up with very sore heads on the first day of the tour.

Max, the FOH engineer from the sound company and I were really just system engineers on this tour. That is; we came with the equipment from the sound company and were responsible for rigging. This means, prepping the whole system including speakers, amps, consoles, cabling, mics, stands and etc. and making it all work the first time . . . hopefully. Hank and Richard were Liza's engineers who came over with her from America. So, we were literally as they are called in the business, "babysitters." This was cool as these guys were so good you had to be impressed. I guess Frank Sinatra would have demanded the best engineers in the world anyway, with not a "cowboy" in sight.

I was somewhat wary at the beginning this was going to be a really boring tour, as it looked like Cabaret to me. It was not like the movie Liza starred in; however, the form of concert where the audience is comfortably seated and politely applaud after each song and in some places where they can eat and drink at tables in the auditorium rang true. The band looked pretty cabaret. They were all very smartly dressed. The leader / musical director seated at the piano was in a dinner jacket and bow tie. The horn section, string section and all the others were reading from sheet music.

Liza sang lots of "standards." These were old time songs your Mum and Dad would have loved, but that's where similarity ended. Although the audience did start off polite and reserved, they soon got rowdy.

It was a kicking band, orchestra or whatever it was. Elliott Randall was on guitar and he was a legend in his own lunchtime. He had literally played with everybody from Steely Dan to Paul McCartney and everyone else on either side of them. They were tight and what a big sound! The audiences were only reserved until Liza's voice cut loose. She had them standing in the aisles and screaming their heads off after fifteen minutes. By the time she got to "New York, New York," they wouldn't let her off the stage and went on to do encore after encore every night.

As a sound engineer I was never that interested in what type of music the band I worked for played. It was just a job I enjoyed doing. I can honestly say with Liza, it may not have been the type of music I was into at the time (I was a "rocker!"), but this women was just so good you just had to be impressed. Even to this day I don't think I have ever seen such immense performances, EVERY FUCKING NIGHT!

This was not going to be a boring tour after all. We were in the best hotels. We were taken out to dinner by promoters. And, we were really well looked after by everyone. Everything was first class. The band and the crew were a pleasure to work with and Liza was a breath of fresh air every day. Being a worldwide superstar she still had the time to sit and talk to any of us about friends, families, our childhood . . . anything. Even years after I had worked with her she still used to send my girlfriend and me, a Christmas card every year, what a nice person! You may think that this all sounds a little grown up, well it is, but Liza had many sides to her personality.

Of course, with a name like Minelli it's not too hard to guess she has some Italian heritage in her family. We did quite a few shows in Italy. I remember one specific day off "somewhere" in Italy; the whole band and crew numbering about thirty-five people were invited to a family lunch by some distant relatives of Lisa's. This was a beautiful summer's day. It was a typical outdoor Italian lunch at a huge long table with enough food and wine on it for a thousand people. This lunch went on all day and well into the evening. I met distant aunts and uncles and cousins and nephews. We were all treated like family. Fabulous day out!

As I said earlier, I believe at that time that Liza was very much rumored to be "her Mother's daughter" in many respects. She would be the first to admit she had a few of her own demons, though to see and hear her performances you would never guess it.

I know she liked hard liquor but I would never assume or intimate she had any more serious demons. On a couple days when she turned up at the venue for a sound check, I was talking to her backstage and she asked me, "Have you seen Mr. Zoom today Mick?" This confused me for all of about thirty seconds until I realized that was her code for cocaine. I said "I had," and that it was awful stuff.

I would never intimate, as I have said, that Liza had anything to do with cocaine. I could never afford the lawsuit. In a way though, I think it would have been her kind of drug.

On another day off on the tour, this time in San Remo, an Italian resort on the Riviera just down the Mediterranean coast from Nice and Cannes, Liza invited all the band and crew to have breakfast with her in the hotel at the very sociable time of noon. Our Liza knew what mornings were for, they were for staying in bed; so about thirty-five of us took over the restaurant for "breakfast."

"Ok guys order whatever you like. I'll order the champagne for you. I've gotta have a couple of large Bloody Mary's before I touch the champagne." Liza knew how to do breakfast!

After the delights of the food and drink of Italy, with the odd gig thrown in just to break up the monotony of champagne breakfasts, we moved on to Paris. Now, this really was Liza territory.

We were doing a week of shows at the old Olympia Music Hall. It was built in the 1880's in the Montmartre district and played host to every big French star there ever was. Stars like Maurice Chevalier, Sacha Distel, Johnny Hallyday and probably the most evocative of all . . . Edith Piaf. It has been a big venue for international acts for over a hundred years now, although a capacity of only just over two thousand. The likes of The Beatles, Jimi Hendrix, Led Zeppelin and The Rolling Stones have all played in the beautiful auditorium and international acts of today still fill it virtually every night.

I think Liza wanted to play the Olympia due to the fact Edith Piaf virtually made it her home for many years. There's certainly a whole bunch of history in the place. Liza played there for seven nights and could have probably filled it for a couple of months.

Playing the same venue for seven nights can sometimes be quite dangerous as you find yourself with too much time on your hands, especially after the show. When the only work you have to do is flip a big switch to turn off the engines, you have the rest of the night to go out and get into trouble in Paris. Luckily, most of the next day is allowed to sleep it off.

Occasionally, we had a guide to help us after the show, to show us where to go for a good time. Not the kind of guide you would ever imagine, but an *International Superstar*!

One night, maybe, I think it was after the second show Liza had probably got sick of hanging out with the great and the good of the Parisian glitterati. When five or six of us were walking past her dressing room door on our way out of the theater Liza stuck her head out and yelled, "Hey guys wanna go out to a bar?"

Somewhat dumbfounded by an *International Superstar* inviting us out for a drink, we collectively agreed it was a great idea. I think by now we were realizing Liza was no ordinary Superstar. There was nothing she liked better than slumming it with the boys. "Let me just call the limo driver and we'll go," she said. So seven of us piled into the big Daimler limo, which dropped us all off at a small bar in the Montmatre and waited for us outside and it waited a long while. I think we left about 4.30 a.m. Liza was still up for more, but we, been the lightweights we were, thanked her and disappeared off to our rooms.

I wouldn't have been surprised if she hadn't have gone out again rampaging around Paris, but maybe she just went up to her suite to her very, very patient new husband.

I worked with a few girls singers that year. American singer Phoebe Snow, famous crooner Nat "King" Cole's daughter Natalie and 1960's British legend, Dusty Springfield.

The other two were just one off gigs in London, but we did a small British tour with Dusty, which all felt a little weird. In the 1960's of course, Dusty had been huge, probably regarded as the second best "soul" singer at the time behind the great Aretha Franklin. Dusty had a somewhat chequered career. After a few hit records, along with her brothers in The Springfields, Dusty left the trio in 1963 to embark on a solo career. For the next seven years she had many hit records both in the UK and America, this left her with Grammies and Hall of Fame awards. However, in 1970 she disappeared from the music scene with rumors about her health and problems in her personal life. The tour in 1981 was I guess a part of her comeback after so many years. Although a great singer and really nice person, she seemed to be quite a sad person. She did have some chart success again in the late 80's but was diagnosed in 1995 with breast cancer and died four years later.

1982 was a real quiet year for me. The sound company I had been working for since 1977 was going through some changes. Although it had been one of the big three sound companies in Europe since the mid 70's, Ricki the owner sold the London end of the business to concentrate on his Los Angeles venture. Most of the original engineers from the old days had moved to LA to start TFA Electrosound LA. The company in London was bought up by a large corporate event conglomerate called Theater Projects. It then sold to a large worldwide event corporation called Samuelsons. The company by this time had been losing all of its large clients to the American companies such as Showco and Clair Brothers. They did; however, secure a large contract from a French promoter to go over to France and do some tours with many of the large French acts of the time. It all seemed like second rate stuff compared to some of the clients we had worked with in the past. I only really remember one highlight of those French tours. It was when my then friend, and fellow engineer Steve Connolly, and I spent a whole three week tour trying to teach the French crew how to play the old English game of cricket.

There was another highlight in 1982. It is last story from this period of my career, because from 1983 things were going to be very different. What else to finish this section but a second tour with LIZA.

For the second tour with Liza in two years, nothing had changed. We stayed in the best five star hotels. We were forever taken out to dinner and treated like Royalty. We also played some really interesting venues, from the London Palladium where she had appeared with her mother in 1964 . . . to Teatro Tendas in Italy, which has huge circus tents with saw dust and horse shit on the floor. Even the big famous opera singers played these shows. Another unusual one back in Paris . . . The Moulin Rouge!

The Moulin Rouge was opened in 1889. It is regarded as the first and still the most spectacular, Parisian cabaret venue ever. It was the haunt in the 1890's of the famous 4'6" tall painter, Toulouse Latrec. He would sit in the audience and paint pictures of the Can Can girls.

These days the cabaret stands out, in more ways than one for its half-naked dancing girls and huge productions. These include a couple of girls swimming with a couple of dolphins in a huge tank, which comes up on a big industrial elevator from below the stage. We were going to do a gig there!

We were going to do the rigging overnight as the final floor show finished at 12.30 a.m. There was a lunchtime show the next day at 1:00 p.m. so we could rig sound and lights. We couldn't; however, have anything on the stage until about 4:00 p.m. the next day.

We arrived in Paris in the afternoon. We went to check into our hotel, which we found to be the 5 star Hotel Le Meurice. It is a beautiful early 19th century hotel, which is more of a museum than a hotel. It really is a "Grand" hotel. During World War II, it was the headquarters of the German High Command. Nice place for an office!

We were due to load in about midnight, but being such a strange place to be doing a gig we thought we would go down a little earlier just to plan where we were going to put everything. We got there about 11:30 p.m. The show was in full swing and a pretty glamorous affair it was.

It was like a Las Vegas show, but with style and class and lots of bare tits! I could quite happily do a gig there every day! We were shown through the club by the manager to the backstage area, which was quite a small area with about ten small dressing rooms. There was perfume and feathers all over the place. We were introduced to Madame Doris who had been running the dancing girl troupe since the 1960's and still does.

The show was just coming to an end when we were hanging out backstage and suddenly the backstage area was full of statuesque women. All of them were over six feet tall and "dressed" in spangled, feathered costumes. All of them with BARE TITS! I think we just stood there staring for a few seconds before getting back to the job in hand (?).

When all the punters had left and we started loading in, all the girls were leaving their dressing rooms. They were getting ready to go home and even dressed. They were still gorgeous. Unbelievably, they nearly all had little French poodles (dogs, for the uninitiated). Obviously, poodles were the obligatory fashion accessory for a dancing girl in Paris. I think the dancing girls were as curious to see a bunch of long haired Rock 'n' Rollers in their club, as we were to be there; a few of them were very chatty. I thought I would be Mr. Worldly and try out my very limited Rock 'n' Roll French on them.

"Oh! I can't talk very good French," one blond Goddess told me in a thick Yorkshire accent.

"Where are you from?" I asked her.

"I'm from Bradford and my friend Loretta is from Leeds."

Unbelievable, they were nearly all English. Many of them had really thick Northern English accents, but that didn't matter, they were all gorgeous. Then they all went home . . . *fantasy over guys*.

After rigging all the equipment overnight, which included exploring the club and finding the dolphin tank under the stage on a huge hydraulic lift . . . we trudged back to our five star home about 7:30 a.m. Entering the grand reception hall we crossed to the elevators to go up to our rooms for a few hours' sleep. Just as we were getting in the elevator, Liza with somewhat exhausted looking new husband in tow jumped in the elevator with us. 7:30 a.m. and she was just coming in after a night out on the town!

"Hi guys, wanna come up to my place for breakfast?"

This time we had to turn her offer down. We were just too tired. She just had so much energy. We would have sat there talking and eating and drinking all day, then we would have been in trouble. What a way to tour the world. I could have done Liza Minelli tours for the rest of my life.

The end of that tour was the last time I saw Liza; although we still got Xmas cards every year for a while. She gave us all a great big hug and a big thank you for all we had done on the tour.

It should have been us thanking her. It was such a privilege just to spend time with such a warm, caring, friendly person. She still is the most professional Artiste I ever met in the business.

Liza will make one more appearance later on.

Chapter Nine

LORELEI, WEST GERMANY

17th. June 1978

Waving his revolver menacingly in the air with the trigger cocked, the young and stoned M.P. (Military Policeman) impressed his compatriots and anyone else in earshot . . . "If any of those suckers come near me, they're gonna get a bellyful from this little baby!"

No, this is not an American military war game played out in the fields of West Germany. This is, in fact, a rock concert headlined by 1960's San Francisco band, Jefferson Starship. They were supported by Brand X, a metamorphosis of Genesis, fronted by drummer, Phil Collins.

The day hadn't started too well. We arrived overnight in our crew bus from Amsterdam. Most of us were in a somewhat tender condition after sampling the narcotic pleasures available in Amsterdam. Then we were woken at 8:00 a.m. seeing what was a natural amphitheater overlooking the River Rhine. It was a very beautiful setting for an outdoor rock gig, but heavy dark clouds threatened a huge downpour. In fact, it had been raining most of the night, so it was pretty damp under foot already.

Undeterred by the heavy looking weather, the local promoters decided they had to press on with getting everything rigged.

ROCK 'N' ROLL
It's Better than Working for a Living

10,000 tickets had already been sold. These folks were going to expect to see a show even if a swarm of locusts were forecast.

We started rigging the lights, sound and backline, albeit somewhat reluctantly. The rain had just started to fall very heavily and water and electricity don't mix well. Still we pressed on regardless. Still horribly hung over.

I remember the promoters opened the doors to the punters at 10:00 a.m. They streamed in to grab their piece of real estate for the day and sat there getting soaked. Each of them found their piece of real estate getting increasingly muddy. It was all good festival fun and they were in good spirits when the first band appeared at midday.

There were many US army and air bases in this part of West Germany. With the legendary Jefferson Starship playing in a field just down the road from their base, many tickets had been bought by the US G.I.'s. Until this day, no one actually knows what percentage of the audience were G.I.'s. Suffice it to say, there were a lot of G.I.'s there. There were a lot of M.P.s too watching the G.I.'s didn't get into trouble or cause any; unfortunately, no one was watching the M.P.s.

Many of the M.P.s seemed to have access to the backstage area. They were seen wandering around backstage all day. They frequently disappeared into the bushes with a couple of friends and reappeared looking seriously worse for wear. Of course, they were armed!

The rain still poured down as the afternoon wore on, but the stage remained reasonably dry. We had seen "ARS" (What a catchy name that is for a band.), Brand X and Leo Kottke (Southern folk singer from Athens, Georgia.), who by now was probably into the second hour of his performance. This was quite strange as he was only supposed to be on for one hour.

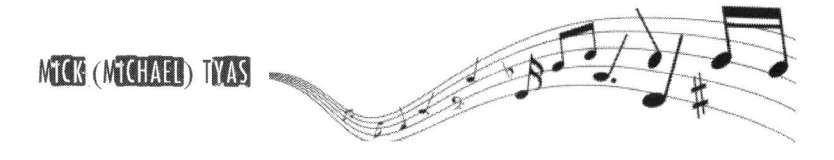

The atmosphere seemed to be getting a little bit tense backstage for some unknown reason. Someone had heard the German promoter on the phone saying the Starship tour manager was having trouble getting Grace Slick to leave her hotel room.

This was not as startling news as you would think as the lady had a history of "illnesses." Grace Slick had an alcohol problem for many years, which caused the band to cancel shows or even appear without her. So the rumor of her "illness" confining her to her hotel room came as no surprise. Grace Slick was back at the hotel, and she was in no condition to sing.

Below are some quotes and revelations of what was actually going on back at the hotel. This information came from Jacky Sarti, who was at the show as a punter. There had been an omen before the band had left the United States. One of their limousines caught fire, giving them quite a fright. This added to a feeling of dread that had already been mounting for some time. A feeling something monumentally creepy was about to happen, soon.

They arrived in Europe and Grace spent a good deal of her time in Amsterdam, a couple of nights before Lorelei, drinking. This was hardly a news flash. More shocking would have been a report of Grace Slick remaining sober for any considerable length of time.

That first show in Amsterdam had shown no signs of any problems, but Amsterdam is in Holland not Germany; once they crossed the border, Grace was off and running. By the time they reached their hotel in Wiesbaden, which was to be the Starship's base of operations, while in the area for the Lorelei show. Grace was in a pathetic state. It wasn't the alcohol, she told her husband, the Starship's lighting director, Skip Johnson. She really was sick this time. Didn't know quite what was wrong with her, maybe a stomach bug. Food poisoning, she thought.

It didn't matter, she wasn't getting out of bed and that was that.

This wasn't like her at all. Skip thought-alcohol usually placed Grace at the centre of the party, not shirking away from it. Something wasn't right. Maybe it really was her stomach. He called in a local doctor, who pronounced Grace too sick to perform. Appendicitis was his guess. But it was nothing to worry about, he informed them. She could still sing.

The doctor neglected to mention, when he made his diagnosis, that he worked for the concert's promoter. Whatever it was, Skip told the crew they would have to cancel the concert or play it without her. Grace wasn't moving.

Paul Kantner, long-time boyfriend, now ex- and also leader of the band was having none of that. Belly ache, drunk, come on . . . she'd always been able to stand up on a stage and sing. He would get to the bottom of this and haul her ass out to the venue. You didn't miss a concert because your tummy hurt and you certainly didn't miss one because you were too high. He'd seen Grace drunk before, many, many times before. He never knew her to be too far gone to make the gig.

She'd been boozing since she was a kid. She'd been drunk for countless Airplane gigs and recording sessions. She had always been able to perform drunk and few outside of the band and crew were ever the wiser. She had a remarkable constitution. Her ability to function even after having consumed enough liquor to put down a large mammal was renowned within the band's circle.

And, even on the rare occasions when Grace was just too marinated to give it her best, she'd always managed at least to entertain in her own inimitable way. She'd make abusive comments about the audience and her fellow musicians. She'd conjure up long, rambling monologues apropos of nothing. And, she'd find new and unusual ways to improvise onstage, keeping the band on its collective toes.

Paul insisted Grace get her act together and get ready for the show, and stop this nonsense immediately. But Skip was standing fast. The doctor said that if she performed Grace could be seriously hurt. She wasn't going anywhere.

Paul wanted to see her himself. He wanted to see a Grace Slick that was too incapacitated to sing. He had known her for more than a dozen years. He had lived with her and he still believed they were soul mates. He knew her better than anyone, especially this lighting director who had wedged his way into her life and now called himself Grace's husband. And, if there was one thing he knew about Grace Slick, it was that she could sing under the most adverse of conditions.

"Why don't you just go on without Grace?" Skip asked Paul.

"Would the Rolling Stones go on without Mick Jagger?" Paul retorted.

"Apples and oranges," Skip said. "You don't need Grace. You still have two other singers."

Paul was through reasoning now. He'd heard enough. He had already graduated to shouting and swearing. Now he was ready for yet another method of persuasion.

Paul jumped him and threw Skip Johnson down a short flight of stairs. He grabbed him by the throat, shocking even those who'd seen Kantner's Teutonic temper at its most virulent.

Bill Thompson, the band's long-time manager, pounced, grabbing at the two men, trying to break up the brawl. "What are you, crazy?!" he shouted.

ROCK 'N' ROLL
It's Better than Working for a Living

As Paul and Skip went at it in the hotel hallway, tearing at each other, Grace Slick managed to rise from bed. Opening the door to her room-she looked like a ghost. Thompson remembers-she stood there in a blue robe, observing a struggle she couldn't believe was taking place. Her long-time lover, and her current husband, was doing a Popeye and Bluto number in front of her eyes.

Which one would she side with? The one who had given her a daughter and had stayed by her side for so long? Or, the one who had become her new companion a couple of years ago . . . who had given her a new outlook on life and gotten her through some difficult times.

"Leave my husband alone!" Grace shouted at Paul, as loudly as a sick woman could.

Paul Kantner, at that moment, knew Grace Slick would not be performing that night. More than that, though, he knew that he'd lost her. She had used the word husband.

By now the Starship crew I think had got some wind of this crisis. They scuttled around and shouted and generally acted like complete dicks.

Leo Kottke had finished at 8.30 p.m. It was now nearly 9:30 p.m. and the crowd was getting increasingly restless. They, after all, could see that everything was set up onstage and wanted the band onstage. It was still raining, probably harder than it had all day. They had been in this quagmire for twelve hours. It was like The Russian Front in World War II out there. They were knee deep in mud, cold and very, very wet. There was no food or drink as the entire lot of concession stall holders had left, probably due to the weather. Did they know something we didn't? It was about to get like The Russian Front on stage, but in a slightly different way.

MICK (MICHAEL) TYAS

One and a half hours after Leo Kottke finished, the situation was critical. One of the Starship crew somewhat gave the game away when he went onstage and took two of the guitars offstage and put them in their cases. This action itself didn't perpetrate what was to follow, but it certainly made the punters suspicious. Also, it alerted the stoned American M.P.s backstage who had probably got word of what was happening and were spreading the rumors eagerly.

One man I still admire to this day was the piano player, David Frieberg. He along with Production Manager Bill Laudner both went on stage to explain in English to an increasingly angry crowd Grace was ill and could not leave her hotel room. He furthered, the band could not do themselves justice by playing without her. This was translated by the promoter into German. Laudner explained everyone would get their money back and another show would be organized; although we were all skeptical he mentioned the bit about getting their money back.

The twenty or so German Police lined up at the front of the stage quickly dispersed. The first beer bottle came whistling overhead and smashed on the stage. This was a pretty bad decision as the band had played many times without Grace due to one of her "illnesses."

I think the crowd would have been more than happy to hear the band play the instrumental section of, *Have you seen the Stars Tonight* for an hour and a half. Anyway, Frierberg was a brave man to stand on that stage. He and Kantner, who had also turned up, quickly got off the stage and presumably off the site. A hail of cans, bottles, rocks, mud pies and anything else that wasn't nailed down started raining onto the stage.

ROCK 'N' ROLL
It's Better than Working for a Living

It was now getting quite dangerous to go out onto the stage. The few security guards there had been in the first place, moved away from the front of the stage. They decided it wasn't worth getting a cracked skull from a flying sun lounger.

Myself and the rest of the sound crew stood way off stage right behind the monitor console. We wondered if it was worth venturing onto the stage to rescue some microphones and monitor speakers. We also came to the decision it wasn't worth a broken head. We did manage to put the lid of the flight case on the monitor console to protect it from any missiles. It wasn't until quite a time later we were to realize what a futile gesture that had been.

One of the Starship crew did actually carry his dedication to the cause just a little too far. He thought he might venture on stage to rescue some of the band equipment. What a stupid bloody idea that was! A glass beer bottle hit him square in the face at such velocity it actually smashed on impact and cut his face very badly in several places. It also broke his nose, his jaw and probably most of his teeth.

This incident produced huge cheers from the now rampant crowd. They wanted blood. This guy was bleeding heavily and he was in pretty bad shape. Somehow two or three people managed to drag him off stage without any more serious injuries; however, this was becoming a siege. It was at this point the situation changed for the worse, just when we thought it couldn't really get any worse. How wrong we were.

Somehow a fire had been started in the middle of the mud bath, which had previously been a grassy field only a few hours ago. How the hell they got a fire going in that weather I will never know. Maybe they siphoned all the gas out of their VW camper vans. I think what these people actually started burning was what remained of their tents and garden furniture. The fire gradually increaseed in size.

Some of the massed hordes had stormed the front of house control tower, which had long since been vacated by the technicians and engineers. Everyone feared for their lives in the middle of this unruly mob who had manhandled the sound console, lighting console and the spotlights onto their now substantial bonfire. This, in itself, was a major development. It meant the majority of the crowd still thought there was more retribution to be exacted on anyone or anything connected with Jefferson Starship. Some had obviously left, but it seemed the majority of the 10,000+ crowd were still here and having fun.

The Starship crew guy who had been hit in the face with the glass bottle had been airlifted to a Mainz hospital by a US Army helicopter. This incredibly came under fire from a hail of bottles and rocks as it tried to land backstage. These people were pissed! They were not going home yet!

The fire out in the field seemed to galvanize the mob. Many were now attempting to climb the security barriers to get onto the stage. We didn't really think they would try and attack the stage. They had a couple of hours to vent their anger and we felt they would probably soon be ready to leave or a huge task force of Polizei would arrive and clear the area. Actually neither happened. The crowd now had some new ideas with regard to the stage and the equipment on and around it . . . including our amplifiers, PA stacks, lighting rigs etc. The Cavalry never arrived.

Apparently, according to the promoter, who was hiding in an underground bunker (Haven't I heard of that before in Germany?) in the backstage area somewhere . . . the Police were not allowed to enter onto private property not even if a war was going on. Sounds a little ironic don't it?

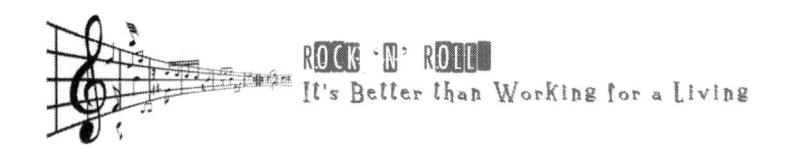

The bonfire out in the field was now lighting up the night sky. You could see the whole of the festival area from the glow. What a strange scene it was. Actually, out in field people were dancing around the fire and throwing more stuff on to it to keep it going. It looked more like some sort of celebration. Yet, if you looked at the stage area and the area around it looked more like some terrible war zone.

The mob had now scaled the security fence in front of the stage. They were now on the stage and systematically trashing all the equipment. Something I thought of quite a few months after this mayhem took place was . . . I never actually saw anyone stealing equipment, except for one item. You could have never imagined anybody stealing in such a situation and I will mention that in a moment. The crowd was so genuinely angry at not being able to see the band after all those hours in the rain, they seemed quite happy to make their point by just breaking everything.

The scary thing though was people were scaling the large PA stacks at either side of the stage. They were also climbing up the thirty feet high lighting system hanging over the stage. It appeared someone was going to be very seriously injured as they ripped the speakers off of the PA towers and lamps off of the lighting rig. These were now crashing down onto the stage below, which was populated by hundreds of people. It was a very dangerous escalation of violence. We realized someone could quite easily get killed. All this carnage was now lit up only by the huge fire burning in the middle of the field.

Someone must have gotten hold of another can of Volkswagen juice as a fire had now been started on the stage. It was stoked with amplifiers, keyboards, speaker cabinets and etc.

We were now standing way off of the side of the stage. It was getting very dangerous on stage with people smashing up anything in site. The equipment had been thrown off the PA towers. There were pieces of lighting rig ripped from the aluminum steel sections above the stage. There was also the worry anyone connected with the band or connected with the organization of the concert could quite feasibly be physically attacked by the mob if they were spotted.

A few moments later, we watched in amazement as four guys lifted the monitor console in its flight case on to the now increaseing blaze in the centre of the stage. There was actually so much confusion and so many people on the stage; four of our crew guys were able to rescue the console off of the fire without anyone noticing.

With the PA system dismantled and thrown down onto the stage to be added to the blazing fire; incredibly we saw once again, four guys pick up the monitor console and throw it onto the fire. The situation was getting so much out of hand we thought better of being heroes a second time. We decided not to go near the fire as it was getting so out of control the flames licked the thirty foot square aluminum truss section of the lighting rig. Being it was thirty feet in the air, very quickly the canvas roof of the stage caught fire. We decided then and there we had to get away from the stage area.

As we backed away from the carnage on the stage, I looked out into the field. The whole area looked like some weird medieval battlefield scene from a movie. It was lit by huge fires in the field and on the stage, which were now burning out of control. It was then I saw the strangest scene I can ever remember.

ROCK 'N' ROLL
It's Better than Working for a Living

In the weird half-light of the fires in the field, still in the pouring rain, I saw about ten people. They were soaking wet from head to toe and covered in mud trying to push a 6 foot Bechstein baby grand piano up a muddy track at the side of the field. This was a surreal sight. It was almost like something from a music video. They were succeeding and it was uphill.

I don't know what ever happened to the Bechstein. I guess they must have succeeded in their quest as it wasn't there the next day, but who had happened to have a van big enough to put it in and how did they get it in there?

We could see white hot molten material was now dropping onto the stage. The aluminum lighting truss melted in the intense heat. We now had to back off away from the carnage on the stage towards the dressing room area. The entire aluminum structure of the stage was white hot and molten. It was about to collapse in on itself as if it were a scene from the newsreel cameras of the doomed Hindenburg airship at Lakehurst Naval Air Station in New Jersey in 1937.

People were running every which way from the stage area. It now being far too dangerous to be any nearer than about 50 yards from it. Most of the mob decided they would hit the dressing room area to see if there was any fun to be had there.

It was time to ditch the Jefferson Starship Access All Areas passes we had around our necks. The marauding horde was heading in our direction. I hadn't actually witnessed any physical violence toward anyone as yet. Once the crowd got into the dressing room area and discovered the production office stacked with kegs of the best German ale and hundreds of bottles of wine and spirits . . . there was a pretty scary thought they could maybe turn into a lynch mob. It was not a good time to be someone associated with the Jefferson Starship organization.

MICK (MICHAEL) TYAS

All of our crew had gotten split up at this point. Seeing as we were about twenty years too early to use mobile phones to locate one another; no one really knew were each other was.

With no electricity, only the huge flickering fires on the stage lite the area. I retreated back away from the oncoming crowd toward the outside edge of the backstage compound. It was marked by the start of a steep forested slope, which dropped steeply to the access road about two hundred yards below. From this point on my recollections all become a little blurred as it was almost pitch black at the rear of the compound by the forest. I was getting a little apprehensive about the situation, especially when I heard . . . "IF ANY OF THOSE SUCKERS COME NEAR ME THEIR GONNA GET A BELLYFUL FROM THIS LITTLE BABY!"

A stoned or drunk or both, young soldier appeared at the side of me waving his Colt 38 in the air. Whether he would have been able to hit anything, considering the state he was in, is debatable. It definitely wasn't worth hanging around to find out. I backed further away from the mayhem into the tree line.

It was then I slipped on the top of the muddy slope disappearing into the tree line. I went careening down the incredibly slippery slope, now in almost complete darkness with just a huge glow visible way above me. I didn't know how far I had slid, but at one point I smacked into what I assumed to be a branch of a tree. I eventually came to a rest close to what I knew to be the bottom of the slope as I could see cars leaving the site on the access road not fifty yards away.

I don't know how long I sat there trying to decide what had happened and what I was going to do next. There was something sticky running down the side of my face, which I rightly presumed to be blood. It came from hitting the tree I'd guessed.

ROCK 'N' ROLL
It's Better than Working for a Living

I tumbled down to the access road winding its way down the gorge from the festival site, which was pretty busy by now with cars. Quite a lot of wet, muddy, bedraggled people were on foot.

I guess I must have looked like one of them. I was wet, very muddy and had blood running down my cheek from the wound on my forehead. The decision of what to do next was now a no brainer . . . GET THE FUCK OUT OF THERE!

This was no longer Rock 'n' Roll. This was a matter of getting away from the carnage. There was nothing I could do back at the top of the hill. I was down at the bottom of the hill. Decision made.

I joined the now increasing line of bodies leaving the site. I headed down to the main Koblenz - Mainz highway, which runs parallel to the River Rhine along the gorge.

I decided the only thing I could do was hitch a ride into Mainz where our hotel was situated. Remember, those were the days when you could still hitch hike around the world without being dismembered and your bones found at the bottom of a lake twenty years later.

I amazingly got a ride within about five minutes with a young couple on their way home to Mainz after visiting relations in Koblenz. I thought them very brave to even pick me up at all. I guess I must have looked disheveled at best, but they seemed unperturbed. They made very polite conversation like, "Terrible weather for the festival." and "Was it fun?" and "Who was playing?" They proceeded to tell me how beautiful it was around here in the summer. I have the heart to tell them . . . it didn't look too beautiful right now to me. I really didn't want to get into a conversation about, "How nice a day it had been."

I was delivered right to the door of the hotel, which was pretty cool as after a day like that; I just wanted to get to the bar.

It was now nearly midnight. I was thinking the bar may close before the rest of the crew made it back to the hotel. If they all made it back of course; I ordered a dozen beers just in case and quickly drank six of them. I thought I better order some more, at which point the rest of the crew arrived almost immediately.

All of us were still somewhat in shock. Each of us related our stories for over two hours until we got asked to leave the bar. We arranged to meet for breakfast at 6:00 a.m. and then travel back to the site to see what the place looked like in the daylight. We were to meet a couple of the directors of our company who were catching the first flight to Frankfurt.

A hot, beautiful day and a very muddy field with piles of smoldering rubble; something I found incredible was there were hardly any people about as the site was almost deserted. I expected police, firemen and still, for some reason, a hardcore of pissed off punters. I suppose you can only be pissed off for so long before you get tired, hungry or just want a beer. Anyway, there was the six of us and two of the directors of our company rummaging around and feverishly taking photos for insurance reasons I guess. There were not many other people, not even security. Still, there never was any Security, which is one of the reasons it all kicked off.

We had four trucks on the site that morning, which were luckily not parked on the site the day prior. It would not take long to load them with equipment to take back to England. In fact, what I saw left were a couple of burnt out dimmer racks, which are voltage supplies for the lighting rig. They were just charred metal boxes really about three feet square. There were three or four pieces of aluminum truss section each piece about a foot long, which was part of the lighting rig. In all, at the start there was more than one hundred and twenty feet of it. I still have in my office a piece of molten aluminum truss section take from the ashes. It is only the size of my hand. The fire had gotten so hot the lighting rig had melted and this was the remains. The sound system consisted of one wooden very charred, HF horn box still in one piece, which had come from the top of one of the PA stacks. When we got it back to London, it still worked!

In total, the sound system, which consisted of more than two hundred boxes and miles of cabling and four mixing consoles when it had left London; took up one and a half 40' trucks. 99.999% of it had disappeared. And, of Jefferson Starship, there was no sign.

Chapter Ten

MY FESTIVAL WORK

Lorelei was really the first festival I ever worked on. It wasn't exactly a festival; it was four or five bands on the same bill, playing outdoors. I can't believe that they still do shows there to this day after all that shit that we went through. It may have been the first festival type shows I ever worked on, but it wasn't my first experience of festivals.

My ex-girlfriend Joan and I were experienced festival goers. We attended from the mid 1960's onward. This is when the outdoor show moved on at last from the Pimms and lemonade on the lawn brigade in the local park, to thousands of stoned hippies in a field. I think I preferred the first example thinking about it now. Then again, I passed the sitting in the middle of a muddy field for ten hours age many moons ago.

The first festival style events in the UK were started by the National Jazz federation in 1961 in a field at the back of Richmond Athletic club in West London. It was suitably called the National Jazz Festival. At that time, it was truly a JAZZ festival. It was both modern and traditional. They weren't exactly stoned hippies yet. They were more real ale swilling, bearded and quite likely over educated. I suppose those early festivals still had the

ROCK 'N' ROLL
It's Better than Working for a Living

Pimms on the lawn feel about them. They carried it on in this format until 1963.

Strangely enough, America was lagging behind the UK in staging music festivals outdoors. Each state does have its own state fair every year, but these are more family affairs with outdoor performances from various Artistes. The first rock festivals did not really appear until 1966 or 67 mainly in and around San Francisco catering to the flower child explosion.

The Knebworth festivals were probably the most organized of all the festivals and Glastonbury as the longest running of all festivals. I never actually went to Knebworth as a punter. By the time the first one came around in 1974, I was now making my way as a sound engineer quite successfully, albeit with very limited knowledge of the job. I was becoming quite successful. Noting the fact I didn't really have a clue what I was doing, I seemed to be making quite a good job of convincing people I did. It's at this point I need to thank Peter Edmonds who really gave me my first chance as a sound engineer.

My first Knebworth Festival was in 1978. In fact, the second one of 1978 billed as "Oh God, not another boring old Knebworth." I was involved in three Knebworths and believe me none of them were boring to work on.

On my first one Frank Zappa and The Tubes seemed to have co-headlining on the bill. I thought it patently obvious that Zappa should be top of the bill. For some reason The Tubes were last on.

Unfortunately, Zappa went on stage about thirty minutes late, which, of course, stressed out all the organizers. They needn't have worried too much; I think the massed hordes had enough introverted guitar solos after ninety minutes. Zappa's sound engineer had a bit of a hearing problem . . . he couldn't hear. Everyone involved seemed quite relieved when the set ended after ninety minutes. The Tubes took the stage, late, of course. I don't believe anyone possesses a watch in the Rock 'n' Roll business, except me.

Anyway for anyone reading this book under the age of fifty The Tubes were an outrageous wacky theatrical band formed in San Francisco in the early 1970's. The lead singer was called Fee Waybill. He sometimes went under the stage persona of Quay Lewd (Which is a play of words on the drug Quaalude, a very popular recreational sedative in the 1970's, but also known as an elephant tranquilizer.). He roamed around the stage in a drugged out state.

Always putting on a wacky theatrical show, this show started with Fee driving on stage in a borrowed 1960's Ford Consul convertible car. It was very spectacular. Well, it nearly was.

This maneuver had been rehearsed many times at the sound check the day before. When it came down to doing it during the show, everyone closed their eyes including the driver. The front wheel ran along the front edge of the stage and threatened to run the car into the security pit. Now that would have been fun and was probably the nearest we came to any sort of disaster at that event. This was a really well organized festival.

The bands were a bit of a mixed bunch though, Peter Gabriel was mind numbingly boring, as to be expected. Wilco Johnson from British rock band Dr. Feelgood and Dave Edmunds and Rockpile played some good rock n roll in the sun. Of course, being an outdoor event in England, it had to rain at some point. It waited till after the show, which made for a pretty wet and miserable load out.

The 1980 Knebworth Festival was by far the most entertaining to work on. After the excesses of the previous year, which I had

ROCK 'N' ROLL
It's Better than Working for a Living

missed . . . there were two hundred thousand turning up on two weekends to see Led Zeppelin for probably the last time or so we thought at the time. Keith Richards and Ron Wood were out for a jolly time with their band The New Barbarians. Legendary bass player Stanley Clark was a little less frantic and more homely.

The Beach Boys topped the bill. They were probably at their pinnacle as a touring band. It was the last concert with the original Beach Boys line-up before they all started dying.

Mike Oldfield turned up with a fraction of under three quarters of his recording studio on stage. This included some floor monitors they could have sold as garden sheds. He also brought some bouncing fluffy rabbits with him?????????????

One of my favorite ladies in the world, Elkie Brooks was also on the bill. I had worked with Elkie in 1976, when she'd just got a record deal after leaving husband Pete Gage and the band Vinegar Joe. Elkie at the time was living on the New Kings Road in Fulham, West London just over Putney Bridge from where we lived in Putney. So, rehearsing at the Harrodian Club in Barnes a couple of miles away, she would pick me up at my house on the way to rehearsals and drop me off home after, now that is a real star.

That same summer of 76, was the hottest on record I believe in the UK. I was in Air recording studios with Elkie for three months of that roasting summer. Instead of travelling on the unbearably hot Underground system I was provided with an air conditioned car to collect me from home and deliver back in the evening. Elkie is to this day, one of my favorite people in the business.

In the couple of years since I had last seen her, Elkie had married her new sound engineer, a chap called Trevor Jordan. He was a nice enough guy known for being a little anal in his approach to the job. He was a little too serious even before he married the star.

Trevor had bought himself some old recording studio that was closing down with two Neve analogue mixing desks. These desks were probably built in the early sixties and had huge knobs and switches on them. They resembled something from a 1950's science fiction movie and Trevor insisted on using his desks for mixing Elkie's shows whenever she did a concert. Trevor became the butt of everyone's jokes as he turned up with these huge leviathans and consequently tried to get them working, which took forever as they were never supposed to be used in the middle of a field.

The Beach Boys were obviously the stars of the show. They were really, really good. It's not very often I actually liked or disliked or even took much notice of the music of the band I was working for. It was purely a job, but just occasionally one band came along and made you sit up and take notice. This was one of those times.

The leader of the band from their inception, Brian Wilson was back playing live. This was after a few years travel into the world of drink, drugs and mental trauma. I'm not sure how much he knew about it after his mental breakdown.

The day before the show was Brian Wilson's birthday. The rest of the band had organized a surprise for him. This should be interesting we all thought and so it turned out to be.

This was 1980, and even after his LSD experiments and all his other drug abuse of the late 60's and 70's, Brian Wilson was still not playing with a whole deck of cards. All these years later . . . amazingly, he could still function as a musician and sing close harmonies. He sat at the piano as a vegetable though.

ROCK 'N' ROLL
It's Better than Working for a Living

So after the sound check on that lovely June day, Brian was sat at the grand piano. The rest of the band had gone off to get their presents and surprises for Brian's birthday. He just sat there. It seemed he barely did anything unless someone told him to do something, which is why he was probably such a good musician still. It was almost as if he were hypnotized. If Carl said play the piano like you did on the "Pet Sounds" album he did.

The band came back on stage with a huge cake and placed it on the Grand piano. Brian just stared into space. Then his brother Carl gave him a large carving knife at which point various members of the crew were heard to say, "Fuck me they've given the vegetable a fucking knife." There was no cause for concern though, as Brian just stood there holding it not understanding what to do until his brother held his hand over Brian's and they cut the cake together, at which point we all broke into Happy Birthday. Brian just turned around and walked away to the back of the stage and was helped down the stairs to the dressing room.

It was quite sad as the man was obviously a genius, but he seems to have come through it all quite well and is still in the business to this day. He is the sole surviving Wilson.

There was one thing I took from that day. That is I can say I once sung with The Beach Boys. I was working for a company called Electrosound now, who were only of the big three sound companies in the UK. I had just opened a shop in LA and now getting lots of American clients and big UK acts. I was in a good place and getting quite established as a sound engineer. I still didn't have a clue what I was doing technically, but I seemed to be able to make things sound ok.

The company was owned by a guy called Ricky Farr who was son of a boxer called Tommy Farr who had come into some money when his father died. He also had a brother called Gary who has a band in the sixties had called Gary Farr and The T Bones.

Ricky had started Electrosound in 1974. He had quickly picked up some good engineers and some good contracts. He quickly became established as one of the country's top sound companies. We had contracts like Rod Stewart, Beach Boys, Tom Petty, Rush, Bette Midler, Liza Minelli, and etc. so this company was going places and it was a good place to be.

I didn't do too many festivals with ElectroSound, as I was mainly touring eight months a year. I would come off one eight week tour have ten days off and then go back out so those were busy days. We played lots of the European festivals that were going on with the bands we were touring with. Germany was probably the biggest festival market along with established European festivals like the Turku festival in Finland and Roskilde in Copenhagen both are still in existence. We did run a few festivals with ElectroSound. These were mainly one day affairs.

A classic one I remember we did every year was in Nurenberg in southern Germany called Rock im Park. It was held on what is called the Zeppelin Field. It was the sports ground next door where a certain Mr. Hitler used to rally and inspect his millions of Hitler Jung, as can be seen from the photographs.

ROCK 'N' ROLL
It's Better than Working for a Living

Zeppelin Field in 1941.

Every member of the crew, and the bands made a point of climbing onto the Fuhrer's podium from where he viewed his 200,000+ followers flanked by ten thousand of his top brass in the main stone grandstand.

Zeppelin Field in 1981.

MICK (MICHAEL) TYAS

Of the big weekend affairs in the 1980's I was only really involved with one of them from beginning to end. That was Glastonbury 1983, which really was not a memorable affair for me at all. This was a week of work before hand with trucks and trucks of gear. What used to piss me off about large systems at large events like this was it takes a whole week to put it all together for the weekend shows. At the end of the festival, you're expected to derig the whole fucking thing over night after a very arduous weekend of concerts.

In fact, the most time I can remember having to derig was the next day after the show. Even then, that was starting straight after the show! That's the economics of it.

Anyway, I was in a field with a bunch of audio hippies setting up the PA. We were doing sixteen to eighteen hour days over the weekend, with no hotel. The nearest hotel to the Glastonbury festival is miles away. We would never have made it through the traffic every day, so we lived on a sleeper bus on site.

This wasn't an ideal solution. There was always lots of noise. There were no proper toilets or showers except in the temporary ones backstage, which were usually disgusting after a couple of days.

I never enjoyed it. It was hard and dirty work. I could always think of somewhere better to be in following years whenever anyone asked me to do it again. I did actually do a gig at Glastonbury the year after with Ian Dury and The Blockheads, but I was working for the band. We arrived the same day, did the show, and left to drive back to London. I didn't even stay for the post gig festivities as I had to be at Whitesnake rehearsals in London at 10:00 a.m. the next morning.

ROCK 'N' ROLL
It's Better than Working for a Living

There were, and still are, of course, many festivals across Europe. I have probably worked at most of them at one time or another with lots of different bands. One of the highlights that stand out for me was at the Roskilde Festival just outside Copenhagen in 1981.

I was mixing monitors for Ian Dury and The Blockheads again. When we arrived at the site it was raining heavily and everyone was thinking this is going to be horrible. Again, water and electricity do not mix! A couple of hours later, the weather were beautiful and very hot, which cheered everyone up.

The Roskilde main stage is covered by a tented structure the promoters bought from the Rolling Stones in 1978. The Stones had used for the Knebworth Festival in 1976. It appears to be a half a circus tent. It opens at the front with two large poles holding up the covering. It goes over the top as a roof and covers the back of the stage.

We followed UB40 and Robert Palmer on stage. I wanted to see Robert Palmer. I was stage left behind the monitor console with an old mate of mine called Bruno. He was working for the sound company, which was useful. I could reset the monitor desk for myself for the Ian Dury set after Robert Palmer had finished. So while Bruno did the equipment change over on stage, I set to work resetting the console. Time was very tight. It was only a fifteen minute changeover. I was up against it to get all the settings done (There was nothing digital in those days.) before the band walked on stage. Just as I finished, I saw the band standing at the side of the stage just about to walk on stage. I turned the console back on ready for the show, which seemed strangely to coincide with loudest clap of thunder I had ever heard in my life followed by a monsoon like rain shower.

MICK (MICHAEL) TYAS

It all seemed surreal as the band walked past me onto the stage, a huge torrent of water came down through the stage roof straight onto the monitor console. I tried to stop the band going on stage, but to no avail. Once Ian Dury started walking you daren't stop him quickly, he had a tendency to fall over. Much as it was hilarious to see as he floundered about like a fish out of water, I didn't want an electrocuted singer.

I obviously had to power down the monitor console to try and dry it out. Luckily, the band spotted what was happening and played on gamely with no monitors. The only way to dry a console out is to take all the channels out. The channels are numbered 1 to whatever, depending on how big the console is. Each channel is an input from a specific microphone. You have to start by drying the channel with a towel to get most of the moisture off and then use a hair dryer! To get it completely dry. So there was Bruno and I, with our towels and hair dryers (Essential equipment for a sound engineer.) sat at the side of the stage like a couple of mothers at bath night for the children. We reckoned we could get by with seven good channels: kick, snare, bass and four vocals. Kick snare and bass so the rhythm section could keep time. The four vocals so the singers could hear themselves. We got seven channels back in the desk and powered up; then another big flash. This time it wasn't lightning. The console blew a fuse. There was still water in it somewhere. We had to repeat the whole process again. This time, we had to take a lot longer over it so we didn't blow any more fuses.

Eventually, we got seven channels working. What a relief. Then, what happened, the band went off stage and then they came back on. It was the encore! We had missed the entire set and only caught the two encore songs. Even the band thought it was funny . . . more of Ian Dury later.

In 1983, I was working for Thin Lizzy, which was a whole lot of fun . . . which I will also relate to later on in the book. At this time though, we were playing the Reading Festival, just outside of London. I hadn't done this for many years. The last time I did it, I was working for the PA Company, so not much time for socializing and eighteen hour days. This time I was working for the band, so easy peasy. Arrive the day before the gig. Do the sound check. Go home and then cruise in next day for the gig.

It was a good day. A very social day with lots of people I knew in the business. The whole Lizzy thing was a very big social club anyway. After all, Philip was a very sociable man and everybody knew him.

The sun was shining. The gig went really well. Lots of post gig drinking . . . lots of everything really. Philip invited all the band and crew and various significant others and hangers back to his house in Kew in West London for an after gig party.

Everybody was pretty well out of it even then. It was only about 9:00 p.m. Salli and I lost our flat mate Heather (Heavy metal Heather!) so we decided to head off to Phil's house. I don't know how much I had had to drink or how much racket (cocaine) I had had. I remember looking at the speedometer of my beautiful 1974 Jaguar XJ6 as we sped back down the M4 back towards London. It was just touching 120mph; considering the police presence in that area and the amount I had drunk and etc. that is still scary to this day.

Of course, there were no speed cameras or any of that intrusive stuff you get today. You just had to keep your eyes open. We reached Philips' house really quickly. Not amazingly . . . it was a big Mock Tudor detached house opposite Kew Gardens. We were let in by the nanny and/or housekeeper.

Philip, ever the sociable host, even though he wasn't there told us to help ourselves from the drinks cabinet. We also helped ourselves to a little white packet in the top drawer he really was the most hospitable host. Only about ten people ever turned up in the end. Consequently, we continued to drink our way through the liquor stock. They nanny went to bed and left us to it. About 3.30 a.m. I think it was, we ran out of racket and we ran out of brandy, whisky, vodka and etc. so Salli and I decided to drive home. We were very cavalier about drinking and driving in those days. It was only about three miles to our flat in Putney, although you wouldn't dare attempt it in today's fascist state.

Philip never turned up to his party. Our flat mate wasn't at home either, which was no surprise as she was famous in heavy metal circles. She had lots of "friends" you could ask. Cozy Powell, if he were still with us, David Lee Roth, Gene Simmons and Phil Lynott to name a few.

Philip was shagging Heather in the Holiday Inn at Heathrow airport whilst we savored his hospitality at his party.

R.I.P. my friend.

The last real festival I ever worked on was the Monsters of Rock at Donnington in 1988. I have since worked on a couple of the big Hyde Park shows in Central London, but they're not really festivals, just big outdoor shows.

I was working for Iron Maiden, I had been since 1985. Lots more of that later; this was Maiden's first really big outdoor show in the UK for many years. In fact, probably their biggest ever apart from Rock in Rio and this was their show, they controlled everything about it.

At this time with Maiden, I was a pampered beast. I had an assistant, the only physical work I did was set up my monitor desk. I had single hotel rooms, hire cars when I wanted them and was one of the top five paid engineers in the world. As usual, when working for the band, I just had to turn up for the sound check, go home. I'd come back two days later for the gig and get fucked up and then be post gig in the Novotel in Derby, which all happened satisfactorily. I also drove up to the site on Wednesday just to make sure the crew was rigging everything in the correct position. I took my 4 year old son Morgan with me. On the following pages can be seen Morgan Plays Donnington.

A darker side of the festival reared its head the following day. We heard on the news two fans had been trampled to death during Guns and Roses set. As usual on these occasions, I was only mixing the one band. Iron Maiden in this case. I was hanging about at the side of the stage during the support bands sets. It was during Guns and Roses set I was standing behind the monitor desk when I saw the crush at the front of the stage and a gap open up as a number of people collapsed from the weight of people pushing them from behind. I saw them go down but I never saw them come up again.

Luckily, there haven't been too many bad injuries and more so deaths, in the history of Rock Festivals. This is quite amazing when you consider the logistics involved and just the sheer numbers of people.

Unfortunately, one of the worst accidents that ever happened was not that long ago, in 2000. It was during the Pearl Jam set at the Roskilde festival in Denmark. Fifty thousand people started pushing toward the stage. The weather had been very wet. The festival site was very muddy. In the crush, the same problem happened as at Donnington, people started stumbling under the weight of being pushed from behind and went down with others on top of them. This time nine people died with countless others hospitalized.

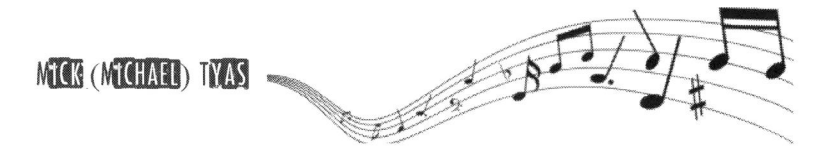

Festival organizers have tried to address this problem since these events. There are lines of barriers now to break the audience into smaller groups to avoid the weight of several thousand people pushing down on the people in front.

In conclusion, Rock Festivals in general have a happy party atmosphere for the audience, for the Artistes, and for the crews who put in such hard work. The instances of this atmosphere been ruined either by the authorities by accidents or just by human nature are rare. I have been witness to a couple of these instances and I don't ever want to witness them again. Most of the festivals I attended as a punter in the late sixties and my days working on them, I gotta say I had some fucking fantastic fun.

Chapter Eleven

1983

1*983. This is what I do best!*

At the beginning of 1983, I was looking and needing work quite desperately. For the first time since I started in the business in the early 70's, I was unemployed. The company I had worked for the last six years had been sold and stripped down to the bare bones. There was no upcoming work on the horizon. I called an old friend who had given me some work when he had set up his own sound company with an associate at the end of 1975. I did Rory Gallagher, Dr. Feelgood, Lou Reed and a few other tours for him in 1975/76. His name was Mike Lowe. He himself is a bit of a legend in the audio business in the UK.

Mike Lowe was originally the bass tech for Greg Lake in British Progressive Rock band Emerson, Lake and Palmer, better known as ELP. When the band split up, Mike decided to form his own sound company with former ELP truck driver, Keith Ferguson. The whole thing only lasted about four years. Since that time, Mike had been associated with a company called Turbosound. It was owned by an independently wealthy hippie called Tony Andrews who was building new sound systems incurporating revolutionary new concepts in design and production. He used all sorts of strange shapes and pipes and tubes and configurations. Many of these new ideas were a little off the wall. I think

ROCK 'N' ROLL
It's Better than Working for a Living

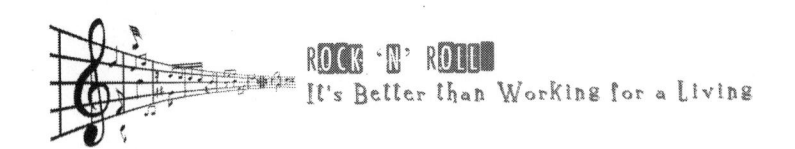

Tony and his cohorts probably smoked a little too much dope on the days they designed some of his new products. Some worked, some didn't. He thought some worked other people disagreed. I'm afraid I was one of those skeptics. I have to hand it to Tony though, he came up with a design which was probably the first sound reinforcement speaker design where all the different components of a large speaker system were enclosed in one box (i.e., the bass, midrange and hi frequency speakers were all in one box). Up until this time, each frequency range of speaker had been in a separate box. This integration of the separate units made the system not only much tidier and aesthetically pleasing to look at, but it was also compact and saved on truck and storage space. But did it work?

I am now going to bore you with some technical stuff. You are not only going to read about the glamour of this business, you also have to know a little of the nuts and bolts involved; albeit, some of those things did get in the way of having a good time.

The product Tony came up with was called the *Turbosound TMS3* cabinet. I personally hated it. Everybody wanted to use them as they were state-of-the-art at the time. I didn't like them as I don't think they made a big enough sound. My approach was always very old school. If you wanted big sound you needed big boxes. The new whiz kids like Tony were out to disprove that theory. They managed to do that with lots of people, yet . . . I did manage to prove my point to him.

MICK (MICHAEL) TYAS

Thin Lizzy Thunder and Lightning Tour. 1983.

I was operating onstage monitors and had the new Turbosound TMS3 cabinets as sidefill speakers. When using sidefill speakers, especially with a loud rock band, you need to be able to create a loud clear vocal sound. With a normal old school speaker system, you would have, maybe, a bass bin with two 15" speakers with the cone or sound area of the speaker made out of cardboard or some similar material. This will handle frequencies up to around 200 Hz (low frequencies).

Next, you would have a mid-range enclosure with maybe two 12" speakers again with cardboard cone areas and a smaller diameter speaker for handling higher frequencies. These were up to around 1250 Hz or 1.25 kHz. For the frequencies above this, you would have something far different. This would be a compression driver, which is a metal enclosure about 6 inches diameter, totally enclosed apart from either a one or two inch hole at the front for the sound to come out of. Inside would be a metal diaphragm about 5 inches in diameter, much like a small plate, which is fed electronically with all the frequencies above 1.25 kHz. The sound coming from the metal diaphragm is compressed (hence the name) and forced out of the one or two inch hole in the front of the driver. This is a much more efficient way of producing high frequencies, especially when a horn arrangement is attached to the front of the driver.

This arrangement only really improves the efficiency of high frequencies. Lower frequencies do not respond so well to this arrangement, due to the laws of physics, which I am not going to start on in this book or it will be a million pages in length.

Most people's voices are composed of higher frequencies than lower frequencies. Higher frequencies cut through large amounts of ambient noise better than lower frequencies. Therefore, the horn loaded compression drivers are highly efficient when trying to get a person's voice to cut through thunderous guitars, bass and drums. That is why we use them in onstage monitors especially, so the singer can hear what he or she is singing through all the noise been generated on stage by a band.

Tony designed his TMS3 cabinet with 2 x 15" speakers for bass, 2x10" speakers for mid-range (Slightly different in size from the normal mid-range, but not too radical.) and a 2 "compression driver" for the highs. In all, not too radical design, except he had his mid-range cardboard cones reproducing frequencies up to 5000hz, 5khz!, which made the sound coming from the cabinet much smoother. It was all but useless for my application of a loud harsh vocal sound to cut through all the noise on stage. It was just too smooth. Tony argued with me the cabinet had a smooth and perfect response when connected to their test equipment in their laboratory. I argued maybe it had, but I was on Hammersmith Odeon stage in London with a very irate Irishman, who wanted to hear his voice, I was not in a laboratory.

I was summoned to a meeting with Phil Lynott, the singer, after rehearsals. Phil was a very strong character, he was irate, he was used to getting his own way and he was not happy. I was in fear of losing my job for not been able to produce what he wanted. Here is my first and not last praise for the man. He sat me down and gave me a glass of champagne, so . . . I had hopes. You don't give champagne too someone you are about to fire, surely. "I don't blame you Mick, I blame the pucking equipment! Can you pucking fix it?"

"Philip it will be my pleasure." I replied.

"Pucking" is the southern Irish pronunciation of that beautiful old word; Fucking!

MICK (MICHAEL) TYAS

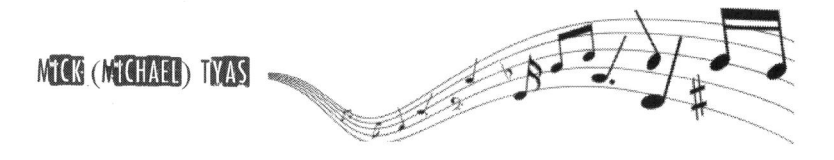

The man had my respect from then on. I called Tony Andrews, "Take those stupidly expensive compression drivers off that you have fitted to those cabinets and just put the normal ones back. I want the mid-range speakers reproducing only up to 1.25 KHz. I want that harsh, barking vocal sound back."

I got it.

Philip was happy and I was still in a job . . . now for the continuing tale of the last ever Thin Lizzy tour.

Now the fun, not the work . . .

Thin Lizzy were formed around 1969 / 1970 by old school friends in Dublin, Ireland, Philip Lynott and drummer Brian Downey. The biography of the band is well documented elsewhere, but I first came across the band in about 1974 playing a small club in London. Phil was writing some great songs and the band was building a big reputation. Around about 1976, Salli and I met a couple of their roadie's whilst drinking in The Golden Lion pub in Fulham, London. The Golden Lion was a major hangout for bands and crew in London in those days.

Philip Lynott was a bit of a "man about town" in Rock 'n' Roll circles. He was the leader of a hugely successful rock band and a good looking black man with lots of attitude and lots of money. He also had a taste for the ladies and for the narcotics.

We met his right hand man, Charlie McLenhan or "Blond Charlie" as he was known. At the time was he was Lynott's road manager, chauffeur and procurer of all things he required. I also think he wanted to be Phil and he was pretty close . . . apart from the fame and talent.

Charlie had acquired money by marrying an heiress to a large department store chain, who no one ever saw. It meant Charlie could always acquire the finer things of a Rock 'n' Roll lifestyle.

ROCK 'N' ROLL
It's Better than Working for a Living

He could always be found hanging out with the band. There was a whole big charisma about the band at that time.

After spending hours talking to "Blond Charlie" we found out that Scott one of the band's guitar players only lived about half a mile away from us. Salli managed to get us invited to one of his parties and so into the Thin Lizzy clique we were. It was a very exclusive clique at that time. Salli was more involved in it socially than I was, but I also knew Phil and Scott and Robbo, the other guitar player, from gigs I had done in the past.

So in 1983, Mike Lowe who was now running Turbosound asked me if I wanted to do a Thin Lizzy Tour. It was the last one ever, to coincide with the last album titled, *Thunder and Lightning*.

"Ooohhhh, that'll be fun," said Salli when I told her I had been offered it. The phrase "Sex and Drugs and Rock 'n' Roll" had been coined a few years earlier by Ian Dury, but this phrase could have described what this band were all about. Shame it was a bit of a sad on occasion too.

We did rehearsals at a studio in West London for three weeks. Phil actually turned up for rehearsals sometimes! Which was useful, for as well as being the leader of the band, he was also the bass player and lead singer. It's pretty hard to rehearse songs if the writer, singer and bass player don't turn up very often.

I say it rather incredulously about Phil turning up sometimes. Because of his own social habits, which were many, he was much of the time at odds with working. So . . . when he was supposed to be rehearsing, he was sleeping. And, when he was supposed to be sleeping, he was out raging. The reality was, the crew and the rest of the band would have been at the studio from 2:00 p.m. until 10:00 p.m. and Phil wouldn't arrive. Then he'd come in just as we were leaving. We'd all be there till 3:00 a.m. on those occasions.

MICK (MICHAEL) TYAS

As I said in an earlier chapter, I used to have a penchant for speed. I had a very good contact for acquiring it. Phil found out about this. Speed was one of his favorite drugs. I say one of, he had quite a few. Phil was no drugs snob, most things would interest him. He asked me one day at rehearsals to get him a quarter of an ounce of Amphetamine sulphate, which is seven grams and quite a lot for any normal person. Even if you took it daily, you wouldn't need to go and see the dealer again for at least another week. Only two days later, Phil had run out and I had to go get him some more!

So we went off on the tour and soon as we got going I was given a warning by Peter. He was the long time FOH engineer. He stated, "You have to be careful with Phil and not overstep the line of "working relationship or your so called friendship with him could come back and bite you in the arse and you'll find yourself out of a job . . ." Phil did have a reputation for been unpredictable and moody. Despite Peter's warning I never really had any problems apart from the equipment related one I had at Hammersmith Odeon.

With a big reputation as a womanizer and always having plenty of good drugs, there was always lots of "hangers on" back stage at Thin Lizzy gigs. This included my girlfriend and our housemate, Heather. "Heavy Metal Heather," as she became known in the business; she had a big reputation and could list among her "intimate friends" the likes of Gene Simmons from Kiss, Cozy Powell from Whitesnake, and etc. There was also, some guy from Manowar, an occasional Motley Crue person and Philip; although I believe Philip was her new "friend," introduced by Salli.

ROCK 'N' ROLL
It's Better than Working for a Living

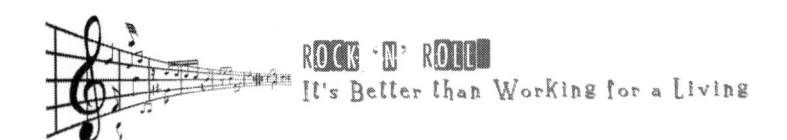

In the festival season of 1983, Thin Lizzy was booked to do quite a few festivals throughout Europe. This was the last tour and the band was being split up. I think the management was trying to get as much from their product as possible before the final curtain. Strangely enough, I just thought of something, the band's management company. Morrison O'Donnell went on to manage big Britpop band Blur in the 1990's. Blur was another band that seemed to split up at the height of its fame.

I didn't do all the European festivals with Lizzy or the few Japanese gigs they did as they couldn't afford to take a monitor engineer with them. I missed their last ever gig at Monsters of Rock Festival in Nurnberg, but I did do the last ever British gig which was at the Reading Festival on August 28th. 1983.

Looking back, I suppose that gig was pretty sad actually. It was the last time anyone in England would ever see Thin Lizzy (Although in 2009, there was a remake, without Phil.). Really, though, that day at the Reading Festival was anything but sad.

I arrived at the Festival site about 1:00 p.m. in my big old Jaguar XJ6. I spent most of the afternoon in the backstage beer tent socializing with the "good" and the "bad" of the British Rock 'n' Roll business, except for a brief sortie to the stage to make sure the rental company had enough equipment for our needs. This took all of about five minutes and then it was back to "socializing." It was the most important part of the day backstage at a Festival in those days.

Salli and Heather arrived about 5:00 p.m. with a gram of speed for me. So . . . it was back to more "socializing."

I don't actually remember much about the gig itself, which means it must have gone fine. Nobody wanted to take it too seriously anyway, there was much more fun to be had, back in the beer tent.

Phil announced he was having a post gig party at his large mock Tudor house in Kew, West London. This was really convenient for Salli, Heather and I . . . as it was only ten minutes down the road from where we lived.

A little while later, as we were getting ready to leave, Phil told us that if we got there before him, press the bell on the gate and the nanny would let us in. He shared there was lots of booze and goodies in the cocktail cabinet and told us to help ourselves.

Salli and I were ready to leave, but couldn't find Heather anywhere. After a while we decided she was old enough to look after herself and left without her and gave a couple of other people a lift.

The fact that I had been drinking and taking speed since one in the afternoon didn't seem to come into my thinking. And, we weren't done yet, as I drove down the M4 motorway into London at 100mph. We were very cavalier in those days. Today, we'd probably be in prison.

When we got to Phil's house, we pressed the bell and the nanny let us in the automatic gates. She was obviously under instructions from her employer. She showed us into the large den where the drink cabinet was. She then disappeared off somewhere else in the house. We never saw her again! It was a big house, so she was probably in the back wing where she lived and where the children were well out of the way of the lunatics that frequented Phil's house.

ROCK 'N' ROLL
It's Better than Working for a Living

Phil's wife Caroline was also nowhere to be seen. I guess she'd gone out of town for the night, so Phil's gang had run of the house.

If I remember rightly, only about ten people actually turned up that night. I think we only managed to drink our way through a bottle of brandy, a bottle of Vodka, and a gram of coke Phil had left for us in a drawer. He was always a very thoughtful and sociable man.

Salli and I left about three, and I actually drove home. I must have been fucking crazy, if I'd have been stopped by the local constabulary they'd have locked me up and thrown the key away.

When we left, Phil still hadn't arrived and never did. He was at the Holiday Inn at Heathrow airport shagging HMH (Heavy Metal Heather).

What style that man had, organize a party for everyone, then don't bother turn up. Instead, go and shag a woman at a hotel, that's pretty good style.

Unfortunately, Phil's style sometimes was a little too close to home and probably cost him his marriage. Heather once told me he used to invite her over to the house and meet her at the gate. Then they'd go down to his recording studio at the bottom of the garden to drink, take drugs and shag whilst the rest of the family was in the main house.

Caroline and Phil were married on Valentine's Day 1980. Caroline was the daughter of British TV presenter; Leslie Crowther. Caroline and Phil had two daughters, Sara and Cathleen.

Phil was one wild, crazy, unpredictable guy. He was also a caring, doting father and one of my favorite people I ever met in the music business.

MICK (MICHAEL) TYAS

Phil died of an overdose in a Wiltshire hospital on 4th. January 1986 after a drink and drugs binge and his estranged wife Caroline was with him.

Chapter Twelve

1984

Things just keep getting better

By 1984, I had got a name for working with loud rock bands or heavy metal bands as they were now been called. One day, I had a phone call from a guy in Hannover in Germany called Olaf, who I had met somewhere along the line.

Olaf was running a sound company called Rocksound, which was actually owned by German metal band, The Scorpions. This was a trend started by Pink Floyd in the UK. They bought a huge touring sound and light system and formed a company called Britannia Row, because that was where their equipment was stored in a warehouse in Britannia Row in North London. When Pink Floyd weren't touring, Britannia Row rented out there sound and light systems to other bands. Thus they owned a sound and light rental company.

Britannia Row Ltd. is now the biggest rental company in the UK. Thus Olaf was running the Scorpions Rocksound Company. He called and asked me if I wanted to do a European tour with American rock band Kiss.

Kiss had been one of the biggest rock bands since the mid 1970's. They were famous, of course, for the make-up they wore in the early days.

I said, "Yes."

ROCK 'N' ROLL
It's Better than Working for a Living

We agreed on a price and I was to be setting up monitors and "babysitting" the German guy who was actually going to be operating them. Two weeks into the tour, and I was never so pleased to be only second in charge of the system. I saw the German guy Rolf, having huge problems. Three quarters of that band were major assholes, more of which later, about six years later.

The front of house engineer was a guy called Achim. He was a bouncy, jovial blond haired German. Probably the only German I ever met with a sense of humor. Let's face it, how many famous German standup comedians can you name?

Rolf's nightmare was continuing on monitors. Even with the support act, a new band called Bon Jovi!

The reason Rolf was having monitor problems, even with the support band, was that Jon Bon Jovi (What a strange name I always thought.) has no voice whatsoever. He never has had. He had the quietest singing voice I had ever heard. Sorry, if never heard that. You should have. Their fame is borne out by the fact when they actually made it into the big time and became a worldwide Platinum selling band in 1986 / 87; they started rehearsals for the tour in Los Angeles and contracted one of the biggest sound companies in the world to do their World tour.

I think Showco out of Dallas Texas were the first. Showco brought in probably three or four monitor engineers. They all got fired one after another, as nobody could make Jon Bon Jovi's voice loud enough for him to be able to hear it. They then started firing companies, not just engineers. There would actually be different Company's equipment on the stage day after day. In the end, legend has it that they went through six different sound companies before they settled on one for the tour. I think they had to go with them as there was nobody left to try!

Shame they didn't have in-ear monitors in those days, which would have done the trick. It wouldn't have been as much fun though as watching all those clever engineers squirm.

I did actually do a couple of shows with Jon Bon Jovi, when they supported Iron Maiden on the World Slavery Tour in 1985. I had no problems. I did make a point of telling him he had the quietest singing voice I had never heard, which got a laugh from him and then he apologized!

I can breathe louder than Bon Jovi can sing!!!!!!!!!

It was summertime in England, I went off to do the Glastonbury Festival with the "Fluffy White Rabbit Sound Company" aka, Turbosound. Remember, these were the hippies that gave me such problems with their equipment on the Thin Lizzy tour.

I met up with Ian Dury and The Blockheads again there. I did their show on Saturday and had to be back in London at Shepperton Film Studios on Sunday morning for rehearsals with Whitesnake.

Whitesnake were a famous British rock band of the 1980's. They were formed by ex-lead singer of Deep Purple, David Coverdale. And, Deep Purple, of course, was an even more famous rock band. The early line up was made up of various characters of the British late 70's rock scene, including Bernie Marsden, and Micky Moody and many other reprobates.

Bass player was Neil Murray, who was the only constant member until Coverdale went all American in the late 80's. Neil came from Scotland originally, but first made his name with legendary drummer Cozy Powell in Cozy Powell's Hammer and alongside guitarist Gary Moore in British Jazz Rock band Colloseum II.

ROCK 'N' ROLL
It's Better than Working for a Living

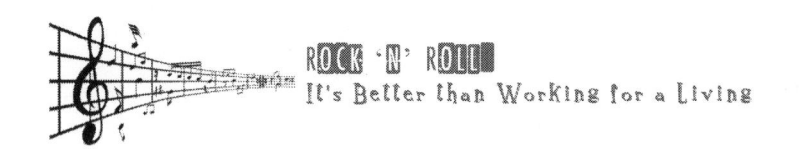

Neil was the bass player in the band in July 1984, when I turned up for rehearsals at Shepperton Film Studios. I knew Neil personally, having met him a few years earlier in the famous music biz pub in Fulham West London, The Golden Lion in various after show parties, in various back stage bars. This was one of Neil's specialties, hanging out in backstage bars. That is, apart from been an excellent bass player.

The aforesaid Cozy Powell had also been brought into Whitesnake by Coverdale. Cozy, a legend on the 1970's British rock scene, started being noticed when he met people like Robert Plant and John Bonham. At the time, they were in an unknown band in Birmingham called Listen. He also interested Tony Iommi from Black Sabbath.

Cozy was recommended to a guy called Ace Kefford from 1960's Birmingham band, The Move when Ace was forming his own band. Cozy started picking up session work, but his big break was when he got the job in The Jeff Beck Group. He went on to play with Richie Blackmore's Rainbow, Black Sabbath, and had his own band. In 1973, he had a chart hit with the *Dance with the Devil* single. He was probably the busiest session drummer of all time. It's estimated he played on in excess of 66 albums over the years. Cozy died in a car crash in April 1998.

Coverdale had also brought in another dinosaur of 1970's British rock. Although a somewhat less assuming figure, but none the less a huge character, in the shape of Deep Purple keyboard player . . . Jon Lord. He could entertain you for many hours with his stories of life on the road with Deep Purple. Jon was a true gentleman of the road.

The two guitarists in this line up were relatively unknowns next to their illustrious friends. John Sykes, the young guitar hero of cult British rock band, Tygers of Pan Tang. He was the hottest guitarist on the British rock scene at the time and had followed me from the last Thin Lizzy line up. Well, not exactly followed me, but we both ended with the same band. John was a bit of a mouthy upstart at the time. Unfortunately, he believed his own hype. I was just as mouthy and plenty more experienced in these situations, so our paths never really crossed.

John moved to Los Angeles, formed his own band Blue Murder and then re-joined the remaining Thin Lizzy boys in 1996 to tour to play the songs of Phil Lynott again. Since 2000, John has been doing his own solo stuff.

Lastly, in the Whitesnake lineup was guitarist Mel Galley. He was another from the Midlands heartland of Black Sabbath and Led Zeppelin.

Mel was not hugely famous, but he knew everybody that was. He was an excellent guitar player and a thoroughly nice guy. He played in a Midlands band called Trapeze, which he formed with Glenn Hughes, bass player for Black Sabbath and also a couple of versions of Deep Purple. Mel died of cancer in July 2008.

So that's the band. I'm just sitting back here thinking, how many people I used to know in this business who are now DEAD!

I better get a move on with this book; time is obviously not on my side.

9:00 a.m., first day of Whitesnake rehearsals at Shepperton Studios, we set up a truck full of sound gear. Quite a lot of it was not working. No surprise there then! That's what happens when you take the cheapest quote for the job in this business.

Eventually, we got most of it working. Coverdale arrived early and started fussing as he always did . . . nice enough guy, but a bit of a dick; still, his prerogative, his band.

ROCK 'N' ROLL
It's Better than Working for a Living

John Sykes also arrived early, being the new boy. He also started fussing about. Mel, Jon Lord, Neil and Cozy arrived and went to the pub!

Mel, Jon, Neil and Cozy come back from the pub, John Sykes and Coverdale were still fussing. Instead of getting on with rehearsing, Jon Lord started on some of his Deep Purple stories about hookers on airplanes and God knows what else. Everybody was entranced.

We had managed to get all the equipment working hours ago. It is now about 8.30 p.m. and Dorothy (The band's pet name for Mr. Coverdale.) suggests they should play a song or two. Dorothy obviously knows all the songs, as does Neil and Jon. Mel has learned them. John Sykes, being the new boy has memorized every note and every chord of every song. Cozy can play anything, anytime.

After about thirty minutes, someone remarked, I think it was Jon . . . he was late for a dinner appointment and had to leave. Cozy also realized he had to go. So that was that. It was a wonderful day of rehearsals, leaving the new boys, I think, a little shell shocked by the older members' lack of urgency.

Nothing stands out too much about that week of rehearsals apart from the lack of urgency maybe to rehearse. I must admit I didn't really see the point either.

After the first day, John and Mel were usually first in, both arrived by cab I think. Neil would get the tube and train of course. A frugal man was Neil. Cozy and Jon would roar up in their big motors from the stockbroker belt of Berkshire and Dorothy would arrive in his limo with driver. Dorothy always had to have a limo.

There was one discussion I remember, which made everyone laugh, except Dorothy, who obviously took things very seriously. Once again it was the ace story teller Jon Lord.

Dorothy was discussing the release of a documentary movie made of the band at The Donnington Festival in the summer of 1983. It was strangely called, *Whitesnake Commandoes*, for a reason known only to Dorothy himself. He started handing out tee shirts to everyone at which point Mr. Lord quipped, "I don't know about Whitesnake Commandoes, it's more like Dad's Army (Famous British wartime Home Guard spoof TV series.) . . ." at which point everyone fell on the floor laughing, including Dorothy.

Out on the road, on the tour, the sound crew was made up of a pretty motley crew of individuals (And you'll be able to read about them later [Motley Crue that is!].). Most of the sound crew was regular employees (which I wasn't) of Tasco Inc. Or, the Trans America Sound Company, which was a very grand name for a sound company formed in London in the early 1970's by a guy with a very dubious reputation, called Joe Brown. I did experience proof of his reputation when I had to sue him after not been paid for a Judas Priest tour. The company got a lot of work, in the late 70's and 80's. They were doing almost all the heavy rock and metal bands, although they did have a reputation for not treating their crews very well. In essence, you were either one of Joe's boys or you weren't. I wasn't!

Front of house engineer was Laurie Quigley. He was a big brash Australian guy. He was really a big softie. The third man, and rigger, was a Belgian (Very unusual in Rock 'n' Roll.) called Charlie, who was trying hard to be one of Joe's boys and fourth man. This was a little unusual on British tours, as you usually only went out as a three man crew. But . . . I was glad to have this man along. He was Phil Wilkey, a longtime monitor engineer and Guru, and still at it. He was a guy I had met in about 1971 working

ROCK 'N' ROLL
It's Better than Working for a Living

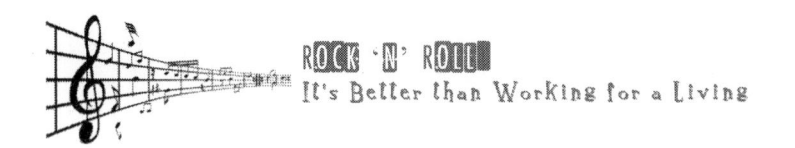

with a British band called String Driven Thing. Phil and I came from the same place, the same time and our careers had run parallel for many years until I retired from touring. We've been mates since that time. Occasionally, we lose track of each other for ten years at a time, but catch up again. Phil is one of my all-time favorite work mates.

That Whitesnake tour in 1984 was one of the easiest jobs I ever had in the business. This was due to it being with some old pros who just wanted to get this gig thing over and get to the bar. Dorothy was still on a huge ego trip dating back to 1973 when he was asked to join Deep Purple. And, John Sykes, still the new boy, was still trying to impress.

There were a couple of other characters on the tour. There was a guitar tech called Clive. He was a Geordie boy with an accent very difficult even for an English person to understand. He had come with John Sykes from Thin Lizzy. There was a Welshman in a woolly hat called Ashley. Clive was a nice guy, and he liked his drugs (Well, who didn't you may well ask.). He smoked quite a lot of weed (Although he always professed to, "Not really put much in the joint." but it still took him about four hours to clean each guitar every day. In fact, he spent all day cleaning guitars.). Clive liked speed also, which unfortunately made him totally incomprehensible. It sounded as if he were speaking some strange foreign tongue, which no one had ever heard before. He also liked cocaine, which basically had the same effect as the speed. He seemed to get back to the guitar cleaning a little bit quicker with the cocaine. On top of all this, Clive was a diabetic, quite a serious diabetic by the look of things. He had to inject himself with insulin on a regular basis each day. My one endearing memory of Clive was a quite regular drama that used to happen. This was of Clive dropping his last ampoule of insulin and begging everyone in sight to quickly get him some chocolate to keep his blood sugar up before he passed out. It wouldn't have been funny I know if he had have passed out, but this scene seemed to happen every other day.

Ever think you were in the wrong business Clive? For someone with such a serious medical condition, did all that dope have anything to do with it?

Never heard of him since; hope you're well Clive.

Then there was Ashley! Ashley was actually Cozy's drum tech. He was also the one Cozy used to throw stupid ideas at regarding his drum solo. Like pyros in the drums and upside down drum kits and drum kits on wheels. Unfortunately, for Cozy, none of that stuff actually got done. Of course, a few years later . . . Tommy Lee of Motley Crue did all that stuff and more.

Ashley once professed to be a monitor engineer. In fact, I met him on a gig at the old Rainbow Theatre in London in 1979, where he was . . . Whitesnake's monitor engineer. Here, I was the system tech for monitors and Ashley was the bands engineer.

The entire band came on stage. Ashley was talking away to me (He did do quite a bit of talking.) about how good the band were to work for. Dorothy went to shout in the mic, screaming feedback from the monitors, which filled the theatre. This didn't seem to panic Ashley. He casually asked me, "I wonder where that's coming from."

"I don't know Ashley, but I think you'd better find out pretty sharpish as there's a titanium shafted mic stand heading in the general direction of your head."

Luckily for Ashley, Dorothy's aim with the super light mic stand that night wasn't that good. It landed a few feet in front of me. Ashley asked, "What the fuck's wrong with him then?"

ROCK 'N' ROLL
It's Better than Working for a Living

I wonder Ashley.

Unfortunately, the production manager was a guy Steve Payne, who was very aptly named, but spelt wrong. He didn't like me, God knows why. But, I didn't like him, so we got on fine.

Sometimes a production manager can be your best friend and really organize the production to run like a well-oiled machine. Payne was cutting all the corners he could find though, getting his own suppliers in. He was getting back handers from them and cutting down on crew costs. He made us drive ourselves in cars instead of having a sleeper bus and we had to share hotel rooms. He actually didn't want to take me on the American tour, as he could have got an engineer in America and saved on my air fare. Dorothy insisted; however, so I went. So . . . "Up yours Payne!"

There were always quite a lot of women hanging around backstage at Whitesnake gigs, as there were with all rock bands . . . especially in America. Not so much in the UK. I must give a name check to one girl I met in a nightclub in Newcastle on the UK tour. Jackie . . . she went home with me to the hotel and I met her for about four years every time I was in Newcastle. I just recently discovered her on Facebook and we speak all the time now some 27 years later.

In America, things were much more serious. On the second half of the American tour, we were supporting Dio. We would get into the gig late, about 2:00 p.m. and finish early at about 9:30 p.m. We had lots more time to get into trouble, than if we had been the headliner.

Fortunately, on this leg of the tour, Payne had to get us a sleeper bus as the distances between gigs were too big to be able to drive ourselves. Of course, these American busses all had the infamous "Back Lounge." This was always where deals were done; drugs were taken and they were a general den of iniquity.

MICK (MICHAEL) TYAS

Before, I move onto the back lounge this particular day . . . just a word about earlier on in the tour when we had to drive ourselves in a car between gigs.

We usually had to leave after the gig, so not the ideal time to drive 400 miles after a twelve hour day at work. There were four of us in a Chevrolet Caprice station wagon. We had just left the gig in Sacramento and were off to I think Eugene, Oregon (Hub of the universe, of course!). I started off driving and think I was still driving four hours later. I screeched to halt in the center of the road, which woke everyone with a start. "Someone else is gonna have to drive," I said. "I'm hallucinating; I just saw a fucking moose in the middle of the road."

As I got out of the driver's seat and headed into the bushes for a piss, I turned around and . . . fuck me! There, in the middle of the road stood a fucking moose about the size of a small fucking house! Now, that was scary!

Meanwhile, back in the back lounge, there is a ritual carried out by some of the crew with time on their hands in the afternoon. Pretty young ladies, and sometimes some not so pretty, happen to be hanging out by the busses and are always hassling the crew for back stage passes. They know that crew guys always have passes . . . so a barter system developed whereby the girls could negotiate for the passes. The unofficial going rate for these passes was set many years prior at the exchange rate of 1 backstage pass = 1 blowjob, which seemed a very fair rate of exchange and seemed to please all parties. This exchange deal usually took place, where else, but in the back lounge. Some of the ladies I have seen doing these deals I wouldn't let them touch me with a barge pole, but occasionally one stood out.

ROCK 'N' ROLL
It's Better than Working for a Living

This particular afternoon I went in to the back lounge to find a video to watch as I had some spare time on my hands. I came across two girls and two crew guys involved in a backstage pass deal. One of these girls was outrageously dressed in not much of anything. She was incredibly pretty. When I walked in, I was asked by her if I wanted to give her a backstage pass, but declined as I like my sex in private. A strange thing happened later on that day.

Firstly, we had a hotel after the gig, which was unusual as we usually drove straight to the next gig. Secondly, I had a single room, once again unusual. Thirdly, the outrageous girl ended up in my room (?) and quickly divested herself of what little clothes she was wearing.

After about an hour of general messing about, there was a knock at the door. The girl jumped out of bed totally naked and opened the door to her friend who she had lost during the gig. Unfortunately, her friend had not lost her. She came into my room followed by a couple of crew guys and a couple of the band. This all looked a bit set up as the girl was extremely excited by the fact a couple of the band had appeared. She started dancing all over the room. At one point someone asked if she could smoke a cigarette in her ass! That is when I stepped in and asked everyone to get out of my room. I heard murmurings of, "Come on let's go to my room." So everyone left, including the girls, which was not exactly what I had planned.

The rest of the night passed peacefully. I never saw the girls again. The next morning when I woke up, the girl's clothes were still on my bedroom floor, so I called one of the other guys who told me that they had left hours ago. They just called a cab and left. That must have been an early morning surprise for the cab driver and I thought she was such a nice girl.

Later on that year, I also went to Japan for the first time. This was with Whitesnake again. And, Payne didn't want me to go, tough again! And, Dorothy overruled him again.

We did a Festival called Super Rock in Japan 1984, with The Scorpions, Michael Schenker Group, Bon Jovi and Anvil. We did six shows from the 4th to the 12th of August. Whitesnake headlined, then Scorpions headlined, then Michael Shenker headlined and Bon Jovi and Anvil were just support bands. I remember we did a show in the southern city of Fukuoka and after the gig we all went back to the hotel, which I guess was about a twenty or twenty-five story place. It was pretty new, as most of Japan was. As was the usual practice, we sat in the bar until it closed and then retired to our rooms. We had single rooms also. There was no sharing in Japan as the promoter was paying all expenses.

I think I passed out pretty quickly. The Suntory Japanese whiskey had the desired effect. I woke in the middle of the night sometime. I have no idea what time. I awoke because the bathroom door was banging open then closed, which I thought was a little unusual. I thought I better get out of bed and close it. I put the overhead light on and it also was swinging from side to side on its chain. Now, that was unusual. So, I got out of bed and noticed the room was swinging from side to side. Now, that was even more fucking unusual. So, I sat down on the bed and thought. It soon became obvious within a couple of nanoseconds, we had either put to sea in our hotel and were been tossed about by a rough sea or it was a fucking EARTHQUAKE. The latter option seemed the more likely unfortunately. I had to think about this, not for very long though. Being on the twelfth or fourteenth floor or whatever floor I was on didn't seem very advantageous in an earthquake. Thinking about it at the time, if I went to the top floor

ROCK 'N' ROLL
It's Better than Working for a Living

of the hotel and the building did collapse, hopefully I would ride down on top of the rubble in a sort of surfing manner; whereas, if I went down to the ground floor, I might make it to the bottom and be crushed by twelve million tons of hotel collapsing on top of me. I did think this through two or three times very quickly. I wasn't able to reach a decision. To get out of the building was probably the more sensible, but it might be raining or something. I didn't really want to go and stand outside in the middle of the night. I just wanted to go back to bed, wake up in the morning and find everything alright. This is exactly what I did. I slept like a baby and everything was alright. Happy ending!

The next morning I was told all the Germans, The Michael Shenker Group and The Scorpions were seen running down the stairs (Remember no elevators in an earthquake!) in their underwear and assembling in the parking lot (Ah!, those wacky Germans.), and it was raining!

The papers the next day reported it as 5.7 intensity on the Richter scale. Just a slight shake really. Don't know about that . . . it was about 10.0 on the Rectum scale as it scared the shit out of me!

I did have another similar seismic experience on an Iron Maiden Tour in 1987. We were driving overnight in the bus from somewhere (?) to San Bernadino California. As normal there were the usual suspects in the back lounge, trying to take as much cocaine and drink as much beer before the sun came up on another day. Day meant work and work interrupted our partying.

I don't exactly remember going to bed. I guess it must have been somewhere around 5 or 6 a.m. as usual. I did have the usual wrestling match with the pillow and the duvet (comforter) for most of what was left of the night. I also remember the bus stopping for a long time, which meant we must have arrived at the gig.

I must have then dozed off again. I was woken by the bus moving again and couldn't think where we were going as some of the bunks were empty. This meant some people had gone into the gig. I was left to wondering if I was the only one left on the bus and somebody had missed me. Was I now on my way to a bus wash or a tire shop or some other repair shop?

I got up and went through the door to the front lounge and I was on a ghost bus!

There was nobody in the front of the bus. There was nobody driving the bus. We weren't even moving except moving from side to side. So was the rest of the planet. It was only slight movement but enough to make the bus move on its air ride suspension. I quickly got dressed and went into the gig. Not one person mentioned "the shake." It was pretty normal in San Bernadino I guess.

So 1984 came to an end with more of those gigs with Kiss (Who we will meet again later, though somewhat briefly.) and Bon Jovi, who will also pop up again.

Chapter Thirteen

1985 SERIOUS ROCK 'N' ROLL!

On the 14th January 1985, I flew from London Heathrow airport to Hartford Connecticut byway of New York's Kennedy airport. On their return to their American tour after playing Rock in Rio, metal band Iron Maiden had been looking for a new monitor engineer. Their previous engineer, Horace, had just been fired. Although, Horace was a nice guy and a competent engineer; I don't think he was Rock 'n' Roll enough for the band. A guy called Nick, who was running Tasco sound company in London at the time, called me and told me Maiden were looking for a new monitor engineer. He asked if I interested. Apparently, he had given them a glowing report of my talents. They were interested in employing me, but I had to make a quick decision. This was a Thursday and I had to be there on the following Monday. Having nothing else on at the time, I said yes. I picked up my ticket from the Maiden office on that Friday morning.

A few years later, I flew the same route en route to meet up with the American Tasco crew at the beginning of the American leg of a Judas Priest tour. The night before I left, Salli and I had been out on the town at the Marquee Club in London. We were later at the St Moritz, which was a restaurant come bar just opposite the Marquee. It was also a favorite late night hangout for music biz people, as you could drink until about four in the morning. We took a gram of coke out with us and, of course, kept dipping into it during the night.

The next day I was wearing the same jeans I had on the night before when I boarded the flight to New York. When I arrived in New York I cleared Immigration and Customs with no problems. Nobody was looking at my baggage. I then went off to find my connecting flight to Hartford. My flight from Kennedy to Hartford was about eight in the evening so I didn't arrive in Hartford until about nine thirty that evening. I went straight to the baggage carousel to watch the baggage go around and round. I watched all the baggage go around and around until there was none left. The baggage claim people assured me that my baggage would be delivered to me at my hotel.

I believe WHEN, was the only question I asked. I had heard of baggage following people around the country for weeks until it finally caught up with them. They assured me as soon as they found it, I would have it. Which wasn't particularly reassuring; so ... somewhat pissed off I got a cab to the hotel and was somewhat cheered up to the see the bar still open. I quickly checked in, but could see no sign of any of the American crew who were already here apparently. I quickly went up to my room before heading back down to the bar to cheer myself up with a couple of large Jack and cokes. I put my room key (As they were keys back in those days.) in my front right hand jeans pocket, but I felt something in the little ticket pocket as I did so. At that moment I felt two differing emotions, one of exultation and one of complete horror. There in a small white wrap was about half a gram of cocaine.

For some unknown reason, this was something that had never ever happened before. I don't recall it ever happening again. Salli and I had gone through a whole night and not finished off the gram, which was unheard of in modern history I believe! I had put the wrap, with what remained of the cocaine in it, in my pocket. And, I put on the same pair of jeans the next day and flown to America. I had walked through American fucking Immigration and Customs with half a gram of fucking cocaine in my pocket! I was horrified. I would never ever have attempted to do that, ever! I was also very pleased, because that and a couple of large Jacks and I wouldn't care about my baggage. To my huge surprise the baggage arrived on the next flight and was delivered to the hotel about 1:00 a.m. everything turned out very nice, if not somewhat scary.

I arrived at Hartford Civic Center about 8:00 p.m. I was met by Dick, Iron Maiden's production manager, who I knew from another Judas Priest tour a few years earlier. We went to the production office for a chat. Dick was one of my all-time favorite production managers, if not THE favorite. Always fair, always helpful, always organized; he never cut corners. He was all-in-all a good guy. As we were having a chat, Bruce the singer with the band came in and introduced himself. I had heard some stories about this guy. I heard how demanding he was and knew he essentially was the reason I was there . . . to keep him happy. I think though, he just needed a friend on the tour.

Known to the rest of the crew as "The Chimp" for his onstage antics, Bruce would stand no nonsense from the (his?) monitor engineer. Although, he would get some from me a few years later, but everyone else in the band had their own techs to look after them and even hang out with sometimes. I think Bruce felt a little left out, but now Bruce would have me, how sweet.

I didn't actually do monitors that night, as I wanted to observe the show to see what I had to deal with. Also, because I had jetlag and a bit of a hangover as I had drunk quite a lot on the flight over. I didn't do much observing as I spotted a girl backstage I knew from a Whitesnake gig in the area. She promptly asked me if I wanted to buy a gram of coke. Weeeeeeell! Ok! You twisted my arm; I think maybe she was the local dealer.

So that was my very first gig with Iron Maiden. It had started just as it was about to carry on for the next four years.

That night after the load out, I experienced my first night on the bus with the Iron Maiden crew. Well, with the back line crew and Dougie the FOH engineer.

Maiden had five crew busses out on that tour, one for the lighting crew; one for the sound crew; a production bus, with the carpenter; set crew; and Dick the production engineer and a production assistant . . . usually an inexperienced girl delightfully lightheartedly referred to as "the bus mouse." She was basically Dick's gofer. She was responsible for keeping the busses stocked with beer, soft drinks, ice and food. So, she was a very important person and also more often than not, ended up in some romantic (or not) situation with one of the crew. There was also another bus with assorted riggers, lighting people and set guys.

These busses were stocked with different departments in the production intentionally as not everybody had to be up in the morning at the same time. For instance, those poor lighting pukes were first in to rig in a morning. Usually, somewhere around 7:00 or 8:00 a.m., which was pretty hard for them as the usual time for finishing the load out the night before would be somewhere around 1:30 to 2:00 a.m. That is if you were lucky. Of course, everything had to be done the reverse way round on the load out. So, first in . . . last out. It didn't leave much time for partying, but they get paid well for it.

Production people were also up about the same time as Dick. They usually had to go find the promoter's rep and make sure everything was in place, like a stage! Before work started, the young set guys on the bus were usually the victims of Dick having to get up early. If he had to get up, they were getting up also!

The sound crew (Minus FOH engineer and monitor engineer.) usually went in a couple of hours after the lighting people when enough rigging had been done to allow them to rig the sound system. The riggers, who went in with the lighting people, were probably the most extreme people on the tour. They had to swing about in the rafters a couple of hundred feet off the ground to hang the electric motors that lifted and dropped lighting and sound rigs. They were usually the most extreme in other ways too. They always seemed to drink the most and take the most drugs in the small off time they had between the end of the load out and the start of the load in. They had the most responsible jobs on the tour, but they always seemed to make it look easy even after copious amounts of substances the night before and hardly any sleep. The one concession they did have was that they were usually finished rigging by lunchtime and didn't really have anything else to do until the end of the show, except sleep or party, of course!

Being on the bus with the backline crew and the FOH sound engineer Doug, meant I didn't have to get up early. The sound crew knew exactly how to hang the sound system to Doug's satisfaction. He only had to plug up his console. I would, more or less have the same situation with the monitor system. Of course, we had to make all that shit work that had been rigged earlier on

Rock 'n' Roll
It's Better than Working for a Living

in the day by the "workers" and make it work to the band's satisfaction and needs. We were basically the frontline contact with the band during the show.

The four backline crew was also in the same situation. Although, they only had half a dozen guitar cabinets and a drum kit to rig. Once again, they were closest to the band during the show, so usually they got all the flack if anything went wrong. We would usually go into the gig around 1:00 p.m., which was a very sociable time of day to rise from one's slumbers.

The main panic in a morning for us was . . . Were the showers still hot . . . and, had they kept breakfast on for us until that time?

We were first out of the gig on the load out of course, as everything was done in the reverse order to the load in. Our record I think was about forty-five minutes after the band finished. So . . . with all that time ahead for partying and getting fucked up, we had to stress to the management getting a good hearty breakfast in the morning (afternoon!) was very important to us.

We would actually find some evenings / mornings we were staggering off to our bunks just as the lighting crew were going to work; *poor fuckers*. Of course, that meant we still had about five hours left to get some sleep, although there would never ever be much chance of that after six or so hours of beer and cocaine. It was usually just enough time to wrestle with the bedding for a few hours.

I must admit there were some days when I had really been suffering from the night before. I really wished I was one of those worker guys, instead of being a member of the "Country Club." I must admit those thoughts didn't arise too often and probably only lasted for a fraction of a nanosecond. I had devised a small test for myself when I went into the gig in the morning / afternoon. It was . . . if the caterers could understand I was speaking English and I could read the writing on the cereal packet I knew I was ok. If I couldn't I knew was in trouble.

Being only a two hour drive from Hartford Connecticut to the next gig in Worcester Massachusetts, meant all the buses and trucks had arrived and parked up at the gig before we. Our bus had gone to bed, a long time before. Which meant, trying to get any sleep, which was a pretty long shot anyway after large amounts of beer and cocaine was fairly impossible; especially when one eventually conceded they really ought to try and get some sleep. It was even harder as we weren't being rocked by the gentle motion of the bus.

I think we only once persuaded a rookie driver to drive around the city until we had finally gone to sleep.

My first actual working gig with Maiden turned into a huge success. Anything I did that was new, or even all the things I didn't do, scored me points with the band. Well, with Bruce anyway, this was why I was there, of course. Mind you, after I'd seen what the other guy had done, that wouldn't have been so hard to achieve. Sorry Horace.

Of course, we celebrated another hard day at the office with the nightly party in the back lounge. This was to become a regular occurrence over the next four years of touring with the band.

Before I go any further I should point out that these back lounge "soirees" really only consisted of drinking gallons of beer, snorting loads of cocaine and talking absolute garbage all night. That is, until we couldn't think of any more garbage to talk about.

From Worcester Mass we had a day off the next day (We needed it of course, all that partying is very hard work.). There was only 180 miles to drive to New York and I think if I remember correctly (which I must admit is unlikely most of the time) we had a fairly quiet evening in the back lounge that night as everyone quite liked the idea of having a good day off in New York instead of spending it in bed after a busy night of partying. Not that it was a particularly good day for having a day off in New York.

When we checked into The Mayflower Hotel on Central Park West it was about -20C with about a foot of snow on the ground. I did manage to meet up with an old friend who had lived with us in London. I had a really nice day with a few drinks in the evening and early to bed about midnight. I was recharging my batteries for my first really big important show with Iron Maiden.

Radio City Music Hall is a beautiful Art Deco movie theatre built in 1932 in the Rockefeller Center at the intersection of W 50th St and 6th Ave. or Avenue of The Americas. It has a capacity of 5933 people. At the time it was built, it was the largest movie theatre in the world. Even now it's fucking big and it is fucking beautiful. If you ever have a day to spend in New York, go and see Radio City Music Hall.

Radio City is not really a venue you associate with a metal band. It is a little like putting Metallica on at the London Palladium, which wouldn't work at all and would never be allowed. In New York, in the beautiful period charm of Radio City, it seemed fine. Besides seven nights of sold out shows would have been much needed revenue to keep such a place going in the center of Manhattan.

MICK (MICHAEL) TYAS

We weren't all having a restful day in Manhattan. I think Dick got the lighting crew in to rig on their day off. As rigging thirty tons of lights in a 1930's theatre is hugely different to rigging in all those basketball arenas that we had just played; also trying to center the whole rig and stage set, which was normally considered quite large at 60 feet in width, on the enormous Great Stage's 144 feet width was a feat.

When we went in on the first gig day, everyone was blown away by the whole place. Such a huge difference to freezing (or sweating, depending on the season) your nuts off each working day in a huge warehouse environment. So much so, the band even did a sound check, which was rather unusual as they normally only did one at the beginning of each leg of the tour. The environment was so different from a sound perspective. Still, I didn't change any of my settings as it worked yesterday, why shouldn't it work today. Anyway, if you change it, you have to change it back again, which is more work!

Four of the seven nights gigs were pretty uneventful. Surprisingly, we didn't get into too much trouble after the gigs considering the spare time we had on our hands. I believe there were a couple of small after show drinks events. So, it was hanging out at the theater for a couple of hours and then earliest to bed. It is quite strange we did seem to get into more trouble at small town gigs than at the gigs in big cities.

On the fifth night's gig, The Chimp was having trouble with his voice, which was not unusual. Especially as the band that had only been back from their trip to Brazil for Rock in Rio for four days . . . coming back to -20c temperatures resulted in a few people developing heavy colds.

ROCK 'N' ROLL
It's Better than Working for a Living

One of Bruce's endearing little foibles during a show was he would come running over to me behind the desk. He did this every night during Adrian and Davy's solos in some song or other. These visits usually consisted of Bruce waffling instructions and opinions on how to solve any problems he was having with the sound that particular night.

There was quite a large amount of bullshit used in these exchanges between us. Bruce was convinced his knowledge of sound engineering was good enough to talk on the level as me. Fortunately, my bullshit was of a much better quality than his. The conversation usually ended with me telling him, "No problem, I'll sort it." In fact, 90% of the time, I changed nothing. This is all part of the art of the psychology of been a monitor engineer. In fact, some nights Bruce would even run over to me again and say . . . "No, change it back to how it was Mick, it was better like that." Job done I think!

There was one fateful night towards the end of my Iron Maiden career, which maybe contributed to me not lasting past the end of 1988 with the band. At the time I thought nothing of it. In fact, that night I was in no condition to think very much at all still having the hugest of cocaine and alcohol hangovers ever at 10:00 p.m. the following night!

Bruce came running over to me in his usual manner at the usual point in the show and started his usual waffle about mid-range frequencies and other such garbage. Whilst all the time I was having trouble standing up; in fact, if the desk hadn't have been there, I think I may fallen over. Instead, of my usual bright, articulate, confident answers, designed to convince Bruce I was on to the problem, I'm afraid I just blurted out, "Look, just fuck off Bruce and get on with it will you?" Bruce just replied, like any other night, "Yeah, cool!"

I thought I'd got away with it that night, but I knew I was in trouble. Not from anyone in particular. No call in the dressing room from the boss (Steve Harris). I think some people had noticed I was getting more and more fucked up night after night. My cocaine bills were definitely going up. I was spending $300 a week on top of my $100 a week per diems, all on cocaine. I was laying three or four lines in the edge of the desk every night to craftily snort during the two hour plus show. That incident that night with Bruce showed I was losing patience due to my lifestyle.

I don't know where exactly that incident took place, but it was one of the American gigs near to the end of the tour. I don't know to this day. I think Bruce had seen what was happening to me.

Meanwhile, back at Radio City Music Hall, Bruce was having genuine problems with his voice due to a heavy cold, rather than the normal gig situation of just requiring some attention during the show. So the next gig day, which was the sixth, we all turned up about 4:00 p.m. just to diddle about and make sure everything was working (no sound checks!) We also wanted to make sure we were in time for dinner. We were told by Dick, the production manager, they might have to cancel the show as Bruce's cold had got much heavier overnight. He could hardly speak. We sat down to dinner and prayed. Our prayers were answered about thirty minutes later when Dick announced the show had been cancelled.

Most people stayed and had dinner in catering and then walked back to the hotel, which was only about six blocks. It was -20c!

ROCK 'N' ROLL
It's Better than Working for a Living

Myself, and the rest of the backline bus, hung around in the dressing room to drink some of the beer that had been put in there for the band. We waited for Warren the assistant tour manager to arrive, because we had an unexpected night off. He was going to come around with a present for us (Wonder what that could have been?).

Warren's job description as assistant tour manager was somewhat misleading. It consisted of making sure the band's baggage got on to airplanes or buses and into hotel rooms. He had to put out towels and drinks on stage for the band. The most unusual facet of his job was as "walk-on" Eddie!

Eddie, as most metal band fans will know, is a mascot adopted by Iron Maiden from the artwork of their first single in 1980. Over the years it appeared on all their album covers in various guises. They also brought him into the live shows. In the 1980's, there was usually on each tour a static Eddie head built into the stage set, which came up by electric motors behind the set and breathed fire from its mouth or shot lasers from its eyes, or some such nonsense. Then there was also a "walk on" Eddie, which once again was in various guises depending on the tour. It was a man and a half size costume with a man inside it who lumbered onto the stage to harass the band during the song *Iron Maiden*, then was eventually kicked of the stage by the band. This was Warren!

Warren liked his cocaine. He had usually had some each night before he did his "Eddie" act. He probably had quite a few beers also. So his appearances some nights were worth the entrance money itself, whilst he tried to control the huge costume he was dressed in, which often succumbed to the forces of gravity and left him helpless on the floor.

Warren arrived back at the gig about sevenish. He sat down at the big round table in the dressing room and produced a glittering white crystal type ball about the half the size of a golf ball. He placed it on the table and said, "Should I start?" What he had was an ounce of cocaine worth about $2000 sparkling away in the middle of the table. Frankly, I had never seen so much in one lump.

Whilst Warren constantly shaved off bits of this rock and fashioned it into a line for each of us . . . we sat and talked and drank and smoked for at least another two hours. That is, until someone suggested we ought to go back to the hotel or we were in danger of getting locked in the theatre all night. So, we gathered ourselves together. Warren shaved of a piece of the rock for us to take with us and ordered a cab to take him back to the band's hotel whilst we ventured out into the freezing New York night.

As we were leaving, there were still a few girls around the stage door. Our resident predator, Michael latched onto two of them and convinced them a walk in the snow back to our nice warm hotel would be a good move for them. When we got back to the hotel, we headed to Michael's room as he had the women. The other three or four of us were now in a party mood and had the cocaine. As we all got into the party mode, ordering $60 worth of drinks from room service every hour or so, there was still plenty of coke left. Things were getting noisy as everybody tried to talk to somebody else, about something really important, all at the same time. With of course no one listening to anyone else; it was a fairly typical cocaine discussion really.

A couple of guys dropped by the wayside in the early hours and decided to go to bed. I was getting really interested in one of the girls now. Michael had his eye on the other one. Still the coke kept coming out. We all turned into gibbering mindless machines, talking complete and absolute crap for hour after hour. The girls were not really joining in that much, until at one point I turned around to Michael and said; "Where'd the women go?"

This must have been about four in the morning. The women had left. I never saw them leave. Michael never saw them leave. They had just vanished!

They weren't in fact supernatural beings, we were just so wrapped up in our conversations between ourselves that they actually got up and left without us noticing. "We scared them off," said Michael. "No we didn't," I said "We just fucking bored them to death; they must have been near suicidal." At least the coke didn't cost us anything.

The last show at Radio City was cancelled due to Bruce's suffering vocal chords as well. So, we all moved on to Bethlehem (Pennsylvania that is.). This is where, once again we all got practice in rigging all the equipment (Practice we didn't really need.) only to take it down again and put it all back in the trucks as Bruce was still on the DL.

We were going down the East Coast of America. The familiar pattern of post gig excess continued in the back lounge of our bus every night only interrupted by having to do a gig every night. The drug taking and drinking and to a point the womanizing was all getting pretty out of hand. Of course, we didn't realize it at the time. It was all becoming very predictable about what was going to happen every night. So, I am not going to bore you with too much more of it at the moment, EXCEPT for one night off that we had in Columbia, South Carolina.

We were staying in the Holiday Inn in Columbia and expecting a really dreary evening as it looked like the kind of town where they rolled the sidewalks up at 10:30 p.m. However, looks can be so deceiving. As usual, we cruised down to the hotel bar about 7:30 p.m. Once again it didn't take any great observer of human behavior to notice it was completely fucking empty. A feeling of dread once more engulfed us. An evening of football on the TV and Pizza seemed on the cards, apart from that I noticed two girls seated at the bar. One of whom was definitely my style, with long blond hair and good tits. Well, actually, I must point out at this time in my life anything with the correct number of tits and the other bits that go with them was usually my style. Maybe even not the correct number of tits!

"Hi you guys. Are you guys from Australia?"

"Why is it, some Americans are always thinking a non-American English accent is Australian?"

Yeah right Australian! So, in our best English accents we put them straight, bought them a drink. They knew a rock club that was open. AND, one of them even knew someone who had some coke to sell who just happened to be meeting her in the Holiday Inn bar in about thirty minutes. Wow! What a stroke of luck (I don't think so.). They were the bait and we were hooked.

A few more of our crew turned up in the bar alerted by the fact the local Pablo Escobar was due to arrive. Forty-five minutes later, we were all on our way to the club in cabs and the girl's car. I couldn't believe it, the place was heaving. We almost had to queue to get in, until we said we were with Iron Maiden. Suddenly, we turned into VIP guests.

I don't have much recollection of our night out at what was obviously THE place to be in Columbia. That is, except not being able to get in the bathroom to stick some cocaine up my nose. There were so many people in there and they were probably all Pablo's clients. At which point, I turned into a raging bull and steamed past the queue, into the ladies bathroom. I dragged the blonde Lisa behind me.

ROCK 'N' ROLL
It's Better than Working for a Living

I believe we made quite a few visits to the Ladies that night. The next morning I awoke when Lisa, who ran a flower shop said she had to go to work. I left quietly about 8:00 a.m. I saw her at the gig later and saw her for the next two or three years every time I was on a tour that went through South Carolina.

I shall forever be amazed when you were touring in the 1980's every shit ass town in America always had a great club, beautiful women and at least one coke dealer. Don't know whether they still do. Even if they do, shouldn't think it's as much fun as it was then though.

We carried on down into the South, through the Carolinas, Georgia, Tennessee and eventually into Florida at Jacksonville. My girlfriend Salli flew out with our 11 month old Morgan. What a fucking nightmare journey that must have been for her. Even taking into account Morgan was the best behaved child I have ever seen, he was getting very tired after a nine and a half hour flight to Miami with an hour stopover and another hour flight to Jacksonville. Salli was really fucked up when I met her at the airport.

This was going to give me a rest from the mayhem of our back lounge. Salli and Morgan were staying with me through to St. Petersburg in five days' time. We were going to be driving ourselves and staying in hotels every night. Then, Salli was off on a flight to Houston to see my sister who had been living there for a couple of years. I was going to meet up with them again at the gig in Houston. So, it was a very welcome break, especially for my head and my wallet.

We had two great days off in Houston until I flew to Waco to join the rest of the crew. Salli and Morgan flew back home to London.

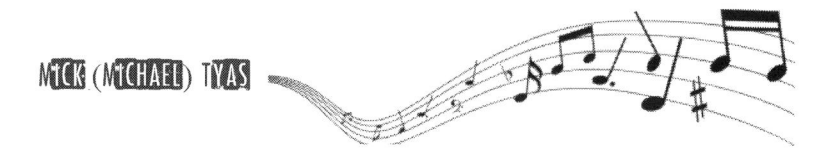

The flight to Waco was interesting, Houston to Waco, about 190 miles. I could have actually driven it, but I got a cheap flight on this little local airline. Although, I think the description of it being an airline was pushing it a little.

A twelve seater something or other; it was a very small prop airplane with me and about four local farmers on board. There was a pilot and co-pilot who also handed out bottles of water. And, there was a curtain between the pilot and the passengers, which was really interesting as you could see everything the pilot was doing. In fact, he was doing everything possible to keep the fucking thing airborne as we approached Waco through this big scary thunderstorm. The actual experience would have made a great roller coaster ride. It was pretty scary in a 12 seater aircraft. All praise to the pilot, he eventually landed it, albeit with a bit of a belly flop onto the tarmac.

Don't know why, but I like Texas. I especially liked meeting some of the Dallas Cowboys cheerleaders, which we did at the gig in Dallas. They were lovely girls. Of course, some of them are only about 15 or 16 years of age. Thinking what I was thinking would have been Statutory Rape.

A town in Texas I always wanted to visit was Lubbock, birth place of Rock 'n' Roll legend, Buddy Holly. Coincidentally, Buddy Holly was killed in a small plane about the size of the one I had been in a couple of days earlier. There was another coincidental event I remember and I'm talk air crashes here!

I was on a Commodores tour and I was on a British Airways flight which took off from Munich airport in the then West Germany bound for London Heathrow Airport on the 6th February

ROCK 'N' ROLL
It's Better than Working for a Living

1978. In a blinding snowstorm, twenty years to the day, the Manchester United soccer team's aircraft crashed on takeoff on the same runway killing 23 players and staff.

Downtown Lubbock is a very small area and as with many cities situated in the middle of nowhere. Nobody lives in the city. Most of the 200,000 or so official inhabitants live outside of the city limits.

We had a day off and were staying at the Downtown Holiday Inn. I was determined to have a Buddy Holly tourism day. I checked with the desk clerk at the Holiday Inn to find out where the famous Buddy Holly statue was located, and surprise, surprise! It was within walking distance, which is weird as I didn't think anything was within walking distance in the US, even if you were stood next to it, which I almost was.

"Out of the hotel, take a right, take the first right which is Glenna Goodacre Boulevard, (which is a grand name for a small side street between Highway 84 and Avenue O). "It's also known as the Buddy Holly Walk of Fame honey." (It's actually now known as the Lubbock Walk of Fame as the money grabbing widow of Buddy Holly upped the price for using her dead husband's name so much that the city father's told her to stick it!") "And, it's just there honey, you can't miss it."

You could actually miss it quite easily. It is barely life-size and sits on a circular plinth, not unlike a roundabout or rotary in the middle of the road. It is not actually a roundabout now as it is on the "Walk of Fame." I never saw anybody walking on it except me. All very disappointing, still I did see it . . . so that was my tourism morning over, took about twenty minutes.

In 1997, the Buddy Holly Center was opened in an old railway station, portraying his life and work. I was 12 years too early for that, so that was the highlight of my first time in Lubbock, pretty dull stuff!

That was the cultural section of the tour, now back to the dirty Rock 'n' Roll part of the tour. Four days later, we were in Long Beach California. The home of the Queen Mary, so maybe just a touch more tourism; we did go see the Queen Mary. Big ship, old, British, nice paintwork, now a hotel; there! That's got that done with.

We were doing four nights at the 10,000 seat Arena and Maiden was making their *Live after Death* video. It was quite a busy four days, for some people. Luckily, for the animals on our bus, nothing really got too much in the way of our partying. We even had two days off before the first gig day so there was plenty of time to get into trouble.

After our quick tourist trip to see the Queen Mary on the first day off, I was sitting in the bar of the Holiday Inn later that evening. A couple of the younger guys who were set builders on the tour came into the bar with this beautiful young chick. I guessed she was nineteen or twenty years old. These guys were like bees around a honey pot. I can't blame them. I think I must have been sat there with my tongue hanging out. I had seen this chick before on other gigs in Southern California. I asked Chris, one of the set guys, who she was. Her name was Kiki and she was a coke dealer. She was gorgeous with a pocketbook full of cocaine! This chick had everything! No wonder there were so many bees around that particular honey pot.

There were lots of these female groupie / coke dealers on the American touring circuit. I guess it gave them good access to the

ROCK 'N' ROLL
It's Better than Working for a Living

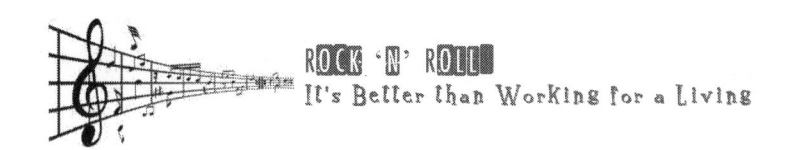

Rock 'n' Roll lifestyle. My memory of Kiki gets a little cloudy here, but I was seriously lusting after Kiki. Being only about 18 or 19 years older than her didn't seem to me to present any problems. It certainly wouldn't when she had a pocketbook full of cocaine, but she seemed pretty friendly also. A situation which was to repeat itself in Toronto a few months later – only that particular chick was only eighteen years old.

Four days after Long Beach, we had a day off in San Diego. I arranged with Kiki to bring me an "eight ball" (An eighth of an ounce of cocaine or three and a half grams.) to the hotel in San Diego. The travel agents, actually owned by Iron Maiden, had a lot to answer for with this hotel. In fact, it wasn't a hotel it was a motel . . . circa early 1960's vintage with outdoor corridors and no bar. This, of course, is a cardinal sin on a day off. Kiki arrived at the hotel early evening and called me in my room from the lobby phone, so I went down to the lobby to meet her.

I must admit she was probably one of the most nervous coke dealers I had ever met. This time she had even brought a minder with her (which was not how I had scripted the evening). She had a broken leg with a big cast on it. This was all looking a little bizarre and disappointing. Still, we went up to my room, which was on the second floor and entered from the outdoor walkway (which is very important in this story).

When we were in the room, Kiki emptied a bag onto the glass topped table forming a small white mountain of cocaine. She made a point of telling me her "friend" couldn't stay very long, but hinted that she could. So . . . things were looking up. We had a few lines when suddenly there was a really loud noise from the room next door which shook the room. Then there was lots of shouting and screaming, which then moved outside onto the outdoor corridor. Then there were more noises and loud voices and slamming doors and arguments. Kiki's friend was looking very nervous and got up to leave. The guy was obviously holding lots more coke and this commotion had spooked him. It sounded as if someone was trying to demolish the room next door. As he opened my room door to leave I heard Police car sirens wailing, getting nearer and nearer, at which point Kiki got up and followed her friend out of the room. In a fucking instant they were gone!

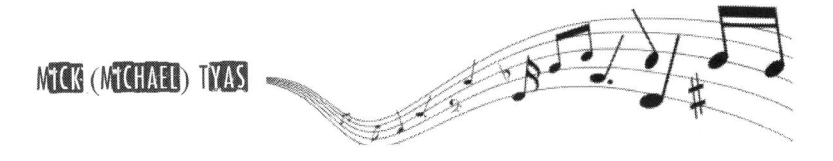

What was going to be a night of sex and drugs with this twenty year old Goddess had quickly turned into a nightmare.

The noise and commotion carried on next door, although now it was just raised voices. I was quickly shoveling the coke into a small packet. I think I was almost ready to flush it down the toilet as I heard what was definitely someone getting arrested in the room next door. Then, it suddenly went quiet. There was always the chance if it had been some of our crew causing the trouble, which it undoubtedly was, the cops would bang on all our room doors and possibly search our rooms.

I sat there for half an hour to maybe an hour not daring to look outside my room. Thankfully, all remained quiet and nothing happened.

I don't think I ever saw Kiki again, what a fucking waste. I found out next day what had happened and who had caused it. I was fucking furious with certain parties.

The guy arrested was the lighting designer, a guy who called himself, Dave Lights. Dave had been with the band since they started. He had been bugging me since I started as monitor engineer. This guy was always telling people I was been paid too much money (I have no idea how he found out how much I was been paid.). He thought he should be getting paid more than me as he had been with the band from the start. My reply to his protestations were, "You have a tongue in your fucking big mouth, make your own deal."

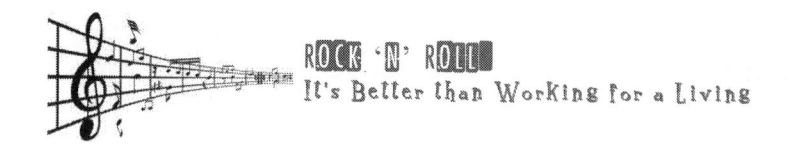

On days off, Dave and a couple of his buddies, used to like to get drunk. He always used to get very rowdy. There was a small clique of them that used to take acid occasionally on a day off, which sounds to me much more stupid than just getting drunk. That fateful night, Dave and his mates were in his room, unfortunately next to mine. They were getting pretty rowdy, as I can testify, but I have no idea what the fuck they were doing. A couple of chairs ended been thrown over the wall of the outdoor corridor and landing on some guy's car in the parking lot below. The guy, of course, was not best pleased. I think one missile even smashed the car windscreen, which resulted in the cops been called and Dave been arrested.

Fucking great shame they didn't lock him up and throw the fucking key away!

Dave and I never really got on with each other all the time I was with Iron Maiden. We kind of made up about ten years later. Dave was eventually fired for his continuing antics a couple of years later.

What took so fucking long?

Back in Long Beach, the second day off, was rigging day for lights, sound and set people. In my executive position, I was getting a little bored by this time. I remember just taking a walk down to the gig to see what was going on. As I was walking back to the hotel on my own, two chicks in a red Mustang stopped me. They asked if I could get them some backstage passes for the gig tomorrow, which, of course, I could. They gave me a lift back to the

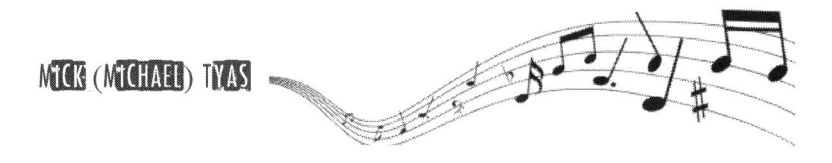

Holiday Inn, where we went up to my room and did a few lines. Then, we went down to the bar. About 9:00 p.m. they decided going to their hotel, which was just up the road was a good idea; so . . . all three of us piled into the Mustang again.

One of these chicks was pretty hot and the other one was a reasonable backup I guess. They took me up to their room, which they shared. In fact, they shared a bed!

The hot one started stripping off her clothes and got into bed and gestured me to do the same. I did. Then, her friend got into the bed. This was looking like a real interesting scenario, but it went downhill rapidly. As all best laid plans always do. The hot one would not shag me whilst her friend was in the bed. The friend pretended to be asleep and would not move. The friend reckoned she wasn't interested in me either. They weren't even interested in each other, least not while I was there . . . I am sure it was all a setup. I think they were lesbians and it was all a windup. They took all the cocaine and then didn't want anything to do with me. Either that, or the friend of the hot one, <u>was</u> interested in me so wanted to spoil it for the hot one.

I don't know! Who fucking cares? I didn't get shagged and left!

I didn't get shagged the next night either! But something similar happened.

Of course, the next night was a gig night. Thank God for that, all this partying was getting tedious. Except . . . because we were doing four nights and making a live video someone thought it would be a really good idea to have an after show party. What a fucking great idea! How many parties can you handle in one week?

ROCK 'N' ROLL
It's Better than Working for a Living

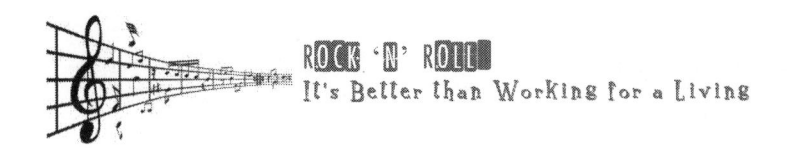

The party was backstage at the Arena and was for band, crew, families, friends and staff of the Iron Maiden office in Los Angeles. This included Platinum Travel, who was the agents who had booked all those shit hotels, well some were ok. Platinum Travel was run by a Californian chick called Karen Pebley, who I had spoken to a few times when she had arranged my extra hotels when Salli and Morgan flew out to see me.

I'd been told she was a pretty good looking chick, perhaps a little old for me as she was in her late twenties. She seemed to know who I was at the party and came over and introduced herself to me. She was a good looking chick. She was very flirtatious. About an hour and a half later we were in my room at the Holiday Inn. As with all these California girls in the music biz she was weaned on cocaine from an early age. She flirtatiously managed to work her way through the gram I had before the sun came up. She then made an excuse she had to be at work in the morning and had a two hour drive in front of her and left!

I have been struck again by the fact there does seem yet again to be a recurring theme in these stories. Maybe it wasn't my animal magnetism or my boyish good looks attracting them. Maybe something else was attracting all these women to my room. I wonder what could that be?????????

We were very nearly done with this leg of the American tour and everybody was getting a little stir crazy. I was having a great time, but even I was feeling a little jaded. Still, I was glad to get away from California.

Original guitarist with the band and all round nice guy, Dave Murray, was getting married to his girlfriend Tamar in two weeks' time in Hawaii. Dave had a house near Honolulu and Tamar was a native of Hawaii. The band had arranged a gig in Hawaii to coincide with Dave and Tamar's wedding. We were all going to get two weeks off in Hawaii, staying at the Hilton Hawaiian Village right on Waikiki beach!

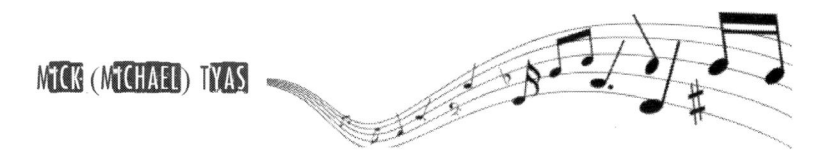

Although this seemed like it was going to be a paid vacation in paradise, the two weeks' vacation bore a stunning resemblance to being on the road for two weeks. Excepting, we didn't really move and we only did one gig. Apart from that, nothing much really changed.

We flew into Honolulu on the 27th March and the gig wasn't until the 31st. We had to wait around those four days for the equipment to be flown from Los Angeles. So, the first three days in Hawaii were pretty chill, including a little hanging out at the beach and around the pool. All of which seemed very weird as we weren't used to this pace of life. Still, we had a gig on the 31st and luckily we managed to ferret out one of the local dealers at the gig who sold us drugs and showed us the local club life. So . . . normal service was resumed.

Dave wasn't getting married until a few days after the gig. He decided to take the whole band and crew out for his stag night. Where better to go than a strip club and titty bar!

Dave had booked The Broadway Club in Honolulu for the night. This was going to be a very silly night, free drinks, drugs and naked women. We were all actually quite reserved for a while, but after a few trips to the toilets and large amounts of J D it was getting a little noisy.

I don't remember too many of the strippers or "acts," but I remember two that did stand out; if you'll pardon the pun. One was a mother and daughter act, allegedly. Hard to tell which was which though - this was actually quite a small club and you sat quite close to the stage. The mother and daughter took off all their clothes. They then took it in turns to sit in a large armchair with

ROCK 'N' ROLL
It's Better than Working for a Living

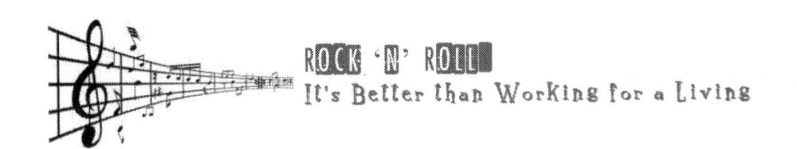

their legs wide apart over the arms. The other one would then shove ping pong balls into the other one's orifice. Then the girl with her legs over the chair arms would fire them out into the audience. What a trick, it was amazing. This was the first time I had seen this done, but I've since been informed it's quite a regular trick in clubs of a certain type. I was also informed by a girlfriend once it wasn't that hard to do. Didn't have any ping pong balls though that night unfortunately.

This also was a club where the acts were able to fraternize with the audience. Well; they were tonight anyway as Dave had hired the whole place for the night. I ended up at one time with a totally naked Mum and daughter sat on my knee.

Next act on stage was a tall blonde chick, which was a fire eater, not much to this really. She took off her clothes and breathed fire.

After this chick had finished her act, I went into the men's room for a quick line of the white stuff. Just closing the door of one of the cubicles was the fire eater with a little wrap of something in her hand. By the way she was female I can assure you of that. She invited me into the cubicle with her and offered me a line out of her little wrap. I almost accepted until I noticed the brown tinge of the contents and said, "I'll stick to the white stuff, if you don't mind."

Smack was not my drug and never has been. We stayed in that cubicle for quite a while though. Eventually, as all the entertainment had finished for the evening, I decided to get a cab back to the Hilton with the fire eater in tow. That was a first; I'd never pulled a fire eater before. When we got back to my hotel room, I ordered a bunch of drinks on room service. She stuck her fingernail in her little brown packet and I stuck mine in my little white packet.

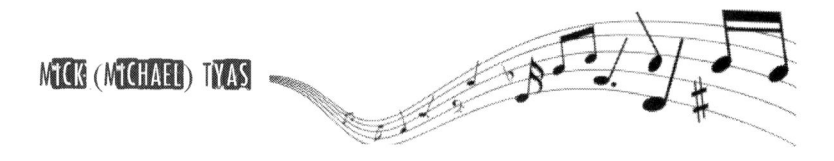

I was just thinking, what a fucking weird life I was leading in those days. A horny drug addled vampire existence with as much sex and drugs as I could handle, living in the best hotels all around the world, AND GETTING PAID FOR IT!

Once when I lit a cigarette, the fire eater (I have no idea what her name was.) immediately took off all her clothes. She told me to light another cigarette and then took both of them from me. She then balanced a lighted cigarette on each nipple and danced around the room with them stuck like glue to her tits.

She also showed me a few more tricks that night before she disappeared the next lunchtime. Well, it was lunchtime when I opened the curtains and she'd gone never to be seen again!

This was all getting a bit like "Fear and Loathing in a Hawaiian Paradise." Still, we had the sanity of the Dave's wedding to look forward to; although, to be quite truthful, I wasn't expecting much sanity at that event if the stag night was anything to go by.

The reception after the wedding probably went on for about two days I think. I seem to remember spending most of those two days in what was a kind of hayloft / small apartment in one of the outbuildings at Dave's house. It was equipped with a bottle of J D a couple of packs of cigarettes and a girl from the record company in New York who had flown in especially for the wedding. Still, at least we had the sanity of a trip to Japan to look forward to. Once again, I wasn't holding my breath with regard to the "sanity clause"!

We had nearly two weeks in Japan, which is almost two weeks too long. If I were a tourist, which we were sometimes, I would do Japan in three days. I'd do Tokyo in a morning; fuck all to see in Tokyo, except your bank balance diminishing rapidly. Next day, I'd do Hiroshima, takes about half an hour. Third day, try

ROCK 'N' ROLL
It's Better than Working for a Living

and get Mount Fuji in. This would have to be in the afternoon . . . you catch it for about ten minutes on the Bullet Train, so that's plenty. Any longer in Japan, and you are in serious danger of not only losing vast amounts of money (Even to buy a hamburger.), but serious amounts of brain cells. It is very foreign and feels a long way from home!

We had a week in Tokyo, which is very dangerous. A different danger than being in London, New York or Hollywood for a week; there are no bums on the streets, no drug dealers (or so I thought), but there are lots of places to lose that money.

We were staying in the Roppongi Prince Hotel, which was not surprisingly in the Roppongi district of Tokyo. It is akin to staying in Soho in London or downtown Manhattan in New York or Sunset Strip in Hollywood.

When we were on tour, we always got a per diem from the management for daily expenses. On gig days, we got fed three meals a day and free beer and soft drinks. If you were able to use your credit card on days off, these per diems virtually became cocaine vouchers. Of course, we only got $20 dollars a day so you can't buy much cocaine with that in a week. This is how lots of us got into trouble and are still paying for it now over twenty-five years later. It takes a while to pay off $60.000 worth of credit card debt.

You didn't need your cocaine vouchers in Japan of course as there are no drugs in Japan (Or are there?). Even if you found cocaine in Japan, you would need to be the leader of a small West African country or a computer software mogul to be able to have enough cash to buy it.

Our $20 a day per diem was raised to $30 a day for the Japan trip. We could afford breakfast on days off. In fact, I had a full cooked English / American breakfast in the Roppongi Hotel on a couple of occasions. It cost me about $25, which left enough for a small whiskey in the bar that evening.

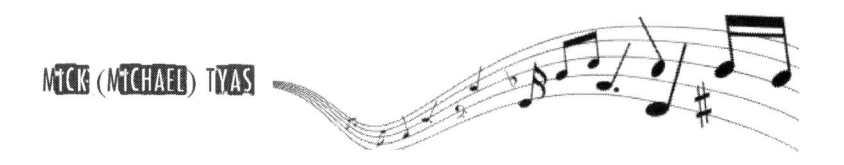

When you're with an English or American rock band in Japan the crew is almost as famous as the band. We were much more accessible to the hordes of groupies who followed us around all the time while there. It's strange as they chase you for autographs and to have their photograph taken with you. You start thinking, "Do they actually do what groupies are supposed to do"? Well! The answer is some do and some don't! The younger ones just follow you around. They are always at the train station when you go to catch the Bullet Train and they are always outside the hotel. The more serious, older and richer ones are usually staying in the same hotel as you, AND THEY DO!

Band and crew were taken out to a nightclub on one of the first nights we were there. We were treated like Royalty. Everything was on the house and those serious groupies were there also, these were not silly little girls, they were real Rock 'n' Roll chicks. One of them seemed to be holding court herself at her own table . . . she was this stunning Filipino looking chick with waist length brown hair. She had her own table with her friends. They had bottles of champagne on their table. It may have been Japanese champagne, but nevertheless still not cheap in Japan. They didn't seem particularly interested in a bunch of noisy Western long haired drug fiends (Unfortunately, of course, we were drug fiends without drugs.), or were they interested?

They didn't show much interest in us, but we were certainly interested in them and when the place was about to close, about 2:00 a.m. Three or four of us went over to their table. They all spoke reasonably good English and offered to take us to another club that was still open. So . . . off we went with them to another

ROCK 'N' ROLL
It's Better than Working for a Living

club in Roppongi, which was in a cellar underneath a restaurant about four blocks from our hotel. This place was packed. It was packed with women. The Filipino seemed to know lots of them and she had money. She bought the four of us lots of drinks, which was fortunate as large vodka was about $20 in 1985! How much would that be now?

This bar closed at 6:00 a.m., which seemed like a very sociable time for a bar to close.

The Filipino's entourage and we were the only ones left, so we suggested that we all go back to our hotel.

Not usually an easy thing to achieve, sneaking lots of girls into your hotel room in Japan. This lot all seemed to have their own rooms anyway, so no problem.

Most of us ended up in my room, I think by this time we were down to three of us and four women. We were ordering drinks on room service!

No surprise then I'm still trying to pay off the credit cards!

I was mad for the tall Filipino chick, but she didn't seem to be very interested. One of the others was and eventually the Filipino and two of her friends went back to their own room. I was left with this other little chick that was very cute. Eventually the two other guys left, so I was quite happy with the outcome of all that in the end, but, extremely drunk.

We eventually got around to doing a gig in Tokyo. The Japanese crews were quietly efficient. They did everything for you as they always did, apart from actually doing your job itself. Due to a steaming hangover, I was quite willing to give someone a quick lesson. As the Japanese did all the rigging and de-rigging we were usually out of the gig within an hour of the show finishing. This meant lots more time to get fucked up. Of course, fucked up didn't mean staying up all night snorting cocaine, but staying up all night drinking. We spent a lot of time in that 6:00 a.m. bar.

We went off on the Bullet Train to do some other gigs in strange looking cities with strange sounding names, namely Nagoya, Fukuoka (Where I was in the earthquake with Whitesnake.); a city they reckon is going to disappear one day, and Osaka, a city that almost did disappear in the earthquake in 1995.

We went back to Tokyo, to do one more show before we left Japan. Once more the Filipino and her gang turned up. Once more we went and sat in the underground bar, drinking until the early hours. This time, I was determined to get my hands on the Filipino, and I did. I managed to get her into my room without her friends, including the little chick I had shagged when we were in Tokyo before. Unfortunately, a rather nasty scene transpired, when she found out I was in my room with the Filipino. She came hammering on my door and shouting lots of unmistakable abuse. No matter what fucking language it was in. I opened the door and she raced into the room. She carried on screaming, aiming the tirade at the Filipino. Then she started screaming at me. Then she started crying. Then she screamed at us both once more and then she left.

Official translation, "I was a bastard and would rot in hell." I was not doing the honorable thing, as Japanese people always expect of you. Apparently, I should have kicked the Filipino out and apologized and let the little girl in, hoping she would accept my apology. I may as well have done, as the spell was broken and the Filipino got up and left also. I bet those two got together later and had a real fucking go at me. Fucking Westerners! I maybe

ROCK 'N' ROLL
It's Better than Working for a Living

ought to have been a little worried at their obvious anger, as the Filipino seemed to know some pretty dodgy people. This was a fact I noted earlier on in our visit. I'm still not convinced she was just a regular Rock 'n' Roll chick.

The myth about drugs being difficult to find in Japan is all but true. That is, unless you know where to get them of course. This is where my suspicion of the Filipino chick came in. She seemed to know anybody that was anybody in the Tokyo nightlife, waitresses, club owners and even the gig promoter. So I was talking to her one day about drugs and how easy they were to obtain in America, especially cocaine. She suddenly said she could get some speed . . . some amphetamine sulphate, which suitably impressed me. She made a phone call and arranged it! Amazing! And the guy was coming round this afternoon, but I had a feeling this was not going to be like any drug deal I had ever done in the past.

A couple of hours later the phone rang in my room, it was the dealer! Calling from his car! Who had a fucking cell phone in their car in 1985? Politicians and Gangsters! I had a hunch this guy was no politician.

I had to take the money downstairs and he would be waiting for me outside in his car. I was to get in the passenger seat and we would do the deal. Fuck me, this was interesting! I went into the parking lot outside the hotel doors, fuck me, this was a movie!

Directly outside the hotel front door was probably the biggest black Mercedes I had ever seen in Japan. The windows were totally blacked out so I couldn't see who was in it.

I got in the passenger seat and sat next to this huge Japanese guy in black shades and a leather coat. He held out a black leather gloved hand, which I put the money into. Just shy of a million dollars I think it was for a gram of speed. Well . . . maybe not quite that much, I think it was about $160.

He took the money and handed me a small white wrap, then gestured for me to leave. I got out of the car and he drove off. That was a movie! I couldn't believe it.

I got back to my room and tried the goods. It tasted right. I found out later it was right, it was good, and it was a good sized gram, it was an honorable deal. The first time I had ever met an honorable dealer. The guy could have easily ripped me off. He would know there was no way I would have gone looking for him to get my money back, unless I fancied been buried in a concrete overcoat. That is not the Japanese way. I still can't believe it, an honorable drug dealer, eat your heart out . . . Pablo Escobar.

That Filipino was one well connected chick. Never saw her again or the little doll who wished me a life in hell.

A couple of days later we were flying to Sydney Australia. The two weeks in Japan had been a welcome change from the sex and drug mayhem of the American tour. Well, maybe a little change. In fact, thinking about it, a very minor change. It was hardly any change at all really, but I was glad to be leaving. Two weeks is too many in Japan.

We arrived at Sydney Kingsford Smith airport about 7:30 a.m. It was about a ten hour redeye flight, but we decided a real breakfast was what we wanted. We were staying at The Southern Cross Hotel. When we arrived we went straight into the restaurant and ordered a full English breakfast and a large pot of tea. When the breakfast arrived, after having spent the last two weeks in Japan, it was close to sex. Fried eggs, sausage, bacon, tomatoes,

ROCK 'N' ROLL
It's Better than Working for a Living

mushrooms, fried bread (A very English thing.)!!!! There was real tea with tea leaves!!!! It was truly one of the highlights of the tour.

This was as near to England as I had been in nearly six months, although it was 12,000 miles away. It felt really good for some unknown reason. I think it was because I enjoyed living in England. Now, it's the fucking pits.

The Australian leg of the tour was altogether a pretty mellow and well behaved experience for me, which I think was a welcome change. Sure, I did a little womanizing and a little drinking, all pretty normal behavior for your average Australian, but nothing excessive. In fact, we did nothing to excess. After the excesses of the American tour and the weirdness of the time in Japan, we even did some sightseeing. I went to see the Sydney Harbor Bridge, the Opera House and the Outback. I even saw a kangaroo and a koala bear. I think that's enough of that, you can overdo this sightseeing stuff.

The gigs were kind of non-events. I mean there are only about ten gigs in Australia and we did seven of them. Everybody more or less lives in six or seven cities around the coast. There are a few weirdoes who live away from the coast, where it gets hot and hostile, for some fucking odd reason.

We played the old Hordern Pavilion in Sydney, which is a great old gig. That's about as excited as I can get about the gig. Built in the 1920's, on the old Sydney Showground site it stands right next to Sydney Cricket Ground. It was another sightseeing opportunity and there really ends the Australian tour. Short on highlights, a little bit of a rest I guess, but of course a couple of days later what we had to come was . . . The Worst Journey!!!!!

We went back home to the UK for about ten days off. Except for seeing Salli and one year old Morgan, it wasn't much fun at all. It's so difficult to get back into normal life for only ten days after been away for almost six months. Thinking about it now, it must have been really fucking weird for Salli also. I don't think Morgan was old enough to notice yet, but I must have been away for almost nine months of his first year.

The highest divorce rate in the world is in the Submarine Corps and it is nearly 80%. Those guys can be away on duty for 6, 9, 12 months at a time; the second highest must be in the Rock 'n' Roll business.

We only had about another six weeks of this tour left and it was back to America. This time for the "B" circuit.

We started out on the East Coast, New York and New York State. Although, we did some of the regular "A" circuit gigs and we also did some real shit holes. Poughkeepsie, New York State is a real old arena built in the 1950's. This gig is where I was stood at the board and turned around and there was a firefighter standing next to me in full firefighting kit with a hatchet!

"Where's the fire at?" he said.

I know I did feel really bad that day. I think I was in the middle of a two day hangover. I immediately thought he might be the Grim Reaper in fancy dress.

"What fucking fire?" I replied.

It turns out The Chimp wouldn't have the AC on in the arenas during the show, because he sweated buckets during the show and then got cold. Allegedly, this gave him a cold (Poor little fucker!). It had got so hot in the venue the automatic fire alarm had gone off in the firehouse and all these firefighters turned up in full kit. I noticed one had some oxygen with him, which I could have done with myself.

Glens Falls, also in New York State is another fucking shit hole. Another was in Evansville, Indiana. They should fucking demolish some of these places; luckily now in the 21st century they are replacing some of these broken down old places. We did do New Haven Connecticut, which is not the prettiest town in Connecticut at the old Coliseum, which is a real dump. It's gone now. Of course, New Haven is the home of Yale University and also the home of a world famous club called Toad's Place, which has been a rock club since the dawn of time.

One of the worst gigs of the whole tour was at Allentown Fairgrounds, Pennsylvania. This was a horse racing track and it was hot, very hot and dusty, very dusty and very fucking windy, and there's an obvious reason for that, which I'll let you know of in a minute.

Bruce, the singer, didn't like playing outdoors as he couldn't hear his own voice echoing back at him in the arena off of all the reflective surfaces. Fortunately, all the rest of the band loved playing outdoor shows. Outdoors the acoustics are perfect, so it's much easier to hear the sound. But . . . you couldn't hear that beautiful voice of Bruce's soaring above the band in the vast echoing spaces. Well . . . Bruce couldn't. What you could hear was what sounded like another band playing about 400 yards away right in front of the stage and they were playing the same song! Except they were playing it about three seconds later than Iron Maiden, how fucking spooky!

Bruce was not a happy little chimp, as he heard this other guy singing his song about three seconds after him!

What was happening was some fuckwit had built this stage at this fucking ridiculous gig at the side of this racetrack. It was across the course from a fucking grandstand, which probably held two thousand people. It was probably built in the 1920's with a sloping shiny tiled roof and the front of it like a big open mouth. There was no other ambient noise to hear in the open air. The sound was echoing back from the open front and roof of this grandstand.

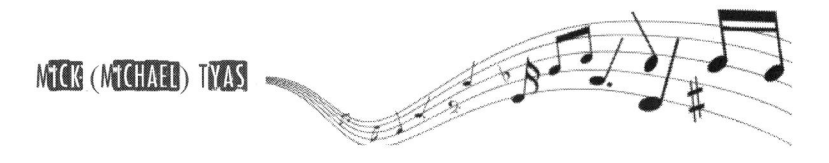

I thought it was really funny, the slap back (technical term) from the grandstand was nearly as loud as the band's backline. However, Bruce was not amused.

"Do something!!!!" he repeated twice.

"Yeah right Bruce, I'll go and knock the fucking grandstand down shall I?" *Dickhead!!!!*

As I've already said, it was very windy that day. So that wasn't helping the sound either. Especially if you'd paid to see the band as one minute you can hear them, then next minute the people half a mile to your left can hear them, pointless in paying really. You may as well suss out which way the wind is blowing and park your car half a mile downwind!

As the set came to an end, and we started the load out, the weather was getting increasingly rough and the rain started. It always seemed to on load outs on outdoor shows. Not that it bothered us much of course. As an hour after the show finished we were back in the back lounge as usual.

The next day we were in Providence Rhode Island. We saw on the TV, in the early hours of the morning a small hurricane had passed through Allentown Fairgrounds and trashed the place. So . . . there is a God after all and he picked his spot well.

As the tour plodded on we were kind of heading out into what is called in America, the Midwest. It is rather weirdly named as most of it is not in the West at all. In fact, it's nearer the East than the West and its North. So, it should really be called the Mid-Northeast.

The Mid-Northeast encompasses the states of Illinois, Indiana, Iowa, Kansas, Ohio, Michigan, Minnesota, Missouri,

ROCK 'N' ROLL
It's Better than Working for a Living

Nebraska, North and South Dakota and Wisconsin, which are lots of places where people don't really want to live. Unfortunately for them, they have to. America has some really interesting places for the tourist to visit in its 9,540,000 square miles (est.). None of them are in these states. This list of States is not really a definitive list as different people have their own ideas of what and where is the Midwest. You get some pretty interesting weather out there though in the middle of fuck all.

To carry on the theme of outdoor concerts and weather, we drove to Fargo, North Dakota. This is right in the middle and way north in that Fuck All region. Just a little further on down the road you bump into the Canadian outback, or whatever it's called.

The population of Fargo is allegedly 95,500 people. To be honest I didn't see ninety-five people while I was there. We were heading for Red River Fairgrounds, now that sounds to me like a shit gig before you even see it. In fact, you didn't need to see it to know it was going to be a shit hole. I remember the bus driver saying, "Well, here we are then."

"Where?"

We were smack in the middle of absolutely nowhere! In one direction, nothing! In another direction, nothing! In fact in every direction, fuck all! That actually ought to be the name of this state, North Fuck All! Which, is, of course, just up the road from South Fuck All.

The "gig" itself was actually about four or five Portakabins, a few Portaloos for the audience, a fucking dirt race track for driving stupid old souped up cars on and a stage. Using the word "stage" as a noun, very loosely indeed; it was actually six flatbed trailers parked side-to-side, end-to-end. Looking on the positive side it did have a roof, which is very useful especially when it rains because as we all know, water and electricity don't mix together very well. Unfortunately, it doesn't always rain in a straight line top to bottom. In fact, out in this wilderness in summer it tends to rain more sideways driven by that old wind. This "roof" didn't have any walls to stop the rain coming in. Once again the word "roof" was a very loose description of the structure. It was more like a very large tarpaulin sheet (which is probably what it was) suspended from two fucking cranes each with their jibs extended about 100 feet in the air!

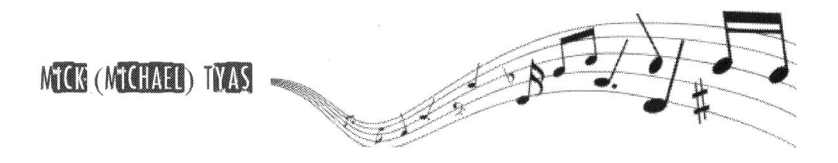

This was probably about one of the most dangerous looking structures I have ever seen in over thirty-five years in the business. It would look dangerous on a calm sunny day. Now that old wind was getting up again and this place was a dust bowl. It was not the place for a gig. Nobody had opened the backs of the trucks yet. In fact, I believe Dick the production manager had made his mind up about this place as soon as he saw the stage and roof structure. Negotiations were in progress in one of the portakabins.

I think Dick had also pointed out to the local promoter that it looked like the end of the world was blowing in from the North.

The sky was black, big and black! It was getting even windier. One of the truck drivers heard on the local radio a tornado had touched down about thirty miles north of us.

"Ok! Let's go," said Dick, there were no more negotiations. Everyone jumped back on the buses and the trucks were rolling quicker than I'd ever seen them move before.

"Where are we going," I asked the bus driver.

"South, very quickly," was his answer.

They didn't actually have a tornado touch down at the fairgrounds but it was mighty windy and mighty wet. They had to dismantle the roof thing to stop the whole thing from being blown over.

ROCK 'N' ROLL
It's Better than Working for a Living

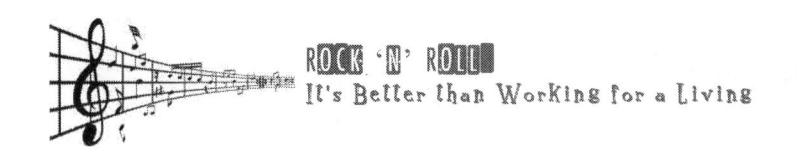

We were heading for Des Moines, Iowa nest. Oh, my God! The State Capitol of Iowa . . . and still a shit hole.

As you've probably guessed I don't like the Midwest very much. I totally understand why the settlers wanted to get to the West Coast as soon as possible. There are just hundreds and hundreds of miles of fuck all. It wouldn't be so bad if it had mountains and stuff like they do further south and west, but it's as flat as my first girlfriend's chest. It was 500 miles from Fargo to Des Moines, so it was going to take us all day and well into the evening to get there. So the evening would be a couple of hours in the hotel bar and off to bed. How healthy is that?

Next day we did have a whole day off in Des Moines due to the cancellation of the Fargo gig. What to do? I think a few of us went through the usual day off ritual of heading for the nearest shopping mall or staying in bed most of the day and only coming out when the sun was going down. Then there was Bill, Davy's guitar tech, who would head out into the town in search of thrift stores and junk shops looking to find a bargain old guitar or amplifier. He would invariably come back with a 1920's National steel guitar or a 1950's Fender amplifier that had only cost him ten million dollars!

We would normally find a local club on an evening off, mainly from information given to us by the hotel staff. Tonight they weren't very enthusiastic about anywhere in town, but nevertheless gave us a couple of names of local clubs.

The first place we went to was more of a supper club with some cabaret band playing. The second was a club with just a DJ playing records. At least it was rock music. The place was pretty empty. We did start chatting to a couple of chicks who knew a coke dealer who just happened to be there.

I still find it truly fucking amazing, even in the smallest one horse town anywhere in America; you can always find a coke dealer and a woman!

The night developed into the familiar pattern of play. Tonight I got the cocaine and the woman. As you've read previously a combination not always easy to keep together. The coke was good and so was the woman. Move on!

We were just over a week from the end of the tour and we were heading west. Thank fuck! We had four outdoor shows at the end. Three were in California and one in a place called Red Rocks Amphitheater, just outside of Denver Colorado.

Red Rocks was created out of the red sandstone rock formations that make a natural amphitheater, which holds about ten thousand people. The first concerts at Red Rocks were over a hundred years ago. This is when, of course, they didn't have six 48 foot trucks full of sound and lighting equipment. And, therein lays the problem with Red Rocks.

Nice auditorium, nice big stage and it never rains in summer. There's a nice dressing room area, but! You access the whole site up a small, narrow, steep rocky mountain road, which large semis cannot get up or they won't let them up. Consequently, all the equipment has to be trans-shipped onto small flatbed trucks to be taken up the mountain to the stage. It takes fucking hours. Also, they won't let you take the buses up there, which was a bad situation as we always used the buses all day as our own dressing rooms and homes basically.

So nice place, shame they built on the side of a mountain.

The last gig of the tour was at Irvine Meadows Amphitheater in Orange County California. It is another one of what are called "sheds." It has a full proscenium arch stage as with any indoor

ROCK 'N' ROLL
It's Better than Working for a Living

theatre and a covered amphitheater with no sides. It's a very nice gig. The weather is always beautiful. The place is about five miles north of a major US Marine base at Pendleton. There are always low flying F15 and F16 fighter planes passing over, which is pretty spectacular sight.

Kiki the young coke dealer with whom I had been in a sticky situation with, or wanted to be in a sticky situation with, a couple of months earlier turned up and spent all day on the bus with the young set guys not venturing near the crazy old bastards on the backline bus. This was probably a good move.

So, for the first time in a while the band comes back into the book (I know you'd almost forgotten they were on the tour, so did I sometimes!).

For the first encore of the set, the band dis one of their "anthems" called *Run To The Hills*, which has a guitar break in the middle and then Flat nose (Nicko) comes in with a role across the toms (God!, I hate all this technical artistry stuff, still I have to put a little of it in somewhere I suppose.). As I was standing behind the monitor board at the end of the roll on the toms I heard a whooshing sound that went past my right hand side. Something landed on the floor behind me, it was a drumstick!

At the end of the song, the band goes off and then come back on for another encore, of course. As they were going off flat nose came over to the monitor desk directly in front of me and said angrily, "Turn that guitar up in that fucking break, I have to hear that solo." At which point, myself seething with anger also I grabbed a hold of the neck of this ridiculous jumpsuit suit thing he was wearing and dragged him across the front of the board and said . . . "If you ever, ever, throw a drumstick at me again I will come and drag you off of that fucking drum stool and stick it up your fucking ass, sideways!"

At which point, the band's manager, Rod, came and put an arm around him and pulled him away. I heard Flat nose walking off saying, "The monitor guy just threatened to stick a drumstick up my ass."

I heard Rod say, "I know its ok."

Then Rod turned around and looked at me as he walked off and gave me a look that said, "Yeah, and he fucking deserved it."

Nicko and I would clash again.

That was The World Slavery Tour; I hadn't done all of the tour. I joined about a third of the way in, but it was still a hell of a fucking ride and I had survived. There were times when I thought I wouldn't but I made it to the end and now we were all going home. Back home to a life I hadn't known for a while. I had my life on the road and Salli had her life back in London. Although I had been making really good money on this tour, it wasn't enough to sustain both our lives. I had $500 a week cocaine bills. Salli had to have her interest and kicks back home; these included, Gucci, Donna Karen, Yves St Laurent, a Harrods store card and her membership of a couple of fancy clubs so she was able to maintain her hectic social life. It wasn't such a bad life, being a Rock 'n' Roll widow. I know Salli loved it and I wouldn't have denied her one minute of it. I knew we could never afford it. I am still paying for it today, but it was worth every penny.

I was able to fit some more work into this year as we were only in July when the Maiden tour finished. I needed to do as much work as possible to keep up with the costs of our somewhat expansive lifestyle.

I used to do some work for a theatre sound company who would employ me whenever they had any proper music jobs on

ROCK 'N' ROLL
It's Better than Working for a Living

their books. One of these occasions was in late 1985. When they called to ask if I wanted to go out to Jordan for six days, not a part of the world you associate with Rock 'n' Roll. This job wasn't Rock 'n' Roll at all. In fact, it was doing two concerts. One in a large arena in the capital city of Amman and the other on a beach on the Red Sea in the Gulf of Aqaba with Brazilian Latin, jazz, funk band called Sergio Mendes and also Brasil 66.

Sergio Mendes was a huge act all over the world. It was the particular favorite of King Hussein of Jordan. These two concerts in Jordan were being put on to celebrate the King's 50th birthday. The band had been booked exclusively by the King's wife, Queen Noor as a surprise gift for the King.

Derek the head sound guy at Theater Projects, the company responsible for producing these concerts, made me an excellent offer for the weeks work. It sounded almost like a vacation, an offer I couldn't refuse really.

We flew to Jordan on a Royal Jordanian Airlines jet. We flew First Class, which was a surprise. I couldn't believe Theater Projects were paying for that, in fact they weren't!

When we arrived at Amman International airport we were taken aside by some official looking guy and shown into a private waiting room. This was a little disconcerting. I thought we were in for a little hassle with getting into the country. Especially, when the guy took all our passports and disappeared out of the room for about twenty minutes. Fortunately, he came back smiling and gave us all our passports back. He showed us out of a side door of the airport towards a line of waiting Mercedes cars, with the parting words... "Enjoy your stay in Jordan gentlemen, your cars are waiting for you."

We had been given VIP diplomatic treatment! Derek did actually mention to me in the car all the equipment had been shipped as Diplomatic baggage. There was no Customs for it to go through. Derek said he had hidden a little treat in the equipment for us, knowing that it would not be searched when it arrived in Jordan.

It was the first Arab country I had ever been to, except for a two week vacation in Tunisia. It was hot and it was dusty. It was somewhat similar weather to what you would get in Las Vegas; unfortunately, that is where the similarity ended.

The center of Amman is the same as most oil rich Arabian capital cities which all now have the chic stores you would see if you were driving around New York or Paris. There was plenty of Gucci, Prada, Armani and etc. and lots of other fine designer stores. It is a pretty rich part of the world these days. In Amman, unfortunately it all changes once you get a mile or two out of town. It goes from affluence to poverty in the blink of an eye. I suddenly see guys walking the dusty streets with AK47 assault rifles over their shoulders. There were pickup trucks with machine guns and cannons mounted on the back. I realized this area has long been a war zone between various Arab factions and Israel. Although Jordan has been pretty much an onlooker in this struggle, Israel ain't that far over there.

We were staying at the Amman Intercontinental Hotel the first night we were there and then heading down to Aqaba on the Red Sea the next morning. When we arrived in Aqaba we were driven to the Holiday Inn (Don't they just get everywhere!). We were staying there for the next four days. It was then, I found out we would have no extras to pay on our room bills as we were staying "carte blanche." We were guests of King Hussein. He was paying for everything or rather his wife was or the peasants who pay their

ROCK 'N' ROLL
It's Better than Working for a Living

taxes. What wonderful people! With literally a free bar there were a few sore heads around for the next few days.

The next day was a production day where we basically went to suss out the gig and rig as much of the equipment as we could. Although there wasn't much to rig as the gig was on the beach. There were only going to be fifty people in the audience!

We were driven in our fleet of cars to this high walled compound outside of town and driven straight through the gates, past the guard post into what looked like a small army camp. In fact, it was. They were just the army guarding the King and this was his camp. The camp itself probably covered a square mile or two with lots of barrack type looking buildings where soldiers lived by the looks of it. There were office blocks, warehouses and a couple of aircraft hangers. I'm guessing there was an airstrip over the other side of the camp. Also, on our left were obviously the King's private quarters and offices, which were in a typical Arabian style. It looked like a bloody big bungalow, which was essentially what it was . . . but it was big!

I sort of guessed these were the Royal private quarters as there was a brand new Aston Martin Lagonda supercar sitting in the driveway. I casually asked our liaison guy if the car belonged to the King. Stupid question really, it was hardly going to belong to one of the many soldiers walking about in the compound. The retail price at the time was about $180,000. To make it now would probably cost in the region of a quarter of a million dollars. The liaison guy replied "Yes." to my stupid question. "It is another present the Queen has bought the King for his birthday!" he furthered.

These people had serious money, not only had she paid for the band to fly to Jordan for a week to entertain the King at his birthday party. They must have cost big money plus flying all the equipment and also all our equipment and six of us out there for a week. She'd also bought him what was one of the most expensive cars in the world at the time.

Why couldn't they discover oil in my backyard?!!!!!!!!

Another strange thing I noticed I asked Mr. Liaison about was I had seen lots of ordinary soldiers all driving about in what looked like almost brand new Mercedes cars. Lots of them from family size 190's to sporty 500 SEC's. Surely they didn't get paid that well!

Mr. Liaison was a really nice guy and was basically giving us a quick tour of the facility. "Ah! The Mercedes," he said, "Let me show in this aircraft hangar."

There were no aircraft in this aircraft hangar. There were just wall-to-wall Mercedes cars from one end to the other and every model you could imagine. I thought there must be at least five hundred new cars in that one hangar alone.

"These cars are part of the oil deal the King has with West Germany. Every year they give him a certain number of Mercedes cars as part of that deal." He didn't say how many.

Mr. Liaison then took us down the side of the Palace (bungalow), through the beautiful gardens. We eventually came out on to the beach with the beautiful blue Red Sea (?) in front of us. I'm not going to try and explain why a blue sea is called The Red Sea as there are a million anoraks out there in cyber land who will all give you an explanation. This is not a book about nature, except human nature of course.

The beach was nice. The sea was blue and The Palace was a bungalow! Quite a nice bungalow though.

Our tour of the estate was over. Our equipment still hadn't arrived; although we were assured it would arrive first thing in the

ROCK 'N' ROLL
It's Better than Working for a Living

morning. I'm sure heads would have rolled in the King's offices if it hadn't. So there was nothing left for us to do but to go back to the Holiday Inn, lie in the sun, and eat and drink. Hotels, of course, being one of the few places in Jordan (being a Muslim country) where you could buy alcohol. Except we weren't buying it! Thank you Queen Noor.

The next day we were up bright and early. We were driven down to the Palace where our equipment was being manhandled off of Army trucks by what looked like half of the Jordanian Army. They then pushed and carried it out onto the beach in front of the Palace where a flat stage affair had been built facing out into the Gulf of Aqaba. It was about fifty feet in front of a large Bedouin type tent, which had been erected. This is where guests would watch the concert from. These where extremely high profile guests. Kings and Queens and Princes, Princesses, Sultans, Sultanas and etc.; whatever the big knobs were called from around this part of the Arab world.

Our liaison man was with us most of the time. He was very attentive to our every need . . . drinks, food, man power and bathrooms! The bathroom is where Derek and I were off to now! We had been told by Mr. Liaison we could use the bathrooms in the Palace, which were attached to the kitchens.

Derek who had promised me a surprise when we got here; he suggested we should go to the bathroom.

"Okay" I said. This usually meant one of three things . . . 1) you needed a piss; 2) you needed a crap neither of which you usually needed an invite for; nor 3) Derek was offering me some cocaine! In Jordan!

Derek had been very clever knowing all the equipment was been shipped by Diplomatic Baggage from the UK to the King's Palace. It was never ever going to be searched by Customs so he had stashed a gram in the equipment. It was still, pretty risky I thought. He had gotten away with it. So we were off to do a line of cocaine in the King of Jordan's fucking bathroom. How fucking decadent is that?

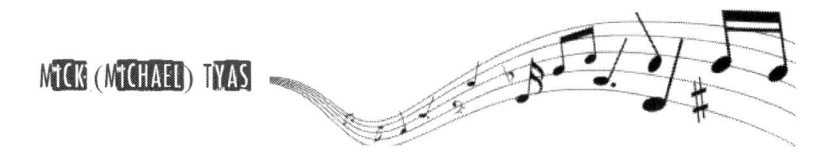

I had actually done a line in one of the offices in the Reichstag in West Berlin, when we were there doing a gig. It had allegedly been one of Hitler's offices during World War II, but I think this topped that in the bragging stakes.

To get to the bathroom we had to go into the Palace through the French windows, which looked out onto the beach where we were setting up the gig. Derek and I walked up the garden and through the doors into a large lounge area where two beautiful young chicks were sitting on a sofa talking.

"Hi girls," we said nonchalantly.

"Hi guys," they replied.

It wasn't until after we got back from the house the liaison man told us they were the King's two daughters, Princess's Aisha and Zein.

They were fucking Princess's, now that could have been a life changing experience, pulling one of them.

Derek and I sneaked into the bathroom adjacent to the kitchens. I had a really stupid thought . . . we should have invited the girls! Except we would probably end up going home minus our hands and probably our heads!

One thing I did notice whilst we were in the bathroom, was even the toilet paper had the King's crest on it. These people had money.

When it actually came to doing the show, we were on the beach with a beautiful sunset and about $23 trillion worth of Sheiks and Kings and heiress all sat sedately in their lawn chairs

ROCK 'N' ROLL
It's Better than Working for a Living

in front of the stage before the band went on. The show itself was pretty unspectacular except it was good Latin cabaret music. The assembled glitterati and Royalty applauded politely.

After the show, we went back to the dressing room with the band as we weren't allowed to do any de-rigging work on the stage until all the assembled guests had retired to the Palace.

The dressing room was actually the King's private cinema. It was literally almost as big as some public cinemas. Laid out on tables was as much food and drink as a small Army would consume in a day. A pleasant surprise was to see beer and wine on the table also. As I discovered from Liaison Man, although Jordanians are Muslim and do not drink alcohol, they don't force these restrictions on foreigners visiting their country. That is a very fucking sensible philosophy, which of course is why all the big hotels have bars. I guess the King can do as he likes in his own Palace, so we had beer and wine.

There was one problem that popped up, and it was I couldn't find any glasses to drink the wine out of. So being the road animal I was I just popped the cork and drunk out of the bottle. Suddenly, there was a tap on the door behind me and in walked Queen Noor. A very pretty and impressive looking woman who I found out was only about the same age as me. So why did the Queen choose the King over me? I guess because she hadn't met me yet! What other reason could there be?

She was, and still is, a very successful American business woman. When she met King Hussein, I think he had a few dollars more than her. Anyway, as she walked in she apologized, "Sorry guys carry on what you were doing."

So I did.

She then handed each one of us a small blue box and thanked us all for coming over for the King's birthday. Inside was a gold

Longines wristwatch with an Arabic inscription on the dial, which Liaison Man told us read; "Presented on the occasion of King Hussein of Jordan's 50th birthday."

I found out later the watch itself was worth around $2000, but with the inscription, who knows? It's anyone's guess. My watch was stolen two years ago when my house was broken into.

That was pretty much the last work I did in 1985. It had been a very good year. I had made lots of money, but I had spent lots too. In fact, we both had. We both had some serious demons to keep at bay and one big bright shining light was that Morgan, my stepson, was only just 18 months old and he had already been on tour to America.

So, onward to 1986!

Chapter Fourteen

THE MAYHEM CONTINUES

1986.

I did go into some extreme detail in the chapter on 1985, but that was how my life was going at the time. It was interesting, exciting and crazy. When I was home I was the typical family man and much of the craziness disappeared. Perhaps not all of it, but I was much calmer at home. Well, at least I thought I was. Unfortunately, Salli was finding it hard to adjust to me being at home again. She had to lead two lives. One whilst I was away on tour. The other when I came home. She was feeling it hard to cope with the second one sometimes; still we battled on. Sometimes . . . literally battled, 1986 though, looked as though it was going to be another busy year. I was getting offers of work from all over the place.

One tour I took on was with British jazz, rock, funk outfit or whatever you want to call them, a band called Level 42. This proved to be one of the most boring tours I had ever done. There is only one highlight, which stands out for me from that tour. My fellow sound engineer on the crew was a guy called Gary Hughes, who had a bit of a celebrity girlfriend called Sam Brown.

Sam was the daughter of 1960's British rocker Joe Brown. Sam had just signed her own recording contract.

ROCK 'N' ROLL
It's Better than Working for a Living

We were doing a show in Paris and had the night off before the show. Sam came over to Paris to see Gary.

The three of us went out to dinner that evening. As is the norm in France, dinner took about three hours to get through with endless bottles of wine and port and cognac. By about 10.30 p.m., Sam was looking a little worse for wear. This can happen in these circumstances. She was having a little trouble with the English language, not only forming the words but getting them in the correct order. We eventually decided to leave the restaurant as Sam's connection between her brain and her legs seemed to have malfunctioned. In the end, Gary and I more or less had to carry her back to the Holiday Inn. I've worked with Sam a couple of times since then over the years, but I've never mentioned that evening to her.

So that ladies and gentlemen was the Level 42 tour . . . instantly forgettable!

My star was still shining bright in the Heavy Metal market in 1986 after the big Iron Maiden tour. I was called one evening from Los Angeles by a guy called Terry who ran The Trans American Sound Company, otherwise known as Tasco. This was the English company that opened a big operation in Los Angeles, and the company that I had worked for on the Whitesnake tour in 1984.

As I think I mentioned before, there were many people in that organization that I didn't like. As I said previously, you were either one of Tasco's boys or you weren't. I don't think I ever was and this was to be proved so over the next few years. Problem was they had all the work . . . lots of it.

I flew out to New York yet again. Then up to Glens Falls in New York State to start the American leg of Motley Crue's "Theater of Pain" tour. The most perfect name for any tour I had ever been on. All English crew again, because as everyone knew we were the best in the business at the time. American crew talked a good gig, knew all the numbers of every single piece of equipment, and still do; whereas, I didn't have a clue what half the shit was called, but I knew what it did and how to do it.

This tour was seriously understaffed in the sound department. My old mate of forty years and fellow crew member on the Whitesnake tour, Phil Wilkey was on the tour; plus we had the band's American sound engineer who was going to be the fourth member of the crew.

We had a huge arena sound rig. It took up two 48' trucks. We were to start the get in at 8:00 a.m. in the morning by hanging the two huge clusters of speakers obviously went left and right of the stage. I was to rig and hang one side assisted by Phil. Before he got to rig his monitors, the band's American sound engineer offered to hang the other side assisted by the third English guy Arthur. Of course, after this operation the sound engineer had to go out front of house to rig his mixing console. Rigging these left and right PA clusters was a very heavy and long process. There should have been a permanent four man crew to do this part of the job, plus the monitor engineer and the sound engineer. That was why Tasco got all the work, as they could undercut everybody else by having only a four man crew instead of a six man crew. Unfortunately, we suffered for it.

After the luxury I had been afforded on the Iron Maiden tour of being one of the main men and even having an assistant, I had been able to wake up late and stay up all night . . . this tour came as a bit of a shock.

I had to be up at 7:00 a.m. to start work at eight. I couldn't get to bed at night. There were still lots of cocaine and alcohol about; unfortunately, my habit had to be fed. There never seemed to be enough hours in the day. I was starting early and finishing the load outs much later than I was used to. And, I was still trying to get in lots of cocaine, lots of alcohol and lots of talking. I would get to bed at four and get up at seven. This was never going to work for very long.

No one else on our crew seemed to be having any problems. Arthur was very sensible. He had two large vodkas and went to bed every night. Phil had good nights and bad nights. On a good night he was sensible and was in bed thirty minutes after load out. On a bad night he was worse than me. He always seemed able to handle the misery of the next morning better than me. Perhaps it was the cocaine I saw him sprinkle on his bowl of cereal at seven in the morning. Believe me, that is not a good way to start a day, but it always seemed to work for Phil.

My main compadre on "Dawn Patrol" on the bus was Mark, the band's sound engineer. Mark was very adept at snorting as much of my cocaine as possible before he went to bed. He was a good talking companion. I talked shit and he talked even more shit, for hours!!

There was one big problem with this scenario apart from the fact we were very understaffed. The problem was Mark could not get up at 7:00 a.m. after snorting all my cocaine and going to bed at four in the morning. We were both responsible for rigging either side of the PA and it was left to me to try and wake him every day.

Of course, the lazy fucking bastard never got up. He thought as the band's sound engineer he did not have to take responsibility for rigging the PA, although that was part of his deal with the sound company. This, of course, put loads of pressure on me as I now had to try and rig both sides of the PA after just three hours of trying to get some sleep every night. Arthur and Phil were helping as much as possible, but this was never going to work. Three hours late Mark would come strolling into the gig, laughing and sarcastically asking if I had finished yet.

After a week or so of this behavior, I had to say something to the production manager. I was told Mark was the band's sound engineer and could basically do what he wanted. I also called the sound company and complained. They more or less told me it was our problem to sort out as they were not sending out any more crew.

Thank you very fucking much!!!!

I was the new boy. I was just winging in their eyes instead of just getting on with the job.

I was fucked up, both mentally and physically. This guy's attitude just got worse when he found out I had been complaining about him. His facetious comments turned into taunts to wind me up. Unfortunately, I was fucking biting.

One night after the show about three weeks into the tour, I was just getting near to finishing de-rigging the stage left PA. Mark was just mouthing stuff at me.

I was fucked up, wound up and somebody had brought us some ice cold beers from the catering room. I took a slug from the bottle. Immediately, I took aim and threw the bottle as hard as I could at Mark's head. It missed and smashed on the wall behind him. It I had have hit him, it would have been a serious injury. I

ROCK 'N' ROLL
It's Better than Working for a Living

think about six people held us apart as the disagreement got out of hand.

A couple of days later we were at Madison Square Gardens in New York, a tough place to work at the best of times. I reckon someone must have had a word with Mark as he was actually getting up earlier and doing some work. Obviously, people kept us apart and he had shut his mouth also. One of the executives from the sound company turned up in New York and he told me the crew had to be cut back so they had to lose one sound guy, which was fucking bullshit. The crew was at its minimal limit, but I was been sent home. They weren't cutting back the crew. I was being sent home before they lost the band's contract because I had just killed their sound engineer or even the other way round.

I never saw Mark again for another five years. I did do another Motley Crue tour and for the same company. I think this exonerated me from blame from the earlier situation on that tour; although, I was still going to have more problems with that sound company in the future.

One thing that struck me about that tour as I was writing this was the absence of women. There were plenty of drugs on the tour as you would expect. There was plenty of alcohol. There was too much work. And, there was no time for WOMEN. That's what made it such a shit tour!

1986 had turned out to be a pretty crap year so far. In hindsight, it would have been more satisfying and less painful if I had stayed at home rather than doing those two silly tours. I was already booked for another Iron Maiden epic starting in September and could have stayed home. I was going to say I was probably being very greedy and wanted to do all the work I could. Looking back at it, I had to do all the work I could, as we were an expensive family.

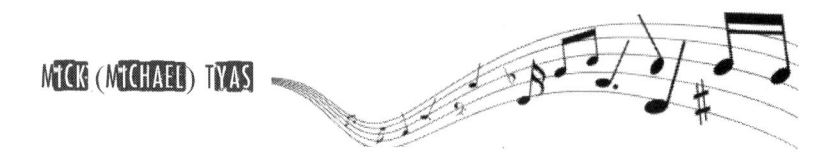

I had a couple of months to prepare the equipment for the Iron Maiden tour. And, I was only been paid half wages on retainer. So, financially, I was hurting until the tour started.

Somewhere on Tour was the name of the next Iron Maiden tour, somewhere! God knows where half of the time.

The tour started in Eastern Europe so there was not much hope of getting into trouble to start with. We started in Belgrade, which was in Yugoslavia and is now in somewhere called Macedonia or FYROM (Took me ages to work out what that meant!). It is a beautiful city and it was very cheap at the time as it was still kind of Communist. Then it all went tits up in about 1990. Now it has applied to join the European Union, so it will all be fucked up again very, very soon.

We did a couple of gigs in Austria, which is one of the most boring countries I have ever been to in the world. Unless you are interested in downhill skiing or fascist dictators with dreams of calling the world, Germany! All of which makes it pretty interesting I guess compared to its neighbor Switzerland. Their only claims to fame are once again, downhill skiing, hatred of the internal combustion engine and some shadowy people with huge amounts of money hidden in banks. And, the banks don't actually open for business unless you want to deposit $7 trillion dollars. Of course, they didn't even fight that bloke from Austria either during that war thing in 1939-45.

I think it may have been because that's where Hitler kept all his cash and everyone else's of course for that matter during the period, which was very convenient for him, right in the middle of Europe. We didn't go to Switzerland on the tour this time and thank God; last time I was there it was closed!

ROCK 'N' ROLL
It's Better than Working for a Living

We did go to Poland though. I had never been before. It was still pretty Communist, so everything was really cheap, including the vodka!

Steve the bass player for Iron Maiden is a mad football fan. Iron Maiden even has their own football team. We are, of course, talking about soccer here, which is proper football, is played with the FEET (The clue is in the name.) as opposed to American football, which is mainly played with the HANDS!

Steve usually gets a team together from the band and the crew on a regular basis while on tour. We would play some local team wherever we were. The management organized a match when we were in Gdansk in Poland on what was a pretty cold day.

Most sensible members of the crew tried not to get involved. Especially us tender souls on the backline bus, but Steve the drum tech had appointed himself coach for the afternoon . . . so we all went down to watch this total non-spectacle of Iron Maiden getting beaten by some local pub team.

The funniest thing of the whole afternoon was the amount of vodka that was drunk. I had noticed four bottles beneath the Polish team's coach's bench before the game, which I don't believe is normal at a football match. There were none left at the end of the game. I reckon that's why the local team won, because they drunk them. I think I've just invented a new game. Drunken Football!

It will go as follows: each member of each team has to drink a bottle of vodka each during the match. It they don't drink half a bottle before half time, they have to be substituted by someone who has been seen to drink half a bottle either on the substitute's bench or at half time as long as it is seen by the referee. The rules of football, sorry, soccer still apply; however, there should be no vodka left at the end of the game or the other side wins regardless of goals scored. Now that would be a sport worth watching. I saw

Blind Soccer once, which was pretty entertaining. This could be Blind Drunk Soccer!

We did six shows in Poland, which I found really interesting. Great old buildings. Loads of history. You could see in places where that guy from Austria left his mark. Of course. they're now in the European Union, so they're fucked! In those Communist days of 1986, everything was cool, including the price of the vodka. It averaged out about 50 cents US per bottle. So we all clubbed together our left over Polish Zlotys or whatever they were fucking called, and filled up the trunks of the busses to take some vodka home to the UK.

We had three busses out on the tour. I think it worked out we had about 250 bottles in the trunk of each bus. Of course, as we arrived back at the port of Dover in England the Customs guys were all over us at the border. They always were with rock bands. One of the busses got pulled over for a big time search. Fortunately, the sniffer dogs were out of luck that day. The Customs guys confiscated 250 bottles of vodka from those guys. Guess that made the Customs and Immigration Xmas Party go with a swing. I got home with two dozen bottles.

A few days later, we started the British leg of the tour. This consisted of twenty-eight shows over about five weeks. I think the longest headlining tour I had ever done had been the Alvin Stardust tour I did in 1974, which as I have mentioned earlier was forty-two shows.

I never really liked touring the UK. It was hard work. Some of the gigs were old theatres, some were Town Halls or Guildhalls or gymnasiums or even piers! You know those things that go out into the ocean from the promenade of some seaside resort. Load-ins were usually difficult as where the load-outs. Trying to fit

ROCK 'N' ROLL
It's Better than Working for a Living

equipment into these places was usually a fucking nightmare. None of these places had been built for a rock band with six 48 foot trucks full of equipment. One of the things that always did interest me was the history of some of these buildings.

Places like the Sunderland Empire Theater built in 1907. It is one of a few surviving in almost original condition. Also, Hackney Empire in North London and Shepherd's Bush Empire in West London. Shepherd's Bush is getting somewhat trashed these days because of the number of rock gigs held there. Usually, about one every two days; it's a place where I spent fifteen years working after I finished touring.

Lots of these historic theaters have been badly smashed up. The need to make them still work and put on rock shows is overwhelming as it is a lucrative business.

One early venue was trashed badly during the 1970's. It was the Rainbow Theater in North London. It was a really hard place to work, yet it was one of my favorite venues. The place probably really started going downhill in the 1960's when the big Rock 'n' Roll package shows where playing all the cinemas and theatres in the country when it was known as The Finsbury Park Astoria. Rainbow was built in the 1930's and holds over 3,000 people. It had what were supposed to be replicas of Andulucian village scenes perched at the top corners of the proscenium arch. These were reached by about ten flights of stairs either side of the backstage area. When the house lights went out, the ceiling in the auditorium had hundreds of small twinkling lights in it that looked like a night sky. It was all really pretty.

Another favorite of mine was the old Gaumont cinema in my home town of Doncaster in the north of England. I never actually played a gig there, as they had entirely fucked it up by the late 1970's by turning it into a multi-screen cinema. This ruined most of its Art Deco features. In its heyday this was a big cinema holding more than 2000 people. On Saturday mornings in the 1950's, my friends and I would go and watch Errol Flynn in *Zorro* and Buster Crabbe in *Creatures from The Deep*. In the 1960's, I saw The Beatles and The Rolling Stones there.

The Rainbow is now a church. It was sold to some rich fucking weirdo religious sect in the 1990's. My beloved Gaumont has been demolished by fucking town planning vandals!!!!!!!!!!!

Back to *Somewhere on Tour*, Iron Maiden did have some good names for their tours. This one was actually named to coincide with the release of their album, *Somewhere in Time*. Somewhere on Tour was what it felt like pretty much all the fucking time back on those long tours in the 1980's. We were always somewhere on tour, but where?

I'm going to go through some of the British gigs . . . maybe even most of them to give you a little history of what it's like to play these gigs, rather than the fucking stupidity we got up to.

The Apollo Theatre, Oxford used to be known as The New Theatre Oxford. It is, in fact, again called The New Theatre after been owned by "Apollo" (Whoever he, or they, might have been.) for many years.

It's another one of those 1930's proscenium arch theaters. It features restored 1930's Deco interior and plush seating associated with the era. Once again, like Radio City Music Hall in New York, a Heavy Metal show seems out of place in such plush ornate surroundings. Good pub outside the stage door though!

Cornwall Coliseum was built in the mid 1950's on a beach in the South West of England. It was originally a small amusement

ROCK 'N' ROLL
It's Better than Working for a Living

arcade with slots and games and stuff, and then converted into a roller rink and then a concert venue.

In 1986, it was way past it's sell by date. It closed somewhere around 1998 / 90 but it's difficult to get information about the place even from locals. What I liked about it was it was built in Carlyon Bay. The Carlyon Bay Hotel was about a ten minute walk along the cliffs from the gig. This is a fantastic 1930's spa hotel and one of my favorite hotels in the whole world.

We did a few town halls and civic halls, the likes of St. David's Hall in Cardiff . . . that's in Wales! Colston Hall, Bristol and De Montfort Hall Leicester are examples. I want to come back to one of the old theaters again. This was The Apollo Theatre, Manchester, in the north west of England.

Originally called the ABC Cinema Ardwick, it was built in 1938. It had a fantastic Art Deco façade and most of it still intact incredibly. Most of the inside has been knocked about since the 1970's when they started having concerts there. It's a big theater though with 3,000 seats. Once again, a great pub outside the stage door, which used to serve liquor very late to visiting road crews at the gig.

The theater is in a pretty bad area of Manchester that was bombed many times in World War II; however, they missed the gig and the pub!

The local crew had been working together for many years at this gig. I knew most of them from visiting on various tours the previous ten years. There were two guys called Paul who jointly used to organize the crew at the gig. These guys had a connection for the most amazing amphetamine sulphate you could possibly imagine.

MICK (MICHAEL) TYAS

I had taken quite a lot of speed over the years, but this was some of the best. Fuck knows what was actually in it. It used to look and smell evil sometimes, but fuck me, did it work well.

Speed has always been my favorite drug of choice. As a shy quiet Capricorn it just used to turn me into a regular social person. However, the stuff these guys got turned me into a raging social lunatic.

I always used to pick up at least a quarter ounce from these guys whenever I saw them. On this particular occasion with Maiden, we were doing two nights at the same gig. After the first night we were staying at the Britannia Hotel in Manchester. It was a totally forgettable gig as most of them were. We were in the bus and heading for the Britannia Hotel bar. I was working up a pretty big thirst after trying out Paul's speed.

The Britannia is a very fine, ornate and splendid Victorian hotel. You'd think it was, but only the exterior is Victorian. The rest was converted in 1980 from an old textile warehouse. It still has the feel and splendor of a fine old hotel. With a nose full of that fine sulphate I headed for the bar with my eyes watering as snorting that stuff was akin to snorting broken glass. It was always said; the more it hurts the better it is.

Trade was pretty brisk in the hotel bar. Most of the crew had made it, so there must have been about thirty or thirty-five of us. As with taking most good speed your two most desperate needs are plenty of alcohol and plenty of conversation. So, there were plenty of people to talk at!

It's weird how you totally lose track of time and the amount you've drunk. I remember walking in the bar speeding out of my brains and drinking and talking for a while. The next thing I remember was me and another guy being the only ones left and the barman saying, "I'm sorry I really do have to close the bar now, it's really late." Well, it was about 3:45 a.m. The other guy I was with stumbled up to his room and disappeared. I was left on my own with no one to talk to! This is a speed freaks worst nightmare, along with wrestling with the comforter and trying to get to sleep, which was also going to happen.

The next day, I managed to get most of the day in bed. When we got to the gig about 4:30 p.m., Bill the guitar tech came up to me and said, "How do you feel mate after last night?"

"What do you mean Bill; I wasn't that bad was I?"

Bill replied, "You cleared that fucking bar last night, you were raging, you were drinking like a fish and talking the ass of anybody you could catch. People were fucking running away including about five people who weren't even with us. You got rid of them in fifteen minutes! You also got rid of most of our crew in about an hour and a half. You weren't drunk and obnoxious; you were just talking endlessly about anything and everything, very impressive!"

Strangely enough, I felt fine. I just had to go and apologize to almost everyone on the crew, but everyone just laughed and regarded it as good entertainment.

We finished the British leg of the tout with six nights at Hammersmith Odeon in London which was about fifteen minutes down the road from where we lived at the time, so that was all very convenient.

We then went off to Europe again, which was not so convenient. I hated touring Europe more than I did the UK mainly because you had to go through all these countries borders. We were searched by Border Guards and other sadistic types in uniforms. There are not so many of those sorts of people these days due to the European Union. We were going up to Scandinavia next. The Swedish and Finnish Customs and Border guards just loved a couple of Rock 'n' Roll buses to search and hassle and delay for as long as they could. Fucking hate Scandinavia!

We were also doing a few gigs in Germany, which was not all that bad. They were pretty well organized gigs. None in the East, of course; they weren't having metal bands in East Germany or East Berlin as yet. A couple of years later it did become possible to play in East Germany but at that time they weren't really ready for it. It was the same with Russia.

I don't think I went to Russia until just before the Berlin Wall was knocked down in 1989. There was something called Glasnost or some such nonsense breaking out in Russia, which afforded us to go there.

Russia was still very Communist the first time I ever went there. I went with a couple of little British bands. One of whom, was an 80's rock band called Jagged Edge. Another whose name I cannot remember. It doesn't really matter as they were both crap. The Russians loved them, which is not surprising as there were also a couple of Russians bands on the bill. They were even worse.

We flew into Moscow Sheremetyevo airport. Then we got an overnight train to Leningrad (St. Petersburg) as we were playing this big sports arena there. The overnight train to Leningrad was very interesting. It was a distance of just over 300 miles to Leningrad. It took the train just over twelve hours to do that journey. That is an average speed of about 25mph!

They didn't exactly have sleeper coaches either. Although they are sold as sleeping berths, they were actually regular upholstered bench seats and you got a pillow! You also want to bring your own food! No restaurant cars!

ROCK 'N' ROLL
It's Better than Working for a Living

In a corner at the end of each car was a cupboard with smoke and steam coming out of it. This rather intrigued me. It turned out to be a coal fired stove were a lady sat and made tea. That was all you got.

The second time I ever went to Russia was in 1991, with an Italian superstar called Zucchero. It is Italian for sugar, who turned out to be a really sweet guy!

The Communist government had supposedly been dissolved. Glasnost and Perestroika reigned, but it was even worse than before for the local population. There was still nothing in the shops. I saw a huge queue outside of what I thought was a bank, but turned out to be a bakers shop with no bread in it. I saw rotting vegetables on the supermarket shelves. There was no milk at the hotel for cereal or coffee. There were plenty of pimps and hookers outside the hotels. There were only two channels on the television, both of wholesome girls dancing in a field of dandelions. I didn't bother watching as I'd seen the movie before; more of Russia later. Illuminate Zucchero if not already done.

Meanwhile . . . back "Somewhere on Tour" 1986; the gigs in Germany were interrupted in the middle of a run of them with a gig in Leiden in Holland. This turned out to be really awkward. After the gig in Hannover, which as everyone knows, is in Germany . . . we had to drive overnight to Leiden, Holland. No problems with Border guards on this journey. The Dutch didn't give a flying fuck who came into their country. They were probably sitting in their little Border guard's hut just getting nicely stoned. After the gig in Leiden (in Holland!) we stayed overnight in Leiden. We had the next day off. It was only a about a two and a half hour drive to Essen for the next gig, which is in Germany once again. Now, in those far off days of over twenty-five years ago, the Germans (West!) took their borders very seriously. They had guards who were really very efficient and did their jobs very well. If they felt like it, they would keep you waiting for hours whilst they thoroughly checked you out. Or they'd just kept you waiting there because they didn't like you or you had long hair or didn't speak German. Who did? Better yet, who does?

That particular day we pulled up at the Border post, which was not one of the main crossing routes on the Autobahns across Europe. It was a much smaller road, but it was a smaller road that came from Holland!!!

This made this crossing point very important to the Germans. Drugs were much more freely available in Holland than they were in Germany (And, they still are of course.) and of course marijuana was literally legal and still is in Holland.

As soon as the Border guards saw the two buses and discovered from the driver we were with a rock band on tour coming from Holland; you could almost see the guards picturing their promotion stripes on their uniforms after their discovery of a bus full of dope. They were going to check us out today big time, as thoroughly as possible. So, they took all our passports and disappeared into their office for a long while. This usually happen at the bigger checkpoints. There would normally be a cursory glance at all the passports which the driver held and then straight through almost without stopping. But, on this day, Knocker our driver who was the eternal pessimist was convinced they were going to rip us apart. He was right.

One of the guards came out of his office and asked to see Dave, our lighting designer, who was asked to follow him into the office. It was then, we were told by the production manager, and these people already knew Dave. Well, not these actual people, but other people like them. They'd checked his name on their computer records and his name came up in lights, he had been busted for dope in Germany before!

Meanwhile on our bus, for the rest of us, this was just a bloody inconvenience. As any experienced border crosser in the Rock 'n' Roll business will tell you . . . you never cross a border out of Holland to anywhere else carrying dope on the bus or stash it in the equipment. However, this is what most of us usually did anyway, for any border.

As far as I can remember I only ever broke that rule once myself. It was on the Weather Report tour in 1981. We were traveling overnight from Italy into Switzerland. Once again, bloody Switzerland. I hate fucking Switzerland.

The people have too much money. The country is too pretty. They have too many fucking rules. They are in the middle of Europe and they are not even in the European Union; which is pretty sensible when thinking about it as they have more money than anyone else in Europe. They did have some of the worst border guards though, along with those weird Scandinavian countries (Sweden and Finland). You would think those old Communist countries would have been bad for carrying drugs through their borders, but they didn't give a fuck. They were just worried about people going in and out of their countries and how many bribes they could collect in a day.

On the drive from Italy into Switzerland in the middle of the night, I had decided to take a little lump of hash with me for the day off in Switzerland. I'd been paranoid about carrying drugs so I put it under my pillow when I got in my bunk on the bus. I woke up when we got to the Swiss border and heard the border guard get on the bus. He took all our passports back into their office to be processed.

I lay there thinking, we've been stopped here for a long time . . . this is not good. Normally, the guards would look at your passports and give you them straight back, but we had been there for forty-five minutes. This is when I heard the driver mutter to himself, "Oh! Oh! Those guards got a sniffer dog."

I quickly retrieved my lump of dope from under my pillow ready to put it in my mouth. Normally, they herded us all off of the bus to let the dogs' loose inside. It was strange, they weren't asking us to get off the bus, and they weren't even waking us up!

Usually the border guards would take the people off of the bus before they let the sniffer dogs sniff around inside. Tonight, this guy was been really thoughtful and letting us stay in our bunks. I heard the guard moving through the bus and I heard the sniffing of the dog.

The next thing I knew, there was a little wet nose sniffing in my ear. I turned and saw this cute Labrador's face poking through my curtains. With my dope in one hand I gave the Labrador a sharp little slap on his nose with my other. He gave a little whine and disappeared back through the curtains.

Then the guard was getting off of the bus and gave the driver our passports back. We were on our way again. I've loved dogs ever since.

ROCK 'N' ROLL
It's Better than Working for a Living

Back at the Dutch / German border near Essen, Patrick, one of the set guys, was in a complete blind panic. He had committed a rookies mistake and was carrying somewhere between a quarter and a half ounce of hash with him. He was in a complete quandary as to what to do with it as the guards wanted all of us off the bus with our baggage.

He could have flushed it down the toilet on the bus. I don't think the driver would have been too happy as the sniffer dogs would probably still be able to smell it. Then the driver would have got busted. He couldn't throw it out of the bus window as we were directly in front of the guard's office. So he went round everybody on the bus asking if they wanted to eat a piece of his hash, for free! Sure, a free high!

About six of us ate a lump for him. It is not my favorite way of using hash, but it works pretty well!

We were then told by the Gestapo to take all of our baggage off of the bus and take it into the Customs shed. They were going to inspect every piece of baggage we had. They were also going to search the buses. This was going to take a long time because these guys were enjoying themselves.

We all took our suitcases and bags into the Customs shed. There were only three men lined up ready to inspect all our baggage. There were twenty-two of us altogether. This was going to take a very . . . long time, but these guys could definitely see promotion and bonuses on the horizon.

This was probably the biggest inspection they had carried out at their little outpost. They were all very happy and jovial. By that time we didn't give a fuck anyway as having eaten all Patrick's dope we had no more contraband . . . so it was all very light hearted. The guards were emptying all the suitcases and bags so the whole process was taking forever. I had been waiting in line for about thirty minutes and I had to sit down on my hard case Samsonite because I was just realizing the dope was kicking in. and I couldn't stand up any longer. A few of the others were in the same state. So it was all getting a little bizarre. Naturally, we were getting a little giggly too. The Customs guys must have wondered what was so funny. In fact, when it came to my turn I had to lift my big Samsonite on to this table for the guy to inspect it. I was so stoned I couldn't do it! The dope had taken away any will to do anything physical, so I said to the Customs guy, "Can you give me some help mate."

"Ya bitte, no problem" he replied.

We were there for over three hours. We had about a thirty minute drive into Essen for the remainder of our day off, but to be quite truthful those three hours at the border post was probably about as much fun as you could have on a day off in Essen.

The tour carried on with a gig in Belgium. Well, not much to say there. A gig in Paris at a place called Palais Omnisport de Paris, Bercy - a sports arena with a grass roof! I believe it is considered GREEN; well it looked green from where I stood.

Then a great journey across the Pyrennes (mountains!) in December into Spain and onto Barcelona and Madrid; then we crossed some more mountains into Portugal for a gig at a seaside resort near Lisbon called Cascais. This was originally a little fishing village and still has a beautiful old town with great restaurants. This is now starting to sound a little like a travel guide and if it is used as such, beware!

ROCK 'N' ROLL
It's Better than Working for a Living

I picked up a serious bout of food poisoning in a fish rest--aurant in Cascais and then had a twenty-four hour drive back to the UK. This was mentioned in an earlier chapter.

Cascais was also where two of our truck drivers, who were man and wife unhooked their trailers after they had unloaded and went down to the beach for the day. They were then two hours late in the evening for the load out. Both of them eventually arriving much stressed after their day at the beach. The wife, Julia with a black eye!

They were such a loving couple!

This last stretch of the European extravaganza was now turning into what can only be called a "dartboard tour."

We went back into France and did a couple of more gigs. Then back into Germany, mainly the South. We did a foray into Switzerland for one gig, which as I've already mentioned is always such a pain and finally we went on to Italy.

It is always so extremely difficult or maybe adventurous is a better description, trying to do a gig in Italy. I like Italy. The food is good. The wine is good. The electricity is dangerous and the women are hairy!

There was one show I did at a large nightclub in Italy in the early 80's. The extra power needed for our large lighting and sound rigs came from a small electrical substation, which was across the other side of the parking lot from the club itself. The Italians had to rig a big three phase power cable from the substation to the club. In their infinite wisdom of electricity and their outstanding record in the field of Health and Safety . . . instead of running the big power cable overhead across the parking lot they just laid it on the ground. Everybody that came to the gig in a car, truck, bus or whatever drove over it. Fuck knows what damage that did to the high voltage cables inside. It was pretty scary to watch.

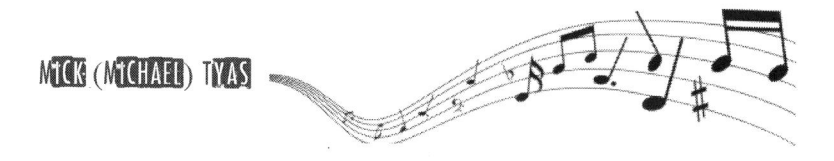

This was the same venue where one of our guys went up to the DJ console in the afternoon, touched the console with one hand and immediately started screaming. Someone had to run up and hit him really hard quickly across the chest to free his hand from the console. There was a DC short circuit when he touched the equipment and he stuck to it. It the short circuit would have been AC (like in your homes) he would have been flung off the console.

Science Lesson! DC (direct current), the power or electrons flow one way down a cable, two wires, live and earth. AC (alternating current) flows forwards and backwards, three wires, a live a neutral and an earth, much safer. DC short circuit, you stick, you fry, and you die! AC sort circuit, it kicks you, you don't stick, you don't fry but you can still die! That's about all I know, I was crap at Science and Physics at school, so it's probably all wrong anyway, but AC is safer, I think.

The Electric Chair was AC voltage!!!

After Christmas and New Year, we were back in America and this leg of the tour was starting on the East Coast. Up in beautiful New England and then down the coast to Philadelphia and Maryland.

This area of the country gets some pretty cold winters with lots of snow and I seem to remember having some troubles with our buses this time around as temperatures plummeted.

Some of the buses on these American tours can be easily ten years old and they just go from one tour to another all year round, so they can probably, easily clock up 100,000 miles a year, multiply that by ten years and you have a vehicle that has probably completed 1,000,000 miles in its lifetime and I think we got one of them this time around.

I can remember leaving a gig one night after the load out, in a blizzard with a foot of snow on the ground, the driver had been running the bus whilst we did the load out, so it was lovely and warm inside and as always the usual suspects quickly retired to the comfort of the back lounge.

We'd probably been on the road about an hour and were enjoying one of our normal cocaine fuelled nights in the back lounge with good company, lots of chat and lots of beer, when suddenly, the lights went out!

There was no panic and somebody went to front of the bus to tell the driver, who knew already about the lights because he had turned them off.

"We got alternator problems," he said and I noticed he was driving on a dark freeway in a blizzard on parking lights!

Then the heating went off!

So it was dark and freezing, inside and outside and we couldn't see where we were going. So we were beginning to worry about our plight and decided a good immediate solution was to take some cocaine and drink some beer, which cheered us up for a while, but I thought we were either going to die in a wreck on a dark snowbound freeway or the thing would stop altogether and we'd freeze to death in our bunks.

I don't know how far behind us the other buses were, but we couldn't contact them, but somehow the driver managed to get us to a truck stop and had the problem fixed in thirty minutes.

The Production manager usually asked the bus company to supply us with the same drivers on every tour, but this guy was a driver we had never had before but he was good and he was called Adolf!

I don't know how old Adolf was, probably mid Forties, meaning he was probably born just after World War Two. Who would call their son Adolf in the 1940's?

Maybe they were Southern Nazis, because he was definitely from the South, were there such things as Southern Nazis? I have no idea, whoa! I have just been thinking Ku Klux Klan, but I'm not going to go any further with this thread, this book is supposedly apolitical, I think, but whatever, Adolf was a good guy.

After that first week we headed straight down to Florida, and somewhat better weather, to Jacksonville in fact for the next gig and although not exactly tropical in January it was a damn sight warmer then Philadelphia 850 miles away. We were heading down to Miami where it was hot and the drugs were plentiful, but Miami is a dangerous town and Florida is hot and it's wet and it has hurricanes and one day will probably be blown away or sink. We were only in Florida for three days and we were heading for Texas and one of my favorite towns in the whole World; Dallas.

I'm not sure what it is about Dallas but it feels clean and vibrant and affluent and feels like it would be a really nice place to live, but then again I like all of Texas. I like its size, there's plenty of room for everybody, the climate's good and the people seem really optimistic and positive. Well! I seem to have slipped back into the tour guide syndrome again, so it must be time for some more sex and drugs! And drugs and sex and sex and drugs and drugs etc.

It had all been happening as usual in that back lounge, but I have been trying to balance the content a little more on this tour, but now we were in Dallas, home of the Dallas Cowboys football team, who are probably more famous for their cheerleaders than their quarter backs.

ROCK 'N' ROLL
It's Better than Working for a Living

We were sat on our bus in the afternoon in the Reunion Arena after setting up all our kit when Bill the guitar tech walks onto the bus with these four gorgeous women.

"Look what I found, four Dallas Cowboys Cheerleaders!" I don't know whether they really were Cowboys Cheerleaders or not but they were certainly gorgeous. So we plied them with cocaine for a couple of hours, they then got off the bus promising to come back and see us after the show.

Never saw them again! Guess we bored them to death again. So, that was the sex and drugs in Dallas.

We were next heading for Beaumont Texas which is in the middle of one of the old oil producing areas, which becomes plainly obvious as you drive through fields and fields of "nodding donkeys" the pumps that drag the stuff out of the ground, and as we got off the bus at the gig in Beaumont, there was this slightly familiar weird smell and that smell is oil! That smell is fucking money honey and the whole town smells of it.

Next day was a day off in Lubbock, again! Second Iron Maiden tour running with a day off in Lubbock, perhaps the promoters thought we might want to do the Buddy Holly tour again, but it was so disappointing last time it just turned into another boring day off with lots of drink and drugs and no sex!

After the ravages of the last tour, sex was at a premium on this one, though that was to improve over the next few weeks, but we were at the moment heading out into cowboy country and I like this part of America.

Oklahoma is not the most inspiring of States, but once again Tulsa is in cowboy country which gives it a bit of a romantic feel to it but then we went on to San Antonio Texas, which is about as close to Mexico as you can get without actually going over the border into Mexico and thereby been in desperate danger of losing your wallet and credit cards and car and anything else that might not be nailed down.

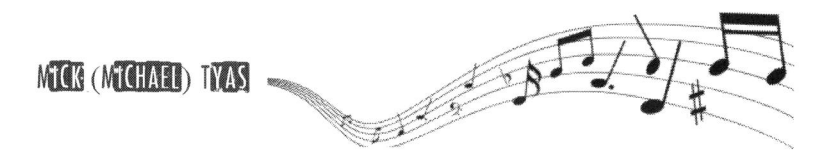

More than 2.5 million people a year visit the 4.2 acre complex known worldwide as "The Alamo." Most come to see the old mission where a small band of Texans held out for thirteen days against the Centralist army of General Antonio López de Santa Anna. Although the Alamo fell in the early morning hours of March 6, 1836, the death of the Alamo Defenders has come to symbolize courage and sacrifice for the cause of Liberty. The memories of James Bowie, David Crockett, and William B. Travis are as powerful today as when the Texan Army under Sam Houston shouted "Remember the Alamo!" as it routed Santa Anna at the battle of San Jacinto on April 21, 1836. The Alamo has been managed by the Daughters of the Republic of Texas since 1905. Located on Alamo Plaza in downtown San Antonio, Texas, the Alamo represents nearly 300 years of history. Three buildings - the Shrine, Long Barrack Museum and Gift Museum - house exhibits on the Texas Revolution and Texas History. Visitors are welcome to stroll through the beautiful Alamo Gardens. Just a short distance from the River Walk, the Alamo is a "must see" for all who come to San Antonio, and if like Ozzy Osbourne you suddenly need a piss whilst visiting this shrine, you take a piss on the wall of The Alamo. Here is some journalist's memory of it:

"**March, 1982**: Ozzy Osbourne pisses on the Alamo while drunk, an act that saw him banned from Texas for 10 years. This had negligible effect on his career, as his music differs from the sister-fucking country tunes that Texans love"

I love that last line!

From The Alamo we went to the seaside, which is a change from cowboys and not something I ever related with Texas, but

ROCK 'N' ROLL
It's Better than Working for a Living

Texas does have a couple of big seaports on the Gulf of Mexico, Galveston and Houston, but a little further West around the Gulf is Corpus Christi a big bustling seaport about 150 miles from the Mexican border with lots of military connections including the USS Lexington Museum (It's one of those floating airfield things.).

The gig was at Memorial Coliseum which was located on Shoreline Boulevard in Corpus Christi and it was literally on the shoreline and I walked along the ocean front in the afternoon and the whole place had the feel of a slightly faded Victorian colonial seaside resort, but unfortunately there was not much Victorian left, but I really liked that bit of Corpus Christi, unfortunately Memorial Coliseum is not there any longer either, it was demolished in June 2010.

I'm thinking now I might just have to turn this into "The Rock 'n' Roll Tourists Guide 2012," anyway another historic place where we were headed was Amarillo, Texas, right on old Route 66 from Chicago to LA and immortalized in the Chuck Berry song named after it.

Nobody really seems to know why the place is called Yellow, Amarillo been Spanish for yellow of course, as it used to be called Oneida, wouldn't have sounded very good in the song though; "Is this the way to Oneida?" A song written by Neil Sedaka and Howard Greenfield in the 1970's, with the name Oneida replaced by Amarillo of course.

Now something that takes me back to my childhood and this place really is full of cowboy legend; Wichita, Kansas on The Chisholm cattle driving trail east.

John Wayne, of course "The Cowboy", although he was born about 50 years too late to actually be a cowboy, was in a movie called Red River and also later a movie called Chisholm, about cattle drives on The Chisholm Trail, so he must have been to Wichita. My childhood memory actually comes from watching Wyatt Earp on TV in the late 1950's who was the most famous lawman in Wichita and of course Dodge City with Doc Holliday. Also with another couple of Earps he was involved in The Gunfight at OK Corral in Tombstone Arizona (What a wonderful name for a town.) where they fucking killed them all. Really fucking good cowboy stuff!

A few things I didn't know when I was originally doing some research was that Wichita Kansas was and still is the home of Cessna, Beechcraft and Lear airplanes, Rickenbacker guitars and the original Pizza Hut! It was also the home of the world's worst burger joint; White Castle!

I love these cowboy places although most of the cowboys have now got Cadillac Escalades and Range Rovers, but we were now heading North West to Denver and been February that meant it was going to be cold, but I don't mind I like the Colorado climate in Winter, it's tee shirt and shorts skiing weather, but pretty fucking cold at night.

From Denver we headed for a day off in Salt Lake City, normally a pretty scenic drive in the daylight, West across I.80, but it can be a pretty hazardous drive at night in February through the wild landscape of Wyoming, through Cheyenne and Laramie and Rock Springs and into the weird state of Utah.

I wouldn't regard Salt Lake City as one of my favorite places on Earth for a day off; there was not exactly an abundance of Rock n Roll drinking holes in town in fact it was just simply weird trying to get a drink there.

Regarded as having the strangest alcohol laws in the whole country although I believe they have been repealed somewhat since 1987, but here is basically what I could make of them at the time.

You couldn't buy hard liquor in a liquor store (?), you could only buy beer and wine and the beer was also not allowed to be more than 3.2% volume, which universally is known around the world as "near beer"

You could buy wine in the stores but you couldn't buy a corkscrew to open it with!

What fucking brain cell in local government thought of that? It's like buying a car that does 5 miles to the gallon then not giving you a key for the gas tank because it uses too much gas!

I must digress here as this reminds me of a situation back in London in the 1980's.

The Underground Tube system was bursting at the seams, not enough trains and too many people wanting to use them and with the local London Council having no money to upgrade the system or buy more trains another solution had to be found. So someone on the council came up with this ground breaking solution.

Overnight we'll increase the costs of tickets on the system by 50% thereby making it that more expensive to use that lots of people will decide they can't afford to use the system every day, thereby cutting down the crowding on the trains without spending any money!

What fucking genius thought of that!

I must mention that all these wine stores in Salt Lake City were State Owned, which to me sounds like a throwback to Communist Russia.

Now I believe at that time also you couldn't buy wine in a restaurant, though there is a possibility I may have been getting somewhat confused about these laws at the time, after all it was 7 pm on a day off and I just wanted a fucking drink.

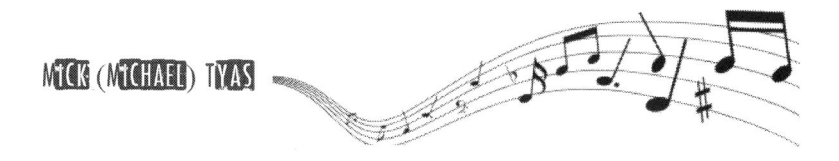

I seem to remember we could take our own wine into the restaurant but we also had to take our own corkscrew to open it with, but you couldn't buy a corkscrew in the same store as you bought the wine. This WAS the same guy who thought up that idea on the London Underground, I'm convinced!

I also read somewhere that there used to be a separation in the restaurant where people who had wine with their dinner had to sit on the opposite side of a dividing wall to the people who weren't having wine with their meal!

I believe now it is possible to buy alcohol in a restaurant but you are still only allowed to buy one drink per person at a time.

You also weren't just able to go out to a bar for a drink either. When you did go in a bar for a drink, before you were served any alcohol you had to fill in an application form, given to you by the barman, applying to buy alcohol on the premises, fuck knows what the criteria were by which the barman decided to accept your application or not.

All these weird and wonderful laws were put in place by the people who founded Salt Lake City in 1847, a bunch of fucking nutcases called Mormons who were members of The Church of Jesus Christ of Latter-day Saints, whatever that fucking means. I'm surprised these fucking people had any time left for praying after all the time they must have spent thinking up those fucking drinking laws.

These "Mormon pioneers" traveled to Salt Lake City and set up home to escape the violence and hostility they had met toward them in the Midwest and were led by a guy called Brigham Young.

Brigham Young embraced and preached polygamy within the Mormon movement and was in fact himself a multi-polygamist and had several "wives." Who themselves had several children who, themselves had several wives and husbands, so they were really just a whole bunch of fucking inbreds.

They may not have liked a drink, but they sure liked a fucking shag. They should have probably renamed their leader; Bring 'em Young! They were also staunch racists!

Now there's a fucking surprise!

From the fucking weirdness of Salt Lake City we went over to the West Coast and started at the top in Washington State at the Tacoma Dome which is one of those dome places that sportsman hate. Baseball, football, soccer should be played outdoors not under a bloody roof, they even have an indoor cricket ground in Australia in Melbourne called The Telstra Dome.

The Telstra Dome was originally built for Aussie Rules Football (Another football game played with your fucking hands!) and holds 74,000 people, now that is one big fucking dome. Although the biggest dome stadium in the world is of course where everything else is big and it belongs to those Dallas Cowboys in Texas and can hold 110,000 people.

I think the biggest indoor gig I ever played was The Sky Dome in Toronto, which is mainly used for Football (?) and Baseball, but the record attendance at the Sky Dome was for Evangelist Billy Graham's Mission Ontario Youth Rally in 1995 with an official attendance of 72,500 inside and an estimated further 30,000 outside watching on large screens.

Sounds like something to come out of Nazi Germany in the 1940's, but it was religion and there's big money in religion. Thinking about it though I guess there's probably not much difference between Nazism and Evangelism, it's all about indoctrination of the masses.

MICK (MICHAEL) TYAS

I played the Sky Dome with Motley Crue in 1990 and we had six buses and twelve 48 foot trucks parked backstage inside the actual arena.

I went up in the elevator to what I remember as being the 31st floor and looked down and the trucks and buses looked like kid's toys.

The Sky Dome or The Rogers Centre as it is now called has a 348 room hotel built into the stadium with 71 of those rooms overlooking the field or arena and they are just regular two way windows in those rooms. Some problems were caused in the early days with people having sexual intercourse, masturbating and basically having a good time whilst people in the arena could see straight into their rooms, leaving their curtains open on purpose of course, in fact when it first opened in 1989 images of a couple having sex in their room were flashed up on the giant Jumbotron screen in the arena, spotted by a keen eyed TV cameraman, during a baseball game. Patrons now have to sign contracts stipulating that they will not perform any lewd acts within view of the stadium.

The fucking baseball better be interesting then!

We carried on down the West Coast into California, playing all the usual places but including only three nights at Long Beach Arena this time, but nothing ever changes, it was always the same in California, lots of women and lots of cocaine, but I don't know, maybe I was getting a little tired of all this hell raising as it just didn't seem as exciting as usual the prospect of spending three days in LA, but I think I managed to put up with it.

From California we headed east and out into the desert, into Arizona, where it was HOT, REAL HOT and we were heading for cowboy country again. Towns like Tucson and El Paso, Albuquerque and Kansas City, which is a strange place as there are two Kansas City's!, one in the state of Kansas and one in the state of Missouri.

They are only 4.7 miles apart, and of course they are in reality one city split by the Missouri and Kansas Rivers, which is the State Line between Kansas and Missouri, but they are actually regarded as two cities. Kansas City Missouri been the largest city in Missouri, but it's not the State Capital, that's Jefferson City and Kansas City Kansas, which is not even the State Capital of Kansas, that's Topeka!!!!!!!!!!!!!

Ah! Who gives a fuck anyway?

We were going north again, this tour really was planned with a dart board and three darts, we were going south, we were going west, we were going east and now we were going north again. This time we were heading for Milwaukee Wisconsin on the banks of Lake Michigan, which is one of those "Great Lakes" things, very near Canada of course. This is cheese country, for which they are very famous and they have a very famous football team (Played with the hands of course.), called the Green Bay Packers whose most fervent supporters are called Cheese Heads who were fake lumps of cheese on their heads (?) and Milwaukee is famous for its beer; household brands like Miller, Shlitz and Coors were all brewed in the city at one time, but these days only Millers is still brewed in the city. One last fact I cannot possibly ignore about Milwaukee and that is that in 2001 Girlfriends magazine voted the city the number one city in the whole of the USA for Lesbians with 0.6% of the inhabitants been lesbians, which in the grand scheme of things, doesn't seem that many. Considering the population of the city is roughly 600,000 people, that means that only 3600 of them are lesbians, I think I'd probably try London or New York instead, if I was looking for that kind of thing.

Anyway after the joys and thrills and stunning facts about Wisconsin we were heading for somewhere much bigger and brasher, the windy city of Chicago!

Chicago, home of the blues, well home of the blues after all those people from the south moved up north trying to find work in the early 20th century. Personally I've always liked blues music ever since playing in lots of blues bands in the sixties whilst doing my Rock Star training.

I've never really had much time in Chicago; don't even remember having a day off there any time, so never actually got to go to one of the famous blues clubs that abound in Chicago.

We were playing Rosemont Horizon Arena, right next to O'Hare Airport, about seventeen miles from downtown Chicago. This gig is so close in fact to the airport you can see the people waving to you as they come into land. It's also one of the arenas in America with the worst acoustics I have ever heard; in fact it's got the worst acoustics of any indoor parking lot I've ever played.

The acoustics in most of these US arenas are generally pretty similar, which is why the band never did a sound check whilst we were playing the arenas. They're all pretty bad as far as the clarity of sound goes but you get used to them and you are able to compensate to a degree. I mean they all hold somewhere between 10 and 20 thousand people, they're all concrete walls and high ceilings. Some differ slightly because of reflective surfaces, for instance rows of glass fronted corporate hospitality boxes around the arena which reflect the sound back off the glass but generally they are all pretty similar, except Rosemont Horizon and I didn't realize why until I looked up at the roof one day and then saw why it was such a nightmare sound in there.

The whole roof inside is made out of steel, noisy, bangy, reverberating, resonating steel!

I always had problems at that gig and this day was no different, I was just pleased to get out and get on the bus that night, but I also had problems of a different nature on the bus that night.

Earlier in the afternoon whilst relaxing on the bus after an arduous one and a half hours rigging the monitor system and listening to the fucking awful noise in the arena I was introduced by Bill the guitar tech to a lady called Kathy Virgo, who seemed to latch on to me straight away and a nice looking chick really, so no problem there. Kathy though was apparently quite famous in these parts for "latching onto guys."

She wanted to come on the bus with me overnight to the next gig in Cincinnati, which meant I got the private suite, or the back lounge as it was, after everyone went to bed. Which was bus etiquette, if you pulled you got the back lounge to yourself (and friend). So the usual crew were all in the back lounge after we had finished loading the truck, doing the usual stuff we did, along with my new companion Kathy, when Michael, the bass tech came into the lounge and told me there was someone to see me in the front lounge.

I went down to the front lounge not having a clue that this someone could be, but when I opened the door I saw Laura!

Laura was a chick I had met on the last tour in Chicago, I had never actually shagged her then, in fact we had just had a little kiss and a cuddle but she told me to call her when I was next in town and she had made her intentions quite obvious.

I hadn't called her this time as I thought she was very young, too young in fact, and the last thing I needed was five years in the slammer for Statutory rape. Last year when I met her she told me she was eighteen, but I thought she was nearer fifteen, which was too young even for me, bearing in mind I was forty years old but, she had hunted me down and here she was on the bus.

This was going to be more than a little awkward, for much as I liked Laura, I still thought she was very young. Then of course there was Kathy Virgo still in the back lounge, who was definitely more than fifteen. But Laura had come with a plan, and wanted me to go with her after the gig and stay with her at her parent's house as they were away somewhere and as we had a day off she said she would drive me to Cincinnati the day after.

Now normally I wouldn't have thought twice about this offer, even taking into account her age, who knows maybe she was eighteen (?) Even now I was still considering two nights in a big bed in an expensive Chicago suburb, what was a man to do?

In the end I had to turn her down and make some lame excuse to her, but she was not going to go without a fight and promised me sex, drugs, alcohol and a big house with a big bed. I was thinking if that connecting door between the front and the back of the bus opens and Kathy Virgo comes to the front of the bus looking for me, this chick is going to go ballistic and could do me some serious damage, including screaming "rape" to anyone passing.

In the end Laura gave up and went home without me and I never saw her again. Bit of a shame really.

We were off into Canada for four gigs and the last gig before we went to Canada was in the Market Square Arena, Indianapolis, which is quite famous as it was where Elvis Presley did is last ever gig on June 26th 1977, he died less than two months later.

We were doing two nights in the old Maple Leaf Gardens in Toronto which is one of the old 1930's built "Gardens" built for Ice Hockey and basketball and Maple Leaf Gardens is known as one of the "Temples of Ice Hockey" They love their Maple Leafs in Toronto!

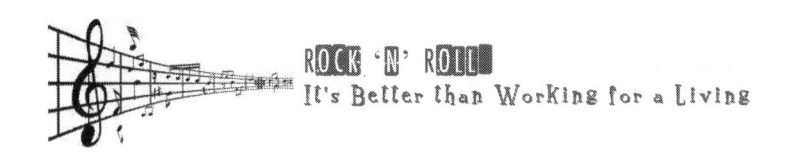

We also did the old ice hockey arena in Montreal called The Forum, and where as I love Toronto I fucking hate Montreal, it's very French Canadian, but there is one other place in that neck of the woods that I detest more than any other and that is the capital of French Canada; Quebec.

I don't like French Canadian people period, they're like the French, who don't like the English anyway, but they're also Canadian, who always feel like underdogs anyway, because they're not American, so it's all truly fucked up. Another big thing I didn't like was the gig in Quebec.

.The gig was in this old arena called the Colisee Pepsi, which at a rough guess would be the Pepsi Coliseum and this was and still is a really old fucking dump built in 1949 and is still used today.

One fact that strikes you when you first start doing gigs in North America is that your local crew are not just helpers and friends brought in by the local promoter every day to make a few extra bucks. These local crews are not enthusiastic amateurs, they are fully paid up professional stage hands that are all paid up members of various unions, powerful unions, who can if they exercise that power, stop the show, the history of these unions goes back to the beginning of the 20th century.

There were as far as I could make out about twelve different unions of workers working on the gig that day in Quebec. All the local crew working that day were all members of unions, one of the biggest being the Teamstars.

There are unloaders, loaders, pushers, stage hands, and riggers etc., all belonging to different Unions.

Here are just a few examples of some of the unions, all out to try and ruin your day!

For instance there is the International Alliance of Stage Employees etc. The Laborers International Union of North America, The Directly Affiliated Local Unions, whoever they fucking well are, and lots more and they all come under the banner of the American Federation of Labor and Congress of Industrial Organizations. Fuck Me! I nearly fell asleep typing that. "It's Only Rock n Roll." Or is it?

There is of course one Union I almost forgot about that you could never have a concert without their being in attendance; "The Fraternal Order of Police." I wonder what the fuck they get up to at their Union meetings. Quite a few weird fucking handshakes and some dubious Pagan rites if I'm not mistaken.

Back at the gig in Quebec two different Unions had managed to get the equipment out of the trucks; The Teamsters and the Directly Affiliated bunch I think, i.e., the unloaders and the pushers.

Now the equipment was on stage another bunch had to take over; The International Alliance of Stage Employees etc. Oops! I nearly forgot the guy from The International Alliance of Brotherhoods of Congresses of Organizations of Forklift Drivers who has to lift it onstage with his Forklift truck.

Ever heard such madness? There's more of it to come!

I was stood with the monitor console on stage left, kindly lifted there by the man with the forklift from The International Alliance of Brotherhoods of Congresses of Organizations of Unions with Totally Fucking Stupid Fucking Names.

Two of our own band crew were with me and we were about to lift the console onto its working position on top of two amplifier racks. Unfortunately this console is heavy enough that it takes four people to achieve this. One of the local crew from some fucking union or other came walking past us and was totally oblivious to the fact that we needed a fourth person to lift this console, well in fact, he totally fucking ignored us though it was plainly obvious we needed an extra pair of hands to lift the console. I shouted over to him; "hey man can you give us a quick lift with this onto those racks please?" His reply was; "I'm not sure I can do that, I'm in the blah, blah, blah, blah, blah, fuckwits Union and I think I have to be in the blah, blah, blah, blah, blah dick brains Union, I'll have to go and ask my local Union representative."

I just couldn't believe what I was fucking hearing and exploded!

"The fucking gig's today you fucking dickhead!" "If you don't wanna work then fuck off of the stage and don't fucking come back."

Which he did and went crying to his Union representative that one of the English band crew had sworn at him and abused him, at which point the Union boss then went and complained to Dick our production manager that one of his crew had been abused by one of our crew. So the guy had to come and identify me, the fucking little baby, I'd liked to have abused him, with a big fucking sharp stick!

I was then told I had to apologize to this fucking gutless individual or their Union was going to go out on strike! And the other Unions would follow their lead and do likewise.

I had to apologize to the fucking wimp and strangely enough I never saw that guy again all day. I think perhaps that was a good thing, or there may well have been a strike, a fucking big strike, probably from me!

We were now all over the place on this tour and thankfully we were back in the US and on our way down the East Coast to the

Brendan Byrne Arena which was right across the road from the old Giants Football Stadium in New Jersey.

I once did a gig at Giants Stadium with a band called Little Steven and The Disciples of Soul, and they were as serious as there name suggests, Steven himself been guitarist in Bruce Springsteen's band and was nonsmoking, non-drinking and non-humorous, so I didn't last long with that lot.

We were supporting U2, and in the afternoon during the U2 sound check I went up into the top tier of the stadium, which must have been 30 story's in the elevator and standing in the back row at the top of the stadium almost looked like a sheer drop down to the field below and the people were like little ants scurrying around, why the fuck you would want to watch football from up there I don't know, you would hardly be able to see the players never mind the fucking ball.

The record attendance at Giants Stadium was actually for a U2 gig in 2009, with an attendance of 84,472, closely followed by his Holiness Pope John Paul II in 1995 with an attendance of 82,948.

So on to Madison Square Gardens in the heart of Manhattan, which was another notoriously difficult arena to work in with about twenty five different Unions taking the equipment from sitting in a truck to making a gig, but this time I kept my mouth shut, one of the rare occasions.

We were now getting near the end of the tour and we were literally all over the place, both personally and physically.

We went back down to the Carolinas, up and over to the Midwest again, back into Canada again, this time out into the wilds of Manitoba and Saskatchewan, Alberta and finally over to British Columbia on the West Coast, which was all really pretty ride. We

ROCK 'N' ROLL
It's Better than Working for a Living

then finished off the tour by going down into California and Nevada and my favorite city of Las Vegas and after playing the stinking Cow Palace (The name, of course gives away what the stink was.), in San Francisco we ended up at another of my favorite gigs, the outdoor amphitheater known as Irvine Meadows in Orange County about 45 miles South of Los Angeles, and the gig where I almost strangled the drummer last time we played there.

Rod Smallwood, the longtime manager of Iron Maiden was now running his highly successful empire from the new house he had just bought in Hollywood and with the gig at Irvine Meadows been the last gig of the American tour, Rod was going to host a party for band and crew at his new house the following evening.

With the gig at Irvine Meadows been on the 2nd May and the next gig been the start of yet another Japanese tour on the 11th. May, all the band and crew had a choice between staying in Los Angeles for a week at The Hyatt House Hotel on Sunset (Known in the business as The Riot House, for obvious reasons.) or flying back to London for the week with the band paying for the return flight back to Los Angeles to connect with the flight to Tokyo. I decided that it would probably be much safer if I went back to London for the week, as will be shown by my behavior on having just one night off in Los Angeles.

Rod's new house was just off Sunset Boulevard, on Wetherly Drive, which was the last turning on the left heading East on Sunset before you came to the infamous watering hole known to everyone in the Rock 'n' Roll business as The Rainbow Bar and Grill, or simply The 'Bow.

There were many of these Rock 'n' Roll watering holes around the world, but mainly in the UK and US, I've already mentioned The Peppermint Lounge in New York and there was a club in the centre of London where I went many times, called The

Speakeasy. These clubs were where you would find the off duty Rock 'n' Rollers on days off or after a gig. There were three specific nights I remember down the "Speak'" as it was fondly known, and as always with these long gone legendary clubs, everybody who was anybody played there.

It was in the centre of London town just off Oxford Street in a very respectable part of town and was just a glass entrance door between a row of shops leading down into the basement, but this was no grubby, dirty basement, the place was clean and well furnished.

It was no good going down to the Speak until at least 1am, when all the musos and crew were on their way back from the gig or had got thrown out of the pubs.

The first time Salli and I went down there was with my old mate Graham Reynolds, Motorhead's roadie, who was a member. You had to be a member of course as it was a private drinking club, or you had to know somebody or even be somebody, but once the reception people got to know your face and knew you were in the business they would always let you in.

A part of the furnishings was a polished wooden coffin stood upright in the reception area and one evening when we went down there, there was this guy sat on the floor leaning against this coffin with his head in his hands. This was a weird looking long white haired guy, white haired but not old only a young guy, an albino in fact, now I'd seen an albino rabbit but never an albino human, this was American guitar player; Johnny Winter.

The club had a restaurant area which apparently served really good food, and a bar/performance area, though nobody really listened to the bands, people down here at this time of night were either out of their heads on speed, alcohol or cocaine or usually

ROCK 'N' ROLL
It's Better than Working for a Living

all three and conversation was the most important thing, so the bands usually only played about 45 minutes and lots of famous bands played early sets there with nobody listening to them; Hendrix, Deep Purple, Pink Floyd, Thin Lizzy, Marc Bolan etc.

We stayed for about three hours that night and saw Jeff Beck, John Bonham, Phil Lynott, Lemmy and lots of other nighttime Rock 'n' Roll people and as we were leaving we walked through the small reception area and Johnny Winter was still motionless on the floor leaning against the coffin, probably wishing he were in it.

After a few visits we were now members and spent a lot of time and money down there and one night Salli and I went down there after the pubs closed and met Graham sitting at the bar talking to Jeff Beck and all the other regular suspects were there, Bonham, Lynott, Bolan, Lemmy etc.

Salli and I had had a lot of speed that night so we spent a lot of time drinking and talking to anybody and probably everybody.

Salli was off chatting up some rock star or other and I was sat next to Graham at the bar when he stuck a little brown medicine bottle under my nose and said; "have a good sniff of this stuff," "go on take a good sniff," Wow! "What the fuck is that I said," "Amyl Nitrate," said Graham.

Amyl Nitrate is a drug that has been used in the treatment of Angina, but has been used as a stimulant on the club scene since the 1970's and these days are sold in the guise of "poppers." It was associated with the Acid House club scene in the 1990's but is now more associated with the Gay scene.

It is a drug that vaporizes on contact with air and sniffing it gives you an instant "hit." Your heart starts beating a thousand beats to the minute and you suddenly feel fantastic and invincible, the problem is like many drugs you've got to keep doing it because the high only lasts a couple of minutes, but along with all the speed I had consumed that night, I was almost shaking and drinking like a fish and couldn't stop talking.

I only ever took Amyl that one night when Graham gave me some, because that shit felt fucking dangerous, even at 27 years of age I felt like a heart attack waiting to happen.

These nitrates or nitrites including Amyl are still on sale legally and are sold as "Room Deodorizes," they don't smell very nice and of course that's not what they're used for, but sold as "Room Deodorizes" they're legal.

It's a fucking weird state of affairs isn't it? Something you drink and makes you incapable of standing up and makes most people really aggressive and makes people believe they can drive and then crash and kill people, something that you can sniff as much as you like of and could cause serious heart problems and instant death are LEGAL!, yet something that you smoke and relaxes you and makes you sleep well and eat well and makes you genuinely a nice person is ILLEGAL!!!!!!!!!!

Do these people who regulate these things know what they are doing? I don't fucking think so!

Another time we went down to The Speak, we were told that Neil Young was going play a set down there, he had that night done a gig with his band Crazy Horse at The Royal Festival Hall.

As we went into the club we looked in the restaurant to see if there was anyone we knew in there and saw Neil Young sat at a table with a bunch of other people, but we didn't see anyone we knew so we went into the bar.

About thirty minutes later a band and a couple of roadies appeared on the small stage and started plugging in guitars and tuning up. This went on for a little while as you can imagine, then they seemed to be ready. This was Neil Young's band of course and they were obviously waiting for Neil to come up on stage, and they stood there for about twenty minutes until someone announced; "As soon as we find Neil you'll here Neil Young and Crazy Horse at The Speak." Couldn't be that hard to find Neil, it wasn't exactly a big club, but eventually someone did find him. The reason he had been so elusive was that he had been sat at the table in the restaurant, but when the rest of the band got up from the table, Neil been on his own and as drunk as a funky skunk he had slipped off of his chair under the table and was passed out on the floor under fucking the table!

They eventually managed to get him out from under the table and on to stage and a roadie handed him his guitar, which he had already tuned for him but Neil insisted on re-tuning it himself, which proved to be an impossible task in the state he was in.

After about another forty minutes of inane and incomprehensible waffling into the mic and his continued attempts to tune an already in tune guitar, which he had by now comprehensively detuned again, he said he was satisfied and the band launched into Cowgirl in The Sand.

A world famous Neil Young anthem, played tonight without Neil Young! But with some drunk guy shouting into the mic at the front of the stage and trying to play a completely out of tune guitar, very badly.

This piece of musical phenomena lasted a whole 45 minutes, by which time everyone in the club had long ago lost the will to live and Neil was helped off stage and thankfully that was the culmination of the night's entertainment.

Back in Los Angeles in May 1987, "Somewhere on Tour," the crew that were going to Japan and the band were at Rod Smallwood's new house for an end of tour party, which were usually affairs where you found you usually had to apologize the next day for your behavior the night before, but tonight seemed a more sedate affair.

Rod was immensely proud of his new house, which put most people on their best behavior, and rightfully Rod should have been proud of his house as it had once belonged to famous Hollywood movie gangster; Jimmy Cagney.

It was all a very polite scene with drinks and canapés and it didn't look as though there was going to be much Sex and Drugs and Rock 'n' Roll going on tonight.

Wetherly Drive where Rod's house was swung to the right a hundred yards or so after turning off Sunset and Rod's house was right on the corner. I don't know whether he was aware of this when he bought it, but the garden at the side of the house backed on to The Rainbow and The Whiskey (which was next door) parking lots. I just thought about this as I wrote it, of course he knew it did!

Bruce, the singer had the same idea as me, as there was not much action at Rod's place, about 10.30pm we both decided to go to The Bow, so we jumped over the fence at the side of the garden, and we were there! How fucking easy was that?

I was originally employed as monitor engineer to keep Bruce happy with the on stage sound but also I became his ally in the noise power struggle I saw on stage between Steve's bass guitar volume and Bruce's voice.

Bruce was a happy bunny as I was a good enough engineer to make his voice as loud if not louder than Steve's bass guitar and we even became sort of mates, in fact our respective partners even socialized when both Bruce and I were away on tour. Bruce and I

ROCK 'N' ROLL
It's Better than Working for a Living

didn't really socialize that much on tour, but tonight we decided to go to The Bow together.

The waitress had recognized us as been from Iron Maiden, maybe the accents were a bit of a giveaway, so we got a table immediately even though it was pretty busy. Our waitress introduced herself to us, although she didn't have to me.

I knew who she was; I'd been in here and seen her before.

Her name was Loretta. Loretta was a legend at The Bow; she'd been there since the dawn of time although she was only about thirty years of age.

You come to the Bow, you want some cocaine, you see Loretta, you order your drinks and your cocaine comes back with your drinks, what fantastic service.

I don't know if it was a management thing or whether it was Loretta's own self-made business, but everybody came to see Loretta, except Bruce, who didn't take drugs.

I went upstairs to the restrooms to stick some of Loretta's finest up my nose. I'd forgotten though none of the toilet cubicles in the Bow have doors on them, so no one bothers using them anyway, they just stand in the restroom and stick it up their nostrils.

Bruce's company was getting pretty boring as he tended to talk about himself quite a bit, but there was what seemed to be some kind of record company party going on in the Bow that night and I had noticed a lovely blonde chick sitting in one of the booths with about eight other people. After a little eye contact she came over and asked if we wanted to join them, so we did.

At this point my memory gets a little sketchy and large lumps of time go missing.

I remember Bruce holding court with a couple of people and waffling on about himself and going on and on and on and on I wasn't interested of course; I wasn't interested in anything except the blonde chick. I remember taking a few sniffs in the restrooms, I remember drinking a lot, I remember this chick had a car, I remember us getting back to my room at The Hyatt, I remember drinking and sniffing quite a bit more, the rest I don't remember at all.

Well actually that's not bad really, seems to cover everything except the gory details, don't know what happened to Bruce.

I woke at about 9am when the blonde chick was leaving; she had to go to work. Never did remember her name, so if you're still out there, Email me!

9am! Fuck me! I had a flight to London at 11am. With a swift check out and some skillful, scary taxi driving somehow I made the flight, but that was just an example of the kind of trouble I would have probably got into every night if I had have stayed in LA for a week, I would have been fucked, fucked up and broke!

So seven days later and I was back in LA with just a hint of jetlag and then a quick overnight in The Hyatt and next morning off to Tokyo, which was going to be somewhere around 15 hours with a stopover in Hawaii, so it was going to be painful but not quite as painful probably as staying in LA. For that week.

The first gig in Japan was in Nagoya and about a three hour trip on the Bullet Train from Tokyo and then the same trip back the next day for a day off in Tokyo.

We had two gigs in Tokyo in different venues with another fucking day off in between. I hated those days off in Tokyo, all you do was spend lots of money, if it wasn't on breakfast it was on the latest Sony Walkman yes a Sony Walkman!, down in the Akihabara district, which was an area of about ten square blocks in the center of the city which was just all electronics shopping

ROCK 'N' ROLL
It's Better than Working for a Living

malls. I'd love to go around there now; I'd probably spend a year's salary in a couple of hours.

The first gig was at the world famous Budokan arena which was probably the most famous gig in Japan. Originally built in 1964 as a Martial Arts venue, the first band ever to play there were The Beatles in Summer 1966 and since that time it became synonymous with bands doing live recordings there including; Bob Dylan, Ozzy Osbourne and Deep Purple's legendary "Made in Japan" album.

Amazingly we played The Budokhan on 13th May 1987 and I was back home in London just over a week later. The day after I got home Salli and I were walking around Camden market in North London and I stopped at a stall selling audio cassettes (no C.Ds in those days remember) and I was looking at the titles and they were all bootleg albums, all illegally recorded of course, and I came across one called; "Iron Maiden Live at The Budokan 13th May 1987." How cool was that? Eight days after the gig, 9000 miles away, to a live album commercially on sale on a Camden market stall.

After the gigs in Tokyo we were back on the Bullet Train on our way down to the gig in the old capital city of Japan, Kyoto and another fucking day off.

Personally when in Japan I'd just like to do the gigs back to back without any days off and get the fuck out of there, but no, we had a day for sightseeing in Kyoto, which is quite pretty in places, in a kind of Japanese kind of way.

The next day though we did have a gig and a flight this time, on All Nippon Airways, which still makes me, laugh. All Nippon this end, then All Nip off at the other end.

We were on our way to the historic city of Hiroshima. Hiroshima as everyone who hasn't been on another planet for the last

100 years knows, was the first and one of only two attacks ever with a nuclear weapon, when a US air force B29 Super fortress bomber dropped an atomic bomb on Hiroshima on August 6th 1945 and a second one was dropped on the city of Nagasaki three days later. It's estimated 200,000 people may have died in the two attacks. Nuclear weapons have never been used in warfare since that time.

Although Hiroshima is a comparatively new city obviously as over 70% of it was destroyed by the bomb, it's pretty spooky when you walk around The Peace Memorial and park.

After the gig in Hiroshima we went back to the hotel to find that the rooftop bar was still open, well only just open, there were just some American voices coming from one corner and nobody else in the place, so we went up to the bar and ordered enough drinks to keep us up for a couple of hours, when there was suddenly this shout from across the room; "Hey!, my man." I turned around to see Lionel Richie approaching with outstretched hand, "How are you doing my man?" I'd worked with Lionel in The Commodores eight years before and he'd remembered the best monitor engineer he'd ever had, of course. He was doing the same gig we'd just done, the next day.

"Of all the people, in all the bars, in the entire world!" A lovely guy!

We only had two more gigs to do on the whole tour, with the obligatory day off of course, just to make sure you didn't go home with any money in your pocket.

So it was back on The Bullet Train this time to Osaka, where we were doing two shows at The Festival Hall. After another ride on the Bullet Train and another day off it felt great to be going to the last gig the next day.

ROCK 'N' ROLL
It's Better than Working for a Living

In Japan there is a strange phenomenon whereby the crew with a band are almost as famous as the band and do have their own fans and today as we arrived at the Festival Hall in Osaka a large crowd of girls crowded around our bus and as we got off we all had to sign autographs on shirts on hands and on tour programmes.

Just as we were going through the doors into the arena I heard my name called; "Mick, Mick." I turned and saw this tall gorgeous Japanese chick who was calling my name and I wondered if I knew her, but I would have definitely remembered if I knew HER. Then I realized she knew my name from the photographs and names in the tour program, as Iron Maiden always put the names and photographs of the crew in the program. I stopped to talk to her; I mean you had to really.

She wasn't like the other girls hanging around the gig, for a start she was tall and with an amazing body, which is different from most Japanese women who are small and petite and she was also a bit older than the other kids that were around. She told me her name was Hiromi or Ria and it was definitely love at first bite as I arranged to come and find her after the gig.

I spent two days with Ria and she was just a little bit different from all the others on the road, she gave me her address, but I never wrote, but I think maybe I could have left home for her, not to live in Japan of course, but she was very sweet.

Two days later I was back home in London.

Iron Maiden's manager Rod also managed a new band called Zodiac Mindwarp and The Love Reaction (which I thought was a very catchy name) who were a greasy, rockers, bikers type of band with boots and leather and studs and Nazi helmets, but were in fact a bunch of normal educated guys who all took on alter egos like; Cobalt Stargazer, Trash D. Garbage etc., and of course Zodiac Mindwarp.

Dick the Maiden production manager was going to take them out on a small promotional tour of the US, just doing small clubs and using house sound systems and he'd asked me if I wanted to go out and do the monitor sound for them, it wasn't going to be the same money as I was making with Maiden, but using house systems there wasn't much work involved either and as I was free until September until Maiden went on tour again, so I agreed. We also did a few crappy gigs in England which were quite fun. This band had no rock star egos, probably average talent but was a lot of fun and really nice people.

We flew to Toronto for the first gig and had a day off there before we played the at a famous little club called El Mocambo, which has been a venue since the dawn of time and still is and is probably most famous for a warm up show there by The Rolling Stones before the start of a tour in 1977.

The day off in Toronto was good, I like Toronto, there's still a little bit of England there, Branston Pickle, Tetley tea bags, HP Sauce and Marks and Spencer's. That night we decided to go out to a rock club of course, what do rock n roll people do on a night off?, go to a rock club.

This was Rock n Roll Heaven, quite a clean, tidy place for a rock club; it was modern and even had a restaurant. We got talking to a couple of chicks and the blonde one was interesting me (of course) and we managed to persuade them to come back to our hotel with us and of course we asked them if they knew anyone who could get some cocaine, and of course they did!

Kathleen made a call to this guy who was round within an hour and a half.

ROCK 'N' ROLL
It's Better than Working for a Living

Kathleen was the blonde and Paul was the guy that came around, Kathleen and I had plenty of connections over the next couple of years and I still speak to Kathleen and Paul now 25 years on, though he is now a much respected Real Estate Agent and Kathleen is a successful restaurateur and mother of two boys.

That night when Paul came around to my room it seemed to fill up very rapidly and I think there must have been a dozen people there, all talking at the same time of course and nobody listening to what anyone else was saying.

Of course I just wanted them all to fuck off and leave me alone with Kathleen but that was never going to happen for a few hours, then suddenly there was a loud banging on the dividing wall between the adjacent room and everyone went quite or quieter anyway. There were also various visits from room service of course, keeping up the supply of alcohol and during one of these visits a couple of the band managed to sneak in at the same time.

God knows what time it was by then but it must have been around 3:00 a.m. Then there was some more scary banging on the wall from the room next door, so we all tried to quieten down a bit and then we heard a shout from the room next door; "Hi, it's me Cobalt" who was the guitar player, and I replied, "sorry about the noise man, I'll try and keep it quiet now"

Shortly after I managed to break up the party as it was getting daylight and we had a gig that day, luckily Kathleen stayed and her friend left with Paul I think.

I found out later that Kathleen was eighteen years old and I was thirty nine, Jackie in Newcastle had been twenty and I was thirty seven, there was a theme developing here and I thought it was pretty good for my ego.

The next day at the gig there were a lot of not very well people and I think I was one of the worst, but the Zodiac Mindwarp gig was easy and I could do it with my eyes closed so it wasn't too stressful and I went and apologized to Cobalt who was banging on the bedroom wall the night before and he said; "I wasn't complaining about the noise, it sounded great I wanted to come in!"

We only did nine or ten shows on this little promotional tour, but we did a few famous shit holes like The Bayou Club in Washington, The Cat Club in New York, the old Pony in San Francisco one of the early venues played by all those San Francisco psychedelic bands of the 1960's, The Whiskey in Hollywood where any Rock n Roller worth his salt or his cocaine must have hung out at some time in his career, and of course right next door to the "Bow," my personal favorite bar in the whole world. We also played the first gig I ever did in America; The Paradise Club in Boston.

There were a couple of other gigs but all instantly forgettable and I didn't get into too much trouble on this little tourette but did manage to have a couple of nights with friends with a small pile of white powder on the table.

In April 1988 Iron Maiden started rehearsals for the next world tour at a rehearsal complex in Koln, Germany. It was actually an old factory complex which had been converted into various rehearsal rooms and also a club by a German musician called Dieter something or other.

We had a whole month there before setting off for the start of The Seventh Tour of a Seventh Tour, loosely named after their current album called Seventh Son of a Seventh Son, which makes slightly more sense than Seventh Tour of a Seventh Tour.

We settled into the daily ritual of turning on the amps at the start of the day and turning them off after rehearsals had finished

ROCK 'N' ROLL
It's Better than Working for a Living

and trying to find some mind numbing tasks to perform whilst the band got some sort of show together.

Some of the most boring days of my life have occurred in rehearsal studios and this was no exception. We had tried to spice life up a little by getting Dieter to find us some cocaine to pass the time; of course Dieter was up for this task and came up with lots of promises but never seemed to come up with the goods.

At the end of the rehearsal period the band had asked Dieter if he would like them to do two shows in the little club in the complex, free of charge, and everyone decided that would be a fantastic idea and give a good indication of how the show would flow.

As we were off to America for the first leg of the tour and were going to be away for over three months and flying straight from Frankfurt to New York, lots of wives and girlfriends had come over for the last week of rehearsals and the two gigs in the club.

My girlfriend Salli and I were in the club on the first night, which was filling rapidly and as there was no support act and the band didn't go on until about 9pm, we had lots of time to stand at the bar and drink, and we did and drinks were free for us, which Salli took advantage of.

When she was drunk Salli was the happiest drunk you have ever seen, but if something upset here, you didn't want to be in the same room. Nicko the band's drummer came over to the bar for a chat and recognized Salli as they had met before when he was in the English band, Streetwalkers.

As the conversation progressed and the drinks flowed I became aware that Salli held the same views about Nicko as I did; that he was a bit of a dickhead, in fact a lot of a dickhead!

The conversation got around to the stick throwing and dragging the drummer over the console incident from the first tour I did but I never saw this coming at all. As Nicko was trying to justify why he threw the stick at me and then got dragged across the console by me, I could see Salli listening and then she suddenly said to Nicko; "sounds like you deserved to be dragged over the console, asshole."

I was cringing now as Nicko said; "fucking hell, you're as bad as your old man."

Then I thought no Nicko leave it, you're never going win this one.

The next thing I knew I turned to pick up my drink from the bar and heard a thump and a scream of pain from Nicko as Salli's boot hit Nicko's genitals with the force of a club hammer.

The guy was bent over in pain and cursing as Salli said; "Now fuck off shit head!"

She was such a tender flower.

I never had a cross word from Nicko ever again and I kept the job!

We had to pack up all the equipment after the club gigs as we had a lunchtime flight from Frankfurt to New York the next day, but we had it all done by about 12.30am. It was at this point that Dieter honored is promise and dropped a quarter of an ounce of cocaine in our hands, what timing!

We had seven grams of cocaine between about six of us to get through by about 9.am the next morning and get some sleep and pack to get on a flight at midday. I can honestly say that was one of the most confusing nights of my life as people were throwing white powder out all over the place in everybody's room. Whilst some people tried to pack their luggage, nobody seemed to pick

ROCK 'N' ROLL
It's Better than Working for a Living

the sleep option and we managed to get through seven grams by the time we left for the airport at 9am, but I didn't feel too well on that flight at all, along with quite a few others.

Charlotte and The Harlots was a pseudonym Iron Maiden used when they did little club gigs, usually as warm up gigs before a big tour.

We were going to do a famous old rock club called; L'amours in Brooklyn. I knew it was going to be a shit gig and it was.

The watch word for the day was "compromise" It was a small stage with not enough room for all the backline obviously and the huge drum riser. I didn't have my own console, I didn't have my own monitors and as is always the case with American club systems, half of their monitors didn't work.

So everybody agreed to compromise to help us all get through the gig without too many traumas, and this is what happened.

Although the stage was only a little over 20 feet wide each guitar player and the bass player had two Marshall stacks each and the full drum riser and I had half a fucking working monitor system!

Consequently the guitarists played almost as loud as normal, Steve's bass was just about the loudest thing on stage and Bruce couldn't hear his vocals. Nobody fucking compromised, everybody got upset and it was a fucking shambles. Kel Surprise!!!

To spare the reader the day to day nuts and bolts of our life on the road with a big rock band I just intend to pick out highlights and some lowlights of the next seven and a half month tour (It's that seven thing again, never noticed that before.) as I think you all get the picture by now.

We started this time in Canada, which is going to bring me quickly to a highlight.

I called Kathleen as soon as we got to the hotel in Toronto on a day off before doing the old Exhibition showground in Toronto. Kathleen arrived in the afternoon with a wallet full of cocaine and we went out and met a few friends of hers and did a pub and club crawl around downtown Toronto and probably ended up back at my hotel at about 4.am. We did the gig the next day at the old showground and it was a lovely hot Spring day and I felt like shit, but by the time I met Kathleen again after the show I had recovered enough to be able to manage a little more partying.

It was a two day drive to the next gig in Winnipeg Manitoba and a really scenic drive but I decided I was going to stay in Toronto with Kathleen for another two days and get a 28 dollar Wardair flight from Toronto to Winnipeg on the day of the gig. 28 dollars! How mad is that?

The next two days were a bit of a blur really, Kathleen and friend Paul just arrived at my hotel both days with bags full of cocaine and off we went, we were out until daylight and I didn't realize it at the time but I think Kathleen had dug herself into a nasty cocaine habit from what she's told me since then.

I have one abiding memory from those four days and that was sitting in a Mexican restaurant on Yonge Street in the middle of the night drinking huge jugs of Margaritas, maybe because it was the only place open selling alcohol.

We were doing quite a few outdoor shows and "sheds" on this tour which was never fun with Bruce, as I said earlier he likes to hear his voice echoing around an arena, so I was having to use reverb and echo on his voice in the monitors, which went against all my own rules of keeping the signals in the monitors clean and to be truthful, I don't think it ever really worked properly.

ROCK 'N' ROLL
It's Better than Working for a Living

Most of the outdoor shows were in the West like; Cal Expo in Sacramento, which was the California State Fair, Shoreline Amphitheater outside of San Francisco, built by legendary local promoter Bill Graham who was responsible for all the famous Filmore concerts in the 1960's and 70's and Shoreline was supposed to be opened with a concert by the infamous Grateful Dead in 1986, but guitar player Jerry Garcia was hospitalized and in a diabetic coma, so guess they didn't make it.

We were also doing Irvine Meadows Amphitheater again, scene of the stick throwing/drummer's ass kicking event and a place called Compton Terrace in Arizona, owned by singer from Fleetwood Mac Stevie Nick's father and probably the hottest outdoor show I have ever done. Temperature recorded in the afternoon was 126degF/52degC.

I would have the chromium mic stands standing out on the stage in the afternoon, in order for me to EQ the mics and Bruce's had been standing out there about 15 minutes, with no shade, I just went up and grabbed it to get the mic and immediately let go and looked at the burn marks on my hand, that was a hot day.

Alpine Valley Amphitheater in Wisconsin (just) was the biggest outdoor amphitheater holding 37,000 people up until 1993 when the San Manuel Amphitheater was built in San Bernardino California and holding 65,000 people and is still the largest in the US.

I actually played Alpine Valley a couple of years later with Motley Crue and only four weeks before Stevie Ray Vaughn's helicopter hit a ski jump whilst leaving the gig.

Because we had done so many gigs in the US on the last two tours and on this one also, we were drifting into a few "B" circuit gigs, which were still arena sized gigs but in different towns from what we had done before, a few examples are; the Five Seasons

Center in Cedar Rapids, Iowa, Battelle Hall, Columbus Ohio, the Dow Events Center, Saginaw, Michigan and my personal favorite, the Mid-Hudson Civic Center in Poughkeepsie, New York, where a very strange thing happened.

Poughkeepsie is a small city in New York State and the Mid-Hudson Civic Center is the shit hole we played in that city.

It's a 1970's concrete convention center and only holds about 3,500 people and was probably the smallest place we played on the whole tour. It was in July when we did this gig and it was a really hot day, but Bruce would not have the air conditioning on at gigs, as he would sweat profusely whilst diving around during the show and then when he stopped diving around he would start feeling cold from the air conditioning and thought he would automatically catch a cold. I have never completely been convinced by his logic on this matter as it has never been proven in research on the common cold that being cold contributes to getting a cold as the common cold is actually a virus that you catch from someone else or spores in the air that you breathe.

I also believe there was another solution to this problem he had with air conditioning. If you had the air conditioning on from the start it would be much colder in the arena therefore you wouldn't sweat so much anyway therefore when you stopped diving around you wouldn't be so hot so the air conditioning wouldn't feel so cold. Makes sense to me! I didn't like it either been so hot in the arenas, it used to melt my cocaine, or whatever was in it used to melt!

This day in Poughkeepsie you really needed the air conditioning; it was a roasting summer's day and really hot in the gig during the afternoon when setting up the equipment. I know some of these arenas you either had to have the A/C on all the time or

ROCK 'N' ROLL
It's Better than Working for a Living

off all the time, which was hilarious when they couldn't turn the AC off, just to watch Bruce going ballistic because there was a breeze blowing.

Unfortunately this day I think he had the last laugh as they had to have the AC off all day, so it was off for the gig, so it was fucking hot to start with. I walked on stage after the support band and it was roasting, it must have been 120 degrees Fahrenheit or whatever that is in Euros. I could even see the normally bouncing Bruce flagging a little with the heat during the show and about halfway through the show I just happened to look at my effects units in a rack to my right when I saw a firefighter standing next to me!

"Where's the fire at man?" he asked.

"What fire?" I replied. I then realized that the heat in the gig had set off the fire alarms and automatically called out the local firefighters. That was a fucking hot day!

As we were nearing the last few weeks of the tour it was also getting hotter and hotter as we headed down to Georgia, Texas, Louisiana and Florida. We did a gig in Tampa, Florida called the Sun Dome, which I remember was one place where they would not turn off the A/C for Bruce. Nobody turns off the A/C in Florida, you die!

The Sun Dome was the first major permanent arena with a blow up roof. It had what looked like a canvas roof which was kept inflated by the whole place been pressurized, bit like been in an airplane. That might not have worked too well if the A/C had been turned off and all that cool pressurized air been replaced by hot air from the arena. The place might have fucking exploded! It was replaced in 2000 by a Teflon coated roof supported by a steel space frame.

When we arrived at our hotel in Daytona Beach on a day off before the gig there was a message for me. Kathleen from Toronto was in the same hotel. She had flown down from Toronto to see me and had even guessed what hotel we were staying at.

No she hadn't! Somehow she found out what hotel we were at. I don't know how, but it used to happen a lot.

We spent five days together as she came on the bus with me through Florida and back up to Maryland. We were like boyfriend and girlfriend, which was not what I had planned at all. She did tell me later that was what she wanted, but would that ever have worked out? She was 19 and I was 41, who knows? She would now be living with a really old guy now.

She flew back to Toronto from the gig in Maryland. I've never seen her since, although we do speak now thanks to Facebook. She still talks about those times together, and that is the last fucking sad story I am ever going to tell!!!!!!!!!!!

Four days later I was back in London. Although Salli and I were having yet another rough period, it felt good to be home.

Chapter Fifteen

MONSTERS0

The Monsters of Rock Festival at Donnington Park in the Eng-lish countryside was going to be the big event of this tour. The gig was only nine days after we had left America, so it was a very tight schedule to get all the equipment shipped back from America and rigged at Donnington.

I made a couple of journeys up to the festival sight to make sure they had my console position in the correct place on the stage. I took my four year old Metalhead stepson, Morgan with me. He is in the photos on pages 411 and 412. He resembled a born Rock 'n' Roller with his shoulder length hair. He had a great day. It is one he's always remembered when he took the stage at The Monsters of Rock Festival. His legs astride, mic in hand and Pussycat Willum under his arm!!!!!!!!!!!!

Pussycat Willum was Morgan's toy cat / teddy bear who went everywhere with him . . . even to the Monsters of Rock Festival. At twenty eight, Morgan is still an Iron Maiden fan.

We did a warm up gig with Charlotte and The Harlots at Queen Mary's College in East London two days before the show, which I absolutely hated. I had lost patience with Bruce and his silly ways and told him to fuck off during the show. I had spent too much money on cocaine and I had got too fucked up every

ROCK 'N' ROLL
It's Better than Working for a Living

Morgan at Donnington - 1988.

Morgan earning his stripes at Donnington – 1988.

night. Salli and I were once again having problems with our relationship. I felt I was self-destructing somewhat, but I still had the job. Surprisingly, and I loved the job. I also think I may have been in love with the idea of a 19 year old girl in Toronto.

The Monsters of Rock gig was a huge success. That is . . . apart from the sight of the two guys trampled to death in the moshe pit in front of the stage during Guns and Roses set.

I got disgustingly off my head after the show in the bar at the Novotel and in various peoples rooms. Salli was disgusted with my behavior. It had been a long harrowing day. It's not every day you see two people trampled to death during a gig!

My head hurt for a few days after the indulgence at Donnington. We had a week off before we set for Europe and still had about two and a half months to go on the tour; which was going to include about six weeks around Europe and a month in the UK, so there was still quite a bit of work to do.

Touring Europe is so much harder than touring the US. Every day you are in an arena holding somewhere with between 8 to 15,000 people. They all sound like indoor parking lots. So, you know what you're going to get before you walk in there, except Rosemont Horizon of course. And, each day in Europe could be a basketball arena, could be a theatre, and could be a convention center or a city hall. Plus on this tour they'd thrown a few festivals in just to confuse our ever diminishing little gray cells.

I don't think my heart was really in the job it after the Monsters gig. This was really strange for me as it was a job I'd always loved doing and is still a great passion for me.

There's just a great feeling of achievement and satisfaction after a good gig, doesn't really matter who the band is. I just wanted to get Europe out of the way as quick as possible and get back to the UK. The UK was going to be fine. I knew the venues. I knew many of the people at the venues. I wasn't that far from home, anywhere in the country.

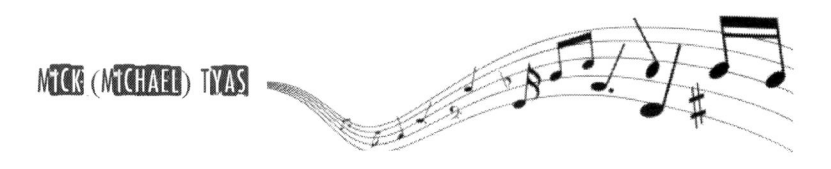

Three nights in Edinburgh was going to be nice. A nice city and I knew the crew and the venue. Two nights in Manchester, I knew the venue and one of the crew guys got the best speed in the world . . . a testament to my hotel bar clearing performance the last time we were there.

There were a couple of "wildcard" gigs in there. The Newport Leisure Center, a small sports hall in a small town in Wales was one. It was a nice easy gig. Then, the shitiest most horrible gig I have ever done in the UK in my life . . . Whitley Bay Ice Rink! It was now the middle of November and this place was cold, dark, and dirty. And, half of the equipment wouldn't fit in there.

Whitley Bay is just north of Newcastle in the North East of England. I've seen it described in articles and blogs as a "seaside town" suggesting people spend some leisure time there, by the sea. When I was there, I never saw any sea or holidaymakers; all I saw was this rundown ice rink in the middle of a rundown housing estate. The show was awful and I just wanted to get back to London.

We had a week in London at the end of the tour. This was unusual as European tours usually finished at the gig furthest from home such as Helsinki or Athens or Palermo. It was usually a three day bus ride home afterwards.

We were doing two days at Hammersmith Odeon, fifteen minutes drive from home. Then we were moving to Wembley Arena for two days and then some bright spark added another final day back at Hammersmith Odeon.

I didn't care, it was fifteen minutes from home and it was the last gig. Literally, the last gig.

Chapter Sixteen

WAS THIS THE END?

The 12th of December 1988, was my last ever gig with Iron Maiden. Maiden were off the road for a long time so everyone was laid off except the guitar techs and drum techs who worked in the recording studios with them.

So 1989 was going to be tough financially for me. I had to go out and find some work. I'd been out of the market place for four years with Iron Maiden taking up 99% of my time. I was hoping a little time together would give Salli and me a chance to get our home life back together again.

We were a few months into 1989, and I was picking up bits and pieces of work, but not enough to pay the ever increasing mortgage. The mortgage rates in the UK rocketed to 15%, which doubled my mortgage payment within 6 months.

We were well and truly in a mess financially. Also, we had big credit card bills from the last four years when we were living the highlife (I am still paying for it!), thinking we could afford it.

One day, I got a call from Dick, Iron Maiden's production manager, telling me I wouldn't be needed on the next tour. I had been fired! Apparently, I had upset too many people on the last tour. I'm still not sure about that statement and who I had upset. I don't really recall upsetting anybody, I was maybe getting a little too big for my boots, but I don't think I seriously upset anyone. I did have that one occasion during the show where I had told Bruce "To shut the fuck up and get on with it . . ." but I don't think he even noticed. Anyhow, that was over six months before. I had dragged the drummer over the console, but that was over three years before.

I think I was just getting too expensive. I was the highest paid member of the crew and I had demanded to have an assistant as I had too much work to do. I had even threatened to resign if my assistant wasn't taken on the last Japanese tour. I think I was just costing too much money. So they got a Kiwi guy in from a sound company, who had been on the Monsters gig. I knew he wanted the job. He was probably willing to do it for half the price. I think he also did a small solo tour with Bruce, so Bruce already knew who he was. He was probably quite an attractive option financially.

I also read a headline a few months later that said; "Adrian Smith leaves Iron Maiden." That's not exactly what I heard from a couple of members of the crew.

I was told Adrian asked to have more of his songs included on the albums, to which Steve had told him, "If you write some better songs, they'll probably get on the album."

Adrian responded, "I have written some good songs, but they never get on the albums."

Then, on the spot, Adrian was fired!

Only one voice in that band!

Chapter Seventeen

1989 LIFE AFTER DEATH

Of my Iron Maiden career
Through an old friend I got the number of a guy that ran an Italian sound company called Nuevo Services. They were looking for a British monitor guy (Yes . . . because they are the best, and that's what the Artiste said to me!). They wanted me to go out on tour with a big Italian superstar called Zucchero. They were going to pay pretty good money, nothing close to what I was getting with Iron Maiden, but still pretty good.

This guy had a couple of English musos in the band and a couple of Americans. He spoke English so there were no language problems. The equipment was pretty crappy, but I managed to make something of it.

One thing I had to sort out was the travel arrangements. The first tour, which mercifully was no more than about six weeks, saw six of us were traveling in a Fiat van. We were doing three hundred mile drives every day. It was a fucking nightmare. Just trying to get the Italians out of the gig was a nightmare.

One of the big problems was that no one ever seemed to know what time the show was going to start. After the sound check, which usually ended about six thirty we would go to a local bar for some pasta and wine.

ROCK 'N' ROLL
It's Better than Working for a Living

I would ask Paulo the main sound guy, at what time the band was going on. The answer would come back, "Oh, maybe 8:00 p.m. or 8:30 or maybe 9:00 or 9:30, when Zucchero is ready." It was a two hour show, so at the end of the show we just derigged the equipment and some other crew guys loaded it. We would usually get in the van about 1:00 p.m., as the show never started before 9:00 p.m. Then then the Italians had to say Ciao! To just about every local guy left in the gig before we eventually got out of the gates.

We would go to a restaurant then for another meal and would sit there guzzling food and wine until about 3.30 a.m. before retiring to our hotel, which we could never find. So we never ever got to bed before 4:00 a.m. We had to be up at eight to drive 300 miles to the next gig. Maybe they could have fitted the food and wine in somewhere else in the day, maybe while we were waiting for the fucking show to start, instead of when we were supposed to be sleeping.

The start of that first tour, I was picked up at Milan airport the day of the gig by the local Italian sound guys. We drove up North up to Bergamo heading towards The Alps and Swiss border. We got there about lunchtime. Although it was a beautiful place, there were high winds blowing at the gig site. It was a great site in a big open field with mountains in the background.

As we drove into the site there was a big scaffolding stage with what was called a Thomas tower at each corner. It was about 40 feet high with a large square aluminum structure attached to it covered with a canvas roof and bracing struts underneath the roof that you would hang the lighting rig off of.

I'd seen the same structure many times at outdoor festivals. They were completely safe structures. There was an electric motor at the top of each tower with a long chain attached to the roof structure. The four motors would be started simultaneously and lift the roof structure up the four towers until it was as high as you wanted it.

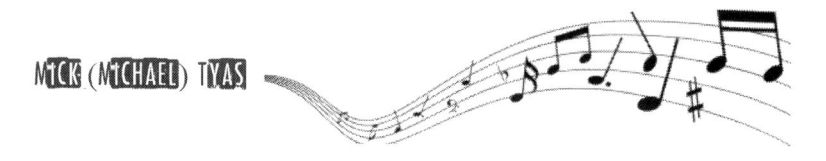

Normally, this is a very safe piece of kit. On this day, the crew was very worried about lifting the roof with the high winds blowing. So . . . the roof was sat on the stage when we arrived; however, you cannot rig the sound and band gear with the roof sitting on the stage. So, everyone who was anyone on the site stood and talked and discussed the situation for a couple of hours, as they do love a discussion in Italy. Everybody was a fucking expert and this went on and on.

At about 4:00 p.m. they were thinking of postponing the gig until the next day, but no decision had been made. By this time in the day I was fucking starving. I hadn't eaten since 7:00 a.m. So Paulo suggested we go into the town to a local bar for some food and wine (of course).

We did expect the gig to be postponed, as it was really fucking windy. We'd only been in the bar about twenty minutes when one of the local crew came running in shouting "Disaster! Disaster!" or Italian words to that effect.

He garbled something I didn't understand and Paulo said we had to leave. We piled in the van and quickly drove back to the site and what I saw just made me really angry. Two of the Thomas towers had collapsed and the roof laying halfway on the stage and half on the ground. What the fuck!

Apparently the local promoter had been told very sternly by the local Communist council, there was no way they could postpone the show. The site was being used for a big Communist rally the next day. "Either do the show or face the consequences," whatever they may have been. There was talk that the council would impound all the equipment if they did not do the show until the promoter paid something like 100,000,000,000,000 lire or fifty dollars!

The crew was told by the promoter to winch the roof up and carry on with the rigging. As they got it maybe twenty feet off of the stage a strong gust of wind got under the roof and just lifted it. The wind pushed it against two of the towers which collapsed under the strain. The roof smashed down on the left front corner of the stage where the PA was being stacked by the local crew. The roof smashed a few sound boxes; however, the worst news was one of the local crew was crushed under the roof and died instantly.

My next sentence was going to be and still is:

"It wouldn't have happened in a civilized country of course. They wouldn't have been able to have been pressurized to lift the roof in such a dangerous situation."

Unfortunately, this has not been true. There have been two major roof collapses at outdoor shows in North America, both in 2011.

One was at the Ottawa Bluesfest in Canada. The roof detached in a high gust of wind and landed on the stage whilst Cheap Trick was playing on stage. Luckily, there were no serious injuries. Once again this was down to wind and construction.

The more serious occurrence was at the Indiana State Fair in August 2011. This time a high gust of wind just virtually lifted the whole roof and wall structure of the stage and threw it in to the audience. There have been many technical reasons and excuses given for this tragedy. Managers and promoters and technicians knew what the weather forecast was, "There was a possibility of high winds." Someone in authority should have stopped the show. Many believe it was promoter pressure to get the show on so as not to lose money. In the end all they lost was five fucking lives and over forty injured!

The gig in Italy was, of course postponed, which proves the gig could have been postponed before the tragedy. Nobody fucking won. The promoter didn't get paid. The council didn't get paid. And, a family lost their son.

Zucchero contributed all proceeds from the re-arranged gig four weeks later to the family of the young local stagehand.

On the second tour in 1990 the Italians managed to get a little more organized. They rented a sleeper bus from England. I was the only Englishman, apart from the driver on the bus with eleven Italians, which was fine really except for days off.

The Italians were quite happy to live on the bus for the whole tour (They didn't have any choice.). I think the tour was only about two weeks, but I was used to having a hotel provided on days off. Someone at the management company forgot to organize it. So, they told me to find my own hotel on the days off and pay for it . . . they would reimburse me.

So, being one to take advantage of a favorable situation when it presented itself. In that small two week tour, I stayed in some of the best hotels I have ever stayed in, because I was booking them myself!

We actually did a full European tour with a totally British crew a few months later. That wasn't as interesting and entertaining as working with fifteen or twenty Italians, running around like chickens with their heads cut off.

I actually worked a really good deal on this tour and made a whole load of money from the Italian sound company and Zucchero's management.

The sound company was paying me independently for rigging the equipment. The management was paying me as Zucchero's monitor engineer. So . . . I was getting paid almost as much as on an Iron Maiden tour.

We also went to Moscow on this tour where they were going to do a live album called, *Zucchero Live in The Kremlin!*

This was two years after the alleged "Fall of Communism." Moscow didn't look much different to me than when I went there in 1989. The hotels still had pimps and hookers in the lounge and bars. The carpets still had holes in them. There was still nothing on the TV and nothing in the shops. There were still armed guards outside Pizza Hut and MacDonald's and the taxis still had no suspension.

There were a few more Mercedes and BMW's around the streets, but most people who could afford a car were still driving Czechoslovakian and Russian rust buckets.

Chapter Eighteen

MEANWHILE — BACK IN THE KREMLIN

Going back to one of my hobbies of reading Cold War spy novels, I was now actually going inside the fucking Kremlin. How cool was that?

The gig was going to be in The Conference Hall of Deputies within The Palace of Congress. This is the place you always see on TV with these hundreds of stern faced, evil eyed delegates sat listening to some tyrant ranting on about Western civilization or whatever it is they rant on about these days.

The auditorium has about 3000 seats and a 130 foot wide stage. Seated on the stage is the hierarchy of the Russian political system, The Politburo. In front of their seats, high up in the ceiling out of sight is a three foot thick concrete and steel armor plated "bomb" curtain. This could be lowered in front of the Politburo seats and separate them from the rest of the Hall if ever there were any attack on the Russian parliament, which I believe there has been occasionally in the last two hundred years.

Positioned right in the center of all the Politburo chairs on the stage is the chair or rather throne. It looks much more regal than the other chairs. This is where the President or whatever he's called sits. At this time, it was Mikhail Gorbachev. On this day, I

ROCK 'N' ROLL
It's Better than Working for a Living

sat in the chair! I sat on the President of Russia's fucking throne, more coolness I believe!

We had stashed about a half ounce of dope from England in one of the flight cases. It was a little worrying on the first rehearsal day when we saw the local militia turn up with sniffer dogs. This would not be cool if these little pooches sniffed out half an ounce of best Moroccan hashish resulting in twenty years in the Gulags of Siberia. It was not a very comforting thought. Luckily, the little terriers were only looking for nasty firecrackers planted by men with strange sounding names, from strange sounding places.

They were explosives dogs.

I really enjoyed going to Russia a couple of times though. After all I had read in spy novels over the years it was really interesting to see the Lubyanka prison where the notorious KGB would hold and torture the supposed enemies of the state. The GUM department store, which looks more like a palace than a store which used to be just full of garbage in the Communist days was interesting too. These days it encompasses lots of Western designer goods.

I remember walking around there one day and coming across the electronics department. There weren't many X boxes or computers around. You could buy a build it yourself TV set. What a fucking clever idea that was! This did actually look quite a lot like the first TV my parents had in 1953. It was a wooden box, with a hole in it for the screen. They included a cathode ray tube, a chassis, lots of valves and resistors and rectifiers and other electronic crap. There was an instruction booklet about the thickness of the Old Testament. All you had to do was glue it all together, fantastic idea! It probably cost a year's salary to buy it and about another year to put it all together.

I wonder if anyone actually got one to work without it fucking exploding and killing half the family watching *I Love Lucy*.

I did actually come across the Art department whilst walking around that huge store that day. I wouldn't say it was exactly bursting to the seams with Rembrandts and Van Gogh's. I did see one interesting painting which caught my eye. This was a big picture, perhaps six feet wide by four feet deep, roughly about the size of your average Moscow apartment at the time.

It was a pastoral scene with lush green meadows in the foreground and beautiful rolling hills disappearing into the distance. There was a beautiful deep blue lake in the center. Sitting serenely on the surface of the beautiful stretch of water was a big black nuclear Akula Class fucking submarine! Only in Russia.

Actually traveling through Sheremetyevo airport in Moscow was another reminder of the romantic days of the Cold War. The amount of bureaucracy involved to actually get you on and off of a flight was astounding, Russia, of course, being the bureaucratic capital of the aviation world was followed closely by India. The US comes in a very poor third. There were probably nine or ten different pieces of paper you had to get stamped and signed by various "officials" before you could get on or off an aircraft.

I did actually ask one of our minders why there were so many different pieces of paper that had to be distributed to passengers and then collected by another bunch of people two hundred yards further on down the corridors. The minder's reply was, "Well, if they didn't have these documents to issue and collect, these people would have no jobs!"

That is typical Russian logic.

ROCK 'N' ROLL
It's Better than Working for a Living

Another first whilst in Russia was flying on the Russian state airline, Aeroflot or Aeroflop as it was sometimes known in the business. There is also the famous Aeroflot passenger joke . . .

Passenger to flight attendant, "Could I have a blanket please?"

Reply from attendant, "I'm sorry sir it's already being used by someone else."

We flew from St. Petersburg or Leningrad as it was then to Moscow. It was just over an hour's flight time or most of the afternoon by Aeroflot.

Leningrad airport was like a little local airport rather than the airport of the second biggest city in Russia. Of course, we needed all the bits of paper handed out by one person and collected by another, two hundred yards away. We eventually were herded into the lounge by the departure gate and sat waiting while they prepared the aircraft. It was then I noticed people jumping over a perimeter wall into the airport. I pointed this out to our minder and he just said, "People do that all the time."

Unbelievable, we go through ten different checkpoints with different documents collected and handed outside there are people jumping over a wall air on the side of the airport and nobody takes any fucking notice.

I noticed they had lots of buses at Leningrad airport also. Whilst we were sat in the departure lounge you saw them every couple of minutes whizzing past the windows. Weirdly no people were on them. All the aircraft seemed to be parked about 400 to 800 yards from the terminal. These buses were obviously to transport you from the departure gate to the aircraft.

When our aircraft was ready for boarding we were led out on to the tarmac and had to walk the four hundred yards to the aircraft. What was all that about? What was the fucking buses doing?

I didn't even bother asking our minder about this as I'm sure the answer would have been totally logical, to a Russian.

Inside the Aeroflot Tupolev TU 154, it was pretty much like any other aircraft I had ever been in. I had never ever been in an aircraft with holes and rips in the carpet. As I walked down the cabin I noticed brush strokes in the paintwork on the overhead lockers, it was hand painted on the inside!

I want to get on to food in Russia in a moment but I must first say that we weren't offered any on the flight to Moscow. I was actually very pleased about as this as it was the first aircraft I had ever been on where there were flies flying about inside the cabin. Still, it saved, flying all the way to Moscow yourself I suppose. The only refreshment we were offered on the flight was a bottle of mineral water. Rusty fucking mineral water, guess it must have had a load of iron in it, because there was fucking rust in the bottom of the bottle!

I have a couple of other little stories about food in Russia, I never actually ever came across anything so diabolical I couldn't eat it but nothing was ever fresh. We stayed in the Finlandia hotel in Leningrad, one of the best hotels in Leningrad. It would typically have chicken and fries and salad on the menu. Nothing ever seemed very fresh. The salad was always wilting. I'm sure the chicken was long since deceased.

A couple of days there was no milk in the hotel. A couple of us decided to take a trip to a local supermarket, which we soon found had nothing on the shelves. There were a few rusty tins of something or other and that was about it. The worst thing about the place was it just reeked of rotting food. There must have had some food there at some time or other.

ROCK 'N' ROLL
It's Better than Working for a Living

We were once taken out to dinner by the local promoter when we were in Moscow to what was reputably a top class restaurant in the city. I don't remember too much about the food that night, perhaps because of the amount of consumption of wine and vodka. Except perhaps there seemed to be quite a lot of beetroot, cabbage and certain mystery meats; all in all I think it was a pretty decent meal.

What I do remember was there were cats roaming around the restaurant picking up scraps dropped from the tables. Some people were even feeding them. There was cat pooh on the floor, pretty disgusting for a restaurant!

Being a smoker, I liked a cigarette with my vodka or brandy during and after the meal. There were no smoking bans in Russia in public places, so during the meal I asked a waiter for an ashtray. Sorry no ash trays sir, please use the floor!

I'd bumped into that good Old Russian logic again . . . if they had ash trays they would have had to pay someone to empty them. If the customer just used the floor as an ashtray, they had to sweep the floors anyway one presumed whilst cleaning the place, so two jobs done in one.

I once had what was called steak, fries and vegetables at a restaurant in Sheremetyevo airport in Moscow whilst killing time waiting for our flight back to the UK. It was a fabulous clean restaurant with ashtrays and no cats roaming around featuring fantastic early 1960's furniture. The food was ever so slightly misrepresented. The steak was once again some sort of mystery meat cooked to within a second of its life as food. The fries were like peelings from the potatoes, which had been thrown in the garbage. The half a dozen green beans were the nearest to the description in the menu. I loved this restaurant. It was situated right alongside the main runway. You could sit there all day and watch the aircraft scream down the runway then "rotate" as their wheels left the tarmac and shoot into the air over the trees at the end of the runway. Well, it was what the British Airways, American, JAL and Lufthansa 747s and DC10s did. It was rather more interesting watching the Aeroflot Tupolevs and Ilyushins trundling down the runway trying desperately to build up enough speed to barely clear the trees at the end of the runway.

Pizza Hut opened their first restaurant in Gorky St Moscow in 1990. The Golden Arches of McDonalds were first visible in the Russian capital on 31st January 1990.

Feeling rather adventurous one evening four or five of us decided we'd check out a Russian Pizza Hut. Hailing an ancient Volga cab outside our splendidly named Cosmos Hotel, which was very aptly named as it was very near the Russian Space Museum. It was one of the biggest hotels in Russia with over 1800 rooms, but dwarfed by The Rossiya with over 3500 rooms. The Rossiya was demolished in 2006 but there are plans to rebuild it near the Kremlin. The Cosmos is still there. I just read some reviews stating the rooms were dirty and outdated. The lobby was infested with pimps and prostitutes, which proves nothing changes in Russia. It was like that in 1990!

The cab of course had suspension that would bounce your head into the roof, when it hit the man sized pot holes in the Moscow streets. So, after a harrowing forty-five minute journey, we arrived at Pizza Hut. The first thing that struck me was this was not like any Pizza Hut I had ever been to in the past. There were soldiers with Kalashnikov assault rifles guarding the entrance! This was because of the riots that took place when McDonalds first opened in the capital earlier in the year. A reported 30,000 people stood in line to sample their first Big Mac, which cost about a week's wages each. Average waiting times to get served were reportedly three to four hours . . . we opted for Pizza Hut instead.

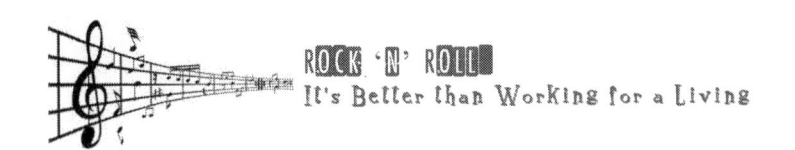

There were two entrances to get into the restaurant both guarded by soldiers. We went up to the first one and the soldiers barred our way. They wouldn't let us in and pointed to the other entrance, where they did let us in. It was only once inside we realized there was one entrance for the local population and one for foreigners. I guess this was to stop foreigners having to wait so long if there were a big queue like there was at McDonalds. Or did they just feed them different food. Whatever it was, segregation lived on in Russia. Strangely enough when you were inside, you sat on one side of a dividing wall from the locals who had come in a different door. You could quite easily sit and talk to people across the dividing wall, if you spoke Russian of course. The menu when it arrived looked just like a normal Pizza Hut menu, with the normal selection of pizzas; Margarita, Pepperoni, Hawaiian etc.

We all plumped for a different variety and I went for my usual that I order in a pizza place . . . pepperoni, with extra pepperoni and anchovies. I seem to remember it taking an age for them to arrive, probably almost an hour. When they arrived they looked just like any other pizza you would expect to find in the West. One problem I did find was that my pizza didn't really taste too much of pepperoni and not at all of anchovies. One of the other guys couldn't really taste any pineapple in his Hawaiian.

We tried a piece of each other's and it then became abundantly clear, that they all tasted exactly the fucking same!

Never went back to Pizza Hut after that.

Chapter Nineteen

INTO THE NINETIES

The three years from 1989 to 1991 in the end turned out to be really busy for me. We were still up against it financially. In 1990, I accepted a week's work in Romania (With the British I might add.) A few months earlier a full blown Revolution was in full swing.

The whole thing been set up by the British Council who were trying to open up these backward ex-Communist, ex dictatorial states to show them there was a world out there beyond the grip of these dictators and tyrants.

Even now, though six months after the revolution, it didn't feel particularly safe. We were first doing a gig in Timosaura, where the whole fucking thing started.

The "revolution" was widely acknowledged as a coup against the tyrannical government of Nicolae Ceausescu, but there were student revolts and all sorts of crap going on. Security guards were stationed at the airport. In fact, they were in flat caps, leather coats and armbands all toting Kalashnikov assault rifles. A circle of tanks still surrounded the Government buildings.

The gigs were instantly forgettable. They were three crap UK bands in crumbling venues. Once again men in leather coats and

ROCK 'N' ROLL
It's Better than Working for a Living

arm bands were there. They were smoking cheap shitty smelling cigarettes, part of the image I guess.

The country was in a complete fucking mess. So were some of the people, including our pilot who flew us from Timosaura to Bucharest. At the set time for takeoff he was nowhere to be found. I remember thinking at the time' this is pretty fucked up. I soon realized everything was fine as they eventually found the pilot in the airport terminal bar!!!!!!!!!!! We had two or three days sightseeing with no gigs, but I was really fucking glad to get out of there.

I did a little Xmas / New Year tour at the end of 1989 with young Mr. Kilmister and his Motorhead with supporting act Girlschool.

This was a tried and tested formula. Girlschool were essentially a female Motorhead. Only, they weren't very good, which didn't really matter. They were cheap to have on the show. They always had good drugs and were real good fun. I was "baby sitting" Motorhead's longtime monitor engineer, a Scottish guy with a really heavy Glasgow accent, nicknamed Eagle. I had known him for years. I can't remember why he was called Eagle. It may have been the shape of his nose, I don't really know. Forgive me mate.

Eagle was not a great monitor engineer. He seemed too able to put up with Lemmy. And, Lemmy seemed quite happy to put up with Eagle.

How it used to work was, I would rig all the system and EQ it all for Eagle and he would stand behind the board for the show so that Lemmy had somebody to shout at or bounce off or whatever. It didn't matter I did all the clever stuff, as long as Eagle was there during the show, everything was fine. This was fine by me as it also gave me an hour and forty-five minutes to hang out in Girlschool's dressing room during Motorhead's show taking speed and drinking beer. This turned the whole thing into a thoroughly satisfying and enjoyable little two week tour.

Early in 1990, I did a small European tour with Judas Priest as a system tech. Once again, this was hard work, which I had not been used to. During that tour Terry Price from Tasco sound company in LA, called me and asked if I wanted to do an eleven month tour as monitor engineer with Kiss. This was to be a big worldwide tour. The money was almost as good as what I was used to getting with Iron Maiden.

This was all coming about because of the reputation I had gained in the last five years with Whitesnake and Iron Maiden. I was now regarded as one of the top monitor engineers in world. Now, I was going to make yet another big mistake in my career!

I was scheduled to do a six week tour with Swedish rock guitarist Yngvie Malmstein, which I still decided to do even knowing I would have to leave the tour after about four weeks to fly to America to join rehearsals for the upcoming Kiss tour, which I did. Not knowing this was a mistake that rated third on the all-time list behind turning down the Lionel Richie job, twice!

Yngvie had a reputation as an asshole and a drunk. He was almost impossible to work with. He and I were getting on fine. I was doing some of my best work ever and enjoying the tour. It was nothing like the money been offered for the Kiss tour, so I made my excuses and left the Yngvie tour.

I flew to Lubbock Texas, again (I was beginning to know this place.) for a week of rehearsals before the first gig of the *Hot in The Shade Tour*.

ROCK 'N' ROLL
It's Better than Working for a Living

I knew Gene Simmons in Kiss was a complete asshole, but I had dealt with lots of assholes. However, I never really knew guitar player Paul Stanley was such an ass.

The week's rehearsals weren't very productive. It didn't really help the sound crew, as most of the time was spent putting the set and lighting rigs up and down. There was no time at all for sound. I think we had two afternoons with the band and these weren't very promising or very interesting.

I was also been hampered by some of the equipment the company had sent out. The console was not the best. It was not the one I was led to believe I was getting. There were two different types of floor monitors, which sounded totally different to one another. I was getting totally fucked up the ass here (as they say in the trade). My ability compromised by the fact the side fills, which are a hugely important first line of attack with a loud rock band were not the ones I wanted. They were not half as big enough. They had to be placed where I didn't want them under the stage set, which hugely compromised their ability to produce the required level of sound. With Iron Maiden they would have been out on stage, the bigger the better.

The bottom line was the sound was being compromised for the look of the stage set. That just isn't the correct way round to do things. Without sound you don't have a rock show!

After three or four gigs I was struggling, I couldn't get the sound I was wanting. I couldn't get the sound the band was wanting, the band were losing patience. I was losing patience. I didn't care that the band never said please or even a thank you or that they even walked past you in a corridor and never even spoke to you. They were complete assholes I knew that. I still wanted to do the best job possible.

I wasn't able to do my job properly. I was limited by the stage set and I was let down by the sound company supplying the wrong equipment. After two weeks of winging and complaining by the band and by me, I quit. I blame the sound company and the set designers for stitching me up.

I heard there were another six monitor engineers after me to take on that job that were either fired or quit. Surely they can't all have been wrong.

Meanwhile my replacement on the Yngwie tour was out touring with him for the next twelve months, in America, Japan, Australia etc. "White gloving it," as it's called in the business (i.e., just mixing, no rigging, no truck loading). Boy! Did I ever fuck up, big time. AGAIN!

I don't know if I ever learned from any of those big mistakes, I don't think so. If I had I would probably be a rich man now.

I flew back to LA from Terre Haute Indiana after the debacle at the start of the Kiss tour. Terry the boss of the sound company had gone to Hawaii on vacation and wanted me to hang out in LA. He told me to join the crew for what would be the third leg of a big worldwide Motley Crue tour starting in two weeks' time. This time, I was a system tech, which once again was going to be hard work and long hours.

Instead of putting me in some crummy motel for two weeks Terry left me the keys to his house in Ventura County and the keys to his BMW 745, with a note saying, "Look after these for me."

Two weeks off in LA with a nice car and house thrown in, better than been on tour with Kiss any day! I flew up to Boise Idaho at the beginning of June to hook up with the rest of the Motley

ROCK 'N' ROLL
It's Better than Working for a Living

Crue crew. I knew instantly this was going to be much nicer than all that crap that was going down with Kiss.

These guys had already been out on tour since October the past last year when I joined up with them in June. They'd already done Europe, the UK, Japan, Australia and just about every arena in the US, including some weird and wonderful ones I'd never even heard of like . . . Amway Arena, Orlando, Florida; the Murphy Center, Murfreesboro, Tennessee; the Dean E. Smith Center, Chapel Hill, North Carolina; and the Redbird Arena in Normal, Illinois. Can you believe there is actually a place called NORMAL? Wonder how they happened on that name?

There is a town called Boring in Oregon, wonder what it's like there, boring?

The Boring city website calls it: "An exciting place to live." Hahahahaha!

Whilst I'm on this theme, I thought I'd do some research and see what other strange (Could find one called Strange though.) names I could find for towns and cities, mostly in the US, in fact exclusively (Couldn't find one called that either.), except for one.

The longest one I found was in Massachusetts called;

Chargoggagoggmanchauggagoggchaubunagungamaugg Lake

Ok, it's a lake, but it's a fucking long lake.

There are quite a few place names which I found that are actual descriptions rather than names. If I remember any of my English tuition at school, which was a few years ago admittedly, makes them adjectives rather than nouns; fuck me! What are we getting into here? Between, Georgia . . . Guess that's between a couple of other places.

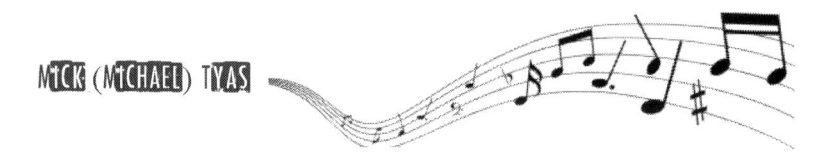

There are two places in Mississippi called, Chunky and the other one is Short. Wonder where Smooth and Long are?

There's a really nasty place in Nebraska called Gross, sounds horrible there. You could live in Difficult, Tennessee or it may be easier living in Only, which I guess is nothing to shout about.

I'm not quite sure what goes on in Wanker's Corner, Oregon. I'll leave that to your imagination, but how embarrassing to live in Big Butt, North Carolina. I should imagine there are a few of those around those parts.

You got lots of Licks in Kentucky, if you want them. There's Big Bone, Deer, Big, Flat, Knob, Paint and they're all Licks, but my all-time favorite is Beaver Lick!

Don't know what they get up to down there in Kentucky, but they seem to have fun. Indiana has a French Lick, which sounds much more erotic; they also have Floyd's Knobs, lucky them!

California of course has to have a town called, Cool and also Weed. There's also Weed in New Mexico, luckily. My favorite town in the whole of California is totally unpronounceable and it's magnificently called, Zzyzx. Fuck knows what it's called but it's about a million at Scrabble!

There's Love in Arkansas as we all knew there was, there's Pee Pee in Ohio, and wouldn't you just love to live there?

There's a Virgin in Utah, which I find surprising. With a Nipple just down the road and it seems those wacky Mormons had only one thing on their minds.

With variations on a theme you could also either live in Intercourse in Alaska or in Pennsylvania, personally I think I'd go for PA. It could be a little chilly around the gonads in Alaska, but what I think is the funniest named place in North America is also in Alaska, and its name is Unalaska!!!!!!!!

Unalaska is called that, because the people didn't want the town to be in Alaska. Where the fuck did they want it to be, fucking Florida? Why not just be done and call it West Palm Fucking Beach!

Internationally, you can go to Fucking in Austria, probably means something like beautiful view in Austrian.

My totally all-time favorite name place in the whole world though has to be in The Republic of The Marshall Islands, which you have probably never heard of. They are an independent nation in the Compact of Free Association with the United States and they are somewhere in the Pacific, near Papua New Guinea. So, they're fucking American and there is a town there called ANAL!

In all my research, I've never been able to find a town called, Just Fucking Weird!

I'd love to live there!

I was doing the last three months of this Motley Crue ten months World Tour and once again there were huge amounts of equipment twelve 48 foot trucks in all. We only had two trucks of sound, so what was in all the rest of them I have no idea, so no white gloves for me this time. It was really hard work and I had to rig one side of the flown sound system again and hook it up to a huge rack of amplifiers.

Then, on this tour I was in charge of the electricity also. I mean you could not have put a more wrong person in charge of electrickery than me! I knew fuck all about electricity and still don't, apart from the fact that it can hurt you. Electricity is all do with electrons?????????????

MICK (MICHAEL) TYAS

Apparently electrons whiz along a bit of wire and electricity comes out of the other end, fuck knows how that happens, but there are magnetic fields and there are watts and amps and ohms as well.

There are ways of working out with scientific formulas how many watts equal an amp or how many ohms are in one watt, or some such nonsense. It's Physics, and I found Physics really complicated at school, as you can see from these ramblings.

Sound is made by electricity, how????????? Light is also made by electricity, or some of it is. There are Alternating currents and Direct currents, don't know how you tell the difference, but they both fucking hurt.

I don't know who the brain cell was that decided I should be in charge of electricity, but he certainly wasn't having one of his best decision making days.

Luckily, I managed to plug in this huge transformer (What the fuck that did I have no idea, transformed something I guess!) every day and managed to get through the remainder of the shows without actually killing anybody.

Although Motley Crue had already done almost a hundred shows in the US on this tour, we still had to go up to Canada again and then back down into the US. It was summer so there were plenty of outdoor shows and "sheds."

One of the first outdoor shows totally new to me was The Seashore Performing Arts Center in Old Orchard Beach, Maine. This was a small Minor league baseball park, which held about 6,000 people in a town of only about 8,500 people.

Old Orchard Beach was a real old school early 20th century seaside resort. What the fuck were we doing playing it with Motley Crue? In fact only a couple of years later the place was

ROCK 'N' ROLL
It's Better than Working for a Living

closed down (The gig, not the town.) after the local residents complained endlessly about the music being too loud and the town was full of drugged up drunken kids every time there was a concert in town. No shit Sherlock! Who'd have thought that would ever happen? I do have one little afterthought about this ballpark.

When it closed down the local franchise was relocated to MOOSIC Pennsylvania! What a perfect name!

The band decided it would be really nice to do a gig in a little club in New York. One of the worst things you can do in the music biz is to let a band or musicians make a decision. Never give a guitar player an amplifier to play with either.

We did do The Ritz in New York City, which I had done with British band, Adam and The Ants in1981. It had now moved from its original 11$^{th\ St}$ location. I believe it's now a Gay club. Don't think you'd get Motley Crue playing there now.

This was a really good summer tour for me. It was very hard work. I think we did every outdoor show and shed I think you could possibly do in America. There were lots of drugs around and lots of women. I guess this tour was probably good for me as I didn't have the time for womanizing. I still had the time for the cocaine though, but this tour was probably my swansong in the Sex and Drugs and Rock 'n' Roll lifestyle.

Chapter Twenty

WHAT NEXT?

I went back to the UK. The phone didn't ring until well into 1991. I really thought I had burned all my bridges and my touring career was over. A guy called John Tinline who owned a small sound company in London called and said he was having major problems with monitors on a tour with a band called Color me Badd.

It seemed like a pretty stupid name for a band plus I had never heard of them. They were a young American hip hop group. The four front guys were singers and dancers, very much in the boy band genre. This was a big step in a different direction for me; however, a good engineer should be able to turn his hand to most jobs.

The problem the current monitor engineer on the tour was having was that the four singers had a live band behind them who weren't terribly loud. The front guys were singing very quietly and actually had some pretty good harmonies going. They were dancing all over the stage so the monitor engineer had to put all their voices in all the monitors at the front of the stage. This created a situation where one guy would come over and say, "Turn my voice up," another would say, "Turn his voice down." Then they would each say, "Turn the other guy down."

ROCK 'N' ROLL
It's Better than Working for a Living

So it was an impossible situation. This way of doing the monitors was never going to work. When we were in London an old friend of mine called George Glossop brought me over a new system invented by a Front of House engineer called Chris Lyndop.

It consisted of a radio transmitter which took the mixed signal from the mixing console and sent it to a small receiver that the Artiste wore with a pair of "Walkman" style earphones plugged into it. Thereby, each member of the band got his own personal monitor mix in his own ears and also had complete freedom of movement on stage.

The problem was solved we didn't need big lumpy speakers all over the stage; they each just had their own earphone setup. The four singers loved their in the ear monitors and immediately ordered four systems. This reminds me I never did get my commission for selling them to them. I did get asked to do an American tour with them though.

Well, I was back on tour in America but this was not going to be anything like the excesses and mayhem of 1984 thru 1990.

Color Me Badd was to be the opening act on the Under My Spell Tour by Paula Abdul. She was a huge international star at the time and who has since been a judge on American Idol. We'll keep away from all that kind of crap.

This tour was going to be the least work I think I have ever had to do on any tour. I had one rack with four wireless mic systems and four in ear monitor systems in it. These plugged into the monitor console provided by the sound company on the Paula Abdul tour. The musicians just had six floor monitors provided by the sound company. I individually mixed the band and the singers vocals into their own ear systems. It was so fantastically easy.

No getting up early on this tour. We never used to get into the gig until about 4:00 p.m. and never got on the stage until about

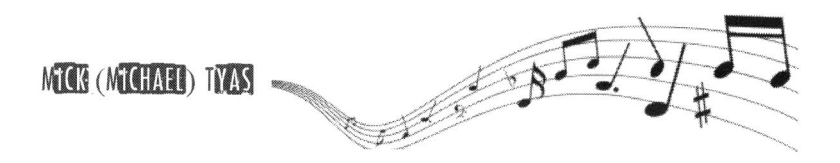

6:00 p.m. as opening act we were finished by 8:30 p.m.! So plenty of time for Sex and Drugs, but times had moved on somewhat, there was no sex on this tour, these people were fucking Christians, practicing fucking Christians.

The band would stop there tour bus at a local church wherever they were on a Sunday morning and go to church.

Fuck me! What was happening to the world I knew? I was getting buried under a blanket of normality. Help!

We weren't allowed to smoke on our bus so we had to go and stand outside to smoke a cigarette (A sign of the times to come of course.). It made it rather tricky when you were doing 70 mph down the freeway!

We were allowed some beer on our bus, but if you were caught with any drugs it was instant dismissal. Still, I guess I must have saved some money. Although on some days off when we were in the same hotel as the Paula Abdul crew there was the occasional cocaine party.

Mark Dowdle, the guy I had had a big ruckus with on the first Motley Crue tour was brought in as Front of House engineer. We made up and became good buddies. We would have a little weed now and again but we were essentially clean living boys now.

It was all quite weird at first. I had to adapt myself to the circumstances and I managed to get through the tour. After that Color Me Badd tour I went back home to London for Christmas. I only made it by the skin of British Airways teeth as will be revealed later on.

Things were pretty good at home as well and Salli and I were probably more together than we had been for ten years. And, I was asked by Color Me Badd to go out and do the rest of the Paula Abdul in the US in February 1992.

ROCK 'N' ROLL
It's Better than Working for a Living

This work was really sorting us out financially. I also had a Zucchero toured lined up which had been postponed from 1991, which worked out fine as 1991 had been really busy.

The Zucchero tour was going to start in the spring of 1992, straight after the Color Me Badd tour. Unfortunately, the two overlapped by a couple of weeks. As the Paula Abdul / Color Me Badd tour was drawing to a close . . . the Zucchero thing was supposed to be a World Tour. I elected to miss the last two weeks of Color Me Badd and fly back to London for the start of Zucchero rehearsals.

That was the last ever American tour I ever did.

The Zucchero rehearsals were to be in a hotel on the seafront in Viareggio a short drive from Pisa; that's the place with that tower thing that's falling over. It was an all English crew (because they're the best obviously). I was getting paid really well as Zucchero loved my work. He had employed Mick Shrieve on drums. He was the drummer on the early Santana albums. He's a fabulous drummer as can be seen in a famous cut of Santana at the Woodstock festival, and a really nice guy.

We all had single rooms for rehearsals at this hotel, which was right on the fashionable Viareggio seafront. The backline crew was to go home for a couple of weeks after all the gear was set up, to save money presumably.

I should have heard the warning bells ringing then.

I was Zucchero's main man, in audio terms. I was to stay on for the full rehearsal time. An English guy called Tommy Winstone was the production engineer. He was somebody I had met on previous Zucchero tours and had no problems with him. That is, except one day he called a crew meeting before the backline boys went home, just to give us a quick rundown on how things were going to work on the tour. Not that we needed telling we had all done this before, once or twice!

One of the first points Tommy made was that nobody would be getting a single hotel room on this tour. We would all be sharing, except him of course!

This was like a red rag to a bull to me; I had been at this game for over twenty years. I worked my way up to become one of the best monitor engineers in the world. Part of my deal with the Zucchero management was that I always got a single room. Now this little shit, who had nowhere near as much experience as me, was telling me I had to share a room.

The crew meeting didn't go any further. I was raging and shouting and threatened to leave the tour if I didn't get my single room. He didn't change his mind. Perhaps I should have gone and told Zucchero how I felt as I did on an Iron Maiden tour when Dick said they couldn't take Michael Jache, who was my monitor assistant, on the Japanese leg of the tour.

I went and complained to the singer Bruce and said, "If they don't want Michael on the tour, then I would resign, as we were a team and worked together." Amazingly, Dick told me a few days later that they would be able to take Michael on the tour.

I'd gambled and gone and complained to the boss. He in turn, used his influence and I won. Weirdly, I've only just thought of this maybe was why I got fired from the Iron Maiden job. I'd played Dick, who was the Production Manager off against the band and won. Maybe it was Dick I had upset and ultimately stitched him up to the band on that tour, and that's why I got fired!

A situation that never happened in Viareggio, I didn't bother going to Zucchero.

I regret it now; I should have done instead of letting that little shit Tommy Winstone gets away with it. Instead, I packed my bags and next morning went to the airport, and never went back to Viareggio.

Chapter Twenty-One

IS THIS THE END?

I had literally come to the end of the road, I went home on that flight from Pisa and I never went back to the tour. I was missing out on about £1000 per week by resigning, but that didn't seem to matter.

I remember getting yelled at by Salli saying stuff like; "Are you fucking crazy, you quit the tour and you have no other work, that's probably about £26000 we're going to lose."

I didn't care. They hadn't kept their word on our contract. Why should I keep mine? It was their loss. Now they had to find someone else as good as me to do the job. Sadly, I guess they did as I never heard from them again

I was never in this game to make millions that would never happen. The only way that would have happened was if I had become that rock star.

As a "roadie" or sound engineer, there were still moments of glamour, plenty of sex and all the drugs I could handle. I don't know how many miles I traveled but I did twenty eight tours of America, I went to Japan four times, I went to Australia four times and did endless tours to every corner of Europe including Russia, Romania and the former Yugoslavian republics and the old East

Germany and I went to Africa, to Nigeria and Jordan in the Middle East.

I'm not going to come out with the old cliché that; "I wouldn't change a thing." I would have changed lots of things over that twenty-year period. I fucked up plenty of times and I'd probably liked to have reversed a few of my decisions, but maybe that wouldn't have made it as much fun. I made a lot of money and I spent it all and more, with a little help from Salli Jane Holgate, my soul mate.

Chapter Twenty-Two

BACK HOME 1992 TO PRESENT

Well, that was a whole lot of fun but now I was back in London with no desire to go back on the road again I have no idea why though. In the twenty years I'd been doing it I'd become really successful. I could have gone on much longer than I did.

My old friend Phil Wilkey is still touring and he started the same time as me. Strangely enough, I have noticed something about myself again just recently. A couple of years ago I gave up my job as head sound engineer at Shepherd's Bush Empire, a major venue in London. I'd been there fifteen years and I could do gigs there with my eyes closed and one arm tied behind my back. Then one day, I just decided to give it up. There were quite a lot of political pressures working at one venue all the time though. The lack of money was one pressure; there was never any money to do upgrades to the system or even repairs. The hours were also very long. The salary was not great. In the end I put the decision down to quit as, "Being too old for this job these days."

I think I'd lied to myself as I still go back and do occasional gigs there. Once again, I'd made a success of something and then quit. Maybe I just get bored; maybe I need a new challenge.

For fucks sake this book is probably one of the biggest fucking challenges I have ever had.

So 1992, I had no job, no money and no prospects. Luckily, I had no cocaine habit, which I still find a minor miracle after that last twenty years. I was still smoking dope and in fact still am. So that was never going to kill me. I would still take cocaine but only if someone gave me it. I could no longer afford a $600 a week habit.

It was definitely only a "for kicks" habit and it had been really fun at times but now been back at home with the family there were so many other things to keep me occupied.

Salli and I were still doing well and agreeing on most matters though the odd raging argument did occasionally occur.

I was trying to spend as much time as possible with Morgan. We had a new addition to the family. This was Lulu a beautiful six month old Border Collie / Spaniel cross. Lulu was the best behaved most intelligent dog I have ever come across. She was with us for sixteen years and the heart of the family.

Having no income I was really rooting around for any job in London. Once again, I still can't understand why I didn't go after any touring gigs. I think I must have just got too comfortable at home and enjoying family life after all those years.

One day a guy called me who I had known since my early days in London. He asked if I could go down to The Marquee Club in Charing Cross Road in central London to sort out their PA system for them.

This was not the original world famous Marquee Club were all the 1960's bands like Jimi Hendrix, Pink Floyd, The Rolling Stones, Eric Clapton and The Yardbirds etc. played. It was the new address it moved to when they tore the old place down as local councils do.

They even tore down The Cavern where the most famous and influential bunch of musicians of the 20th and 21st centuries started, The Beatles.

I never went to The Cavern. It was too far from my home town of Doncaster at the time. I did go to the old Marquee many times and boy! Was it a shit hole, it was dark (all painted black), it was damp (Especially when it was full of people.), the bathrooms were disgusting, and the bar was basic. You didn't go there for a shit or to brush your hair. You went to drink and listen to loud music.

I even did a couple of gigs there, which was an experience. You couldn't load in before 2:00 p.m. and you couldn't make any noise until after 6:00 p.m. as there were offices above.

With the lights on during the day it looked much worse than at night when it was full of people. The walls were bare brick painted black; under foot was an uneven concrete floor, painted black or maybe just black from dirt. There was no air conditioning, no heating and the sound system was almost as old as the building I think. The mixing position was on a scaffolding structure at the back of the room with people standing underneath. The front of the room to the back was only about thirty feet away so you were almost on the stage anyway.

I did a gig there with The Pretty Things in 1976. The Pretty Things were a 1960's band who had come up on the back of The Rolling Stones success and developed into a decent Rock 'n' Roll band and were signed to the Swansong record label which was owned by a larger than life character called Peter Grant who just happened to manage another band called Led Zeppelin.

Grant had an uncompromising style of management.

In 1977, Grant gave his approval for Led Zeppelin's tour manager Richard Cole to hire a guy called John Bindon to act as security coordinator for the band's concert tour of the United States. Bindon had previously provided security for actors Ryan and Tatum O'Neal.

Towards the end of the tour, a major incident occurred during their first concert at the Oakland Coliseum on July 23, 1977. Upon

ROCK 'N' ROLL
It's Better than Working for a Living

arrival at the stadium, it was alleged that Bindon pushed a member of promoter Bill Graham's stage crew out of the way as the band entered via a backstage ramp. Tension had been simmering between Graham's staff and Led Zeppelin's security team during the day. As Grant and Bindon were walking down the ramp near the end of the concert, words were exchanged with stage crew chief Jim Downey, which resulted in Bindon knocking Downey unconscious. Within minutes, a separate off-stage incident involving Graham's security man Jim Matzorkis (He was accused of slapping Peter Grant's 11 year-old son Warren over the removal of a dressing room sign.), escalated into an all-out brawl.

Led Zeppelin's second Oakland show took place only after Bill Graham signed a letter of indemnification absolving Led Zeppelin from responsibility for the previous night's incident. However, Graham refused to honor the letter because, according to his legal advice, he was under no obligation to agree to its terms.

Members of the band returned to their hotel after the concert, and were woken the next morning by a surprise police raid after Graham had decided to press charges. Bindon, Cole, Grant and Bonham received bail and continued the tour to New Orleans on July 26. When all four finished the tour, a suit was filed against them by Graham for $2 million. After months of legal wrangling, Led Zeppelin offered to settle and all four pleaded *nolo contendere*, which basically meant they didn't contest the charges, receiving suspended sentences and fines.

Bindon had already been dismissed by the band upon return to England. Grant later stated allowing Bindon to be hired was the biggest mistake he ever made as manager.

I met John Bindon in The Golden Lion in Fulham a couple of years later, not knowing his reputation. It was said he was a hard man. There were allegations of his being connected to organized crime and connections with big time drug dealers. I found him an amiable if imposing character. John also claimed to have had a steamy affair with Princess Margaret.

Peter Grant learned his management skills from one of the best, the so called Mr. Big of the 1960's music business; Don Arden.

Don Arden was a legendary no nonsense manager who first started by bringing over to the UK the young American Rock 'n' Roll stars of the day like Gene Vincent, Bo Diddley and Chuck Berry. He later went on to manage The Small Faces, Electric Light Orchestra and most famously, Black Sabbath, whose lead singer Ozzy Osbourne later went on to marry Arden's daughter Sharon Osbourne.

Sharon went on to take over management of Black Sabbath and Ozzy from her father, which started a twenty year feud with him after a family incident.

Below is a little account I found from Small Faces drummer, Kenney Jones, which typifies Arden's and for that matter Grant's management styles:

In 1966, Arden, and a squad of 'minders' turned up at impresario Robert Stigwood's office to 'teach him a lesson' for daring to discuss a change of management with the Small Faces. This became one of the most notorious incidents from the 1960s British pop business.

Arden reportedly threatened to throw Stigwood out of the window if he ever interfered with his business again. The band was never entirely convinced Arden had paid them everything he owed them. Kenney Jones has mixed memories of the band's stormy relationship with Arden:

"Without Don, the Small Faces may not have existed, without his sort of vision at that time, be it short-lived or what. The fact is, we became known and we got a break through Don. So if you think of it like that, and I think all of us are prepared to swallow what went on, leave it, fine, its history. We all learned from each other, he gave us our first break, fine, fair enough, you know, leave it. I've got good and bad memories. Mainly I think of Don with affection, surprisingly enough."

The Golden Lion pub in West London as well as being a hang-out for off duty rock stars and crew also attracted a slightly criminal element. There has always been a tenuous connection between successful bands and Artistes and crime. You can take it back to the days of Frank Sinatra and his connections with "The Mob."

Now here's a little known fact, film actress, TV star, singer and ex-wife of Liam Gallagher of Oasis . . . Patsy Kensit's brother James is the Godson of Reggie Kray of the Kray Twins. And, they are infamous gangland villains and nightclub owners from the 1950's and 60's.

The Kray Twins were reported and recorded to have lifestyles aligned to crime and corruption in the 50's and 60's. They were also nightclub owners, although this also provided them with cover for some of their more unsavory underworld dealings. They still liked to hang out with the rich and famous of the entertainment world, the likes of Frank Sinatra; English actresses, Diana Dors; Barbra Windsor; and also Judy Garland. The Krays were also involved in band management, though not Reggie and Ronnie, they had an elder brother called Charlie who took over management of London band Stray in 1975; shortly after his release from Maidstone Prison in the south of England.

MICK (MICHAEL) TYAS

A regular customer in The Golden Lion pub was a guy called John Miller a friendly ex-British soldier and a veteran of the Falklands War. He was to become famous in 1981. He kidnapped British Great Train Robber, Ronnie Biggs from his exile in Brazil to Barbados. He handed him over to the British Government who had put a bounty on his head after his escaping from Wandsworth Prison in South London. Biggs had served sixteen years after been sentenced to thirty years in prison for robbing a mail train in 1963 of £2.3 million, the equivalent of £40million today. Unfortunately, Jonny Miller and his mates hadn't thought the abduction through very carefully. Barbados had no extradition treaty with the UK, so Biggs was released and sent back to Brazil.

You were always able to get a drink in The Golden Lion after closing time, which in those days was 11:00 p.m., as long as you were inside at the time (but strictly for the regulars). All the normal punters were kicked out at 11:00 p.m.

The lock-ins as they were called in the pub trade never caused a problem for Sean the landlord. However, if caught a landlord could lose his license and his livelihood. Sean had some influential customers, not rock stars or gangsters, but the London Metropolitan Police Force!

The Golden Lion was literally across the road from the new Fulham Police Station. Sean soon discovered the cops going off duty at, or before, or after, pub closing time liked a drink after their shift. Some would be already in the pub. Some nights there would be a knock on the private apartment about midnight and there would be a couple of cops looking for a drink. This kept the Golden Lion protected.

Back to The Marquee Club in 1976 the billing for tonight's band read: "Live, Mystery Swansong Band." People around town

ROCK 'N' ROLL
It's Better than Working for a Living

soon started jumping to conclusions and the word went out that Led Zeppelin were playing at The Marquee, Swansong been manager Grant's own record label. By early afternoon there was a queue of people down Wardour Street and round the corner into Old Compton Street. The Marquee had a legal capacity of 400 people for concerts but by 8:00 p.m. it was reckoned there were 1400 people squeezed in there and they were still letting them in.

I had seen the Marquee pretty full before but maybe not quite this full. I was stood behind the monitor console, which was situated just off stage right. There were so many people squeezed in some were actually standing next to me behind the console.

I don't remember too many boos as The Pretty Things took the stage. Too bad if you were disappointed it wasn't Led Zeppelin and you wanted to leave. If you were in the middle of the crowd, you couldn't move anyway.

That night was my lasting memory of the old club. Then they fucking knocked it down and built a fucking restaurant.

The Marquee I was involved with was the Mark 3 version in London's Charing Cross Road. It was as dark and dirty just like the old one. Even the sound system was a pile of shit, and that was why I was there.

The Marquee Club by now was owned by one time Rod Stewart manager Billy Gaff. Billy seemed pleased someone cared enough to come and fix his sound system for him. He'd managed to make some money available to buy new amplifiers and some new speakers. Everything sounding good and during the next two years I was even made a licensee, which meant I could manage the club also. This also meant I could help myself to drinks behind the bar. Unfortunately, there were also many others doing the same thing and not only helping themselves to drinks. There was a little clique there of about four or five people, couple of them were managers. One was a girl behind the ticket counter; one was the lighting guy and his brother, who had also been a manager. He had been fired a couple of years before. There was this little clique of people, there may have been more, it was hard to tell. There was a bit of a drug culture there, which seemed to revolve around a couple of employees. There was money going missing. There were break-ins at the premises on regular occasions and some highly suspicious behavior. There were quite a few people helping themselves to the profits.

There was one guy employed by Billy called Tim who was employed as accountant but also took on the job of general manager for no extra pay. Tim really tried to keep ahead of all this pilfering and waste that was happening. He was fighting a losing battle. Billy was never anywhere to be seen so he had no control. Tim and I had lots of conversations on the subject. We both knew what was going on and knew who was involved. Try as we may, we couldn't prove anything. The club was losing money big-time. It looked as if Tim and I were the only ones who cared. Eventually, when equipment started to disappear or repairs needed doing there was suddenly no money available to spend things just got worse and worse. I left in 1994, the club eventually closed in December 1995. It has never really been replaced.

It was in 1994, I started my relationship with MTV Studios. I was working as freelance monitor engineer for all the live bands they recorded until their closure in February 2011.

In the same year I also started working at Shepherd's Bush Empire. The hundred year old theatre, which was opened as a live music venue in 1994 after being owned by the BBC since 1953; it was used as The BBC Television Theater for live TV shows.

ROCK 'N' ROLL
It's Better than Working for a Living

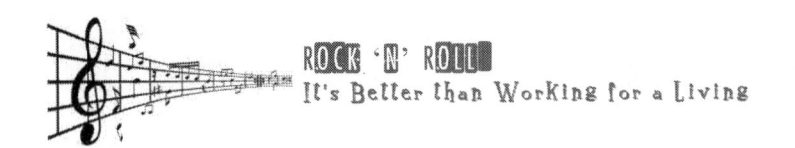

I personally have done almost 1500 shows there with: The Rolling Stones, David Bowie, The Who, Oasis, Paul McCartney and many other big acts. Nothing very interesting about these shows very much workaday gigs. You turn up, you do the gig, and you go home. Although on The Rolling Stones show there was an interesting incident.

They played The Empire as a warm up show for a Wembley Stadium gig in June 1999. The Empire has its own very good top notch sound system, which is always kept in very good condition. The Stones crew decided they wanted to bring in one stack a side of their own PA including amplifiers to augment the Empire system. They were also bringing their own monitor console . . . a state-of-the-art fiber optic multicore system. This is the fat cable that goes to the Front of House Console carrying all the mic signals (In this case it's not so fat, as its fiber optic, so it's much thinner.). They also brought in their own digital mic splitting system, which splits the signal from each mic to the monitor console and the multicore to the Front of House console.

The Stones sound system for the tour and for this gig was been supplied by Db audio from Chicago. They were a surprise choice to the industry to supply the biggest touring band in the world, as they were one of the smaller companies.

As with most American engineers these guys come into the gig with all the numbers and all the knowledge and all the waffle. Generally, trying to give you the idea they know everything and you know nothing. They had to convince you they were the superior beings (I've never known what that attitude was all about.). Unfortunately, they don't have the talent except for a very few and include my old mate Mark Dowdle in the talented category.

So they came in with their new PA and their attitude. Luckily, the guy mixing the band was another old friend called Robbie

McGrath. He wasn't really interested in new PA's and digital, fiber optic blah de blahs. He wanted to mix on our old Yamaha console, have a few drinks and go home with 1000 bucks in his pocket.

The hot shot Db system technicians insisted on using their digital fiber optic multicore plugged into our old Yamaha console at FOH. As soon as they did the extra PA they brought started buzzing really loud. The hot shot technicians decided to unplug their new PA for the sound check and just use The Empire's own system. After all they didn't want the most important clients in the Rock 'n' Roll world thinking there was something wrong with their equipment.

So eventually it got around to Show Time and the Empire was packed as you would expect. We had to put up with Sheryl Crow as the opening act and then half an hour later the most famous Rock 'n' Roll band in the world would be on stage. Unfortunately, the Stones had other ideas and came on an hour and a half late.

All the time we were waiting for the band to appear, Robbie and I had been standing behind the console at FOH, drinking beer and wine from Robbie's stash of cold drinks supplied by the caterers. I think we must have been pretty drunk by the time the band appeared, which is the way us old timers did our best gigs, no Red Bull or water!

After a couple of songs, Robbie turned to me and said "What do you think of the sound?"

I replied, "To be quite frank old mate, it sounds like a sack of shit. It sounds like listening to an old 1960's record."

"Good." said Robbie, "It's supposed to. They want that authentic 60's sound." At which point we thought another drink was in order, job done.

ROCK 'N' ROLL
It's Better than Working for a Living

This sound engineering business is not that difficult, as long as you know what you want and how to get it. Just as we were relaxing the intercom from the stage rang. It was a very earnest and panicking hot shot technician on the other end.

"Robbie we forgot to turn on our extra PA, we're just using the Empire system, should I turn it on now?"

"No! Fuck off!" said Robbie, "I never fucking wanted it in the first, it sounds great as it is."

At which point we had ANOTHER drink. Job done!

I still love the old Empire and as I said I still do the occasional gig there.

I also worked on some corporate stuff from 92 onwards, exhibitions, conferences, award ceremonies etc., but this really wasn't for me. It wasn't Rock 'n' Roll. It was downright boring and far too regimented for me. It was almost like having a proper job and some of the people working for these companies were so fucking anal.

On a typical medium size conference gig, you would probably have a top table on the stage. There would be with maybe six to ten of the management or owners of the company and twenty or thirty tables of employees. They were either lecturing them, or discussing or maybe telling them, they were all fired. Some of these conference things started at ridiculous hours. They have breakfast conferences starting at 7:00 a.m.! Then they go off to work in the office until 5:00 p.m.

Sometimes they are all day affairs. They'd discussions and seminars and question and answer sessions. I once did one of these things for a company that made cardboard boxes. They talked all day about fucking cardboard boxes! Unbelievable.

Of course, the management sitting at the top table always had either mics placed on the desk in front of them or personal radio mics attached to their suit or tie or something. There would be a hand held radio mic on the floor for questions and answers. It always sounded like shit. You had a bunch of people who didn't know how to use a microphone and a bunch of speakers facing the mics and people. I was not ideal in the world of physics, just to hear what each other were saying.

There was one conference gig I did enjoy doing. It was the First Annual General Meeting of British Telecom, to decide if it should be turned into a public company or some such nonsense. All the shareholders were invited. Seeing as this was the first such meeting, nobody knew exactly how many people would turn up on the day. There were hundreds of thousands of shareholders or investors so British Telecom decided to rent all the three exhibition halls at the National Exhibition Center in Birmingham in the UK.

They were going to rig the biggest which held about 15,000 people and have a big stage with the top brass answering questions from the punters. As a safety measure in case more people turned up, they rented the next hall which held about another 7,500 and a third one which held another 5,000 people. All these halls had to be linked together with both audio and video.

Myself and an old engineer friend of mine called "Roadent" were employed by a company along with about another twenty people to do the audio installation. So we had to rig three separate sound systems and then link them all together. This way, mic signals could be sent from one hall to the other and back again.

ROCK 'N' ROLL
It's Better than Working for a Living

So Roadent and I were given the task of rigging the third hall which was farthest from the main hall. It was, in fact almost half a mile away I guess. So, they gave us bicycles. All the equipment had been dumped in the hall. We all had breakfast about 8:00 a.m. and at 9:00 a.m. we set out on our bikes to Hall 3 arriving at 9:30 a.m. By 10:00 a.m. we had sorted out what we were going to do. By about noon, we were getting a little thirsty, so we decided to cycle over to our hotel where we were staying, which was in the same complex and go and have a beer in the bar.

At 1:00 p.m. we cycled back to the main hall for lunch. At 2:00 p.m. we started the same sequence again arriving back at the main hall for dinner about 7:00 p.m., then after dinner at 8:00 p.m. we would all go back to the hotel and the bar.

This was a pretty good day's work, out of a twelve hour day we had managed to get easily four and a half hours work in. It was a very steady schedule that we adopted. It worked. We got all the work done over the two week period we'd been there.

Then the big day arrived, how many people would turn up?

Roadent and I were in our hall, Hall No.3. We sat there most of the morning, went to the pub about noon, had lunch, and sat there in the afternoon. Went to the pub and at 6:00 p.m. it was all over. Nobody turned up in our hall. It was all for nothing. A wonderful two weeks work and another week to take it all down.

In 1997, I was employed by the same production company to go out to Delhi, India to do the monitor sound for the Indian Channel V TV Awards show. It was a little like Indian MTV and sounded like a very interesting job.

I had never been to India before, never mind done a gig there. We flew Emirates Airlines, which is a pretty cool airline and renowned for good service.

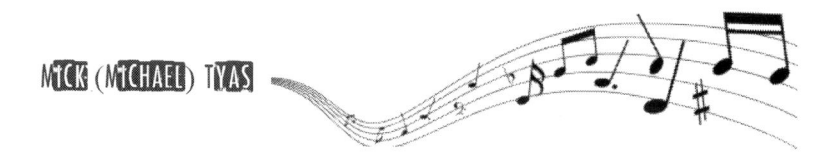

We flew London Heathrow to Dubai. With an hour stopover we checked out lots of really expensive stuff at the duty free shop we couldn't afford because we came from a country that bought oil, not one that sold it.

It was only a three hour flight to Delhi from Dubai. We were due to get into Delhi at 2:40 a.m., which seemed like a pretty stupid time to arrive. Luckily, we had a day off next day to rest up or go sightseeing, which I thought might be interesting.

Arriving at Delhi airport felt a little like arriving at a small local airport in the African bush, not in one of the world's biggest cities. The airport arrivals area was dark and dingy and smelly. I don't remember seeing any Customs officers, who can blame them at that time of night. Somebody did stamp our passports. Don't know who the fuck he was. He didn't look like an immigration official, but then there are many things in India that didn't look like they should.

When our baggage arrived at the carousel, I considered it a minor miracle looking at the state of the airport. I know it was the middle of the night but there didn't seem to be anyone else in this airport except us. It was a bit of a weird feeling, until we got outside. Once again it didn't look like the arrivals building of a major International airport. No matter what time it was.

There was a bunch of about six really dodgy looking guys talking quietly and looking at us as if we had just landed from another planet. There were a couple of rundown old taxis, two dowdy looking buses and a rabid dog! Not exactly what I would expect to see outside LAX at 3:00 a.m.

The street lighting was almost nonexistent. There were just a few poles with yellow orange glows on the top. They gave the

ROCK 'N' ROLL
It's Better than Working for a Living

whole scene a bizarre out in the middle of the bush feel about it, again.

A guy got off of one of the buses and came to point us towards his bus. After leaving London more than nine hours ago, we were all exhausted and just flopped on the seats in the bus. The driver went back to talk to the six dodgy looking guys stood around in a group chatting.

Why did he have to go talk to them? Were they planning, where they planning where they could stop the bus and rob us of all our valuables? The rabid dog prowling about outside the open door of the bus didn't make me feel any easier either.

Eventually, the bus driver returned and was a really jolly little man. Far too jolly for this time of day, but he didn't look like a robber. He had probably just been discussing the football results with those other guys.

We didn't have to tell him where we were going, he knew already; "The Metropolitan Hotel Sahibs, very nice hotel." After a forty-five minute drive through the dark, dingy streets of downtown Delhi we pulled up outside this big bright shining birthday cake, The Metropolitan Hotel.

Even at this time of the morning, there was a sentry on duty at the door. I suppose he was the doorman really but dressed magnificently in gold lame and a big gold headdress all topped off with a huge handlebar moustache. He looked like something from the time of The Raj and Maharajas, which I guess was the impression they were trying to convey.

He saluted us as we entered into this huge marble and gold reception area. Even though by now it was still only 5:00 a.m. this place was really busy. Guess they get up early in India to avoid the heat of the day.

MICK (MICHAEL) TYAS

Derek our leader and crew chief suggested we all try and get a few hours' sleep, in the afternoon we would take a leisurely ride down to the gig just to have a quick look. We wouldn't be able to do any work as the sound equipment wasn't arriving until the next day. This was because the majority of the equipment was in Bangalore doing a Beach Boys gig.

Derek had booked us a wakeup call for noon to leave at about 1:30 p.m. after some lunch. I woke up about 11:00 a.m. dealing with a little jetlag.

I woke up in this beautiful plush hotel room and gingerly opened the curtains a little as I could. There was a blazing sun out there. Luckily, the big picture windows had tinted glass so it didn't hurt too much. What I saw out of the window took me aback.

My room was at the back of the hotel facing across a dirt road onto some shaky looking old two story houses. I was on the sixth floor and I could see right down on top of them.

The ground floor of one of the houses seemed to be lived in. I saw people coming out and wandering around in the small dusty courtyard at the back where a few scrawny chickens and a couple of rabid dogs (They do a good line in rabid dogs in India.) scratched around in the dirt. It was the top floor that caught my attention. It just seemed to be a flat roof with a couple of small temporary shelters on it. On the roof were a man and a woman sitting around a fire cooking lunch while a couple of children jumped around and played. The roof seemed to be "furnished" with a couple of broken down chairs a chest of drawers and even a couple of tall lamps. It actually looked like an open air room on the roof, which is exactly what it was. These people lived on the fucking roof!

ROCK 'N' ROLL
It's Better than Working for a Living

One of the small shelters on the roof was probably a shelter if it rained, which it didn't do very often. The other was probably the bathroom. I can only guess what that was like, but I would see something similar later on in the day.

This was real poverty right outside my five star hotel bedroom window. I was going to have breakfast in my room, but that kind of put me off food seeing just outside the window. I went down to the restaurant for lunch. After a somewhat safe attempt at lunch of ham and eggs (Always remember India is the food poisoning capital of the world.), we set off from our five star luxury accommodation once more saluted by our guardian at the front door into what looked and felt and smelled like a fucking "war zone."

Outside of our Crystal Palace it was hot and dusty and smelled strangely agricultural since we were in the center of a major city. I guess it must have been handed down to cows wandering up and down the highway or the occasional bullock cart I spotted lumbering down the wide boulevard. There was also a deep haze hanging over the city, which made the pollution over Los Angeles look like a fluffy white cloud on a bright summer's day. There were also some really large black birds swooping about in the sky. These were the biggest crows I have ever seen in my life. When you saw one on the ground they were as big as chickens, big chickens! They were actually vultures! Don't see many of those in Los Angeles, actually thinking about it, you do, but not the feathered variety.

This place really did look like what was left over after a nuclear blast, except of course our shining palace. We asked our doorman to call us a taxi, which was already waiting on the forecourt. This beautiful black and yellow 1958 Morris Cowley trundled up. Although this wasn't made in 1958, this one was almost new as they were still been made in India from the original blueprints of the vintage British car. They are now called the Hindustan Ambassador.

The cab was of course adorned with all the usual Indian tat, sorry finery, with frilly curtains. There were gold Shiva's and bright colored plastic Gods. You needed a few fucking Gods on your side driving a cab in Delhi.

Five of us managed to squeeze into the cab. It was roasting hot inside and he had all the windows open. Somebody asked him to close the windows and put the air conditioning on, "No air conditioning sahibs."

So we were in a country where it only rains one week a year. It that week deposits the equivalent of the entire contents of the Pacific Ocean on the land. The other fifty one weeks of the year the sun shines. It is 40C even at night. We were in a brand new cab, albeit designed in 1956, you would have thought someone by now might have thought it might be a good idea to have a little cooling system fitted for the passengers.

I had obviously forgotten that India was still a Third World country. There were more important things in the world than air conditioning, like food and trying to stay alive.

A small percentage of the population of India did have air-conditioning in their cars. The other 99% didn't. Many of them were starving, fuck me! I'm starting to sound like a humanitarian or ecologist or some such nonsensical being.

Before I go any further there is one observation I have to make. I had only been in the country for about twelve hours when this observation struck me. India is a shit hole!

Whatever else I say, India is a shit hole. If you live there or did live there, my advice is still the same as it was in 1997. Leave!

ROCK 'N' ROLL
It's Better than Working for a Living

So we set off in our steaming cab, with the smelliest wind blowing into our faces from the open windows that I have ever smelled. As we traveled down the wide boulevard, obviously built by the British, we were getting into a busier part of town and the roads were getting more crowded. In fact, they resembled the crowded streets of Central London or Manhattan (You have to use your imagination a little here.). The roads were very similar though, they were crowded, they were pot holed, they were very noisy with people blowing their horns and there were lots of people shouting except there were a few subtle differences. There were probably about three million more vehicles on the road in this particular part of town than in London or New York.

The pot holes were about three feet deeper. They were easily big enough to swallow one of the three wheeled motor bike type taxi things called Tuk Tuks; or as they call them now, auto rickshaws, which were all over the street.

There were also three million more people blowing their horns, all at the same time. In fact, if it were me driving on these roads every day I would do away with the horn button completely and join the wires together so the horn would sound constantly. It would save a lot of messing about with a button.

There was also what sounded like about a thousand people screaming their heads off. Maybe because they had just been crushed trying to cross the road, by a truck or bus. And, coming up to the first roundabout I had seen in India, I can understand why.

In the center of this roundabout is the biggest sign in the world, which gives all the information of the daily, monthly and yearly statistics of the casualties and fatalities on the roads of Delhi. This is updated daily, which makes you wonder how many people died trying to read all that fucking information.

MICK (MICHAEL) TYAS

I made a point of studying the daily figures on this sign every day we went past it. There was something like an incredible forty or fifty deaths a DAY, just in Delhi, fuck me. In ten years there'll be nobody left (Stupid! Of course there will they breed faster than rabbits.).

There were probably room for four lanes of traffic coming up to this roundabout, but the Indian drivers had managed to squeeze this into seven lanes. What you have to be aware of on the roads is there is no such thing in India as a queue of traffic. It is a crowd of traffic. The same as there is no such thing as a queue of people for train tickets. It is a crowd of people, the noun queue, does not exist in India.

I soon learned after about ten minutes in the cab the golden rule in India when approaching a road junction or roundabout is not to stop. If you stop you'll never get going again. So, you just pull out into the traffic whether they stop or not, blowing your horn furiously (You see with my idea you wouldn't need one hand to blow the horn, it would be on all the time, leaving you a spare hand to light a cigarette, drink a beer or call a prostitute on your phone.).

Once you are blowing your horn, you have the right of way. It is the other driver's responsibility to avoid you driving straight at him. It you hit him, it is his fault for not getting out of the way! What a wonderful system, sounds like my kind of driving. In fact, the second day I asked the cab driver if I could drive to the gig. He told me it would be too dangerous. Too fucking dangerous? He should try driving around the M25 around London on a Friday evening.

If you do happen to get stuck in a traffic queue; the sorry traffic crowd it is usually unbearable. It is stifling hot with the win-

ROCK 'N' ROLL
It's Better than Working for a Living

dows closed in the cab in Delhi. You have to have them open, but when you do open them you feel your chest heaving. You gag on the noxious fumes of cheap gasoline emitted from every vehicle (no emission testing here) and also the fragrant odors of rotting garbage and excrement from the open sewers.

Between the hotel and the gig, every day we drove past the quaint inner city suburb of Cardboard City. It is a sizeable piece of real estate which stretches off into the distance. I've seen people living in cardboard boxes under arches of bridges in London and under freeway underpasses in New York, but not in the thousands. This community comes right up to the side of the road. You can literally put your hand out of the cab window and shake hands. People run business outside their boxes; I even saw an antique barber's chair outside one where the guy had set up in business.

There was probably business going on inside the boxes also. Like the two beautiful girls I saw sitting on a dining table not more than four feet from this chaotic highway.

This was probably quite a good place to set up in their business. There was certainly no shortage of passing trade. I thought it quite a strange way to advertise their services though, one sat cross legged behind the other on a dining table. Perhaps, it was an Indian take on the displays to be found in the windows in the Red Light districts in places like Amsterdam or Hamburg. Until I saw the girl siting at the back running her fingers through the hair of the girl sitting in front, then! I realized she was running her hair through her fingers and pulling out all the bugs that had nested in the other girl's hair! Aaaahh! I've looked at the ladies of Amsterdam in a totally different light since that day.

We eventually arrived at the gig. The magnificent Indira Gandhi Stadium, an indoor 25,000 seat stadium. It is the largest indoor facility in India built to host athletics, basketball, netball, gymnastics and they've even played one game of cricket there.

It's not quite Cowboy Stadium or the Amsterdam Arena, but it looked quite impressive.

As with many buildings in this country, it looked a little run down. They should have cleaned up the outside space a little, like cut the grass and weed the paths occasionally.

From a beautiful hot summer's day we walked into a huge dark cavernous space when we went inside. I couldn't believe how dark it was. It was bright enough to see that nobody had cleaned up after the last event they had here. Nobody even collected the garbage it was still laying where all the punters had dropped it. So the place smelled really bad, which seemed to be a recurring theme in India, especially in the heat. You need to keep things fucking clean. Don't get me fucking started on the rest rooms. When I eventually found the rest rooms, there were probably five or six rest room areas around the arena, for 25,000 people! They were the smelliest, dirtiest rest rooms I had ever seen anywhere in the world.

I'd been to run down Eastern Bloc countries and some horrible places in Africa, but I had never seen anything as dirty as this. The squatting hole in the floor toilet is not to everyone's taste but it is something you can put up with if you have to. Not they're never been cleaned and these were never cleaned.

I needed a toilet pretty badly. I went outside and got a cab back to the hotel, did what had to be done and got a cab back. The precedent was set for the rest of the week; we could not leave the hotel in the morning until everyone had had a crap!

The second day, after we had all had a crap of course, we left the hotel and went to the gig. Another thirty people dead on the roads, according to the sign on the roundabout; we went into the gig and saw some equipment, a few monitors, a few amp racks and a monitor console. Well, it was a start I guess.

We also met a couple of the Indian sound crew, who seemed like okay guys. There didn't seem to be much of a sound system. Apparently, it was on its way from Bangalore and wouldn't arrive until the next day. There wasn't a stage yet either. There were about two hundred people constructing something that, if you used your imagination looked vaguely like a stage. There was a lot of wood being used, which made it look more like a bridge. Anyhow, we got the monitor system working on the floor and it sounded fine. When I set the digital equalization for the speakers one of the Indian guys deleted my settings. I had to start all over again.

Day Three, still no sound system, it was still on its way from Bangalore. Thirty more dead on the roads, but we had a stage. It was a bit of a flimsy looking affair. You could feel it moving when you walked about on it but the Indians seemed confident it was strong enough and would hold together when they built the PA wings either side. Of course, they were still doing this, with bamboo scaffolding! It was pretty scary to watch. It was going to be interesting putting thirty tons of sound equipment on there?

Day Four, had a crap, left the hotel, thirty more dead on the roads, some of the PA arrived . . . no mixing console. We couldn't make any noise. Still no PA wings, just lots of bamboo and lots of people.

Day Five, was supposed to be a rehearsal day, but actually turned into a PA stacking day. Normal start to Day Five, had crap, people dead again, but this time we had a hundred boxes music comes out of and two hundred crew. There were no ramps or fork lifts to get the boxes onto the stage. There were only two hundred people and some bamboo scaffolding. This was going to be a job for Indians, Europeans please stand clear!

Shortly after lunch with the Indian sound crew directing operations they started the operation. This was going to take forever, although four quite normally built guys should be able to lift one sound cabinet. Some of these guys were skin and bone, living on rice and vegetables. They would try and get ten people around one box and could still hardly lift it.

They would lift on to one level of scaffolding, then on to another level and finally on to the PA wing. The boxes then had to be stacked five high. This was going to take all day and all night. Somebody had to get injured as the whole structure rocked about as they were building the stack.

I think I would rather trust the Italians rather than this lot; I just had a weird flash of the movie "Bridge on The River Kwai."

About 9:00 p.m. we left them to it and headed back through the dingy dirty streets of Delhi for the safety of the hotel bar.

Day Six was the last rehearsal day, not that we had even had one yet, so we were going to get to the gig especially early today. This meant getting up extremely early to get your body's natural functions dealt with before you committed to a day at the gig. Usual mayhem on the streets of course, no matter what time you drive around.

When we got to the gig we found that not all the PA had been stacked on the PA wings, due to the fact they had to dismantle some of it and rebuild during the night as it turned out to be too weak to carry the load. Well there's a fucking surprise!

They were now stacking the PA again though. It looked as if we may get some rehearsals in, but there were some very "dead" looking local crew wandering around. They still hadn't got the FOH console onto the FOH mixing position.

We went back to the hotel for lunch instead of hanging around in the shitty gig worrying if these people would ever be able to get a show on. It did take us nearly four hours to get to the hotel and back.

When we did get back around 4:00 p.m. we were surprised when we were walking towards the doors to the gig to hear music coming from inside. The Indian PA crew had actually managed to get the entire PA stacked and the FOH console in place. They'd joined all the wires together and noise was coming out of the boxes. It was a miracle!

I did have faith in the sound guys they were pretty well on the case. It was just the rest of the organization that was a complete shambles.

Bon Jovi had even got their band gear on stage and the sound crew was plugging mics in. By 8:00 p.m. we had a sound check in progress and by 10pm we had a completed sound check. Wow!

Things were really moving fast now. A couple of Indian Artistes and the presenters were going to rehearse their bits. We had no interest in them whatsoever. We were only there to deal with Bon Jovi, Savage Garden and The Spice Girls and Savage Garden who weren't due for a sound check until the next morning. The Spice Girls were not doing a sound check at all, as they were miming (of course)! We left for the bar!

Day Seven dawned in Paradise, sorry, India, please don't confuse the two.

I had a strange feeling that morning at breakfast it was going to be one big fucked up day. It turned out to be not a million miles from reality.

We were all lasting the course quite well. We had no cases of fucked up stomachs and everybody had got away without having to use the disgusting facilities at the gig.

As we left the hotel that morning we gave a wave and a big thank you. And, a big tip (Well big in Indian terms, it was probably about $3, but it looked much bigger in rupees.) to our guardian angel at the door. We received in return an especially extravagant salute as we headed for the last time into the "war zone."

We had checked out of the hotel as we were leaving for the airport straight after the gig. Our flight was leaving at 4:15 a.m., which is a strange time to catch a flight, but I didn't give a fuck I just wanted out of there.

Of course, the accident sign on the roundabout told us that another fifty or more souls had been stupid enough yesterday to attempt to drive their cars on the streets of Delhi or even try and cross the road. Due to the weekend traffic on the roads (As if it were any different to weekday traffic.) it was around about 11:00 a.m. before we got to the gig. The sporadic mayhem was breaking out both inside and outside the gig. Event staff was erecting fences and barriers, trucks were delivering food, whilst the TV people attempted to get their trucks somewhere near the gig so their cables would reach.

Inside there was a general air of milling about with camera people, news presenters, directors, producers and God knows who else.

Savage Garden managed to get their band gear on stage about 1:00 p.m. and eventually after a few false starts managed to get through their sound check by about 4:00 p.m.

That was really the end of our involvement until the gig got started. Savage Garden were the first band on, or so we thought.

ROCK 'N' ROLL
It's Better than Working for a Living

Due to the extra traffic chaos outside, as people were already arriving for the show, we had to have lunch in the gig. It was not a very appetizing thought. We were pleasantly surprised by the excellent spread laid on for us, except that the whole place still stank from all the garbage still lying around from the last gig. Whenever that was, probably about 1979!

The doors were due to open at 6:00 p.m. so we still had to sit through two hours of Indian Artistes' sound checks and presenter rehearsals, just to make sure the whole thing ran like clockwork Hahahahahahahahahahahah!!!!!!!! !!!!!!!!!!!!!!!!!!!!

Just before the doors opened about a thousand coolies descended on the place to eventually clean up the garbage left from the last gig. I wonder if they ever cleaned those toilets.

They were expecting 15,000 people. As the hordes came through the gates and gradually filled the arena the air conditioning started to struggle. I didn't even know it had air conditioning as it was always hot in there.

Of course, very loud Indian walk in music was playing. The show was due to start at 7:00 p.m. with a couple of Indian TV presenters doing the MC duties.

By 7:30 p.m. the presenters had still not appeared. The place was getting hotter and hotter and noisier and noisier. This was not the way to run a slick TV Awards show.

At 8:00 p.m. the presenters appeared. Obviously, they weren't broadcasting live until 8:00 p.m., but this male and female presenter waffled on and on. Then they brought out two people who were doing some karaoke stuff, screeching along to backing tracks. Two people we didn't even know were on the show, and they carried on until about 10:00 p.m.!

Savage Garden eventually went on stage about 10:15 p.m. until about 11:00 p.m. They, they were supposed to be on at 8:00 p.m. This show was over two hours fucking late already!

There was then to be a thirty minute break before The Spice Girls went on. It was actually after midnight before The Spice Girls eventually went on stage after the demon presenters shouted and screamed at the audience. They introduced another woman squealing along to another fucking backing track. This show was now running three fucking hours late! How can you run a live TV show like that? They probably turned off the feed in the control room hours ago.

Mercifully, for all concerned The Spice Girls only did a seven minute show, even though they were only miming it was still fucking painful.

Although their radio mics were turned off at the console during the songs, their mics were working. You could listen to what they were putting into them through something called a Pre Fade Listen facility on the console even though they were not live to the stage or the audience. They were just turned on for what's called "topping and tailing."

"Hello!" We'd like to do a song called etc. "Thank you that was a song called etc."

When we listened on our Pre Fade listen speaker coming from the monitor console they were actually singing along to the track themselves during the show. Obviously, only heard by us, but it was the most painful noise I have ever heard in my life.

I have since done other TV shows with some of The Spice Girls separately over the years. I did a big popular show in England called T.F.I. Friday with Emma Bunton (Who I believe was

ROCK 'N' ROLL
It's Better than Working for a Living

called Baby Spice.). I must say I was terribly impressed as she did actually sing and it wasn't that bad a performance.

I also did a Prince's Trust show in Hyde Park in London in 2001. This was sponsored by the Prince Charles for charity with Gerri Halliwell, also known as Ginger Spice. It was an elaborately glamorous show with male and female dancers. She was dancing and "singing," except that she wasn't of course. She can't and anyway there is only one master of that type of show and that is Madonna, who does sing!

I did a Brit Awards show in London in 1995 with Madonna. I wasn't really looking forward to this experience one little bit as there are lots of crew horror stories about working with Madonna. People had been dragged into her dressing room after the show when something had gone wrong on the show or someone had forgotten to do something. These people got fired instantly. Unfortunately, most of these stories are true. There is one specific incident I remember seeing, which is actually on one of her videos, she actually left in, in the editing of the video, obviously to teach the poor guy a lesson. The monitor guy was a little slow turning her mic back on after a dance routine. Suddenly, she's singing and she can't hear it, neither could anyone else.

The mic was off for a few minutes not just a few seconds. So, the guy did fuck up pretty badly. The video shows him being verbally torn apart in the dressing room by Madonna and fired instantly. He fucking deserved it. That's why you get paid the big bucks, not to fuck up.

When I worked with Madonna on the Brit Awards, she was directing not just the dancers and singers and band, she was also giving the lighting guy his cues and telling the sound guys exactly what she wanted. I won't have a word said against her, I was really fucking impressed.

The only other Spice Girl I worked with separately was the one called Mel C. Who, in truth was not the prettiest of Spice Girls. I have to give her ten points for effort as she did launch a solo singing career after the Spice Girls stopped working together. I just wish I hadn't been in the same room during a couple of her performances. Ok, she did try to sing but when I say "Screaming Banshee!" that about sums up what I heard.

I don't think the remaining two girls actually fancied make a fool of themselves by trying to launch a singing career. Marrying footballers and DJ's seemed more lucrative.

When the Spice Girls had mercifully finished their short show back in Delhi it was about 12:30 a.m. This extravaganza showed no sign of ending anytime soon as another presenter ran onto the stage and carried on the tirade of yelling and screaming. The excited Indian punters were yelling and screaming back at them.

By 1:00 a.m. the presenters were showing no sign of leaving the stage. The punters seemed to be enjoying themselves, but we all made the decision very soon we were going to have to leave for the airport if we were going to make our 4:00 a.m. flight back to the UK.

We were not panicking yet but the airport was twelve miles on the other side of town from the gig. On a Saturday night on the roads of New Delhi, no one really had a clue how long that was going to take to get there. First, we had to find some cabs.

At 1:30 a.m. we decided to leave. The Indian sound crew looked mildly concerned we were leaving them with the whole show in their hands, but we had no other choice. The Bon Jovi crew just stood on stage and looked bemused as the Indian presenters ranted on and on.

ROCK 'N' ROLL
It's Better than Working for a Living

We had no problems finding cabs to take us to the airport as there were lots of them outside the gig. When we asked how long it was going to take to get to the airport, the drivers just shook their heads from side to side as Indian people do and said, "I don't know sahib, I don't know," not a very reassuring answer.

As soon as we drove away from the gig, I could see why he didn't know how long it was going to take. Saturday night 1:00 a.m. and everyone was out on the road for a cruise. They were all around the gig as that was the hottest show in town tonight.

Where the roads were chaos in the day time, at night it was just fucking mayhem. We negotiated one noisy traffic jam after another and half of the time you couldn't see the traffic as driving on dipped headlights was not an option in this town. You drive there with as many lights on as possible.

Surprisingly, we made it to the airport in about an hour. By 2:30 a.m. we approached the dimly lit departure building. Once again there were the same people standing around in small groups, which I couldn't understand at 2:30 a.m. in the morning. Maybe that was their occupation, standing around in small groups at the airport all night along with the odd rabid dog. Inside there were a few crowds at the check-ins. I was going to say queues, but they were definitely crowds. We managed to bustle our way through pretty quickly to the next obstacle in our way, which involved catching a flight out of India, Security!

Well, there wasn't any security really in 1997 in New Delhi airport. There was a man who wanted to look in your carry-on bag and then wrote on a form to tell you he had looked in your bag and then gave that to you. I thought that would really put off the determined terrorist, NOT!

Then there was another guy who wanted to know if you were taking millions or billions of rupees out of the country and why?

MICK (MICHAEL) TYAS

Why the fuck would you want to take billions of rupees out of the country? Rupees are worth fuck all anywhere else but India? So he would give you another form, which confirmed you weren't exporting the whole wealth of the Bank of New Delhi out of the country.

Then there was the Immigration officer who took a long hard look at your passport to confirm you were the person who was leaving the country and not one of the locals who had stolen your passport and was now trying to pass himself off as me and leave the country. I mean I can understand his concern; there must be a couple of billion people in the country who would love to do that; including the Immigration officer probably.

I still had a handful of bits of paper from the check in people. The Security man and the guy worried about his rupees. There was somebody at the last desk to collect all these completed forms. After studying them intensely of course; he probably threw them all in the garbage at the end of his shift.

It's the same the world over. It you are going to have this level of bureaucracy, you have to employ people to deal with it. Otherwise, all those people would be out of work and the forms would never get completed. I then saw the Duty Free shop in front of me and knew we were on the homeward stretch. It was a surprisingly well stocked and cheap Duty Free Area.

Booze and cigarettes purchased, we headed for a sign that read: "Bar." Not before we noticed though that we only had thirty minutes before the flight left. Quickly, we ordered some Tiger beer and sat down at a plastic table covered with a dirty plastic table cloth. We saw the gate number come up on the old digital departure screen for our flight back to the land of the living.

ROCK 'N' ROLL
It's Better than Working for a Living

It was only about a five minute walk to the departure gate. Thankfully, which was lucky because we had only been there about ten minutes when we saw on the screen "Gate Closed." That was a pretty tight window between seeing what gate you had to get to and then the gate been closed. It kind of summed up the whole airport. They herded us on to the plane and into the beautyful bright cream, gold and red splendor of the Emirates Boeing 747. It was heaven!

The flight was only about half full to Dubai so we had plenty of room to spread ourselves out. After a while I found myself drifting off. The last thing I remember thinking was, "How could anybody ever use those fucking toilets?"

My touring career had finished a few years before. I was still doing some big shows. Probably, the last big extravaganza I ever did was again in 1997.

The year 1997, was of course, the year that the UK handed back the Sovereign territory known as Hong Kong to the Chinese who they had stolen it off in The Opium Wars of 1839 – 1842.

Now, I'm not really that big on war myself, as lots of people can get hurt in them, which includes yourself if you're not very careful. I must say The Opium Wars sounded like one of the more interesting ones to fight in.

"Ok, listen up men at 0600 hours I want you all to fix your bayonets. Charge over that hill with your rifles blazing and kill all those ten million little Chinkies!"

"Sir, do we have to do it at 0600 hours? That's really early. I'm really stoned. I'll never get up for that time, can't we leave it until about 4:00 p.m."

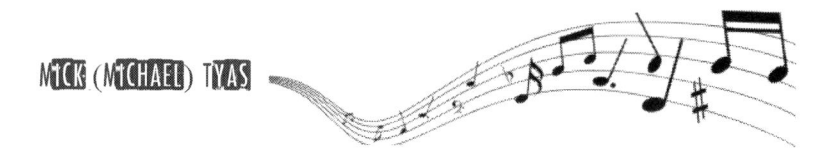

"Yes ok men, I'm pretty fucked myself. Nice bit of hash that. I'm sure the Chinkies won't be very interested either. Pass me the skins someone, I'd better roll another one then."

There was to be an outdoor concert to be held at the Happy Valley Racetrack in Hong Kong to celebrate the handing back of Hong Kong to the Chinese. Fuck knows why the Hong Kong people wanted to celebrate. They were just been thrown back to the lions by the British. I think if I'd have lived in Hong Kong, I'd be getting my money and possessions out of there as soon as fucking possible.

Happy Valley Racetrack sits right in the middle of the financial, capitalist jewel of Hong Kong. It is an amazing place. It's like having a racetrack in the middle of Manhattan. It is surrounded by skyscrapers. I have never seen so many lights on in one place. It's brighter there at night than when the sun is fucking shining.

I was only in Hong Kong for the weekend. We got in on the Friday. The gig was on the Saturday. We left again on Sunday evening, which theoretically gave us Sunday off really for sightseeing and shopping.

All I wanted to do was buy a fake Rolex watch and take a drive up to the old Chinese Communist Border, which still was a border actually.

Unfortunately, the British Government had decided to hold these handover ceremonies in Hong Kong in the rainy season. Probably on purpose, thinking that, "Ok you Chinkies if you want your rich little peninsula back you're going to have to do all the ceremonial parading up and down in the inevitable monsoon rains," which I think shows a good sense of humor.

ROCK 'N' ROLL
It's Better than Working for a Living

We flew in to the old Kai Tak International airport. Anyone who has actually flown into that airport knows is a very unusual experience. On the final approach to the airport it feels as if you're flying down the High Street into the airport. What you are doing is flying very close to dozens of skyscrapers and actually lower than some of them. So, you can actually see people in the windows of their apartments. It is quite fucking scary actually. Probably scary for the pilots as well.

Since that time, the clever old Chinese or Hong Kongians or whatever they are called have built an island from scratch out in one of the bays. They stuck the new Chek Lap Kok International airport on it, which is still quite a spectacular approach. Now you look as though you're going to land in the ocean instead of a fucking skyscraper.

When we arrived in Hong Kong on the Friday it was pissing down, really, really heavy fucking rain. This was not unusual I suppose as it was the rainy season.

I'd done many outdoor festivals in Europe and America where it just rains for a week and it's not very pleasant. You get wet. You get covered in mud and sometimes the sun evens comes out and you get sunburnt. Even the "original" Woodstock, was a Mudfest; however, we were in the tropics. It doesn't just rain here. The sky picks up most of the water in the world's oceans and then dumps it on the land for a month, nonstop!

I'd been employed on this little weekend in the Orient gig to do the monitor sound for Lisa Stansfield. She was a well-known singer from the North of England who had a couple of hit records. She had quite a big band. It was a nine piece band, with two big keyboard set ups, a couple of guitars, bass, drums, backing vocalists etc. It wasn't really the type of band you wanted to be doing at a festival where you were always struggling with the time during changeovers. The money was good. I wasn't looking to base a career on working for this band. I'd never been to Hong Kong before, so it was just a well-paid weekend in Hong Kong.

We sat in the hotel on Friday afternoon after we'd arrived at about lunchtime. The rain was incessant. We were supposed to be doing a sound check in the evening, which was going to be particularly unpleasant in this weather. I decided to try and grab a couple of hours sleep. The tour manager was going to call me when we were supposed to be going to the gig for the sound check. Eventually, I woke up without a call. It was dark outside and still raining. I called the tour manager and was told the organizers had decided to cancel the sound checks tonight. They would do them early tomorrow morning. So it was going to be a nice meal in the restaurant, which of course, was really fucking expensive. Followed by a few drinks in the bar, which was also really expensive.

I got to bed by midnight and was woken by the phone at 7:00 a.m. to be told the organizers had postponed the show until Sunday as the racetrack was flooded. Not surprising really, it was still pissing down.

What would happen if it kept raining on Sunday? Would they cancel the show? We'd go back to London without doing a show? That would be an easy pay day.

I woke again about noon, and it was still raining, but only showers now, which were a little worrying. It might dry up enough to do the gig.

I decided to go for a walk into the city. It wasn't raining that much now. It *was* hotter than fucking hell.

All the shops were selling everything I didn't want or could afford. I discovered a fake Rolex cost more than a regular watch

ROCK 'N' ROLL
It's Better than Working for a Living

in the UK. People were trying to sell me suits. People were even trying to sell me girls. I didn't really want any of that it was too late in the day to try and get up to the Chinese border so I headed back to the hotel.

I realized I was suffering a little with jetlag as I went and had another nap.

I woke up and it was dark again, so went to the restaurant and then to the bar again. I'd totally lost track of what fucking day it was now.

Apparently, if the weather kept as it was it was going to be dry enough to do the gig tomorrow. They arranged a sound check for 8:00 a.m.

"Murphy's Fucking Law," it was a beautiful sunny day at 7:00 a.m. the next morning. So, at 8 a.m. we arrived for the sound check. This was the first time I had seen Happy Valley. There was this amazing horse racing track, still somewhat submerged in places, with huge grandstands surrounded by even huger skyscrapers with a stage set up in the centre of the circuit.

The whole thing looked pretty well put together, big weatherproof stage, big backstage area and dozens of Portakabins for dressing rooms and production offices. I even met a couple of other crew people that I knew.

The stage was actually split into two and we were on the right hand side of it. I recognized some of the sound equipment and realized it was Janus Sound from Sydney Australia providing the equipment and crew. I'd used them before on Ian Dury and Iron Maiden tours. They were really the only company to use in the area (Pretty big area really; Hong Kong, Australia, and etc.).

The sound check and the gig were a complete disaster. The sound company didn't have all the equipment I needed. The band was bitching and I was bitching. The gig was running late. We had to go on second on the bill instead of top of the bill. The band was bitching again. It they went on top of the bill we would miss our flight back to London, which left at midnight. It was a long drive to the airport and even going on second bill we only just made the flight. What a fucked up weekend!

I came back from that little weekend in Hong Kong and never heard from Lisa Stansfield again.

Guess I didn't get the job then!

This has been my story; it's not a history of Rock 'n' Roll. It's not a history of Rock 'n' Roll touring. It's what I did in the Rock 'n' Roll business. It's what happened to me.

Not everybody doing this job has the same experiences. I'm sure lots of people doing this job have managed to avoid doing the same stupid stuff I was doing. I also know lots of people who were involved the same as me and some were involved in even worse things.

I have had lots of success. I've had lots of disappointment too. I've made lots of money and I've spent lots of money. I think my personal life suffered. I think that both Salli and I got engulfed and swept away by the whole aura of the business. There was excitement and glamour but there was also lots of uncertainty. There was a time when I craved a bit of security from the business and from my relationship, but I was in the wrong place for that.

If I wanted security I should have been in a 9 to 5 job, five days a week, but how exciting would that have been? I wouldn't have met all the wonderful people I have met. I wouldn't have been to some of the great places I have been to? I would not have had some of the weird experiences I've had.

ROCK 'N' ROLL
It's Better than Working for a Living

Some great moments

Watching Dee Snider of Twisted Sister when they were supporting Iron Maiden standing in the middle of the stage at Madison Square Gardens in the afternoon while we were rigging the gig shouting, "Hello New York!" This is when there was no one actually in the building except the crew. That was a classic moment.

Having sex in a small room on the stage during an Ian Dury show at a gig in Sweden; all the while someone could have opened the door and all the audience would have seen us.

Traveling to Russia during the old days of Communism.

Meeting King and Queen Hussein of Jordan.

Experiencing what it was like being in an earthquake, twice!

Seeing David Crosby from Crosby Stills and Nash pushed up a ramp onto the stage before a show, due to him been so bloated from his cocaine and alcohol addiction.

Watching my girlfriend talking about babies and housekeeping in the dressing room, at a gig with Rob Halford, who was the lead singer from the Heavy Metal band Judas Priest.

Regularly drinking in a pub with Robert Plant and John Bonham from Led Zeppelin as well as Mitch Mitchell from Jimi Hendrix's band.

Impressing our neighbors because we were personal friends with Brian May and John Deacon from Queen, who lived just around the corner from us.

Receiving personal Christmas cards from Liza Minelli.

MICK (MICHAEL) TYAS

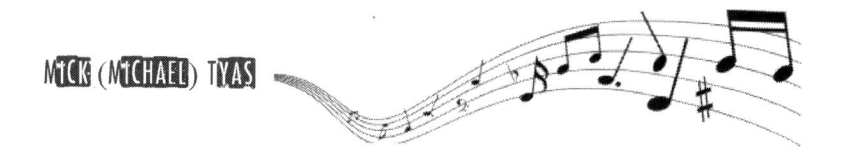

Meeting and working with The Rolling Stones, being surprised Mick Jagger was really short.

Wondering what the fuck Keith Richards was talking about most of the time and noticing that Bill Wyman was also short!

Bumping into Ronnie Wood coming out of a toilet cubicle at Shepherds Bush Empire with little white rocks dropping out his nose.

Realizing I was probably in a better band than The Rolling Stones when I was fifteen years of age, I was definitely a better drummer!

I suppose the Holy Grail in the music business was meeting The Beatles, well three of them anyway, I never got to meet John Lennon. I did solo shows with Paul McCartney, George Harrison and Ringo Starr, I don't know if I would have liked to work with John Lennon or not, he didn't seem like a very nice guy. The other three were pretty harmless and all nice guys in their own way. I remember asking Ringo during a sound check if the sound was ok for him and he just said; "Don't worry about me, I'm just lucky to be here!" I think I know what he meant. John Lennon was once asked by an American journalist "If Ringo Starr was the best drummer in the World?" Lennon replied, "He's not even the best drummer in The Beatles." I like Ringo and his son's not a bad drummer either.

And, just to clear the air in closing . . . as an author I in no way advocate the use of drugs, be they legal or illegal. These were purely my personal experiences during an era where drugs were a part of life. They didn't say, "Sex, drugs and Rock 'n' Roll" for nothing.

I'd like to finish with three quotes from my all-time favorite writer, Hunter S. Thompson.

ROCK 'N' ROLL
It's Better than Working for a Living

"The music business is a cruel and shallow money trench, a long plastic hallway where thieves and pimps run free, and good men die like dogs. There's also a negative side."

"I wouldn't recommend sex, drugs or insanity for everyone, but they've always worked for me."

"Maybe it meant something. Maybe not, in the long run, but no explanation, no mix of words or music or memories can touch that sense of knowing that you were there and alive in that corner of time and the world."

"Whatever it meant."

~ Mick Tyas.

Part II

FESTIVALS

Chapter Twenty-Three

SOME FESTIVAL HISTORY

The Monsters of Rock juggernaut thundered back onto the British festival circuit on the 3 June 2006 at Milton Keynes Bowl after an absence of 10 years. For more than fifteen years it held the crown as the UK's loudest festival. Monsters of Rock played host to the greatest names in metal. It courted controversy and forever turned Donington Park into the 'spiritual home of rock.' It ultimately spawned Download festival, which takes place the weekend afterwards. So what's it all about?

Between 1980 and 1996 it was the colossus of the rock festival scene. It became legendary worldwide. It gave heavy rock and metal fans of the time a festival, which was all their own without compromise. Sure, there was the Reading Rock Festival and Glastonbury, but these festivals also appealed to a mainstream audience. Monsters of Rock and Donington Park were synonymous as a Mecca for those who liked it hard and heavy.

For those who used to make the annual pilgrimage, an early start was usually in order. Some would ignore the "No Camping" message printed on the tickets and pitch up in tents anyway. Others would set off the night before and get a head start at an all-nighter in Nottingham's Rock City, a few miles down the road. Most tended to get picked up early in the morning by a minivan

ROCK 'N' ROLL
It's Better than Working for a Living

full of hairy assed metal heads who had already made a hefty dent in the obligatory bottle of Jack.

Queuing at the gates there was always a bunch of people downing the drink they'd brought with them that they weren't allowed to take into the arena. Some year's security handed out water bags, which you could pour your beer into. These made you look like you were drinking out of bags of piss all day, but it was bought and paid for. It wasn't getting left behind! Such precautions never seemed to stem the legendary bottle fights though.

There was only one stage for most of the festival's life. Once in the arena you made for a good spot and stuck with it. The hardcore would pile down to the front for a good mosh but otherwise it was a case of getting settled for the day and having a drink. A storming headline set was usually capped off with a giant fireworks display. This must have caused alarm to any late flying jet pilots who had to fly directly over the arena and stage from the nearby East Midlands airport.

Originally conceived as a way for Richie Blackmore's Rainbow to round off their 1980 world tour with a big flourish, race circuit Donington Park was chosen as the venue and a line-up of seven bands put together. The event got off to an explosive start before it even began whilst testing the pyrotechnics on the night before. A miscalculation resulted in £18,000 worth of damage to the backline and PA speakers. Nevertheless, for the thirty-five thousand attendees that first year, it was a day to remember. So began a cycle, which would last for sixteen years missing only the odd year here and there.

The eighties were the heyday of Monsters of Rock. Many defining moments occurred during the decade. In 1984, David Lee Roth played what would turn out to be his last performance with Van Halen. 1985 saw ZZ Top suspend their "Eliminator" custom car from a helicopter and fly it over the waiting crowd. Def Leppard proved a one armed drummer was more than capable of delivering the goods in 1986. Kiss used to boast that they would "never open for a band that ever opened for us," but precisely that happened in 1988 when they played second from the top, leaving Iron Maiden (A one-time Kiss support act.) to headline. Iron Maiden also were to give a glimpse of the future in 1992 when Adrian Smith joined his once and future band mates performing in a line-up, which became permanent seven years later.

Many big rock and metal acts had their names linked almost inextricably with Monsters of Rock. Iron Maiden headlined twice, Ozzy Osbourne played three times and AC/DC took the top slot three times. But surely the band who worked hardest to earn their position at the top of the bill were Metallica, who first appeared fourth from the top of the bill in 1985 and worked their way up, finally attaining the coveted headline status in 1995. Late rock DJ Tommy Vance compered the event for six years from 1981. His appearance would be greeted with a chant of "Tommy is a wanker" and hails of projectiles from the seldom-sober crowd, but his appearances were always met with a great deal of good cheer.

All good things come to an end and, after the 1996 Kiss/Ozzy Osbourne co-headliner; Monsters of Rock departed the UK festival scene. This was in part as a result of the changing face of rock music. The fall-out from grunge in the early '90s, along with the emergence of Britpop, was beginning to make metal a dirty word for those in the music industry. Anal band managers no longer wanted to be seen associated with what was seen as a dated brand in Monsters of Rock.

Ozzy returned with Ozzfest in 2002, and the three day, three stages Download Festival is now the current incumbent.

Chapter Twenty-Four

NATIONAL JAZZ AND BLUES FESTIVAL

The 1960's

When Harold Pendleton began the National Jazz Festival in 61, he probably had little idea that his brain child would rapidly mutate and turn into a mixing bowl chock full of blues, folk, pop, and rock. Its jazz ingredient declined until it had virtually disappeared by the end of the decade. But then again, perhaps he did have some idea that things would, inevitably, change.

The history of the festival shows is that the organizers were willing to adapt and go with the rapid fire changes that enveloped the British music scene in the 1960s and 70s. They were, after all, businessmen. Although they shared a genuine love of jazz music, they were not about to let that love get in the way of profit.

The first festivals featured the likes of Chris Barber, Johnnie Dankworth, The Clyde Valley Stompers and Alex Walsh. These were real British jazz musicians. However, changing tastes meant jazz alone could not satisfy the needs of the new generation of teens who were discovering new sounds such as R & B. Gradually, more pop and R & B Artistes were added to the bill, such as Georgie Fame and Long John Baldry. In 1963, the as yet relatively unknown Rolling Stones (Apparently playing the gig for the lowly sum of thirty pounds.) performed and for the first time the

ROCK 'N' ROLL
It's Better than Working for a Living

air rang to the screams of thousands of teenyboppers who had come to the festival solely to see their idols play outside the confines of a steamy club.

Those screams marked the end of an era.

By 1964, The Stones were top of the bill, netting a cool 50% of the night's takings (By 1965, they had outgrown the festival and were never to play a British festival again until Knebworth in 1976.).

There were also overseas blues Artistes in the form of Mose Allison, Memphis Slim and Jimmy Witherspoon. It was inevitable the title of the festival was changed from the National Jazz Festival, to the National Jazz and Blues festival.

By 1965, the festival had outgrown its roots. Instead of attracting a couple of thousand to see and hear jazz on a balmy summer evening . . . they were now attracting tens of thousands. The noise levels had also gone up as had the disruption with traffic and people. This had now all become too much hassle for the local Richmond council and its inhabitants. For the next five years the festival moved around the horse race tracks of Southern England from Windsor to Kempton Park to Plumpton Park finally arriving in Reading in 1971.

Over those five years, the National Jazz and Blues festival emerged into the weekend festival we know today. Joan (My girlfriend at the time.) and I went to most of these gigs. We drove down from Yorkshire, as we were relatively wealthy in weekend hippy terms. I owned a late 50's MG car and we had a large ridge tent. We would arrive in the south of England in the early hours of Saturday morning.

Over those six years, of The National Jazz and Blues festival the likes of Pink Floyd, John Mayall, Stevie Winwood, Fleetwood Mac, Fairport Convention, Jeff Beck, and Joe Cocker all made regular appearances. As you can see, just by the few names I have mentioned they were almost all British Artistes and it carried on like this until 1971. Lindisfarne, Wishbone Ash, and a very low key Genesis were some of the highlights of the British bands.

Following the move to Reading, the festival had not exactly been welcomed by some of the denizens of the Plumpton local council. I expect the move was prompted by the heat generated by the Tory MP who had tried to place injunctions to prevent the festival going ahead. Specific details now become very sketchy. I have to rely on a few short press articles for details of the festivals from 1971 -75.

My own opinion is, that by now the Festival was past its glory years and was a on a long slow downhill path. Not only musically, but in its festival spirit, which had always been pretty friendly and laid back in the 60s and early 70s. However, others may disagree. I'm sure the new audience got as much out of the festival as we did in the 60s. It's just the experience was a different one.

Reading, forty miles from London is a hard, red brick town with little beauty. Whereas, previous festivals had been held near villages or the upper crust areas such as Richmond and Windsor, this move was not one that placed the festival in the midst of verdant countryside. The organizers gradual movement towards specializing in booking mainly heavy bands, which would cater for the burgeoning Heavy Metal audience, seemed to somehow go with the turf. Certainly, the move did not deter the punters. The change proved to be very successful, as the festival is still going to this day, albeit with a changed name. The very concept of including jazz in the title would alienate the crowds who attend the event nowadays.

ROCK 'N' ROLL
It's Better than Working for a Living

In some ways, it's a shame we now have to offer a limited range of music at festivals. They have to be genre specific. The concept of having a mix of music on the bill is only really used at the Womad festivals. Although the PA's and facilities are generally much better then these early festivals, we have regressed to some extent in the open mindedness of crowds towards accepting a wide range of music. Although, I can think of times in the early festivals where crowds were ugly towards certain types of acts; so perhaps it's just promoters playing safe and giving the punters more of what they know they want. However, the chance of a non-genre specific band like Mungo Jerry breaking out to stardom from the Reading Festival is practically zero; whereas, it would have been possible in the National Jazz fests of the 60's.

As the bill changed towards the more heavy acts it attracted a younger, new generation who had a different idea of what was acceptable festival behavior. Their drug of preference was booze, not dope. Increasingly, the optimism and relatively open mindedness of audiences of the 60s was being replaced by a partisanship, which became increasingly ugly. With excessive booze consumption being the order of the day; can throwing at the acts and other audience members was so bad by 1974 many veteran festival goers no longer attended.

By 1978, the transformation was complete. Uriah Heap was the headliners and hard rock bands dominated the entire weekend. I remember seeing a documentary about Reading from this era and the entire field was a sea of cans, several layers deep.

Chapter Twenty-Five

THE WOODSTOCK FESTIVAL

Historical Importance of the Woodstock Festival of 1969
The Woodstock Festival was a three-day concert (which rolled into a fourth day) that involved lots of sex, drugs, and Rock 'n' Roll - plus a lot of mud. The Woodstock Music Festival of 1969 has become an icon of the 1960s hippie counterculture.

Dates: August 15-18, 1969.

Location: Max Yasgur's dairy farm in the town of Bethel (outside of White Lake, New York).

Also Known As: Woodstock Music Festival; An Aquarian Exposition: Three Days of Peace and Music.

Overview of the Woodstock Festival of 1969:

The Organizers of Woodstock.

The organizers of the Woodstock Festival were four young men: John Roberts, Joel Rosenman, Artie Kornfeld, and Mike Lang. The oldest of the four was only 27 years old at the time of the Woodstock Festival.

Roberts, an heir to a pharmaceutical fortune, and his friend Rosenman were looking for a way to use Roberts' money to invest in an idea that would make them even more money. After placing an ad in *The New York Times* that stated: "Young men with unlimited capital looking for interesting, legitimate investment opportunities and business propositions," they met Kornfeld and Lang.

The Plan for the Woodstock Festival

Kornfeld and Lang's original proposal was to build a recording studio and a retreat for rock musicians up in Woodstock, New York (Where Bob Dylan and other musicians already lived.). The idea morphed into creating a two-day rock concert for 50,000 people with the hope that the concert would raise enough money to pay for the studio. The four young men then got to work on organizing a large music festival. They found a location for the event up in an industrial park in nearby Wallkill, New York. They printed tickets ($7 for one day, $13 for two days, and $18 for three days.), which could be purchased in select stores or via mail order. The men also worked on organizing food, signing musicians, and hiring security.

Things Go Very Wrong

The first of many things to go wrong with the Woodstock Festival was the location. No matter how the young men and their lawyers spun it, the citizens of Wallkill did not want a bunch of drugged-out hippies descending on their town. After much wrangling, the town of Wallkill passed a law on July 2, 1969 that effectively banned the concert from their vicinity.

Everyone involved with the Woodstock Festival panicked. Stores refused to sell any more tickets and the negotiations with the musicians got shaky. Only a month-and-a half before the Woodstock Festival was to begin, a new location had to be found.

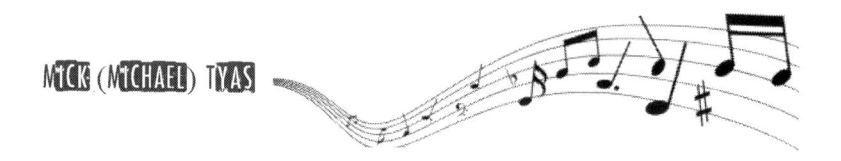

Luckily, in mid-July, before too many people began demanding refunds for their pre-purchased tickets, Max Yasgur offered up his 600-acre dairy farm in Bethel, New York to be the location for the Woodstock Festival. As lucky as they were to have found a new location, the last minute change of venue seriously set back the Festival timeline. New contracts to rent the dairy farm and surrounding areas had to be drawn up. Permits to allow the Woodstock Festival in the town had to be acquired. Construction of the stage, a performers' pavilion, parking lots, concession stands, and a children's playground all got a late start and barely got finished in time for the event. Some things, like ticket booths and gates, did not get finished in time.

As the date got closer, more problems sprung up. It soon appeared that their 50,000 people estimate was way too low and the new estimate jumped to upwards of 200,000 people. The young men then tried to bring in more toilets, more water, and more food. However, the food concessionaires kept threatening to cancel at the last minute (The organizers had accidentally hired people who had no experience in concessions.) so they had to worry about whether or not they could airlift in rice as a backup food supply. Also troublesome was the last minute ban on off-duty police officers from working at the Woodstock Festival.

Hundreds of Thousands Arrive at the Woodstock Festival

On Wednesday, August 13 (Two days before the Festival was to begin.), there were already approximately 50,000 people camping near the stage. These early arrivals had walked right through the huge gaps in the fence where the gates had not yet been placed. Since there was no way to get the 50,000 people to leave the area in order to pay for tickets and there was no time to erect the

ROCK 'N' ROLL
It's Better than Working for a Living

numerous gates to prevent even more people from just walking in, the organizers were forced to make the event a free concert.

This declaration of a free concert had two dire effects. The first of which was that the organizers were going to lose massive amounts of money by putting on this event. The second effect was that as news spread it was now a free concert, an estimated one million people headed to Bethel, New York. Police had to turn away thousands of cars. It is estimated that about 500,000 people actually made it to the Woodstock Festival.

No one had planned for half a million people. The highways in the area literally became parking lots as people abandoned their cars in the middle of the street and just walked the final distance to the Woodstock Festival. Traffic was so bad, the organizers had to hire helicopters to shuttle the performers from their hotels to the stage.

The Music Starts

Despite all the organizers' troubles, the Woodstock Festival got started nearly on time. On Friday evening, August 15, Richie Havens got up on stage and officially started the Festival. Sweetwater, Joan Baez, and other folk Artistes also played Friday night.

The music started up again shortly after noon on Saturday with Quill and continued non-stop until Sunday morning around 9:00 a.m. The day of psychedelic bands continued with such musicians as Santana, Janis Joplin, Grateful Dead, and The Who . . . to name just a few.

It was obvious to everyone that on Sunday, the Woodstock Festival was winding down. Most of the crowd left throughout the day, leaving about 150,000 people on Sunday night. When Jimi Hendrix, the last musician to play at Woodstock, finished his set early on Monday morning, the crowd was down to only 25,000.

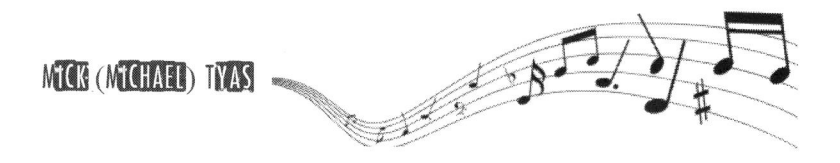

Despite the thirty-minute lines for water and at least hour-long wait to use a toilet, the Woodstock Festival was a huge success. There were a lot of drugs, a lot of sex and nudity, and a lot of mud (created by the rain).

After the Woodstock Festival

The organizers of Woodstock were dazed at the end of the Festival. They didn't have time to focus on the fact that they had created the most popular music event in history. They first had to deal with their incredible debt (over $1 million) and the 70 lawsuits that had been filed against them.

To their great relief, the film of the Woodstock Festival turned into a hit movie and the profits from the movie covered a large chunk of the debt from the Festival. By the time that everything was paid off, they were still $100,000 in debt.

Woodstock has been idealized in the American popular culture as one of peak events of the hippie movement — a festival where nearly 500,000 "flower children" came together to celebrate. Hippie activist Abbie Hoffman crystallized this view of the event in his book, *Woodstock Nation*, written shortly afterwards.

Although the festival was remarkably peaceful given the number of people and conditions involved, there were three fatalities: one from a drug overdose; another due to an occupied sleeping bag accidentally being run over by a tractor in a nearby hayfield; and a third when a festival participant fell off a scaffold. There were also three miscarriages and two births recorded at the event, along with many colossal logistical headaches. Furthermore, because Woodstock was not intended for such a large crowd, there were not enough resources such as portable toilets and first-aid tents.

ROCK 'N' ROLL
It's Better than Working for a Living

Yet, in tune with the idealistic hopes of the 1960s, Woodstock satisfied most attendees. Especially memorable were the sense of social harmony, the quality of music, and the overwhelming mass of people, many sporting bohemian dress, behavior, and attitudes.

Sound for the concert was engineered by Bill Hanley, whose innovations in the sound industry have earned him the prestigious Parnelli Award.

Listed below are the Artistes and playing times.

FRIDAY, AUGUST 15

Artist	Time	Notes
Richie Havens	5:07pm – 7:00pm	
Swami Satchidananda	7:10pm – 7:20pm	Gave the opening speech/invocation for the festival
Sweetwater	7:30pm – 8:10pm	
Bert Sommer	8:20pm – 9:15pm	

FRIDAY, AUGUST 15

Artist	Artist	Artist
Tim Hardin	9:20pm – 9:45pm	
Ravi Shankar	10:00pm – 10:35pm	Played through the rain
Melanie	10:50pm – 11:20pm	
Arlo Guthrie	11:55pm – 12:25am	
Joan Baez	12:55am – 2:00am	She was six months pregnant at the time

SATURDAY, AUGUST 16

Artist	Time	Notes
Quill	12:15pm – 12:45pm	
Country Joe McDonald	1:00pm – 1:30pm	Joe later performs with Country Joe and the Fish.

MICK (MICHAEL) TYAS

Artist	Time	Notes
Santana	2:00pm – 2:45pm	
John Sebastian	2:00pm – 2:45pm	
Keef Hartley Band	4:45pm – 5:30pm	
The Incredible String Band	6:00pm – 6:30pm	
Canned Heat	7:30pm – 8:30pm	
Mountain	09:00pm – 10:00pm	
Grateful Dead	10:30pm – 00:05am	Their set was cut short after the stage amps overloaded during *Turn On Your Love Light*.
Creedence Clearwater Revival	00:30am – 1:20am	
Janis Joplin with The Kozmic Blues Band	2:00am – 3:00am	

SATURDAY, AUGUST 16

Artist	Artist	Artist
Sly & the Family Stone	3:30am – 4:20am	
The Who	5:00am – 6:05am	Briefly interrupted by Abbie Hoffman.
Jefferson Airplane	8:00am – 9:40am	

SUNDAY, AUGUST 17 – MONDAY, AUGUST 18

Artist	Time	Notes
Joe Cocker and The Grease Band	2:00pm – 3:25pm	After Joe Cocker's set, a thunderstorm disrupted the events for several hours.
Country Joe and the Fish	6:30pm – 8:00pm	Country Joe McDonald's second performance.
Ten Years After	6:30pm – 8:00pm	
The Band	10:00pm – 10:50pm	

ROCK 'N' ROLL
It's Better than Working for a Living

Johnny Winter	12:00am – 1:05am	Winter's brother, Edgar Winter, is featured on three songs.
Blood, Sweat & Tears	1:30am – 2:30am	
Crosby, Stills, Nash & Young	3:00am – 4:00am	An acoustic and electric set were played. Neil Young skipped most of the acoustic set.
Paul Butterfield Blues Band	6:00am – 6:45am	
Sha-Na-Na	7:30am – 8:00am	
Jimi Hendrix/Band of Gypsys	9:00am – 11:10am	

There were some notable performances during the weekend. First on Friday opening the festival, Richie Havens played an intense set, but was never meant to open. Everyone else was stuck in traffic jams.

The Grateful Dead only played for an hour and thirty five, instead of their normal six hour set! After technical reasons forced them to shorten it and Jefferson Airplane's set was mercifully shortened to one hour forty minutes at 8:00 a.m. on Sunday morning due to rain and the amount of water on the stage. How did Sha Na Na feel going onstage at 7:30 a.m. on Monday morning before Jimi Hendrix? I thought they were fantastic.

Jimi Hendrix's set was fantastic, but there was no one there to see him at 9:00 a.m. on Monday morning. I suppose Crosby Stills and Nash were the most polished act on the bill.

The two most outstanding performances for me though, were on the Saturday when Janis Joplin sang her heart out for an hour. I never ever tire of watching Mick Shrieve play drums in Soul Sacrifice with Santana. Thirty years later when I met him, what a lovely guy he was.

Bob Dylan

There were a few bands that actually declined the offer to play at Woodstock. Probably the most noticeable being Bob Dylan, in whose backyard the festival was placed; getting the poet laureate of the counterculture to come out and play was never in serious negotiation. Instead, Dylan signed in mid-July to play the Isle of Wight Festival of Music, on August 31. Dylan set sail for England on the Queen Elizabeth 2 on August 15, the day the Woodstock Festival started. His son was injured by a cabin door and the family disembarked. Dylan, with his wife Sarah, flew to England the following week. Dylan had been unhappy about the number of hippies piling up outside his house in the nearby town of Woodstock.

The Beatles

There are allegedly two scenarios as to why The Beatles did not perform. The first is that promoters contacted John Lennon to discuss a Beatles performance at Woodstock. Lennon said the Beatles would not play unless there was also a spot at the festival for Yoko Ono's Plastic Ono Band, whereupon he was turned down. Other people claim the more likely explanation is, Lennon wanted to play but his entry into the United States from Canada was blocked by President Richard Nixon. The Beatles were, in any case, on the verge of disbanding. Also, they had not performed any live concerts since August 1966, three full years before the festival (Not including their impromptu rooftop concert given on January 30, 1969 a few months before in London.).

ROCK 'N' ROLL
It's Better than Working for a Living

Led Zeppelin

Led Zeppelin was asked to perform. Their manager Peter Grant stated: "We were asked to do Woodstock and Atlantic (record company) were very keen, and so was our U.S. promoter, Frank Barsalona. I said no because at Woodstock we'd have just been another band on the bill." An attitude typical of Grant's style of management; however, the group did play the 1st Atlanta International Pop Festival on July 5, as one of twenty-two bands at the two-day event. Woodstock weekend, Zeppelin performed south of the festival at the Asbury Park Convention Hall in New Jersey.

History was made that weekend.

Unfortunately, darker history was made a few short months later on the West Coast.

Led Zeppelin Performances

Led Zeppelin accepted an offer from Bannister to headline the festival at a fee of £20,000. They took the stage at about 8:30 p.m. as the sun was setting. The band's performance is widely considered by music critics, and members of Led Zeppelin itself, as being one of the most important of their career. It represented a turning point in terms of the amount of recognition they received in Britain; until that point their on-stage success and popularity had largely been borne out on numerous United States concert tours. At Bath, the band played five encores. Their set list from the show is as follows:

1. *Immigrant Song*
2. *Heartbreaker*
3. *Dazed and Confused*
4. *Bring It on Home*
5. *Since I've Been Loving You*

6. *Thank You*
7. *That's the Way*
8. *What Is and What Should Never Be*
9. *Moby Dick*
10. *How Many More Times*
11. *Whole Lotta Love*
12. *Communication Breakdown*
13. Classic Rock Medley (*Long Tall Sally, Say Mama, Johnny B. Goode, That's Alright Mama.*)

Pink Floyd Performance

At the concert Pink Floyd premiered their new suite, "Atom Heart Mother," which at that time was announced as the "Amazing Pudding." The performance featured a complete brass band and twelve strong choir and took place at precisely 3:00 a.m., due to major delays. As well as the Atom Heart Mother suite, the band also played tracks from *Ummagumma, Music from the Film More*, and *A Saucerful of Secrets*. The band's set list from the show is as follows:

1. *Green Is the Colour* (Waters)
2. *Careful with That Axe, Eugene* (Waters, Gilmour, Wright, Mason)
3. *A Saucerful of Secrets* (Waters, Gilmour, Wright, Mason)
4. *Set the Controls for the Heart of the Sun* (Waters)
5. *Atom Heart Mother* (Waters, Gilmour, Wright, Mason. Geesin)

Chapter Twenty-Six

ALTAMONT FREE CONCERT

The Altamont Free Concert was a famous rock concert held on December 6, 1969 at the then-disused Altamont speedway in Northern California between Tracy and Livermore. Headlined and organized by The Rolling Stones; it also featured, in order of performance: Santana; Jefferson Airplane; The Flying Burrito Brothers; and Crosby, Stills, Nash and Young with the Stones taking the stage as the final act.

The Grateful Dead were also scheduled to perform between CSNY and the Stones, but cancelled at the last minute owing to the ensuing circumstances at the venue. Approximately 300,000 people attended the concert, and some speculated it would be "Woodstock West." Filmmakers Albert and David Maysles and Charlotte Zwerin shot footage of the concert and incorporated it into a subsequent documentary film entitled *Gimme Shelter*.

The event is best known for having been marred by violence, including one killing and three accidental deaths (Two of the deaths were caused by a hit-and-run car accident, another death was the result of a drowning in a drainage ditch.). There were also four births.

Planning Altamont Free Concert

The concert originally was scheduled to be held at Golden Gate Park in San Francisco. However, the permits were never issued for the concert, or were revoked after the fact. This was a result of Mick Jagger of The Rolling Stones announcing in a press conference that they would be performing at the event; they were to be a surprise appearance; their American Tour of 1969 had recently concluded.

With the public revelation that the Stones would be performing, San Francisco city officials feared a repeat of the crowd control problems that occurred at Woodstock. Accusations have arisen that Jagger made this announcement to ensure a large crowd for a planned concert movie. The venue was then changed to the Sears Point Raceway. After a dispute with the owner of Sears Point, Filmways, Inc. regarding film distribution rights, the festival was moved to the Altamont Raceway at the suggestion of its then-owner, local businessman Dick Carter.

The concert was to take place on Saturday, Dec. 6. The location was switched on the night of Thursday, Dec. 4. This resulted in numerous logistical problems. Most importantly, facilities such as portable toilets and medical tents were lacking in number. The stage, which was only four feet high, was surrounded by the Hells Angels, led by Oakland chapter head Ralph 'Sonny' Barger who acted as security. The sound system was hardly sufficient for such a large audience.

Hells Angels

By some accounts, the Angels were hired to be security by the Rolling Stones on recommendation from the Grateful Dead for $500 worth of beer. This is a story Carter and Barger both vehemently deny. According to Stones' road manager Sam Cutler, "The only agreement there ever was . . . was for the Angels would make sure nobody fucked with the generators, but that was the extent of it. There was no 'They're going to be the police force' or anything like that. That's all bollocks. Hell's Angel member Sweet William recalled this exchange between himself and Cutler at a meeting prior to the concert, where Cutler had asked them to do security . . ."

"We don't police things. We're not a security force. We go to concerts to enjoy ourselves and have fun."

"Well, what about helping people out - you know, giving directions and things?"

"Sure, we can do that."

When Cutler asked how they would like to be paid, William replied, "We like beer."

Other accounts verify that the initial arrangement was for the Angels to watch over the equipment. However, Cutler later moved the Angels and their beer, nearer to the stage in order to settle them down or to protect the stage. Hells Angels had provided security at Grateful Dead shows in the past without reported violence. Some have speculated the Rolling Stones thought their experience with the Angels would be a peaceful affair.

Crowd management proved to be difficult: many spectators were injured and four died. Over the course of the day, the Hells Angels became increasingly agitated and violent. They had been drinking alcohol and taking drugs. They may have been concerned at having to control such an enormous crowd. The Angels used sawed-off pool cues in order to control the crowd. After one of the Angel's motor bikes was knocked over, the Angels became even more aggressive, even toward the performers onstage. Marty Balin of Jefferson Airplane was knocked unconscious following an altercation with an Angel on stage as seen in the documentary film *Gimme Shelter*. The Grateful Dead refused to play following the Balin incident, and left the venue.

ROCK 'N' ROLL
It's Better than Working for a Living

The organizers hoped to ease tensions in the crowd by having the Stones perform early, but it took hours before the Stones could take the stage. Accusations that Mick Jagger did not want to take the stage during daylight hours due to the filming of the concert have been voiced in the past. However, in the commentary on the official *Gimme Shelter* DVD, it is reported that Stones bassist Bill Wyman was having difficulties reaching the venue.

The Death of Meredith Hunter

The most famous death was that of Meredith Hunter. Hunter, an 18-year-old African American, became involved in an altercation with some Hells Angels and drew a long-barreled revolver. It is disputed whether or not Hunter drew his weapon before or after he was stabbed the first time. He was stabbed five times in total and kicked to death during the Rolling Stones' performance. His graphic death near the stage was clearly captured on film by three separate cameras. The killer, Alan Passaro, was arrested and tried for murder in the summer of 1972. He was acquitted after a jury concluded he acted in self-defense because Hunter was carrying a handgun, drew it, and allegedly pointed it at the stage. It was also alleged that Hunter was under the influence of methamphetamine.

Footage from *Gimme Shelter* shows that while the Rolling Stones were ending *Under My Thumb*, Hunter was approaching the stage and drawing his gun. Passaro subsequently parried the gun with his left hand and stabbed Hunter in the upper back with his right. The same footage also gives a glimpse of audience members and some of the Angels on the Stones' stage at the time. This incident is detailed in Rolling Stone magazine.

There have also been rumors, over the years that a second, unidentified assailant had inflicted the fatal wounds. As a result, the police considered the case still open until 25 May 2005. This is when the Alameda County Sheriff's Office announced it was officially closing the stabbing case. Investigators, concluding a renewed two-year investigation, dismissed the theory that a second Hells Angel took part in the stabbing.

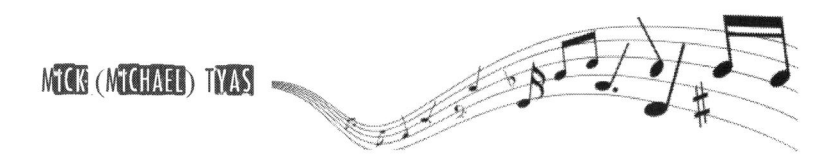

Reactions

Various news agencies reported the event as a "drug induced riot." The Rolling Stones had to interrupt their performance numerous times. At one point, Keith Richards tired of the events taking place said "fuck this" began to take off his guitar and walk off the stage. An unidentified Hell's Angel allegedly then pulled out his gun and stuck it in Richards gut and ordered him to "play or die." Richards began playing. Unaware Hunter's stabbing was fatal; they decided to continue to prevent a possible riot. The Altamont concert is often contrasted to the Woodstock festival that took place four months earlier. It is sometimes said to mark the end of the innocence embodied by Woodstock, or the de facto end of the 1960s. Critics called the tragedy the "Death of the Woodstock Nation." All future rock concerts were banned at the site.

Several Grateful Dead songs were written about — or in response to — what lyricist Robert Hunter called "the Altamont affair," including *New speedway Boogie* (Featuring the line "One way or another, this darkness got to give.") and *Mason's Children*. Both songs were written and recorded during sessions for the early 1970 album *Workingman's Dead*, but *Mason's Children* was viewed as too "popular" stylistically and was consequently not included on the album. A later Dead song, *My Brother Esau*, contains the line "My brother Esau killed a hunter / Back in 1969," perhaps a reference to the death of Meredith Hunter.

ROCK 'N' ROLL
It's Better than Working for a Living

In the famous song *American Pie* by Don McLean, there are some lines which have been claimed to refer to Altamont: "And as I watched him on the stage / My hands were clenched in fists of rage / No angel born in hell / Could break that Satan's spell / And as the flames climbed high into the night / To light the sacrificial rite / I saw Satan laughing with delight."

That was a *Day the Music Died*.

Chapter Twenty-Seven

THE ISLE OF WRIGHT FESTIVALS

The Isle of Wight Festival is a music festival which takes place annually on the Isle of Wight, England. It was originally held from 1968 to 1970, the venues being Ford Farm (near Godshill), Wootton and Afton Down (near Freshwater) respectively. The 1970 event was by far the largest and most famous of these early festivals; indeed it was said at the time to be one of the largest human gatherings in the world surpassing the attendance at Woodstock. The most notable of over fifty performers were The Who, Jimi Hendrix, Miles Davis, The Doors, Ten Years After, Joni Mitchell, Melanie, Donovan, Free, Chicago, Richie Havens, John Sebastian, Leonard Cohen, Jethro Tull and Tiny Tim. The unexpected level of the attendees (mostly non-ticket holders) was beyond that which the festival organizers and local authorities could supply adequate amenities and guarantee public safety for. Such concerns led in 1971, to Parliament passing the *Isle of Wight Act* preventing gatherings of more than 5,000 people on the island without a special license.

The event was revived in 2002 at Seaclose Park, a recreation ground on the outskirts of Newport. It has been held annually since that year, progressively extending itself northwards beyond Seaclose Park along the fields of the eastern Medina valley.

ROCK 'N' ROLL
It's Better than Working for a Living

Many notable Artistes have performed since its revival including The Rolling Stones, Donovan, Ray Davies, Robert Plant, The Proclaimers, David Bowie, The Who, R.E.M., Coldplay and Bryan Adams. It was sponsored by Nokia from 2004 to 2006. The promoters of the event now are Solo Music Agency and promotions. Apart from being held somewhere on the Isle of Wight, and featuring the now customary artwork of Dave Roe, there is no connection with the festivals of 1968–1970.

1968

> Held August 31, 1968.
>
> Attendance - 10,000 (approx.)
>
> Site - Ford farm, near Godshill.
>
> Headline Acts - Jefferson Airplane
>
> Other Acts - Arthur Brown, The Move, T. Rex, Plastic Penny and Pretty Things.

1969

> Held August 30 - August 31, 1969
>
> Attendance - 150,000 (approx.)
>
> Site - Wootton
>
> Headline Acts - Bob Dylan, The Who
>
> Other Acts - The Band, Joe Cocker, Free, Richie Havens, The Moody Blues, The Nice, Tom Paxton, Pentangle and Pretty Things.

1970

> Held August 26 - August 30, 1970.
>
> Attendance - 600,000 (approx.).

Site - Afton Down.

Headline Acts (Wednesday) – Redbone.

Other Acts (Wednesday) - Rosalie Sorrels, Kris Kristofferson, Mighty Baby, Judas Jump, Kathy Smith.

Headline Acts (Thursday) - Tony Joe White

Other Acts (Thursday) - Supertramp, Black Widow, The Groundhogs.

Headline Acts (Friday) - Procol Harum.

Other Acts (Friday) - Fairfield Parlour, Lighthouse, Melanie, Chicago, Taste, Family, Cactus.

Headline Acts (Saturday) - The Doors and The Who.

Other Acts (Saturday) - Sly & the Family Stone, Free, Joni Mitchell, Ten Years After, Emerson Lake And Palmer, Miles Davis, Mungo Jerry, John Sebastian, Cat Mother.

Headline Acts (Sunday) - Jimi Hendrix and Joan Baez.

Other Acts (Sunday) - Moody Blues, Jethro Tull, Leonard Cohen, Richie Havens, Everly Brothers, Pentangle, Donovan and Tiny Tim.

Chapter Twenty-Eight

THE GLASTONBURY UK FESTIVALS

The first festival, a small scale event of 1,500 people called the Pilton Festival, was created by Michael Eavis in 1970. The first artist to perform was the group Stackridge. This was followed by the larger scale Glastonbury Fayre of 1971, now also with the help of co-organizers Andrew Kerr and Arabella Churchill.

The 1971 festival featured the first incarnation of the "Pyramid Stage" conceived by Bill Harkin, built from scaffolding and metal sheeting. It was paid for by its supporters and advocates of its ideal, and took a medieval tradition of music, dance, poetry, theatre, lights and spontaneous entertainment.

The 1971 festival was filmed by Nicolas Roeg and David Puttnam and was released as a film simply called *Glastonbury Fayre*. Although there were unofficial events during the 1970s, the festival was not fully held again until an unplanned event in 1978 and a planned festival the following year which lost money. The festival has been an annual fixture since 1981, albeit with breaks in 1988, 1991, 1996, 2001 and 2006.

I'm just going to run through the first twenty years of this festival. This festival is still an annual event and as such as become a bit of a corporate baby with large multimedia companies getting involved in organization and sponsorship. Presently, it no longer embodies the spirit of festival, rather more akin to corporate greed.

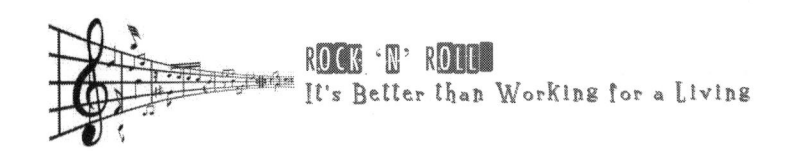

**ized with
the Campaign for Nuclear Disarmament (CND). That year a new Pyramid Stage was constructed from telegraph poles and metal sheeting (Appropriately, repurposed from materials of the Ministry of Defence.). It was a permanent structure, which doubled as a hay-barn and cow-shed during the winter.

In the 1980s, the children's area of the festival (which had been organized by Arabella Churchill and others) became the starting point for a new children's charity called Children's World. 1981 was the first year that the festival made profits, and Eavis donated £20,000 of them to CND. In the following years, donations were made to a number of organizations. Since the end of the Cold War, the main beneficiaries have been Oxfam, Greenpeace, and Water Aid who all contribute towards the festival by providing features and volunteers who work at the festival in exchange for free entrance.

Since 1983, large festivals have required licenses from local authorities. This led to certain restrictions being placed on the festival, including a crowd limit and times during which the stages could operate. The crowd limit was initially set at 30,000 but has grown every year to over 100,000. In 1985, the festival grew too large for Worthy Farm, but neighboring Cockmill Farm was purchased.

1985 was a wet festival with lots of rain. Worthy Farm is a dairy farm and what washed down into the low areas was a mixture of mud and liquefied cow dung. This didn't prevent the festival-goers from wallowing in the knee-deep slurry in front of the pyramid stage.

1990s

1990 saw the biggest festival yet; however, violence at the end of the festival between the security guards and new age travelers - the so-called Battle of Yeoman's Bridge - led to the organizers taking 1991 off to rethink the festival. The festival returned in 1992 with an expanded festival, which proved to be a great success. 1992 was the first year that the new age travelers were not allowed onto the site for free and a sturdier fence was designed. This success was carried through to 1993, which like 1992's festival, was another hot, dry year.

In 1994, the Pyramid Stage burned down just weeks before the festival. A temporary main stage was erected in time for the festival. The 1994 festival also introduced a 150 kW wind turbine which provided some of the festival power. This festival also included the setting of a new world record on 26 June when eight hundred and twenty six people, juggling at least three objects each, kept 2,478 objects in the air. This was also the year the festival was first televised by Channel 4 in the UK; concentrating on the main two music stages. It provided a glimpse of the festival for many who knew little of it. Channel 4 also televised the following year as well, which proved to be very successful.

The following year saw the attendance rise drastically due to the security fence being breached on the Friday of the festival. Estimates suggest there may have been enough fence-jumpers to double the size of the festival. This aside, 1995 proved to be a highly successful year with memorable performances from Oasis, PJ Harvey, Jeff Buckley and The Cure. This was also the first year of the festival having a dance tent to cater for the rise in popularity

ROCK 'N' ROLL
It's Better than Working for a Living

of dance music, following the success of Orbital's headline appearance the previous year. The dance acts of 1995 were led by Massive Attack on the Friday and Carl Cox on the Saturday.

The festival took a year off in 1996 to allow the land to recover and give the organizers a break. This would be a pattern which would be followed every five years from now on. 1996 also saw the release of *Glastonbury* the Movie which was filmed at the 1993 and 1994 festivals. In that year, local artist Paul Branson established his Glastonbury Arts Festivals to provide a platform for classical works and put on a highly successful production of Rutland Boughton's opera *The Immortal Hour* at Strode Theatre as well as an art exhibition and a *son et lumière* at Glastonbury Abbey. These festivals, however, were short-lived.

The festival returned in 1997 bigger than ever. This time there was major sponsorship from The Guardian newspaper and BBC TV, who had taken over televising the event from Channel 4. This was also the year of the mud, with the site suffering severe rainfalls which turned the entire site into a muddy bog. This caused many festival goers to leave early on the Friday, or not even bother to attend after radio and television reports gave details of just how muddy the site was. However, those who stayed for the festival were treated to many memorable performances, including Radiohead's headlining Pyramid set on the Saturday, which is said to be one of the greatest ever Glastonbury performances.

In 1998, the festival was once again struck with severe floods and storms, again some festival goers departed early but those who stayed were treated to performances from acts such as Pulp, Robbie Williams and Blur. 1998 was also the first year that attendance officially broke the 100,000 mark.

1999 was a hot dry year, much to the relief of organizers and festival goers. Memorable performances from R.E.M, Fun Loving

MICK (MICHAEL) TYAS

Criminals and Al Green were among the highlights. Again, the festival was overcrowded due to fence-jumpers; this however would not be a major problem till the following year when the festival suffered from massive numbers of fence-jumpers. This surge increased the attendance to an estimated 250,000 people. The 1999 festival is also remembered for the Manic Street Preachers requesting and being given their own backstage toilets, however it was revealed by the band this was a joke. The 'reserved' sign on the toilet was not at the authorization of the management.

2000 saw a new Pyramid Stage introduced as well as several new features such as The Glade and The Leftfield. The festival was headlined by David Bowie playing thirty years after his first appearance. The Pyramid Stage also hosted an unusual event on the Saturday; with the wedding of Chelfyn & Helen Baxter conducted by actor Keith Allen (Whose daughter Lily would perform at the 2007 festival.). This year also saw an estimated 250,000 people attend the festival (Only 100,000 tickets were sold.) due to gatecrashers. This led to public safety concerns and the local District Council refused any further licenses unless and until the problem could be solved.

Glastonbury festival is now a British institution but I went to the first one in 1971.

My abiding memories of this festival are that it was a really nice sunny weekend (There didn't seem to be that many people there.) and of taking loads of LSD. They say Glastonbury is a mystical place; well it was bloody mystical and mysterious that weekend. I remember sitting around a camp fire in the pitch black. All the bands had finished playing. I was just sat talking away with a lots of other people. Did I know any of them? I can't remember, but my next recollection was waking up in a bed in an apartment I did not recognize, with a girl I did not recognize. I say did not recognize but I do remember her from the night before around the camp fire. Well, I think it was the night before. How did I get there? Apparently, we had got a ride back to London with some other people. Whether I had passed out due to the amount of LSD and various other drugs; or "teleported" back by the acid and Glastonbury mysticism, I have no idea. The girl's name was Beverley Pitchford. We were in an apartment in Earls Court in West London where she lived. When I woke she told me she was going to Coventry in the Midlands where she came from and asked, "Do you want to come?"

"Guess so??? I remember going to a high rise apartment in the centre of Coventry with her. What happened after that, did she come back to London with me? I have no idea, but I never saw her again. Was she my Glastonbury guide??????????"

Chapter Twenty-Nine

THE NEXT BIG BRITISH FESTIVAL

K *nebworth*
Here is a potted history of the Knebworth Festival, now truly an international affair.

1974, THE BUCOLIC FROLIC: The Allman Brothers, The Van Morrison Show, The Doobie Brothers, The Mahavishnu Orchestra, The Sensational Alex Harvey Band, and Tim Buckley - attendance: 60,000.

For the first time, we face the logistical problems of a crowd the size of a small town arriving in a field for the weekend. Food, water, toilets, camping, rubbish . . . from the outset there were protests from local residents. Chief Superintendent Tom Oliver of Hertfordshire Police thought the day "Would be good exercise for the men." A toilet block full of people sank into a sewage ravine . . . the sixty thousand Watt PA was the largest sound system ever heard in England.

1975 KNEBWORTH PARK: Pink Floyd, The Steve Miller Band, Captain Beefheart, Roy Harper, Linda Lewis. Attendance: 100,000.

The fences had to be pulled down to let in thousands of extra people. The fly past by RAF Spitfires arrived out of sync with

Dark Side of the Moon. They drug squad arrived in sync with the party afterwards at Knebworth House . . .

1976 KNEBWORTH FAIR: The Rolling Stones, 10cc, Hot Tuna, Lynyrd Skynyrd, Todd Rundgren, The Don Harrison Band. Attendance: 120,000.

Circus clowns invaded Wimbledon Centre Court (tennis!) clutching a banner reading, "The Stones at Knebworth." All very well, but Lord Cobbold's father, who owned the Knebworth estate was Lord Chamberlain to the Queen. He had accompanied The Royal Family to the event (The tennis event that is!). At Knebworth House, Mick Jagger left his Y-fronts at the bottom of Queen Elizabeth I's four-poster bed; they're still in the House safe.

1978 A MIDSUMMER NIGHT'S DREAM: Genesis, Jefferson Starship, Tom Petty, Devo, Brand X, Atlanta Rhythm Section. Attendance: 60,000.

The first concert at which a baby was born. . . Where are you now?

1978 OH GOD NOT ANOTHER BORING OLD KNEBWORTH!: Frank Zappa, The Tubes, Peter Gabriel, The Boomtown Rats, Nick Lowe, Dave Edmunds, Wilco Johnson. Attendance: 45,000.

A new breed of fans with a new level of amplified swearing . . . while the Red Cross tackles magic mushroom season.

1979 KNEBWORTH FESTIVAL: Led Zeppelin. The New Barbarians, Todd Rundgren, Southside Johnny, Marshall Tucker, Commander Cody, Chas & Dave, Fairport Convention. Attendance: 200,000 over two weekends.

The largest stage ever constructed; also 570 toilet seats, 750 feet of urinals and the biggest rock band in the world. Led Zeppelin played their last ever concerts at Knebworth (or so we thought). It was the end of an era for the Knebworth shows. Both concerts overran noise complaints were received from seven miles away. The garbage team struggled to cope with clearing the arena between the shows. The Police believed that two hundred and fifty thousand people had turned up each night. One local supermarket lost one hundred and fifty carts. Another, 75% of their stock and Lord Cobbold ended up in Court.

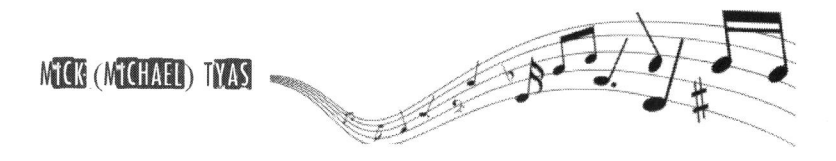

Here are some other major concerts at the park:

On 30 June 1990, the park was the location for The Silver Clef Award Winners Concert, a big live show which was recorded and released on DVD. It included the performance of Artistes including Paul McCartney, Cliff Richard & The Shadows, Pink Floyd (with Candy Dulfer), Tears for Fears, Eric Clapton, Dire Straits, Elton John, Robert Plant (with guest Jimmy Page), Status Quo and Phil Collins with Genesis.

In 1996, The Charlatans, Kula Shaker, Manic Street Preachers, Ocean Colour Scene and The Prodigy supported Oasis at two shows with a combined audience of over 250,000.

Over 10 Million people applied for tickets for the shows, making it the biggest demand for concert tickets in British history. The 1985 event was the first UK gig by the re-formed Deep Purple. It was very muddy.

In 2003, Robbie Williams performed at Knebworth over a three day period, drawing crowds of over 375,000, and a further 3.5 million who watched live on television and online.

This was reputedly the biggest UK pop concert ever and caused a huge traffic jam on the A1 (M) motorway as an estimated 130,000 cars tried to reach the venue. A subsequent album, entitled "Robbie Williams – Live at Knebworth," was released.

Chapter Thirty

CONCERT HISTORIES

> The following details all the major concerts held to date on the grounds of Knebworth House.

Date, Name, Artists and the Attendance...

20 July 1974: The Bucolic Frolic. The Allman Brothers Band, The Van Morrison Show, The Doobie Brothers, The Mahavishnu Orchestra, The Sensational Alex Harvey Band, Tim Buckley. Audience: 60,000.

5 July 1975: Knebworth Park Pink Floyd. The Steve Miller Band, Captain Beefheart, Roy Harper, Linda Lewis. Audience: 100,000.

21 August 1976: Knebworth Fair The Rolling Stones. 10cc, Hot Tuna, Lynyrd Skynyrd, Todd Rundgren, The Don Harrison Band. Audience: 120,000.

24 June 1978: A Midsummer Night's Dream. Genesis, Jefferson Starship, Tom Petty, Devo, Brand X, Atlanta Rhythm Section, Roy Harper. Audience: 60,000.

ROCK 'N' ROLL
It's Better than Working for a Living

9 September 1978: Oh God Not another Boring Old Knebworth! Frank Zappa, The Tubes, Peter Gabriel, The Boomtown Rats, Nick Lowe, Dave Edmunds, Wilco Johnson. Audience: 45,000.

4 August 1979: Knebworth Festival. Led Zeppelin, Todd Rundgren, Southside Johnny, Marshall Tucker, Commander Cody, Chas & Dave, Fairport Convention. Audience: 200,000 (over two weekends).

21 June 1980: Knebworth '80. The Beach Boys, Santana, Mike Oldfield, Elkie Brooks, Lindisfarne, The Blues Band. Audience: 45,000.

1981 & 1982: The Jazz Years. Ella Fitzgerald, Chuck Berry, Muddy Waters, Sarah Vaughan, BB King, Jimmy Cliff, Dizzy Gillespie, Benny Goodman, Lionel Hampton. Audience: 50,000 (over a few days).

1982 & 1983: Greenbelt Festival Cliff Richard. Audience: 65,000 (over two separate years).

1985: The Return of the Knebworth Fayre. Deep Purple, Scorpions, Meat Loaf, UFO, Blackfoot, Mountain, Mama's Boys, Alaska. Audience: 80,000.

1986: It's a Kind of Magic Queen. Status Quo, Big Country, Belouis Some. Audience: 120,000.

30 June 1990: Knebworth '90. Pink Floyd, Paul McCartney, Mark Knopfler, Eric Clapton, Elton John, Genesis, Robert Plant &

Jimmy Page, Cliff Richard & The Shadows, Status Quo, Tears for Fears. Audience: 120,000.

2 August 1992: Genesis at Knebworth. Genesis, The Saw Doctors, Lisa Stansfield. Audience: 90,000.

11, 12 August 1996: Oasis. Oasis, The Prodigy, Manic Street Preachers, Ocean Colour Scene, Charlatans, Cast, The Chemical Brothers, Dreadzone, Kula Shaker, The Bootleg Beatles. Audience: 250,000 (over two consecutive nights).

11 August 2001: Ministry @ Knebworth 2001. Jamiroquai, Bent, Lo Fidelity Allstars. Audience: 50,000.

1, 2, 3 August 2003: Robbie Williams Live at Knebworth. Robbie Williams, Moby, Ash, Kelly Osbourne, The Darkness. Audience: 375,000 (over three consecutive nights).

30 June 2007: Wild in the Country. Renaissance 15th Anniversary. Underworld, Hot Chip, Sasha & John Digweed, Simian Mobile Disco, Justice, Erol Alkan, 2ManyDJs to mention. Audience: 40,000.

2009: Sonisphere Festival. Metallica, Linkin Park, Nine Inch Nails, Heaven and Hell, Limp Bizkit, Bullet For My Valentine, Avenged Seven Fold, Anthrax, Lamb of God, Airbourne, Alice In Chains, Killing Joke, Feeder, Mastadon . . . and many more. Audience: 50,000.

2010: Sonisphere Festival. Iron Maiden, Rammstein, Alice Cooper, Motley Crue, Iggy and the Stooges, Placebo, Pendulum, Good Charlotte, Alice in Chains, Papa Roache, Slayer, Anthrax, Gary

Numan, Skunk Anansie. The Cult ... and many more. Audience: 50,000.

2011: Sonisphere Festival. The Big 4, Metallica, Slayer, Megadeath & Anthrax, Slipknot, Biffy Clyro, Limpbizkit, Motorhead, Weezer, Bill Bailey, The Mars Volta, Diamond Head, Opeth, The Sisters of Mercy, Killing joke, You Me at Six ... and many more. Audience: 50,000.

27-28th June 1970: The Bath Festival of Blues and Progressive Music. A British music festival held at the Bath and Wells Showground in Shepton Mallet featured a line-up of the top American west coast and British bands of the day, including Donovan, Mothers of Invention, Santana, The Flock, Led Zeppelin (headlining act), Hot Tuna, Country Joe McDonald, Colosseum, Jefferson Airplane (set aborted), The Byrds (acoustic set), Moody Blues (unable to play), Dr. John (acoustic set), Frank Zappa, Canned Heat, It's a Beautiful Day, Steppenwolf, Johnny Winter, John Mayall, Pink Floyd, Fairport Convention, and Keef Hartley.

27 August 1970: Isle of Wright Festival. The Bath Festival of Blues and Progressive Music line-up eclipsed the more famous Isle of Wight festival held in August of the same year, but as it attracted less press coverage at the time and was a smaller affair, it has generally received less attention in the years since. The show started at midday on the 27th (a Saturday) and finished at about 6:30 am on Monday morning.

Bath Festival was the brainchild of promoter Freddy Bannister, who had held a smaller Blues festival within Bath itself in 1969. The 1970 show attracted a significantly larger crowd of 150,000, but, like the Isle of Wight festival, an audience of such magnitude created some serious on-ground difficulties. The logistics proved to be too vast for Bannister's small team to adequately cope with, and his security staff stole large amounts of gate receipts, resulting in a far smaller profit than expected. The festival also suffered from inclement weather on the Sunday night, with Jefferson Airplane being rained off half way through their set and The Moody Blues not playing at all due to the wet stage.

Actually, getting to the festival itself was another problem for many of the throng of fans. The country lanes leading to the site were swiftly blocked by cars, also meaning that many of the bands' equipment trucks could not get to the site. As a consequence the festival ran behind schedule and many bands had to play to diminished crowds in the small hours of Monday morning. The last act, Dr. John, hit the stage at dawn on the Monday

The festival featured many innovations, including projections of the bands on screens on the side of the stage; also, a good quality PA system, on-site tents for the patrons to sleep in and larger tents which projected films such as King Kong throughout the night. The expenditure on these items ate into the profits. Many people decamped with the tents, which were hired. This was another expense that had to borne by the promoters.

The festival was captured on both film and on video, in varying quality. A lack of post-festival organisation led to the footage being lost for many years. Much of it has now been recovered. The black and white footage is of poor quality and is in many different hands. It is considered unlikely that it will ever see the light of day as a legitimate release since no one can agree on who owns the copyright. This situation could be contrasted to the Isle of Wight Festival, which was professionally recorded and filmed in colour.

The festival was widely bootlegged, and several audience tapes are now in circulation. It is rumoured that excellent soundboard tapes also exist, though to this point they have not publicly surfaced.

The Author

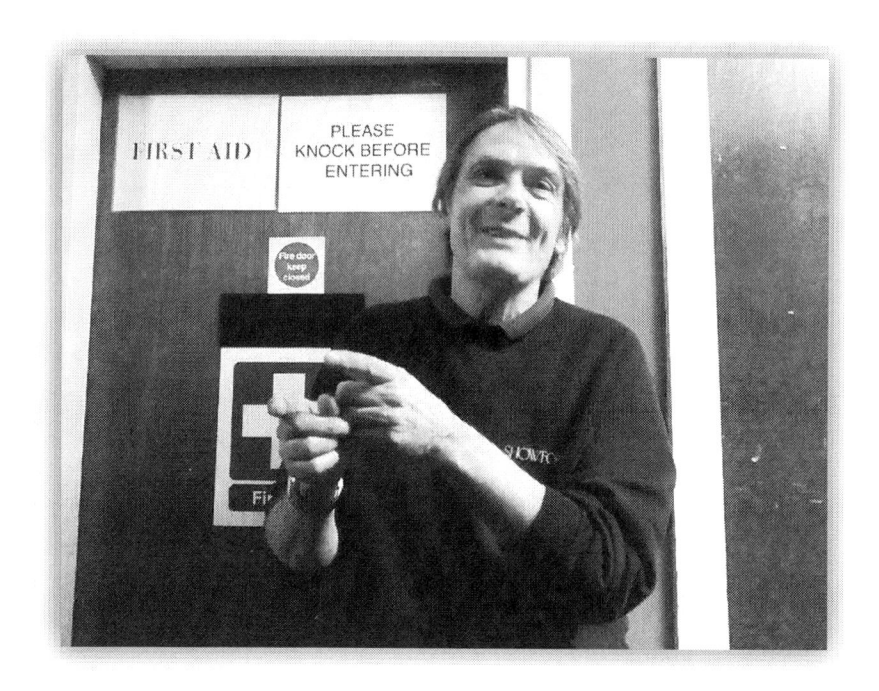

MICK TYAS

Visit the Author

WEBSITE

PUBLISHER
DonnaInk Publications, L.L.C.: www.donnaink.org

SOCIAL MEDIA

FACEBOOK
https://www.facebook.com/pages/Author-Michael-Tyas-Publisher-Page/158781370935711

LINKEDIN
uk.linkedin.com/pub/mick-tyas/2b/258/57

TWITTER
http://www.twitter.com/AuthorMikeTyas

WORDPRESS BLOG
http://authormicktyas.wordpress.com

dpInk

Donnalnk Publications, L.L.C.
www.donnaink.org

CW01267269

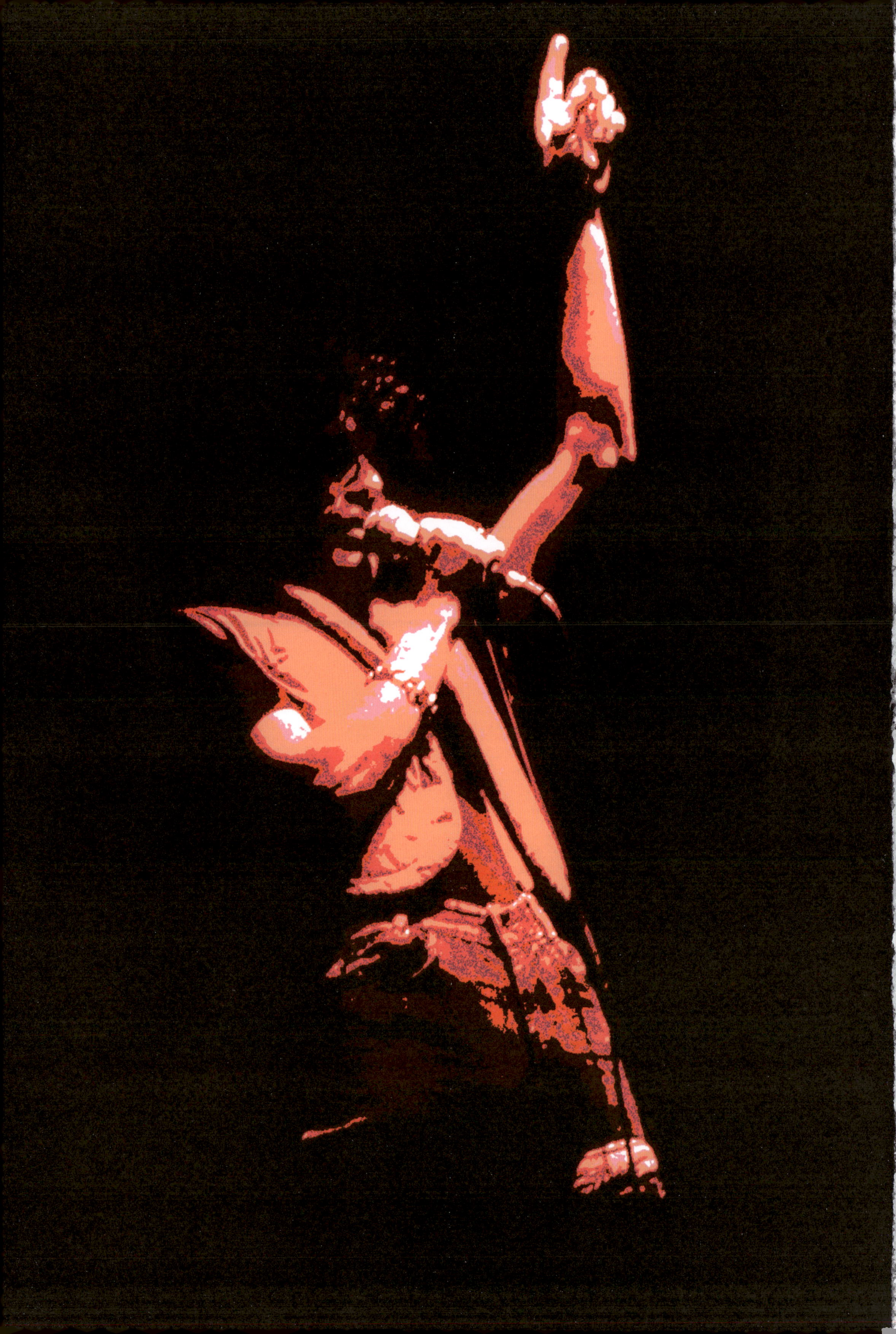

Loud 'n' Proud
50 Years of
Nazareth

Martin Popoff
with Roni Ramos Amorim on Images

Loud 'n' Proud
50 Years of
Nazareth

Martin Popoff
with Roni Ramos Amorim on Images

WP
WYMER
PUBLISHING
Bedford, England

First published in Great Britain in 2021
by Wymer Publishing
www.wymerpublishing.co.uk
Tel: 01234 326691
Wymer Publishing is a trading name of Wymer (UK) Ltd

Copyright © Martin Popoff /Wymer Publishing.

ISBN: 978-1-912782-71-0

The Author hereby asserts his rights to be identified
as the author of this work in accordance with sections
77 to 78 of the Copyright, Designs & Patents Act 1988.

All rights reserved. No part of this publication may be
reproduced or transmitted in any form or by any means,
electronic or mechanical, including photocopying, or any
information storage and retrieval system, without written
permission from the publisher.

This publication is sold subject to the condition that it shall not,
by way of trade or otherwise, be lent, re-sold, hired out or
otherwise circulated without the publishers prior consent in any
form of binding or cover other than that in which it is published
and without a similar condition including this condition
being imposed on the subsequent purchaser.

Every effort has been made to trace the copyright holders of the
photographs in this book but some were unreachable. We would
be grateful if the photographers concerned would contact us.

Design by Andy Bishop / 1016 Sarpsborg
Printed by Imago Group.

A catalogue record for this book is available from the British Library.

Loud 'n' Proud
50 Years of
Nazareth

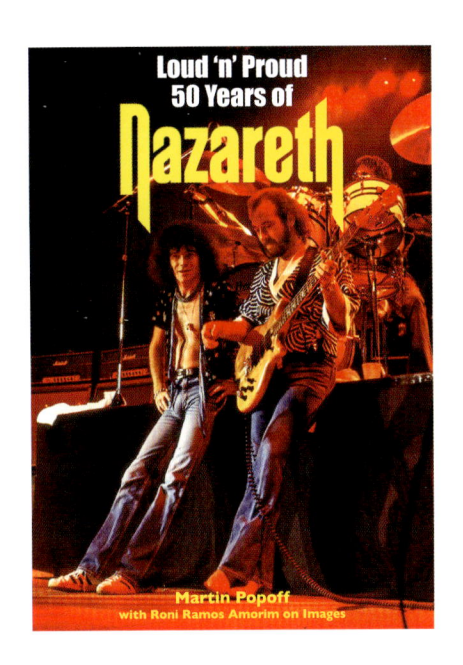

Martin Popoff
with Roni Ramos Amorim on Images

ROLL OF HONOUR

Wymer Publishing duly acknowledges the following people who all put their faith in this publication by pre-ordering it:

Bjørnar Andreassen
Bruce Ashcroft
Jason Barber
John Bell
Sandy Brands
Jules Brazeau
Ralph Palma
José Ailton Claudino de Bastos
Arne Dahl
Bjørn Dalvang
Russ Evers
John Fell
Grant Finlay
Keith Fitzgerald
George Galloway
David Gauger
Ulrike Graber
Mike Grieshaber
James Griffis
Derek Hall
Steve Haynie
Sharon Heath
James Hoffmaster
Roy Hutchinson
Ron Lewis
Julian Lewry
Danny Lucas
Pål H. Lund
Edenil Osmar Marques
Larry McGuffin Jr
Altair Antonio Muraro
Alan Murray
Bill Nelson
Andrew Newberry
Raymond Niemelainen
Mark Porrovecchio
Robert Pratt
Alex Pritsker
Susanne Rashed
Paul Robertson
Jan Harald Roset
Richard Schultheiss
Vadim Grigorievich Shatskiy
Nigel Sheppard
Mark Skaar
Darla Soich
Karl Stanka
Jan Atle Steinsland
Chryssi Stout-Yonkins
Eric Sweetwood
Werner Temmel
Lee Thomas
Martin Thompson
Wes Waschuk
Brian Wilson
Karel Zdenovec

Nazareth

CONTENTS

Introduction	9
Origins Through 1974	13
1975 – 1979	49
The 1980s	101
The 1990s	155
The 2000s	189
The 2010s and 2020	211
Acknowledgements	239
About the Author	239
Martin Popoff – A Complete Bibliography	240

© Wolfgang Gurster

INTRODUCTION

Welcome one and all to this celebration of Scotland's finest, a band that surprisingly hasn't seen much elaborate pictorial presentation in the past. It took long enough, but here we are, 50 years since the self-titled debut album, extolling the virtues of Nazareth, a band near and dear to my heart because it was the favourite band of my deceased brother, Brad. But the reason my brother and I grew up listening to Nazareth is because, in addition, I'm pretty darn sure that Razamanaz was the first properly heavy rock record I ever owned, even if something tells me that either Led Zeppelin II, III or the untitled fourth was the first properly heavy rock record I ever heard.

And what would that make howler monkey Dan McCafferty? Well, he would be the first extreme rock vocalist I ever heard, although now it gets complicated: I did indeed own Steppenwolf Gold and a couple of Creedence Clearwater Revival records *(Cosmo's Factory* and *Pendulum)* before metal became my unceasing biggest hobby, and one could argue that John Kay and John Fogerty are somewhat extreme atop each's not very extreme musical backing, i.e. dated, pre-Nazareth-type music from the late 1960s and in CCR's case, the late 1860s!

But man, dropping the needle on *Razamanaz* and specifically "Razamanaz" back then in the summer of 1973, at ten years old, my world changed, and not just because of the unholy screech emanating from the spaces between Manny Charlton's stacked wall-of-sound power chords, but also because of Darrell Sweet's double bass drum madness. It's possible that right there something wormed into my subconscious that made me take up the drums, which I did immediately.

Not long after, me an' my buddies were lowering the needle on "The Ballad of Hollis Brown," and our brains were wrecked, forever destined to be metalheads, as Nazareth became the second band after Black Sabbath to wallow in what would become known as doom metal, not that these guys were ever deliberate about their heaviness, much less any obscure subgenres of heavy metal. That's one of the cool things about Nazareth: anything goes. And as the years piled up, anything went, much to the detriment of their career. It might be argued that all that '80s stuff made the '70s stuff sound even more special, but that one is up for debate. In fact, I really only thought of that now.

Another cool thing about doing this book is that besides the personal connection that my brother and I had with this band, there's an extra level of personal attachment, and that's because I'm from Western Canada, now living in Toronto, and Nazareth were a big deal in Canada, playing back and forth across the country regularly, and in later years, really staking an uncommon claim in BC and Alberta and Saskatchewan. Quite remarkable, really, to the point where my dad and my brother, long after I'd moved to Toronto, actually went and saw the band in a small bar in Nelson, BC.

But yes, the Great White North was a territory where most of those '70s records went gold and platinum. Now, something I just recently figured out. If you aren't particularly impressed with Canada's certification levels of 50,000 sold for gold and 100,000 sold for platinum, the wider point is that Nazareth could headline hockey arenas for years across Canada, meaning

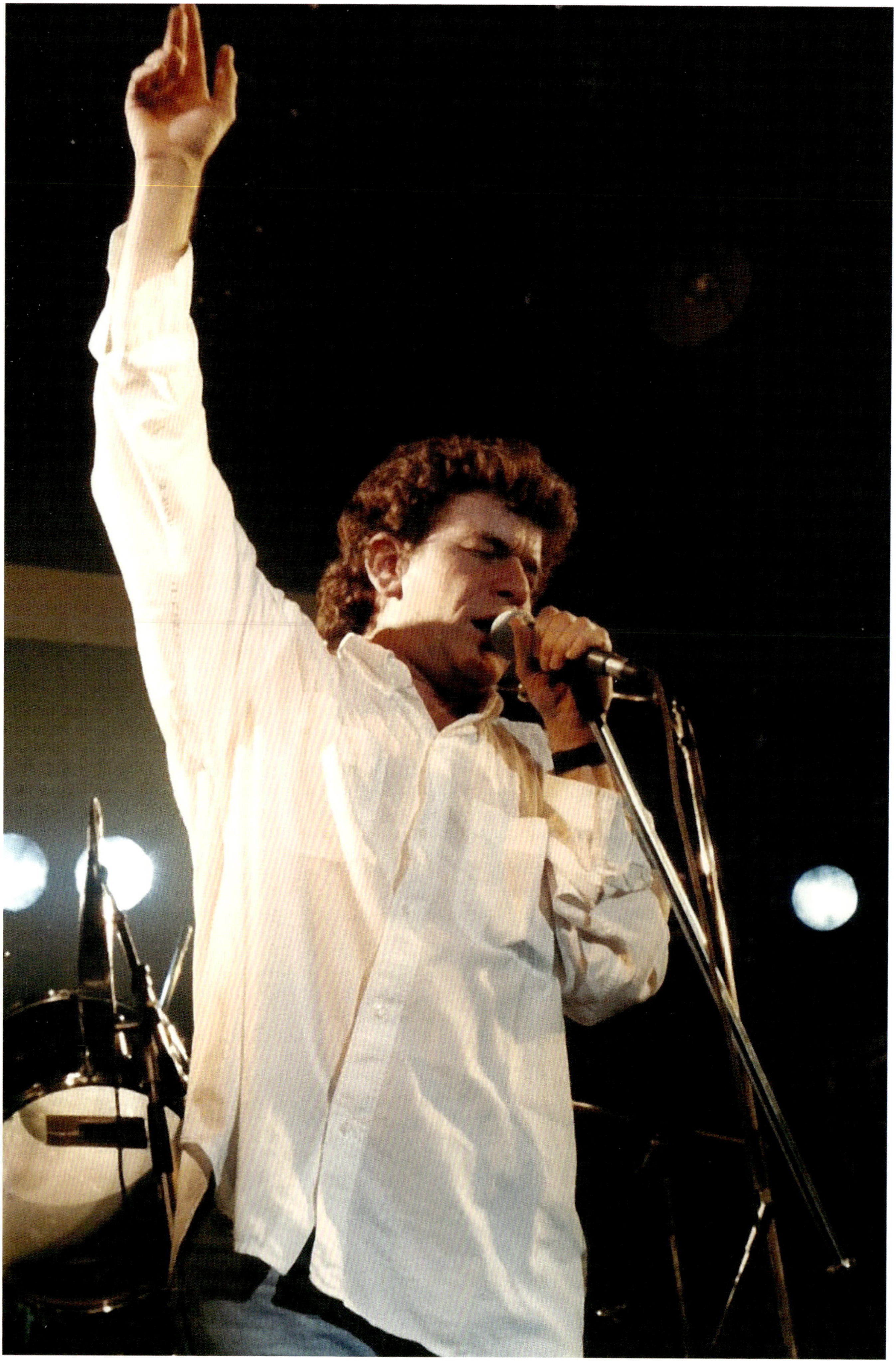

that the upside impression that Canada had on the band's success was actually quite large. The band expresses as much, with the fond memories that they hold for this territory made clear in interviews across the ages, enhanced also by the fact that they made three records at Le Studio in Quebec, famed for its association with local heroes Rush.

Of course the other cool thing is that Nazareth are one of these world-travelling bands, particularly big in Germany and Brazil and Russia, besides the well wishes they receive across Canada. Good stuff, and it's made for an interesting life, even if that pirate lifestyle has come to a close for Dan, who literally can't catch his breath after years on the road breathing in both second- and first-hand smoke. After McCafferty had reluctantly bowed out of the band, bassist Pete Agnew soldiered on, hiring on first Linton Osborne and then Carl Sentance, with whom the band has actually made one studio album already. But the story doesn't end there: Pete's son Lee and guitarist Jimmy Murrison have been part of the band for what amounts to decades now, and so we shouldn't be so quick to declare Nazareth over when Dan has had to, quite literally, take a seat.

Crack open the pages of this book and these story points are all explained, in a format with which I'm familiar, and which readers of my books should, by now, also be familiar. What I've done is create a detailed timeline, just as Wymer Publishing and myself have done across four other books similar to this in recent times, as well as many other books I have done outside the Wymer umbrella. What makes this a little more special over and above my recent similar books on Blue Öyster Cult, Thin Lizzy, Van Halen and Uriah Heep, is that I've liberally marbled in quotes from the band, making this better than a timeline book, better than an oral history, because it's… both a timeline book *and* an oral history.

In other words, there should be more than enough literary substance to satisfy as you graze these pages filled with the band's fantastic album cover art, 45 sleeves and demonstrations of live camaraderie and friendship between each and all the various lineups of this band, even if—and they would agree with a chuckle—the mugs on the front of the Nazareth guys aren't exactly the most photogenic in the world. As well, this wasn't a band surrounded by stage props and pyro—they just kind of went up there and played, and so there's not a lot of drama in the live shots you're about to see, even if there is a more than ample display of the rainbow of human emotion and experience that comes from a bunch of Scottish lads plying their trade since the mid-1960s.

But like I say, the live photography is supported ably by the band's artistic flourishes in the graphics department, as well as the special fact that among the books in this series, with this one you really get to hear the guys explain their 50-year career in their own humble and bemused words. Finally, I've got to say that one of the crowning joys of doing this book besides the reasons cited so far is the fact that I find myself very surprised that the final three albums with Dan—in my heart of hearts, swear to God—are probably three of my favourite six albums the band has ever crafted, along with *Razamanaz, Loud 'n' Proud* (hence the title of this book), and *Hair of the Dog*. I love that! And I love this band. And I love the fact that we're about to share our love for Nazareth together. So let's do that.

Martin Popoff
martinp@inforamp.net; martinpopoff.com

"It had never, ever even crossed my mind to play bass and the only times I strapped on a bass guitar was when our bass player would turn up late for gigs and I had to play 'til he arrived. When I listened to records it was always the singers and the songs that I concentrated on and never any particular instrument and certainly not the bass. I ended up playing bass because there was nobody else in our hometown that we wanted. Up until then, Dan and I used to do twin vocals and before that I was on rhythm guitar and vocals. But when we eventually fired the bass player the guys said to me, 'Why don't you play it? You play the guitar so why not the bass?' I thought, 'Well, I don't know.... and then again, it's only got four strings so why not?'"

"So I really got the gig by default, and since they never found anybody else I just kinda got stuck with it for the last 50 years.(laughs). Like I said, I always concentrated on singing rather than bass playing and have never consciously studied other bass players, although I have had and still have many excellent players as good friends. Guys like Roger Glover, Glenn Hughes, the late great Trevor Bolder—Uriah Heep and Spiders from Mars—and of course my own son Chris. But we never really talked about bass playing. We're not like drummers who are always talking about nuts and bolts when they get together. Bass players... they're usually talking about the quality of the beer."

Pete Agnew

ORIGINS THROUGH 1974

Nazareth

© Rich Galbraith

Just like their good buddies in Uriah Heep, Nazareth set themselves up for life across the span of two or three action-packed, sleep-deprived years in the early '70s. But it almost went pear-shaped before it got going. There was a debut that didn't make much of a dent, even if its considerable heaviness raised a few eyebrows. Then there was the career stumble that was Exercises, a bit like Deep Purple's classical album debacle, Zeppelin with III, Rush with *Caress of Steel* and even more similar to what Uriah Heep did with *Salisbury.* As Mick Box is wont to say, Heep found their sound with *Look at Yourself,* while across London town, Nazareth just as forthrightly found their sound with *Razamanaz.*

And again, like Heep and many other '70s greats, Nazareth found themselves putting out two records in one year, following up their heavy metal barnstormer of a third album with a fourth called *Loud 'n' Proud* before 1973 was out. Unlike Heep and Deep Purple (but more like Black Sabbath), there wouldn't be a live album, with Nazareth getting right back to work in 1974, issuing *Rampant*, which took a wee bit of wind out of the band's sails, although, fortunately, the decline was not to last.

An interesting question is to what extent Nazareth paid their dues, so to speak. One might say that they emerged relatively quickly onto the scene and became a working band, i.e., off to America with their very first album. But the fact is, through their origins as The Shadettes, the guys really did spend years learning their collective craft, even if these woodshedding years were relatively tranquil, having been spent close to home.

But yes, as soon as we got to the '70s, and especially 1973, the band got very busy, playing at home, to be sure, but also on the mainland and also in Canada and the United States, helped along by support slots with Deep Purple, sort of like Elf, although the residuals of that situation would take a much different turn than that of Nazareth's. Within the context of this story, what would happen is that Deep Purple bassist Roger Glover would produce the band, seizing upon their "live for today" material, teaching them the reality of reality, and framing the likes of *Exercises* as just that, exercises, or, conversely, the type of material one might save for a Roger Glover solo album.

The resultant explosive records, along with the cock-sure live shows, honed from years of experience playing covers and seeing what works and what doesn't in front of a demanding penny- and battery-chucking Scottish pub audience, resulted in a not insignificant amount of media buzz about this band, in the local UK music weeklies, but also rock and pop magazines on the continent. The fact of the matter is, in the early '70s, Nazareth were executing, bringing both quality and quantity, again, building a sturdy foundation upon which decades of rock was about to be piled.

February 13, 1692. The Massacre of Glencoe takes place, in the Scottish highlands, pitting government forces against the Clan MacDonald. Nazareth would write a song about it called "1692 (Glencoe Massacre)," which would appear as the last track on their second album, *Exercises*.

1935. H. Kingsley Long sees publication of his novel *No Mean City*, which would inspire a 1979 Nazareth album of the same name.

July 25, 1941. Manuel "Manny" Charlton is born in La Linea, Andalusia, Spain.

1943. The Charltons immigrate to the UK, settling in Dunfermline, Scotland, where Manny would make his way through Commercial Primary School and Queen Anne High School.

September 14, 1946. Pete Agnew is born in Dunfermline, Scotland.

October 14, 1946. William McCafferty is born in Dunfermline, Scotland.

May 16, 1947. Darrell Antony Sweet is born in Bournemouth, England.

May 4, 1949. Alistair MacDonald "Zal" Cleminson is born in Glasgow, Scotland.

1957. Pete Agnew's first show is a skiffle contest at the ABC Cinema in Kirkcaldy, which he won.

> **Manny Charlton:**
> "Originally Pete was a guitar player, and then he didn't play guitar and he just sang for a few years. And then when we lost our bass player—he left—Pete said, 'I'll play the bass.' So that was it. He became the bass player. Yes, Pete the happy bass player. Yeah, Pete always has a big smile on his face, bobbing around the stage; he's probably happiest when he's on stage. He's the original… It was kind of his band, because he started it way back, in the early '60s, and they were called The Shadettes. It wasn't until I joined that they changed the name to Nazareth. And that was Pete, Dan and Darrell and another bass player at the time, and the keyboard player was the original Shadettes. And they asked me to join when they lost their guitar player. They were all from the same town."

1957. Darrell Sweet's first public show is with The Fife Pipe Band, Burntisland.

1959. Manny Charlton plays his first gig, the Cowdenbeath Palais, with his band The Hellcats.

1961. Pre-Nazareth band The Shadettes open for business, with Pete playing guitar. Manny Charlton, who would join right at the end, had already been in bands, most notably Mark 5 and the Red Hawks. Dan says their first gig was at the Kirkcaldy YMCA.

> **Pete Agnew:**
> "In Scotland in the '60s, all the bands were heavily into soul music, as were the people who came to dance. The vocalists on the Stax and Tamla labels were—and still are to a great extent—the best in the world. To this day Dan and I would name Otis Redding as the best singer the world has heard. Also the great riffs that peppered soul music were an inspiration in later years to the

creators of heavy or 'hard' rock: many a' soul riff has been changed around a wee bit and used as the basis of some of our best known rock songs. The songs themselves were fantastic, and there seemed to be about five classics released every week. I still get a buzz when I hear Otis sing 'Mr. Pitiful,' when I hear Sam & Dave sing 'Hold On I'm Coming,' or Bob & Earl do 'Harlem Shuffle.' We used to do all those songs back then, and I suppose it must have rubbed off a bit when it came to writing and performing our own songs. At least, I hope it did." (w/ Dmitry Epstein, dmme.net)

1962. Bill McCafferty becomes Dan, at least to his buddies.

Pete Agnew:
"Everybody thinks it's William Daniel McCafferty. But Dan was Bill, Bill McCafferty, and Dan doesn't come from a middle name because he never had a middle name. We grew up with Bill—Bill and the boys. When he went to start work, when he was 16, he got this nickname Dan, from the guys. God knows how he got it, but we all started to call him that and it just stuck and he became Dan McCafferty. So it was just an old nickname. He was Bill McCafferty everywhere he went. I mean, his whole family, his wife calls him Bill (laughs). And I know his sisters and brothers, and everybody, the whole family, they all call him Bill. My wife still calls him Bill (laughs)."

1962. Bonnie Dobson includes her song "Morning Dew" on her live album *At Folk City*. Nazareth will cover the well-travelled classic on their first album.

Early 1964. Darrell Sweet is now part of The Shadettes, replacing Alan Fraser, and Des Haldane joins on guitar.

Pete Agnew:
"When The Shadettes started in '61, it was my band, and I was the singer and a rhythm guitar player and there were the four of us. And then when it got to 1964, the end of '63, the beginning of '64 the drummer, Darrell and Des Haldane joined. Des played guitar and he could sing. Up 'til then, I was only guy that could sing in the band; the other three guys couldn't sing at all. When Des came in it was great because it was another guy who could sing so we could do all these harmony things and I got to really like that. And when he left, it was really strange not having another singer."

November 8, 1964. Future Nazareth guitarist Jimmy Murrison is born.

1965. Keyboard player Ronnie Leahy is in a band called The Pathfinders, at which time he makes the acquaintance of Dan, Pete and Darrell. Later, Leahy would play with Stone the Crows and White Trash before becoming a member of Nazareth in the '90s, appearing on the *Boogaloo* album from 1998.

Early 1965. Dan joins The Shadettes.

> **Pete Agnew:**
> "When we lost Des, I always said it would be nice to have another singer again, and at the time, Dan used to travel around in the van with us, just as a pal. He was my mate from school; he used to come to all the gigs. And somebody just said, 'Well, Dan sounds good, he can sing.' So we thought why not? Let's give him a shot. And so we said, 'Dan, fancy a go?' 'Certainly, let's have a go.' So it was great to have another singer in so we could do the two-vocal things again."
> "Now Des used to play guitar but when Dan came in, he was just a singer standing on his own—he doesn't play guitar. So what happened was, for the first six or nine months of Dan in the band, he only did something like six, seven songs—because I was still the lead singer in the band. And of course he had to go off the stage, because he didn't sort of play guitar and wasn't singing and playing guitar like Des did. But we wanted more and more and more to get Dan to become the lead singer. I was still playing guitar and what happened is, later on—actually later that year—we added a keyboard player. At that time, '65, you've got to realize that around here the big thing was the Tamla soul stuff. That was going everywhere in the dance halls and was what the bands were all playing in Scotland. So we got a keyboard player in and what happened is that I stopped playing guitar. Because you had Sam & Dave, Bob & Earl, all these soul things, Four Tops, so we figured we'd just have the two singers then and I stopped playing the guitar altogether. So we had the keyboard replace my rhythm guitar, if you like—I never played guitar and it was just Dan and I as the two lead singers."

November 2, 1967. Cream issue their second album, *Disraeli Gears,* which helped set a new hard rock standard that would inspired bands like Nazareth to turn up the volume.

February 1968. Tomorrow issue their one and only album, a self-titled, on Parlophone. Opening track is "My White Bicycle," which Nazareth would cover and take to moderate hit status.

> **Pete Agnew:**
> "The secret of a good cover is not to think of the song as a cover. A great song is a great song and can be performed in a number of different ways. When we do someone else's song, we probably loved the original but would never think of doing a version of that version. If you can't change it enough to make it yours, don't do it." (w/ Dmitry Epstein, dmme.net)

July 1, 1968. The Band issue their debut album, *Music from Big Pink*. It includes a song called "The Weight" which would soon become part of the story of the band discussed in this book.

Pete Agnew:
"We loved The Band—as did almost every other musician on the planet—but I wouldn't say they particularly influenced our music, although everything you listen to must subconsciously influence. Being a rhythm 'n' blues-based 'hard rock' band, Nazareth have always listened to every other kind of music except hard rock, so our influences are wide-ranging. What we call Scottish rock—and that goes for most of the Scottish rock bands of the '60s and '70s—is heavily influenced by American music rather than the English rock bands who tended to influence one another. The Scottish settlers who went to America tended to move to the south and were largely responsible for what we know today as country music, which with black blues influence became rock 'n' roll. So in a roundabout way, you could say our ancestors had a great deal to do with creating Scottish rock. Little did they know what they were starting!"

"There have been a lot of good bands come out of Scotland, and indeed are still coming—Simple Minds, Texas, Travis, to name but a few—but although they play excellent contemporary music, I don't think you would describe them as rock bands. So yeah, I suppose you could say we are the only ones flying the Scottish rock colours—and certainly the oldest." *(w/ Dmitry Epstein, dmme.net)*

November 1968. The four members of the classic Nazareth lineup play together for the first time, although the band at this point is still called The Shadettes and there are six members in the group.

Dan McCafferty:
I went to school with Pete and I've known Manny and Darrell since I was 16. We all come from similar backgrounds. We have the same basic values, so it's much easier for us to get along together. Plus we're all coming from an identified prime musical influence, which was the original Jeff Beck Group, the lineup which had Ron Wood and Rod Stewart in it. Now *that* was an incredible rock 'n' roll band!" *(w/ Ritchie Yorke, Star-Phoenix, January 13, 1978)*

Pete Agnew:
"When Manny joined the band at the end of '68, the lineup was still Dan and me as the two lead singers, and we used to do one song apiece and that kind of thing. And then what happened was our bass player at the time, he just really wasn't interested. He'd come up when he felt like coming up. He'd never come to rehearsal for ages, and when we went to start a gig—we played in Dunfermline's Kinema Ballroom as a resident group—he was never there in the beginning of the thing. I would just put the bass on and I'd play the first two or three songs until he turned up. And eventually we got fed up with that and said, 'Look, you may as well not bother coming anymore. We're fed up with this.' And then we thought, well, who's gonna play the bass? And then Manny said, 'Well, there isn't anybody else in town so you could just play the bass, Peter.' I never really intended being a bass player; I was thinking of getting somebody else. Anyway I thought, well, it's only got four strings, I could play a guitar with six strings, so let's give it a go. So that's how I became the bass player—the job just became mine."

"As the year went on, the keyboard player went the same route as the bass player. He was one of these guys, when we were playing the Kinema, we'd go on break and he'd disappear to the bar. We'd come off the break and go back on and he was never there. We'd do two or three songs without him and so we said, 'That's it. You, off you go' (laughs)."

"By the way, the Kinema was one of the main stop-off points for big touring bands when they came to Scotland. For example, we played here with Cream,

The Who, Deep Purple, David Bowie, Jeff Beck, Rod Stewart... the list goes on forever. Before The Who went to tour America with Tommy, they did some warm-up dates 'up in the sticks' (laughs) to try it out. When they played the Kinema, we, as the resident group, had the dubious honour of playing before and then after their set! This was after Mr. Townshend spectacularly smashed his guitar to smithereens, as was his wont on any given evening. Yep, as resident group we had to open and then follow every guest band that came. Good training for our future career and it probably contributed heavily to the 'cavalier' approach we have to playing festivals—bring 'em on!"

"But yes, at this time, now we were definitely just a four-piece, and Dan was definitely the lead singer. Because we weren't doing Sam and Dave stuff anymore. Through '69, that all started to go, where we started to have Dan as our proper lead singer. Thank God we did, by the way, because he started to develop his own style as well then. He wasn't imitating people or copying people so much. He was starting to be the Dan McCafferty that the world got to know."

1970

Early 1970. The Shadettes change their name to Nazareth.

Pete Agnew:
"At the beginning of 1970, that's when the keyboard player, got the chop. So then it was very much, well, we had the same lineup as The Who and bands like that then, didn't we? It was a three-piece with a singer. And that's when we thought, well, we definitely have got to get a name change here. The Shadettes just doesn't cut it. Especially these days with other bands like Cream and Blodwyn Pig and all the strange names that people had. It was all what we called modern names, if you like (laughs). The Shadettes was so old-fashioned, like The Ronettes, that type of thing. So we thought it's definitely got to be changed."

"By this time, we had started playing at a place across the road from our old regular gig called the Belleville Hotel, and we started talking about changing the name, putting out all these different suggestions. And we were having a pint and 'The Weight' by The Band came on the radio, with 'I pulled into Nazareth.' And I said, 'What about Nazareth?' It just sounded good—'What about Nazareth?' And nobody said no, you know? But they didn't say, 'Oh yeah, that's great.' So we said, 'Let's write it down and see what it looks like.' So we wrote it down and it was pretty punchy, that. We went, 'Ah, that's good, that's it, that's it—Nazareth.'"

"But, you know what was funny? I've been watching that film that they did with The Band, *Once Were Brothers*, with Robbie Robertson, and I never realized that until then, he was telling the story of 'The Weight,' and he said that he was just diddling away trying to write a song and he's just thinking and he looked inside the Martin guitar, and of course it said 'Made in Nazareth, Pennsylvania' and he saw the word Nazareth and he just thought it sounded good. And I thought that's funny, that's exactly what happened to me (laughs). I got it from him, but he got it from the same kind of vibe as I did—the name sort of punched him the same way it punched me."

June 3, 1970. Deep Purple issue *In Rock*, while Uriah Heep and Black Sabbath also issue very heavy albums in 1970, two in fact from Sabbath. Hard rock is on its way, with Nazareth soon to participate in the movement boldly.

Dan McCafferty on *In Rock*:
"I just thought it was amazing. The Deep Purple before, they were a good band, too, but when Ian and Roger joined up, it was like oh, hello, this was something else altogether. The excitement. There was such a good vibe about it and energy that was like, whoa. The electric guitar, and the way Ian drummed, it was just new. And then Black Sabbath with that sort of anger, it was like whoa, these guys are not kidding. It was pure, raw energy that nobody had before. Ten years after Deep Purple came out, every band I heard was trying to sound like Ian Gillan—heavy metal was about singing like Ian."

1971

1971. Nazareth relocates to London.

Dan McCafferty:
In Britain, in that time in the music business and the early days, if you weren't from London and you didn't go to London, you couldn't get arrested. You would have to play the Marquee and all these places. But the Beatles came along and changed all that because they were from Liverpool. So everybody's like, 'Wait a minute, there's bands north of the Thames.' That's when it started to open up for everybody."

January 13, 1971. Lee Agnew is born in Dunfermline, Scotland. Lee is the son of Pete Agnew and became Nazareth's drummer when Darrell Sweet died in 1999, after first serving as drum tech. Pete has two other musician sons as well, Stevie and Chris.

May 3, 1971. Leon Russell issues his second album, *Leon Russell and the Shelter People*, which includes a song he wrote called "Alcatraz," soon to be covered by Nazareth.

June 1971. Joni Mitchell issues her *Blue* album; it contains "This Flight Tonight," which Nazareth will cover.

November 4, 1971. Nazareth issue their debut, a self-titled, on Pegasus Records, a Vertigo-like offshoot of B&C Records. The album, recorded at Trident, is produced by David Hitchcock with Roy Thomas Baker engineering. Also engineering on the record is John Punter, who will produce 1982's *The Fool Circle*. Pete takes a lead vocal on a song called "I Had a Dream."

Pete Agnew:
"We recorded this first album at Trident Studios in London. Neither ourselves nor our management had any experience of recording studios up until that time so we just went for somewhere famous and expensive. I remember we were told Elton John used Trident so we reckoned if it was good enough for him… you get the idea. I didn't like the place because of the layout and cramped control room but on the plus side the resident sound engineer was Roy Baker—soon to be Queen's producer with an added 'Thomas' in his name—who not only introduced us to the intricacies of recording but also became a good friend and producer of our next album. First albums are like the first time for anything, that is you mainly learn what *not* to do. It was recorded over 11 days and mixed in three days."

Dan McCafferty on the heavier songs on the debut:
"That's just what we wanted to play. We were young and full of piss and vinegar, and rock music had to be aggressive because that's how you felt. You know, you went to join the national 'blank' party or something. It was the energy and anger that went on with a lot of things that was going on politically in your home place. It was a difficult youth, really, and that's where that came from. I have no regrets about it, by the way. I have no regrets about it at all. But we were starting up at the same time as a lot of the other bands and heavier music was popular at the time. In the clubs and stuff, not too much on the air waves, but in pubs and clubs. But then people like Sabbath and Zeppelin came out and it was like whoa, what's this, then?"

1972

January 1972. Mountain/Pegasus issue a first UK Nazareth single pairing "Dear John" with "Friends."

Dan McCafferty:
"The decision to go professional was a hard one, because we are all married and have kids, and we had to have some kind of guarantee that when we were away, the wife didn't get evicted. We were writing our own songs and our manager brought the tapes to London and started taking them around the record companies. It was really nice. Because you read about bands that have been flogging their tapes around for ten years before they got anywhere, but we got right in, the first kick at the ball."
(w/ Rosalind Russell, Disc, June 9, 1973)

Pete Agnew on the Nazareth logo, in place already on the band's debut:
"For years we had no idea who did that logo. But then what happened was this: Dave Field, an artist who designed both our *Razamanaz* and *Loud 'n' Proud* album sleeves, contacted me last year a few months into this plague lockdown to let me know he was putting out a new book of his work. It's a big pictorial book something like this one you're doing but displaying all the album sleeves he's designed. I had a look at Dave's website to check out all the sleeves he'd done. It turns out that not only did he do loads of beautiful sleeves, he also did loads of great logos and, yep, you guessed, there was our logo right at the beginning of the bunch. I've known Dave for years and it never clicked that he was the guy our original record company had hired to design a logo for the first album because I never met him until he did the *Razamanaz* artwork. So there you go: now I know, and better late than never."

February 1972. The band play the Rainbow supporting The Faces. Dan and Pete consider this the band's first important public appearance.

April 5 – 8, 1972. The band play multiple shows at the Whisky a Go Go in West Hollywood, California.

May 1972. Little Feat issue their second album, *Sailin' Shoes*, which includes "Teenage Nervous Breakdown" soon to be covered boisterously by Nazareth.

June 1972. Nazareth's cover of "Morning Dew" is issued as a single, backed with "Spinning Top."

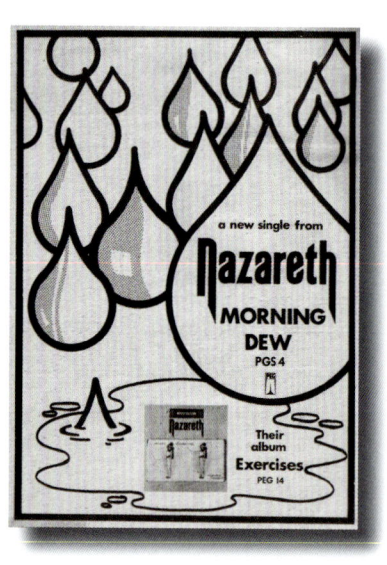

July 1972. Nazareth's first single in the US, issued by Warner Bros., pairs "Morning Dew" with "Dear John."

July 1, 1972. Nazareth issue their second album, *Exercises*. The record marks only the third project for producer Roy Thomas Baker, soon to be famous for his work with Queen. It is recorded and mixed at Trident Studios.

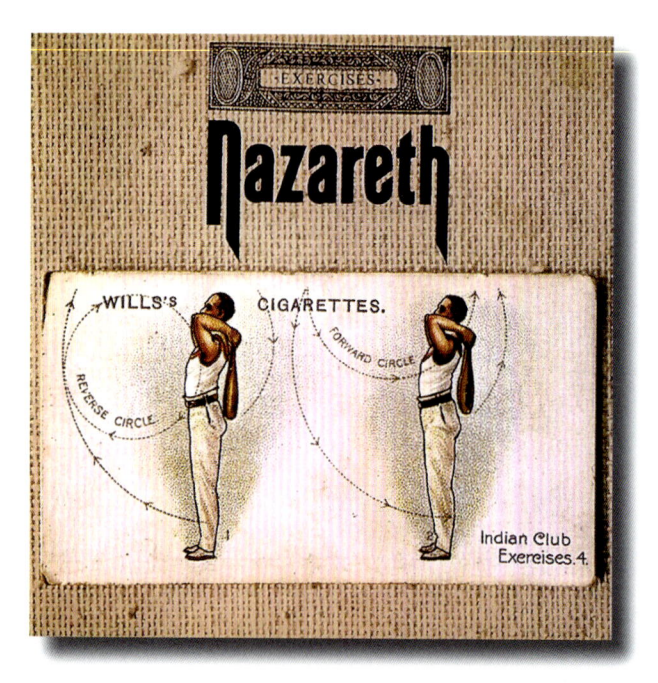

Dan McCafferty, on why *Exercises* was so mellow:
"I know, I think it was just because that was the stuff we were writing at the time. And because we were Scottish, and really the first band ever to succeed internationally from Scotland, I think we got a bit ethnic for a bit there (laughs). We were trying to create Scottish rock. I don't think it was a conscious decision, but looking back and analyzing it, that's what we did. At the time I liked it. Looking back that's the way it

worked. Do you like the songs? Yes. Do you think we should record them? Yes. Do you think people will like them? Yes. Well then let's do them!"

Pete Agnew:
"We'd done *Nazareth*, the first one, which was just a mix of songs that we did. Some were rock, some were… When we did *Exercises*, at that point we were listening to Poco, The Grateful Dead, all these kinds of bands, and we thought, 'What do we want to be?' What were we going to be as a recording band? We weren't a cover band anymore. So we saw ourselves at that point as playing acoustic stuff, electric, different things. And we did that album and it was a fucking disaster. But it was a learning curve. Roy Baker produced that album, the great Roy Thomas Baker. He was just an engineer then. So we did that album and the record company—and our management company—said, 'Well, boys, you got one more chance.' Because that record did nothing."

"Interestingly, we never named this album, never even had a say in the matter. It went like this: the album was recorded over 13 days. We finished recording on the Thursday night at 11:00PM, went back to the band's apartment and had a quick sleep, got up and packed our bags for an American tour, took our bags (and bodies) back to Trident at 8:00AM and began mixing the album. After a straight 21 hours of mixing, the album was proclaimed finished at 5:00AM (and so were our ears) so we picked up our bags and headed out to Heathrow airport, had breakfast and hopped on a plane to New York. If any of you think the mix on the album sounds 'not wonderful,' this might go some way to explain maybe why. During the fifth week of our American tour we got a phone call from our management to tell us that the album was to be named Exercises and that they had designed the record cover. We said, 'Eh?'"

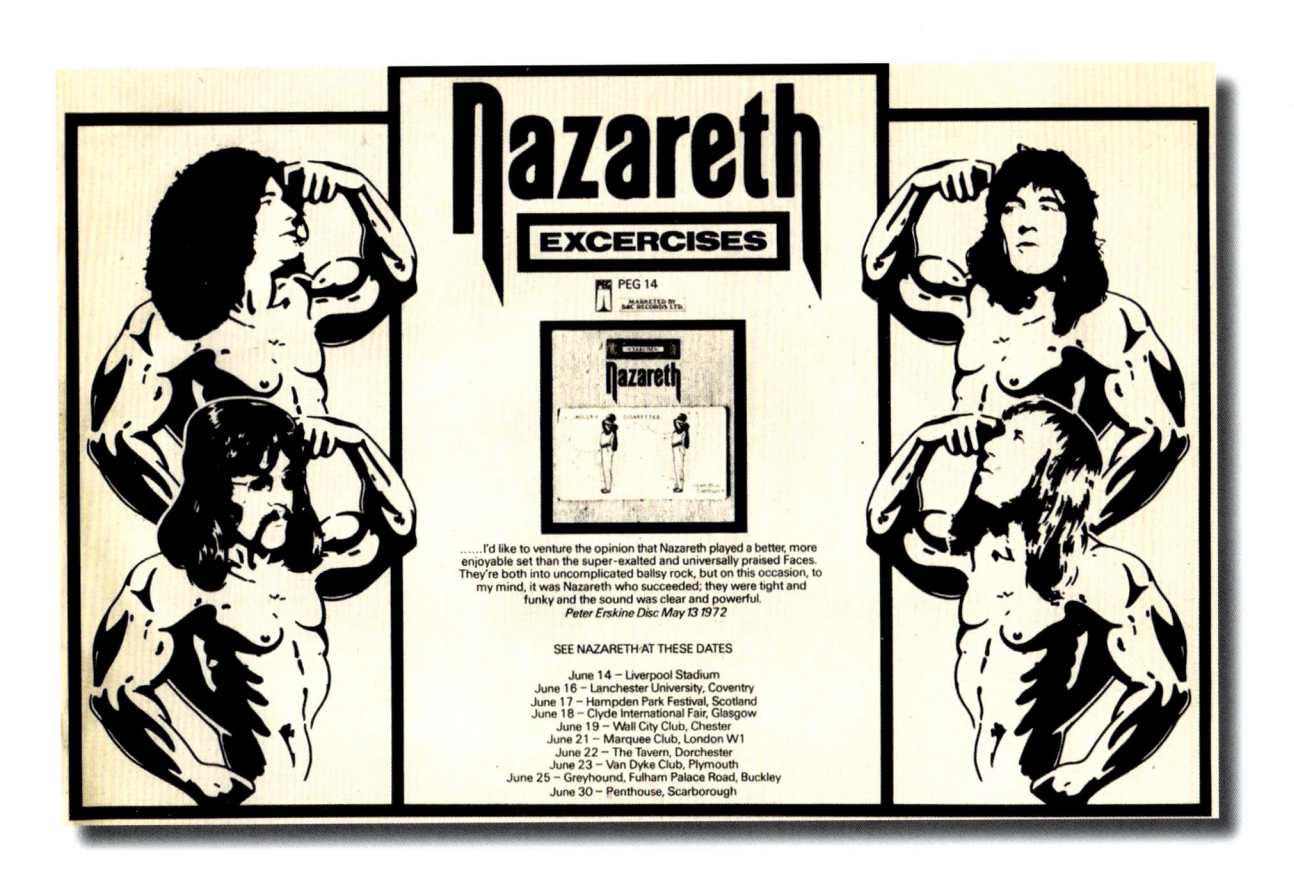

September 1972. Mountain/Pegasus issue a non-LP single from Nazareth pairing "If You See My Baby" with "Hard Living."

Dan McCafferty, comparing *Exercises* with the debut:
"I still think *Exercises* is good music. But there were things we just couldn't get over. For our first album, we had only been professionals for two weeks, so we were lost then. It was our first time in the studio and it was a lot of fun because they put the drummer in a box. Darrell was like a big tomato in this box and we couldn't feel the drummer. And Manny and Pete were behind the screens, and I had to sing with cans and I hated that. I was really disappointed. That's why we changed the whole policy with *Razamanaz*."

"But there is one thing that Nazareth's first album has that I still like: excitement, which is another thing that we are about. We are excited when we play and try to shove it in plastic. Whereas with *Exercises* we were relaxed, because we were terrified of falling into the Black Sabbath riffy-type of thing. There was a lot going on at the time, and we didn't think it was for us. We were in a bit of a mess actually. I didn't think *Exercises* hurt us, because if we hadn't done that, we would still like to follow that direction. Now we can look back at this and think, 'This is where we go wrong, and we will have to avoid that in the future.'"
(w/ Tony Stewart, New Musical Express, August 18, 1973)

December 1972 – March 1973. Nazareth work with Deep Purple's Roger Glover at The Ganghut, Jamestown, Scotland utilizing the Pye Mobile on tracks to comprise their proposed third album.

Pete Agnew:
"After *Exercises*, we were writing these songs and they were all rock songs. We were heavily influenced by the rock bands and we were playing them live. You had Deep Purple, Zeppelin and all that thing. And funnily enough, we did a British tour with Deep Purple and we were playing songs from *Razamanaz* on the tour, and Roger Glover heard us every night, and we were looking for a producer to do the album. He said, 'I'm your man; I want to do this.' And of course we worked with Roger for the next three albums and it was a great, a match made in heaven."

"We were looking at Jimmy Page and Pete Townshend, but the thing is, Roger really, really wanted to do it. He actually said to us, 'I really, really want to do it.' And that makes a difference, rather than we were just hiring someone to do it and I think you can see that the few albums he did with us, he was a great producer for us. Hats off to the guy. He definitely helped to make those albums, and those were the albums that got us into the big time."

Manny Charlton on The Ganghut:
"We had turned professional and we needed some place at home as our rehearsal facility. And that's basically what it was. It was two rooms that we used to rent in this warehouse. They were maybe ten, twelve feet square, and we had one room for all the equipment. It was concrete walls and high ceilings though, and we had Marshall stacks in there and the drum kit and it was deafening. We used to come out of there after working all day and my ears would be ringing for hours. And the other room we had set up for mixing. We had a little Revox and we did our demos in there."

"When Roger came to produce the band, he said, 'Where are you guys happy playing?' 'Well, we're happy in our little rehearsal place in Scotland.' And he said, 'Well, then that's what we'll do. We'll record there and we'll bring a little mobile studio. We'll record in the place that you're happy.' And we thought that was so neat, to think of something like that, rather than put us in a commercial facility. He just brought the studio to us."

1973

April 1973. Nazareth, through their new label Mooncrest, issue "Broken Down Angel" paired with debut album track "Witchdoctor Woman." The single reaches #9 on the UK charts. In 1974, Dan calls this the band's first big break—as well as biggest disappointment, when the track didn't reach #1.

Pete Agnew:

"It's very funny with 'Broken Down Angel.' It was the first big, big hit, and how it came about, I remember the night it all happened. We played at a ballroom in Cardiff. It was a horrible night and we were sitting in the dressing room and our two roadies were taking the gear out and we were just sitting around waiting. Manny was playing the acoustic guitar and we were singing different songs and stuff, and we started doing Marianne Faithfull's 'If You'll Come and Stay with Me.' We used to love that song. And Manny started playing this chord sequence and it developed from that and soon we had the shape of 'Broken Down Angel.'"

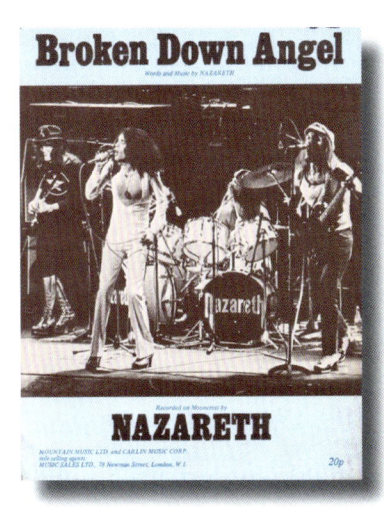

Manny Charlton on "Broken Down Angel:"

"We just thought it was a really good tune. We kind of modelled it after Rod Stewart, who was big at that time. I wrote the chorus, and between the rest of the guys in the band we wrote the verses. The two producers we had from previous albums, we didn't really feel were getting things right. We did a lot of dates with Deep Purple, supporting them, and we asked Roger if he would try producing us, for a single. 'Broken Down Angel' was specifically recorded as a single. And he said, 'Sure, I'd love to do it.' And he did a great job on that. And then it was full steam ahead."

"So again, the first thing that we came up with and gave Roger was 'Broken Down Angel.' We went, 'Look, we want to do like The Faces, but make it sound like a Rod Stewart record at the time.' That was kind of how his audition was with us. We went in and did that single and got on so well that it was sort of automatic that we said, 'Yeah, do the album.' 'Woke Up This Morning' we had actually done on our second album, and we were playing it live, totally different from the album version, of course. That was one of the songs right away we knew from the inside out. We had 'Razamanaz' and 'Broken Down Angel' and several other songs."

"You see, even Zeppelin, at that point, weren't making singles; they didn't want any singles. So automatically they didn't go to Top of the Pops and they didn't get airplay during the day on mainstream radio. So that's where the kind of underground connotation came around, because basically they weren't visible, or as visible as, say, T. Rex and other bands that were on Top of the Pops. And in Britain, a band would appear on Top of the Pops and then instantly they'd be headliners. They're the main musical outlet. We didn't get played that much until we came down with 'Broken Down Angel' and they decided that yeah, that fitted the radio format and we were on Top of the Pops and our album nearly went Top Ten."

July 22nd, 1973, Frankfurt, Germany.

May 5, 1973. Nazareth's third album, the Roger Glover-produced *Razamanaz*, is issued in the UK; it reaches #11 on the UK charts.

Dan McCafferty:

"*Razamanaz* I really like a lot, because I think that's the point where we found out what we wanted to do. Because *Nazareth* and *Exercises* before that were kind of varied. But we found out what we liked to do, and we found out what we were good at. We did Exercises and we thought, well, this is not what we like doing very much. So we started writing all this stuff for the stage and went out playing it on the road and it was going down really well with the crowds. Roger had just finished working with Elf, which was Ronnie James Dio, God rest him, and so we said to Roger, would you like to do it? Yeah. So we did *Razamanaz*, *Loud 'n' Proud* and *Rampant* with Roger. But that kind of band had established itself as a rock band anyway. See, *Exercises* was actually the one that was different because Nazareth's original album was a lot heavier as well. So *Razamanaz* was normal for us."

Pete Agnew:

"*Razamanaz* was so much fun to do. We loved playing that music. That was the album where Nazareth became Nazareth. And you've got to remember, that record was recorded in nine days. Same with *Loud 'n' Proud*—it was nine days as well. It's incredible when you think about it. They're almost like live albums, basically a live album with an overdub (laughs). And when we made *Razamanaz*, you know what it's like, Martin, it's a feeling that you get. When we did *Razamanaz*, we went, 'That's a hit. That album is going to make people take notice.' We knew it. You had no doubts about it when you finished it, that you'd done something really good. You just can't wait for it to come out. We were going, 'Release it, release it, release it!' (laughs)."

Manny Charlton:

"Roger was great. If it wasn't for Roger, I don't think we would have gotten anywhere. Because we had done two albums and we didn't know what we were doing. We wanted to be Elton John, we wanted to be Deep Purple, we wanted to be Led Zeppelin, we wanted to be The Band—we went through everything, all our influences, Neil Young. We just wanted to write songs like all our favourites and play them, and we could (laughs) but we found out that wasn't too smart. The albums didn't sell; the albums didn't do any good at all."

"And it was two different producers. The second album was by Roy Thomas Baker; that was his first production, by the way. No, they were just all over the place, basically. And when we went in with Roger, he said, 'Look, your albums aren't selling, but you always get great live reception when you play live.' 'Yeah, we're always going down well.' When we played live, we were something else. We were a hard rock trio, you know? Blues, that's what we were when we played live. And Roger said, 'That's what you do live. You've got to do that on the album.' So fortunately we had a great bunch of songs. And Roger produced it and it was great. Because he knew what he was doing. He was a musician. That's what we needed. We needed a musician to help us translate what we were going to do musically and get it on record."

"But yeah, the first two albums that we did, we were all over the place musically and genre-speaking. But when we played live we went out as a four-piece and basically played hard rock, with Marshall stacks and a lot of drums and stuff and Dan screaming his head off. And that seemed to go over really well. So we were puzzled at the time as to why our records weren't selling but we were doing well live. And so we decided the best thing we could probably do was get a musician that understood what we were trying to do. And we'd been playing dates with Purple in the States and Europe so we knew Roger. And there were these guys that were producing their own bands, and we knew Roger was producing Purple at the time. And Pete Townsend was an influence working with The Who, and Zeppelin and Jimmy Page, so basically we asked the three of them if they would be interested in producing the band, and Roger got back to us first and really wanted to do it. So we went yeah, well we know the guy anyway; we were mates."

July 20, 1973. Nazareth gets on Top of the Pops, with "Bad Bad Boy." The next day they play the Buxton Pop Festival, after initially having withdrawn from the show, followed by a trip to Germany to play the second night of the Summer Rock Festival in Frankfurt.

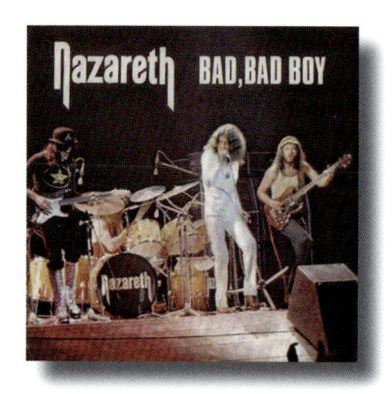

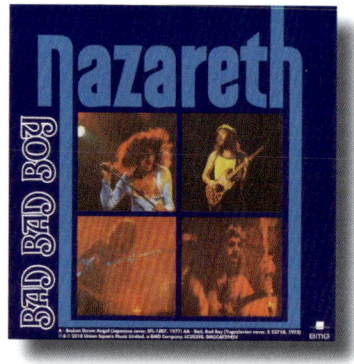

July 1973. Mooncrest float a second single from *Razamanaz*, "Bad Bad Boy," which rises to No.10 on the charts. On the flipside are non-LP heavy rockers "Hard Living" and "Spinning Top."

July 27, 1973. Nazareth play the London Music Festival, at Alexandra Palace, as part of many UK shows throughout 1973.

August 1973. *Razamanaz* gets belated issue in the US and Canada, the latter eventually sending the record to platinum status for sales of over 100,000 copies.

Reviewer Jim Miller:
"Displaying some small flair for contemplating disaster, 'Woke Up This Morning' cheerfully recites a litany of murdered dog, dead cat and crispy burnt homestead. The title tune, nonsense vocals and all, gets the pagan raucous fuzz-zap treatment. 'Sold My Soul,' on the other hand, toys with satanic capitulation, a muddy guitar line accenting McCafferty's earnest confession of sin. And finally 'Broken Down Angel' widens the stylistic spectrum to include Rod Stewart overtones, Purpled C&W passages and a song of lost virtue. As for the band's performances, McCafferty croak-talks rather than sings, and Manuel Charlton's guitar playing proves something less than innovative. But the four Scottish lads rarely avoid an opportunity to turn a stale cliché to their slender advantage. When Nazareth hits snide stride, they turn out enough pop staples to match any modest band: a subdued cheer for Scotch rock."
(Rolling Stone, October 25, 1973)

September 1973. "Broken Down Angel"/"Hard Living" is issued as a single in the US.

September 23, 1973. Nazareth play a gig on the shores of Lake Spivey, just outside of Atlanta, Georgia, with Blue Öyster Cult and hard southern rockers Hydra.

September 29, 1973. In the annual Melody Maker Music Poll, Nazareth take top spot for "Greatest Hope," beating out Wings and Genesis.

October 18 – November 10, 1973. The band mount a short UK tour, just as their new album—and single "This Flight Tonight" (backed with "Called Her Name")—is hitting the shops. The single reaches #11 on the UK charts and #27 as the band's first charting single in Canada.

Dan McCafferty on "This Flight Tonight:"
"You know how you're on the road and everybody's got tapes? Well, that song just kept showing up all the time on somebody's fave-raves tape, off the *Blue* album. So eventually we decided to give it a go. Obviously we wanted to make it as far away from Joni as we possibly could, 'cause you could imagine how it would sound with me trying to sound like Joni Mitchell! It's a good song, and if you start with a good song it should be able to be played any way you want it." *(w/ Steve Newton, Ear of Newt)*

Record and Radio Mirror on "This Flight Tonight:"
"The rhythm on this Joni Mitchell song suggests a galloping Western, with John Wayne or somebody equally stone-faced, in the saddle. Or putting it another way, Nazareth see it as a) a hit and b) some kind of space-age presentation. It's very good indeed, packed with lead-voice power and a lot of galloping. No crash-landing, but a ruddy great hit. Very together, Nazareth."
(Record and Radio Mirror, October 6, 1973)

October 18, 1973. Nazareth get on Top of the Pops with "This Flight Tonight." The guys had great respect for Joni Mitchell, and would play her music on long van rides between gigs. Fortunately, Mitchell was over the moon when she heard Nazareth's heavy metal treatment of the song.

Manny Charlton:

"'This Flight Tonight' was absolutely killer. We were really happy with that. One thing about that one is that Pete asked me when we were recording it, he said, 'Are you going to do the solo on that?' I said, 'The solo is done. That's the solo (laughs). It's that slide solo that I did on it.' And he went, 'That's the solo?!' And I went yeah! (laughs). Basically, I turned my guitar up an octave so all the strings were single note. And I like playing slide a lot, so what was going on was, the guitar was extremely loud and it was feeding back and you were getting these resonances. The feedback would alternate sometimes, and from the high register, sometimes it would drop an octave out of the blue, you know? So I just put a slide on it and I played what I thought were cool notes. I tried to basically imitate a jet, just to give the song some atmosphere, not play a conventional pentatonic scale blues thing. And it sounded great. Roger was knocked out with that."

"The gallop, that was our idea; I liked that rhythm. But Roger helped us a lot in the construction of it, the drumming mainly. He helped out Darrell a lot, pretty much telling him what to play and where to play. That rhythm was familiar to us anyway, because we did 'Morning Dew' like that anyway, on the first album."

October 19, 1973. Nazareth's fourth album, *Loud 'n' Proud*, is issued in the UK, managing a #10 placement on the UK charts.

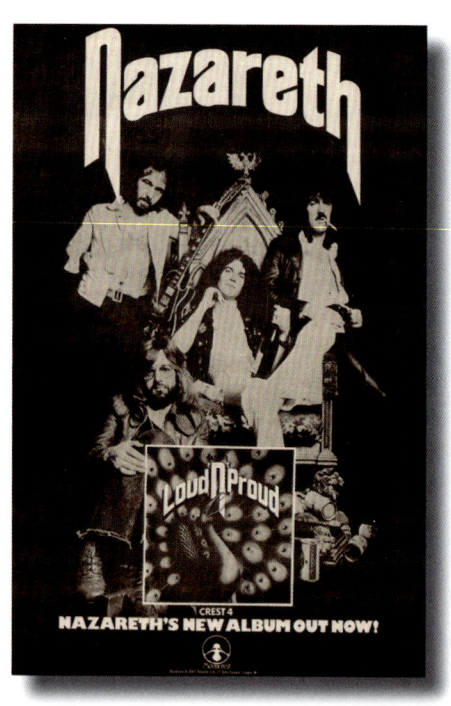

Pete Agnew:

"Back to the Gangy and the Pye mobile again, which had only 13 of 16 tracks working by this time. I think they scrapped the studio after we finished the album. Anyway, we didn't have enough time to finish recording the album because we had to go on tour so we arranged to do the one remaining track (and all the backing vocals) at Apple studio in London."

"The problem was that we didn't *have* the one remaining track. Here's how things were back in those days. You had two sides on the vinyl record and you aimed at having a total minimum of 36 minutes for the record, or approximately 18 minutes a side. We were about seven-and-a-half minutes short on original

July 22nd, 1973, Frankfurt, Germany.

July 22nd, 1973, Frankfurt, Germany.

PETER BOWYER
presents
Nazareth
IN CONCERT
THE APOLLO
Renfield Street, Glasgow
SUNDAY, 21st OCTOBER, 1973
at 7.30 p.m.

BALCONY

L   Nº   15

Ticket 80p inc. V.A.T.
To be retained

PETER BOWYER
presents
ON TOUR
NAZARETH
with special guest stars
SILVERHEAD

18th October	Stadium, LIVERPOOL
19th October	City Hall, NEWCASTLE
20th October	Empire Theatre, EDINBURGH
21st October	Apollo, GLASGOW
22nd October	Free Trade Hall, MANCHESTER
23rd October	Town Hall, BIRMINGHAM
24th October	Town Hall, LEEDS
25th October	Top Of The World, STAFFS.
26th October	Victoria Halls, HANLEY
27th October	City Hall, SHEFFIELD
28th October	Locarno, BRISTOL
29th October	De Montfort Hall, LEICESTER
31st October	Top Rank Suite, SOUTHAMPTON
1st November	Civic Hall, DUNSTABLE
2nd November	Corn Exchange, CAMBRIDGE
3rd November	Kursaal, SOUTHEND
4th November	Top Rank Suite, READING
9th November	Rainbow
10th November	Guildhall, PRESTON

Jens Van Houten / Frank White Photo Agency

material so we had no idea what to fill this gap with. It was decided that Darrell should go into the studio and lay down eight minutes of a heavy plodding rhythm and we would come up with some ideas to overdub.

I went in after him and stuck down this big fuzzy bass part, and although this was all sounding like fun, we still didn't know what we were going to sing."

"That's when Dan came up with the idea of singing Dylan's 'The Ballad of Hollis Brown.' Not because he loved the song especially, but because it had eight verses and he reckoned he could space it out over the time we needed. It's weird that under the circumstances of how that track was eventually conceived and completed, people still come up to me and tell me that it's their favourite Nazareth track of all time. Go figure."

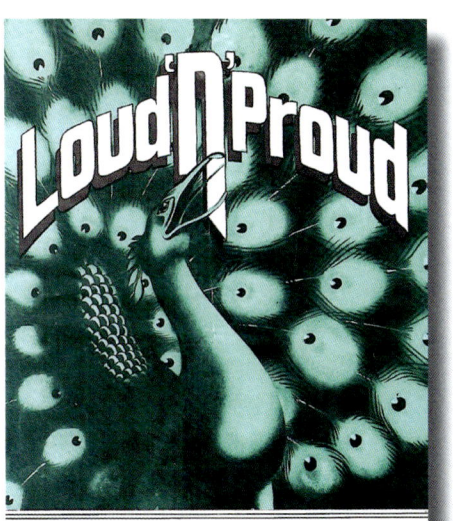

Dan McCafferty on the *Loud 'n' Proud* cover art:

"That was done by a kid in London. The band was really starting to take off. We had done *Razamanaz* and of course we were doing *Loud 'n' Proud*, so we wanted something that would represent that, and we sent out feelers to see what people could come up with. And they came up with this young artist who did that, and it was perfect for what we were doing at the time. He actually did it the size of the album sleeve. The management company got it, at one point."

Darrell Sweet:

"Individual and collective performances are much better. The numbers are great. Production is also a step forward. ('The Ballad of Hollis Brown') is the biggest thing we've ever covered. For four, it's an achievement. It synthesizes sounds without a synthesizer."
(w/ Steve Clarke, New Musical Express, October 27, 1973)

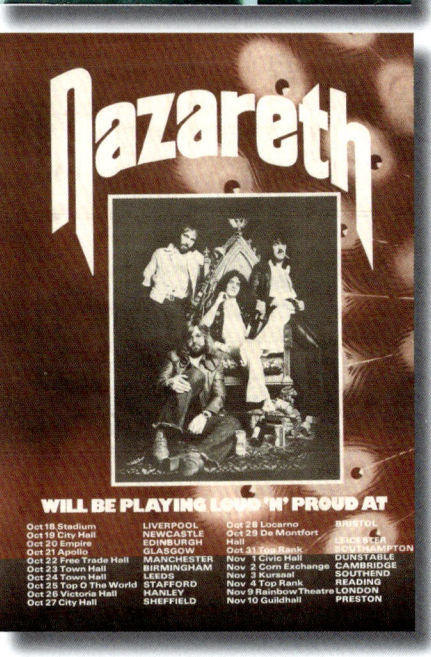

Reviewer Greg Shaw:

"Much as I enjoy the fast numbers, it must be noted that Nazareth are occasionally as monotonous as Status Quo or Uriah Heep, as on 'Not Faking It,' which is all strut and preen, but with none of the substance of their earlier remarkable heavy metal C&W 'Broken Down Angel.' The non-originals provide the best moments. Little Feat's 'Teenage Nervous Breakdown' picks up in power what it loses in subtlety; Joni Mitchell's 'This Flight Tonight' is shocking when heard in a Led Zeppelin arrangement. The clincher comes with a nine-minute version of Bob Dylan's 'The Ballad of Hollis Brown.' An over-long drone of a song to begin with, it's stretched to the limits with every repetitious device known to modern rock, and drowned in a haze of feedback fuzz. Strangely enough it works. And that leads me to the conclusion that Nazareth, in bridging the gap between folk and heavy metal, could easily become the Turtles of the '70s. They are a group worth watching." (Rolling Stone, May 9, 1974)

November 1973. "Bad Bad Boy"/"Razamanaz" is issued as a US single.

Dan McCafferty on working with Roger Glover:
"Roger was a great lad, and still is. Pete and I just went to see Purple before Christmas when they were in Glasgow and we went out for something to eat and that was great fun. He's a really nice guy and a dedicated musician. He's a great arranger and knows how to get you to do stuff. He'd say, 'Well, your songs, guys, you know how to do that,' and if there's something he doesn't like, he'll say, 'I don't necessarily like that, but if you guys are crazy about it, fine. It's your stuff, you know I mean?' But he was good at things like, 'Well, there are too many of those bits; you don't need all those.' And as a person, he's a lovely man. He's just a good mate."

Pete Agnew on "Razamanaz."
"Need you ask? Did you ever hear 'Speed King?' (laughs). Actually, when Roger produced the album and we went to them with the album and album cover all done, and they started playing it, all the guys in Deep Purple, Ian Paice said, 'Oh, come on' (laughs). And Roger, 'No, no, no…' I mean, that's obviously what we were thinking about when we did it. Of course it's a different song, but the vibe and the structure, it's practically 'Speed King' part two. But it was Nazareth's 'Speed King.' For us, those kinds of songs came from jams, like Deep Purple did it. They'd jam and then a song would come over the top. We kind of did that with 'Razamanaz.'"

July 22nd, 1973, Frankfurt, Germany.

© Laurens Van Houten / Frank White Photo Agency

1974

February 1974. "This Flight Tonight"/"Go Down Fighting" is issued as a single in the US, concurrent with the belated issue of the source album, *Loud 'n' Proud*, also this month. The record would receive platinum certification in Canada, fuelled by repeated radio spins of "This Flight Tonight," which was classed as Canadian content given that it was written by Joni Mitchell. The "CanCon" rule at the time in Canada was that 30% of what was played on the radio had to be "Canadian content."

Roger Glover:
"I got the Judas Priest job on the basis of Nazareth's 'This Flight Tonight,' which was basically my arrangement. Nazareth had run out of songs. They were going to do 'This Flight Tonight,' but they were going to do it the way, I don't know, Rod Stewart might have done it on a solo album. And I said no, that's kind of boring, let's do something different. So I came up with this whole chugga concept and the arrangement for it. And it was on the strength of that that Judas Priest wanted me to do 'Diamonds and Rust,' which, if you listen to it, you see the similarities."

Pete Agnew on working with Roger Glover:
"When people listen to Deep Purple, they don't realize the arranging and all that stuff—it's all done with Roger. He's the guy that runs the recording sessions, you know? This is how it gets done; he's the man. And when he got with us, he taught us structure of the song, structure of the solo, how to actually record the thing. We learned a lot about recording studios with Roger. Although we'd been in them and used them, this was, 'Do this, do that.' And he's still a great friend. I'm eternally grateful to Roger Glover. He was a big, big influence in making Nazareth believe in themselves as a rock band. Plus he was the first guy in the studio to really spot Dan's potential as a vocalist, a great rock singer."

"It's funny; we learned a lot from him but he learned a lot from us. See, he was all about heavy rock and that was it. He didn't see any farther than that. Deep Purple was 'all.' Well, Deep Purple were never our favourite band. We liked them, but they're not songwriters. They're an instrumental band that's got some vocals over the top of it. So we introduced Roger… and in fact he'll tell people this to this day, that Nazareth introduced him to Little Feat. He'd never listened to them, never heard of them. And we went, 'Roger, this is the best band in the world.' And, 'You've got to listen to them.' And we used to play Little Feat to him every day and every night and he became a huge fan and his actual musical tastes started to spread out a bit. So he kind of thanks us, in a roundabout way. So we helped each other. But no, he was the man that actually put us on the road to success."

"But he could bring everything together; he was a good arranger. And he was a disciplinarian. We would do one track every day, and at the end of the day, when everybody was pretty much tired, he would say, 'Okay, we're going to routine the track for tomorrow.' So we would just start messing around with the track, and we would play for about two hours every night and work out what we were going to do the next day. We wouldn't record it that night, because we were too tired to record it. But he used to go around with his drumstick, you know, like a conductor (laughs). And one of the things that he really loved, when we did the albums, he loved the vocals. Because we have a lot of harmony and he never had that in Deep Purple. Ian was always just singing; Deep Purple wasn't a harmony band. So he had a great time saying, 'Can you do this? Can you do that?' And of course we could. He really enjoyed that."

Darrell Sweet:
"We are fans of Joni Mitchell. I don't care if Joni Mitchell fans like it—Joni Mitchell does and that's the main thing. She thoroughly enjoyed it, especially the phone part." *(w/ Steve Clarke, New Musical Express, October 27, 1973)*

March 1974. "Shanghai'd in Shanghai" reaches #41 in the UK charts; the single issue is backed with "Love, Now You're Gone." Jon Lord is a guest musician on the A-side, playing on "Glad When You're Gone" from the *Rampant* album as well.

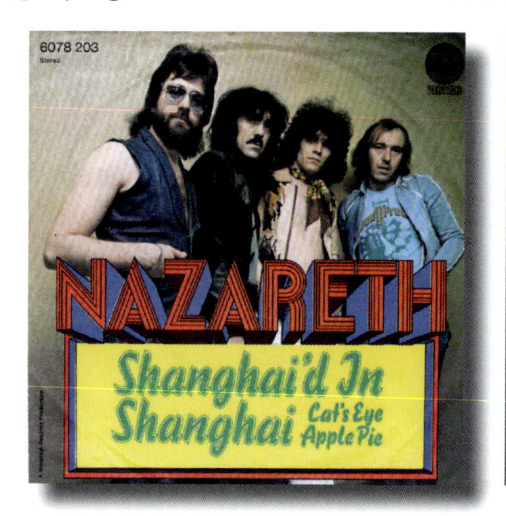

Dan McCafferty, on singing the high ones:
"What I found was, if you can make the notes, fine. Then you can find a way to get your personality into them and make it your own. But if you can't make the notes physically, then that's very odd. Because you get some producers making albums by trying to piece takes together, and I would hate that; I wouldn't know how to handle that very well. So I guess everybody's got to handle it differently. I've had troubles in the studio but I've always overcome them, thankfully, he says, touching wood. But I've got no advice for anybody else how to do it, to be honest."

"I had to go to a specialist in Austria—once—but I just had a terribly sore throat. I got a cold; it was like bad laryngitis. My vocal cords were swelling. He gave me a bunch of really ugly-tasting stuff to take for a couple of days and it was okay. So I've been very lucky. I know some wonderful singers who've had so many problems. But see, I never let it bother me, Martin, because I always figured, if it's gonna go, it's gonna go. I've met so many singers that were paranoid: it's too hot, it's too cold, it's too smoky, it's not smoky enough (laughs), and they just worry themselves into giving themselves a sore throat. But I didn't really worry about it that much, because I figured if it goes, well, it's served me well. It maybe deserves a couple weeks off. What can you say? (laughs)."

Pete Agnew on getting Jon Lord to play on the album:
"We were in Montreux, in Switzerland, and we were recording. Funny enough, we were recording on the Rolling Stones mobile, same as Deep Purple did with 'Smoke On The Water,' down in the Convention Centre. Roger wanted us to go over and do the same thing that they did, so we did that. And it just so happens that Jon was in the area. All of a sudden we needed a piano player. He came

along for a drink with us, and we said, 'Well, since you're here, pal, come down here, we've got a big grand piano, come in and hit it.'"

"But that mobile, the thing was parked in the basement in what's called the Convention Centre. It's still there, I think. And Roger suggested it would be good, because we made a couple of records with him and they were both on mobiles. He liked us working with mobiles, because we didn't like working in studios at that time. We just liked to play our guitars and whenever we felt like it, rather than in a closed-in studio. And he said, 'This will be good for you' and it worked out really, really good; we had a lot of fun."

April 4 – May 26, 1974. The band tour the UK.

NAZARETH U.K. TOUR
MAY
12th. Apollo — GLASGOW
13th. Caird Hall — DUNDEE
15th. City Hall — NEWCASTLE
16th. City Hall — SHEFFIELD
17th. Town Hall — BIRMINGHAM
18th. The Stadium — LIVERPOOL
19th. Top Rank — SOUTHAMPTON
20th. Top Rank — SWANSEA
21st. Free Trade Hall — MANCHESTER
22nd. Top Rank — BRIGHTON
24th. Rainbow — LONDON
26th. Coulston Hall — BRISTOL

Pete Agnew, on stage clothes:
"I tried the jacket and costume stripes when we played at Watford, and I threw a bummer because I was self-conscious about what I got in. I'm used to jeans. You go in jeans and you sweat and you go out and think, 'Yeah, so I'm going to get batteries.' But it's good because you're playing in what you're used to. If Dan imagines himself in a suit, good luck to him, but I feel really stupid. You get guys that go on stage and get really neat—and then they go out and put on a pair of jeans. What's the point? Who are they trying to fool? At least when Dan and Manny started using flashy gear, they used it all the time. Apparently, Elton and the like are the same."

(New Musical Express, June 1974)

April 24, 1974. Nazareth get on Top of the Pops with "Shanghai'd in Shanghai" and then again the following month with "Shape of Things," both *Rampant* tracks. On the record, Roger is credited with synthesizer on the latter, as well as on rousing opening track "Silver Dollar Forger."

Pete Agnew:
"We lost the first place by 40 places—it crossed out at 41. If you don't do Top of the Pops, then forget about it. And why not do it? I care that it doesn't get on the charts. I feel really bad about it. (As for radio) I think the BBC producers are pretty hip guys who get quoted for records and evaluate their merits. But it's the panel that picks the records. Have you seen the guys on the panel? It's quite amazing. They must be the guys who choose people for Coronation Street. They are the ones who really say, 'Yes, this is a good record—it will be played.'" (New Musical Express, June 1974)

April 26, 1974. *Rampant,* Nazareth's fifth album, is issued in the UK, managing a #13 placement in the UK charts and, after a couple years, gold status in Canada.

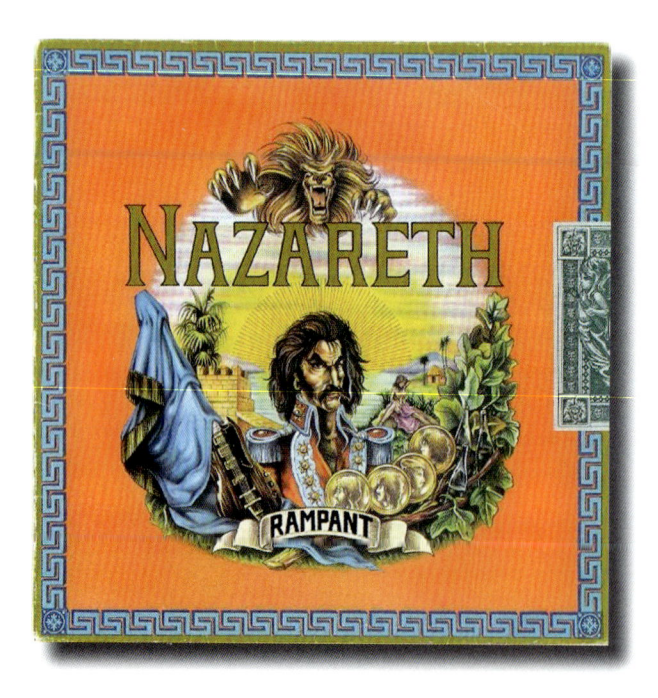

Dan McCafferty:
"Good album, but it was a transition album for us. It's the last one we did with Roger. He wanted us to do son of *Loud 'n' Proud*. But we were like, 'No Roger, we have this other stuff and we want to move along.' And he was all like, 'Well, Deep Purple do it this way,' and this that and the other. And I don't mean that as nasty toward Deep Purple, but he was more about stick to what people recognise you for. And our attitude was we think that people can think for themselves (laughs). Okay, they like *Razamanaz,* but they might like this as well. But we didn't fall out because of it. Roger was like, 'Okay lads, that's no problem,' and he was a big help on the record. I like it because it was a transition album, but when I look back, I think we were trying to do too many different things too quickly. And again hindsight is an exact science. We were excited about the stuff at the time and it was fun to do. We had the mobile and were in the Swiss mountains and it was a lovely place to work."

"But I love *Rampant*. I mean, I like all our stuff. You look back years later and perhaps for some things, you say, 'Oh that was a bit dumb. Maybe we shouldn't have done that.' But there wasn't an album we didn't like at the time. It's easier in a year's time to go, 'Oh, wrong!' But rock 'n' roll should be spontaneous and instant. Because by the time we get something in the studio that we all agree on, it's been through all the fights. At least we all agree we should record that. And then you do the best job that you can. If it doesn't work, well, you gave it your best shot."

Roger Glover:
"We were always on good terms, but it was definitely the end of the road. They wanted to produce themselves. Manny, I know that every time I made a move in the studio, he was like, 'What are you doing that for?' And you can always tell that when someone is that keen, they really want to be in charge. And eventually it happened, of course, and they did very well with it."

Pete Agnew:
"As I say, the studio was parked in the basement of the convention center and we used a big work/storage room upstairs to actually play most of our parts as overdubs although we had a setup with the drums and some amps next to the mobile. I can't remember exactly how long it took to do my bass parts but I reckon I walked 20 miles up and down those stairs and lost 20 pounds in the process. I also can't remember why we did all that running around because you can overdub in the control room whilst sitting on your ass! Hmm… Anyway, we eventually finished the backing tracks in 14 days, lost weight, got fit, and returned to the UK to do the vocals in Ian Gillan's studio in London. Dan sung all the lead vocals in three days and we did all the backing vocals in one night. When I think back, that album was more of a workout than a recording."

May 14, 1974. Nazareth get on The Old Grey Whistle Test with "Silver Dollar Forger" and "Loved and Lost."

June 7 – August 3, 1974. The band mount a North American tour, supporting Blue Öyster Cult.

July 1974. *Rampant* is issued in the US. Concurrently, "Sunshine," backed with "This Fight Tonight," gets floated as a US single from the album.

July 7, 1974. Nazareth play second on a bill to Blue Öyster Cult, supporting in the third slot is Kiss.

September 14, 1974. In Stockholm, Sweden, the guys are presented with *Loud 'n' Proud* gold record awards for sales of over 30,000 copies.

At the Sheraton Hotel, Stockholm, 1974 receiving gold records.

© Roger Tilberg / Alamy Stock Photo

September – November 1974. The band conduct a twenty-date Canadian tour, with a few of the Ontario dates in late October supported by Rush.

November 8, 1974. Non-LP Everly Brothers cover "Love Hurts," backed with non-LP original "Down" is issued as a single in the UK. On November 30th, the guys present the song on Top of the Pops.

43

44

August 30th, 1974, Rotterdam, Netherlands.

© Laurens Van Houten / Frank White Photo Agency

August 30th, 1974, Rotterdam, Netherlands.

© Laurens Van Houten / Frank White Photo Agency

August 31st, 1974, Amsterdam, Netherlands.

"For *Hair of the Dog*, that was a guy who was recommended to us by the people that do the sleeves at Hipgnosis, it was at the time, and he said, 'This guy is great.' And they showed us a kind of rough sketch and we thought, well, that's pretty cool. So he delivered the sleeves (laughs) but he'd drawn it on the wrong size of paper, so that's why there's a black band down the side of the back of the album, right? And we thought, no, we can't ask this guy to do this again, because you never know, it could be worse. So we thought, well, we'll just put that on the back and use it for the titles. Nobody met the guy. He doesn't like to meet people and stuff. You know, you see what he draws through the day—what does he come up with at night, man? (laughs). We called him and said, 'Great job,' and he kinda whispered, 'Thanks very much, man; love your music' and that was that."
Dan McCafferty

1975-1979

April 1st, 1976,
London, UK.

© Laurens Van Houten / Frank White Photo Agency

The latter half of the 1970s found Nazareth essentially touring in support of their two hits, a song called "Love Hurts," and an album called *Hair of the Dog*. The fact that there were fully four other records released during the multiple national and international legs of the *Hair of the Dog* campaign is neither here nor there.

I'm being facetious, but there is some deep music business truth to that concept. In fact, to take the proposed interpretation further, during this five-year span, the band was touring in support of *Razamanaz*, *Loud 'n' Proud* and "This Flight Tonight" as validly or relevantly or significantly as they were *Close Enough for Rock 'n' Roll*, *Play 'n' the Game*, *Expect No Mercy* and *No Mean City*.

In other words, the impressive platform the band had engineered for themselves in the early '70s, as well as the bona fide hit album they had in 1975's *Hair of the Dog*, had set the band's reputation so profoundly that, although things could have conceivably got better and better, they didn't, which, as a feedback loop, puts even greater emphasis on past glories. As the guys spread their wings fearlessly exploring quite jarringly different music styles across the records of the late '70s, the bloom on this period—most pertinently, the fact that they could headline large venues—in actuality resulted from the evergreen sales of the band's two 1973 albums as well as *Hair of the Dog* and the AM and FM success of their cover of rote ballad "Love Hurts."

Further proof of this proposal is that the guys were able to notch to their belts impressive sales for *Greatest Hits* and *Hot Tracks*, a sure sign that a band had reached the institution stage, en route to being a successful and working heritage act. And even though none of the records of the late '70s yielded that next big hit single, four out of five of them went gold in Canada, meaning that the band could continue to headline all the A-level and B-level hockey barns dotted across the country.

April 20th, 1975, Amsterdam, Netherlands.

© Laurens Van Houten / Frank White Photo Agency

1975

March 14, 1975. "Hair of the Dog," backed with "Too Bad, Too Sad" is issued in the UK as a single. On tour dates in support of the new album, the band would be augmented with ex-Tiger keyboard player Tommy Eyre, later of the Ian Gillan Band and The Sensational Alex Harvey Band.

April 30, 1975. Nazareth issue their sixth album, *Hair of the Dog*, produced by Manny Charlton, recorded at Escape Studios in Kent, mixed at AIR London. The US edition switches out Randy Newman's "Guilty" for "Love Hurts," propelling the record to RIAA-certified platinum status, aided by second hit, "Hair of the Dog." The album reached #17 on the Billboard charts and also certified gold in Canada.

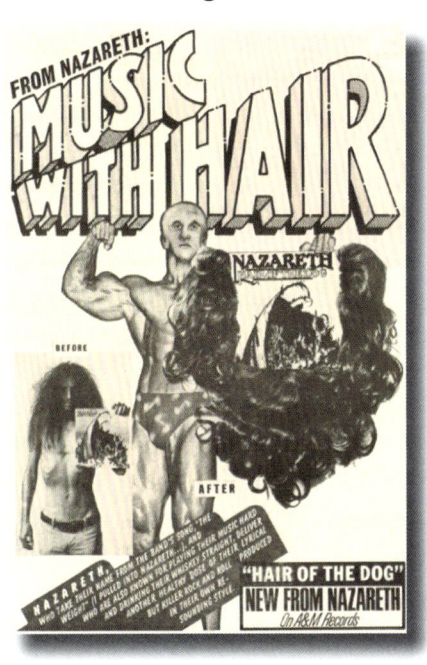

Dan McCafferty:
"Hair of the Dog was a particularly busy time. We had been working flat-out for three years straight and I think everybody was like needing a break. Maybe that's why it sounds so desperate (laughs). I think also when you tour a lot you start to get a bit more cynical, less trust in people, so maybe the album is a bit cynical. It was the first one that Manny Charlton produced; the three before that, Roger Glover had worked on, which was great fun. But then we decided we wanted to go in this direction and Roger just thought we should stay with what we had. So we said, no, we want to try this. We want it to be really quite raw and quite sort of heavy. Because that's what the music we were writing at the time demanded, you know?"

"And I remember it very well. It was a case of the guys going in and doing the backing tracks. I would do the vocals, and we would say, yes, that's fine but we'll change this a little bit. We had it sort of worked up before we went into the studio, so we knew what we expected to hear. And the main thing for us was getting the sound we were getting in rehearsals, which we managed to get. We recorded it in a studio that's no longer there, and then we finished it off in Air London and it turned out really well. Jeff Beck was there every night, because he just lived around the corner. And Jeff used to drop by and give us his grade, 'Oh, six out of ten, four out of ten; you can do better than that, boys.' And he used to sit and talk about cars 'til four in the morning. We kept saying, 'Come on, Jeff, play something on it.' But he didn't (laughs). Because he's tied up by more record companies than a rodeo cow."

"We did it in somewhere like ten days or something (laughs). It was Manny and a guy named Tony Taverner did it and John Punter worked on the mix as well. So we knew that we would get the sounds that we wanted. We had most of the songs together before we went into the studio so it was a case of just getting the best performance. 'That's the one, guys,' you know? We hadn't played any of those songs live. It was just a case of having rehearsed them up quite a bit at sound checks and little rehearsals."

"When we tried to do the vocals, the studio we were in, they didn't have any compressors (laughs) and you couldn't do any vocals in there. You could only do guide vocals and take them somewhere else to do them because they would just crack up all over the place. So it wasn't all that well equipped for doing voices, which was kind of a hassle. But everything worked out okay."

"'Please Don't Judas Me'… we were going through a bunch of stuff at the time with management companies and record companies and so-called friends. We found ourselves in a lot of trouble, unbeknownst to us, of course. And that was kind of a reflection on that. If you're going to sell me out, just tell me about it, you know? Let's not get a bunch of lawyers to have to work it all out. And then there was 'Changin' Times,' which was a case of, we just loved the riff. Manny and Pete played it so well and we thought, let's get something for this. And it turned out quite nicely with the odd time signature and everything."

Pete Agnew:

"By this time we had had our fill of mobiles for the time being and decided we would use a studio that didn't have wheels. The place we ended up in was on old 'oast house' down in Kent in England. The house was where we lived, and outside there was a barn that these guys had converted into a studio. Problem was, they never told the local authorities that they had converted the barn, so when neighbours complained about the 'noise from the studio,' the local authorities replied, 'What studio?'"

"However, no matter how basic the studio was—and it was basic—we managed to get a great sound on the backing tracks and instrumental overdubs. They were all done in nine days but we had to move up to AIR Studios in London to record the vocals. What I remember most from the AIR sessions was coming into the control room after Dan had just sang 'Miss Misery' for the first time and it was on playback so we could have a listen and see where it needed any fixing. When the track finished, the band members were completely silent having been stunned by this incredible performance. It was at this point that one of our managers broke the silence with, 'That will be great when Dan gets the vocal right!' We never discussed music with that guy again."

May 1975. America sees a single issue for the cheeky title track of the new album, backed with "Love Hurts." At the same time, back home, Mooncrest issues "My White Bicycle" as a single. The non-LP Tomorrow cover (featuring Steve Howe on guitar) manages a No.14 placement on the charts and is backed with metallic *Hair of the Dog* rocker "Miss Misery."

Dan McCafferty:

"We said, 'Who the fuck are Sears?' I had been in the States and I had even heard John Wayne say son of a bitch. So we just changed the meaning behind it to get past the false modesty of Americans. Hair of the dog really means the same thing. But really, the whole band is involved in the lyrics. We do a lot of things like a band. It saves a whole lot of arguing down the road. There were a couple of occasions where Manny wanted to have his name on stuff. We said, fine. Nine times out of ten, when we write something it was credited to everybody. Later on in life, it makes it better."

"But 'Miss Misery,' everybody gets excited during that one. We used to have to use an electric metronome to keep us from going too fast. Some nights we get carried away with it. Some nights it's hard to keep the timing slow enough. Lyrically, it was based on more than one person. Everyone has had their own Miss Misery. If not, then you are a lucky boy."

Pete Agnew:

"We were going to call the album *Son of a Bitch,* because where we come from, 'son of a bitch' is not even a saying. That's just a thing John Wayne said in movies; it's not a British thing. We took it to A&M in California and they said no. So we thought, fair enough, we'd be really smart and we'd call it *Heir of the Dog,* HEIR. And basically, the guys said, 'Oh, we're all Scottish; let's call it *Hair of the Dog.*' So once the dog was mentioned, we went to this guy to draw it and we actually never met the guy. We saw the finished album sleeve and you've got to realise, I'm not really a monster guy; I'm a little more laid-back. They're not my favourite thing (laughs). But I was outvoted and the band loved it. It's a fantastic painting, I've got to admit. Management just showed it to us after the guy did it and the guys thought, 'Yeah, that's punchy.'"

June 19, 1975. Nazareth get on Top of the Pops with "My White Bicycle," with a repeat airing two weeks later.

Dan McCafferty, on "My White Bicycle:"

"When it first came out, we were playing on the Scottish circuit of bars and ballrooms. I mean, to stay alive in those places, you just had to play the current hits of the day, you know, all the Beatles and Stones stuff. But what we tried to do was choose songs that we thought would be hits and make them. This satisfied everyone. So we chose 'My White Bicycle' and we have enjoyed it ever since. In fact, it's one of the most requested songs we've ever had."

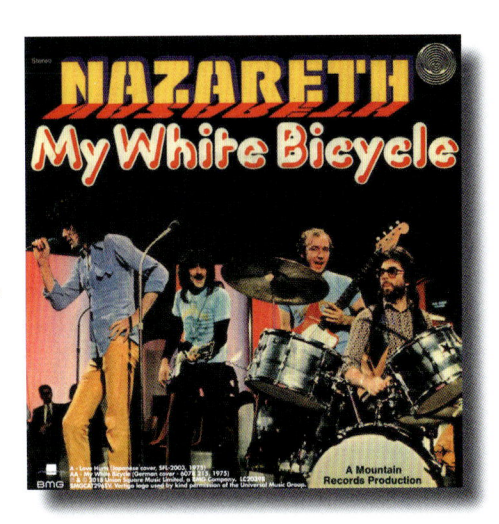

June 26 – September 26, 1975. Nazareth conduct a cross-Canada tour, many of the dates supported by Rush.

October 1975. Mountain issue "Holy Roller"/"Railroad Boy," both non-LP, as a UK single, with the A-side reaching #36 on the charts.

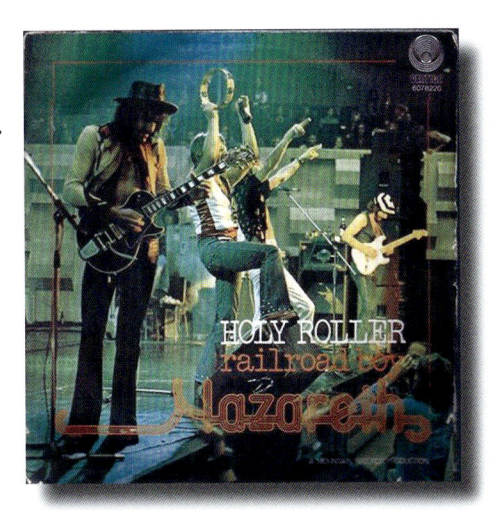

October 1975. Mountain issues *Dan McCafferty*, Dan's first solo album. It's a record of covers, recorded at Basing Street Studios. Five singles are floated from it across a number of years, with only Rolling Stones cover "Out of Time" charting, at #41. Roger Glover plays bass and Manny Charlton plays guitar, as does future Nazareth member Zal Cleminson. Manny also produces the record. The cover art is an early Joe Petagno, renowned for his Motörhead covers.

Dan McCafferty, on the guest stars on his record:
"There are three basic reasons for this. I know them all and they are all good companions. What I didn't want was that kind of horrible superstar thing where people just played for a credit up their sleeve. Second, they are all good musicians, and that is very important. And thirdly, they were all available (laughs). (Zal Cleminson) is amazing. When we were here listening to the reproductions, he was writhing and doing all the hand actions and everything. God, he's incredible. What we wanted was to be kind of happy with the album. We didn't want it to sound segmented like, you know, here comes Eric's solo and everyone is quiet. But at the same time we didn't want it to sound like Dan McCafferty and his new band or anything. Yes, we are quite satisfied with it. They're all big numbers and it's just something I've wanted to do for a long time."

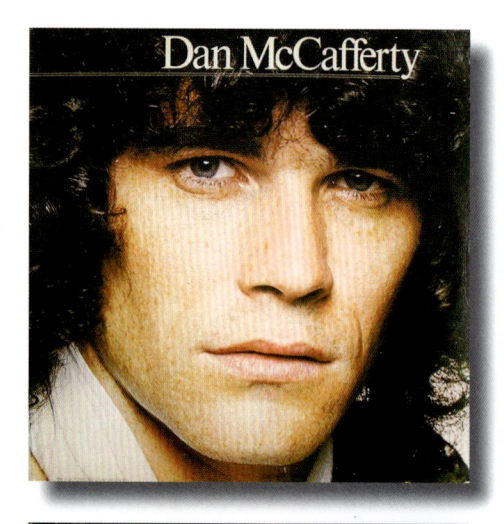

"When the band was doing *Loud 'n' Proud*, which was our second successful album, I wanted to do a solo then. But we had to take a tour of the States and then there was Canada and then Germany and then the States again, so you can see that it was a little bit difficult. Then, all of a sudden, there was this month out of nowhere, so I took the chance. That was back in June. While I desperately wanted to do this, I didn't want to be selfish, but the rest of the boys couldn't have been more helpful about it. Manny produced my album and he plays a little bit of rhythm guitar in 'Out of Time.' As a band, we are very much into what the rest of the guys want to do as their own little pet projects And Nazareth is going to do some things from my album on stage. Why not? Because it is another facet for us and it will help to broaden our musical horizons a little." (Melody Maker, 1975)

November 1975. Ballad "Love Hurts" sees success as a single in the US, reaching #9 on the Billboard charts. It is included on *Greatest Hits*, also issued this month. The album is reissued on CD in 1989, 1996 and 2010, each with an increasing number of bonus tracks. Greatest Hits zooms to the #1 spot on the Canadian charts. The album is not issued in the US, with that territory in its stead getting *Hot Tracks* the following year.

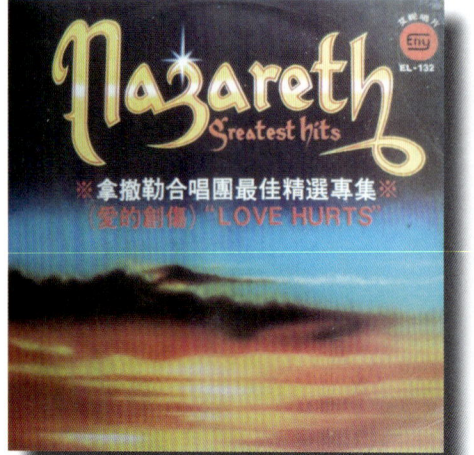

Dan McCafferty on "Love Hurts" being added to the US version of *Hair of the Dog*:

"It was only put on the American version. We had a Randy Newman song called 'Guilty' on it in Europe and we did 'Love Hurts' as a B-side (laughs). Shows you what we know. And we sent it to the States, and Jerry Moss from A&M said, 'No, no, no, boys, this is a chance to really get some airplay here.' So he said, 'We'll take off "Guilty" and we'll put on "Love Hurts,"' and God bless him."

"We've always love that song. We used to do it as kids. We covered it when we were in bar bands, like the Everly Brothers version, and Pete and I used to sing it. Emmylou Harris and Gram Parsons did it on the *Pieces of the Sky* album, and we thought, oh, man, that's still a great song, let's do a version of that, so we did! And when we were recording it, Pete and I were at a wedding in Scotland and Manny and Darrell—God bless them—at the time did the guitar part and the drums, and then we came down and Pete did the bass part and I did the vocals and that was kind of that."

"We loved the version. 'That's a really great version of it, guys.' But we had no idea what it was going to do. And it came out in the States and nobody played it. And it was a place down in Texas that just kept playing it and playing it and playing it and eventually it started to spread from there. But it was a year after that song came out that it became a hit. It's an amazing story. And actually, the guy who wrote the song came and saw us in Los Angeles. He told us that the guys had heard it and they thought it was great. It's not like he was going to tell us that he thought it was a load of shit. We also got asked to sing the song at Axl Rose's wedding. We were in Germany so we couldn't do it. I think it was just as well because I think the song lasted longer than the marriage."

"We also covered 'Guilty' and 'Beggars Day' and we just loved those songs too. We still love them today and we're still fans. We just thought that any song we took, we could do our own version of it. The way Nils Lofgren did 'Beggars Day' was different than the way we did it."

November 12, 1975. Nazareth get on Top of the Pops with "Love Hurts."

November 27, 1975. The BBC air a Nazareth set from London's Paris Theatre; the recordings will be included as bonus material on the 2010 Salvo Records reissue of *Hair of the Dog*.

Dan McCafferty, also in 1975:

"It boils down to being a people's band. They have to get off on the music as well as the band. It's spoiled if there's a guy up there on stage preaching about his religion and telling the kids how cosmic it is. That's not where it's at. When we tour, we still keep things like 'This Flight Tonight' and older old numbers because people want to hear them and that's what they pay for. Christ, you can't say, 'Right, we're going to play all new material; forget the old stuff.' We consider ourselves as an old-style band. We play for the people and give them what they want. In doing so, we hit the odd high spot. That's what good rock is all about. I don't think the media is that impressed by what we do because we're not into something outlandish. The music is rock 'n' roll and it doesn't make for good comic books. Nobody is going to call us the saviours of rock 'n' roll." *(Melody Maker 1975)*

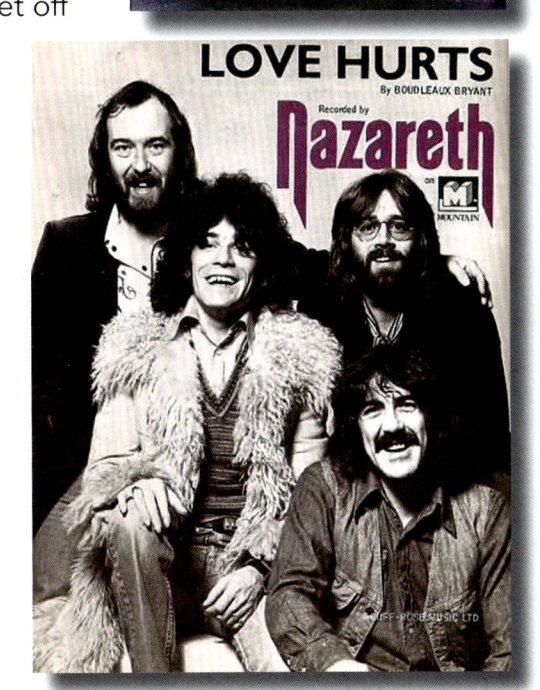

58

Performing on the Austrian TV show Spotlight in 1975.

Pete in Sweden: the epitome of rock 'n' roll.

April, 20th, 1975, Amsterdam, Netherlands.

© Laurens Van Houten / Frank White Photo Agency

60

61

April, 20th, 1975, Amsterdam, Netherlands.

© Laurens Van Houten / Frank White Photo Agency

1976

January 14 – March 4, 1976. Nazareth tour the States, supporting Deep Purple, followed by UK dates and a return to the US in May.

Glenn Hughes:
"I befriended Nazareth in '72, about a year before I joined Purple, and I befriended Dan McCafferty and the bass player, Pete Agnew. I was living down in London, and we hung out quite a lot together. And then a couple of Purple tours, they opened for Purple. Dan and Pete were very close friends of mine. Dan has an incredible voice. I remember that 'Love Hurts' song, and when were doing Mark IV, that was the No.1 song across America. I have a certain amount of love for a lot of Scottish musicians. There are some amazing Scottish singing/songwriting musicians out there. But Dan, what an incredible, incredible voice. There was a lot of very strong camaraderie with those guys; it was great."

Late February 1976. "Carry Out Feelings," backed with "Lift the Lid," is issued as a single in the UK as well as the US.

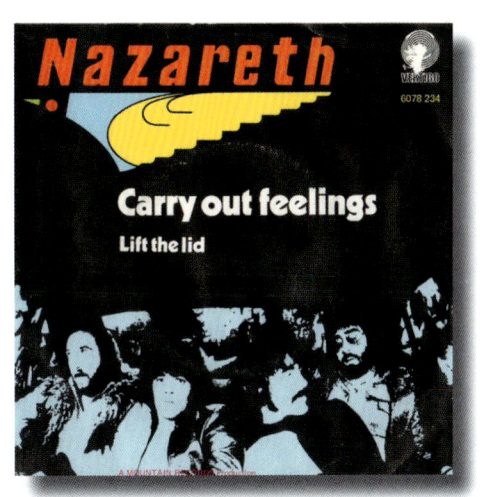

March 25, 1976. Nazareth issues a seventh studio album, entitled *Close Enough for Rock 'n' Roll*. The album would mark the first time the band recorded in Canada, using the legendary Le Studio, Morin Heights, in rural Quebec, north of Montreal. The record would also mark the first time the band didn't reach a certification level in Canada since the pre-*Razamanaz* days (according to official certifier Music Canada, despite other sources citing not only gold but platinum sales).

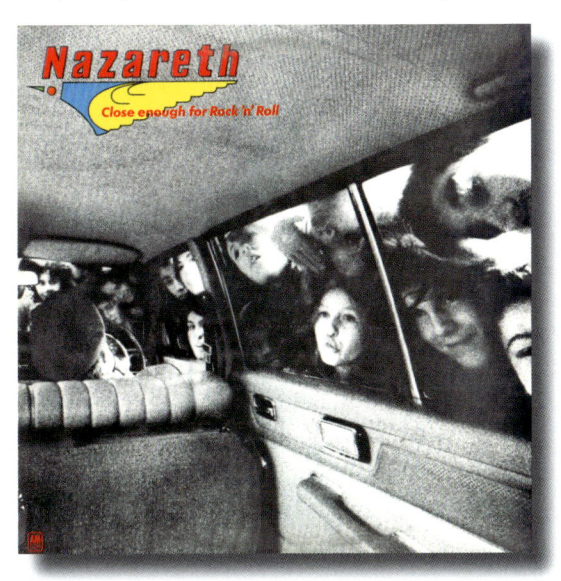

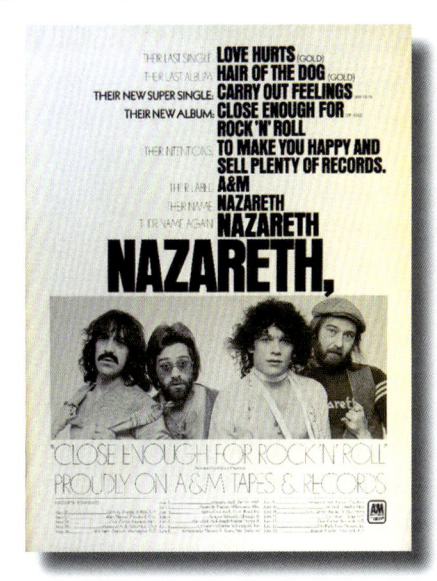

Dan McCafferty:
"I like the covers stuff from *Close Enough for Rock 'n' Roll*. That was another time when we had to make a lot of albums really quickly. Because we were doing really well touring-wise. We were selling out big halls and the record company wanted albums as well. I mean big time. We were doing loads of headlining. We did about three or four years of the halls. 1975 to '77 more or less. It was fine; I liked it. It was no problem. Of course we just got on with it, heads down and let's go! I look back now, and I would have liked to have had a bit more time. But that's the way it was done in those days."

"But Le Studio, that was a great place. See, we always liked recording like that, where you can get away from everything so you can just concentrate on the music. We liked to be in a working environment. And the town was just down the road five miles or something; it was nothing. It was just a lovely place and the people that ran it were cool. It was glass and you were standing in the middle of the Canadian woods with a lake outside. You could plug in near a tree if you wanted and do a guitar solo, if it was a nice day. I didn't sing out there personally, though. I don't think they'd like that, because you'd get bugs twittering and things like that."

"We tried canoeing. They had a wee aluminum canoe and we did try have a go at that. If we would have been the guys trying to find a way across Canada by water, we would've never got past Toronto. We were not canoers, put it that way. The fondest thing for me was playing in places nobody would go and play, but not canoeing there (laughs). We actually played Ulan Bator once, in a football stadium. The capital of Mongolia. That was bizarre, but very, very interesting. It was really good, actually; I enjoyed it. I asked if they'd had anybody play here before. They said, 'We do have a local band; they do "Love Hurts" too.'"

"But no, we always got a good vibe there. I'm sorry to hear that it's gone, but see, the thing is, that's kind of the story internationally. People don't need big rooms to work anymore. Mind you, live drums are coming back. There are a few studios up here that are building a bit on for live drums. But people can make records in their bedroom now. Nobody seems to care about ambience or vibe. I don't know, I'm probably sounding old-fashioned and horrible (laughs)."

Pete Agnew:
"The income tax situation in Britain at that time meant that if you got lucky and your new record was a hit, the government was being so kind that they would save you from having to worry about safeguarding your money by taking it all from you. Most bands found this unhelpful and decided to record anywhere except Britain. We had heard about a studio in the Laurentian mountains not too far from Montreal. Even had an easy name to remember. It was Le Studio and it was beautiful where it sat with its own lake in the woods among the mountains, so quiet it made us wonder if we were actually allowed to cause a disturbance playing rock 'n' roll."

"The studio itself had every latest gizmo that had been invented for recording and was the very opposite of where we had made the last album. We were very well prepared for this album and had written plenty of material so the recording was easy and quite relaxing. We decided that we loved this place and would be back again. Oh, did I mention they had a wonderful little restaurant down in the valley where we ate every night for six weeks? This time I put *on* 20 pounds."

Uncredited record review:

"Finger-in-the-socket rockers Nazareth have arrived again to bring us Gibraltar-solid rock. Side one is preoccupied with the musical diary of a rock band on tour, an inter-blending of their own 'Telegram' and an infectious momentary cover of the Byrds' 'So You Want to Be a Rock 'n' Roll Star.' The clap-along 'Here We Are Again' is a dynamite number with 'short single' potential and the languid tones of the acoustic 'Vicki' are mellow and inviting. Harmonies are dirty-sweet and instruments are clear, giving *Close Enough for Rock 'n' Roll* vast AM and FM potential. This is certainly the richest and most cohesive outing to date." *(Cashbox, May 1, 1976)*

April 1976. "Love Hurts" is RIAA-certified as a gold single in the US.

Dan McCafferty on the band's predilection for doing covers:

"It was the case of touring so much. We always liked doing covers anyway. We've always liked other people's songs. It was usually just a case of working it out, doing a demo and then putting it away. And then when we get to making a record, we found that we had a whole bunch of these things. And we thought, why the hell not? (laughs). Sometimes we had loads of stuff and other times it was like, 'Oh my God!' Back in the early '70s, putting out a lot of product was the big thing. They had you in the studio like twice a year, and then they wanted you to tour for nine months. So it was difficult to get stuff written. But like everything else, we used to manage it."

May 1, 1976. Nazareth enjoys a blanket certification day in Canada. *Razamanaz*, *Loud 'n' Proud* and *Greatest Hits* are simultaneously certified gold and platinum, while *Rampant* and *Hair of the Dog* are certified gold. As well, "Love Hurts" is certified as a gold single.

June 1976. "You're the Violin"/"Loretta" is issued as a single in the UK. Like "Carry Out Feelings," it fails to chart.

July 1, 1976. The band play a show at the Beacon Theatre in New York, supported by the Ian Gillan Band.

Uncredited reviewer:

"Near the end of the 'Hair of the Dog' segment, Nazareth paid tribute to its Scottish heritage with a bit of showmanship, including the onstage appearance of a kilted dancer, a set of bagpipes and a bottle of scotch. McCafferty teased the audience with a two-minute turn on the bagpipes. He also led the crowd in a round of 'Happy Birthday to Nazareth' before the finale, 'Woke Up This Morning.' The ten-minute encore, which featured the band's own 'Teenage Nervous Breakdown,' Cream's 'Sunshine of Your Love' and ZZ Top's 'Tush,' left the enthusiastic audience wanting more." *(Billboard, July 24, 1976)*

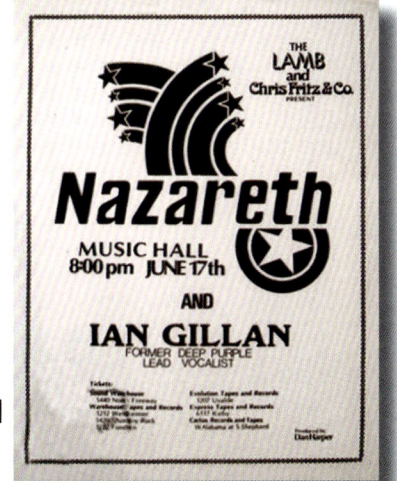

July 27, 1976. The band's beloved manager Bill Fehilly dies in a plane crash, flying in a Piper, en route from Blackpool to Perth, on the way back from a meeting with the band. All six occupants of the plane perished in the crash, caused by engine failure due to an oil leak.

Dan McCafferty:
"Both he and his son were killed. It was horrible. It was very tough to deal with altogether. We had all agreed on everything together. He did really well with us. He was going in the right direction. He had us and he had the Alex Harvey Band. Things were going well for him before his plane hit that mountain. It really took us a few years to get over that. Even business-wise it was tough for us because everything was tied up in court. It got us down for several years but we carried on. With any band, all you have is your talent. If you believe in your talent then keep going. Everyone who has ever been in a band has been ripped off. At some point they have been ripped off or done something stupid themselves. We have been guilty of both. The bottom line is that all we have is our talent. If you don't believe in it then you just go off and say, 'That was fun.' For us it's still fun. We get to see the smiles on people's faces and it really makes you feel wonderful. I know it sounds schmaltzy but it really is true."

August – September 1976. Nazareth work at Le Studio on tracks slated for what will be their eighth studio album.

Dan McCafferty:
"We hadn't seen each other in five weeks before we went into the studio. We decided to just go in and see how our ideas came out. One week we just did little things, changing little bits and just generally messing around. The whole album was actually finished in three weeks. We couldn't believe we'd done it so quick. We kept listening to it to see if there was anything wrong with it, you know? Manny does all the mixing. As far as the instruments are recorded, the band fights it out with him until everybody's happy with it. Seems to work out that way. The new one is much more 'up' than *Close Enough*. The amount of energy that went into *Play 'n' the Game* was incredible. I think it took the band a step forward musically, and communicating with each other as well. There's more energy than *Close Enough*. We've all written from ideas that we've gotten over the last year, from being on the road touring so much. The original songs just came together in the studio pretty much." *(w/ Wesley Strick, Circus, 1976)*

August 1, 1976. "Love Hurts" is certified as a platinum-selling single in Canada.

September 1976. "Lift the Lid"/"Loretta" is issued as a single in the States.

September 24, 1976. Nazareth are presented with a number of Canadian record awards, on a visit to Edmonton, garnering platinum for *Razamanaz* and *Loud 'n' Proud*, gold for *Rampant* and *Hair of the Dog* and double platinum for *Greatest Hits* (plus a platinum single for "Love Hurts"). By this point, the band had sold over 600,000 units across their five albums to date, in Canada. Also on this Canadian tour, at a stop in Vancouver, the front cover image used on *Play 'n' the Game* is shot, courtesy Fin Costello, who captured the band playing poker before the night's performance. The 12-day Canadian tour found the band playing to 100,000 fans, with a ticket gross of $625,000 and Nazareth taking home $250,000.

Dan McCafferty:
"In Canada, almost every album we did was a hit, like a gold record and stuff. And in Europe, we've had ups and downs all over the place. Somebody told me we've sold 70 million records or something crazy like that, but we've had two different managers as well, so who knows how many there really were? (laughs). We've had more court cases than Mickey Rooney. I know *Hair of the Dog* went gold in the States. We even have a gold eight-track for that, if you can believe it. Because that was the format in everybody's truck at the time. And *Greatest Hits* was huge in Canada."

November 1976. Nazareth issue as a single, across a number of territories but not in the US, "I Don't Want to Go on Without You," backed variously with "Good Love" or "L.A. Girls."

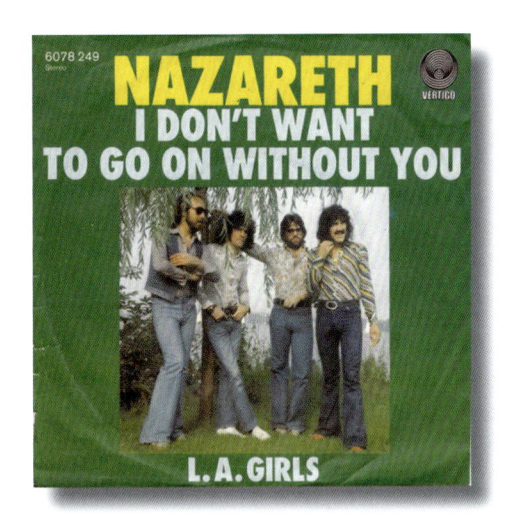

Pete Agnew:
"That's the only time in our career where we did what we said we would never do, which is try to do a single the same as the last one. It was usually, 'No, no, don't give into that pressure.' But we had so little material for that album, we would've welcomed anything, almost, as a suggestion. And that one was to follow 'Love Hurts,' basically; it was to do another 'Love Hurts.'" And Dan did a fabulous job of singing 'I Don't Want to Go on Without You.' I think it's a great record. But it was never going to replace 'Love Hurts.'" Reviewer Angie Errigo:

Reviewer Angie Errigo:
The Wexler-Burns tearjerker, 'I Don't Want to Go on Without You' is handled with such unusual restraint that McCafferty for once has plenty of room to lean his powerful, wide-ranging voice on the emotional possibilities. The stab at being classy is a trifle overblown on the vocal echoes and wringing guitar, but the intensity is mighty impressive." *(Melody Maker, December 4, 1976)*

November 13, 1976. Nazareth issue their eighth album, *Play 'n' the Game*, which would certify gold in Canada. The album finds the band back at Le Studio, Manny producing aided by famed engineer, the late Nick Blagona.

Pete Agnew:
"As promised, we went back to Le Studio to record this new one but this time we were nowhere near prepared for it. What happened is this: *Hair of the Dog* had a big hit single with 'Love Hurts.' When *Close Enough* came out there was no hit single on it. Even though 'Telegram' became probably one of the Nazareth's all-time classic tracks, it wasn't a hit single and as we all know record companies just love hit singles (who doesn't?)."

"This meant it was back to the studio for us within six months of finishing the last album. The only problem with that is, because of touring solidly for six months, not only did we not have time to write a hit single, we had no time to write anything! Now picture four guys in a studio with the tape running and countless cases of beer, jamming for all their worth and hoping some sparks will fly in the right direction to create something worth recording. We ended up putting four cover songs on this album but they were cracking cover versions and we enjoyed every minute of recording what we originally thought was a non-starter. I remember when we arrived we said, 'Well we're here and we're nowhere near ready for this but we'll have to play the game.'"

"But yeah, when the engineer said, 'Okay, what are you gonna record for us?' it was, 'Well, we got nothing, absolutely nothing.' So he'd basically run a half-inch tape and we went into the studio and played all day. You know, just play for two or three hours, come down, listen back to all the stuff, play for another couple hours, listen for another couple hours, 'Oh, keep that, and we can do something with that.' That went on for four or five days, and then we started to go in and take bits of that and add it to a piece of that. Sometimes Dan would sing a vocal; like 'Waiting for the Man,' he came in right away for that thing—that happened right on the spot. But other ones, you take little bits of a backing track and you go, 'What can you do for a vocal on that?' It was all very piecemeal."

Manny Charlton:
"Basically, we didn't really have a lot of material for it at that point. We were touring and recording, touring and recording, and when we got… the management, they didn't care. 'You got a break in the tour; go up to Morin

Heights and record a new album.' 'We don't have any songs.' 'Just go anyway. It's booked.' So they booked it for six weeks or whatever. Like I say, we didn't have a lot of original material, so we did a bunch of covers on that album. We were back up to the Laurentian Mountains, outside of Montreal, and it was a great place. We had the studio to ourselves and they had accommodation for us. That album cover was before a show. A photographer came over from the UK to do it, and we were in the hotel in Vancouver. And he just said, 'Set up like you're playing a game of cards.' That was about the only sleeve that had us on the cover."

Reviewer Angie Errigo:
"There's something about Nazareth that makes them more appealing than just any full-volume, full-tilt blasters. Underneath the apparent abandon, they show an enthusiastic taste. And along with having a first-rate singer, they could pick pleasing songs that make them that little bit more spirited than others in the same basic bag. Charlton's production is a little over-clever at times, with guitar lick sliding busily from speaker to speaker more than a few times. But on the whole, it has vibrancy that is almost startling from a band that's been doing what Nazareth have been doing for as long as they now have. They know themselves well and exploit what they have with consistent dynamism."
(Melody Maker, December 4, 1976)

December 1976. The band receive a gold record award in Brazil for the single issue of "Love Hurts." The award is accepted by Dan, who flies down to Rio with his wife Mary Ann and son Derek.

Dan McCafferty, speaking in 1999, on the sense of family within the band:
"I've been married for thirty years, so has Pete, so has Darrell. We've all got grown-up kids. I've known Pete since I was five. I've known Darrell since I was in my teens. They're like anybody else in the world who've gone through changes in life. I think what kept us reasonably, well, half-sane, was being brought up in the same area and having the same type of parents, I guess. We got taught the same values. I think that makes it easier for us to communicate with each other. I think if you put one guy from Toronto and one guy from LA and one guy from Edinburgh together, you're looking for trouble here. So I think having the same background and the same kind of education helps."

"We've never had any drug problems in the band, not at all. Although we are fond of a jar or two. It has been known for alcohol to cross our lips (laughs). But drug problems, no. Because I think, again, having families and stuff like that, the little man in the back of your head goes, 'You do it and you die.' It just never appealed to us. It's part of the business. The scariest thing though is that you see more of it outside the business than you do in it."

December 1976. A&M issue "I Want to (Do Everything for You)"/"I Don't Want to Go on Without You" as a single in the States. The single is a featured track on US hits compilation *Hot Tracks*.

April 1st, 1976, UK.

© Laurens Van Houten / Frank White Photo Agency

April 1st, 1976, London, UK.

© Laurens Van Houten / Frank White Photo Agency

February 17th, 1976, Oklahoma City Fairgrounds Arena, Oklahoma City, OK.

© Rich Galbraith

© Rich Galbraith

73

February 17th, 1976,
Oklahoma City
Fairgrounds Arena,
Oklahoma City, OK.

© Rich Galbraith

© Rich Galbraith

October 27th, 1977,
Tulsa Assembly Center,
Tulsa, OK.

1977

1977. The band spend much of the year playing North America, sharing stages with the likes of REO Speedwagon, Point Blank, Head East, Lynyrd Skynyrd, The Outlaws, Ted Nugent, The Dictators, Starz, Riot, Uriah Heep, Foghat, The Michael Stanley Band, Foreigner, Utopia and Aerosmith (quite regularly, in June and July).

Manny Charlton on British fans shunning bands who spent too much time out of the country:

"That happened; that did happen. Basically right from the Beatles on. You can only go so far in the UK. You can tour around the UK in a month when you're that size. When you're the size of the Beatles or Zeppelin, there isn't the venues that would constitute the tour. So you did your British tour and then what did you do? You sat on your backside and said what else can we do? Where else can we work?"

"So we went to Europe and we played Germany and France and Sweden and all these countries, and then America. That was the big market. Huge market. I mean even the Beatles eventually had to go and do America. And Canada, when we first started coming over to North America, we treated Canada really seriously because it was a great market for us. They really loved us in Canada. We did full-blown tours right across Canada, and we were one of the first bands to do that. So you just had to play and you became a world band as opposed to a British band. And of course people in Britain would go, 'Oh, we never get to see you any more; you're in America all the time.' Well that's where we work."

January 7, 1977. "Vancouver Shakedown" is issued as a belated single, from *Close Enough for Rock 'n' Roll*, backed with "Somebody to Roll."

Dan McCafferty on "Vancouver Shakedown:"
"We got ripped off twice in Vancouver by the same guy. Everybody over here took it as though we were actually slagging Vancouver to death. And we go, 'No, no, we're not slagging Vancouver; we're slagging this guy who lives here.' But there you go—life's a spit and then you die, isn't it? That's all in the past." (w/ Steve Newton, Ear of Newt)

February 1, 1977. *Play 'n' the Game* is certified gold in Canada.

March 1977. Paice Ashton Lord issue an album called *Malice in Wonderland*. Come 1980, Nazareth didn't clue into this until the last minute, and added to the inner sleeve of their record of the same name, a missive reading, "No malice intended, PAL."

April 1977. A&M issue "Somebody to Roll"/"This Flight Tonight" as a single in the States.

September 1977. Mooncrest issue a seven-inch EP version of the *Hot Tracks* hit compilation. The four-tracker reaches #15 in the UK charts.

October 20, 1977. Lynyrd Skynyrd's plane crashes, killing Ronnie Van Zant, Steve Gaines and Cassie Gaines, along with road manager Dean Kilpatrick and both pilots.

Dan McCafferty:

"The guys suggested we go for a barbecue and it sounded like a good idea. But something came up. Our record company wanted us for some promotion thing or something. They were a great bunch of guys though. We did not understand a word any of them said, and they didn't understand us. But we would go out and get drunk and have a great time." (w/ Jack Lloyd, The Dispatch, April 6, 1981)

Pete Agnew:

"We played Greenville Memorial Auditorium that night and Artimus Pyle, Skynyrd's drummer, introduced us onstage before our show. It was his hometown and it was he that invited us to a barbecue they were going to have at his place."

November 19, 1977. Nazareth issue their ninth album, *Expect No Mercy*, the fourth in a row produced by band guitarist Manny Charlton. The cover art is by famed fantasy artist Frank Frazetta, with the classic image reproduced a second time without text on the inner sleeve.

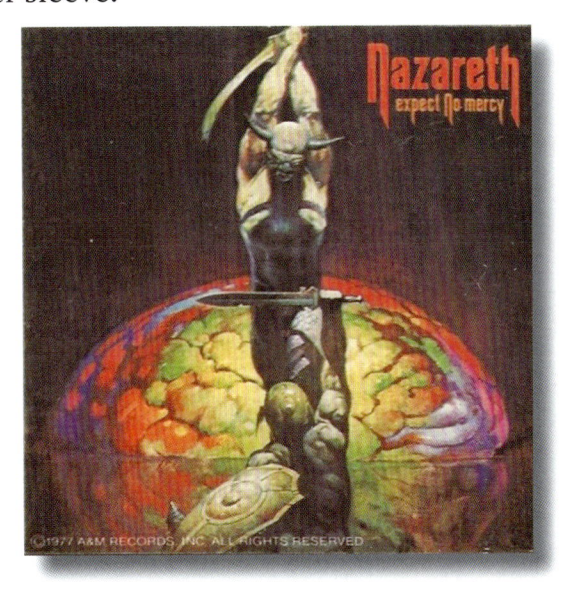

Dan McCafferty:

"At the time we were the first to use Frank Frazetta, who we used for *Expect No Mercy*. We were in the studio in Montreal, and they had a coffee table book of Frank Frazetta's art, and we were flipping through it and we thought that would be perfect for our album. We phoned him up and we said, 'Could we speak to Frank?' And his wife said, 'This is his wife; Frank doesn't like phones. What is it that you want?' We asked him if we could use the sleeve. 'Right, give me a number and we'll get back to you.'"

"So she got back to us and said, 'Yes, sure you can use it, no problem. Thanks for asking.' Obviously there was a fee involved, but fair enough, you know? Still, it cost us practically nothing. Which I'm sure changed rapidly after that, because there were a whole bunch of people using his stuff. But he was cool about it. It just seemed to go with the music: *Expect No Mercy*, you know? The guy's getting his head chopped off (laughs). That sort of said it simply, really. Actually, if you look at it again, he can't chop off his head because his arms would never get past his horns. It's true. We thought that was quite ironic. That's why we picked it, really."

Pete Agnew on tough bass parts:

"The ones that are killer for me are things like 'Morning Dew' and 'Expect No Mercy.' I mean, I was stupid on those, and that's what the guys all tell me. When I come offstage complaining that my hand is going to fall off, they say, 'Well, you were stupid enough to write that part in the first place. You shouldn't have done that.' Those are just really hard work. I like playing them all, really, but I like the more mid-tempo things. I like 'Whiskey Drinkin' Woman' and I like 'Heart's Grown Cold' and 'Beggars Day.' I like playing all the songs, but it's just that some of them are harder to play than others."

"But yes, as Dan says, that album cover, that painting—it's called *The Brain*—it was very funny because the big devil guy that is standing with the sword, and is trying to kill the guys in front of him, he's going to take his own arms off, with his horns (laughs). Of course, after that, people like Molly Hatchet and a whole bunch of people used Frank Frazetta stuff."

"For *Expect No Mercy*, the love affair with Le Studio continued. We were prepared for the studio this time with a bunch of songs that sounded like they were going to work but we were not prepared for a Canadian winter! Anyone who has experienced winter in Canada will know what I mean. We get snow at home and as we all know, Europe gets its fair whack of snow (we hadn't toured Russia at this point in our career) but Canada gets big *giant* snow. We spent most of our money paying tow trucks to pull our cars out of snow drifts and spent most of our time stuck in the studio with snow half way up to the roof. I think we had more playbacks of *Expect No Mercy* than any other album we made simply because of the time we spent as prisoners."

October 27th, 1977,
Tulsa Assembly Center,
Tulsa, OK.

© Rich Galbraith

© Rich Galbraith

82

October 27th, 1977,
Tulsa Assembly Center,
Tulsa, OK.

© Rich Galbraith

October 27th, 1977,
Tulsa Assembly Center,
Tulsa, OK.

© Rich Galbraith

© Rich Galbraith

© Rich Galbraith

October 27th, 1977,
Tulsa Assembly Center,
Tulsa, OK.

© Rich Galbraith

October 27th, 1977,
Tulsa Assembly Center,
Tulsa, OK.

© Rich Galbraith

© Rich Galbraith

89

October 27th, 1977,
Tulsa Assembly Center,
Tulsa, OK.

© Rich Galbraith

1978

January 1978. Issued as a single in the UK is "Gone Dead Train" along with the non-LP "Greens" and "Desolation Road." The Expect No Mercy song gets to #49 on the UK charts.

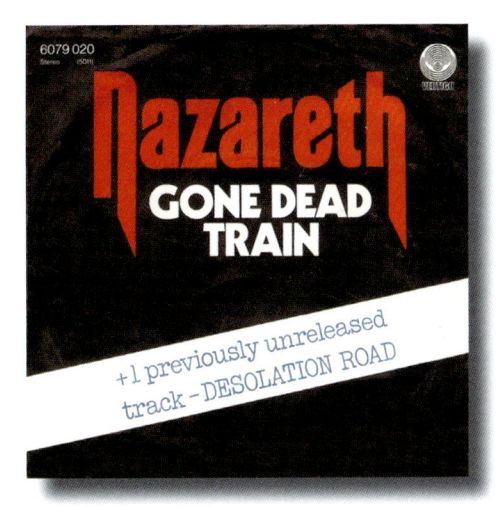

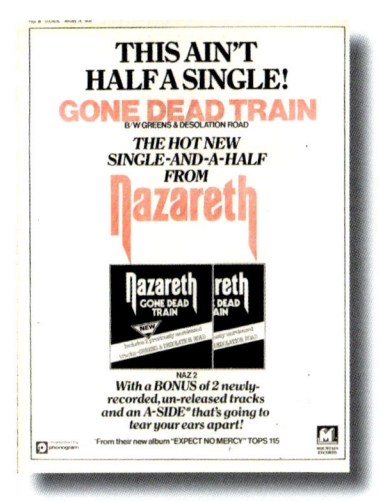

Pete Agnew:
"'Gone Dead Train,' well, we loved the *Crazy Horse* album. I mean, that was a phenomenal album; we loved it so much and played it so much. We did 'Beggars Day,' from that album and 'Gone Dead Train' and it was every intention… you know, Rod Stewart was always a guy that could pick a good song, and he did 'I Don't Want to Talk About It' from that album. We would've done that, but we didn't get to do it because he beat us to it (laughs). In fact at one point we thought about 'Dance, Dance, Dance' and 'I Don't Want to Talk About It,' and 'Dirty Dirty' was another song on that album—we used to play that at sound checks and things like that. But 'Gone Dead Train,' what a great rock song—we just loved the whole vibe of that."

Late January – Late March 1988. The band tour the States, supported mostly by Head East, Frank Marino & Mahogany Rush and Sammy Hagar.

April 1978. Issued as a single in the UK is "A Place in Your Heart" backed with "Kentucky Fried Blues" while the US gets "Shot Me Down"/"Kentucky Fried Blues." The US single doesn't chart but the UK offering reaches #70.

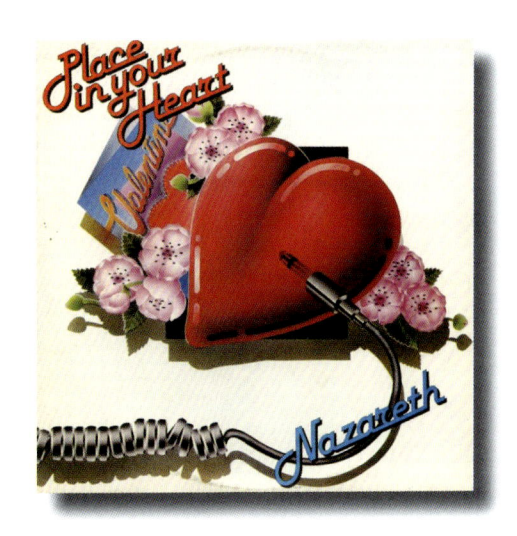

April 25 – May 23, 1978. Following German dates in mid-April, the band mount a cross-Canada tour, mostly supported by The Guess Who.

1979

January 1979. Issued as a single in the UK is ballad "May the Sunshine" backed with "Expect No Mercy," with the A-side notching a #22 placement on the home country chart.

Mid-January – February 20, 1979. Following UK dates in January and into February, the band play Luxembourg en route to a German leg, supported by Whitesnake, commencing February 9th until the 20th.

Pete Agnew:
"We took them on a big long European tour. That was when Jon Lord and Ian Paice were in that band, and they had other people as well, mates of mine, actually. And they had David Coverdale. So we took them out kind of repaying the favours that they did for us.

Same with the Ian Gillan Band. When Ian first put his band together, we actually did a big long US tour, and we took Ian out with us, to break his band, hopefully. Because they did us a big favour in taking us there, we took Ian out with us in the States for quite a long tour, five or six weeks."

January 13, 1979. Manny Charlton is back in the producer's chair for the fifth time, as Nazareth issue their tenth album, *No Mean City*. Cover art is by famed fantasy illustrator Rodney Matthews. It is the first of two albums for Zal Cleminson as part of Nazareth.

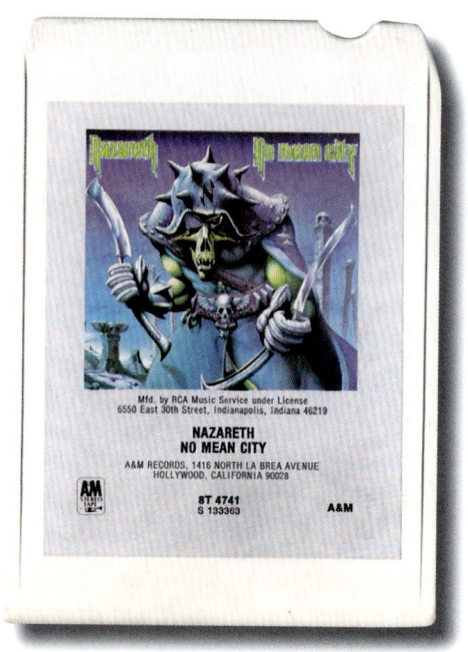

Dan McCafferty:
"We had known Zal since we were kids in Glasgow. He had always been around; he was in a lot of bands, and the Alex Harvey Band split up and Zal was driving a car and we said, 'That's stupid. Why don't you come and be in Nazareth for a bit?' So he did (laughs). He's a great player, so it was obviously easy to bring Zal into the band. It was good to have him for a couple of albums."

"*No Mean City* is actually based on a book that every Scottish student has to read in school. It was about gangs in the '20s and the Depression and stuff. It was standard school reading for children at that time, all about the gangs in Glasgow. And it was after that one being so heavy, and the subject matter being as heavy as it was, we decided subconsciously that we better lighten up a little bit. Looking back on it now, I think that's what we must have thought. Plus at the time we had Manny and Zal in the band, and we got a lot of guitar-oriented stuff because the two of them were playing together. We had evolved, we changed, we go left and right and go off on it, and that's the kind of music we were writing at the time, so that's what we did. And it had to be heavier because the basis of *No Mean City* is the song about razor gangs and they were nasty characters. So we couldn't really make a light album around that (laughs)."

"We were recording on the Isle of Man at the time, so the cover artist, Rodney Matthews, came up there and had a word with us. We gave him a rough tape of the music and that's what he came up with. We were there because we used to like to use mobiles. And at the time, Pete and I and Darrell were staying on the Isle of Man, so it seemed like an appropriate place. We did it at an old farmhouse and just put the mobile outside and did it there. With those things always something goes wrong—a track goes out that takes away all the effects and stuff like that. But generally speaking it was okay."

"The funny part, everybody grew beards. And they sent a photographer out to take these pictures of us and our manager at the time freaked out. He's like, 'No, y'alls have to shave your beards off!'"

Zal Cleminson:

"The Nazareth guys were just friends of ours. We had sort of grown up almost together in Scotland. We started about the same time, in music, and when Sensational Alex Harvey band split up, I was driving a taxi cab in London for a couple of months. I was doing all sorts of things trying to pay the bills. And then I got a call from Manny Charlton and he said do you want to come down and get involved in the *No Mean City* album they were recording at that time. I think what they were looking for, really, was a lot of input and musical songs, some writing contribution. They were looking for songs, basically. I just said yeah, this is cool, okay, let's just see where it goes, and I spent a couple of years with them, touring, recording a couple of albums, and they're good guys. We just worked together. We had the same management company, for example. So, we were like old pals."

"But they were never really my cup of tea, Nazareth, to be perfectly honest. They were never really a band that I would associate myself with musically, which sounds like a contradiction in terms as they're a pretty basic rock band. They just play that stuff and it's great. At that time, as a musician, I had a broad… I was more into the sort of Frank Zappa jazz-fusion thing, all that kind of stuff, compositions and creating soundtrack type music and whatever else. So, the basic rock thing for me was going back to a very, very basic style of playing, and I thought, okay, that's fine. It was good. The albums were okay." (w/ Marko Syrjala, MetalRules)

Pete Agnew:

"Our manager at the time phoned and was thinking we needed a change. We needed someone new. And Zal was driving a taxi. 'What do you think of Zal?' And I remember thinking, hey, that's a great idea. We were at Manny's house that night mucking about, and we said, 'Give him a ring; give Zal a ring.' So it was Manny that made the call—'Phone him and see.'"

"As for the album, there's a book called No Mean City, written way back in the '30s, about the razor gangs. It was a rough place to be at that time. And we all read the book when we were younger. The guy in the book that is the main man, he was The Razor King, and he had two razors, and that's why you've got Fred, as we call him, on the front cover, with his two razors. The song itself was about that, but the rest of the album was… I suppose it does fit because it was a hard rock album. It harkens back to those days. But we didn't really go into the idea with a concept. Zal had just joined, and he came in with a couple of songs and we all had some songs and we just decided to make them into an album. We didn't really say that we were going to do a concept but i suppose when you look at it from a fan's point of view, it does sound a little like that."

"To record it, we got Jethro Tull's mobile and we brought that up. We had a big farmhouse up there. We were all living on the Isle of Man at the time, all the band. And we'd got this farmhouse where we were rehearsing and writing, and it was decided that we loved the place and were very relaxed there, loved the atmosphere. Actually, if you saw where it was, it was so idyllic, and you see the kind of music we were actually playing there, it was actually very funny. Because the place isn't like that (laughs)."

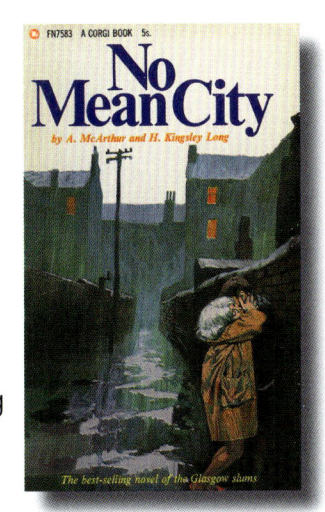

"We didn't record all of it there. We did all the backing tracks and stuff there, but the vocals, you can't do a lot. You can get the tracks down, so we did that there, and then we went to Queen's studio in Montreux, Switzerland and that's where we did all the vocals. Over there at the casino, when Queen owned the studio there. I think we did one or two guitar overdubs there too but most of the album was done in Isle of Man."

Manny Charlton:
"We produced a killer album. I was producing and we had the songs, and we had Zal helping out, and helping out quite a lot, filling out the sound. It's a great record. Zal was a good friend of all of the guys in Nazareth, and myself, and I admired the hell out of him. I thought Zal was a great guitar player, and with his writing and helping out with the guitar playing, I could sit back and concentrate more on the production. We didn't try to make him play anything different. It was just a great team, and *No Mean City*, to me, is one of the best Nazareth albums, a great rock record. Zal played his heart out on it."

Late February – early April 1979. Nazareth tour the States, playing most regularly with Thin Lizzy, who bow out after the March 25th show in Saginaw, Michigan.

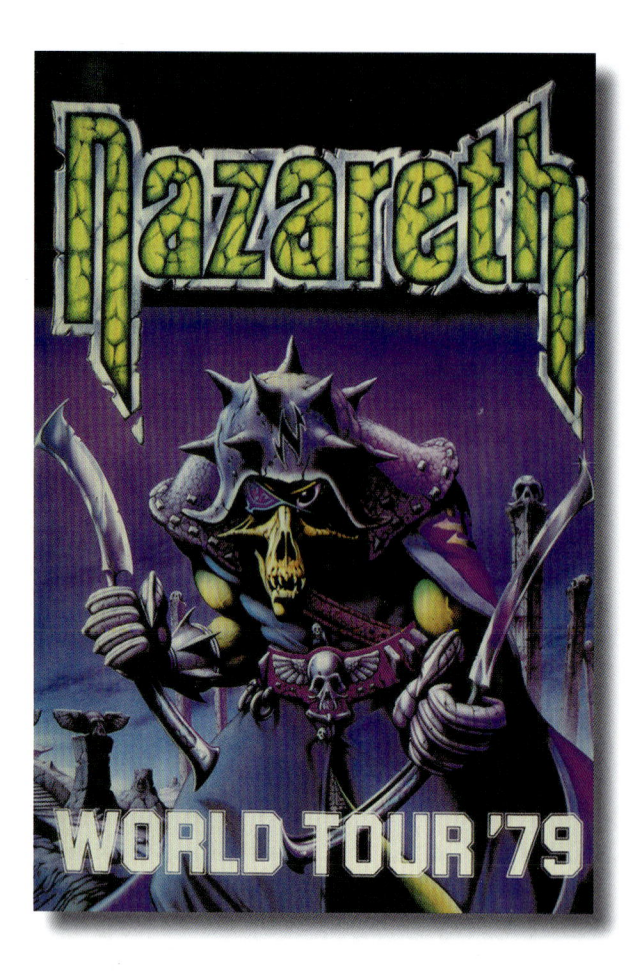

Uncredited record review:
"This could probably be the first Nazareth album that incorporates texture and subtlety into the musical proceedings. The addition of erstwhile Sensational Alex Harvey Band lead guitarist Zal Cleminson might have something to do with why the total sound and feel of *No Mean City* is less heavy-duty industrial strength rock 'n' roll and even less uni-leveled metallic drone. A natch for AOR acceptance, with at least three possible singles lurking around to boot."
(Cashbox, January 27, 1979)

April 1979. Issued in the UK is a picture sleeve single pairing "Whatever You Want Babe" with "Telegram."

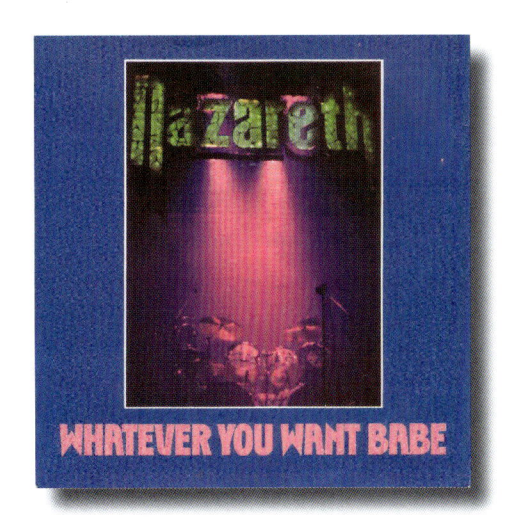

Pete Agnew on "Telegram:"

"When we did *Hair of the Dog*, we started to build a studio here in Scotland. We got a hold of this premises. This wasn't the Ganghut, that we had ourselves in the early days. We never used it as a recording studio, but we used it as a rehearsal place; it was really nice. And when we got there, we were talking about getting this new album done. We'd been touring ourselves stupid on *Hair of the Dog* because of 'Love Hurts' and never really had that much time to think about writing."

"So the first thing we did, in the preparation, was just playing a chug—we just started chugging away, like we used to do. Just chug, chug, chug. And then it developed, as things do—there's no explanation. And the lyric, it was, here we are, you've been on the road, you get your record done and get back on the road again. We were just thinking about the busyness of the whole thing. You're recording, touring, recording—it was all in our heads at that point. We were very, very busy. The whole thing became a song about touring. And once we started, it was one of these where everybody's going, 'What about this bit?, you could say this, oh, and you can say that, you can say this, and what about this line, what about that line?' It was like a complaint almost (laughs), a complaint to your manager and record company. It ended up being a story about touring. And then once we decided what it was going to be, then it became a real fun song to make. Mind you, the times I've had to play it since then… but it became a major favourite for the fans. It's one of those ones where every now and again, you think let's give this thing a rest. In fact, at the moment, it's getting a rest (laughs). But it was an opener for years on end."

May 15 – May 17, 1979. The band play Japan, with all dates in Tokyo, followed by a long North American tour leg into July, including a number of festival dates. Main support is Frank Marino & Mahogany Rush.

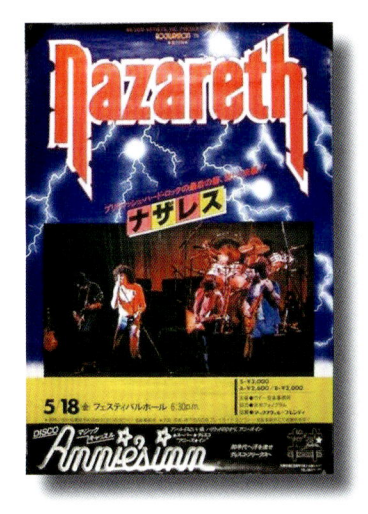

Pete Agnew on the band's new two-guitar team:
"They got on well together but they were totally different players. Manny was into the rough sound thing—he goes for the noise and likes creating noise. Zal is an amazing technician, and a good songwriter as well. The guy is mind-blowing, one of the best guitar players on the planet. It was quite an honour, actually, to play with the guy for a couple of years."

June 1, 1979. *Expect No Mercy* is certified gold in Canada.

Mid-1979: Manny Charlton produces *Under Heaven Over Hell*, the second album from Canadian band Streetheart. The record goes platinum in Canada, for sales of over 100,000 copies.

Matt Frenette:
"You know what? The coolest thing that Manny did was that he let everybody play. Because, he was a producer that came from a band where their sound was vital. With Nazareth, you had the screaming vocals but you had the really raunchy guitar and the straight-ahead drums. Darrell wasn't a flashy drummer but he was very punchy and straightforward. Everybody had their sound, right? The rhythm and bass and drums were very strong, but not complicated. I mean, we played way more chops than Nazareth. But that was their sound, right? You feature the vocal and the guitar in that band, and the catchy hook lines. And McCafferty's vocal was so distinct—it's still distinct today. And he wanted Streetheart to sound the way we sounded live, on vinyl—he wanted to catch the energy. But the cool thing he did was cut us all live on the floor, and do as few overdubs as possible, and erasing as possible, so he caught the energy of the band all playing live together."

July 1979. Issued as a picture sleeve single in the UK is "Star" backed with "Born to Love." The US version (non-picture sleeve) gets "Expect No Mercy" as its B-side.

July 4, 1979. Nazareth play one of Bill Graham's Day on the Green shows, in Oakland, California. Alternately called The 4th of July All American Rock 'n' Roll Show, that package included Journey, The J. Geils Band, UFO and Thin Lizzy.

Pete Agnew on the *No Mean City* tour campaign:
"We did a whole world tour, really, played with Thin Lizzy, Blackfoot. We had the backdrop with Fred on it and everything. It used to drive the road crew mad, putting this thing up every night. It was huge. I mean, you wouldn't do that nowadays. You would do it with a very light fabric. But at that time, the record company had this made up and it was the size of a house and it was made out of cloth and it was almost velvet and weighed a ton, maybe two tons. And we had to suspend this thing every night, off of light rigs and things that we used to bring. We made the crew work for their money."

"Nothing in the '80s was really that much of a big success. It was a pretty bad time for us. Not so bad in the early '80s, but it wasn't until *Move Me* that we even started to get the airplay again. The whole system seemed to be geared towards dance and MTV at the time, and in Europe anyway, rock 'n' roll was on a few obscure shows, late at night. In the States, everything rock was classic rock, so they were playing your old stuff but not your new stuff. Very strange time not just for us, but for a lot of rock bands."
Dan McCafferty

The 1980s

July 5th, 1986, Out in the Green, Dinkelsbuhl, Germany.

© Wolfgang Gurster

Hey, all of our favourite '70s bands, if they made records through the '80s, they were confronted with the results of what they had forged in the '70s through the phenomena of the New Wave of British Heavy Metal—its brief and regional flash—followed by a long golden period for heavy metal in general, juiced by the success of a subgenre called hair metal. Some of these bands embraced it wholeheartedly or to considerable degree, while others ran screaming, arms waving wildly, in the other direction. I'd say foremost in the latter camp would be Rush and Nazareth, both successes in Canada and tour mates, Rush supporting Nazareth in the beginning and then eventually, Nazareth supporting Rush.

I remember quite distinctly when *Malice in Wonderland* came out, and there was indeed some excitement about the new non-hard rock direction. Even myself and my usually uncompromising buddies weren't completely averse to the new sound. Why? Well, through the previous handful of albums, there wasn't much metal anyway, and the new record seemed to mark an uptick in songwriting quality, in sophistication, in all 'round smarts and maturity that even we, as boneheaded metalheads, could appreciate in our teens.

The bloom of novelty quickly wore off, along with any confidence in the band's songwriting abilities, through the following clutch of records. As it turns out, the record-buying public agreed and Nazareth fell out of the public consciousness precipitously. As it turns out, the lack of creative and commercial success would begin to cause squabbles within the band dynamic as well, with Manny Charlton flaming out after the last record of the '80s, the pretty much disastrous *Snakes 'n' Ladders*. Along the way there had been Zal Cleminson and Billy Rankin, as well as keyboard player John Locke. The youth and pop of Billy, along with the very fact that John Locke was a keyboard player, arguably served as gateway drugs toward too much '80s technology being used. Then again, a bunch of that could be blamed on Manny, who was the band's producer as well as a natural gear-head, not to mention just curious about new music.

In any event, it might've gone well, but it didn't. We might have been calling these rock-lite Nazareth records the greatest artistic documents of their career, but we aren't. I know it's 20/20 hindsight, but man, imagine if this band would have seized upon and amplified their heavy metal hobby from the '70s (I say "hobby" because it wasn't all they did, nor particularly deliberate) and hit twice as hard, inspired to riff madly by the NWOBHM. Sabbath and Priest and Scorpions stayed heavy, Kiss got heavy again, Deep Purple came back doing what they did in the '70s, Aerosmith stuck around and did essentially what they did on *Rocks* and *Draw the Line*, and even Alice Cooper came back from the crack years to become a hair metal sensation. And what of Uriah Heep? Fact is, they were closer to their heavier early '70s sound throughout the '80s than they were to their Nazareth-scattered late '70s sound.

So yes, it boggles the mind, given the records we actually got, but Nazareth is certainly a case where nothing much would have been lost had they headbanged their way through the '80s, with potentially vast payoffs to be gained.

May 1980, The Spectrum, Philadelphia, PA.

© Rudy Childs

1980

January 1980. Issued across a number of territories is "Holiday" backed with "Ship of Dreams." The single reaches #87 on the US charts.

February 8, 1980. Nazareth mark the new decade with a change in musical direction, issuing *Malice in Wonderland*, produced by Jeff "Skunk" Baxter, working with the band at Compass Point in Nassau, Bahamas. The album would reach #41 on the Billboard charts, and #43 on the German charts.

Dan McCafferty:
"Jeff was introduced to us by an executive at the record company who thought it might be interesting if we worked together. Jeff had a reputation as a very inventive musician, and even though he had never produced before, his knowledge of the recording studio and his musical background just made him perfect for us. We had always relied on our own ability to produce records before, with Manny handling the controls and the rest of us just playing as hard and as loud as we could, but that just naturally tends to restrict your thinking a little. When Jeff started to work with us, it was like a whole new musical area opened up. We gave him a lot of freedom to work with, and he really helped us. I think it's safe to say that the partnership between Mr. Baxter and these 'nice' Scottish boys has not yet come to an end."

"The songs on the new album show a lot more taste and style than any of our earlier things. We're not scared to try and express a little feeling and emotion in our music anymore. Before, we tried to either just blow everyone away with our energy or slow down completely for a ballad like 'Love Hurts.' Now, we found that we can also have a middle ground where we can still rock, but with a little more subtlety. And honestly, it's nice to really sing for a change instead of just yell as loud as I can. Also, I think that we've become more cohesive as a band on this album and the reason is that we're back to really playing music again."

"I guess we changed as a matter of necessity. We knew we couldn't change so much that we'd lose the long-time fans, yet we knew we had to change enough to make the music exciting again. It wasn't easy, but I think the results speak for themselves." *(w/ Andy Secher, Sacramento Bee, November 22, 1980)*

Zal Cleminson:

"The production wasn't really my cup of tea, the second album particularly. *Malice in Wonderland* I thought was very peculiar from Nazareth as a band. It was like a complete departure in some way. I don't know what happened there. Manny got his head around this idea that his favourite band at the time was Fleetwood Mac, with the *Rumours* album. And Fleetwood Mac, you know what that's like; it's very melodic, a nice rhythmic album, beautiful, lovely musicians, etc. It's full of amazing, classic songs, of course, but it's much more in that vein than Nazareth wanted to be—or that's what I thought. I think he got carried away with the idea of those types of songs and that kind of production that he wanted to try maybe create an album that was a bit more mainstream, let's call it, mainstream commercial." *(w/ Marko Syrjala, MetalRules)*

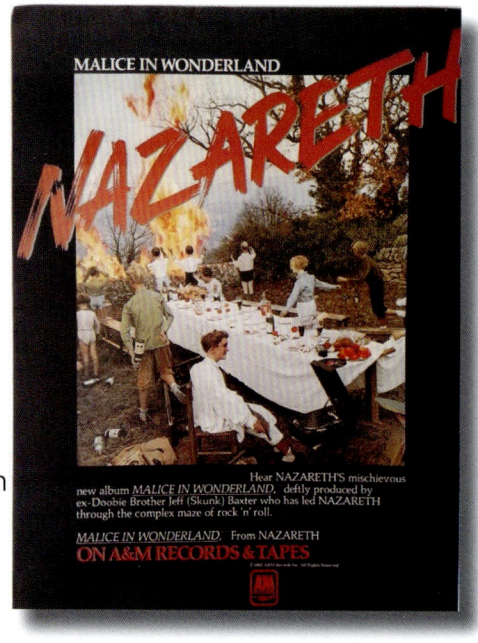

Pete Agnew:

"Our record company suggested we get Jeff 'Skunk' Baxter. You can imagine, we were a bit sceptical but at the time we met him, Jeff was also playing session guitar on 18 hits that were in the Billboard Top 40 that month so we figured he must know a thing or two about making records. We decided to record in the Bahamas at Compass Point studio which turned out to be a bad choice. Although the country is a lovely place with lovely weather, that was not the reason for us being there. We were trying to make a record, and almost every day something or other broke down in the studio and all we did was play pool on the two big tables they had, passing the time while they flew in engineers from Miami to repair the recording machines."

"After a month of this going on, we became almost competition-standard pool players but the record was going nowhere fast. At this point Jeff phoned his friends who owned Cherokee Studios in Hollywood and they fitted us in there to finish the rest of the album. This place had four separate first-class studios and while we were in one of them, they had Neil Sedaka, Harry Nilsson and—Lord save us—the Blues Brothers in the other three studios. As you can imagine, things got pretty mental at times but we ended up with a classic album that sounded nothing like anything we had done before but still appealed to fans who had always favoured the heavier side of the band. It's still one of my favourite Naz records of all time."

Darrell Sweet, on working with Skunk Baxter:

"On paper it was probably the biggest mismatch of all time, but it worked out really well. We'll always be that adventurous, and try to be that melodic, but I think a few of the rough edges were smoothed off just maybe too much on *Malice*." *(w/ Cameron Cohick, Fort Lauderdale News, June 15, 1980)*

Jeff Baxter:

"I was really impressed with the band after I heard the songs they had ready and their live playing. My job was just to give them an album that was technically state-of-the-art. We set out to make the first '80s album, and I think we came as close as anybody could." *(Cashbox, January 19, 1980)*

Uncredited Record Review:
"*Malice in Wonderland* is such a radical departure from this band's musical norm that not until Dan McCafferty's distinctive lead vocals click in do you realise that this is indeed the group Nazareth. It's all very deceptive though, because Nazareth has never sounded better. Their bicep-bursting energy has a crystal-clear focus now that totally excludes the word boredom. The chances taken are nearly shocking in their brilliance. An AOR must." *(Cashbox, February 2, 1980)*

March 16, 1980. The BBC record a Nazareth set at the Hammersmith Odeon in London; these performances would be included on the 2010 reissue of *Malice in Wonderland*.

Pete Agnew on the Malice in Wonderland album cover:
"Kind of a freaky cover, isn't it? It gives me goose bumps, having all these mannequins, and it's mainly really, really young people. Creepy, that one. I was never very relaxed with it."

April 1980. A&M in the US and Canada issue "Heart's Grown Cold" as a single, backed with "Ship of Dreams."

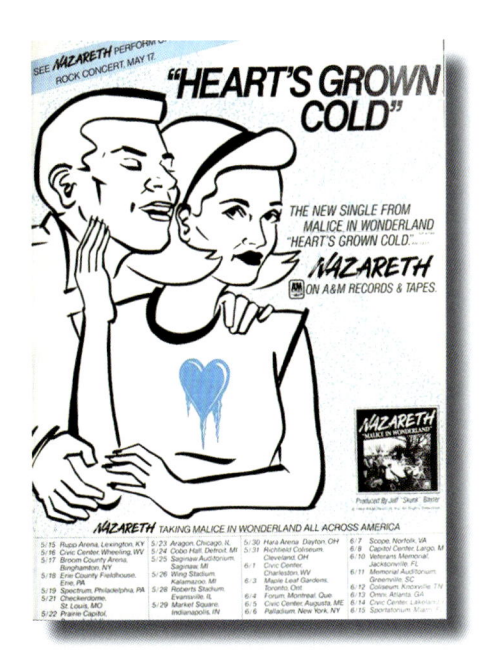

Zal Cleminson:
"We're just trying to take the band in another direction. We must progress. You've got to develop. You listen to what's getting written nowadays, and what is being played by the young groups and you'll see what I mean. You've got to know what you're doing. Jeff is an excellent technician and a very good musician. He was a great help with the arrangements. Obviously he preferred some things and other people preferred other things, so it was always a compromise. The two of us really got off on each other from a musical point of view." *(w/ Zach Dunkin, Indianapolis News, June 6, 1980)*

Dan McCafferty:
"Jeff's smoothed things over a little, but there's still our basic aggression. You should've seen some of the things that went on. Like one day when we were recording, Neil Diamond put his head 'round the door and said, 'I need a guitar solo.' So off popped Jeff. Then the next day, Harry Nilsson suddenly arrived: 'Got a moment, Jeff?' And off he disappears for another five minutes. I'm telling

you, I came running home screaming after three weeks there (in LA, mixing the album). It's just that he demands high standards. 'Feel is real but time is right' is his motto. But at least we know why all those albums by LA acts sound the same. They all use the same musicians, whether it's the Doobie Brothers, Donna Summer or Linda Ronstadt. Jeff's worked with 'em all!" *(w/ Mike Nicholls, Record Mirror, March 22, 1980)*

May – June 1980. Following a UK tour and a mainland European campaign, the band transitions to the States, for a series of shows supported by Blackfoot.

May 25, 1980. The band play Saginaw, Michigan, as one of the stops on the *Malice in Wonderland* campaign. A performance of J.J. Cale song "Cocaine" would be recorded and added to the band's next studio album, *The Fool Circle*.

Darrell Sweet:
"It was a unanimous decision to become more melodic. We had been going the same way for more than a decade, and it was time for us to move on. Hopefully it still has the rock feel, and the melodies add more to the songs. We're too old to be punks" *(w/ Kim McAuliffe, Detroit Free Press, May 23, 1980)*

June 1, 1980. *Malice in Wonderland* is certified gold in Canada.

Dan McCafferty:
I like *Malice in Wonderland*, because it was different, you know? It showed a more melodic side of the band. That cover was by a French artist. At the time we had done quite a bit of the monster-y ones. It was just a photographer really, who wanted to do these art photographs. But we really liked his stuff and I think that worked really well."

Mid-1980. Canadian hard rockers Streetheart issue their Manny Charlton-produced third album, *Quicksand Shoes*.

Daryl Gutheil:
"Manny produced our second album too, and this one. He came in immediately and suggested that we record 'Here Comes the Night,' and we worked on an arrangement for it, and we recorded probably in an evening or something, and we still do that song. So I've always liked that. I think there's a bit more sophistication and style on that second album than there is on the first one. Manny also produced 'Under My Thumb,' later in the year, when we went back for a couple days and recorded that."

"There was a bit of a thing going on with Nazareth at that time. I mean, they were traditionally a hard rock band, and they had a couple of personnel changes, added another guitarist, and they just came off recording an album and it was kind of light rock for them, and it seemed to be getting a lot of attention. I remember they were on the cover of Cashbox magazine, and I think in his mind Manny was thinking, for some of the bands that were playing hard rock, lightening up was the way to go. That was the way he was directing us on that third album, *Quicksand Shoes*, which, you know, in hindsight, I think it was a mistake for him and for us."

December 1980. NEMS issue a double-seven-inch EP called *Live*, featuring "Heart's Grown Cold," "Razamanaz," "Hair of the Dog" and "Talkin' to One of the Boys" recorded at the Hammersmith.

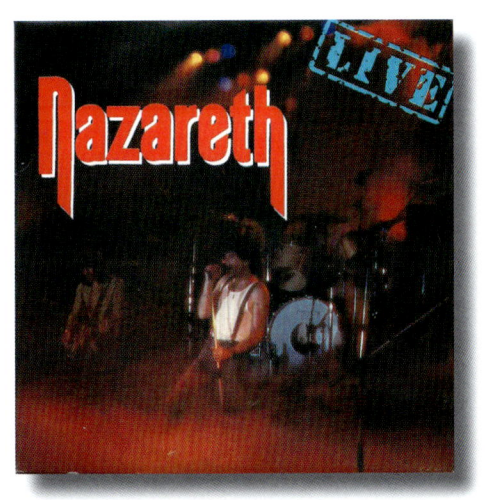

December 17, 1980. The band, introducing new members Billy Rankin (new after the recording of *The Fool Circle*) and John Locke (on the forthcoming album but not as an official member), perform a five-song set for Scottish TV's In Concert. The performance airs the following month.

Dan McCafferty:
"A few years ago, we just felt the need for a change. The rock style was still selling records fairly well, but we felt that we were getting a little stale with it. When the music starts to bore the people who are playing it, well, then it's time for a change. We had no desire to become another Fleetwood Mac, but we had always been viewed as a band that only knew three chords and we just wanted to show off a few of the skills that we had kept hidden over the years."
(w/ Andy Secher, Asbury Park Press, October 11, 1981)

May 1980, The Spectrum, Philadelphia, PA.
© Rudy Childs

May 1980, The Spectrum, Philadelphia, PA.

1981

February 14, 1981. Nazareth issue *The Fool Circle*, their 12th album. It is the first for ex-Spirit keyboard player John Locke, although he is listed as an "additional musician." The album was recorded in Montserrat, with Jeff Baxter producing the band for a second time. Engineering is Beatles associate Geoff Emerick. The album peaks at #70 on the Billboard charts and achieves a #60 placement in the UK. It is the band's first album since *Close Enough for Rock 'n' Roll* not to go gold in Canada.

Dan McCafferty, at the time, on the band's new political stance:

"We are not into flower power or anything like that. But the whole thing is scary. We talk to people. It's not just our opinion. It's what people on the street are talking about. They're scared. And I don't feel too secure about it myself. I live in the country, 40 miles from Glasgow, which is very close to where the US has the largest Polaris missile base in the world. So there we are in Scotland, watching what's going on in the world. All we can do is say, 'Excuse me, why don't you talk all this over and work something out?' It's scary."
(w/ Jack Lloyd, The Dispatch, April 6, 1981)

Pete Agnew:

"By the time we got 'round to writing the songs for this one, our management company had gone bankrupt leaving us in a real mess, having to pick up the pieces and put everything back together again. Zal had left because he had had enough of all this crap and I can't say that I blamed him. Hostages in the American Embassy in Iran had been held for more than a year. Russia had invaded Afghanistan and the Cold War was getting hot. The world in general was going to hell and I can say, it *did* have an effect on the way we were writing. Because of this, *The Fool Circle* became a kind of social commentary but we tried to do it with tongue-in-cheek humour so as to not come across as pain-in-the-ass preachers. I think we were successful in that."

"Anyway, just to cheer ourselves up we picked Air Studios on Montserrat to record. What a place that was and what a studio! Jeff was producing again but this time we had Geoff Emerick as our engineer. Geoff is one of the world's most famous studio engineers. He recorded *Sgt. Pepper* and all the Beatles albums, so say no more. He actually designed the studio in Montserrat with George Martin, the studio owner and Beatles producer. We had worked with Geoff many times in the past at AIR London and knew we were in good hands."

"While recording, we mentioned at one point that it would be good to have piano on a couple of tracks and wondered who we should fly in to play it. The studio manager then told us that a guy named John Locke was living on the island and would probably love to play piano for us. We couldn't believe it: John Locke from Spirit, one of our favourite groups, who made *Dr. Sardonicus*, one of the best albums of all time, and here he was on this tiny island. 'Bring him in immediately' we cried, and in he came and proceeded to blow our minds with some of the best piano playing we had ever heard. John ended up playing on five tracks and before we left to go home, we asked him to join the band. That album had many happy moments but finding John was the happiest. Reagan was elected President of the United States during the recording of the album, so obviously the world was still fucked up when we left Montserrat."

Uncredited record review:
"This is the second time in a row that Nazareth has enlisted the help of Jeffrey (nee "Jeff 'Skunk'") Baxter as their producer. Consequently this album continues a musical trend that finds the band diving even deeper in Doobie Bros. waters. A denuded Nazareth still sounds okay enough for AOR, but several mid-tempo ballads liberally sprinkled throughout the album (plus a token reggae cut) could conceivably find them on A/C playlists." *(Cashbox, February 7, 1981)*

February 16 – May 26, 1981. The band conduct a major North American campaign, supported at first, mostly by Donnie Iris, followed by April Wine and then finally Krokus in May.

Mark Faris, in 1981, in a live review:
"Dan McCafferty's singing is hard to describe. Sometimes it resembles the howling squeal of new tires on hot asphalt. Other times it sounds like a tomcat being garrotted over an inexpensive public address system or a large chimpanzee undergoing a heavy session on the thumb screws. Basically it is a series of guttural, ear-shattering, agonizing shrieks that, more than anything else, evoke utter amazement in listeners."
(Akron Beacon Journal, March 13, 1981)

March 1981. Issued as a single is "Dressed to Kill"/"Pop the Silo," picture sleeve in the UK, non-picture sleeve in the US and Canada.

Dan McCafferty:
"The social commentary and the timing of the Reagan election were coincidental. We wrote the album before Reagan got elected. Iran was holding the hostages and the Russians were in Afghanistan. All Carter said was, 'Boo, hiss, you guys can't do that.' So we wrote that album to say that soon people are going to get fed up and could everybody please try and communicate?"
(w/ Bruce Britt, Detroit Free Press, October 30, 1981)

Pete Agnew:
"*The Fool Circle* was the nearest we came to making a concept album, trying to inject a bit of humour into a pretty heavy subject. I think the fact that we recorded it on the island of Montserrat might account for a teeny bit of reggae poking its way through." (w/ Dmitry Epstein, dmme.net)

May 23, 1981. Nazareth play the Pacific Coliseum in Vancouver, BC. The show is recorded and issued as the '*Snaz* live album later in the year. Or at least that's what the liner notes say (see September 17, 1981 entry).

August 1, 1981. MTV launches. ZZ Top is on board. Nazareth isn't.

Dan McCafferty:
"I hate doing videos. I like doing live concert-type videos, but I've hated the ones where I'm trying to be an actor. I'm not an actor, you know; I'm a rock 'n' roll singer. I suppose we'll eventually have to do another one, but I'm trying to avoid it. I'm hoping that I can make it on the music alone. Remember when music used to sell records?" *(w/ Steve Newton, Ear of Newt, 1984)*

August 7, 1981. The two-LP soundtrack album to the movie *Heavy Metal* is issued. Among a number of non-LP tracks from big bands is Nazareth's "Crazy (A Suitable Case for Treatment)." As well, at his juncture, the UK is in the throes of the New Wave of British Heavy Metal.

Dan McCafferty on the heavy metal genre:
"I liked it when we first started getting into it. But back then it was just rock 'n' roll. Then they changed it to heavy rock, and then they changed it to heavy metal. And it had this image. You had to have long hair and wear spiky metal things and play thrash and make funny faces and stuff, and we didn't fancy any of that. I mean, there was a lot of good, but there was also a lot of poor stuff that came out, just because it had that image, and that got you signed. A lot of it was great, bands like Metallica and stuff; they're the gods of heavy metal sort of thing. But they always had good tunes and they could play."

"But eventually we thought, well this is going a bit farther than we would like to take it. Because we had tried to avoid having anything other than a basic rock image. We've never gone in for a big flash image or anything like that. And heavy metal was definitely going for that, and we decided, no I don't think so. We played a few festivals, and the bands were good and stuff, but unfortunately they all looked the same to me (laughs). I don't know, like with other forms of music, there's good stuff and then there is some absolute crap."

"You see, I'll explain it this way. When we started, we were a band. And then we were a rock band, and then we were a hard rock band, and then we were a heavy metal band. So this wasn't us that was making up these titles. This was journalists that were making up these titles (laughs). Because in the '70s, when I first started, we were signed to the same label as Genesis. You could like Genesis, Jethro Tull, Nazareth, Led Zeppelin, Deep Purple, Uriah Heep—you could like all of them and nobody cared. But then they had to put you into a box. All of a sudden the press became quite large, in a way. And they had to put you into pigeonholes. So I always just thought of us as a rock band, to be quite honest. But then the other thing in my life that I've been is the new guys in the club, the most promising newcomers, and then I was a dinosaur for a while. And then I was a legend. A legend was a lot easier than being a dinosaur."

September 17, 1981. Nazareth issue a double live album called 'Snaz (or It'Snaz if the carry-over text from the back cover is included). It is Scottish "boy wonder" guitarist Billy Rankin's first record with the band. The album reaches No.83 on the Billboard charts and #78 back home in the UK. Issued as a single from the live album is the band's cover of "Morning Dew" backed with a studio track (which was also included on 'Snaz) called "Juicy Lucy."

Zal Cleminson:
"Billy. Baby Billy Rankin. Yeah, he was a lovely musician and a good writer. I don't recall recommending him, but I might have. Somebody probably did. He seemed to be like the next in line (laughs). He was a substitute sitting on the bench, waiting to get called on. 'Get your tracksuit off, Billy. You're on next.' He was completely shell-shocked to be involved in the Nazareth thing. He was just like, 'What the fuck's happened to me?' and he had to go on and play. But he was talented. He's a talented musician." (w/ Marko Syrjala, MetalRules)

Dan McCafferty:
"The time's right for us to finally release a live album. People have been asking us for years, 'When are you guys gonna finally release a live album?' And quite honestly, I was getting pretty sick of it. The band just really seemed to be happening during our 1981 Spring tour, so we recorded a number of shows and said to ourselves that if everything sounds as good on tape as it does on stage, then this would be the time we finally do that live album. Needless to say, those tapes sounded mighty good."

"We wanted to spread our sound out a bit. We saw the opportunity to do something a little different on our tour, so we added keyboards and an extra guitar. Both Billy and John have added a new dimension to our sound. They've revitalized some of the older songs and given a more expansive feel to some of the more recent stuff. I guess we're always looking for some way to be a little different, and a little unusual. That's what's kept Nazareth healthy for so long, and I sure don't see any reason to change now."

"Getting on stage is still the greatest feeling in the world. Those two hours in concert make up for all the time you have to spend sitting around your hotel room or in airport lobbies. Every time we play, we feel we have to reward our fans, because they're the greatest in the world. They stuck with us over the years, and most of them have accepted all the changes we've gone through.

This album is for them. It's a way of saying thanks and that we love them. The two studio cuts are included as a bonus for those people, 'cause they're the ones who really kept us going over the years, and this is our opportunity to show our appreciation."
(w/ Andy Secher, Asbury Park Press, October 11, 1981)

Pete Agnew:
"After we returned from Montserrat we decided to go all the way and add another guitarist to the band. After having Zal, we had kind of got used to hearing two guitars so a pal of ours who had worked with our management at one time suggested a young man named Billy Rankin. Billy was not only an extremely accomplished guitarist and excellent singer, he was a cracking songwriter who could knock out a new tune in the time it took to boil a kettle. At 21, he was the baby of the group, but only in age. In all other aspects he was a seasoned rocker who had been performing live since he could tie his own shoe laces."

"Now having a six-piece band (including John on piano) this lineup became affectionately referred to by our road crew as the Nazareth Orchestra. Our record company and the people around us had been bitching at us for a while to make a live album and now seemed like the perfect time to do that. With this lineup and instrumentation there wasn't a song we couldn't do live. The band had toured a lot that year and we were playing tighter than a gnat's ass so we lined up the recording to take place on a US/Canadian tour in the cities of Houston and Vancouver. The Orchestra hit it on the button both nights and we have an album that every member of the band is proud of. Our good friend John Punter (another AIR Studios man who we worked with many times, even on our first album) was the sound engineer and ultimately the producer of 'Snaz."

September 17 – October 2, 1981. The band conduct a short UK campaign.

October 15 – November 29, 1981. The guys tour North America, supported at first mostly by The Joe Perry Project and later by Billy Thorpe.

November 28, 1981. The band play Houston, Texas, supported by Trapeze and Krokus. The show is filmed and would be released on DVD in 2005 and again in 2007.

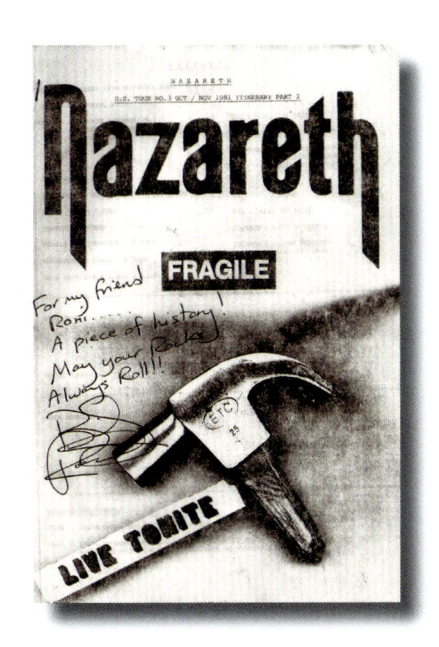

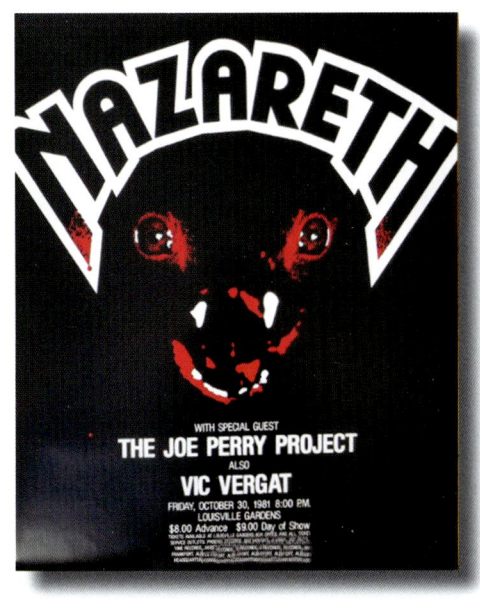

116

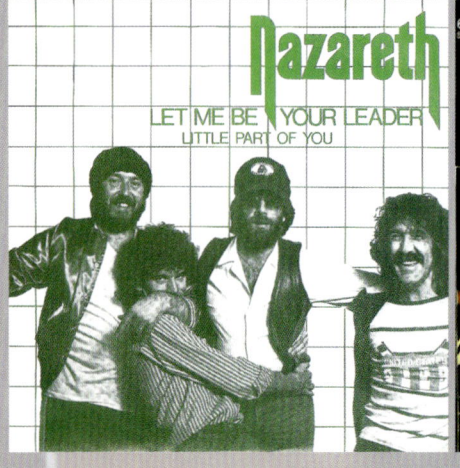

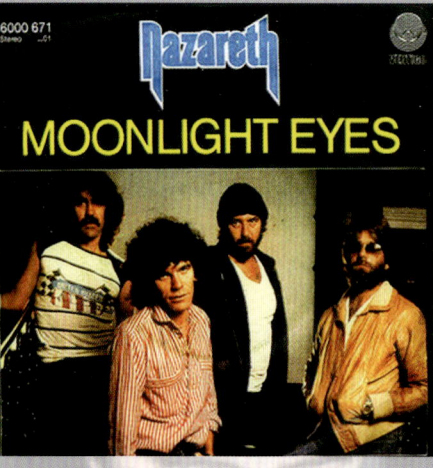

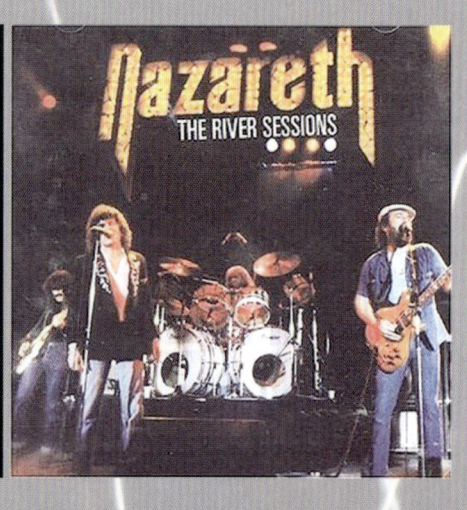

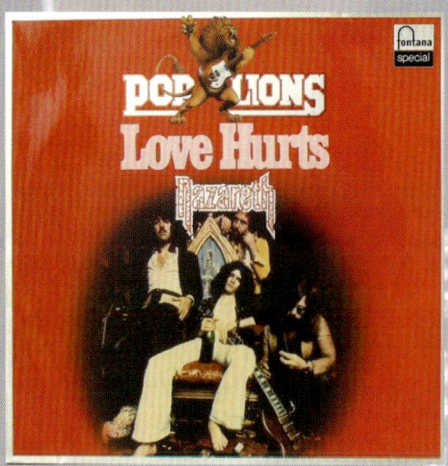

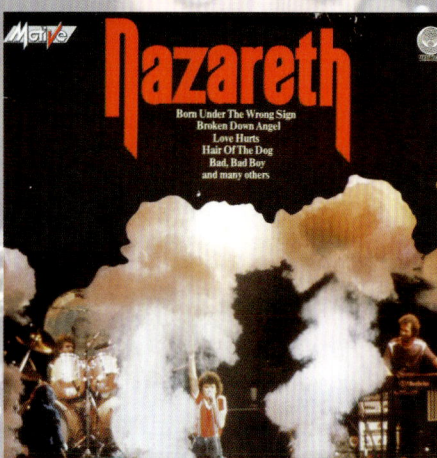

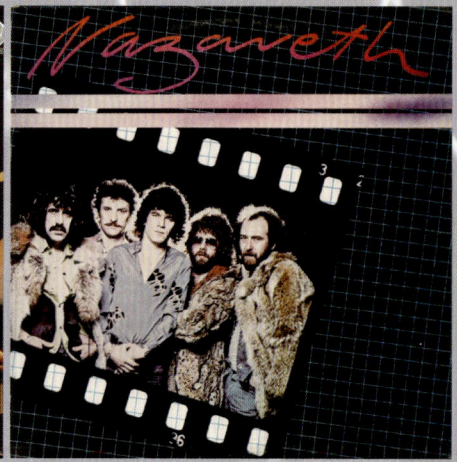

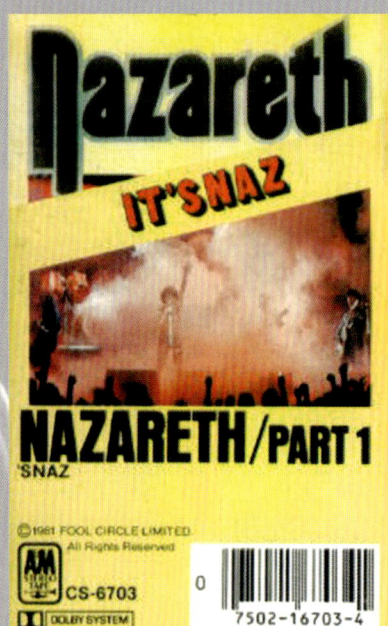

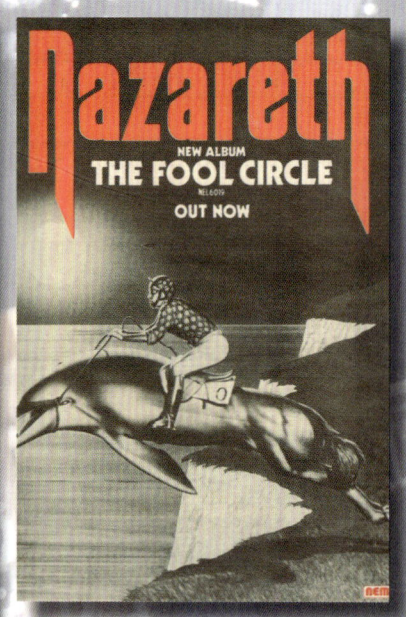

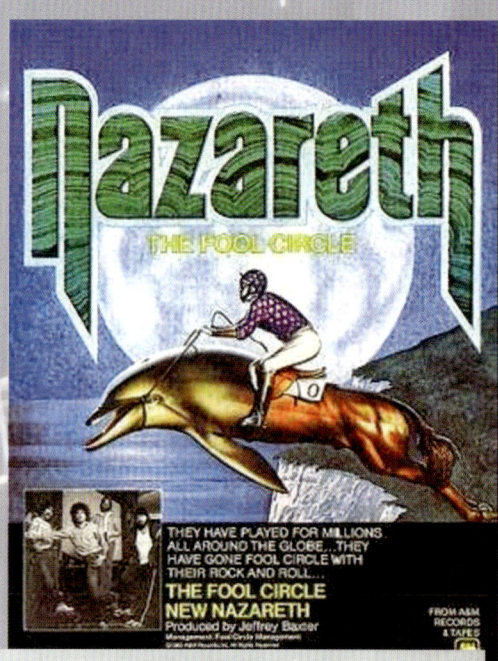

1982

May 1982. Nazareth work at AIR Studios in Montserrat on material slated for the follow-up to *The Fool Circle*. Producing is John Punter, who comes to the band from sessions with Roxy Music, Sad Café and Japan.

May 1, 1982. *No Mean City* is certified gold in Canada.

July 1982. Nazareth issue, on Vertigo, their 13th album, *2XS*, which stalls at #122 on the Billboard charts and #74 on Canada's RPM chart. The band is presented as a six-piece, the original four plus Billy Rankin and John Locke.

Dan McCafferty:
"I think what's going on is that we've already done 15 albums now, we've survived, and rather than get respect for that kind of longevity from radio programmers, we're simply being ignored by them. They go, 'Oh, it's just another Nazareth album. Who cares? Give us something fresh and new and young.' The programmers probably don't even listen to our albums anymore. They probably don't even know there are six of us in the band now, instead of just the original four. What I think it comes down to for Nazareth today is that radio's never really been on our side, except for 'Love Hurts.' But then again, it didn't exactly take a genius to figure out that one was a great car radio song."

"We've always just played the music we wanted to play, and carried on with it. Who knows? Maybe we have too much melody for heavy metal and too much heavy metal for people into melody. But it's simply the kind of rock music we like to play, and we're not about to change and become dedicated followers of fashion or jump on the latest synthesizer bandwagon to make it. That would really be the death knell of this band."
(w/ Jon Marlowe, Miami News, September 10, 1982) for us." *(billyrankin.com)*

Pete Agnew:
"And were we ever sorry for naming this album! We thought it was pretty obvious that it meant 'to excess' but we couldn't believe some of the

pronunciations we heard, 'two times five' being the favourite. Nowadays there would be no problem with everyone doing SMS/text speak but back in 1982 the drugs must have been stronger."

"We went back to Montserrat with the Orchestra and this time we had so many songs written we didn't know where to start. The album was so much fun to make and it's personally one of the highlights of my career. I remember the first time we went to Montserrat in 1980; we walked down inside the volcano which was close to the studio. The smell of burning sulphur made our eyes sting and heated water popped out in little streams all around the walls of the cone. It's hard to believe now that the studio no longer exists since it was completely destroyed in a hurricane not long after we were there, and the main town of Plymouth where we spent many a happy evening, was totally buried in ash when the volcano erupted. I don't think pronouncing our album title wrongly is such a big deal after all."

Reviewer Steve Futterman:
"The spectre of REO Speedwagon's belated superstardom must hang heavy over a band like Nazareth. After flirting with hard rock success during a 12-year, 14-album career, the Scottish sextet can almost taste that long-awaited breakthrough. Unfortunately, 2XS will not be Nazareth's *Hi Infidelity*. Identity rather than inspiration seems to be the problem here. Though it unwisely relies on decibel roar, the group actually sounds more soulful and relaxed on the ballad 'Dream On' and the reggae-tinged 'You Love Another.' When acoustic guitars and keyboards dominate producer and engineer John Punter's precise mix on 'Love Leads to Madness' and 'Games,' Nazareth sound almost inspired. These cuts prove that restraint rather than excess is where Nazareth's talent lies."
(*Rolling Stone*, September 2, 1982)

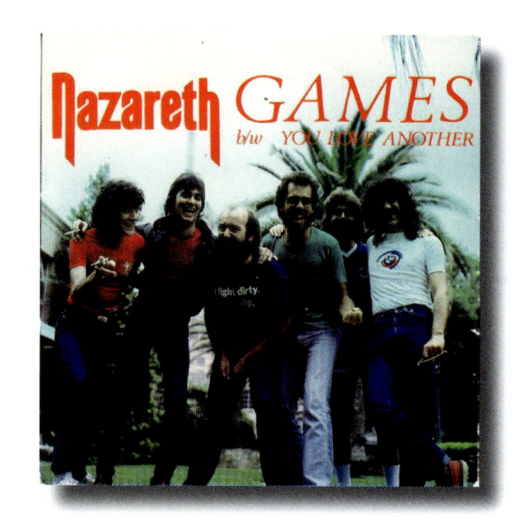

Uncredited record review:
"On their 15th album, veteran Scottish rockers Nazareth have come up with a surprise. The album begins with an obligatory AOR tune, and then goes into a hard rocker, but the next song, 'You Love Another' contains a slinky bass line that sounds like it came over from a Police album. This is followed by a Dave Edmunds-type of rockabilly song and then a big ballad. That is only side one. It is good that Nazareth is willing to take chances and even more heartening that they get away with it so well. This LP is one to cheer for." (*Billboard*, July 3, 1982)

July 1982. "Love Leads to Madness" is issued as a single across a variety of territories, backed with "Take the Rap," followed the next month by "Dream On" with varying B-sides. "Dream On" hits No.1 in Germany.

Pete Agnew, on the hiring of Billy Rankin, composer of "Dream On:"
"Years later, we were actually doing a live album, a DVD thing, in Brazil. One of our biggest songs there is 'Love Leads to Madness,' and it's one of the songs that is so, so big in Brazil, it's almost like an anthem. And of course we forget. We were starting to play this thing, and were recording it for a live album, and then the crowd started singing and it was, 'Scrub it; you can't use this track' (laughs). Because you can't hear the band. So sometimes songs are just that popular, where we were doing it and you just couldn't hear the band."

Mid-September to early December 1982. Nazareth play North America, most dates supporting Billy Squier. As the tour is ending, the band split with A&M, possibly due to the demands manager Jim White had been putting on the label as they negotiated a new contract.

November 1982, Brooklyn Zoo, Brooklyn, NY.

November 1982, Brooklyn Zoo, Brooklyn, NY.

© Kevin Hodapp / Frank White Photo Agency

1983

1983. Keyboard player John Locke leaves Nazareth to reform Spirit.

January 17, 1983. "Games" is issued as a single in the UK, backed with "You Love Another."

February 14, 1983. Nazareth play a charity gig at Coasters in Edinburgh, marking the first time back for a show on home turf in a year-and-a-half. The band was now a five-piece, after the departure of John Locke back to his old band, Spirit.

February 22 – April 6, 1983. The band work at Little Mountain in Vancouver, on tracks to comprise their forthcoming album. While in Vancouver, Billy Rankin befriends Bryan Adams who signed to A&M just as Nazareth were leaving.

May 1983. Blackfoot issue their sixth album, *Siogo*, which includes a cover of Nazareth's "Heart's Grown Cold."

May 1983. Nazareth log a few German dates supporting Rush.

June 1983. "Dream On" is issued in the UK as the third and final single from the *2XS* album. The Billy Rankin song goes to No.1 in Poland and charts well in other European countries as well.

Pete Agnew, on Billy:

"There were umpteen suggestions. You know, 'Get this guy, get that guy.' But we wanted someone that would fit into the band. Billy was perfect because he's still impressionable. Yes, we've fixed him there. He was 21 when he joined the band; he's 45 now (laughs). He just gets battered if he doesn't agree with us. Seriously, we didn't want to have an ever-changing band. Generally, you find that guys that go from band to band are going to do that to you as well. You just get the thing to how you like it, and they're leaving."

"Even though Billy and John have been with us one-and-a-half years, there's no way they're going to know us like the four of us know one another. They see us fighting and they think it's the end of the group. But the next morning it's all blown over. For a few days after the fight, they keep asking if everything is alright. They've now developed the good sense so that when a fight starts, they just leave."
(w/ Barbara Jaeger, The Record, August 22, 1982)

June 30, 1983. Vertigo issues a second Nazareth album for the label—and the 14th for the band—called *Sound Elixir*. Producing is Manny Charlton, who shares guitar duties with Billy Rankin—this is Billy's second and last studio album with the band before returning in 1990. "Where Are You Now" is issued as a single but it fails to improve the poor sales of the record.

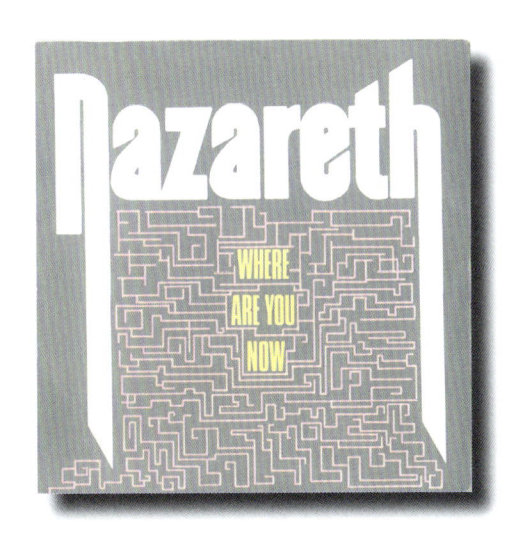

Pete Agnew:

"John left after having had enough of the manager we had at the time—we fired him soon afterward—and he met up again with his old mates in Spirit when they put the band back together after all those years. We wished him well. So now we were a five-piece again and it was time to do another album. Again, as in Montserrat, we had so many songs that it was hard choosing what

May 17th, 1983, Eishalle Liebenau, Graz, Austria.

© Isabella Seefriedt

should be recorded and what should be left out. The problem here is this that when a song is passed over (and I only speak for Nazareth) it is unlikely to pop up at a later date because the writer will probably be tired of it by then and have written other songs to be considered. Okay, enough of that."

"This time we went to another mountain studio but this one was in Vancouver. It was a very nice studio and right in the middle of the city. We did some crazy stuff there experimenting with different noises that weren't created on musical instruments. My personal favourite is when we recorded the studio pinball machine and built the whole track around the pulse that it made."

"Being in the middle of the city, and since we knew a lot of people in Vancouver, we tended to get more visitors than normal at our sessions. I especially remember one young guy who our record company sent along to meet us. They said he was a good songwriter and they wanted to put him and Billy together to write as they thought the two of them would make a good team. Billy and him met at the studio a few times, had a few drinks and promises were made to get in touch. But like most of these things, nothing ever came of it and we never heard from him again. We did, however hear of him quite a lot in the years to come and it seems Bryan Adams managed to write one or two hits without Billy's help. Shortly after the album's release, young Billy left to have a stab at a solo career. As with John, we wished him well."

Dan McCafferty:
"*Sound Elixir*, that's the one from the '80s I'm not really sure about. At that time we were going through yet another record company and yet another management and we were in court at the time trying to get an album done. And again, that was a bad time for us, because we trusted our manager and he screwed us, or tried to anyway. A lot of the material on that album deserves better than it got, to be honest, really."

Uncredited record review:
"Big Country may be Scotland's entry into this year's charts but the band owes a great deal to such relentless and enduring pub rockers as Nazareth, who have kept the fire burning in the land where the guitar plays second fiddle to the bagpipe. Nazareth's latest release is yet another blues scorcher which pays considerable attention to melody as well as energy. One of the band's many noteworthy attributes is its ability to compose inspiring ballads and this record is no exception. 'Where Are You Now' and 'Rain in the Window' highlight Dan McCafferty's ragged yet warm and soulful voice as well as the band's folk influences often not heard on the band's boogie rockers like 'Why Don't You Read the Book' and 'Rags to Riches.'" *(Cashbox December 3, 1983)*

October – December 1983. The band tour Canada in October, followed by American shows to close out the year. Some of the Canadian dates are in support of an Ian Gillan-fronted Black Sabbath.

May 6th, 1983, Sporthalle, Böblingen, Germany.

© Wolfgang Gurster

© Wolfgang Gurster

1984

1984. A&M in Canada issue the two-LP *The Very Very Best of Nazareth*.

Early 1984. Billy Rankin issues a solo album called *Growin' Up Too Fast*, which generates a minor US hit called "Baby Come Back." Also included is a version of "Where Are You Now" last heard on *Sound Elixir*. He's quickly back into the studio to record a second album, *Crankin'*, which is issued the following year, but only in Japan.

Mid-1984. Nazareth work at home in Scotland on tracks to comprise their forthcoming album. It's the first time they've recorded an album in Scotland in eight years. Producing is John Eden. Billy Rankin is now out of the band, due to a maelstrom of legal issues pertaining to publishing, management and his solo career.

Dan McCafferty:
"When you record in, say, Montserrat or Vancouver or France or somewhere, you tend to pick up the vibes that are happening in the street of that particular country. Basically, what we wanted to do was see what was happening at home. Because things are pretty tough at home at the moment. There are millions unemployed, lots of kids just hanging around with nothing to do. Musically, because of that, there's a bunch of things happening. Years ago, these kids could've come to Canada, but no more."
(w/ Ted Shaw, Windsor Star, January 19, 1985)

July 4 – July 14, 1984. The band conduct an extensive tour of Sweden, playing Finland as well.

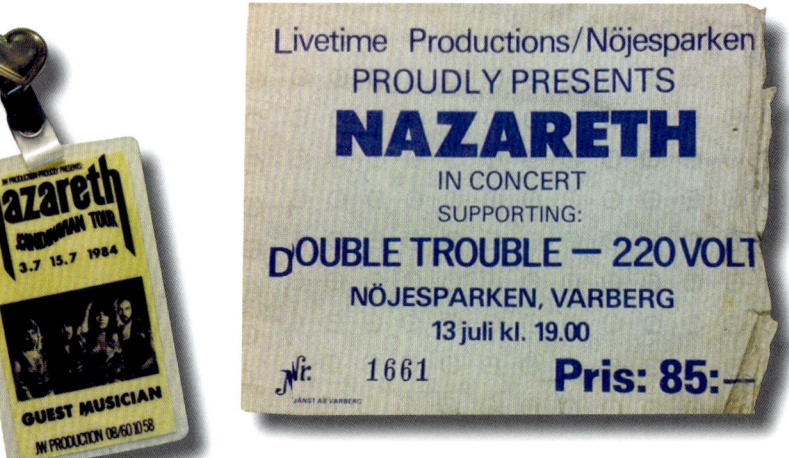

September 1984. "Ruby Tuesday" (banjo part included!) is issued as a single in the UK and Germany backed with "Sweetheart Tree." In Canada the B-side is "This Flight Tonight." For the home territory, Vertigo offers an expanded four-track version.

September 22, 1984. Nazareth sees the release of their 15th album, *The Catch*. The record consists of seven originals assigned a simple full band credit, plus a cover of the Rolling Stones' "Ruby Tuesday" and a version of 1966 Carole King/ Gerry Goffin number "Road to Nowhere."

Dan McCafferty:
"A lot of our earlier albums were made in studios that had an on/off switch, and we didn't know any better either. Plus we were younger and we only knew four-and-a-half chords. I don't think we've ever consciously thought, 'Right, let's change, let's do this.' The reason we've been together so long is because we've always done what we like to do at the time. We just went along with how we felt. It was the only way to go. We like to try other things and we have tried other things. But we like the original four-piece. I think the energy level of the band comes up when it's just the four of us, because everybody's busy, you know. We're back to the real deal." *(w/ Steve Newton, Ear of Newt, 1984)*

Manny Charlton:
"We were now back to the original lineup, and this time, unlike the last four or five albums, we didn't have a surplus of songs to choose from. Except for one song in particular (two at the most) we struggled with the material for this album and I'm sorry to say that it's not an album I would hold up to represent Nazareth at its best. We recorded it back in Scotland in a wee place called Pencaitland whose old schoolhouse had been converted into a studio. It's a great studio and is still in operation, but now with different owners. We recorded several things there other than *The Catch*. For instance, we recorded 'Crazy (A Suitable Case for Treatment)' for the movie *Heavy Metal* and also 'Cinema,' the title track for the album we recorded next."

October 2 – 29, 1984. The band tour the UK, winding up not successful in their quest to get the album to chart. Germany however grants the band a No.60 placement.

November 12, 1984. The band appear on famed German live music show Rockpalast, performing twenty numbers in Bochum, albeit offering only two selections from *The Catch*. Another filming for TV takes place on the 19th in Munich.

1985

1985. The band is forced to take legal action when their ex-manager Jim White issues a spate of Nazareth records on his own Sahara imprint.

1985. A compilation called *The Ballad Album* is issued by Vertigo in a number of territories, foremost being Germany.

1985 – 1988. Future Nazareth guitarist Jimmy Murrison attends the Perth Rock School. He will become a guitar teacher, with his connection to Nazareth coming when he plays with Lee Agnew in the band Trouble in Doggieland.

February 13, 14, 1985. Following scattered Canadian and US shows, the band play two nights at the Viña del Mar International Song Festival in Chile.

February 22 – March 11, 1985. The band conduct an extensive German campaign.

Dan McCafferty:
"Nothing in the '80s was really that much of a big success. It was a pretty bad time for us. Not so bad in the early '80s, but it wasn't until *Move Me* that we even started to get the airplay again. The whole system seemed to be geared towards dance and MTV at the time, and in Europe anyway, rock 'n' roll was on a few obscure shows, late at night. In the States, everything rock was classic rock, so they were playing your old stuff but not your new stuff. Very strange time not just for us, but for a lot of rock bands."

September 14, 1985. The band play a metal fest put on by Metal Hammer magazine. Also on the bill are Metallica, Venom, Heavy Pettin', Wishbone Ash and Warlock. How big Nazareth might have become had they gone the heavy metal route in the '80s is thrown into high relief. Wishbone Ash as well.

February 23rd, 1985, Biberach, Germany.

© Wolfgang Gurster

© Wolfgang Gurster

November 14 – November 25, 1985. The band tour Eastern Europe.

Dan McCafferty, on close calls in the Baltics and around the world:
"There was the time in Yugoslavia. Oh, that was wonderful. A guy rips us off at the hotel and we call the police. The next thing we know, the police are chattering about hash and sticking the muzzles of their machine guns up our noses. We said, 'Hey, you don't understand. *We* called *you.*"

"Then there's Italy. If you don't end up in a communist riot, you'll end up in a fascist riot. When you play Sicily, they shoot the tires off your truck because you haven't paid the 10%. When you ask, 'What 10%?,' they answer you with guns and you suddenly realize you could disappear over there. You realize it's not Scotland anymore."

"And there was Iceland. Procol Harum, Led Zeppelin, Deep Purple and Nazareth are the only bands ever to go there as far as I know. At the end of the night, you discover that the Chief Justice, who's supposed to pay you, doesn't want to turn over any cash. Finally at 4 AM, we held him up against the wall and threatened to pack his head in a suitcase. We got what he owed us."

"We went to #1 in Guatemala and our manager is saying, 'Look, now you gotta go there to support the record.' Somehow we didn't fancy giving target practice to a bunch of guerrillas and turned him down." (w/ Jack Lloyd, The Dispatch, April 6, 1981)

July 21st, 1985, Sporthalle, Linz, Austria.

© Isabella Seefriedt

© Isabella Seefriedt

1986

February 22, 1986. Nazareth issue the Eddie Delana-produced *Cinema* album, recorded (during a freezing winter) at Pearl Sound Studios in Canton, Michigan, except for the title track, which was recorded in Scotland. The album is issued in Canada and various countries in Europe but not in the UK or the US.

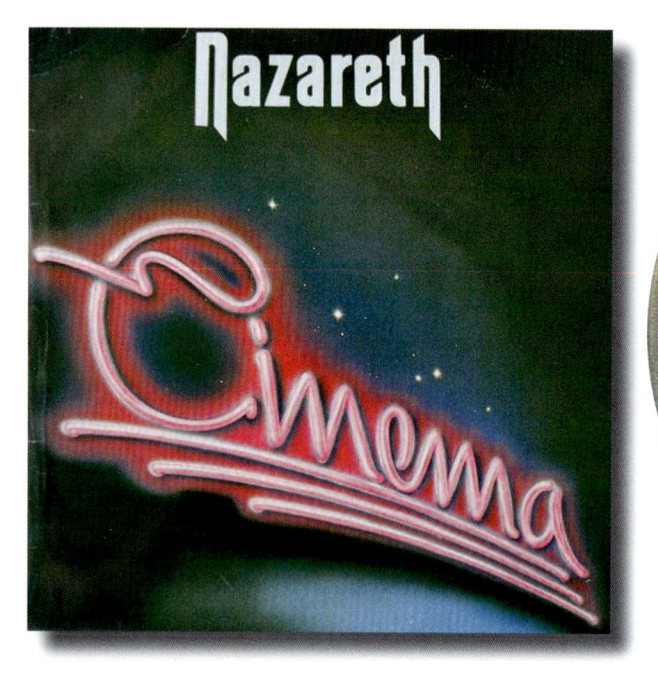

Pete Agnew:
"This was a great Nazareth album but what I remember most about it is the place we made it. Our manager at the time (a really nice guy) had Nazareth and Ted Nugent as his acts. He and Ted lived near Ann Arbor in Michigan and he told us to come over and that he had a nice studio for us to work in. The studio he had for us belonged to one of the guys in Grand Funk Railroad and it was a nice enough place but it was all carpeted—on the floor, up the walls—and the ceiling was heavy with acoustic tiles. This place was deader than your grandma's great aunt, so we said, 'No thanks.'"

"Now our manager (poor guy) had to find a place quick since we were all here and ready to go. He found one. The studio was infested with these crawling bugs, the likes of we had never seen before. It was a dump beyond description. The control room was okay, and so as long as you stayed in there you were fine. But when you weren't playing, they only had this little area—I won't call it a room because that would be a gross exaggeration—with a two-seater couch, which was infested with these bugs, and a Space Invaders machine, and that was your lot, mate! We couldn't wait to get out of the place every night and I have no idea to this day how we managed to make such a belter of an album in there. I won't bother telling you where it is because the local health and safety people have probably burnt it to the ground by now."

Manny Charlton:
"At that point we were looking for management, and we knew of a guy called Doug Banker, from Michigan, who managed Ted Nugent. We were friends with him and he suggested that we come over to America and record in a studio in Michigan. So that's what we did. Cinema was a return to form for us. It's a good

Nazareth rock 'n' roll record, you know? Eddie Delana was basically an engineer, more an engineer than a producer, but he got the band to sound good. Plus we were back to the original four-piece by that time too, just the original four of us. There's a few good songs on that record and like I say, for me, it was a return to form for the band. We were back writing rock 'n' roll and playing in the right pocket."

Dan McCafferty on the '80s album that was the most work:
"*Cinema* actually, because we had to keep changing studios and stuff. There were a lot of technical problems and breakdowns, major repairs in the studio, so we had to go somewhere else for a few days and then come back. We started to lose that continuity. You get in the studio, and then you go, 'God, there's no bottom end here. It sounds different than the last one we were in.' You make little tapes and take it out into the car to see if it sounded good. Probably stress-wise, that was the worst. But I like the song 'Cinema' a lot."

June 4, 1986. After Axl Rose expressed interest in having Manny Charlton produce the first Guns N' Roses album, Charlton records some early sessions for the band at Sound City in LA. Scheduled work with Nazareth had Manny bowing out of the project, with Mike Clink taking over the production duties on what was to become *Appetite for Destruction*.

October 30 – November 28, 1986. The band tour mainland Europe, concentrating as usual on Germany.

July 5th, 1986, Out in the Green, Dinkelsbühl, Germany.

© Wolfgang Gurster

November 20th, 1986, Kammersaal, Austria.

141

1987

1987. Live album '*Snaz* is issued on CD for the first time, however it is pared down by five tracks to fit on a single disc.

1987. Dan sees the release of a second solo album, *Into the Ring*, recorded at Chameleon Studios in Hamburg and issued by Mercury in Germany. Floated as a single is "Starry Eyes"/"Sunny Island." Pete co-writes with Dan on six tracks.

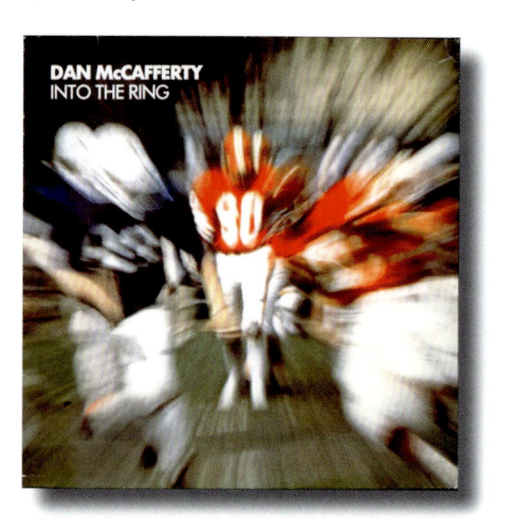

Dan McCafferty:
"Half of it was stuff Pete and I wrote and the other side was a soundtrack for a German movie. There's no reason how you would have known about it. It's one of these obscure things. I think it actually sold one copy in Tokyo or whatever the hell it was (laughs)."

February – May, 1987. The band tour North America, followed by Europe and then a few more North American dates later in the year.

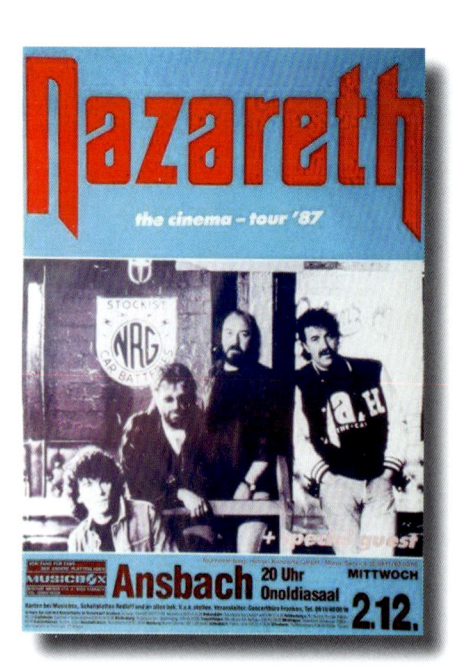

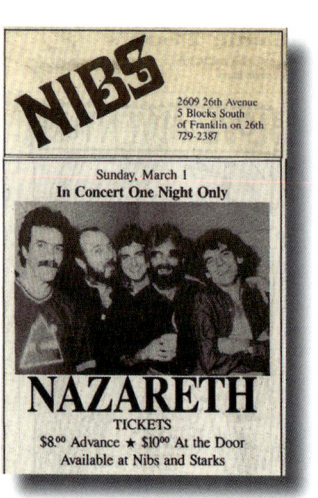

Dan McCafferty on the '80s:
"MTV and all these things started, so it became less of an audio form than a visual form. So we just had to stick with the music. Because we're British, we were very aware of let's do what we do and stick with that. Because Britain changed its mind every three seconds. It was very fashion-motivated and very aesthetic, visual, that kind of thing. So we just stuck to our guns and played rock 'n' roll and survived through all those times."

June 21, 1987. Canadian heavy metal band Helix issue their sixth album, *Wild in the Streets*. On it is a cover of Nazareth's "Dream On," from *2XS*.

July 21, 1987. Guns N' Roses issue their seminal debut, *Appetite for Destruction*, which goes on to sell thirty million copies worldwide. As discussed, Manny Charlton almost produced it.

1988

February – June 1988. The band tour North America, kicking off with a Canadian leg before transitioning to the States.

144

© Wolfgang Gurster

1989

January 23, 1989. Nazareth issue what will be their last album with Manny Charlton in the ranks, entitled *Snakes 'n' Ladders*. Producing is Joey Balin, with the team working at Comforts Place Studio in Surrey, England. Vertigo issues the album in Europe and Japan but not in the UK or North America.

Pete Agnew:
"This was the Nazareth album that Nazareth never made! How's that? It went like this: all of our recording contracts had expired by this time so our German record company (who had us for the world excluding America) offered us a new deal on the condition that we used an American producer who was a big favourite of theirs at the time. No problem. After meeting this guy a few times I get the distinct impression that what he really wants is to do a solo album with Dan, whose voice he absolutely loves."

"Anyway, in the weeks before we go to the studio, him and Manny have become good buddies and they've decided that we will have 'programmed drums' instead of a live kit. Everyone including Darrell—actually *especially* Darrell—is quite happy to go along with this so they arrange a session programmer to handle this. Unknown to myself, and for whatever reason, they have also decided to replace me with a session bass player, but I don't find this out until I have played on a couple of tracks in the studio. By the way, the studio was a beautiful big old manor house near Lingfield in England."

"So that's two of us not playing on the album now. I'm still hanging out at the studio because I have all the backing vocals to do, when three or four days later I'm told that Manny has now been replaced with a session guitar player. Oops, he didn't see that coming! But dear me, can we still call this a Nazareth album? Apparently we can, because the session keeps rolling on. However, after getting the backing vocals out of the way, I don't need to hang around so I hop on a plane home. The album eventually gets finished and at least it has Dan doing the vocals, so we had *one* Nazareth guy that managed to finish the course. I've often wondered what would have happened if this guy had decided he didn't like Dan's voice either. Funny thing is, one track from the album, 'We Are Animals,' became a massive hit in Russia and all the surrounding countries.

This is one of the only two tracks that we—Manny and me—play guitar and bass on together. I guess the Russians must have wanted to hear 'Nazareth!'"

Dan McCafferty, on the record being issued only in Europe and Japan:
"We do quite good in Japan. They think some albums are great and others they think are crap. In Japan, a lot of that is down to promotion. If the record company decides that this is going to be hot, it's going to be hot. That's how the country is geared. They just blast things at people."

July – October 1989. The band tour Europe, with most dates taking place in Germany, supported by Canada's Lee Aaron.

September 1989. Hanoi Rocks singer Michael Monroe issues his second solo album—*Not Fakin' It* contains a cover of the Nazareth song of the same name.

November 9, 1989. The fall of the Berlin Wall.

Pete Agnew:
"When the wall came down, I mean, so much happened. People don't realize that it was a different career, '89 to '90, when that wall came down. That changed rock 'n' roll for the planet. You don't notice it so much in the US and Canada, but over here in Europe, there used to be a big chunk of concrete there and that just disappeared. That opened up the biggest market in the world to us, all these Eastern European countries. What an incredible difference to us that made, and many other bands. I mean, you could write a book on that alone."

December 17, 1989. Hair metal band Britny Fox issue, on Columbia, their second album *Boys in Heat*, which includes a cover of "Hair of the Dog."

July 27th, 1989,
1.Radio Rock Nacht,
Illertissen, Germany.

July 27th, 1989, 1.Radio Rock Nacht, Illertissen, Germany.

July 27th, 1989, 1.Radio Rock Nacht, Illertissen, Germany.

© Wolfgang Gurster

© Wolfgang Gurster

October 11th, 1989,
Longhorn Club,
Stuttgart-Wangen,
Germany.

© Wolfgang Gurster

WE ROCK THE CITIES TOUR '89
Nazareth meets Lee Aaron
+ special guest

© Wolfgang Gurster

"In the '90s, you could always sell tickets. You could always go out and work. It's just that you couldn't get arrested on the airwaves at all. But the end of the '80s, when Guns N' Roses came along, for instance, all those bands, and they started talking about us and Queen and the other influences growing up, that didn't hurt us at all. And then the boys covered 'Hair of the Dog,' which didn't hurt either. In my experience, I've been doing this for 40-odd years now and it tends to go in circles anyway, music. Fashion as well, oddly enough, seems to go in circles. If you just wait long enough it will come around."
Dan McCafferty

The 1990s

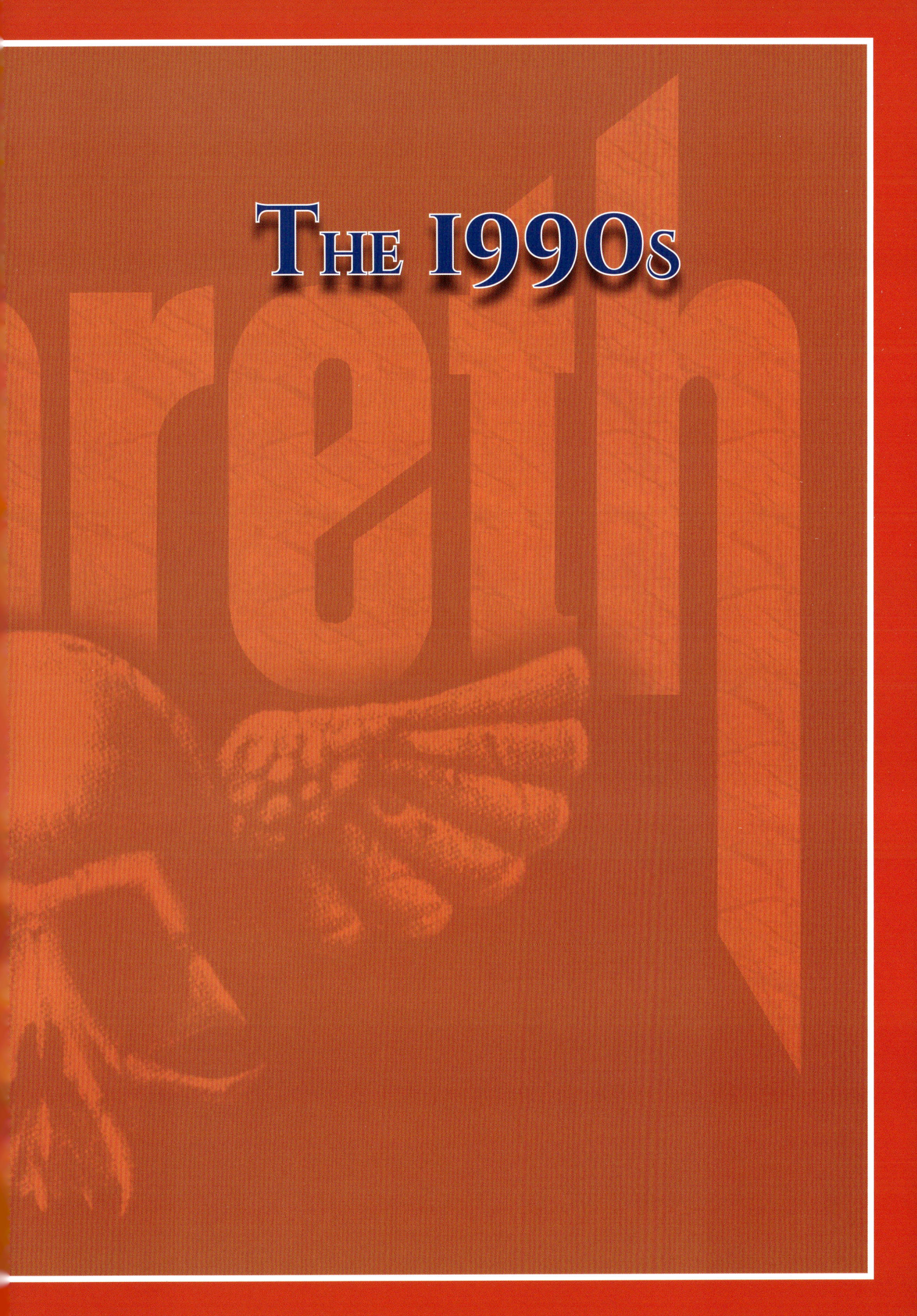

© Isabella Seefriedt

In the 1990s, Nazareth makes the shift away from the record/tour cycle to a band that has touring as its identity, showing up, punching the clock, and then making the odd record not because they're particularly inspired, but because it's about time, or because a record deal with a decent advance happened to materialise.

Still, there's an exciting dimension to each of the records that we got. For the first two, in 1991 and 1994, Billy Rankin returns to the band despite ongoing financial disputes. And not only does he rejoin, but his writing sort of defines the band, with *No Jive* and *Move Me* being a sort of up-tempo pop metal (if you allow the generality), with glossy late-'80s production values making everything behave.

For the third of the three records we got this decade, 1998's *Boogaloo*, Billy is out of the picture again, replaced by Jimmy Murrison. And despite the fact that we are about to embark on the longest gap between Nazareth albums, ending with 2008's *The Newz*, *Boogaloo* is essentially the first of a quartet of bold, swaggering, creatively very much successful Nazareth albums that would serve as a nice surprise this late in the band's career. Ronnie Leahy is brought back as keyboard player after a five-year "retirement," but he's more so emphasizing the band's old school, rock 'n' roll values, much appreciated after years of Nazareth trying to look youthful.

Unfortunately, *Boogaloo* would be the last record for original drummer Darrell Sweet, who would die in 1999, quite unexpectedly from a heart attack while the band was out touring America, in fact. Still, if we are to stress the positive, Darrell was there for the entire decade, clutching his lunch box as Nazareth went to work, at this point more or less delivering a hits-heavy set, but one that nonetheless stressed how rich a history this most famous of Scottish bands very loudly professed night after night from stages all over the world.

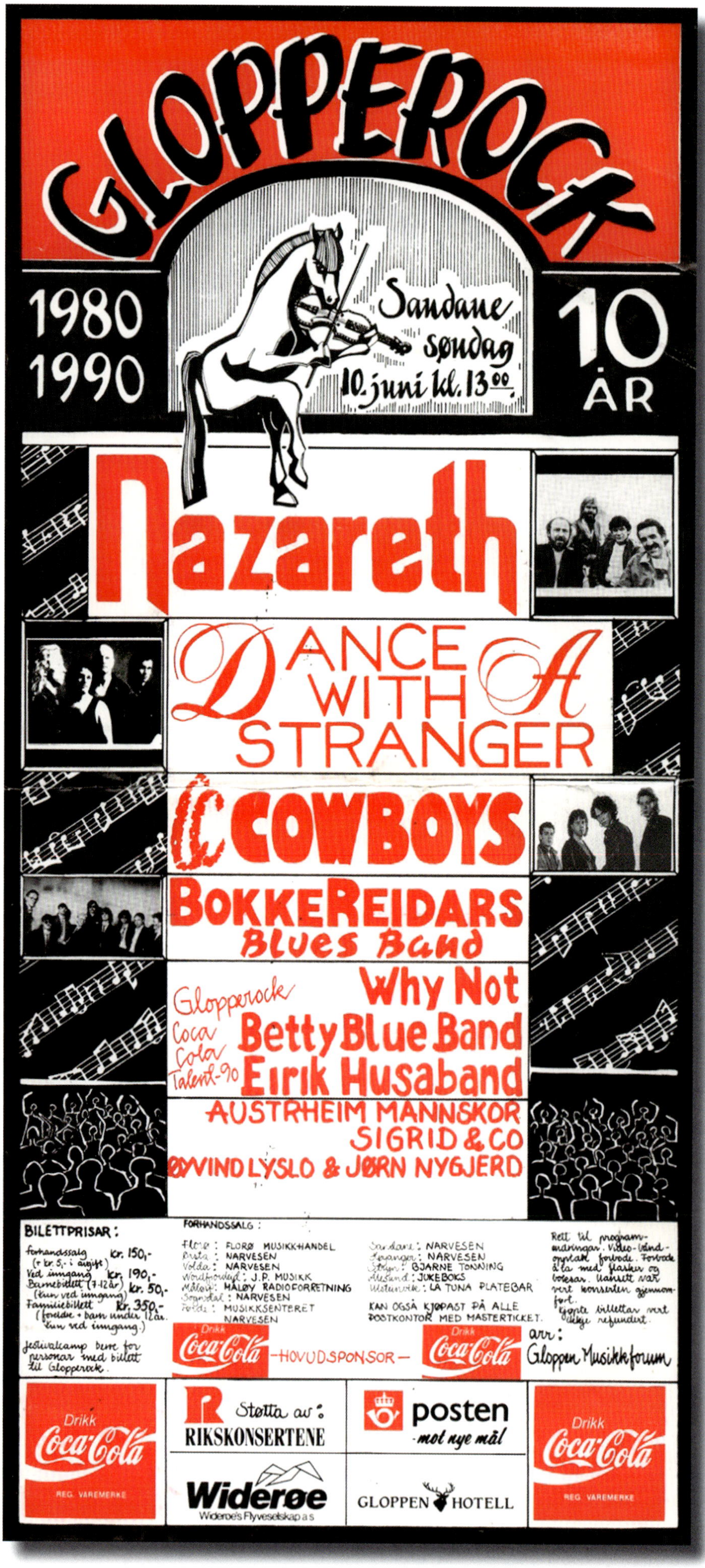
GLOPPEROCK
1980
1990
Sandane
søndag
10. juni kl. 13.00.
10
ÅR
Nazareth
DANCE WITH A STRANGER
CC COWBOYS
BOKKEREIDARS
Blues Band
Glopperock
Coca Cola
Talent-90
Why Not
Betty Blue Band
Eirik Husaband
AUSTRHEIM MANNSKOR
SIGRID & CO
ØYVIND LYSLO & JØRN NYGJERD
BILETTPRISAR:
forhandssalg kr. 150,-
(+ kr. 5,- i avgift)
Ved inngang kr. 190,-
Barnebillett (7-12 år) kr. 50,-
(kun ved inngang)
Familiebillett kr. 350,-
(foreldre + barn under 12 år. kun ved inngang.)
Festivalcamp berre for personar med billett til Glopperock.
FORHANDSSALG:
Florø: FLORØ MUSIKKHANDEL
NARVESEN
Volda: NARVESEN
Nordfjordeid: J.P. MUSIKK
Måløy: MÅLØY RADIOFORRETNING
Sogndal: NARVESEN
Førde: MUSIKKSENTERET
NARVESEN
Sandane: NARVESEN
Høyanger: NARVESEN
Stryn: BJARNE TONNING
Ålesund: JUKEBOKS
Ulsteinvik: LA TUNA PLATEBAR
KAN OGSÅ KJØPAST PÅ ALLE POSTKONTOR MED MASTERTICKET.
Rett til programendringar. Video-bandopptak forbode. Forbode å ta med flasker og boksar. Uansett vêr vert konserten gjennomført.
Kjøpte billettar vert ikkje refundert.
Drikk Coca-Cola
-HOVUDSPONSOR-
Drikk Coca-Cola
arr:
Gloppen Musikkforum
Drikk Coca-Cola
REG. VAREMERKE
Støtta av:
RIKSKONSERTENE
posten
-mot nye mål
Drikk Coca-Cola
REG. VAREMERKE
Widerøe
Widerøe's Flyveselskap a.s
GLOPPEN HOTELL

1990

1990. *Hair of the Dog* is issued for the first time on CD.

May 13, 1990. After twenty-two years faithful service, guitarist and sometimes producer Manny Charlton leaves Nazareth, playing his last show in Nazareth's hometown of Dunfermline, Scotland, at a benefit for wheelchair sports. Opening on the night is Fish, ex-Marillion, with the prog legend also joining the band for a rendition of The Sensational Alex Harvey Band classic, "The Faith Healer."

Dan McCafferty, in 1999:
"We had been together for twenty-six years, and basically we wanted to do what we do and he wanted to do something else. And eventually that starts to get in the way. I mean, break-ups are never pleasant at all, really. Unless the whole band just decides to call it quits. After the band, he was in production for a while and he did a couple things in Europe, and then he was running a studio for this guy and doing a lot of stuff on the side. I think he got bored with that and I believe he has an album that is either out or it's coming out."

Pete Agnew, in 2017:
"We had disagreements—that's it. We totally disagreed with some stuff and that was it. There was no point in staying together. Since then we haven't spoken to each other. We have agreed to be apart. We were doing our own paths, and we never had big fights. So it was just a goodbye and just, 'Go do your thing. We'll do ours.' I've never seen the man for 18 years, since Darrell Sweet died. I've only seen him maybe four to five times in all those years, after he quit with the band. But the last time I saw him was way back when Darrell died."
(w/ Marko Syrjala, MetalRules)

June – July 1990. Nazareth tour the US in a package with Blackfoot and Ten Years After. Manny has been replaced by a returning Billy Rankin.

November 3 – 16, 1990. Nazareth mount a German tour, as part of a package with Saga and Kansas.

November 9th, 1990, Deutsches Museum, Munich, Germany.

© Wolfgang Gurster

© Wolfgang Gurster

1991

Mid-1991. Nazareth work at Cas Studios, Inbert-Schüren, Germany, on tracks to slated for their 18th album.

Dan McCafferty:
"We produced ourselves and did it with as few overdubs as possible, because we wanted it to sound like us live. Mike Ging is a big fan of the band and so he knew our sound really well. It was like having the album mixed from a fan's perspective. *(w/ Tom Harrison, The Province, July 14, 1993)*

November 1, 1991. Nazareth issue—through Mausoleum in German, Griffin in the US and Attic in Canada—*No Jive*.

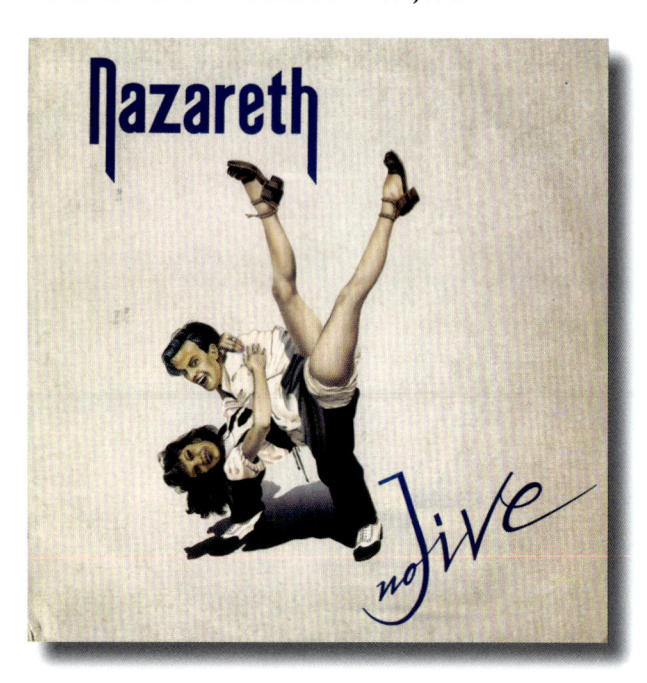

Dan McCafferty:
"It's the best record we've done in a long time. I had a good feel about it. Rock was having a bit of a comeback and it's like everything else in this business: you get the right tune in the right three minutes at the right time, then you are lucky. And if you don't, well, you've just got to keep trying. We still have fun with it. We enjoyed playing and the only way you can do that is if you go on the road. And we enjoy each other's company, and having fun, basically."
(w/ David Howell, Edmonton Journal, July 9, 1993)

Pete Agnew:
"After the dust had settled from Snakes, Manny was no longer in the band and we had Billy back, so this album was always going to be fun and games. Of course with Billy's return we had more songs than you could shake a stick at, and some really great ones at that. We went to a studio in a tiny village (well, not even a village, more a street) near Saarbrücken in Germany. The place had been a restaurant until Frank Farian bought it and made it into a studio. He was the guy who made all the Boney M and Milli Vanilli records. It was a great studio but the resident sound engineer kept disappearing for hours on end so we—well, Billy actually—ended up engineering the sessions. We had such a good time making this record that we were sad when we finished it after six weeks.

The German newspaper, Bild, were following the recordings and doing stories about it every other week as a sort of serialization of the making of an album. This coverage led to all sorts of nutters turning up at the studio with all sorts of instruments, wanting to jam with us. As you can see on the album, we resisted the temptation."

December 21, 1991. Nazareth play a charity gig at home in Dunfermline, upstairs at a bar called Sinky's. The gig was in support of the Darrell Sweet Memorial Fund.

1992

February 1992. The band begin the year playing Germany with Uriah Heep followed by UK dates in April, followed by more European shows and then more UK concerts in October.

February 18th, 1992, Neu-Ulm, Gorki Park, Germany.

© Wolfgang Gurster

CARNIVAL IN ROCK '92
NAZARETH
&
URIAH HEEP
Mittwoch, 19. Februar '92, 21 Uhr
FRANKFURT - MUSIC-HALL
KARTENVORVERKAUF:
an allen bekannten Verkaufsstellen!
Telefonische und schriftliche Kartenbestellungen: Kartenkiosk Sandrock Hauptwache Passage, 6000 Frankfurt 1, Tel. 069 / 2 01 15-6 und Kartenhaus Mainz, Schillerstraße 11, 6500 Mainz, Tel. 0 61 31 / 22 87 29
Tourneeleitung: CBH
Örtl. Durchführung: Shooter Promotions & Classics GmbH
CBH

March 1st, 1992, Orpheum, Graz, Austria.

© Isabella Seefriedt

© Isabella Seefriedt

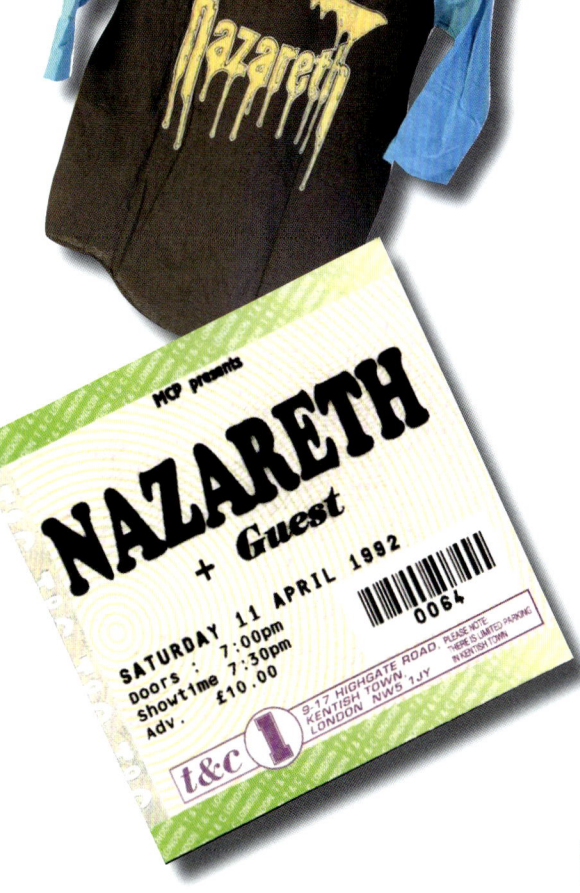

June 26th, 1992, Knittelfeld, Austria.

© Isabella Seefriedt

1993

1993. Sequel Records issues a Nazareth compilation called *From the Vaults*.

February 1993. Once again Nazareth tour Germany with Uriah Heep.

April 30 – December 4, 1993. Nazareth spend much of the year touring North America, including their usual spate of Canadian dates. Much of the campaign is conducted as a package with Uriah Heep and Wishbone Ash.

November 23, 1993. Guns N' Roses issue a covers album called *The Spaghetti Incident?*. Included is a rendition of Nazareth's "Hair of the Dog."

September 13th, 1993, Graz, Austria.

© Isabella Seefriedt

September 15th, 1993, Oberwart, Austria.

© Isabella Seefriedt

© Isabella Seefriedt

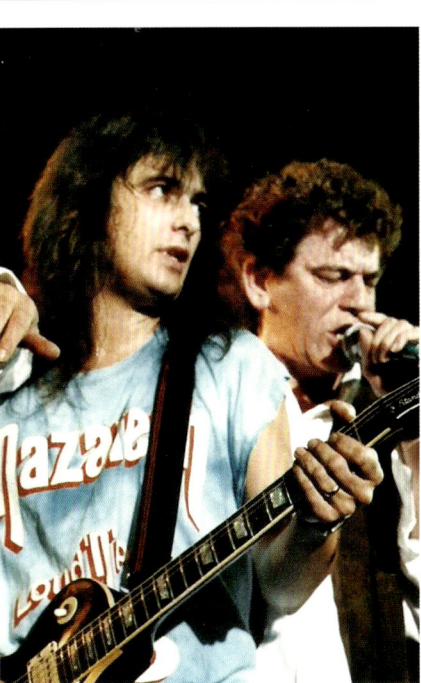

171

1994

June 3, 1994. Lemmy from Motörhead joins the band onstage, at a biker festival in Wiesen, Austria.

Pete Agnew:
"What happened is, we were on the road and we were starting a European tour that was going to last about five weeks. Our agent told us there was this tour that was out there, and it was weird, with Suzi Quatro, Bay City Rollers, Marmalade, The New Seekers, light bands. And the headliner cancelled and there were six shows to go. And they said 'Would you guys go out and play?' Strange bill, but then we thought, well, it was in Austria, Germany, and we only had to play for 40 minutes or something. We said, yeah, we'll go and have some fun."

"We got there and after the second or third date, one of the guys who worked with us turned up at the hotel with Lemmy. And Lemmy was having some fun—Lem had come around to see his pals in Naz. So he came along to the gig and we were doing 'Tush' as an encore type of thing. We did it as a sort of last number of the set and we got Suzi Quatro up and the girls did dance steps and all this and Lemmy had come up and played bass and I was just doing handclaps or something stupid like that. But it wasn't just the playing the bass. After that, Lemmy stayed with us for about three days on that tour, just coming around with us, and I don't think he ever went to bed. I really don't. On one occasion, at 4:30 in the morning, after a gig, I'm saying, 'I've got to go to bed.' And he's going, 'Wimp!' (laughs). But yeah, he hung about for a couple of days with us and stayed at the same hotel. It was fun."

October 17, 1994. Polydor are the label of choice for Nazareth's 19th album, *Move Me*. Producing is engineer Tony Taverner in conjunction with the band, the team laying down tracks in Germany. Chief writer of the material on the record is Billy Rankin.

Pete Agnew:
"*Move Me* was great fun. We decided to program the drums—again—and we got Steve Pigott, who actually had his own recording studio in England. It was great; he wrote a lot of songs, great songwriter and stuff, but he was

a great programmer and he had quite a reputation for it, and he was a pal of Tony Taverner, the engineer/producer on that one. And it was absolutely amazing because it does not sound like programmed drums. I mean, guys that know programmed drums and guys that had recorded a lot, you can tell right away, even if the general public can't pick it up, but with Steve, it's absolutely impossible. It sounds so much like real drums, a real human being playing. And of course Darrell sat with him and they discussed, 'Let's do this, I like that, I like that.'"

"But he was so good that when he finished working for us on that album, the guy who had the studio, they had done reams of these disco dance music records, and when he heard what was going on, he said, 'This guy's amazing.' So he says, 'When he's finished working with you, can he come and work with me?' And what happened was Steve spent the next six months in Germany (laughs), working up in this other control room on these other records with him. Anyway, the actual record itself was good fun to make."

"What's funny, we weren't really sure about what we were going to call the album. In fact, the first idea was *Steamroller*, which was one of the tracks we did. We didn't have any management at the time, we were just doing it ourselves, and we thought maybe we would go for somebody. So we were actually approached by Deep Purple's management—I won't name any names here, but we all know who they are—and he said he was quite fancy managing Nazareth because he heard the album and everything and could hear what was going on and he'd like to manage us. We said, we'll give it a shot. And when he was listening to the album, what happened is, we had done a photo shoot for the front of it. You know, the old Mercury car that's on the front of it? It was a next-door neighbour of mine who had that. He was into cars and stuff and he had this thing all in pieces. And it was Deep Purple's manager who actually suggested we should call it *Move Me*, with the car, which we thought was pretty funny."

November – December 1994. The band conduct a UK tour, playing a number of home base Scotland shows.

Late December 1994. Jimmy Murrison and Ronnie Leahy join Nazareth, more than making up for the departure of Billy Rankin, due to a big dust-up over the divvying of the £50,000 advance on *Move Me* from Polydor.

Pete Agnew:
"Around that time there was a spate of so called 'unplugged' concerts being done by bands that were traditionally loud electric outfits, so Dan, Billy and myself decided we'd like to have a shot at this (Darrell was unavailable at the time) and got together at our rehearsal studio to try it out. Billy was on acoustic guitar and had a 'stamping board,' a raised wooden board with a little instrument mic underneath, so that was guitar and drums taken care of, and I used my acoustic bass."

"We completely rearranged all our songs and did them using three-part harmony vocals wherever possible—yes, even 'Razamanaz.' We thought the combination of this instrumentation and vocal approach sounded wonderful and as it turned out, so did the fans. I think we played about 15 shows, all in the UK, and it was one of the most fun things we ever did."

"It was billed as 'An Acoustic Evening with Nazareth,' a title which suggests a cozy night by the fire listening to tinkling melodies. But itt was in fact a couple of acoustic guitars and a stamping board cranked up through a PA system.

It was acoustic, but we still tripped the decibel meters in a couple of clubs we played. You can actually hear it on YouTube under 'NAZARETH - Live in Scotland 1994.' The recording is taken straight from the sound desk so the audience is very quiet. Great fun, and we finished with a concert in our home town just before Christmas, which turned out to be Billy's last show with the band."

© Isabella Seefriedt

© Isabella Seefriedt

1995

February 15, 1995. The new Nazareth lineup begins touring, playing throughout Europe and into festival season. This is followed by US and Canadian dates with shows in the UK and more German festival dates rounding out the year.

March 1995. Jimmy Murrison joins Nazareth, with Ronnie Leahy to follow two months later, more than making up for the departure of Billy Rankin.

Pete Agnew:
"We knew Ronnie back in the day, when he was with The Pathfinders, when we were a part-time band and just young guys. And then we got to know him pretty well, when he was playing with Maggie Bell and that. We were in London at the same time. And then after he played with Jack Bruce and we used to meet up with Ronnie then. The thing is, he was another Scotsman as well. And this was a good thing: we'd never had just one guitar and piano, never had it like that. When Billy was gone, we got Jimmy and we actually thought of having two guitars but it didn't really work. We had brought in Bruce Watson from Big Country, because he's a good pal and he lives in the town with us. So we thought we would try with two guitars. So Bruce came in and he was playing with us at rehearsals for about two weeks and it looked as if that was going to be the lineup. And then Big Country had some legal things happen at the time and he had to go back and do some tours. Long story short, Bruce couldn't do it."

"Then we thought, okay, he's gone, and we already had our mind on having somebody in again, so what about a piano player? And what happened was, when we were off the road, Dan had been doing this fun thing in Glasgow on a Friday and Saturday night. He'd got this band together called The Party Boys. It was the old Alex Harvey Band, basically, with Dan singing. It was Zal on guitar, Ted on drums, Chris on the bass, and they didn't have Hugh on the keyboards—they had Ronnie on keyboards. And this band, The Party Boys, with Dan singing, was a brilliant band, fabulous. So I used to go off on a Friday or Saturday night and I used to go have a jam with them. Great fun."

"By the way, we'd never played any gigs with Jimmy at this point, but we were sitting and having a drink at some point, and we were talking about how much fun that Party Boys thing was. So we thought, what about Ronnie? Ask Ronnie and see if he would fancy it. So we asked Ronnie and he was up for it. It was the first time we'd had just one guitar and keyboards. Any time we had the keyboards before, it was with Billy, so it was two guitars. I mean, I loved the sound. The stuff we did on *Boogaloo*... 'When the Light Comes Down' is one of best songs we ever did. It's a fabulous record and the keyboard playing on that album is just amazing. So I loved playing with Ronnie; Ronnie was such a nice guy, and a really funny guy too."

"As for Jimmy, well, at the beginning of 1995 we were looking to replace Billy and there was a unanimous decision that Jimmy Murrison was the man. I had first met Jimmy in 1988 when he was a student at Perth Rock College playing in Trouble in Doggieland, that he had asked Lee to join. They actually played on a bill with Nazareth at East End Park in Dunfermline, which was Manny's last show with the band. We saw Jimmy playing many times after that and now we all agreed he was not only a brilliant guitarist but a very good songwriter and an all-around very nice guy, so that was that. So there yo go: Jimmy joined us in March and eventually Ronnie joined in May.

May 21st, 1995, Koeflach, Austria.

© Isabella Seefriedt

May 8th, 1995, Longhorn Club, Stuttgart-Wangen, Germany.

© Wolfgang Gurster

September 16th, 1995,
Aeroanta Curitiba, Brazil.

1996

1996. *Razamanaz* is reissued by Castle Communications, highlight being two non-LP bonus tracks, "Hard Living" and "Spinning Top."

February – March 1996. The band tour Russia, returning for another leg in late September through October.

Dan McCafferty:
"We've played all over Russia, out in Siberia and stuff, which is interesting. The people are great; it's just that getting around there is difficult. Like, with roads just stopping (laughs). 'The road stops, but don't worry about it—it starts again in a couple hours.' 'Okay.' And I remember travelling once in the airplane, and the woman said, 'Fasten your seat belts!' And I said, 'I haven't got one.' 'Well, that's okay then!' I suppose the fans are little more staid than Western fans, because of the years of looking over their shoulders. But nowadays, since 1990, things have changed a lot there. They get MTV and all the rest of it too."

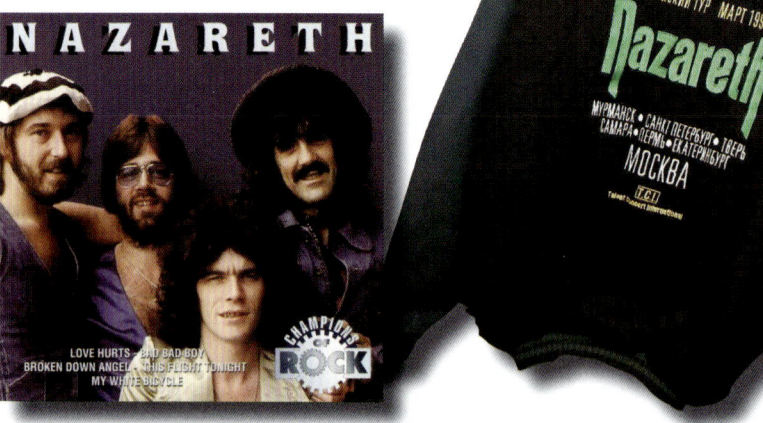

April – July 1996. The band tour the US, taking a break for festival season in Europe.

1997

1997. Manny Charlton issues *Drool*, his first solo album and the only one he assembled when living in Scotland, before he moved to the US.

1997. *'Snaz* is issued on CD for a second time (through Castle Communications), adding "Let Me Be Your Leader" over and above the 1987 issue but leaving four tracks off versus the original vinyl issue from 1981.

Late 1997. Manny Charlton moves to Fort Worth, Texas.

European Tour, October-December 1998.

184

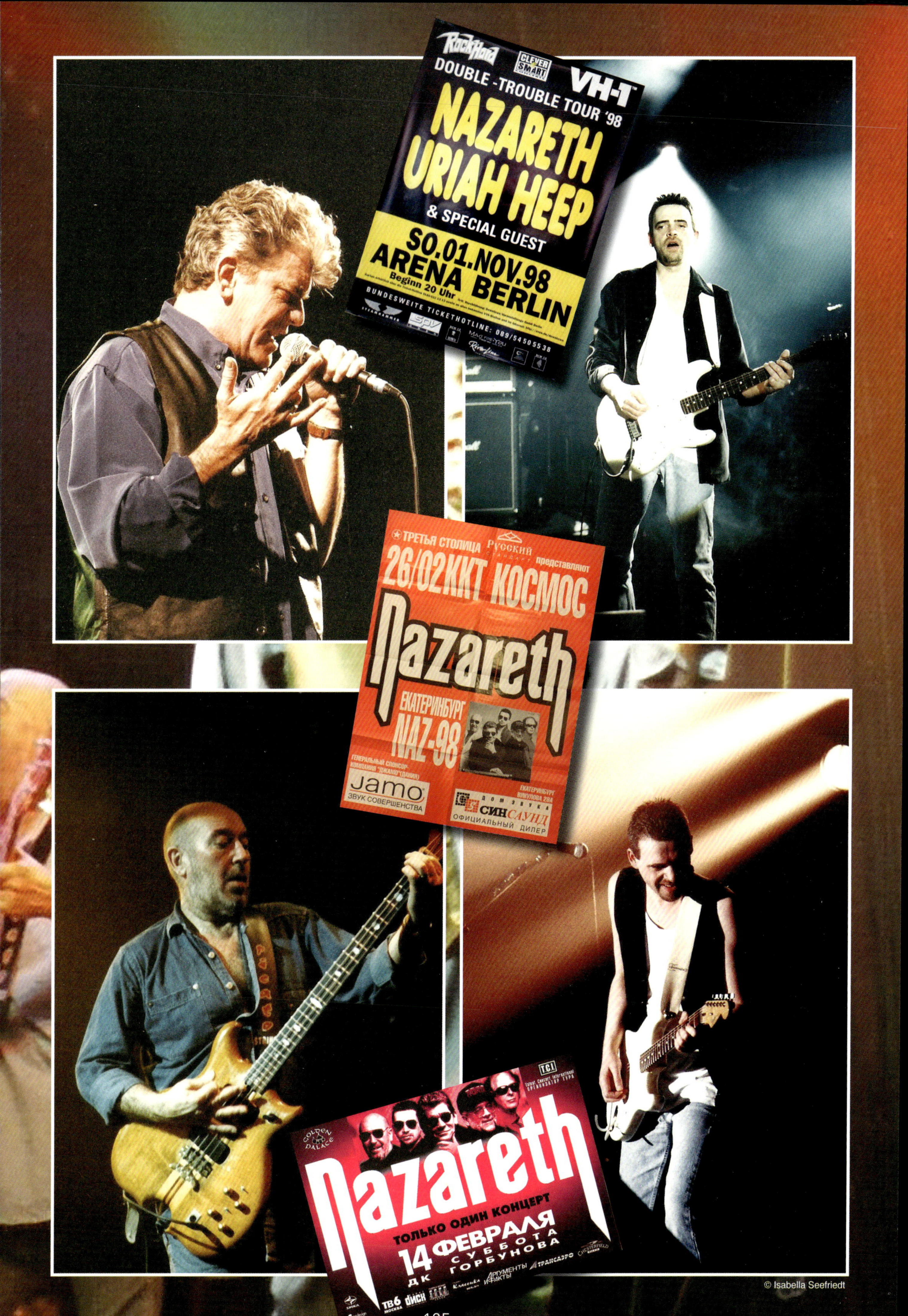

© Isabella Seefriedt

1999

April 30, 1999. Darrell Sweet dies of a heart attack, aged 51, before a concert in New Albany, Indiana on the second leg of the band's tour supporting *Boogaloo*. He is survived by a son, a daughter, and his wife Marion.

Dan McCafferty:
"Darrell was loud, and he liked huge monitors—he really did (laughs). No, Darrell was just loud, in life, as well as a drummer. And he was a very bright guy. He was an accountant, so I guess numbers and drummers... timing and all that. But he was a super guy. He had all these terrible sayings and terrible jokes he used to crack all the time, and people used to just crack up with them. Me, if I tried, 'That's not funny, man.' But when he did it, it was funny. So he was a good lad. Good boy. I miss him."

Pete Agnew:
"Darrell was a great drummer. I've played with Darrell since he was 16, when he joined us, as The Shadettes, so we go way, way back. We got on very, very well together and we played together so much that when you started into any song, we just automatically locked in without even thinking about it. We saw the thing getting played the same way."

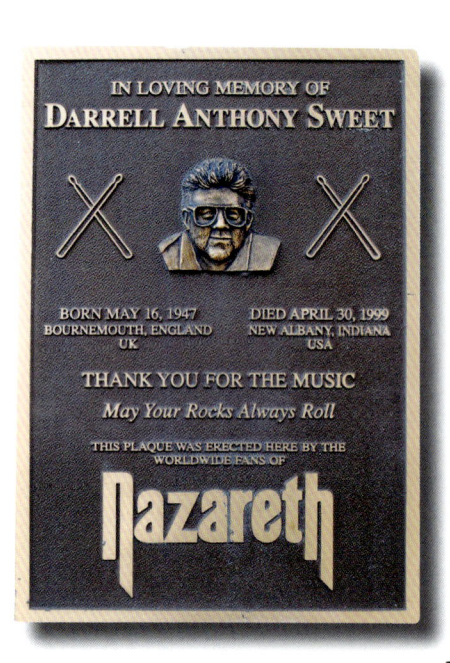

October 8, 1999. Swiss legends Krokus issue *Round 13*, the band's only album to feature future Nazareth singer Carl Sentance on vocals.

МИРОВОЕ ТУРНЕ 1999-2000
ОРГАНИЗАТОР ТУРА СНГ

Nazareth

ЛИ АГНЁВ | ПИТ АГНЁВ | ДЭН МАКАФФЕРТИ | РОННИ ЛИХИ | ДЖИМ МУРИСОН

12 ноября госцирк
Nazareth

"MAY YOUR ROCKS - ALWAYS ROLL" ПАМЯТИ ДАРРЕЛА СВИТА ПОСВЯЩАЕТСЯ

12 ноября, пятница, начало в 20:00
ПЕРМСКИЙ ГОСУДАРСТВЕННЫЙ ЦИРК

КОНТРОЛЬ

ЦЕНА: 350 руб.   СЕКТОР   РЯД 8   МЕСТО 13   ЦЕНА: 350 руб.

"I have five sons, Lee, Stevie, Chris, Blair and Stewart. Lee you already know. Stevie's a singer, guitarist and songwriter who has a couple of albums on release. Chris is a bass player, singer and songwriter who has played on many albums as a session player and is also bass player for the Rezillos. Stewart's a pianist, singer and actor. Blair, although he isn't a musician, can play a wee bit guitar but actually works with Nazareth in our road crew. So you see, when we have a family gathering, we don't need to hire a band!"

"Lee went to college and he met up with Jimmy, our guitar player, and they played in the same band for a few years, called Trouble in Doggieland. And Lee also used to come out with us when we were touring, when Darrell was still alive. And actually Lee was one of Darrell's favourite drummers. He used to go along and watch Lee playing; they had a sort of mutual admiration society. So if he had six weeks where he wasn't working, Lee would come out and be our drum tech and play percussion with the band, over the years, long before Darrell died. So when Darrell died it was the obvious choice, to bring on Lee as the drummer. And when we're on stage, and when we're touring, these days, I mean, you know, I'm going on 65 and he's 40 years old. It's not like, 'Hello dad,' 'Hello son.' It's really, we're on a tour and we're a drummer and a bass player. The only time it's still, 'Hello dad,' 'Hello son,' is when he needs money (laughs)."

Pete Agnew

THE 2000s

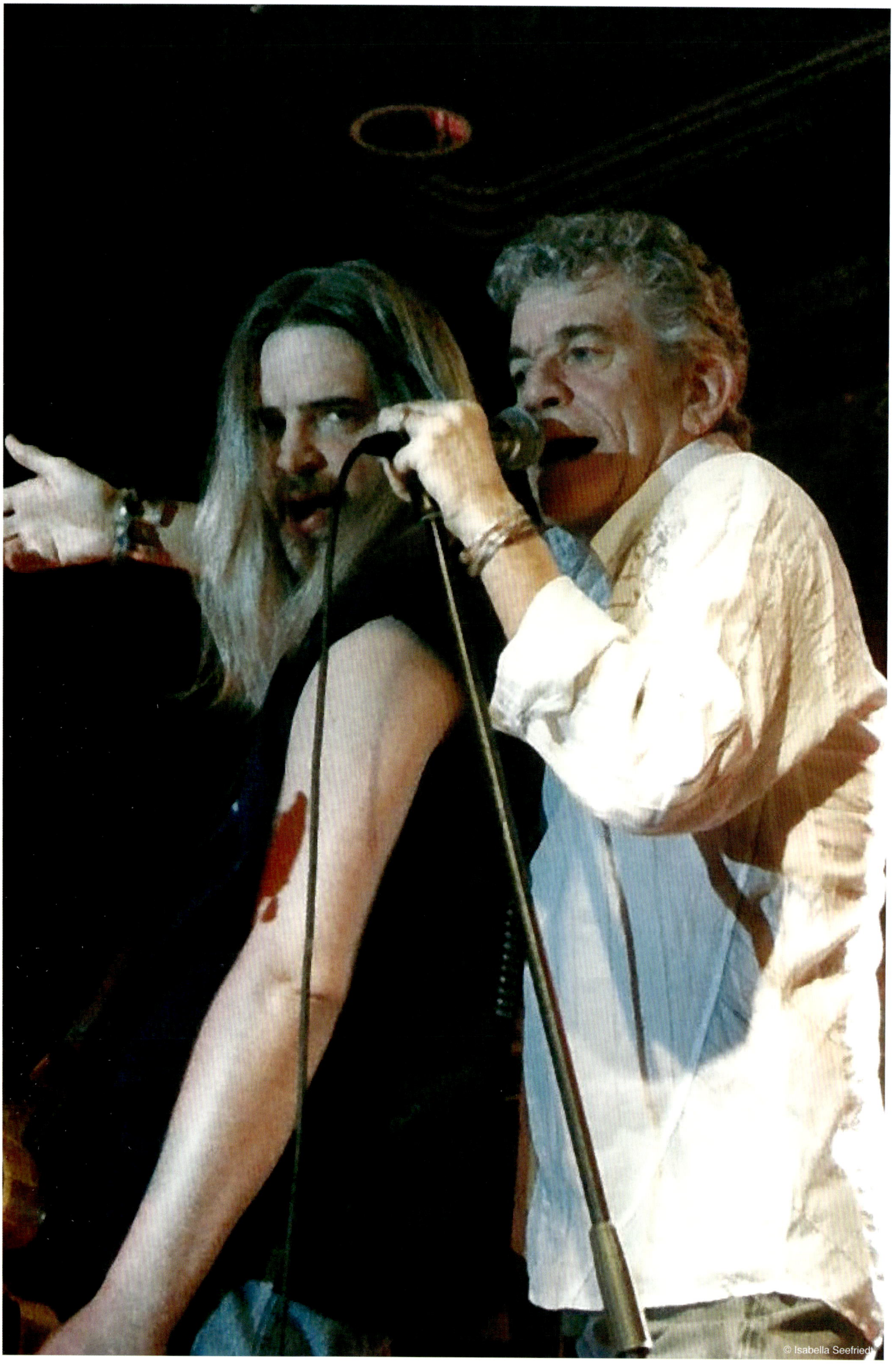
© Isabella Seefriedt

To put it politely, the 2000s marked a period of reflection for Nazareth, first upon the death of drummer Darrell Sweet, but then watching on as all manner of reissues and compilations and video and audio live sets saw the light of day (sometimes dubiously), to keep the guys on the road throughout the decade, despite the band only delivering one new studio record throughout the entire ten years. But *The Newz* turned out to be worth the wait, being the first record of what would become a solid and successful lineup, consisting of Dan, Pete, guitarist Jimmy Murrison and now Pete's son Lee on drums—and actually so much more. In fact, both Lee and Jimmy would pull their weight in the reinvigorated version of the band, writing and injecting youth into the style and arrangements of the impressive records to come.

Otherwise the decade found the band playing to their strengths, hitting Germany, embarking on expected return visits to Brazil and, just as expected, return visits to Western Canada. The guys at this point would play anywhere, resigned to this life on the road they'd known so long, indeed making peace with the fact that this is who they are, town-to-town troubadours presenting songs bigger than the people playing them.

Another happy circumstance of the decade would come with the guys making the acquaintance of producer Yann Rouiller, who would both toughen the band's sound as well as add to it a certain type of Mack Reinhold smack, last heard on Queen albums like *The Game* and *Hot Space* as well as hit records from old Nazareth tour mate Billy Squier. Really, it would be Yann, Lee and Jimmy combined that would help the old warhorses of the band make the following decade so purposeful. Still, Nazareth spent the 2000s essentially celebrating its past, in a bit of a holding pattern until 2008, when a bright future beckoned, if not particularly commercially, most definitely creatively.

2000

2000. Manny Charlton issues *Bravado* while his old band continues to hit the road.

2001

2001. *'Snaz* finally sees reissue of the complete original vinyl album, through Eagle, as a 30th Anniversary Edition. A Salvo Records reissue ten years later expands the set further.

March 2001. The band tour the UK, with Stray and old friends Uriah Heep.

Dan McCafferty, on the new guys on stage:
"We've known Lee all his life. The guy's been around the band for a long time. He was the drum tech for us when he wasn't playing himself. He's part of the family and an excellent drummer. (As for Ronnie Leahy), a rock 'n' roll piano player is what he is. We can do different things now that we couldn't do before, and we're quite happy with the way the band sounds. We've always stuck by the rule that if we like what we play, then there's a good chance the public will like it too." *(w/ Blair S. Watson, Calgary Herald, June 6, 2000)*

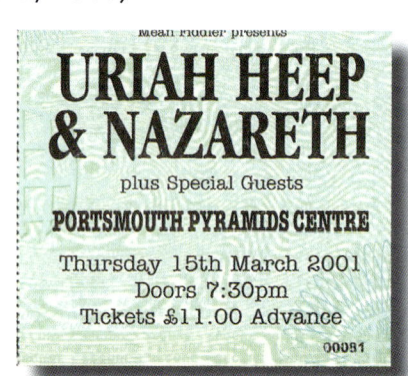

Pete Agnew, further on Darrell's replacement on drums, namely his son Lee:
"Lee and I have been jamming now for close on twenty-three years. Lee has played in a lot of bands but none more so than with his brothers, Stevie and Chris, who he still plays and records with in-between Nazareth tours—they go by the name Satellite Falls. We have a studio at home, and the boys and myself would play together a lot when I was at home."
(w/ Dmitry Epstein, dmme.net)

May 22, 2001. Receiver issues the two-CD *Back to the Trenches: Live 1972 – 1984*.

October 18, 2001. Manny Charlton Band issue *Stonkin'*.

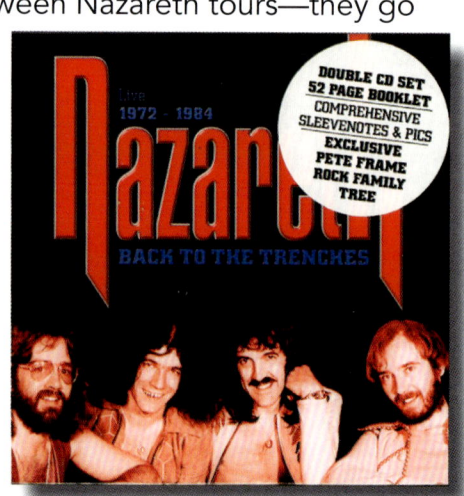

March 23rd, Astoria, London.

© Isabella Seefriedt

2002

2002. The year finds the band concentrating their live performances in Germany and Russia.

2002. Zebra Records issues a star-studded album called *Another Hair of the Dog: A Tribute to Nazareth*.

Pete Agnew:
"Nobody takes part in a tribute unless they like or respect—sometimes both even—the artist or the band. For that alone we thank the guys who took time to work on those albums. It's nice to see what other people do with your songs, but most of all it's a great compliment and we appreciate it very much."
(w/ Dmitry Epstein, dmme.net)

April 23, 2002. Eagle issues a live album called *Homecoming*, which captures the band live in Glasgow from the previous year. The set is also issued on DVD. A pared-down version of the album would be reissued the following year as *Alive & Kicking*.

Pete Agnew:
"This live CD and DVD almost didn't happen. We had a new lineup, with Lee on drums, and as there were no plans to do a studio album in the near future, it was decided that maybe it was time for another live one. The venue was The Garage in Glasgow and we had a sell-out crowd. During the second song there was a feeling onstage that something wasn't quite right but we couldn't place what it was. It was much later in the set that we realized there were no spotlights and this is what had made things feel odd. In the dressing room after the show it was explained that up in the balcony, where all the power was being drawn to feed the mobile studio truck and the stage lighting setup, one of the main cables had burst into flames. By the time our lighting crew had got the fire under control, the balcony and stairs leading to the auditorium were filled with smoke and it looked as if the show would have to be stopped. Meanwhile our crew (who were choking in the fumes) managed to redirect the smoke through a fire door using the electric fans that they have for cooling themselves while operating the spotlights. By this time all the cables to the spotlights had been destroyed, but at least they didn't have to stop the show. Quite a few people have mentioned to us that the DVD seems a bit flat as regards to lighting—well, that's the reason."

May 6th, 2002, Bad Aussee, Kurhaus, Austria.

© Isabella Seefriedt

December 11th, 2002, Orpheum, Graz, Austria.

© Isabella Seefriedt

2003

2003. Manny Charlton Band issue *Klone This*.

2003. The band focus their touring efforts on Germany, Russia and the UK.

Dan McCafferty, in July '03:
"Well, Ronnie left, so we're back to a four-piece band. He just got tired of touring. And him and his missus have got a business going over here, and she was a partner at one point and it didn't work out, so he's between the Devil and the deep blue sea. But mainly, he just got tired of touring. We're doing a lot of earlier stuff… stuff from *Hair of the Dog*, about six or seven new songs. Or I should say, six or seven new old songs (laughs). Half the set is kind of spoken for anyway. There are certain songs that if we don't play them, people get very unhappy (laughs). We don't want to get them unhappy, know what I mean? But we're now doing things like 'Changin' Times,' 'Not Faking It,' 'Turn On Your Receiver,' songs we haven't done for a few years."

"The first leg has been really fun. We have a laugh every day (laughs), but most of that we couldn't repeat on the radio. It was interesting to see what the reaction was to the changes and it's all been very, very positive stuff. I think the band sounds tougher now than it did, obviously with the keyboards gone. You can do things as a four-piece that you couldn't do previous. It's pretty much straight-ahead stuff, more rock 'n' roll than it was."

2004

2004. Manny Charlton issues *Say the Word*.

June 12, 2004. Metro Doubles issues a two-CD compilation called *Maximum XS*.

2004, Vienna, Austria.

2005

2005. Manny Charlton issues *Sharp*, which is mostly covers.

February – Mid-March, 2005. The band play Europe, focussing on Germany.

Pete on his son Lee and his effect on the band:
"He had all the same favourites as me from what he was hearing as a kid. He was a Little Feat fan and Abba fan because he was in the house with me and all his brothers. They came up with the same influences as me. But then, of course, they go into different things, when you start to leave and go to college and stuff. Lee was in a band with Jimmy at the college together and they were into all sorts of different music. Lee's a great drummer but he's also a really good songwriter—that's what Lee added to the band. When we're on stage live, I mean, it's always been myself and Lee doing the backup vocals; we're doing all the harmonies on stage. So he's not just a drummer; he's a singer and songwriter. So he adds a lot to it."

March 21 – 27, 2005. Nazareth put into motion yet another Russian tour, followed by additional European dates.

December 1 – 8, 2005. The band mount a tour of the Ukraine.

2005, Spielberg, Austria.

2005, Spielberg, Austria.

© Isabella Seefriedt

2006

August 4, 2006. Former Nazareth keyboard player John Locke—*The Fool Circle*, *'Snaz* and *2XS*—dies, in Ojai, California, from cancer at the age of 62.

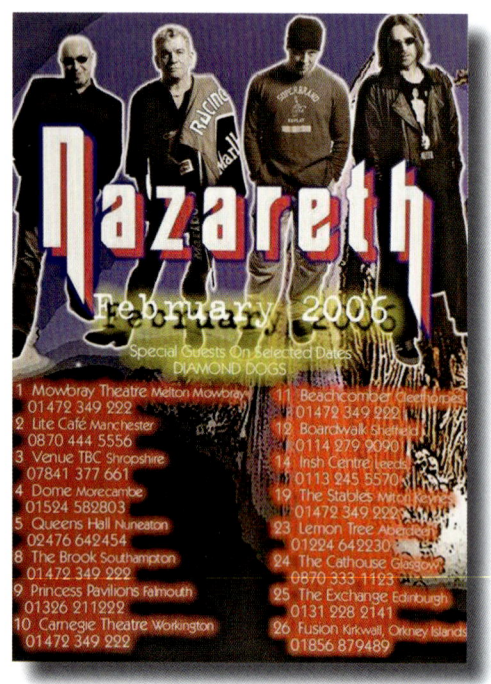

October 28th, 2006, Graz, Austria.

© Isabella Seefriedt

2007

2007. Manny Charlton issues *Americana Deluxe*.

April 18 – 21, 2007. Amidst a typical year of European, Russian and North American dates, the band get back to Brazil for a few shows.

March 16th, 2007, Traun, Austria.

© Isabella Seefriedt

March 23rd, 2007, Feldkirchen, Austria.

2008

2008. Manny Charlton issues *Then There's This*.

January 25 – May 2, 2008. Nazareth conduct an intensive European tour, including at the beginning many UK shows.

March 31, 2008. Nazareth issue, on Edel, album No.21, *The Newz*, the band's first record to feature Pete's son Lee as drummer.

Dan McCafferty:

"With this album, I just think it's the chemistry of the guys in the band—Lee, Jimmy, Pete and myself. It's taken a step forward. We learn from each other, and we're all enjoying it a lot and having a good time. I think that comes across on the record, and it certainly comes across in the live shows. And certainly a lot of writing was done for this album; we came up with the 13 songs that we did, and it was hard to do that. There are a lot of good lyrics on it and everybody wrote. When Jimmy came in with 'Goin' Loco,' we went, oh, this is really different. And we got behind him to make it even better. It was a hearty, very productive album to make."

"I wanted the energy level higher this time, you know what I mean? I think we wanted to do that. And I wanted it to be accessible; I wanted people to be able to understand the songs, think a little bit, but not like *War and Peace*. I wanted these songs to entertain people, but yeah, 'Liar' (laughs), that's probably the heaviest thing we've ever done."

"And Yann, the producer, he really helped a lot too. We wanted it to sound like an album that was made today, but keep the spirit of the band. It was all done by computer, in Switzerland. It took six weeks basically, and maybe Yann did a couple of remixes for us, and that's a couple weeks, I guess. It was done very quickly. He has worked all over the world, but he's based in Switzerland so that's where it was done. I'm quite impressed by the whole thing pretty much. I don't want to sound like I have a big head, but I do like it (laughs)."

Pete Agnew, on Yann Rouiller:

"He's a drummer as well. But he's a studio engineer. This is the thing: a lot of producers are producers. They sit next to the engineer and tell them what they want. Well, Yann is the engineer. He sits there and he's got an assistant if he wants, but again, he does everything. He's recording on his computer, and he sits there and he looks at it and gets all the sounds personally. Yann is excellent. He's a studio man. He's been the fifth member of the band since we met him. Dan and I met Yann in 2006. We went over to see him in a studio there, Zurich, and we spoke to him back and forth for about a year. 2007, we went to record *The Newz*, and he was a very young guy and we thought, I hope he knows what he's doing. But he was great to work with. He's a great drummer, great guitar player, great singer. He's very, very good at everything."

"It's funny, in the studio, when you do a vocal, incredibly high or whatever, a producer will talk to you and maybe play it on the piano and say, 'I want you to sing that.' No. Yann just sings it. You go, hang on a minute; you're singing this impossible thing. So he's a very, very talented man, just brilliant. He's one of these guys that listens to what you've got to say, about how you want the song, and then he's going to get the sounds for you. And he's always got a lot of suggestions."

"He'd never done a rock album with a band like us before, so he was a bit nervous going into the thing. But we told him what we were trying to create. We told him we didn't want to sound flash, with an Aerosmith-type production. It's more nitty-gritty, like they just invented the studio, that kind of thing. And I think we achieved that. It sounds like the record could have been made in the '70s, but it was made now (laughs)."

"There were so many kinds of different things to play on this album. There are a few straightforward things like 'Day at the Beach.' There's the opening track, 'Goin' Loco' and 'Liar.' There weren't actually two tracks the same. It was funny actually, because when we did the album, Roger Glover, who's a good pal of ours, his girlfriend live in Switzerland, so he came up to the studio just to visit for a day. After we had done most of the album, that was one of the things he commented on. He said, 'It must've been a lot of fun playing bass on this album' (laughs). He noticed it right away. And I said yes, it was."

May 14 – 29, 2008. The band mount a pretty extensive Brazilian campaign.

October 8 – November 5, 2008. After the usual European dates and a few shows in North America, the band conduct an extensive tour of The Ukraine, including shows in Russia, Moldova and Kazakhstan. Then it's back to America followed by more Europe to close out the year.

Pete Agnew in November of 2008:

"We've been asked to do another album next year, but I don't know if we're going to manage that. I mean, this year has been unbelievable touring-wise. So far we've done more than 180 shows, and we're finishing in America. We're only doing ten shows or so there but we had to go there, for our 40th anniversary tour. We couldn't miss it out. We're going to do a big North American tour next year, but we figured we'll drop in the ten shows this year."

"We just got back from Russia, and we've come straight out here. We're finishing America, and we got a few dates in Europe in December, then we've got some time off, then we'll go into rehearsals to change the set for next year in January, and then we start all over again touring. So we don't know if we're going to manage to fit anything in. Because we've actually got a lot of material ready that didn't go on the latest album that was very, very good, but we wanted to play around with it a bit more. We've got enough to do an album. We could have it ready, but we just don't think we have the time to prepare it, because of the amount of touring we have coming up again next year. We might get to recording towards the end of the year, but I can't promise that one."

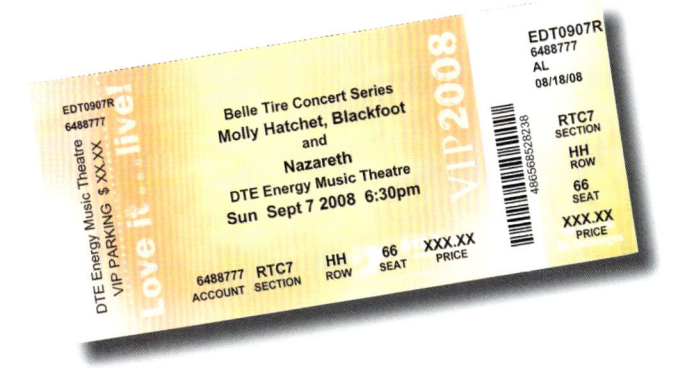

April 18th, 2008, Spielberg, Austria.

© Isabella Seefriedt

2009

February – May 2009. Nazareth play dates across Europe.

May 29 – June 7, 2009. The band return to Brazil for shows.

July 9 – August 8, 2009. The band conduct an extensive tour of Western Canada, with a few shows in the East tucked in at the end.

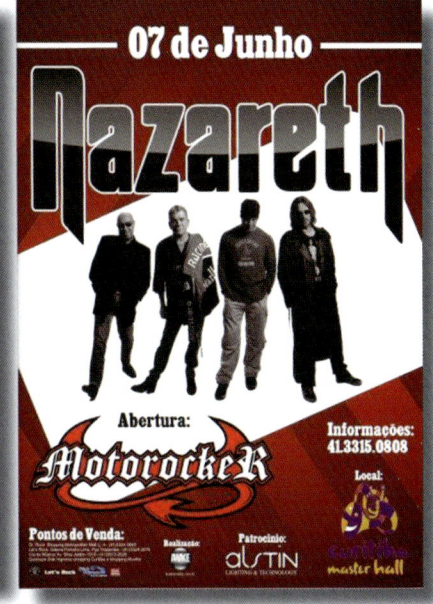

Dan McCafferty: "We're doing four from the new album and the rest is pretty much greatest hits. We do a song called 'Sunshine' which is really big in Canada, so we do that when we come to Canada. But the rest of the set is songs you really couldn't *not* do, because, I mean, you buy a Nazareth ticket, you want to hear 'Razamanaz,' 'Hair of the Dog,' 'Love Hurts,' that stuff, and we're not in the business to piss people off so much."

August 16 – September 4, 2009. The band play shows in Poland and the Czech Republic.

September 8 – November 17, 2009. The guys play Kazakhstan, Latvia, the Ukraine and Russia in what is the band's most extensive tour of the region ever.

Pete Agnew, on playing Russia:
"It's a completely different country, compared to what it was like when we first went. Completely different. The country and the people, there's potential. There is the mega-rich and you've still got the poor, but you've got a kind of middle class now that they never, ever had before. What you would call the middle class, anyway. People have got a bit more money, and everybody's got a mobile phone, cell phone. I mean, if you go to Moscow and St. Pete, it's just about as good as going to any large city in the world—you've got everything."

"And then you've still got places where we play. Deep Purple were out the same time as us playing Siberia and stuff like that. Some of that is still a bit rough. But things are improving. The hotels are improving, things like that. You see a big difference. But when we first went it was just shocking. And the train rides, they can be monumental. You can be on a train for three days. But when you see the airlines, then you see why people would go on the trains for three days. Everybody says to us—they ask you all these questions at press conferences in the places that we play—and they say, 'Do you gamble? Are you a gambler?' And of course Dan was going no, and I'm going, 'Yeah, we are—we get on Russian planes.'"

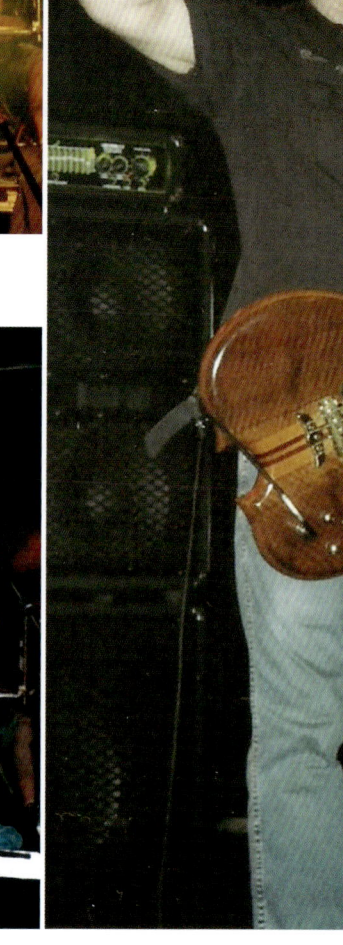

April 7th, 2009, Vienna, Austria.

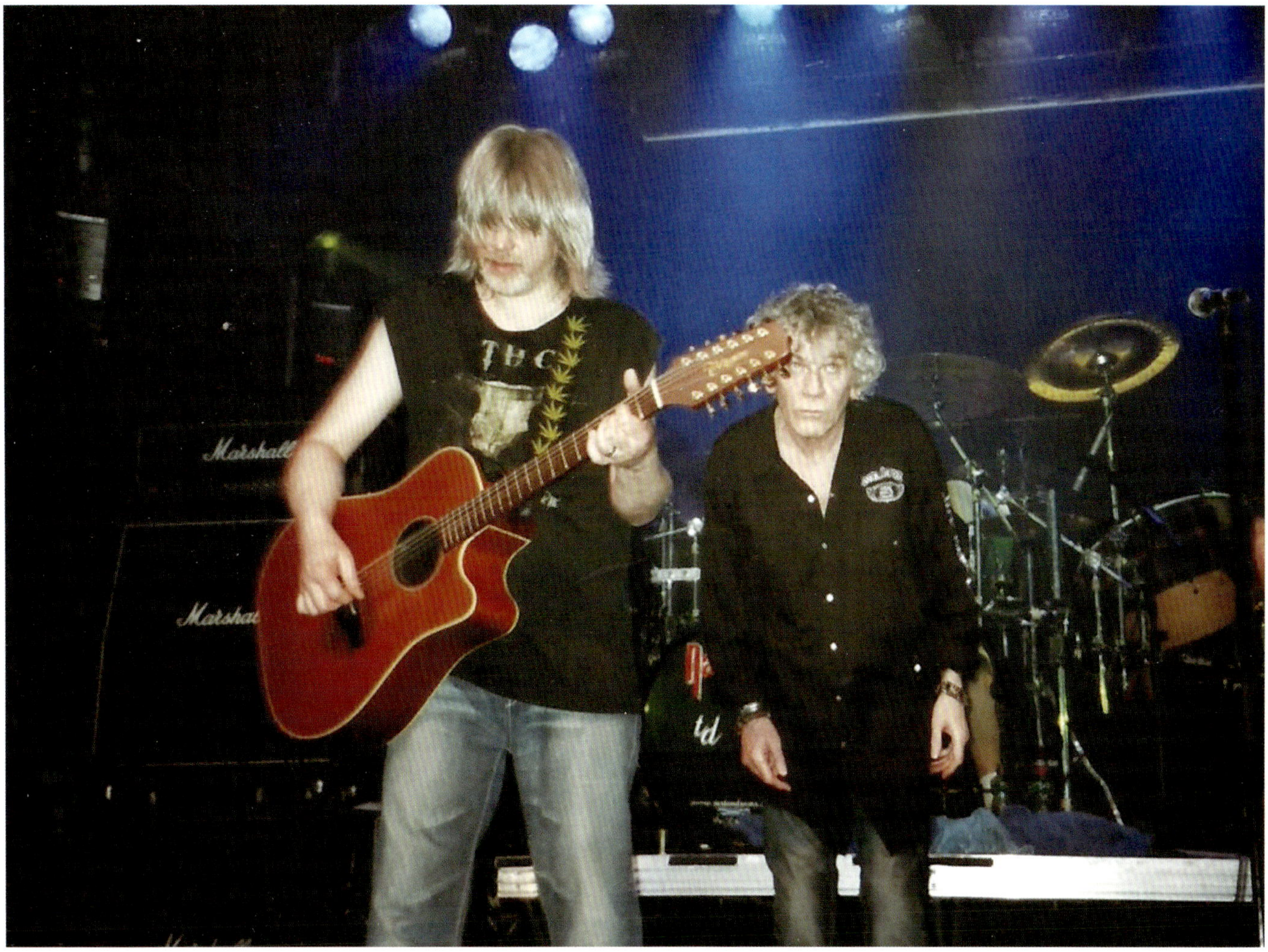
THC
Marshall
Marshall

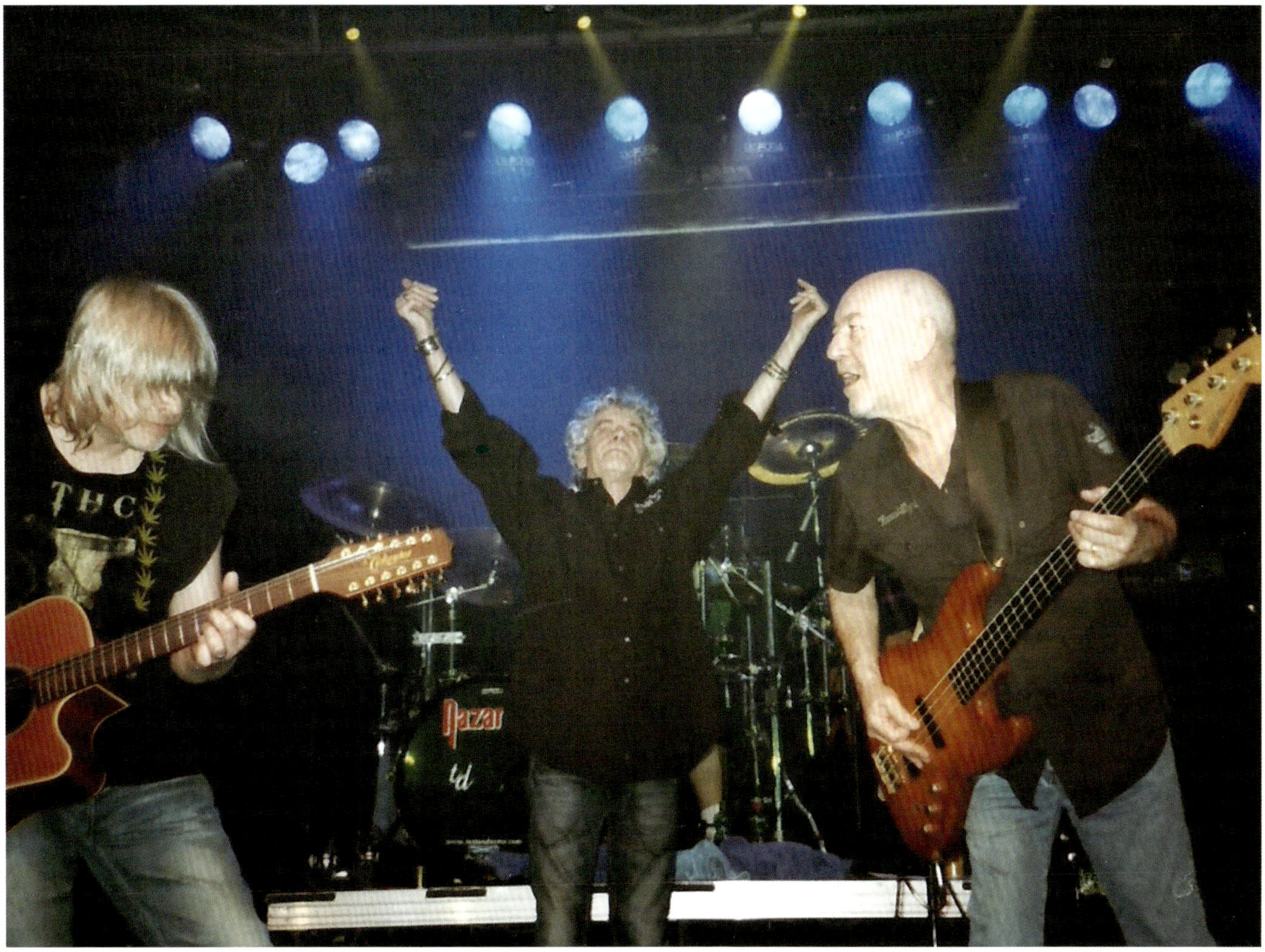
THC

"'The Toast' is a funny song—Lee, our drummer, wrote that. You see, we play a lot in Russia, and when you play in Russia, you play early, you play seven o'clock shows, and then everyone, the promoters, they always want to take you out to dinner. And dinner always takes about four or five hours, because it's very slow service there. Plus they're waiting to make a toast. These guys stand up, speaking in Russian, holding up a vodka glass, 'I'd like to make a toast.' And we have an interpreter and it goes on forever. So that's the other reason the dinners take so long—there are so many toasts. So Lee wrote it. We've always joked about that: 'Oh, here we go; couldn't we just go to McDonald's? It would save a lot of time.' 'No, no, we're going out.' And we have 759 toasts. So that's what the song is all about—it's really about Russia. And doing the talking there, that's Alan, our agent. He's a very funny guy. He's about 65 years old and we gave him a couple of beers and said, 'You've got to put this thing on there.'"
Pete Agnew

The 2010s to 2021

December 2nd, 2018, Graz, Austria.

To reiterate what I said way back in beginning of this book, what made the penning of this tome so delightful is the fact that way up into Nazareth's fifth decade, the band was making some of its loudest and proudest music since the early days, at least as far as this writer is concerned. I'm a big fan of 2008's *The Newz*, but I'm even more invested in 2011's *Big Dogz* and 2014's *Rock 'n' Roll Telephone*, which, sadly, was the last for Dan McCafferty as the lead singer of Nazareth, who was forced to tap out due to crippling chronic obstructive pulmonary disease, or COPD.

In a parallel world, we must give a shout-out to Manny Charlton, on every record from the '70s through to the end of the '80s, who despite being in a self-professed form of retirement for years, found himself making all manner of solo album, all of them very independent and under the radar but joyfully and sincerely delivered nonetheless. He is the only member of the classic lineup to make solo albums besides Dan, who to this point had only done a covers album in 1975 and a pretty strange low-key record in 1987 called *Into the Ring*. However, in 2019 McCafferty would deliver *Last Testament,* a heart-wrenching, earthy and sometimes Celtic record of reflection, and a more than fitting close to a career (at least thus far).

Meanwhile, Pete Lee and Jimmy weren't throwing in the towel, hitting the tour trail after Dan's departure, first with Linton Osborne singing and then settling upon Carl Sentance, who was indeed the post-Dan front man on a surprise new studio album from the band in 2018 called *Tattooed on My Brain.*

As it stands here in early 2021, it's anyone's guess what happens next in the Nazareth camp, or with respect to the very nature of the music industry itself, for that matter. Suffice to say that Nazareth at the 50-year mark have nothing left to prove, quite pertinently on the strength of the music they made throughout their fifth decade, much less the 40 years previous. Part of me wants to see five more records with Carl, so that a new legacy is established, one that perhaps sees Pete replaced by another one of his sons! Another part of me wants to see another solo album from Dan in the vein of *Last Testament,* which affected me deeply, underscored by the poignant hometown videos he made in support of the record.

And then of course another part of me, possibly the largest part, would like to see one more record with Dan at the microphone, howling away, holding the big dogz of death at bay—or if that's too much to ask, at least growling as good as he can. Because as *Last Testament* demonstrated so ably, any amount of Dan McCafferty singing for us is indeed nourishment for the soul that is much appreciated.

2010

February 5 – February 20, 2010. The band conduct a UK tour, followed by mainland Europe, west and east.

June 30 – August 1, 2010. The band conduct an extensive cross-Canada tour.

August 2010. *Malice in Wonderland* is reissued by Salvo Records, who add seven BBC live bonus tracks to the original record. Also reissued in expanded versions by Salvo at this time is *Razamanaz*, *Loud 'n' Proud*, *Rampant*, *Hair of the Dog*, *Greatest Hits*, *Expect No Mercy*, *No Mean City* and *The Fool Circle*.

August 14 – 28, 2010. The guys conduct another tour of Eastern Europe.

October 11 – 23, 2010. The band return once again to Brazil, followed by more European shows.

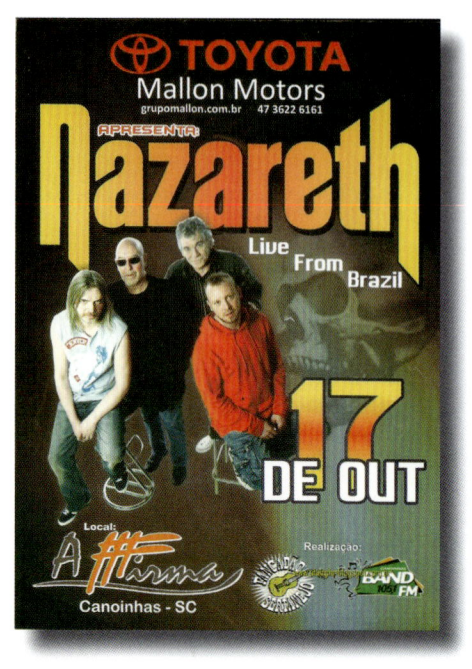

May 6th, 2010, Vienna, Austria.

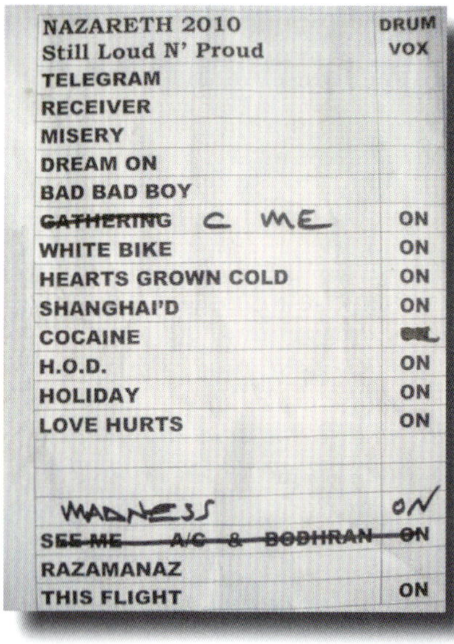

2011

2011. Salvo Records reissues *'Snaz, The Catch, Cinema, Move Me* and *Boogaloo.*

February 24 – March 31, 2011. The band play Brazil, followed by Russia.

April 15, 2011. Nazareth issue, again on Edel, *Big Dogz*, which is produced by the band's guitarist Jimmy Murrison in conjunction with Yann Rouiller.

Pete Agnew:
"We were trying to not do *The Newz* again, but a bit more rhythm and blues, if you like. And we used very, very little overdubbing; it was kind of live in the studio. Obviously you've got to do overdubs for solos and stuff like that, but we didn't go over the top with it. We were trying to make it studio live, if you like, and I think we've kind of done it, because most people who've phoned me have kind of mentioned that."

"We don't ever record unless we all like a song. Because we've written quite a lot of songs, it takes for us to say 'We all like that one.' But I like 'Big Dog's Gonna Howl,' obviously, as it's a good fun kind of track. I love 'When Jesus Comes to Save the World Again' and I like 'Radio,' because it tells you of a time, well, in our lives definitely. 'Lifeboat,' we don't like to get political, but that one kind of comments on how things are going these days politically, and it hits it on the head. 'Time and Tide' is basically Jimmy, our guitar player, talking about his time in the band. I like 'Claimed' because it's a groovy number. I like the whole thing, actually."

"You now, in the early days, what you used to call hard rock, it all came from the blues, rhythm and blues, Chuck Berry, and that's the way we grew up. Our early albums are like that and things changed a bit in the middle, and poppy in some cases. But this time we just felt we'd like to just go back and groove. They're modern songs, but with that approach. We wanted to sound like a three-piece Delta band, really. So we wrote these modern songs, but we thought, how would we play those things in 1973?"

April 20 – June 25, 2011. Nazareth tour Europe, with most dates as usual taking place in Germany.

June 30 – August 12, 2011. The band conduct another impressive tour blanketing Canada.

September 18 – October 14, 2011. Nazareth conduct another quite thorough tour of Russia.

November 11 – 19, 2011. The band return to Brazil for shows almost every night.

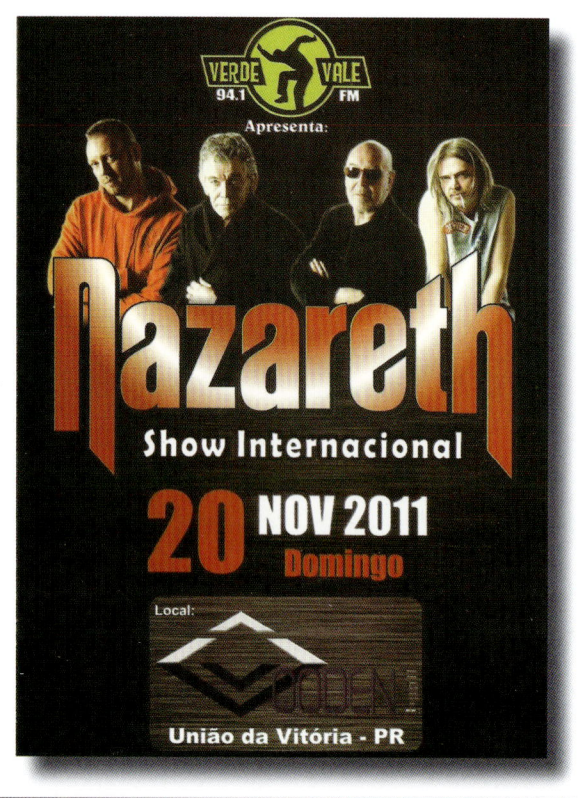

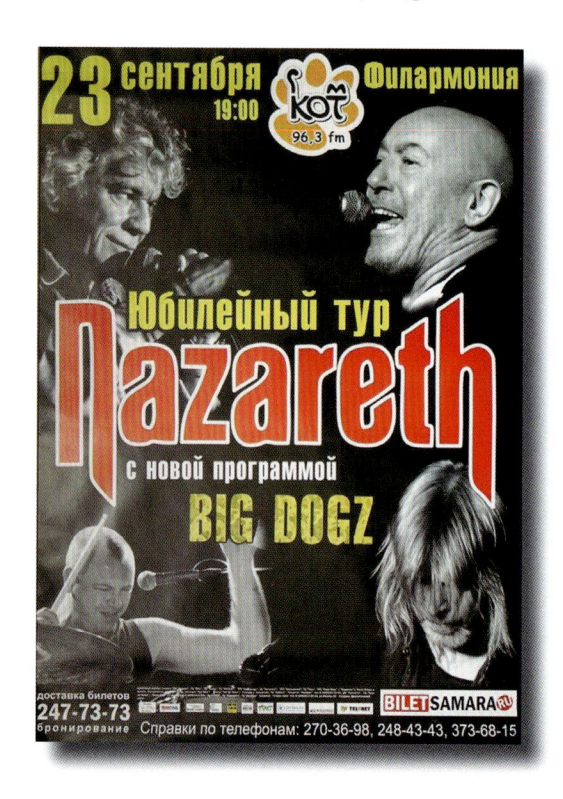

217

2012

February 2 – February 10, 2012. The band play Brazil yet again.

March 10 – March 23, 2012. Nazareth conduct a brief UK campaign.

April 19 – June 29, 2012. The band begin touring in Germany and cover much of Europe once again.

> **Pete Agnew on the intricacies of touring with Jimmy Murrison:**
> "We have a song on *Big Dogz* called 'Sleeptalker' because he's a big-time sleep-talker. I mean, if you get in the room next to him in a hotel, you really don't want to be there, because the guy can talk and talk and talk all night, and he does do this. Jimmy actually wrote the song about himself. And what we did at the end of it, we put a sort of sleep sequence, if you like, a dreamy kind of instrumental part, and we had a whole lot of people who knew us coming in and saying a word here and a word there and a little line there. One of the women who is speaking—that's his wife (laughs). And you've got our agent Alan again, and you've got a drummer mate of ours. There was no other place, Martin, where you could do that on the album—it could only be at the end. You couldn't do it in the middle, because it would be a bit weird. So we thought, well we could either end the album with a great big bang, or we can end the album with, 'Oh, what's this?'"

July 5 – 28, 2012. The band do another one of their intensive tours of Western Canada.

September 20 – October 30. Nazareth conduct another involved Russian tour, with other Eastern European territories covered as well.

November 9 – 24, 2012. The band return for another short tour of Brazil.

2012, Feldkirchen.

2012, Judenberg.

© Isabella Seefriedt

Nazareth

220

2013

2013. The Manny Charlton Band issue *Hellacious*. Vanilla Fudge and Cactus legend Tim Bogert guests on bass plus there are cameos by Vivian Campbell and Steven Adler.

February 22 – March 9, 2013. Nazareth play ten dates in Brazil.

March 27 – June 2, 2013. The band play Russia and other Eastern European territories.

June 7 – July 15, 2013. The guys play the US, Mexico and Canada, with a number of shows cancelled at the tail end. A handful of European shows round out the year.

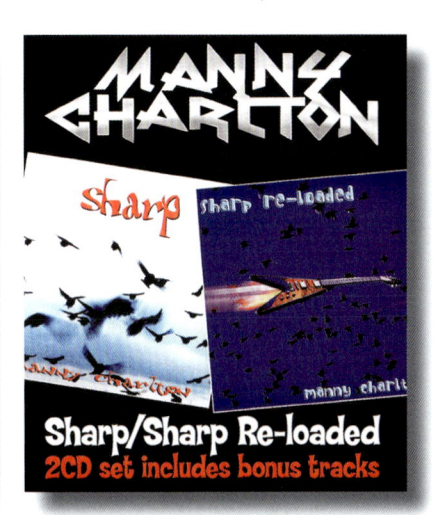

August 2013. Dan has to leave the stage at a show in Switzerland after three songs due to his worsening health. This follows upon an on-stage collapse at a Canadian show in Cranbrook, BC the previous month.

Dan McCafferty on the cause of his ailment:
"Something to do with my misspent youth, I would imagine. And also, well, I didn't help it with the smoking, but I've stopped smoking ages ago. I did my share at the time of many things. But the other thing is, my father died of emphysema. So I've heard the theories from some doctors I've spoke to, that it could be a gene as well. Because I have a friend in the village I live in, she has COPD as well, and she's never put anything in her mouth smoke-able ever. So who knows, you know? You can only play with the cards you're dealt, young man."

August 28, 2013. The band announce the retirement of Dan McCafferty, due to ill health, specifically chronic obstructive pulmonary disease.

Dan McCafferty:
"I've had COPD for a few years. Up until last year I could manage. I was getting through the shows and stuff. Then what happened was, I went in and made the record and I was kind of struggling. I went into it and I was okay, and then

I went to the States, and I had to go to the hospital with an ulcer which is a completely different thing. It sounds like I'm falling apart. And then of course, because you lose so much blood doing that, I wasn't very well. So I only managed to do about four gigs in Canada and then I had to quit. I just wasn't well enough to play. Then we came back home and finished up the album. We had a little bit of a break and then went to do a gig in Switzerland and I couldn't breathe after about three songs. So I decided it was time to hit it on the head. Very sadly, I must say. Because, well, because it's a job I've had for about 45 years (laughs). So it's a bit of a bummer."

"At the moment I'm working on *Rock 'n' Roll Telephone*. I'm doing a lot of interviews, talking to people like yourself, all over the world. But when the album gets released, then I'll go and… there are a couple of offers in the fire, recording and stuff. But I'm trying not to think about that at all. I'll wrap this up and tie it in a bow and say, 'Goodbye, baby' (crying voice) to another one of your children (laughs). It's true. And then I'll think about what I'm going to do next."

2014

February 22, 2014. Scotsman Linton Osborne joins Nazareth as lead singer, replacing Dan McCafferty. A number of shows are cancelled when Osborne contracts a virus.

Dan McCafferty, in 2014:
"We have Linton Osborne, who is a great singer. And he has already performed in Scotland. I think they wanted to see how it was going to go. And then there are two or three shows in Russia. And then they're going to the Czech Republic and Canada in July I believe. Good luck with that. I know Linton well, because he's a local guy. Well, he's local-ish. For the size of your country, he'd be a next door neighbour, but in Scotland, he's local. And he's a good singer. I've known Linton for years; I've seen him in different bands or whatever, so good luck with that, boys, really."

June 3, 2014. Nazareth issue *Rock 'n' Roll Telephone*, their 23rd record and the last to feature Dan McCafferty as the band's vocalist. Producing once again is Yann Rouiller.

Dan McCafferty:

"We just thought it was a great title (laughs). Especially with the old British telephone boxes; these things are a thing of the past now. But what happened was—and this is true story—we were doing gigs in Russia last year, and Jimmy was going through security at the airport and he left his phone. You always take your phone out of your pocket and that kind of stuff. And in Russia, not having a phone is really being cut off. But everybody's got phones now, so it wasn't a problem, really. But he did get wound up about it a lot, of course. A lot of it is like, I'm stuck in Russia and I can't even speak to my girlfriend, or my wife, or whatever—and never both at the same time, by the way (laughs). Sorry, that was a really bad old joke. But anyway, there's humour in the song and I think it's a really cool track. And it just seemed like a good title. There's no reason why you think it's a good title; you just think 'That's a good title.'"

"All through its history, this band has always done what we feel like doing at the time. Obviously people change. I mean, you get older and wiser—or stupider (laughs). You know, I'm not making any claims in which way I got. But still, you do what you think is good, and then hopefully other people will think it's good. That's always been our criteria. So nothing really changed on this album. It's just that on this one, I mean, Lee and Jimmy have been writing a lot of songs last couple of albums, and they just come up with so much stuff and it's all good. So it's a case of pick the ones you wanna do and let's make a job of them."

"We kinda know what we're doing when we go into the studio. Things can change, obviously, but generally speaking we have a plan. As we do in life, we have a plan. And the thing was, we've played together for so long, Pete and I obviously for a million years, but Jimmy's been with Nazareth for nearly 20 years, and Lee's been there for 11. So you can speak to the people. It's like, 'What about trying this? Could you sing that again, Dan?' And nobody gets upset. It's like everybody's got their eye on the gold ring. They want to make a good record."

"As for the songs, I like 'Boom Bang Bang' for obvious regions, nudge nudge, wink wink. You know, you get it; there's a lot of humour in there. And I also like 'The Right Time,' because it's a very hopeful song. 'Speakeasy,' I think is a hoot, really good. 'Winter Sunlight' is about as romantic as it gets for me. Really, it's a pretty varied, interesting album, he says, blowing his own trumpet. But I really do think that."

Pete Agnew:
"A great album that proved to be the end of an era. Sadly, only a week after recording was completed, Dan was forced to quit Nazareth. Throughout our career, other musicians came and went, but Dan's departure marked the end of an era. He knows we wish him well and we know he wishes us well, as he has mentioned on several occasions how delighted is that we found a singer of Carl's calibre to take his place. It's funny though; sometimes I swear I can still hear his voice in the dressing room after a gig going, 'Will somebody shut that fuckin' door?!' I miss him."

June 25 – July 19, 2014. The band, now with Linton Osborne singing, conduct an extensive Western Canadian campaign.

July 26 – August 16, 2014. As expected, the band participate enthusiastically in the European festival season, following up with a German tour.

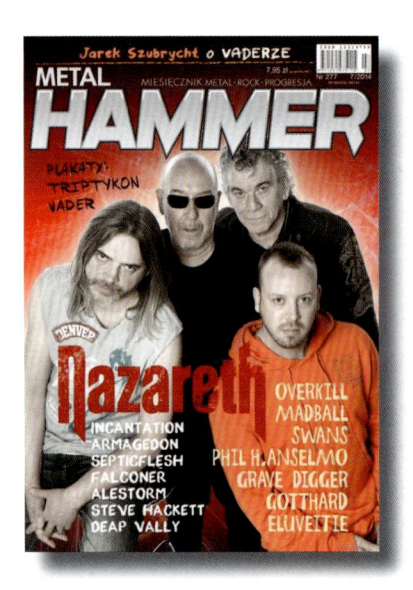

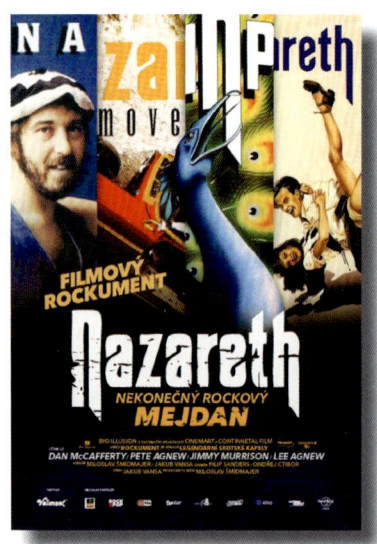

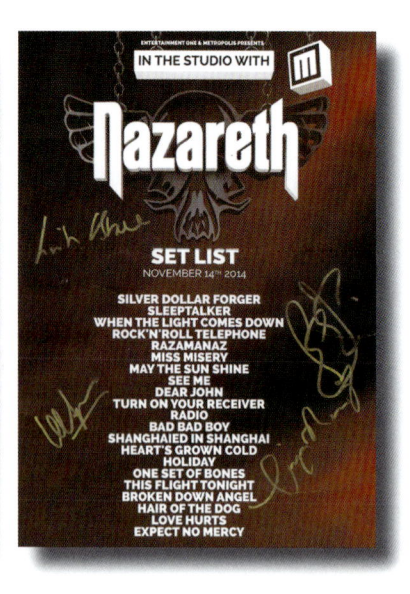

2015

2015. Manny Charlton moves to Cordova, Spain.

> **Manny Charlton, on his reason for leaving Texas and relocating to Spain:**
> "Blood. DNA. I've got family here. I always wanted to come to Spain to retire, so to speak."

January 16, 2015. Linton Osborne announces on his Facebook page that he is no longer Nazareth's lead singer.

February 13, 2015. The band announce Carl Sentance as their new singer. Sentence had sung previously with Persian Risk (Phil Campbell's pre-Motörhead band), Krokus (briefly) and with Geezer Butler's solo band.

Pete Agnew:
"Carl's got a way different sound compared to Dan and this is what we wanted. The stipulation was—well, two stipulations—he had to be a great singer and he had to not sound like Dan. We didn't want a Dan sound-alike because we would've been crucified if we'd done something like that. And you wouldn't want to do something like that. When we did all the auditions and stuff, the stuff that was being sent to me, a lot of people wanted to try to do the Dan sound-alike but it's not what we were looking for. We tried a couple people, tried a couple different things, and that didn't work. And then a friend of mine said, 'There's a guy you want to have a look at, this guy, Carl Sentance.' He was quite keen to join if we wanted him, and when he came to do an audition with us, within a couple of verses of 'Silver Dollar Forger,' we said this is the man, this is great, wonderful singer. So it worked out. And he's good on stage; he's got a wonderful presence on stage, a great act, if you like. And I thought, it all works really fabulous."

April 17 – December 25, 2015. The band tour extensively, with all the dates taking place in Europe.

October 4th, 2015, Graz, Austria.

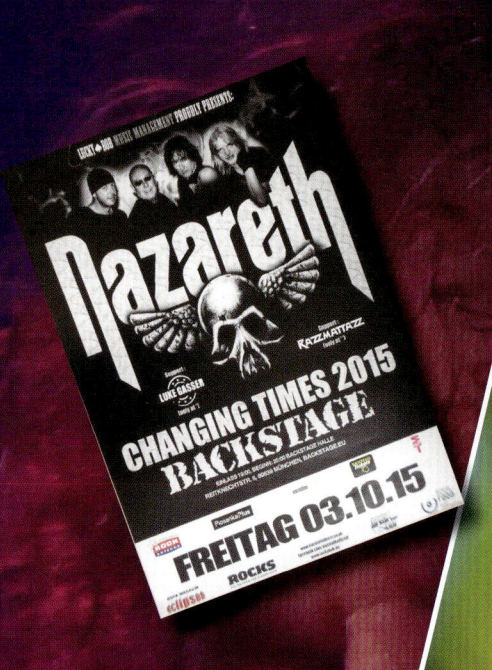

October 4th, 2015, Graz, Austria.

© Isabella Seefriedt

2016

2016. Manny Charlton issues *Solo*.

January 30 – July 17, 2016. The band tour Europe, getting in a few dates in Brazil as well, plus one show in Israel.

Pete Agnew, on the legitimacy of the band's lineup at this point:
"I used to get the question about how we still called ourselves Nazareth having only one original member in the lineup, but I don't get asked that hardly anymore these days and I could give you a few examples why. Bands with only one original member include: The Eagles, Guns N' Roses and AC/DC. That pretty much covers the most famous bands in the world. But you could go on and name a few more, like Status Quo, Whitesnake, Uriah Heep, Foreigner, Blue Öyster Cult, REO Speedwagon, Sweet, Little Feat, and if you want to get really picky, Deep Purple, with Ian Paice being the only original. So there you go—we're in good company."

"I'd even go a step further and say I'd like to think that the guys in the band as it is now would carry on the name even without me and I'm sure there would be very few complaints from the many fans that we're currently playing to in concert. You must remember that Jimmy and Lee have been in Nazareth for 26 years and 22 years respectively (both longer than Manny) and have written songs for, and performed on six Nazareth albums—counting the one we are currently recording)—accounting for almost a quarter of the total output of the band's recordings. You said yourself, Martin, that you put three of these albums in your top six Nazareth albums, so that alone says it all."

"Anyway, time will tell, but I'm 75 this year (ouch) and the fans who used to come to see the original band aren't getting any younger either, so now we're seeing more and more people coming to our concerts who have never seen the original lineup and completely identify Nazareth as the guys who are up on that stage now. Long may that continue even after I've shuffled off to the big bass amp in the sky."

July 19 – July 27, 2016. The guys conduct yet another Western Canadian campaign; then it's an intense blanketing of Europe to finish out the year.

November 21st, 2016, Graz, Austria.

© Isabella Seefriedt

November 21st, 2016, Graz, Austria.

© Isabella Seefriedt

2017

January 19 – 23, 2017. The band play the Rock Legends Cruise.

March 30 – July 15, 2017. Nazareth conduct a tour of Europe but also, in April, execute a couple of shows in India.

Carl Sentance, in 2017:
"I've become a bit more confident, and of course then I didn't know what to expect. It was like rabbit in the headlamp. Now it's just a bit more confidence and it feels like a family now. It's been great. We have been working solid. I only had a chance maybe three months ago to start listening to different albums that I didn't have a chance to listen before. Now I hear all the stuff and I've picked a few songs out there that I like and I thought would work. It might take me another ten years to learn all the other songs, but I'm getting there (laughs)."
(w/ Marko Syrjala, MetalRules)

May 18, 2017. Although Andrew Carnegie had already built a library in the place of his birth, Dunfermline, Scotland, additions over the years included a museum and art gallery that opened on this date. There is a display dedicated to hometown heroes Nazareth, which Pete and Dan have visited, Pete having donated his first bass guitar to the cause.

July 22 – August 5, 2017. The band conduct a Canadian tour, covering the west as usual, but also Central Canada. Then it's back to Europe to close out the year.

2018

January 19 – August 1, 2018. The band play their regular European stomping grounds, east and west, before returning to similarly familiar territory—Western Canada, in August, with a few Ontario dates as well. Then it's mostly Germany for the balance of 2018.

October 12, 2018. Nazareth issue, on Frontiers, their 24th record, *Tattooed on My Brain*. On vocals is Carl Sentence and producing is a returning Yann Rouiller.

Pete Agnew:
"We did almost like three years with Carl live. We all knew each other very, very well by that time. And when we got to the studio, it was a case of, he's never recorded with us, and everybody's got their own way of recording. But it was great, because he's been in the band for three years. We recorded pretty much the same way as we would record with Dan. It's just a different guy coming through the speakers. But I've got to say, he's pretty much an incredible first-take singer. When the guy goes in to sing, every time he does a take, it sounds perfect. He's like, 'Oh, let's try that again,' and I'm thinking, why? (laughs). So he's really easy to record with. And that was it—we'd been with him for three years so we were used to Carl being the singer with Nazareth."

"We did Carl's songs first, because people were still writing and working at home and in other rooms, rehearsal rooms in the studio. So we recorded his songs first. That was great, because when you're recording with Nazareth, if you can't sing your own songs, you're really up against it. So you're singing the songs you're comfortable with because you wrote them, which was a great way to start recording."

"And then we moved on to the other songs that other people had written. There could easily have been 18 tracks. Due to the amount of great material we had, our biggest problem was having to decide which songs were to be left out. Personal favourites for me are 'Secret Is Out,' 'Pole to Pole' and 'Tattooed on My Brain' but I can play this album right through without wanting to skip a track. However, even though we were all delighted with the finished album, there was a definite nervousness in the camp during the run-up to its release. This was the first album without Dan, so we knew that judgement day critics were going to be harsh. The reviews couldn't be just oaky, or even just 'good'—that was never going to cut it. No wiggle room here: our fans had to love this one, and to our great happiness—not to mention relief—they did. Overwhelmingly. The media reviews and fans' comments were ecstatic."

"In these days when music is 'streamed'—or to use the right word, 'stolen'—instead of being bought from record stores, it's sometimes hard to measure an album's success, so we have to settle for the fact that Tattooed on My Brain was streamed untold thousands of times and hit No1 on the Amazon rock chart on and off for a few of weeks. So we rejoiced knowing that by today's standards we had a long-awaited hit record. Although what we all really know is that by today's standards we just handed out a $50,000 business card. And here's the kicker: we can't wait to get started on another one! Go figure."

2019

2019. The band tour extensively, with almost all of it, all year, in Europe. However, the guys play Brazil in late October, into November, and make a return visit to India, for the Shirock Festival on October 16th.

June 25, 2019. The New York Times article on the 2008 Universal warehouse fire lists Nazareth as one of the band who lost original masters in the blaze.

June 21, 2019. Dan McCafferty issues a video for a song called "Tell Me," from his forthcoming solo album.

October 18, 2019. Dan McCafferty issues a solo album, called *Last Testament*.

Manny Charlton, on Dan:
Dan, fantastic vocalist, great writer, great lyrics. I really miss him when it comes to doing music and stuff (laughs). Yeah, he's a fantastic vocalist. And never, ever, ever was a prima donna. I've met vocalists since and before who are complete prima donnas. Ask Jeff Beck about vocalists (laughs). Jeff Beck decided he wasn't going to have any, and he's never worked with another vocalist. Dan was great, just one of the guys, and there was a rumour going around that AC/DC wanted him as a replacement for Bon Scott. But Dan would never have left Nazareth. Him and Pete are joined at the hip (laughs). They've been buddies since schoolchildren; like five years old, they've known each other. I was always the new boy (laughs)."

December 2nd, 2018, Graz, Austria.

© Isabella Seefriedt

December 4th, 2018, Vienna, Austria.

© Isabella Seefriedt

June 29th, 2019,
Eisenstadt, Austria.

June 29th, 2019,
Eisenstadt, Austria.

© Isabella Seefriedt

2020

January 10 – March 7, 2020. The band tour extensively, mostly in Germany and Russia, making Nazareth one of the most prolific of classic rock bands in the months leading up to shows being cancelled due to the worldwide Coronavirus pandemic.

Pete Agnew:
"I'll be seeing Dan tomorrow, because I've not had a chance to see him these last few weeks. I was in Canada up until the end of September. We did the Canadian tour. He lives only five minutes from me. I live in one village and he lives in the next village down at the seashore. So I go to see him every now and again. He likes to be brought up to date with what we're doing and he loves to hear the stories."

"He has good days and he has bad days with the breathing stuff. If he gets the slightest little bug, it's really bad, for his breath and that. But he can't go along too far walking and stuff without being terribly short of breath. But he's done a new album as well. See, he can't travel with our band. He can't come up and do a show but he can still record. Because as you know, when you go in to record, you can record one line at a time. You can record one word at a time if you like. He can sing a verse, a line of a verse, have a cup of tea and then sing again."

"The studio we used for *Tattooed on My Brain*, well, it's the studio we used for *Rock 'n' Roll Telephone*. And the reason we used it, is it's right close to Dan's house. When we did *Rock 'n Roll Telephone*, he wasn't getting any better then. It was good to be just recording around the corner so he could just nip down when he was needed to sing. And it was good. So he's recorded a solo album in there with a guy from Prague, the Czech Republic."

"But he'd been having breathing problems for quite a while. When we did *Big Dogz*, it was probably right around that time, those few years leading up to *Rock 'n' Roll Telephone*—that's when it got worse. But for *Rock 'n' Roll Telephone*, he was fine. We did like about a month of the album and we were supposed to come to Canada. Well, we came and we did some dates in the States, and then we came up to do Canada. And when we were in the States, we had to cancel a couple of shows. And then when we went up to do Canada, I think we only managed about four shows. I think Cranbrook was the last place that we actually got up on the stage, and he just couldn't do it anymore. So we had to cancel that Canadian tour."

"And then we came back and we finished recording. We spent another month recording *Rock 'n' Roll Telephone* and he did the vocals and everything. But then after that, when we finished the record, a few days after we finished it, we went out to do a festival with Joe Cocker and ourselves, and Krokus, which was a band that Carl used to sing with, funny enough. So we went to Switzerland to do that, and we went on the stage that night and he struggled through sort of a few songs and then he just couldn't breathe anymore. He had to come up and say that's it. And that was the day he went. Because he tried to do that a few times and he said, 'No, no, I can't do this to the band anymore. That was my last attempt.' That was five years ago now. Time flies, doesn't it?"

Dan McCafferty on what he's going to miss the most in retirement, playing live or making records:

"Oh, I'm really going to miss the road. Oh God, the two things I love. Obviously I've been doing this for 50-odd years, so I'm kind of fond of playing music. The studio was great, because you are having a bit of fun, taking a punt; if something doesn't work, let's do this, let's try that. Because we were never a formula band, really. But the road I love, because, well, you meet new people on their own turf. And they don't care if you traveled 300 or 400 miles that night to play to them. They'll say, 'Hey man, I paid 20 bucks' (laughs), and you have to do perform and I kind of liked that. It was very enjoyable and it was personal. I mean, you see people's faces and they're smiling at you. Or they're going, 'You suck, man' (laughs). Generally speaking they are smiling at you. So yeah, I'm going to miss them both—very much."

"What am I most proud of? Making 24 recorded albums, I guess. And playing just about every place in the world that had a plug. I mean really, I've enjoyed much it. I thought it was great. And it's funny, since I got sick, the amount of people who run into me from other bands and say, 'Oh, come on, Dan, get better' blah blah blah. So at least you know you had made an impact, that you made a few ripples in pool."

TURN ON YOUR RECEIVER
NEVER DANCE WITH DEVIL
RAZAMANAZ
THIS FLIGHT TONIGHT
DREAM ON
LOVE LEADS TO MADNESS
WHITE BIKE
CHANGE
HEART'S GROWN COLD
BEGGARS DAY
CHANGING TIMES
HOD
TATTOOED ON MY BRAIN
LOVE HURTS
MORNING DEW

MISS MISERY
WHERE ARE YOU NOW
GO DOWN FIGHTING

2021

February 21, 2021. With live gigging a distant memory worldwide and not exactly slated to resume any time soon, the Nazareth clan work toward a follow-up to *Tattooed on My Brain*.

Pete Agnew:
"Because we've been locked in for all this amount of time, there are so many songs. It's going to be hard to decide what to use. I mean, Jimmy, he's sent me 14 songs he's done. And Lee only really started writing last month and Lee's got five. Carl, I'm sure he'll have a few. But Carl, what he did was he recorded a solo album. He's living out in Austria now and he wrote and recorded a solo album, during the summer of last year, and Yann, our producer, mixed it; I think he's still mixing it. But he'll have a lot of material because he writes songs all the time. Put it this way: it's not going to be like it was at Morin Heights when we did *Play 'n' the Game,* when we had nothing, absolutely nothing, and you go into the studio and you're just jamming. It won't be like that with this new album because with no touring the guys have done nothing *but* writing."

"You know, what I always like is that first week in the studio, when you get all the drum sounds but more importantly, you've got everybody in there and you're wondering what are we going to be doing? What sorts of songs are we going to be doing? That's when you listen to all the material that everybody's got and you start to choose. 'We can do that one, change that, change that…' I always look forward to that first week. There's a great buzz. Everybody is going in and you're not really sure what you're going to be doing and it's great. Despite right now going fuckin' stir-crazy (laughs), me and the guys absolutely have that to look forward to."

June 29th, 2019, Eisenstadt, Austria.

ACKNOWLEDGEMENTS

Thanks once again to my faithful copy editor Agustin Garcia de Paredes, who applied his eagle eye to this book and hopefully helped me keep the typos down to an acceptable number. Agustin is also the administrator of the Facebook page for my History in Five Songs with Martin Popoff podcast and has the most complete collection of my books of anyone I know. Plus he's got a whip-smart band and he saw Nazareth in concert in Barrie in 2018.

Digging deeper, Nazareth expert and buddy Robert Lawson (who has his own Nazareth book, Razama-Snaz!), conducted a peer review of the book. His wise and conscientious scholarship on all things Naz applied to these pages made me look less stupid.

I'd also like to thank my good buddy Kevin Julie, who helped assemble a bit of a press archive, handy for the odd key quote.

And yes, cheers to those lovely photographers! Thank you to Roni Ramos Amorim, Rudy Childs, Richard Galbraith, Wolfgang Gurster and Isabella Seefriedt for helping make this book, in a visual sense, sing like Dan. Of course among these fine collaborators, Roni needs to be singled out for his collecting, scanning and photographing of his top-shelf Nazareth collection. His kind contribution in the field of images helped so much to make this a treasure trove in book form.

Special thanks to Pete Agnew for permission to use the official Nazareth logos.

ABOUT THE AUTHOR

At approximately 7900 (with over 7000 appearing in his books), Martin has unofficially written more record reviews than anybody in the history of music writing across all genres. Additionally, Martin has penned approximately 110 books on hard rock, heavy metal, classic rock and record collecting. He was Editor-In-Chief of the now retired Brave Words & Bloody Knuckles, Canada's foremost metal publication for 14 years, and has also contributed to Revolver, Guitar World, Goldmine, Record Collector, bravewords.com, lollipop.com and hardradio.com, with many record label band bios and liner notes to his credit as well. Additionally, Martin has been a regular contractor to Banger Films, having worked for two years as researcher on the award-winning documentary Rush: Beyond the Lighted Stage, on the writing and research team for the 11-episode Metal Evolution and on the ten-episode Rock Icons, both for VH1 Classic. Additionally, Martin is the writer of the original metal genre chart used in Metal: A Headbanger's Journey and throughout the Metal Evolution episodes. Martin currently resides in Toronto and can be reached through martinp@inforamp.net or www.martinpopoff.com.

Sources

Sources cited throughout this book are credited "in situ," i.e. right at the end of the quote. Quotes with no accreditation at the end are from the author's own chats with the Naz guys or other speakers deemed relevant to the tale. The exception are some of the stories from Pete Agnew, who graciously contributed some of his own written musings to the cause. Pete also diligently went through the document correcting for accuracy and conducted a late-in-the-process interview with me to cover some of the gaps. His time and care spent on hammering this into improved shape is much appreciated.